MW00811234

Endgame at Stalingrad

The Stalingrad Trilogy, Volume 3

Endgame at Stalingrad

BOOK ONE:
NOVEMBER 1942

David M. Glantz

with

Jonathan M. House

University Press of Kansas

© 2014 by the University Press of Kansas

Published by the University Press of Kansas (Lawrence, Kansas 66045), which
was organized by the Kansas Board of Regents and is operated and funded by
Emporia State University, Fort Hays State University, Kansas State University,
Pittsburg State University, the University of Kansas, and Wichita State University

Library of Congress Cataloging-in-Publication Data

Glantz, David M.
   Endgame at Stalingrad / David M. Glantz; with Jonathan M. House.
     volumes cm.—(Modern war studies) (The Stalingrad trilogy; volume 3, books 1–2)
   Includes bibliographical references and index.
   ISBN 978-0-7006-1954-2 (book 1: November 1942: acid-free paper)
   ISBN 978-0-7006-1955-9 (book 2: December 1942–February 1943: acid-free paper)
1. Stalingrad, Battle of, Volgograd, Russia, 1942–1943. 2. Soviet Union. Raboche-Krestíianskaia
Krasnaia Armiia—History—World War, 1939–1945. 3. Germany. Heer—History—World
War, 1939–1945. I. House, Jonathan M. (Jonathan Mallory), 1950– II. Title.
   D764.3.S7G5886 2014
   940.54'21747—dc 3

2013049880

British Library Cataloguing-in-Publication Data is available.

Printed in the United States of America

10 9 8 7 6 5 4 3 2 1

To my wife, Mary Ann, without whose support,
assistance, and inexhaustible patience I could
not have written this or any other book

Contents

Maps, Tables, and Illustrations

TABLES

PHOTOGRAPHS

(following p. 52)
Iosif Vissarionovich Stalin
Colonel General Aleksandr Mikhailovich Vasilevsky
Colonel General Aleksei Innokent'evich Antonov
Major General Fedor Efimovich Bokov
Colonel General Nikolai Nikolaevich Voronov
Colonel General Aleksandr Aleksandrovich Novikov

(following p. 380)
Generals Rokossovsky and Batov at 65th Army's observation post during the
    Uranus counteroffensive
Soviet *Katiusha* multiple-rocket launchers firing in the preparation for
    Operation Uranus
Soviet artillery firing the preparation for Operation Uranus
Soviet tanks entering the penetration in operation Uranus
Soviet infantry beginning their assault in operation Uranus
Soviet infantry advancing under a smoke screen
Soviet troops and tanks assaulting Kalach-on-the-Don
Troops of the Southwestern and Stalingrad Fronts linking up at the village
    of Sovetskii

Preface

The Battle of Stalingrad, the epic World War II struggle pitting the *Wehrmacht* of Adolf Hitler's Third German Reich and the armies of his Axis allies against the Red Army of Josef Stalin's Soviet Union, culminated in November 1942 when Soviet forces struck back against their Axis tormentors. About six months had passed since Axis armies first lunged eastward across the southern Soviet Union. During this time, the Axis invaders wrought havoc on the defending Soviets, inflicting more than 1 million casualties on the Red Army and advancing over 600 kilometers (372 miles) to reach the northern slopes of the Caucasus Mountains and Stalin's namesake city on the Volga River. Despite debilitating defeats and repeated futile attempts to contain and strike back at the invaders, the Red Army succeeded in halting Axis forces in the rubble-filled streets of Stalingrad in October 1942. With his and the *Wehrmacht*'s reputation at stake, Germany's Führer ordered his country's most famous army—General Friedrich Paulus's Sixth—to capture Stalingrad at all costs. The grisly fighting that ensued bled Sixth Army white, leaving the frustrated Hitler no choice but to commit the forces of his Axis allies to front-line positions.

As they had done the year before, Stalin and his *Stavka* (High Command) skillfully exploited Hitler's unbridled ambition, which pushed the *Wehrmacht* well beyond the limits of its capabilities. After failing repeatedly to identify and exploit weaknesses in Axis defenses during the summer and fall of 1942, the *Stavka* finally did so in mid-November 1942 by orchestrating Operation Uranus, the most important of a galaxy of counteroffensives designed to defeat the Axis enemy and seize the strategic initiative in what the Soviets now termed the Great Patriotic War. In its Uranus counteroffensive, the Red Army's three attacking *fronts* defeated and largely destroyed the bulk of two Romanian armies and encircled German Sixth Army and half of German Fourth Panzer Army in the Stalingrad pocket, literally turning Germany's world upside down. Within the next ten weeks, the Red Army parried and then defeated two German attempts to rescue Sixth Army, crushed Italian Eighth and Hungarian Second Armies, severely damaged German Fourth Panzer and Second Armies, and destroyed German Sixth Army in the ruins of Stalingrad. With well over half a million soldiers rudely torn from its order of battle in the East, Hitler's Axis watched in horror as its status abruptly changed from victor to vanquished. In short, the Axis defeat at Stalingrad was a turning point in this war because it was a catastrophe from which Germany and its *Wehrmacht* could never fully recover.

The first two volumes in this trilogy describe the antecedents to this catastrophe: first, the Germans' deceptively triumphal march east into the Caucasus and to Stalingrad, and second, the vicious battle of attrition in Stalingrad proper, which proved to be as pivotal in that campaign as the battle would become in the war as a whole. Both volumes exploit copious amounts of recently released archival materials to identify, document, and dispel those myths about the campaign that have prevailed since war's end.

The mythology associated with the Stalingrad campaign is a natural byproduct of the sources on which previous histories were based. The destruction of German Sixth Army in the ruins of Stalingrad has fascinated historians and the general public for seventy years. Despite this fascination and the innumerable books on the subject, many of the causes and events of this tragedy have eluded posterity. As the first two volumes in this study have demonstrated, the fighting in Stalingrad can be understood only within the context of a German campaign that originally had almost no interest in capturing the city. The invaders came within a few miles of their true goal, the oil fields of the Caucasus, only to fail. The broad causes of that failure were almost identical to those that had frustrated Germany in 1941: logistical overstretch, the inability to focus on a single objective, and the increasingly sophisticated organization and conduct of the *Wehrmacht*'s opponent, the Red Army.

A second reason for our collective ignorance about this campaign is that participants on both sides wrote their accounts based on their memories, with little access to official records. Throughout the Cold War, many of the German records appeared to be irretrievably lost, and Soviet participants such as Vasilii Chuikov and Georgii Zhukov were also restricted to their own recollections.

A third and related reason for misunderstanding Stalingrad is the widespread acceptance, at least in the West, of the German mythology concerning the entire conflict. It is human nature to seek excuses for one's failures and even to rearrange one's memories in a way that provides a logical if oversimplified explanation of what is often a complex and disjointed process. Thus, most German survivors of the "Eastern Front" offered as literal truth what was, in fact, their own (perhaps unconscious) alibi for defeat. In this version, the German survivors remembered advancing easily, almost without opposition, until they became entangled in the bombed-out streets of Stalingrad. Then and only then, in the German collective memory, was their fanatical but clumsy enemy able to bleed them to death in a hundred combat actions. Once the German forces were depleted, the Romanian and Italian units on their flanks crumbled in the face of overwhelming Soviet attacks that were able to encircle and strangle Sixth Army. Even then, the collective alibi argues, the *Wehrmacht* might have escaped were it not for the criminal interference of the amateur Hitler and the incredible passivity of Paulus. If nothing else, this final volume should demonstrate that Hitler was not alone in his mistakes and that the Red Army had become so effective and Sixth Army so weak that there was little chance of Paulus breaking out to join hands with the scratch German forces sent to his rescue.

We will leave it to the reader to discover the other causes of German failure and Soviet success, many of which are detailed in these pages and in the two previous volumes. Suffice it to say, despite incredible gallantry and suffering on both sides, the Red Army ultimately won out, beginning the long process of redeeming Soviet territory from the Axis.

Like its predecessor tomes, this third volume tests controversial questions and prevailing myths on the basis of fresh documentary evidence. The principal difference between this and the previous volumes is the sheer quantity of questions and myths associated with this period of the fighting. In short, this period is replete with controversy and unanswered questions, the most notable of which include the following:

- Who was responsible for developing the concept for Operation Uranus?
- Why did the Uranus offensive succeed?
- Could Sixth Army have escaped encirclement or been rescued?
- Why did the German relief attempts fail?
- Who was most responsible for Sixth Army's defeat?

In addition to a wide variety of traditional sources, this volume exploits two major categories of documentary materials that were hitherto unavailable to researchers. The first consists of extensive records from the combat journal of German Sixth Army, which had been largely missing since the war's end; large portions of this journal have now been rediscovered and published. The second is a vast amount of newly released Soviet (Russian) archival materials, including excerpts from the Red Army General Staff's daily operational summaries; a wide variety of *Stavka*, People's Commissariat of Defense (NKO), and Red Army General Staff orders and directives; and the daily records of Soviet 62nd Army and its subordinate divisions and brigades for most of the time fighting was under way in Stalingrad proper.

Because of the persistent controversy and mythology characterizing this period, we believe it is necessary and prudent to include in this volume verbatim English translations of the many documents on which we based our judgments and conclusions. These, along with other detailed evidence in the form of charts and tables, are the substance of the *Companion*. This supplement to volume 3 offers concrete evidence necessary to accept, reject, or simply qualify our conclusions. Thus, like the first two volumes, this one offers unprecedented detail and fresh perspectives, interpretations, and evaluations of the later stages of the Stalingrad campaign.

This volume concentrates only on German and Soviet planning and conduct of combat operations in the immediate vicinity of Stalingrad. Specifically, it focuses on the struggle in and around Sixth Army's encirclement pocket, including the launch and defeat of German relief attempts; the Red Army's efforts to expand its outer encirclement fronts to and beyond the Chir, Don, and Aksai Rivers; and the operations conducted by the Soviet Don and Stalingrad Fronts to reduce Sixth Army's Stalingrad pocket. As such, it briefly describes the Southwestern and Voronezh Fronts' planning and conduct of the Little Saturn offensive and the Stalingrad (later Southern) Front's conduct of its Kotel'nikovo and Tormosin offensives.

Since the Red Army's offensive operations conducted south and west of the Stalingrad region during the second half of December 1942 and January 1943 were so vast in scale, a supplemental fourth volume will examine the military operations outside the limits of the trilogy. Specifically, it will include operations tangential to Stalingrad but that had a major effect on the ultimate fate of German Sixth Army, such as:

- The Southwestern and Voronezh Fronts' Operation Little Saturn against Italian Eighth Army
- The Stalingrad (Southern) Front's Kotel'nikovo and Rostov offensives against German Fourth Panzer, Romanian Fourth, and, later, German First Panzer Armies
- The Voronezh and Southwestern Fronts' Ostrogozhsk-Rossosh' offensive operation against Hungarian Second Army
- Most of the Briansk and Voronezh Front's Voronezh-Kastornoe offensive operation against German Second Army
- The Southwestern and Stalingrad Fronts' offensive in the eastern Donbas region against Army *Abteilung* Fretter-Pico and Army Group Hollidt
- The Trans-Caucasus Front's offensive in the northern Caucasus region against German First Panzer and Seventeenth Armies

A research effort of this magnitude would not be possible without the support of numerous individuals and agencies. In this regard, we must again thank Jason Mark, both for his generous personal assistance and for the groundbreaking tactical accounts of Stalingrad published by Leaping Horseman Books in Pymble, Australia. Likewise, William T. McCroden, who has spent a lifetime compiling detailed and definitive orders of battle for German forces during the war, shared with us the numerous draft volumes produced by his research.

Most important for this volume, we are indebted to two individuals whose keen knowledge of the war and the German language proved indispensable. The accomplished German military historian Dr. Romedio Graf von Thun-Hohenstein generously and selflessly volunteered to critique the manuscript for this volume. He spent countless hours reading it and commenting on all aspects of it, pointing out errors in fact and interpretation, identifying necessary sources, and correcting our frequent mutilations of the German language. Dr. Lothar Zeidler, a veteran of the war who served for more than two years in the *Wehrmacht*'s 168th Infantry Division and was twice wounded, translated many pages of German documents and shared with us his copious notes and other memorabilia from the war. Both generously provided their assistance driven by the desire to make this volume as accurate and objective as possible. We deeply appreciate their help.

As with our previous efforts, we gratefully acknowledge the crucial role Mary Ann Glantz played in editing and proofreading the manuscript.

David M. Glantz   *Jonathan M. House*
Carlisle, PA   *Leavenworth, KS*

Selected Abbreviations

German (Axis)

Higher Commands

OKW (*Oberkommando der Wehrmacht*)—Armed Forces High Command

OKH (*Oberkommando des Heeres*)— Army High Command

AG (H.Gr.) (*Heeresgruppe*)—army group

A (AOK) (*Armeeoberkommando*)— army

Pz A—panzer army

Harko (*Hoherer Artilleriekommando*)— higher artillery command (army level)

Arko (*Artilleriekommando*)—artillery command

AC (A.K.)—army corps

PzC (Pz.K.)—panzer corps

D (Div.)—division

    ID (I.D.) (J.D.)—infantry division

    PzD (Pz.D.)—panzer division

    ID (JD)(mot)—motorized division

    MotD (Mot.D.)—motorized division

    CavD (K.D.)—cavalry division

    MtnD—mountain division

    Sec. D—security division

    LFD—*Luftwaffe* field division

Br.—brigade

    IB (Inf.B)—infantry brigade

    MotB—motorized brigade

    PzB—panzer brigade

Rgt. (R)—regiment

    Sec.R—security regiment

    AR—artillery regiment

    IR—infantry regiment

    PzR—panzer regiment

Soviet

Commands and Forces

A—army

GA (Gds.A)—guards army

TA—tank army

TC—tank corps

GTC (Gds.TC)—guards tank corps

MC—mechanized corps

GMC (Gds.MC)—guards mechanized corps

RC—rifle corps

GRC (Gds.RC)—guards rifle corps

CC—cavalry corps

GCC (Gds.CC)—guards cavalry corps

MAC—mixed aviation corps

RD—rifle division

RDNKVD—NKVD rifle division

GRD (Gds.RD)—guards rifle division

CD—cavalry division

GCD (Gds.CD)—guards cavalry division

AAD—assault aviation division

BAD—bomber aviation division

NBAD—night bomber aviation division

FAD—fighter aviation division

MAD—mixed aviation division

FR—fortified region

RB—rifle brigade

TB—tank brigade

GTB (Gds.TB)—guards tank brigade

MB—mechanized brigade

MRB—motorized rifle brigade

NRB—naval rifle brigade

DB—destroyer brigade

RR—rifle regiment

GRR (Gds.RR)—guards rifle regiment

TR—tank regiment

German (Axis) (continued)

PzGR (Pz.Gren.R)—panzer-
grenadier regiment
EngR—engineer regiment
MotR—motorized regiment
MtrcR—motorcycle regiment
Bn (Btl.)—battalion
PzBn—panzer battalion
MotBn—motorized battalion
InfBn—infantry battalion
EngBn—engineer battalion
MG Bn—machine gun battalion
Co. (kp.)—company
Btry (battr.)—battery

Miscellaneous
Abt. (*abteilung*)—detachment or
battalion
A.A.—reconnaissance *abteilung*
Pz. A.A.—panzer reconnaissance
abteilung
Abschnitt—section or sector
Aufkl. (*Aufklarung*)—reconnaissance
Gp. (*Gruppe*)—group
HKL—front lines (*hauptkampflinie* or
main combat line)
Inf.— infantry
Kpfgp. (Kgr.)—*kampfgruppe* [combat
group]
mot.—motorized
Flak (fugabwehrkanone)—antiaircraft
guns
Jg (Jäg) (Jäger)—light
i. G.—in the General Staff
Pak (panzerabwehrkanone)—antitank
gun
Pi—Pioneer (engineer)
Pkw (*personenkraftwagon*)—personnel
carrier
Pz.Jg. (*panzer*jäger)—antitank unit
St.G. (*Stu.Gesch.*) (*stürmgeschutz*)—
assault gun
IG (*infanteriegeschutz*)—infantry gun
v.—von
z.b.V.—temporarily formed

Soviet (continued)

GTR (Gds.TR)—guards tank regiment
AR—artillery regiment
Gds.AR—guards artillery regiment
ATR—antitank regiment
TDR—tank destroyer (antitank)
artillery regiment
AAR—assault aviation regiment
BAR—bomber aviation regiment
MAR—mixed aviation regiment
RAR—reconnaissance aviation regiment
CAR—corps artillery regiment
GAR—gun artillery regiment
HAR—howitzer artillery regiment
G-MR (Gds.-MR)—guards mortar
(multiple-rocket launcher or
Katiusha) regiment
MtrR—mortar regiment
MRR—motorized rifle regiment
CR—cavalry regiment
GCR (Gds.CR)—guards cavalry
regiment
RAS—reconnaissance aviation squadron
RBn—rifle battalion
TBn—tank battalion
AABn—antiaircraft artillery battalion
ATBn—antitank battalion
MG-Arty Bn (MGArtyBn)—machine
gun–artillery battalion
G-MBn (Gds.-MBn)—guards mortar
battalion
Sep.ArmdCarBn—separate armored car
battalion
ArmdTrainBn—armored train battalion
Co—company
Btry—battery

Miscellaneous
AA—antiaircraft
Arty—artillery
AT—antitank
Cav.—cavalry
CP—command post
DAG—division artillery group
DD—long-range artillery group

German (Axis) (continued)

(R) (r. or ru.)—Romanian
(I)—Italian
(H)—Hungarian
(G)—German

Soviet (continued)

Det.—detachment
FD—forward detachment
G (Gds.) as a prefix with any
    abbreviation—guards
Gp.—group
MTF—motor tractor factory
MTS—motor tractor station
OP—observation post
PVO—antiaircraft defense
RAG—regimental artillery group
Res.—reserve
RVGK—Reserve of the *Stavka* of the
    Supreme High Command
Sep.—separate
SF—state farm

PART I

Soviet Strategic Planning

CHAPTER ONE

Framework for Disaster

FRUSTRATION

By September 1942, Adolf Hitler was acutely aware that his window of opportunity was closing. When Germany had invaded the Soviet Union 15 months earlier, Hitler, as well as his senior advisers, had confidently assumed that they could destroy the Red Army in a series of encirclement battles in the Soviet Union's western border region, battles that would lead inevitably to the collapse of the Soviet regime. Instead, both the Red Army and its parent government had demonstrated remarkable resilience, continuing to fight despite almost 4.5 million soldiers killed, wounded, and captured in the first six months alone.[1] Furthermore, though the Red Army was often suicidal, its penchant for stubbornly attacking into the teeth of the German juggernaut in defense of the Soviet homeland inflicted serious damage on the *Wehrmacht's* advancing forces. By weakening Hitler's vaunted panzer spearheads and causing attrition in his infantry, these hundreds, if not thousands, of small Russian cuts gradually weakened the invaders. This led directly to the *Wehrmacht's* unprecedented defeats at the approaches to Leningrad in the north during September and October 1941, at Rostov in the southern Soviet Union in November, and, in a surprising climax of Operation Barbarossa, in the Moscow region in December. At the gates of Moscow, senior Red Army generals watched in utter astonishment as their desperate counterattacks against the advancing Germans suddenly succeeded. Within a month, these local counterattacks had developed into multiple counterstrokes and ultimately an ambitious general counteroffensive encompassing the entire front from the Baltic to the Black Sea.

These setbacks, however, did little to dampen Hitler's offensive ardor and unquenchable appetite for total victory. The Soviets' winter counteroffensive collapsed in April 1942, and smaller-scale Red Army offensives in the Khar'kov and Crimean region ended in embarrassing defeats in May 1942. Then the German *Wehrmacht* renewed its offensive in Operation Blau (Blue) in late June and early July 1942. Yet victory eluded the Germans, despite their triumphal advances through the eastern Donbas region and across the Don River into the mountains of the Trans-Caucasus region. By

September the Germans were no closer to military victory than they had been in June.

Politically and militarily, Hitler believed that he had to reach some stable conclusion in the East by the end of 1942 so that he could confront the growing strength of the United States, on which he had declared war in December 1941.[2] Economically, the Blau offensive had so far failed to solve Germany's critical need for petroleum.[3] When Army Group A overran the small Maikop oil field in southeastern Russia on 8 August 1942, the Germans found that the retreating Soviets had destroyed all the wells and refineries in the area. Larger oil fields still beckoned at Grozny in Chechnia and in Azerbaijan, but Field Marshal Wilhelm List, the commander of Army Group A, seemed unable to advance the last few hundred kilometers to seize these prizes. Not the least of his problems was that all supplies for the army group had to be funneled through the bottleneck river city of Rostov, then transshipped from railroad cars to trucks or animal carts for the long journey forward to the Caucasus. Moreover, given the difficulties the Germans had in converting and operating the Soviet rail system, supplying the Caucasus would come at the expense of the attack on Stalingrad.

List was hamstrung not only by the long and slender logistical path to his rear but also by the growing effectiveness of the Soviet troops to his front. Almost invisibly to Hitler and his principal advisers, the Red Army had contested every meter of the 1942 German advance, launching incessant if clumsy counterattacks and counterstrokes that slowed and weakened the invaders. Some Soviet units collapsed, as they had the previous summer, and the Red Army still experienced a severe shortage of commanders and staff officers who could orchestrate the combined arms and logistical support in formations the size of a field army and larger. Nonetheless, the Soviet defenders, survivors of the bitter defeats of 1941–1942, were growing in competence and determination every day. What Hitler regarded as the excessive caution of his generals was really a necessary response to the increasing capability of their adversaries. In fact, those adversaries might have been even more dangerous were it not for the fact that the German advances, in combination with Josef Stalin's own impatience for success, had prompted the Red Army to launch many of its counteractions prematurely and without ensuring effective command and control. Such premature attacks had repeatedly sacrificed both troops and arms for want of a few extra days to prepare and coordinate. The sad reality was that attacking Red Army forces still lacked the necessary expertise to overcome prepared German defenses, much less contend with experienced German panzer forces maneuvering on an open battlefield.

List's difficulties in the Caucasus were mirrored and complicated by the problem facing Colonel General Maximilian von Weichs, commander of

Army Group B, at Stalingrad. The original operations order for the Blau campaign (Führer Directive No. 41, 4 April 1942) had barely mentioned this industrial city and transportation hub on the Volga River. Aiming for the Caucasus oil fields, the German planners had intended to bypass Stalingrad and simply neutralize it by aerial and artillery bombardment.[4] Only gradually did the city become a magnet for the Germans, primarily because its name made it a key propaganda goal.[5] Yet Army Group B lacked sufficient forces to take the city and simultaneously deflect a series of Soviet counterstrokes on both flanks of the city. General of Panzer Troops Friedrich Paulus, the commander of Sixth German Army, was able to reach the city and slowly clear it only because his army group commander, Weichs, continually reshuffled and rotated troops to give Paulus enough combat power to sustain the advance. Moreover, to put even a handful of German divisions into Stalingrad and the Caucasus, the Germans had to use other Axis troops to protect their long, vulnerable left flank. Thus, by early October 1942, Second Hungarian Army, Eighth Italian Army, and Third Romanian Army, in that order, were all stretched thin to provide this flank guard along the Don River northwest of Stalingrad, with Romanian VI and VII Army Corps (scheduled to become Fourth Romanian Army on 20 November) continuing to protect the area west of the Volga River and south of the city. Yet the Italians, Hungarians, and Romanians lacked both numbers and weapons to defend against a serious counterattack. Although a few German antitank batteries and other specialized units reinforced these satellite troops, the defenses on both flanks lacked heavy weapons and were vulnerable to a major mechanized attack.[6]

By contrast, inside Stalingrad, the defending Soviet 62nd Army under Lieutenant General Vasilii Ivanovich Chuikov received enough—although sometimes just barely enough—reinforcements to deny the city to the Germans. In two months of bitter, house-to-house fighting through the ruins of Stalingrad, the Germans lost all their advantages of maneuver warfare, and close-quarters fighting limited the use of German fighter-bombers and artillery. In fact, Chuikov's troops deliberately "hugged" the German assault groups so that German aircraft and guns could not fire, for fear of hitting their own troops. By late September, Paulus had succeeded in clearing the southern two-thirds of the city, but only at the cost of bleeding his army white. Each infantry and panzer-grenadier regiment could barely muster a few hundred combat infantrymen to continue the advance, while Chuikov's men clung grimly to the factory district in the northern part of the city. To maintain the offensive, Paulus had to rotate engineer and infantry units between the city center and flanking defenses outside.

All this increased Hitler's sense of frustration and his belief that his subordinates were failing him. Each time field commanders used their own judgment or otherwise ignored Hitler's intent, they only reinforced his suspicions. Nor was his frustration completely unjustified, considering that many of his generals persisted in thinking in terms of destroying Soviet military forces—a tactical or operational goal—while ignoring the designated strategic objective of securing more oil.[7] From Hitler's point of view, Operation Blau had degenerated into a long series of missed opportunities as the small-minded, overly cautious professional soldiers sought to dissuade their Führer from following the correct course to victory. Given the number of times these generals had been wrong in the past, the creative gambler in Hitler was naturally inclined to follow his own instincts.

Weichs had inherited command of his army group after Hitler fired his predecessor, Field Marshal Fedor von Bock, on 13 July for excessive caution during his advance. Two months later, the German dictator lost patience with the rest of his senior military leadership. On 9 September, he sent Field Marshal Wilhelm Keitel, the submissive head of the Armed Forces High Command [*Oberkommando der Wehrmacht*, or OKW], to instruct List to resign. Instead of appointing a new commander of Army Group A, for the next two months Hitler simply had the two field army commanders of that group report to him directly on alternate days! General Franz Halder, who since 1939 had loyally served Hitler as head of the German Army General Staff [*Oberkommando des Heeres*, or OKH], found himself retired on 24 September, and Hitler hinted at further dismissals. Moreover, subsequent chiefs of the General Staff no longer controlled the assignment of General Staff officers, a function that Hitler moved to his adjutant, Rudolf Schmundt.[8] Yet this shake-up simply exacerbated Germany's command problems without producing any improvement at the front. Increasingly, therefore, the German dictator avoided meeting with his staff, preferring to pass orders through the new and relatively enthusiastic General Kurt Zeitzler, who succeeded Halder as chief of the OKH.

Despite his reputation as a supporter of the Nazi regime, Zeitzler was a competent General Staff officer. He quickly became concerned about the same issues that had cost Halder his job, especially the lack of sufficient German units to seize the Caucasus oil fields and Stalingrad simultaneously. He was also acutely aware of the toxic atmosphere at headquarters, where Hitler was openly suspicious and contemptuous of his professional advisers.

In mid-October, the new chief of staff made an appointment to give Hitler a private briefing on Zeitzler's estimate of the strategic situation. Because there were no witnesses to this meeting, we have only Zeitzler's account of what transpired. Still, given his known actions during the following month, it seems probable that the general did, in fact, provide Hitler with an unvarnished appraisal. If so, then two of Zeitzler's main points proved especially prescient:

2. The most perilous sector of the Eastern Front was undoubtedly the long, thinly-held flank stretching from Stalingrad to the right boundary of Army Group Center. Furthermore, this sector was held by the weakest and least reliable of our troops, Rumanians, Italians, and Hungarians. . . .

4. The Russians [*sic*] were both better trained and better led than they had been in 1941.[9]

According to Zeitzler, Hitler heard him out without interruption, but then politely dismissed the general's entire argument, assuring Zeitzler that he was too pessimistic in his appraisal.[10] The dictator was equally optimistic when he spoke with Weichs and Paulus, apparently believing that even those subordinates he still trusted needed encouragement if not outright goading.

It would be unfair, however, to depict Hitler as a blundering amateur who ignored the threat to his flanks. During September, he made repeated efforts to bolster the defenses there. Based on Weichs's recommendations, on 13 September a Führer order directed that preparations be made for limited advances to clear and secure the flanks once Stalingrad was secured, in particular, toward the city of Astrakhan', near where the Volga ran into the Caspian Sea. The plan even allocated scarce reserve divisions, such as the 29th Motorized and 14th Panzer Divisions, to make such advances possible. Unfortunately for Hitler and for the future of Sixth German Army, the tenacious Soviet defense of that city continued for another two months, rendering the 13 September order virtually moot.[11] From the German viewpoint, Stalingrad appeared to be the last operation of 1942. To some extent, in fact, the fight for Stalingrad became a struggle by Sixth Army to acquire shelter for the impending winter.

From September onward, Hitler frequently expressed concern about the Don River flank. He often reminded his staff of Stalin's experience during the Russian Civil War, when Semion Mikhailovich Budenny's 1st Cavalry Army had conducted a rapid thrust from Stalingrad to Rostov. Therefore, Hitler ordered the German *Luftwaffe* (Air Force) to increase interdiction attacks on bridging sites over the Don and on suspected assembly areas along the river's northern bank. Further expressing his disquiet, he issued Operational Order No. 1 on 14 October and a supplement to that order on the 23rd. These directed a number of defensive precautions, including the construction of fallback positions south of the Don. Yet Hitler was intensely human, and he resented his subordinates reminding him of risks he could do little to avert. On 27 October, for example, Zeitzler reported that the Soviet government was generating a massive propaganda campaign about a forthcoming offensive. Hitler dismissed this report and instead worried about reinforcing Army Group Center, the German force opposite Moscow.[12]

Nor was the Eastern Front Hitler's only problem. As the tide turned against him in western Europe and the Mediterranean, he tried to shore up his defenses. This resulted in various efforts to defend Crete, the British Channel Islands, and North Africa, diverting scarce resources from the East. On 3 November, one of his favorite generals, Erwin Rommel, openly disobeyed the Führer by retreating from El Alamein in Egypt. This betrayal only fueled Hitler's anger at the professionals, which he vented by firing several additional staff officers. Six days later, in response to the Anglo-American invasion of northwestern Africa, Germany invaded the previously unoccupied portions of southern France.

Moreover, Hitler was physically absent from his eastern headquarters, code-named "Werewolf," in Vinnitsa, Ukraine, during the crucial two weeks of mid-November. On 7 November, the dictator left Vinnitsa to make his annual speech at Munich commemorating the 1923 Beer Hall Putsch. While in the Bavarian capital, the Führer publicly proclaimed that Paulus's Sixth Army had already secured Stalingrad, in the mistaken belief that this announcement would strengthen the resolve of the troops. His subordinates dutifully reported that this speech had reenergized the exhausted assault forces of Paulus's army. Thereafter, Hitler remained in Germany, traveling or vacationing at Berchtesgaden, until 23 November. Although he received constant reports, this absence isolated him from daily contact with Zeitzler and the OKH staff. It is tempting to attribute this absence to a subconscious desire to avoid an intractable situation, but the dictator certainly had other problems besides Stalingrad.

THE *WEHRMACHT* IN NOVEMBER 1942

The stalemate of October–November 1942 reflected the limitations of the German war machine. When Germany first invaded the Soviet Union in 1941, 19 panzer and 15 motorized infantry divisions had provided the *Wehrmacht*'s cutting edge, but the bulk of the German army still consisted of 118 foot- and horse-mobile infantry and cavalry divisions. This invasion force depended on artillery and supplies hauled by more than 600,000 horses across the Soviet Union's woefully underdeveloped transportation network, and the harsh Russian environment took an even greater toll on horses than it did on motor vehicles.[13] Germany's allies were far more limited in their equipment and mobility; for instance, there was only one Romanian armored division, equipped largely with obsolescent tanks.

For the 1942 campaign, Germany fielded several additional panzer divisions, as well as more *Waffen* (combat) SS motorized divisions, which had the same combat power as army panzer units. Overall, however, the Germans' combat power on the ground was probably less in 1942 than it had been the previous year because of the disastrous loss of vehicles, crew-served weapons, and horses during the winter of 1941–1942, to say nothing of the experienced *landsers* and officers who had perished or been maimed in the Barbarossa campaign. During the first seven months of the Soviet war, in addition to suffering almost 1 million human casualties, the Germans had lost more than 41,000 trucks and 207,000 horses, at a time when horses were the primary means of mobility for artillery and supply units in most infantry divisions. The cost in artillery, antitank guns, and mortars exceeded 13,600 gun tubes, while the *Luftwaffe* had written off 4,903 aircraft as destroyed due to battle damage and accidents.[14]

These losses were never completely replaced. Instead, to prepare for Operation Blau in 1942, the Germans prioritized their shortages. In Army Group South, where the new offensive would occur, mechanized units were supposed to reach 85 percent of their authorized strength; farther north, each panzer division was authorized enough armor to equip only one tank battalion rather than the two or three battalions of the previous year. The same was true even in some panzer divisions of First Panzer Army in the south. These battalions were just a jumble of different variants of the same tank. For example, Panzer IIIs and IVs might be identified as "short" or "long," depending on the main gun barrels; in general, the longer barrels were high-velocity guns with greater armor-piercing capabilities.

Infantry divisions fared even worse in the distribution of resources. In Army Groups North and Center, 69 out of 75 infantry divisions were reduced from nine to six battalions of infantry, and their artillery was cut from four guns per battery to three. These divisions also sustained great reductions in horse and motor transportation, making it difficult for them to redeploy forces in response to an enemy attack. Although the *Luftwaffe* reluctantly agreed to release some of its personnel for ground duty, these potential reinforcements were not transferred to the army; rather, they were formed into separate *Luftwaffe* field divisions, lacking in heavy equipment and staff experience.[15]

To complicate matters further, the majority of divisions in the East were not even withdrawn to the rear to rest and refit; they had to reconstitute themselves while still defending a sector of the front. Thus, even before the 1942 summer offensive, the typical German division was notably less capable than it had been in 1941. Because of its high production priorities, the German *Luftwaffe* began the 1942 campaign at substantially the same level (2,750 aircraft in the East) it had fielded in 1941 (2,770).[16] Still, these figures concealed a decline in the training level of aircrews after nearly three years of active warfare.

Such was the state of the *Wehrmacht* when the second great offensive began in early July 1942. Four months later, it was again only a shadow of its former self. Constant operations, fragile logistics, and incessant enemy activity wore down men, vehicles, and horses. For example, 24th Panzer Division, formed in early 1942 from the former 1st (horse) Cavalry Division, spearheaded the entire offensive and was instrumental in clearing the city of Stalingrad. Between 28 June and 31 October 1942, this division of 11,000 men suffered 5,870 killed, seriously wounded, and missing; in addition, 36 of perhaps 100 tanks were permanently destroyed, and many others were rendered nonoperational by combat and excessive wear. Another 2,791 men had been lightly wounded but remained with their units, while the division received only 2,298 replacements during this four-month period. As it gathered for another urban assault on the morning of 31 October, 24th Panzer Division's actual dismounted rifle strength, including two panzer-grenadier regiments, a motorcycle battalion, and a combat engineer battalion, was only 41 officers and 960 men.[17]

By mid-November, the 16 divisions of Sixth Army were, in the aggregate, understrength by 107,982 men, or an average of 6,748 per division. Frontline infantry units were even weaker than these overall figures suggest. Compounding this numerical weakness, the tenuous German logistical system was unable to meet requirements for ammunition and petroleum products, nor was the army able to build up winter stocks of food. On average, Sixth Army received only about half the required daily trainloads of supplies. With winter approaching on the barren steppes around Stalingrad, German horses were so malnourished that many did not survive being moved to winter recovery centers.[18] The troops were almost equally sickly after months of combat and uncertain rations. Although they suffered fewer combat losses, Germany's air formations also declined under constant use in extreme conditions. Thus, the Fourth Air Fleet [*Luftflotte* 4], the air force unit supporting Operation Blau, started with 1,600 aircraft in early July but had only 950 left in September. On any given day, perhaps 550 of these were operational, a figure that declined with the arrival of extreme cold.[19]

Such problems were not confined solely to the long-suffering troops in Stalingrad. By early November, Army Group A's effort to take the Caucasus oil fields had also reached the end of its tether. On the morning of 5 November, 13th Panzer Division, operating more than 2,000 kilometers from its starting point 16 months before, found itself cut off and surrounded in the outskirts of the city of Ordzhonikidze by the Trans-Caucasus Front's Northern Group, under the command of Lieutenant General Ivan Ivanovich Maslennikov. Although First Panzer Army eventually extricated its forces from this trap, 13th Panzer Division left behind most of its equipment as well as a significant number of casualties. Counting the losses of 13th Panzer Division and two other divisions of III Panzer Corps involved in the same fierce fight for Ordzhonikidze, the Soviets recorded destroying or capturing 40 tanks, 7 armored personnel carriers, 70 guns, 2,350 vehicles, 183 motor-cycles, more than 1 million rounds of ammunition, and countless other sup-plies, while killing more than 5,000 German and Romanian troops.[20]

Acknowledging the overall weakness of its combat forces in the East, on 8 October 1942, the OKH had directed all headquarters above division level to release 10 percent of their personnel as replacements, while all sup-port units not engaged in combat were to form standby "alarm detachments" [alarm abteilung] to respond to sudden emergencies. Six weeks later, these alarm detachments in various sizes and shapes proved to be critical in restor-ing a tenuous front line after the coming Soviet offensive.[21]

In short, by early November, the German forces were exhausted, inca-pable of doing anything more than holding their positions until the arrival of better weather and significant reinforcements. Given Hitler's consistent re-luctance to fully mobilize his economy and population, rebuilding the forces for a third campaign in Russia would be at least as difficult as the second effort had been.

GERMAN FIELD COMMANDERS

Even those German leaders who survived Hitler's housecleaning did not al-ways prosper. Paulus, the loyal workaholic who had dedicated his entire life to gaining acceptance as a General Staff officer, had long been a favorite of Hitler's, but this status would lead him to take a sacrificial role, trying to clear and then defend the city long after his shattered Sixth Army had become ineffective.

Of the many other field commanders in the East, two would emerge as pivotal in the coming campaign. The first of these, Fritz-Erich von Manstein, had just received a field marshal's baton for the brilliant offensive operations that had cleared Soviet forces from the Crimean Peninsula in May and cap-tured the Soviet fortress of Sevastopol' in early July. On 20 November 1942, he was preparing his Eleventh Army for a new attack near Vitebsk when Hit-ler summoned him to deal with the huge breach created by the first Soviet counteroffensive against Stalingrad. Born in 1887, Manstein was a wizened disciplinarian of great ability and great ego. In the coming crisis, he nearly succeeded in his assigned task of building bricks without straw, halting and reversing the Soviet counteroffensive with a handful of threadbare German divisions. Although he was ultimately unable to save Paulus's forces, Man-stein conducted a series of brilliant offensive maneuvers that contained the great Soviet offensive and saved a large portion of the German army in the East.[22]

Manstein's great achievements and unabashed self-promotion have generally obscured the equally brilliant performance of his counterpart, Colonel General Ewald von Kleist. A committed royalist and Christian since his birth in 1881, Kleist had a distaste for Nazism that had led to his retirement in 1938. Recalled when the war began, this superb cavalryman showed a consummate grasp of mobile warfare, commanding First Panzer Army up to the gates of the Caucasus oil fields in 1942. In early November, as noted earlier, Kleist was already stymied in the Caucasus by a combination of desperate Soviet resistance, winter weather, and incredibly extended supply lines. While Manstein tried to halt the advancing Soviet torrent as head of the new Army Group Don, Kleist would have the similarly difficult, if less glamorous, task of extricating the entire Army Group A back to the Rostov area. This feat eventually earned him a marshal's baton.[23]

THE RED ARMY IN NOVEMBER 1942

Soviet forces had suffered even more than their German counterparts during Operation Blau. Between 28 June and 18 November 1942, the Red Army and Navy units defending against the German offensive suffered 694,000 dead from combat and illness, a figure that did not include the nearly 200,000 dead in the Caucasus region.[24] Despite, or perhaps because of, detailed instructions from the headquarters of the *Stavka* (Soviet Supreme High Command) in Moscow, several Soviet field armies had simply ceased to exist during the initial German advance of July–August.

Nowhere were these losses more serious than in Stalingrad itself. Between 14 September and 26 October 1942, nine Red Army divisions and five separate brigades crossed the Volga River into the ruined city, yet by 1 November, Chuikov had no more troops—perhaps 50,000 on a good day—under his command than he had possessed two months before. All the reinforcements had simply melted away in the crucible of warfare, leaving behind only a handful of men in each regiment. Small wonder, then, that the shrunken bridgeheads in the northern part of the city appeared to be on the verge of destruction when Sixth German Army also ran out of troops in early November.[25]

Despite the continued weakness of front-line forces, however, the overall Soviet force structure and combat capability were, if anything, stronger in November than they had been in July. Through a miracle of dedicated effort, the Soviets had first moved hundreds of arms factories east of the Ural Mountains during 1941 and then brought those factories back to mass production in the following spring and summer. This phenomenal mobilization allowed the Red Army to absorb huge materiel losses while still fielding new units, a situation their opponents could only dream of. Of course, creating new units rather than reequipping existing ones carried a price when inexperienced new formations entered combat. However, during 1942, the People's Commissariat of Defense (NKO) mastered the technique of using the headquarters from shattered units to provide the nuclei for new, more sophisticated formations.

Following Soviet doctrine as well as the experience of 1941, the Soviet government continued to generate new or reconstituted armies and other units on a grand scale, holding many of these formations in the *Stavka* general reserve (RVGK) until the Axis invaders had exhausted themselves. On 23 October, for example, the *Stavka* formed the 1st and 2nd Guards Armies in its strategic reserve and earmarked them for employment in the Southwestern and Western Fronts, respectively.[26] For the first time since July 1941, the Red Army began creating two full-strength field armies, each with two rifle corps (of three divisions each) and one mechanized corps, as well as artillery and combat support units. These forces represented a conscious decision that at least some Soviet commanders and staffs could integrate a complex mixture of combat arms and services in combat.

The mechanized corps themselves were the latest step in the process of constructing mobile forces capable of dealing with the Germans on almost equal terms. The initial invasion of 1941 had shattered the huge but poorly equipped and poorly trained armored forces of the prewar Red Army. For the remainder of 1941, the *Stavka* had concentrated the few available tanks in infantry support brigades, some of them numbering only 46 tanks, and separate tank battalions of even fewer tanks. During the desperate battles before Moscow, however, some of these tank brigade commanders had survived and learned how to lead their units. Such men became the leaders of the next generation of mechanized forces, the so-called tank corps of 1942. Despite their designation, each of these corps was in fact the size of a slightly understrength German division. By July 1942, a typical tank corps consisted of 7,200 to 7,600 men and 146 to 180 tanks.[27]

The father of these new units was Lieutenant General Iakov Nikolaevich Fedorenko, chief of the Red Army's Main Auto-Armored Directorate. Fedorenko used the vast new production of Soviet arms factories, supplemented by limited amounts of British and American Lend-Lease equipment, to build 28 tank corps during 1942. When the first units proved too weak to sustain prolonged combat operations, Fedorenko began to organize a related formation, the mechanized corps, which included one or two tank brigades as well as three mechanized brigades, with each of the latter including 39 medium tanks and trucked infantry. Depending on the specific table of organization, a mechanized corps varied between 175 and 204 tanks.[28]

At first, these new tank and mechanized corps experienced a number of teething problems, some due to a shortage of specialized equipment such as tracked armored personnel carriers, recovery vehicles, and radios. Worse still, although there were many competent corps commanders, these corps were often yoked with conventional infantry and cavalry units in an unwieldy structure known as a "tank army," four of which the Soviets fielded in the summer of 1942. Not only did these armies have to deal with the uneven mobility and armor of their subordinate units, but the staffs and commanders were in many ways unprepared for the task of orchestrating such a large and clumsy formation. As a result, some of the early tank corps suffered heavily in the fighting of the summer and fall of 1942, and the first tank armies fell apart under the German offensive. Again, however, the harsh school of combat experience helped develop commanders and technicians capable of operating mechanized forces.

The newfound wealth of weaponry was not confined to tanks or tank units. Across the board, more weapons permitted the creation of more specialized Soviet units. During 1942, for example, the NKO formed 192 new tank destroyer (antitank) artillery regiments, a key component in the Soviets' growing ability to wear down and contain German mechanized advances. Despite losing 31 of these regiments in combat during 1942, by the end of the year, the NKO had increased its antitank strength more than 500 percent, adding 4,117 antitank guns to the inventory.[29] Field and rocket artillery grew apace. Although the Red Army did not increase the number of artillery pieces permanently assigned to each division until 1944, it continued to create huge numbers of nondivisional artillery, rocket, and antiaircraft formations. On 31 October, the NKO prepared for the coming counteroffensive by combining many separate RVGK regiments into 18 new artillery divisions and a like number of antiaircraft artillery divisions. Each of these artillery divisions initially included three howitzer regiments, three gun regiments, and either three antitank or two antiaircraft regiments, for a total of 168 or 144 gun tubes, respectively. Command and control of such units suffered many of the same problems that had plagued mechanized units, but the creation of these divisions marked another key step in enabling senior Soviet commanders to employ their vastly expanded forces.[30]

While Hitler was losing faith in his generals, Stalin was gaining confidence in at least some of his subordinates. As the 1942 campaign progressed, the Soviet dictator retained overall control but increasingly trusted the professionalism of senior Red Army staff officers and commanders. Even commanders who lost battles escaped the kind of draconian punishment that had characterized the peacetime purges and the early battles of 1941.[31]

Stalin's renewed confidence in his commanders took many forms, from the creation of new medals and awards to distinctive uniforms for the officers.[32] Perhaps the most significant sign of this increased trust in Soviet commanders was NKO Order No. 307 of 9 October 1942, which ostensibly restored unity of command [*edinonachal'stvo*] in the armed forces. Soviet commanders at all levels regained full control of their units, with commissars and other political officers being reduced to "Members of the Military Councils" at *front* and army levels or deputy commanders for political affairs [*zampolits*] at lower command levels. This action was a clear indication that Stalin trusted his professional officers both militarily and politically. In the words of the Presidium of the Supreme Soviet decree that justified the NKO order: "The system of war commissars which was established in the Red Army during the Civil War was based on mistrust of the military commands. . . . The present patriotic war against the German invaders has welded our commands together and produced a large corps of talented new commanders who have gathered experience and who will remain true to their honor as officers to the death."[33] Stalin implemented this change at the very time that, on the German side, Hitler was scorning both the competence and the loyalty of his subordinates.

In addition, on 16 October the *Stavka* published Order No. 325 regarding the combat employment of large tank formations. Although signed by Stalin, this was, in fact, a digest of lessons learned in previous battles, lessons that would now be applied to all future operations. Improvement did not come overnight, but under Order No. 325, tank and mechanized corps would be employed as independent formations designated for maneuver warfare, rather than broken up into penny-packet units to support the infantry. Armor commanders were to engage German armor only when the Soviets had clear numerical superiority.[34] The coming winter battles would be the first opportunity to test such ideas, but these decisions clearly demonstrated the growing combat effectiveness of the much-maligned Red Army.

SOVIET FIELD COMMANDERS

There were many competent leaders in this army, and more would earn their spurs during the coming campaign. At least five senior officers had already made their mark prior to the new offensive, and all would burnish their reputations in the ensuing combat.

Georgii Konstantinovich Zhukov, age 45, was Stalin's favorite general. Having served with distinction in the Red Army's cavalry forces during and after the Russian Civil War, Zhukov won a signal victory over the vaunted Japanese Kwantung Army at Khalkhin-Gol, Manchuria, in August 1939. In recognition of his distinguished service, Stalin appointed him commander of the Kiev Special Military District in June 1940, a post he occupied until January 1941, when he became chief of the Red Army General Staff and first deputy commissar of defense.

A charter member of Stalin's wartime *Stavka*, Zhukov became the dictator's favorite "fixer," traveling to many threatened areas to coordinate local defenses and counterstrokes in 1941. In particular, he earned lasting fame for his tenacious defense of Leningrad in September 1941 and Moscow in October and November 1941. He then planned and conducted the Red Army's first great counteroffensive in the Moscow region from December 1941 through April 1942. Despite his single-minded and often ruthless conduct of the campaign, his forces saved Stalin's capital but failed to achieve the *Stavka*'s more ambitious strategic aims.

As Hitler's *Wehrmacht* conducted Operation Blau across southern Russia in July 1942, Zhukov's Western Front launched multiple counterstrokes in a vain effort to divert German attention and forces from their primary objective in the south. After Stalin rewarded Zhukov by anointing him deputy supreme commander in August 1942, the general launched a series of spectacular counteroffensives against German Army Group Center's defenses in and around the Rzhev-Viaz'ma salient west of Moscow. Although this major effort failed before achieving its ultimate objective of destroying German forces in the salient, it severely damaged German Ninth Army. Zhukov had also tied down German operational reserves in the central portion of the front, reserves desperately needed to achieve victory in the Stalingrad region. Then, replicating the feat he had performed roughly a year earlier when he saved Leningrad and Moscow, Zhukov sped south in September to the Stalingrad region, where he orchestrated the Stalingrad Front's multiple counterstrokes against German panzer forces in the Kotluban' region northwest of Stalingrad. Though genuinely bloody and costly defeats, these magnificent suicidal thrusts decisively unhinged German Sixth Army's plan to seize Stalingrad by a panzer coup de main and ultimately transformed Stalin's namesake city into Sixth Army's grave. Thus, by the middle of fall 1942, the ruthless, calculating Zhukov remained Stalin's most trusted field commander and played a major role in planning the series of ambitious Red Army counteroffensives in November and December 1942.[35]

Forty-seven-year-old Colonel General Aleksandr Mikhailovich Vasilevsky, the chief of the General Staff, was equally important to the Soviet conduct of war. Vasilevsky was one of the few soldiers who enjoyed Stalin's trust, in part because he was a key staff officer and had remained in Moscow during the 1941 defense of the capital, when most of the government had evacuated the city. He was a protégé of Marshal of the Soviet Union Boris Mikhailovich Shaposhnikov, the "father" of the Red Army General Staff. Vasilevsky was arguably the most skilled member of the *Stavka* and Stalin's second most trusted general, after Zhukov. A former infantry officer who did not enjoy the benefits of belonging to Stalin's "cavalry clique," Vasilevsky had advanced through merit alone and had joined the General Staff after his graduation from the General Staff Academy in the purge-truncated class of 1937.

Rising from colonel to colonel general in four years, Vasilevsky became deputy chief of the General Staff's Operations Directorate in May 1940, where he played a vital role in developing the Red Army's defense and mobilization plans during the last few months of peace. In the wake of the German invasion, Stalin appointed Vasilevsky as chief of the General Staff's Operations Directorate and deputy chief of the General Staff in August 1941. While he helped plan most of the major operations the Red Army conducted in 1941 and 1942, Vasilevsky also served as a "representative of the *Stavka*," or Stalin's troubleshooter in the field, during many of these operations. He would reprise this role numerous times during the counteroffensives of late 1942.[36]

Andrei Ivanovich Eremenko was another member of the Red Army's cavalry clique during the Russian Civil War. When Germany invaded the Soviet Union, he advanced rapidly to the senior commands of the army and earned the sobriquet the "Russian Guderian." Known for his audacity and tenacity in combat, he temporarily headed the Western Front during the intense fighting in the Smolensk region in July and August 1941, and he led the Briansk Front in its futile attempts to contain Guderian's famous southward advance toward Kiev in September 1941 and during its defense of the southwestern approaches to Moscow in October 1941, when he was severely wounded. Because of his reputation as a fighter, the *Stavka* appointed Eremenko to command the Southeastern Front in the defense of Stalingrad during the climactic stages of the Germans' Operation Blau. In these positions, Eremenko suffered not only several wounds in battle but also much verbal badgering from Stalin. Yet, at various times, Eremenko, together with his political officer Nikita Sergeyevich Khrushchev, controlled not only his own *front* but also the neighboring Stalingrad Front. His retention in such critical positions indicates that the 50-year-old general had earned Stalin's trust as a methodical if not necessarily brilliant commander.[37] Eremenko justified Stalin's trust by becoming the chief architect of the forthcoming Red Army counteroffensive in the Stalingrad region.

The fourth member of this panoply of leading Red Army generals was 46-year-old Konstantin Konstantinovich Rokossovsky, who became the Red Army's most accomplished army commander by mid-1942. Rokossovsky had earned his spurs commanding cavalry battalions and regiments during the Civil War and a cavalry brigade, division, and corps during the 1920s and 1930s. Despite being caught up in Stalin's great purges, with Timoshenko's and Zhukov's help, he was exonerated and assigned to command the Kiev Special Military District's 9th Mechanized Corps on the eve of the German invasion in June 1941. Thereafter, amidst the Red Army's catastrophic defeats in Operation Barbarossa, Rokossovsky earned recognition as the Red Army's premier "fireman" by successfully leading 9th Mechanized Corps in the border battles of late June 1941, Special Group Iartsevo during the two-month struggle in the Smolensk region, and 16th Army in the battle for Moscow. Where countless other senior officers failed, Rokossovsky succeeded. Unlike many other Red Army generals of this era, he earned the respect of his troops for his reluctance to cavalierly sacrifice their lives for the sake of uncertain victory. The *Stavka* rewarded Rokossovsky for his prowess by appointing him to command the Briansk Front in July 1942 and the Don Front three months later.[38]

Finally, Colonel General Nikolai Fedorovich Vatutin, already recognized for his brilliance as a senior staff officer, would prove himself an able field commander during the Red Army's counteroffensive at Stalingrad. An experienced General Staff officer and veteran of the Russian Civil War, this infantry officer commanded at the company level before rising through various key staff positions to become the Kiev Special Military District's chief of staff in 1940 and then chief of the Red Army General Staff's Operations Directorate and first deputy chief of the General Staff on the eve of the Great Patriotic War. A 40-year-old protégé of Vasilevsky, Vatutin, while serving as the Northwestern Front's chief of staff during the initial stages of Operation Barbarossa, won high praise from the *Stavka* for orchestrating major counterstrokes against German Army Group North in the Sol'tsy and Staraia Russa regions in July and August 1941. Although both these actions ended in defeat, they surprised the Germans, inflicted severe damage on several key German divisions, and delayed Army Group North's advance on Leningrad for as much as four weeks, ultimately facilitating Zhukov's successful defense of that city in September 1941. Vatutin further burnished his reputation as an audacious and skilled fighter in October 1941, when he organized and led a special operational group that thwarted German Army Group Center's advance on Kalinin, thereby preventing the Germans from severing Soviet communications between Moscow and Leningrad.[39]

By virtue of these accomplishments, the *Stavka* appointed Vatutin, who was chomping at the bit for a field command, to head the Red Army's Voronezh Front in its defense against German forces conducting Operation Blau. Vatutin, displaying characteristic audacity and ever-increasing skill, mounted multiple counterstrokes in the Voronezh region during July and August 1942, materially slowing the German advance toward Stalingrad and posing a deadly threat to Army Group B's northern flank. As the German tide crested and then ebbed in the rubble of Stalingrad during October 1942, the

Stavka appointed Vatutin command of the new Southwestern Front, which would play a vital role in the forthcoming Stalingrad counteroffensive.

In addition to these five distinguished *front* commanders who had already earned recognition as effective fighters prior to the battle for Stalingrad, the heated and often desperate struggle in the Stalingrad and Caucasus regions in the fall of 1942 produced an entire generation of effective battle-tested, combat-hardened leaders at the army, corps, and division levels within the Red Army. At the same time, 18 months of war saw other generals emerge with branch expertise. Like General Fedorenko, the Red Army's expert on the formation and employment of armored forces, new experts emerged within the Red Army's force branches, including General Aleksandr Aleksandrovich Novikov for the air forces, General Nikolai Nikolaevich Voronov for the artillery, General Mikhail Petrovich Vorob'ev for engineer and sapper forces, and General Andrei Vasil'evich Khrenov, the army's chief logistician. Some of these experts, along with other senior General Staff officers and former *front* commanders such as Vasilevsky and Marshal Timoshenko, later served as *Stavka* representatives tasked with planning and coordinating major operations that required their expertise.[40]

Thus, if success in the Stalingrad counteroffensive required the leadership and expertise of *front* and army commanders who had already proved themselves in combat, the ensuing offensive would produce an entirely new generation of capable and experienced army, corps, division, and brigade commanders. These men, forged, tested, and hardened in the fighting at Stalingrad, would lead the Red Army to ultimate victory in the war.

CHAPTER TWO

Soviet Strategic Planning:
The Genesis of Plan Uranus

While Friedrich Paulus and Vasilii Chuikov sacrificed their two field armies to take and hold individual buildings in the ruined city of Stalingrad, the larger war went on around them. Adolf Hitler, as noted earlier, had to contend not only with stalemate in the Caucasus but also with defeat in North Africa, in particular, at El Alamein during the last week of October 1942, which culminated in a westward offensive by the British Eighth Army in early November. His adversary Josef Stalin was almost equally frustrated, particularly by what he regarded as insufficient support from Britain and the United States. Although Lend-Lease weapons began to reach the Soviets in quantity during 1942, Stalin consistently demanded a true "second front," by which he meant a major British-American invasion of northwestern Europe.[1]

At the same time, believing that the counteroffensive at Moscow in December 1941 to defeat Operation Barbarossa was not just a historical "quirk," the *Stavka* was convinced it could replicate that performance by organizing another counteroffensive to defeat Operation Blau. Therefore, after German forces reached the Stalingrad region in September 1942, Moscow began planning its own major counteroffensive designed to regain the initiative by encircling German Sixth Army and ultimately destroying Army Groups A and B.

The true story of how this plan evolved into the Soviet victory at Stalingrad is obscured by vanity and self-interest on both sides. German participants, seeking to avoid responsibility for the disaster, ascribed the entire failure to Hitler. Accounts by Soviet commanders and staff officers, by contrast, have been warped by the political shifts within the USSR, beginning with Premier Khrushchev's de-Stalinization program of the early 1960s and continuing in the Russian Federation to the present day. At various times, memoirs and other Soviet accounts have either exaggerated or belittled the roles of Stalin, Zhukov, Vasilevsky, Eremenko, and the other major players.

WHO FORMULATED PLAN URANUS? THE HISTORICAL DEBATE

In general, the predominant interpretation follows the assertions of Marshal of the Soviet Union Georgii Zhukov. Specifically, Zhukov claimed that, following his strategic guidance, the *Stavka* began planning for the Stalingrad counteroffensive during meetings held at the Kremlin on 12 and 13 September 1942. According to this account, this counteroffensive was unique, in that it was based on a "different solution" to the dilemma of conducting a counteroffensive—that is, it involved a broad (or wide) envelopment of all Axis forces in the Stalingrad region. In contrast, the "old solution" that the *Stavka* had been pursuing since the end of August 1942 involved a far shallower encirclement operation designed to envelop and destroy primarily German Sixth Army in the immediate vicinity of Stalingrad by attacks from the land bridge between the Don and Volga Rivers north of Stalingrad and the Beketovka bridgehead and lake region south of Stalingrad. The Soviets had repeatedly failed to penetrate the German flanks outside Stalingrad; now they would seek a broader encirclement by targeting the weaker satellite troops northwest and south of the German positions.

As Stalin's trusted deputy commander in chief, Zhukov first claimed authorship of this great plan in his memoirs, which were first published in 1969. Stalin's deputy described a series of meetings with the dictator on 12–13 September 1942 during which he and Vasilevsky developed and then presented to Stalin the concept for a "different solution," which he described as "a large-scale operation that would enable us to avoid squandering our prepared and half-prepared reserves on isolated operations."[2] Indeed, Vasilevsky's memoirs, which were published in 1973, include a similar account. But both these memoirs sharply contradict the description of planning for the Stalingrad counteroffensive by General A. I. Eremenko, the former commander of the Stalingrad Front. Eremenko's memoirs, which were published in the midst of Khrushchev's de-Stalinization program and the associated "thaw" in Soviet historical censorship in 1961, assert that he first surfaced the concept of a broad encirclement of Sixth Army in proposals he sent to the *Stavka* on 6 and 9 October 1942. In fact, this concept, which exploited the clear weaknesses of Germany's satellite armies, became the blueprint for Operation Uranus. Furthermore, Eremenko claimed that the antecedents for the Uranus plan matured slowly over several months before culminating in his October blueprints: "The concept of the counteroffensive at Stalingrad, while first occurring to me when I was still in Moscow (1–2 August 1942), ripened and strengthened and gradually matured into a concrete plan and into practical preparations for a counteroffensive during the defensive fighting for the city. Its preparation began in the most difficult period of the Stalingrad defense, in August–September, when we and N. S. Khrushchev headed the two *fronts*."[3] Eremenko went on to describe the combat experiences on which he based his rationale for a far broader envelopment of Axis forces in the Stalingrad region:

Our first measures were, naturally, to select favorable axes for the strikes and prepare appropriate jumping-off positions for the offensive. To do so, we had to act so that the enemy would not understand our concepts. To that end, at the end of August, the 21st and 63rd Armies on the most distant right wing of the Stalingrad Front successfully conducted an operation to seize and widen bridgeheads on the right bank of the Don River in the vicinity of Rubezhanskii, Kotovskii, Beliaevskii, and also in the Raspopinskaia and Kletskaia region; these actions were aimed at rendering assistance to Stalingrad's defenders. The 1st Guards Army widened the bridgehead in the small bend in the Don, in the Novo-Grigor'evskaia region, reaching the Malo-Melovskii, Malye Iarki, Shokhin, and Sirotinskaia line.

Two important operations were also conducted in the south during the period from 25 September through 4 October:

The first operation was aimed at seizing the defile between the lakes [south of Stalingrad], which was in enemy hands, to create favorable conditions for the forthcoming offensive. The counterstroke carried out by 57th and 51st Armies fulfilled its missions well. . . . 57th Army advanced to the Tsatsa-Semkin line, by doing so securing the exit from the defile between Lakes Sarpa (north), Tsatsa, and Barmantsak.

The second operation, which consisted of an attack toward Sadovoe, was conducted by 57th Army.[4]

Although there were significant differences between Eremenko's proposals in early October and the final plan for Operation Uranus, archival evidence makes it abundantly clear that Eremenko himself suggested the general concept for the counteroffensive.

A host of newly released Russian archival materials, as well as the precarious course of combat in the Stalingrad region, confirms Eremenko's assertions. First and foremost among this evidence are the detailed entries in Stalin's official appointments diary, a schedule of the dictator's daily activities that describes, hour by hour and even minute by minute, all meetings with his key military and civilian advisers and subordinates. Although the diary does not include a record of the matters discussed at these meetings, it confirms who attended them and, by virtue of the posts these individuals held, strongly implies the topics of conversation. This material proves that Zhukov's and Vasilevsky's assertions are patently incorrect.

For example, Stalin's diary reflects no meetings whatsoever with Zhukov between 31 August and 26 September, nor with Vasilevsky from 9 through 21 September. This does not exclude the possibility that Stalin's two trusted subordinates gave him advice by telephone or teletype, but it suggests that the true authorship of the plan lies elsewhere.[5] Certainly, it is unlikely that

Zhukov would have discussed such a risky proposal anywhere but in a direct meeting with the dictator. The meetings to which Zhukov referred actually took place from 27 to 29 September and culminated in early October, when the *Stavka* adopted its concept for the conduct of multiple strategic counter-offensives in the fall of 1942.

Furthermore, the actual course of combat in the Stalingrad region indicates that Zhukov's and Vasilevsky's interpretation are mistaken. Prior to the end of the first week of October 1942, all Soviet efforts to envelop and defeat German Sixth Army's forces in the Stalingrad region adhered rigidly to the "old solution"—that is, the attacks emanated from the land bridge north of Stalingrad and the Beketovka bridgehead and lake region south of the city, striking German units on those flanks of Stalingrad. In fact, a *Stavka* directive mandating continued counterstrokes in the Kotluban' and Beke-tovka regions after countless failures prompted Eremenko to propose an altogether "different solution" to the problem—that is, the broader envelopment. Therefore, the concept for Operation Uranus clearly took shape only after intensive discussions between the *Stavka* and its *front* commanders, and it was based largely on the specific recommendations of those senior commanders.

What follows is an abbreviated description of the strategic planning for the November counteroffensive, based primarily on Stalin's personal calendar and key *Stavka* and *front* directives, orders, and other planning documents. The *Companion* to this volume includes an appendix containing a detailed chronology of this strategic and operational planning and full translations of the most important planning documents.

COMPETING OFFENSIVE CONCEPTS

As clearly demonstrated by the Red Army's response to Germany's 1941 offensive, both Stalin's inclinations and Soviet military doctrine emphasized offensive action, even when operating as part of an overall strategic defense. The disastrous Soviet offensives at Khar'kov and in the Crimea in May 1942, for example, were intended to disrupt the expected German summer offensive by penetrating the enemy front through weak satellite forces.[6] Once Operation Blau began in July, the *Stavka*'s almost knee-jerk response was to unleash a series of counterstrokes, stubbornly seeking to penetrate German Army Group B's left flank at multiple locations stretching from the Voronezh region southeastward along the Don River to Kotluban' and the land bridge between the Don and Volga Rivers. Stalin's determination to halt or at least weaken the German advance by conducting powerful offensive actions elsewhere along the front prompted intense, bloody, and often futile Red Army attacks in the Bolkhov, Zhizdra, Rzhev, and Demiansk regions much farther north. As was the case in 1941, Stalin and his key military advisers firmly believed that only attrition produced by hundreds of small cuts could bring the German Blau offensive to a fatal end.

Given the persistence of these counterstrokes against Army Group B's immediate, close, and distant flanks, as well as the Germans' awareness of what had occurred at Moscow in December 1941, in retrospect, it seems incredible that the Germans were unprepared to deal with the Uranus offensive that began on 19 November. Yet a single overarching factor explains why the Germans remained confident that they could successfully contend with any Soviet offensive effort. Their confidence was based on an innate belief in their own superiority, reinforced by the reality that they had prevailed on numerous previous occasions, usually with relative ease. For example, since Hitler unleashed his Blau offensive on 28 June, *Wehrmacht* and other Axis forces had successfully thwarted no fewer than eight attempts by the Red Army to defeat or at least slow the German advance through the eastern Donbas region toward the Volga at Stalingrad. These included:

- 6–26 July: Repeated counterstrokes by the Briansk Front's 5th Tank, 60th and 40th Armies, and Group Chibisov in the Voronezh region.
- 23–31 July: A counteroffensive by the Stalingrad Front's 1st and 4th Tank and 62nd Armies in the "Great Bend" of the Don River, coupled with a renewed offensive by the Briansk Front in the Voronezh region.
- 23–29 August: Concentric counterstrokes by the Stalingrad Front's Groups Kovalenko and Shtevnev against Sixth Army's XIV Panzer Corps in the Kotluban' sector of the land bridge between the Don and Volga Rivers.
- 3–12 September: An offensive by the Stalingrad Front's 4th Tank, 1st Guards, and 24th and 66th Armies, orchestrated by Zhukov, against Sixth Army's XIV Panzer Corps in the Kotluban'-Erzovka sector of the land bridge between the Don and Volga Rivers.
- 18 September–2 October: An offensive by the Stalingrad Front's 1st Guards and 24th and 66th Armies against Sixth Army's XIV Panzer Corps in the Kotluban' region.
- 29 September–7 October: An offensive by the Stalingrad Front's 57th, 51st, and 64th Armies against Fourth Panzer Army's defenses in the Beketovka and lake regions south of Stalingrad.
- 20–26 October: An offensive by the Don Front's 24th and 66th Armies against Sixth Army's XIV Panzer Corps in the Kotluban' region.
- 24 October–2 November: An offensive by the Stalingrad Front's 64th Army against Fourth Panzer Army's defenses in the Kuporosnoe region.

In the first two efforts in July, the *Stavka* attempted to halt or slow the German forces conducting Operation Blau before they reached the strategic depths. Initially, it sought to do so by collapsing Army Group B's right wing in the Voronezh region and southeastward along the Don River. When these counterstrokes failed, it tried again to assault, defeat, and destroy Sixth Army, the German spearhead, in late July with direct frontal attacks by 62nd and 64th Armies, coupled with concentrated armored thrusts against Sixth Army's flanks by 1st and 4th Tank Armies. Unfortunately, these efforts failed, and German forces reached the Volga River north and south of Stalingrad, isolating 62nd Army in the city. Thereafter, the *Stavka* conducted two offensives in late August and mid-September designed to pierce the narrow cordon of German forces north and northwest of Stalingrad and restore a contiguous front extending northwestward from the city. Subsequently, during the offensives it conducted from late September through early October, the *Stavka* attempted to encircle German forces by achieving a shallow envelopment of the city—the so-called old solution. Each such attempt began with concentric attacks from the north and south, that is, a close envelopment of German Sixth Army's forces in the Stalingrad region by multiple armies attacking southward from the Kotluban' and Erzovka region and northward from the Beketovka bridgehead and lake region south of Stalingrad. Yet all these efforts to break Sixth Army's iron grip on 80 percent of the city failed, often dramatically and with heavy losses.

Therefore, by late September and early October, it was clear to some in the *Stavka* and to many, if not most, of the commanders of Red Army *fronts* and armies operating in the vicinity of Stalingrad that it was utterly futile, if not outright suicidal, to continue to try to drive Sixth Army from the Stalingrad region by the old solution. This realization, particularly on the part of General Eremenko, the Stalingrad Front's commander, ultimately prompted the *Stavka* to radically alter its offensive plans, abandoning the old solution and adopting a different concept involving a far broader envelopment aimed at encircling and destroying all Axis forces in the Stalingrad region—a counteroffensive code-named Uranus.[7]

Since the concept for Operation Uranus differed so radically from that of Red Army offensives conducted since late July 1942, it is important to examine the Soviet planning process in the context of two broad but critical realities: first, the ever-increasing weakness of Army Group B and its spearhead, German Sixth Army, as Operation Blau evolved; and second, the extensive planning time required to formulate Uranus in light of the prolonged struggle for Stalingrad and the extreme difficulties encountered. In the first instance, by November 1942, Army Group B had become woefully overextended; its armies, corps, and divisions had been bled white, and its vulnerable flanks were defended by a thin layer of far weaker and less experienced Axis satellite forces. In the second, unlike the frantic counterstrokes the *Stavka* had orchestrated from July through September 1942 (and, for that matter, unlike some subsequent operations conducted on an almost ad hoc basis in December 1942 and January 1943), the concept for Operation Uranus developed in fits and starts as Soviet fortunes ebbed and flowed. This erratic planning reflected the *Stavka's* persistent uncertainty as to whether Stalingrad's defenders would be able to hold out or would be forced to abandon the city outright. Ultimately, therefore, Uranus involved weeks if not months of constant revision, careful planning, and time-consuming and tedious preparations. Although this uncertainty accorded the *Stavka* and its subordinate *fronts* more time to assemble troops, weapons, and munitions, it also clouded the issue of where and when these forces should be employed.

As for the Red Army's formations and units themselves, those that had fought in previous battles tended to have more experienced staffs and more time to train before the counteroffensive. New units also gained time for training as a result of the *Stavka's* reluctance to commit them to combat before it was absolutely required by the steadily evolving offensive plans. Admittedly, problems persisted in virtually every aspect of offensive preparations and were most pronounced in the vital realm of logistics. However, compared with previous Red Army efforts, Operation Uranus was the first adequately prepared, deliberate Soviet offensive of the war. Despite the 62nd Army's desperate straits in October, for the first time in the war, Stalin and his generals displayed iron nerve in waiting until the Axis was completely vulnerable and the Soviets were completely ready for the counteroffensive.[8]

As indicated earlier and described in the first and second volumes of this trilogy, the General Staff's Operations Directorate, the *Stavka's* chief planning organ, had been considering a variety of offensive options in the southern Soviet Union since late July 1942. In at least in one instance, these options even included a crude attempt to implement the so-called different solution. For example, within days after the Germans began Operation Blau on 28 June, General Vasilevsky, who became chief of the General Staff that month, had established a small cell of staff officers, supervised by Major General Fedor Efimovich Bokov, that was assigned the task of developing alternative solutions for conducting a strategic counteroffensive on the approaches to Stalingrad. Bokov, who had served as the General Staff's chief military commissar from August 1941 through July 1942 and as deputy chief of the General Staff for organizational questions since early August, also became the titular head of the General Staff during Vasilevsky's many absences in the field. At the time, General Sergei Matveevich Shtemenko, the chronicler of the General Staff during wartime, was chief of the Operations Directorate's Southeastern Axis [Direction] Section. Bokov later described

Shtemenko as "a wonderful person and a good Party worker, but not trained for the operational side of staff work."[9]

Under Vasilevsky's tutelage, Bokov and his associates drafted a number of concepts for a counteroffensive. The most significant was a general offensive to be conducted by three *fronts* in late July, described as follows:

> [A] draft counteroffensive operation with the forces of three *fronts*— Briansk, Voronezh, and Stalingrad (1st formation), in cooperation with the forces of the Southern Front, was worked out in the Operations Directorate of the General Staff. The idea of the concept consisted of the delivery of a series of attacks along the 600-kilometer front from the Elets region to Kalach-on-the-Don, with the aim the destruction of Army Groups "B" and "A" and reaching the Shchigry-Volchansk line and further along the Northern Donets River [see map 1]. The main attack was to be conducted by the adjoining wings of the Briansk and Voronezh Fronts toward Kupiansk to reach the deep rear of the enemy's shock grouping. The concept was characterized by the breadth of the operational thought but the Soviet Army did not possess the necessary forces for its realization in this period.[10]

For a variety of reasons analyzed in volume 1 of this trilogy, this offensive ultimately shrank into two poorly coordinated counterstrokes. The first was mounted by the Stalingrad Front's 62nd and 64th Armies and 1st and 4th Tank Armies against German Sixth Army in the Great Bend of the Don during late July. The second was launched by the Briansk Front's Group Chibisov and elements of 60th and 40th Armies in the Voronezh region during the same period. Although both counterstrokes failed, the strategic concept justifying these efforts directly contradicted Zhukov's and Vasilevsky's later assertion that "the concept about the search for a 'different solution,' which would fundamentally change the strategic situation on the Soviet-German front, appeared on 12 September 1942 at a meeting in the *Stavka*." In fact, the *Stavka* had already considered and even planned for a "different solution," even if it faltered after heavy fighting due to the weakness and inexperience of the Red Army's attacking forces.

Thereafter, throughout August and September and into the first part of October, all of the *Stavka*'s offensive planning focused strictly on the immediate need to delay Army Group B's advance and prevent Sixth Army from capturing Stalingrad. By all accounts, Stalin, Zhukov, Vasilevsky, and other *Stavka* members were so preoccupied with these defensive battles that they were unable to develop any overarching concept for a general counteroffensive in the near future. This laser-like focus on absolute necessity produced the four counterstrokes the Red Army conducted in the Stalingrad region

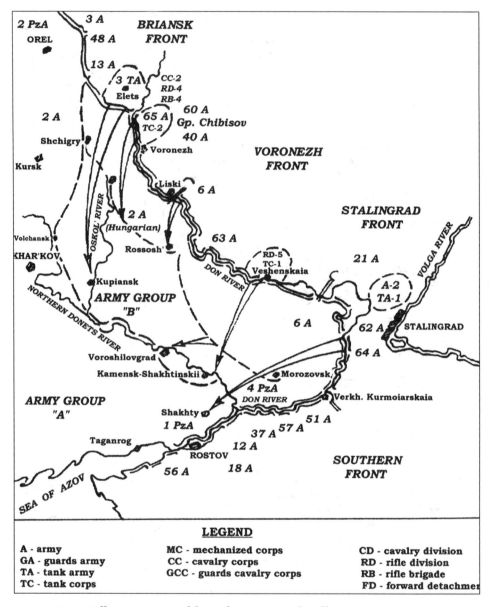

Map 1. Offensive concept of the Red Army General Staff's Operations Directorate,
27 July 1942

from 23 August through 7 October. In fact, Zhukov himself planned, organized, and supervised the first of these efforts after Stalin dispatched him to
the Stalingrad Front's rear area at Kamyshin on 29 August.

Immediately after arriving in late August, Zhukov visited the Stalingrad
Front's headquarters at Malaia Ivanovka, near Kamyshin, to discuss fighting in the Stalingrad region. Later, he visited the *front's* auxiliary command
post, the headquarters of 1st Guards Army, to work with Lieutenant General
V. N. Gordov, deputy commander of the Stalingrad Front; G. M. Malenkov,
Stalin's political representative in the region; Lieutenant General K. S. Moskalenko, commander of 1st Guards Army; Major General D. N. Nikishev, the
Stalingrad Front's chief of staff; and Major General I. N. Rukhle, the Stalingrad Front's chief of operations. Thereafter, Zhukov remained in the region
to help plan, coordinate, and supervise operations until 26 September. Zhukov claimed in his memoirs that he returned to Moscow for a two-day visit
on 12 September and met with Stalin and the *Stavka* to propose his concept
for a "different solution." However, his name does not appear in Stalin's daily
appointments for either date.[11]

During Zhukov's month-long stay in the Stalingrad region, he adhered
strictly to the concept of the old solution, that is, defeating and perhaps destroying German Sixth Army by means of a shallow envelopment. Thus, Zhukov himself planned and coordinated the counterstrokes by the Stalingrad
Front's 4th Tank, 1st Guards, and 24th and 66th Armies from the Kotluban'
and Erzovka regions from 3 to 12 September and by the same *front's* 1st
Guards and 24th and 66th Armies from 18 September to 2 October. Before
he returned to Moscow on 26 September, Zhukov also ordered and helped
plan the offensive by the Southeastern (later Stalingrad) Front's 57th, 51st,
and 64th Armies from the Beketovka bridgehead and lake region south of
Stalingrad between 29 September and 7 October. To his credit, even if these
offensives failed (as had been the case at Leningrad and Moscow in September and December 1941), Zhukov's "old solution" offensives arguably saved
Stalingrad from falling into German hands by utterly confounding Sixth Army's ambitious offensive plan.

Even after Zhukov returned to Moscow on 26 September, he demonstrated his continued commitment to the old solution of a shallow envelopment of German forces in the Stalingrad region in three fundamental ways.
First, because he perceived that the chaotic and ineffective command and
control was the primary cause of the Red Army's previous defeats in the region, he persuaded Stalin and the *Stavka* to reorganize Soviet forces to improve their defensive effectiveness. Acting on Zhukov's recommendations,
the *Stavka* issued a directive on 28 September disbanding the Stalingrad and
Southeastern Fronts, both of which had been awkwardly under Eremenko's

control, and replacing them with two new *fronts*, each with more focused missions and far clearer territorial responsibilities.[12]

The new Don Front would control the six armies situated north and northwest of Stalingrad (63rd, 21st, 4th Tank, 1st Guards, 24th, and 66th Armies). Seemingly, the most logical candidate for Don Front commander would have been General Gordov, Eremenko's former deputy, but Zhukov told Stalin that although Gordov was a competent planner, he had personality conflicts with his subordinates. Given Zhukov's own abrasive style, one can only imagine how offensive Gordov's manner must have been! Instead, the command went to Lieutenant General Konstantin Konstantinovich Rokossovsky, a 45-year-old cavalryman of mixed Polish and Russian ancestry. In mid-September, Zhukov had brought Rokossovsky to Stalingrad to assist him in coordinating the battle. Indeed, according to several accounts, during the 21–24 September crisis, Zhukov had appointed his protégé to replace Eremenko as Stalingrad commander.[13] In any case, Rokossovsky was an experienced *front* commander who performed brilliantly in the coming offensive. The new Stalingrad Front, shrunken in size but still commanded by Eremenko, would control the five armies in Stalingrad and south of the city (62nd, 64th, 57th, 51st, and 28th Armies), thus permitting the former commander of the Southeastern Front to focus on the defensive struggle within the city.

Second, to improve operational planning, the *Stavka* cleansed both *fronts* of what Zhukov perceived as "dead wood" among their command cadre, relieving General Gordov and General Rukhle, Eremenko's chief of operations. Third and most significantly, over the objections of his two *front* commanders, Zhukov insisted that they continue their counterstrokes in the Kotluban' and Beketovka regions well into October. If nothing else, doing so would maintain pressure on Paulus's Sixth Army and facilitate planning for a future counteroffensive by preventing Army Group B and Sixth Army from reinforcing the defenses of their Axis allies on Stalingrad's distant flanks.

Although the counterstrokes did little more than weaken and slow Sixth Army's assault on the city, they served as a vital catalyst in discrediting the old solution based on the shallow envelopment of German forces in Stalingrad. Specifically, the repeated bloody failures convinced Stalin, other *Stavka* members, and, to a far greater degree, his two *front* commanders in the region of the utter futility of attacking in such close proximity to Stalingrad.

Despite the Red Army's repeated failures to weaken Sixth Army's iron grip on Chuikov's 62nd Army in Stalingrad, Stalin apparently authorized the *Stavka* and the General Staff to begin planning for a general counteroffensive to proceed.[14] Meetings with Zhukov, Vasilevsky, Bokov, and other key military planners in Stalin's Kremlin office from 27 to 29 September 1942 produced a series of *Stavka* directives mandating the conduct of major counteroffensives in several front sectors (see appendix 2A in the *Companion* for details on each session with Stalin and the specific directives issued). The topics discussed at these meeting closely corresponded with those Zhukov asserted were discussed on 12–13 September, meaning that planning for the counteroffensive actually took place about two weeks later than previously believed. Immediately after the last meeting in the Kremlin adjourned on 29 September, Zhukov returned to the Stalingrad region to discuss options for conducting Operation Uranus with the commanders of the Don and Stalingrad Fronts. He remained there until 3 October. Therefore, substantive discussions regarding the form, strength, and timing of the Uranus offensive (as well as Operation Mars) began on 27 September and intensified during the first week of October as Zhukov consulted with his commanders at the front. After the deputy supreme commander returned to Moscow on 3 October, he again discussed future offensive options with the *Stavka*, this time with the recommendations of his *front* commanders in hand.

TRIUMPH OF THE "DIFFERENT SOLUTION," 1–13 OCTOBER

The most important developments during this phase of the planning cycle took place on 1–6 October, when initial discussions on Operations Uranus and Mars occurred; 6–9 October, when Rokossovsky, Eremenko, and the latter's commissar, Khrushchev, dispatched their recommendations to the *Stavka*; and 10–13 October, when Zhukov submitted the final draft plans for Operations Uranus and Mars to Stalin for approval (see appendix 2B in the *Companion*). Most significant was the exchange of orders and proposals among Stalin and Zhukov in the *Stavka*; Vasilevsky, the *Stavka's* representative in the Stalingrad region; and *front* commanders Rokossovsky and Eremenko. This flurry of exchanges began on 5 October, when the *Stavka* informed Eremenko and Rokossovsky that, in addition to considering options for conducting a general counteroffensive in the Stalingrad region, it was directing them to mount counterstrokes north and south of the city designed to assist 62nd Army's defense; the *Stavka* also asked to receive their recommendations with regard to the general counteroffensive by day's end on 6 October.[15]

Instead of coordinating their response with Vasilevsky, Eremenko and Khrushchev contacted the *Stavka* directly on the sixth. Their lengthy report not only questioned the wisdom of pursuing a shallow encirclement (the old solution) but also recommended the conduct of a much broader encirclement (a different solution) to avoid the likelihood of future defeats. The *front* commander and his commissar began by asserting, "We need to seek solutions for the mission of destroying the enemy in the Stalingrad region in a strike toward Kalach by strong groups from the north and a strike toward Abganerovo and further to the southwest from the south, that is also toward Kalach from the 57th and 51st Armies' fronts." Their rationale for this different solution included four key judgments based on previous combat experiences:

1. The weak combat capability of enemy forces in the sectors of the intended penetration, which provides an opportunity for a more rapid penetration of the front, and, as is well known, the factor of time in the circumstances of a counteroffensive has exceptional importance.

2. The knowledge of the low combat capability of enemy forces on the flanks, therefore our planned penetration on a broad front eases the securing of our own flanks after the penetration. The fact that we will not go in on a narrow opening but we will instead encroach on a wide front will create a situation such that there is no way the enemy will have sufficient reserves for fortifying a wide breach formed on his flanks as a result of our blows, which, in addition, by reaching far into the enemy's rear, will destroy and disorganize his command and control and logistics of his forces.

3. Those forces that the enemy can employ as reserves will be located far from the planned penetration sectors, especially in regard to the northern flank (the enemy's forces are concentrated primarily close by Stalingrad and in the city itself).

4. The presence of previously specially prepared favorable bridgeheads on the southern bank of the Don and in the region of the defiles between the lakes [south of Stalingrad].[16]

When Eremenko and Khrushchev submitted their proposal to Stalin, they were thinking of a counteroffensive conducted by the Stalingrad and Don Fronts and were clearly unaware of Stalin's decision to form a third *front*, the Southwestern Front. Nonetheless, it was a bold solution that resonated in the *Stavka*. Within 24 hours, at 2305 hours on 7 October, Vasilevsky dispatched two nearly identical directives to the Don and Stalingrad Fronts, directing that they plan for counterstrokes on the immediate flanks of Stalingrad, as the *Stavka* demanded. He did so without acknowledging Eremenko's proposal, probably because he had yet to see it. The short and curt directive to the Don Front, a copy of which was sent to the Stalingrad Front, read as follows:

In order to defeat the forces of the enemy at Stalingrad, according to the instructions of the *Stavka* of the Supreme High Command, a plan will be worked out by the commander of the Stalingrad Front for an attack with its reinforced left-wing 57th and 51st Armies in the general direction of Lake Tsatsa and Tundutovo.

Period—approximately 20 October.

Simultaneously with this operation, a meeting blow must be delivered by the center [1st Guards, 24th, and 66th Armies] of the Don Front in the general direction of Kotluban'-Alekseevka, for which you are permitted to employ the seven approaching divisions above and beyond the forces already situated in the *front*.

Conduct the operation you mentioned in recent days with brief attacks toward Stalingrad irrespective of the orders already given.

I request you submit your decision and notes of the plan of operations for approval by the *Stavka* by 10 October.[17]

Within 48 hours, Rokossovsky and Eremenko submitted draft plans for the counterstroke, both of which complied with Stalin's wishes but also expressed serious reservations about the proven futility of such attacks. The bolder of the two was the report by Eremenko and Khrushchev, which ignored the *Stavka*'s guidance and instead expanded on their 6 October proposal for a "different solution." Dated 1117 hours on 9 October, the Stalingrad Front's response read in part (for the complete report, see appendix 2C in the *Companion*):

In the aforementioned operation for the defeat of the enemy's Stalingrad grouping, the selection of the axis of attack has paramount importance.

I have already thought this question over for a month and consider that the more favorable axis of attack from the Don Front is the axis from the Kletskaia-Sirotinskaia front toward Kalach.

This is the main attack.

The advantages of this axis:

1) We will more easily destroy the weakest of the units of the enemy, which will have great significance for the morale of our forces—it will inspire them.

2) The rapid advance of 21st Army, which at the given time will be successful, will have an influence on this.

3) The arrival on the main communications [lines] of the enemy in the Kalach region and the crossings over the Don River in the Kalach-Vertiachii sector.

With the arrival in this region, we will deprive the enemy most importantly—of maneuvering his mobile tank and mechanized forces which are operating in the Stalingrad region and will isolate them from the main attack, meaning we will destroy the enemy on the western and southern banks of the Don in piecemeal fashion.

The delivery of the attack from the Kotluban' region east of the Don River will not lead to any success since the enemy has the capability here of throwing in forces from the Stalingrad region, and the operation will misfire as we have already experienced many times.

How do I myself conceive of the plan for conducting the operation?

The 3rd Gds. CC and two–three mechanized brigades should play a decisive role in this operation, which should, notwithstanding any sort of difficulties in their march, reach the Kalach region in twenty-four hours, where they can blow up all of the crossings from Vertiachii to Kalach and occupy a front facing toward the east. By this, we can cork up the enemy on the eastern bank of the Don with one cavalry division, screen with a mechanized brigade along the Lisichka River with its front facing west, blow up all of the crossings over the river, and mine the important axes in separate sectors.[18]

A unique aspect of Eremenko's plan was its recommendation to shift the axis of attack away from the Kotluban' region, where German defenses were strongest, and instead exploit the weakness of Romanian forces on Sixth Army's flanks. He proposed conducting penetration operations in the Kletskaia region with the Don Front's 21st Army and in the region south of Stalingrad with his own *front*'s 57th and 51st Armies. Thereafter, raids and diversionary operations by 3rd Guards Cavalry Corps, "special groups of cavalrymen," and a "strong separate detachment with sappers and explosive experts" would capture the Don River line from Vertiachii to Kalach, destroy German airfields and bases at Tatsinskaia and Morozovskaia, and demolish junctions and warehouses at Kotel'nikovo Station.[19] Although it was a plan for a large-scale raid, Eremenko's proposal provided the basis for an entirely new offensive concept.

In essence, instead of providing a draft plan for a counterstroke, Eremenko's message recommended an entirely different course of action—one that challenged the "old solution" and advised the *Stavka* to embark on a "different solution." Although this plan virtually mirrored the one the *Stavka* ultimately approved for Operation Uranus, major differences existed (see map 2). First and foremost, the former retained the current command and control relationships by requiring the Don Front to mount the northern pincer of the envelopment operation by attacking from the bridgehead south of the Don River between Kletskaia and Sirotinskaia with 21st Army and a reinforced cavalry corps. Second, the southward thrust by the 3rd Guards Cavalry Corps, even if reinforced by three mechanized brigades, was far weaker than the full tank army and separate cavalry and tank corps that would launch the deep thrust in the final plan. In fact, as one Russian historian has noted, this thrust amounted to nothing more than a reinforced raid, and its possibilities were limited.[20] Third, although the envelopment Eremenko recommended was broader than previous attempts, it was less broad than the ultimate thrust from both the Serafimovich and Kletskaia regions in the final Uranus plan. Finally, unlike Eremenko's plan, which focused on converging attacks toward Kalach-on-the-Don, the Uranus plan would propel the Southwestern Front's attacking forces to the Chir River line west of Kalach, which also threatened the key German supply bases at Tatsinskaia and Morozovskaia.

Despite the sharp differences between Eremenko's "different solution" and the solution the *Stavka* finally adopted for the Uranus offensive, clearly, Eremenko's plan pushed Stalin and his key advisers toward the radical concept adopted for Operation Uranus. Parenthetically, strong evidence exists that at least some members of the *Stavka* were already thinking about conducting a much broader envelopment. The *Stavka's* decision to conduct offensive operations to seize bridgeheads on the southern bank of the Don River in the Serafimovich and Kletskaia regions during the last week of August 1942 supports this judgment.

If Eremenko's report helped persuade the *Stavka* to adopt a radically different solution, the draft plan submitted by Rokossovsky served to reinforce Eremenko's recommendations. Prepared jointly by Rokossovsky, his corps commissar Zheltov, and his chief of staff, Major General Malanin, the report (dated 2240 hours on 9 October) began by describing in detail the formidable defensive system erected by the opposing 113th Infantry, 60th and 3rd Motorized, and 16th Panzer Divisions. Noting that "the densest grouping of the enemy's combat formations is in the Borodin, Borodkin Farm, Kuz'michi, and Hill 112.7 sector," Rokossovsky and his colleagues pointed out that "the positions the enemy occupy have been fortified for the course of a month. Centers of resistance have been created with the presence of pillboxes, full-profile trenches, communications trenches, mine fields, and barbed wire in separate sectors." For good measure, the Don Front's reluctant Military Council stressed the defense's excessive depth and the presence of imposing enemy tactical reserves.

Before presenting the details of an operation that differed sharply from the concept advanced by the *Stavka*, Rokossovsky provided his rationale for altering the plan: "In light of the insufficient quantity of rifle divisions, it does not seem possible to organize an operation with the main attack delivered toward Kotluban'." He then described candidly the dilapidated state of his *front's* forces:

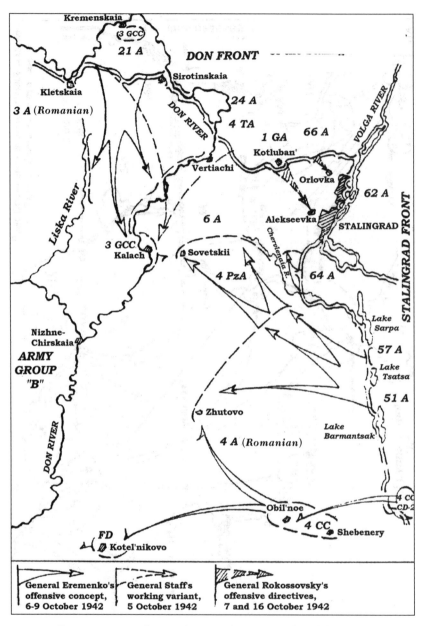

Map 2. Offensive concept of General Eremenko, commander of the Stalingrad Front, 6–9 October 1942

a) As a result of months of fighting, the rifle divisions of 1st Guards, 24th, and 66th Armies are severely weakened and consist of no more than a battalion of bayonets [combat infantry] in each division. The *front* has no replacements to restore their lost combat readiness. This is also not planned by the Center [Moscow].

b) The main force for the penetration and its exploitation include seven rifle divisions that have arrived from the *front*.

c) These forces are completely inadequate for a penetration and the exploitation of the attack recommended by you along the Kotluban'-Alekseevka axis. In this instance, a minimum of four rifle divisions are required to penetrate the front, three rifle divisions to exploit the penetration, and a minimum of three full-blooded rifle divisions are required to protect the shock group against enemy counterattacks from the west and southwest.[21]

Nonetheless, Rokossovsky, Zheltov, and Malanin dutifully presented a new plan of operations to the *Stavka* and insisted that their forces would be ready to attack as ordered early on 20 October.

In the wake of Eremenko's and Rokossovsky's proposals, on 10–12 October, Zhukov, Vasilevsky, the *Stavka*, and the General Staff began formulating the plan for a vastly expended counteroffensive that incorporated the "different solution." As they did so, they issued a flurry of directives designed to solidify the Red Army's defenses in Stalingrad, improve prospective jumping-off points for the forthcoming counteroffensive, and concentrate sufficient forces in the region to ensure offensive success. One set of directives ordered 62nd Army to defend the Volga River islands and the eastern bank of the river, provided reinforcements so that it could do so, and required the Don Front's armies to retain and improve their bridgehead along the southern bank of the Don. Likewise, other directives transferred 4th Cavalry Corps to the Stalingrad Front, anticipated the future creation of 1st and 2nd Guards Armies at full multicorps strength, and withdrew numerous divisions and other formations that would be critical in the future into the *Stavka* Reserve for rest and refitting. A third set of directives, some of which remain obscure, sought to coordinate offensive actions across the entire front by postponing planned attacks against German forces in the Rzhev and Viaz'ma region west of Moscow; in addition, these directives reinforced *fronts* designated to conduct offensives in concert with Operation Uranus—first and foremost, Operation Mars (see below). These actions culminated on 13 October when Zhukov and Vasilevsky submitted their draft concept for Operation Uranus to Stalin. When the dictator approved this concept, preparations for the counteroffensive began in earnest.

PLAN URANUS TAKES SHAPE, 14–31 OCTOBER

From mid to late October, the *Stavka* focused its attention on creating a command structure that could plan and conduct the counteroffensive and on assembling the forces necessary to carry out the operation successfully (see appendix 2D in the *Companion*). Many of the *Stavka* directives issued during this period simply continued the process begun on 10–13 October, that is, they improved existing defenses, rested and refitted active Red Army formations and created entirely new ones, and improved command and control of Soviet forces in the region. However, Directive Nos. 170668, 170669, and 170670, issued on 15–16 October, required the Don and Stalingrad Fronts to continue their futile offensive actions along former axes, from the Kotluban' and Erzovka region north of Stalingrad and Beketovka and the lake region south of the city (see volume 2). As callous as this seemed, these attacks performed a vital function: they ensured that 62nd Army's defenses in the city did not collapse, while deceiving the Germans into thinking that the *Stavka* was still trying to rescue its own 62nd Army or destroy German Sixth Army by means of a shallow envelopment.

Above and beyond these directives, the most significant involved the formation of the new Southwestern Front, its integration into the Red Army's command and control structure in the southern Soviet Union, and the provision of forces necessary for the Southwestern Front, as well as the other *fronts*, to carry out the Uranus counteroffensive successfully. The *Stavka* took the initial step in this process at 0250 hours on 22 October, when it ordered the formation of the Southwestern Front by 31 October. This new force, consisting initially of 5th Tank and 63rd and 21st Armies, was to become the vital northern pincer of Operation Uranus. Later, as Vasilevsky explained, "For the purposes of maintaining secrecy, the official . . . formation of the Southwestern Front was deferred until the end of October."[22] Given the importance of Vatutin's *front* in the overall maneuver scheme of Operation Uranus, this indicates that the planning for Uranus actually began in late September and early October instead of early September, as asserted by Zhukov.

In addition to specifying the composition and territorial boundaries of the new Southwestern Front (along and south of the Don River, between the Voronezh and Don Fronts), the directive ordered that the *front*'s headquarters be formed on the base of 1st Guards Army's headquarters, and it instructed the chiefs of the NKO's most important directorates to provide the *front* with command cadre, personnel, weapons, communications units and equipment, and essential logistical and other rear service organs. Headquartered in Novo-Annenskaia, more than 120 kilometers north of Serafimovich, the *front* was commanded by Lieutenant General Vatutin, with Major

General G. D. Stel'makh, the former chief of staff of the Volkhov Front, as his chief of staff.[23]

The next day, the *Stavka* issued three more directives regarding the Southwestern Front. The first transferred 21st and 63rd Armies to the *front*, effective at midnight on 28 October, and the second established the boundary between it and the Voronezh Front, effective on 31 October.[24] With the infantry nucleus and territorial parameters of Vatutin's *front* established, at 2400 hours on the 22nd, the *Stavka* reinforced the Southwestern Front with cavalry and artillery units from the neighboring Voronezh Front. These included the battle-hardened 8th Cavalry Corps, one rifle division, and five artillery regiments. Emphasizing the importance of secrecy, the *Stavka* ordered the displacing forces to restrict their movement to the hours of darkness, to move under a cloak of air and antiaircraft cover, and to observe total radio silence until they reached their new positions by 3 November. Prior to the transfer, all orders were to be verbal in nature, and the cavalry corps was to leave its radio stations behind to deceive the enemy as to the corps' actual location.[25]

In addition to shaping the new Southwestern Front, the *Stavka* began consolidating existing rifle divisions and brigades into new rifle corps; the goal was to improve command and control within armies by reducing the number of subordinate headquarters. For example, on 22 October, it ordered the NKO to form a new 13th Guards Rifle Corps in the Ranenburg region in Lipetsk District by 15 November. Shortly thereafter, Moscow determined that this corps would help form the nucleus of the new 2nd Guards Army by December.[26] According to at least one source, as of nightfall on 22 October, the Red Army General Staff's general scheme of maneuver was essentially the same as the final map for Operation Uranus on the evening of 18 November.[27]

Capping off all this activity, on 23 October, the *Stavka* ordered the formation of the Red Army's first two guards armies, the 1st and 2nd, which were created specifically to spearhead the forthcoming Uranus counteroffensive and, if possible, expand it into what Stalin hoped would be a successful strategic offensive encompassing an entire winter campaign.[28] Similar in makeup, the two guards armies, formed by 10 and 25 November, respectively, would each consist of two guards rifle corps and a total of six rifle divisions, four of them guards, supported by a powerful new guards mechanized corps. Their organization would be as follows:

1st Guards Army (former 4th Reserve Army)—based at Rtishchevo
    4th Guards Rifle Corps
        35th Guards Rifle Division
        41st Guards Rifle Division

195th Rifle Division
6th Guards Rifle Corps
38th Guards Rifle Division
44th Guards Rifle Division
266th Rifle Division
1st Guards Mechanized Corps (formed on the base of 1st
Guards Rifle Division)
2nd Guards Army (former 1st Reserve Army)—based at Tambov
1st Guards Rifle Corps
24th Guards Rifle Division
33rd Guards Rifle Division
98th Rifle Division
13th Guards Rifle Corps
3rd Guards Rifle Division
2nd Guards Motorized Rifle Division (renamed 49th
Guards RifleDivision)
387th Rifle Division
2nd Guards Mechanized Corps (formed on the base
of 22nd Guards RifleDivision)

On the same day the *Stavka* began reorganizing its forces in the Stalingrad region, it ordered an equally profound reorganization of logistics and other rear services. On order of the *Stavka*, the Red Army General Staff issued a comprehensive directive to the commanders of the Southwestern, Voronezh, and Don Fronts and all the chiefs of the NKO's main directorates, requiring them to reorganize the *front*'s rear areas (see appendix 2E in the *Companion*). Signed by Vasilevsky, this directive established new boundary lines for the Southwestern Front, created administrative stations for all three *fronts* along major rail lines into the region, determined the number of trains per day allocated to provision the Voronezh and Don Fronts, and required the chiefs of the appropriate NKO main directorates to provide specific amounts of ammunition, fuel, and foodstuffs to the three *fronts*.[29]

Strengthening of the new Southwestern Front continued at an accelerated pace until month's end. The most significant step in this process occurred at 0100 hours on 25 October when, after Stalin met with Bokov and Shtemenko, the *Stavka* issued a directive providing the Southwestern Front with additional firepower that would be vital to the accomplishment of its future missions. Specifically, the directive authorized the transfer of sizable cavalry, tank, and artillery forces from Rokossovsky's Don Front to Vatutin's Southwestern Front. These reinforcements included 293rd and 277th Rifle Divisions and 3rd Guards Cavalry and 4th Tank Corps by 2 November, as well as 226th and 333rd Rifle Divisions by 3 November. It also required four

152mm gun–howitzer regiments, one 76mm howitzer artillery regiment, five 76mm tank destroyer regiments, one 45mm tank destroyer regiment, five PVO (air defense) 85mm antiaircraft artillery regiments, and two PVO 85mm antiaircraft artillery battalions, along with all their personnel, weapons, ammunition, and transportation, to be transferred to Vatutin's *front* by 3 November.

As in previous directives, the *Stavka* insisted that the movement take place at night, be reliably protected against enemy air attack, employ the same deceptive radio measures used in previous troop movements, and use only oral orders. In addition, this time, it directed NKVD organs to "undertake measures to cleanse the regions where the divisions are situated and their movement routes of all suspicious persons."[30]

The following day, Bokov notified Vatutin's chief of staff that Stalin himself had ordered the dispatch of three guards tank penetration regiments, each equipped with KV [Klementi Voroshilov] heavy tanks, and two battalions of flamethrower tanks to his *front*'s 21st Army by 28 October.[31]

Finally, on 28 October, Stalin extended the strict security measures he had already implemented to cloak the transfer of forces to the Southwestern Front to all the *fronts* that would be participating in Operations Uranus and Mars. The security practices mandated by this directive would soon become standard operating procedure in the Red Army prior to all offensive actions. For example, the directive sharply rejected requests by some *front* commanders to exempt key facilities in the 25-kilometer security zones behind the front (see appendix 2F in the *Companion*).[32]

FINAL PREPARATIONS, 1–18 NOVEMBER

Thus, by the end of October, the die was cast for conducting Operation Uranus and associated offensives elsewhere across the German-Soviet front. The command and control structure for the forces conducting the counteroffensive was in place, the Southwestern Front possessed most of the forces necessary to carry out its mission, and security measures were in place to ensure that the counteroffensive came as a surprise to the Germans. With this work done, under the guidance and supervision of the *Stavka* and the General Staff, the attacking *fronts* began preparing and refining their final offensive plans and implementing the host of preparatory measures necessary to launch a force of about 1 million men on a successful strategic offensive operation.

The flurry of activity during October took place essentially in Stalin's office, at the *Stavka*, and among the General Staff, but it also included vital participation and input from Vatutin, Rokossovsky, and Eremenko, the

Red Army's *front* commanders in the Stalingrad region. Thereafter, from 1 through 18 November, most of the adjustments and refinements of the Uranus plan and preparations for the counteroffensive occurred in the field (see appendix 2G in the *Companion*). For example, Zhukov and Vasilevsky spent virtually all their time during this period consulting with the commanders of participating *fronts* and their subordinate armies and supervising the *fronts* as they prepared their offensive plans. While in the field, Stalin's two key military representatives were accompanied by an imposing entourage of the Red Army's most accomplished branch experts. These included Colonels General N. N. Voronov and N. D. Iakovlev for artillery, Colonel General A. A. Novikov and A. E. Golovanov for the VVS (Air Forces) and Long-Range Aviation, and Colonel General Ia. N. Fedorenko for armor and mechanized forces. These men addressed every aspect of operations within their specialties, and if they could not resolve some problem that arose, they contacted their branch directorates for a solution. In addition to these experts, Zhukov and Vasilevsky called on Major General P. P. Vechnyi, chief of the General Staff's Department for the Exploitation of War Experiences, to gather, analyze, and utilize previous wartime experiences to improve the Red Army's performance in future combat operations.

More important still, Zhukov and Vasilevsky consulted face-to-face with the *front* and army commanders slated to conduct the counteroffensive, as well as the commanders of the mobile forces that would perform the most vital, complex, and delicate maneuver missions, such as Majors General V. T. Vol'sky and T. T. Shapkin, commanders of 4th Mechanized and 13th Mechanized (Tank) Corps. In addition, as they consulted with key subordinate commanders and identified problems they could not remedy, Zhukov and Vasilevsky turned to the *Stavka* and General Staff for resolutions. This, in turn, generated a whole new series of *Stavka* directives related to command and control, coordination of operations, and the provision of reinforcements for mobile forces.

This new wave of directives began with three issued between 0130 and 0445 hours on 1 November. The first renamed the headquarters of the Southwestern Front's 63rd Army the 1st Guards Army, effective at 2300 hours on 4 November. Led by Lieutenant General D. D. Leliushenko, 1st Guards Army still consisted of 4th and 6th Guards Rifle Corps, 1st Guards Mechanized Corps, and 1st, 153rd, and 197th Rifle Divisions.[33] This directive also appointed the former commander of 63rd Army, Lieutenant General Kuznetsov, deputy commander of Vatutin's Southwestern Front.[34] The second directive, issued at 0415 hours, provided the Stalingrad Front with the armored and mechanized nucleus for its 13th Tank Corps in the form of the new 17th, 61st, and 62nd Mechanized Brigades and their three accompanying tank regiments (44th, 176th, and 163rd).[35] The third directive, issued 30 minutes later, tightened up command and control within General Romanenko's 5th Tank Army by appointing Major General Danilov as the army's chief of staff and Major General Ia. S. Fokanov as its deputy commander.[36]

Sometime during this period, Zhukov requested additional air support for Vatutin's *front* and expressed concern over the coordination of the extensive air operations planned by the Voronezh and Southwestern Fronts during the forthcoming counteroffensive. In response, at 0955 hours on 4 November, Stalin stated, "I am sending you an additional division of fighters for Fedorov [Vatutin's code name]. I am sending you Vorozheikin for coordination of the air operations of the Southwestern and Voronezh Fronts." Stalin ended his message with an urgent appeal for Zhukov to return to Moscow: "I request you call once again to Moscow, and then you can leave to see Alekseev [Purkaev, commander of the Kalinin Front]. It is necessary to speak with you on pressing and urgent matters."[37]

The urgent matters to which Stalin referred were apparently the final approval of the Uranus and Mars plans and the issuing of orders to the participating *fronts*. In fact, Zhukov's work with the Southwestern Front culminated late on 4 November, when the *front's* command and staff worked out a plan graphically on a map and designated the operation "Uran" (Uranus) (see map 3). The actual draftsman of this graphic plan was Major General S. P. Ivanov, chief of the *front's* Operations Department.[38] Then, on 5 November, the Kalinin and Western Fronts ordered their subordinate armies to prepare plans for Operation Mars. Finally, according to Stalin's daily schedule, Zhukov returned to Moscow briefly on 6 November. There, he met with Stalin, Konev, and Bulganin from the Western Front, Leliushenko from 1st Guards Army, and Bokov from the General Staff before returning to the front that evening. This meeting apparently put the finishing touches on the overall concepts for both Uranus and Mars.[39]

Meanwhile, the General Staff accelerated the formation of new rifle corps to improve command and control in the offensive. For example, on 5 November, it ordered the commander of 4th Reserve Army to "unify the commands of 153rd and 197th Rifle Divisions, which are entering the composition of 1st Guards Army," into 14th Rifle Corps by 10 November. The directive ordered the chiefs of the Main Cadres Directorate and other NKO directorates to provide personnel for the corps' headquarters, and it directed the chiefs of the Main Communications and Artillery Directorates and *Gla-vupraform* to add a communications battalion, a headquarters battery for corps artillery, and rear service units and facilities to the structure of the newly formed corps.[40]

Although offensive preparations were well under way, on 8 November, Zhukov sent a message to Eremenko and Rokossovsky postponing the attack date until 13 November (with Stalin's approval). Addressed personally

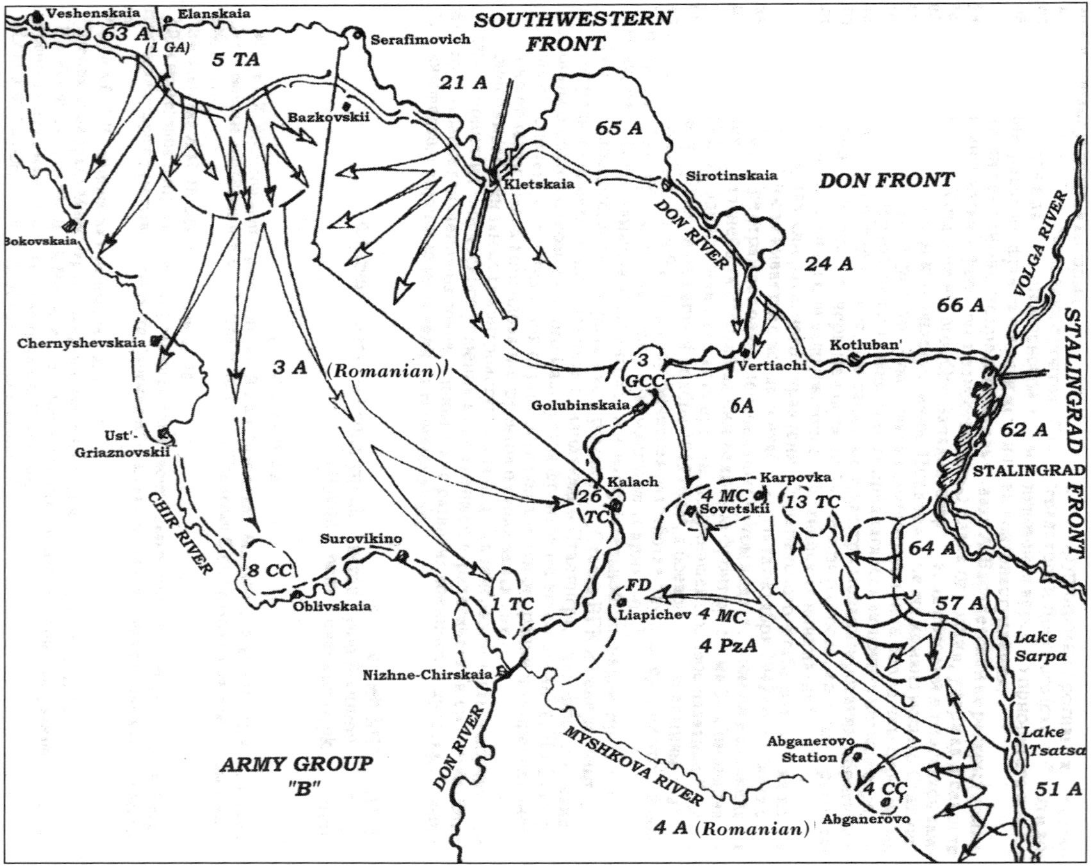

Map 3. Plan for the Stalingrad counteroffensive (Operation Uranus), 4 November 1942

to "Ivanov [Eremenko]" and "Dontsov [Rokossovsky]," these cables read: "The 13th is set as the date of the resettlement." The word "resettlement" [*pereselenie*] was code used by Stalin and the *Stavka* when referring to Operation Uranus.[41] Although the two *front* commanders knew precisely what this term meant, there is no evidence that either Chuikov or Shumilov, his colleague in 64th Army, realized what was about to occur.

There were several reasons for this delay, all of which would become apparent in future messages exchanged among the *Stavka*, Zhukov, and the *front* commanders. These reasons included delays in regrouping the forces necessary to conduct the attack, especially in the Stalingrad Front's 64th Army; requests from *front* commanders for reinforcements and other supporting materials; and apparent shortages in the number of aircraft required to support the counteroffensive. For example, on 9 November, Bokov, deputy chief of the General Staff, responded to a message from Colonel General F. I. Golikov, commander of the Voronezh Front, who had apparently requested reinforcements the previous day. Bokov began his message by indicating that the supreme high commander had approved the request: "After examining your request about reinforcement of the left wing of the *front*, Comrade Stalin made the decision to place three rifle divisions and two rifle brigades at your disposal." In addition to providing information about the timing of the arrival of these reinforcements, the text of the message revealed their combat "characteristics," which were typical of many green divisions and brigades designated to participate in the counteroffensive (see appendix 2H in the *Companion*). The strength of these reinforcing rifle divisions ranged from 7,891 to 9,746 men, and the rifle brigades contained 3,514 to 6,019 men. All these units either were organized on reduced tables of organization or required replenishment of personnel and equipment, all lacked sufficient trained soldiers, and all were assessed as "green" and in need of "additional time for training and cohesiveness."[42]

After Zhukov met with Eremenko and the commander of 51st Army, the Stalingrad Front commander issued orders on 9 November to his subordinate armies concerning their missions in the forthcoming counteroffensive. Subsequently, based on input from the commanders of the armies and the *front's* mobile groups, the Stalingrad Front completed its graphic display of the operation on a map by day's end on 12 November.[43]

Meanwhile, on 11 November, Zhukov sent a message to Stalin by means of BODO [Baudot], a secure teletype system used for communications between the operating *fronts* and the supreme commander and the *Stavka*. He reported on the deputy supreme commander's work with the Stalingrad Front and notified Stalin of another postponement of the offensive's start date, this time to 15 November. This message highlighted some of the reasons for the repeated delays:

I have just spent two days working with Eremenko. I personally examined enemy positions facing 51st and 57th Armies. I ironed out the details of pending Uranus objectives with divisional, corps, and army commanders. The inspection showed preparations advancing the best in Tolbukhin's [*front*]. . . .

I have ordered the conduct of combat reconnaissance and finalization of the combat plan and the army commander's decision on the basis of intelligence already obtained.

Popov is working well and knows what he is doing.

The two rifle divisions (the 87th and 315th) assigned to Eremenko by the *Stavka* have still not entrained because they have not received transport and horses up to this time.

Only one of the mechanized brigades has arrived so far.

Things are going poorly with regard to supplies and the delivery of ammunition. The troops are short of shells for "Uranus."

The operation will not be ready on schedule. I have ordered readiness by 15 November 1942.

We must make 100 tons of antifreeze available to Eremenko immediately, without which the advance of the mechanized units will be impossible; dispatch 87th and 315th Rifle Divisions as rapidly as possible; and provide warm [winter] uniforms and ammunition to 51st and 57th Armies immediately so as to arrive no later than 14 November 1942.

Konstantinov [Zhukov][44]

Stalin dispatched another order to Zhukov at 0400 hours on 12 November, revealing yet another reason for delaying Uranus—insufficient aircraft:

If the air preparations for the operation are unsatisfactory at Ivanov [Eremenko] and Fedorov [Vatutin], then the operation will end in failure. The experience of the war with the Germans shows that operations against the Germans can be won only in the event we have superiority in the skies. In this case, our aviation must fulfill three missions:

First—concentrate air operations in the region where our shock units are attacking, suppress German aviation, and reliably cover [protect] our forces.

Second—open the roads for our attacking units by systematic bombing of German forces standing in our path.

Third—pursue the withdrawing enemy forces by means of systematic bombing and assault actions in order to destroy them completely and deny them time to dig in along close defensive lines.

If Novikov thinks that our air forces are not now in a state to fulfill these missions, then it would be better to postpone the operation for some time and accumulate more aircraft.

Speak with Novikov and Vorozheikin, explain this matter to them, and report your general opinion to me.

Vasil'ev [Stalin][45]

The General Staff played an active role in preparing the Uranus counter-offensive, providing advice and concrete support to the participating *fronts* and inspecting and critiquing their preparations to identify problems and suggest appropriate solutions. Two examples will suffice, both issued by the General Staff on 14 November and both signed by Bokov. The first directive was addressed to the Don Front and sharply criticized the regrouping efforts in Rokossovsky's *front*:

Based on its sources, the General Staff knows:

1. 4th TC's units moved during the daytime while being transferred to a new concentration area.

2. Prisoner of war interrogations indicate the enemy knew about 65th Army's preparations.

3. During the transfer of 252nd and 258th RDs and 27th Gds. RD to 65th Army, the transport means were meager and the *front's* transport means assisting 65th Army were also inadequate: [specifically] on 6 November, 29 of the 50 allocated vehicles turned out to be inoperable, and the transport of all kinds of supplies is being carried out with interruptions (owing to poor supply, 252nd and 258th RDs and 27th Gds. RD have only 62–63% of their required combat load, and 3 men in 252nd RD's units and 6 men in 27th Gds. RD have perished because of the absence of warm clothing).

The replacements being sent to the armies' units are not being provided with winter uniforms, and 2 men among the arriving replacements have frozen en route.

I request you inform the General Staff about the measures you are taking to eliminate the indicated shortcomings.[46]

The second directive indicates that the General Staff's critiques were not limited to operating *fronts* and armies. This one excoriated 10th Reserve Army for its role in the delayed forward deployment of 87th and 315th Rifle Divisions to the Stalingrad Front (see appendix 2I in the *Companion*).[47] Apparently, these and other corrective measures taken by the *Stavka*, its representatives Zhukov and Vasilevsky, and the General Staff satisfied Stalin with regard to the pace and nature of preparations. The supreme commander indicated as much in a cable transmitted to Zhukov at 1310 hours on 15 November. It read:

> You can set the day for the resettlement [offensive] of Fedorov [Vatutin] and Ivanov [Eremenko] at your discretion and subsequently report back to me upon your arrival in Moscow. If the thought occurs to you for either of the two to begin the resettlement one or two days earlier or later, I authorize you to decide that matter too at your own discretion.
>
>   Vasil'ev [Stalin][48]

Contrary to Zhukov's account in his memoirs, in which he claims he returned to Moscow on 13 November, Zhukov actually arrived back in the Soviet capital on the 16th.[49] He stayed for three days as he worked with Stalin and the *Stavka* to put the finishing touches on the plans for Operations Uranus and Mars. These meetings, which lasted through 18 November, involved virtually every senior general officer who had any role in the twin counteroffensives and generated a host of directives and other orders making last-minute changes to the strategic plans, providing the attacking *fronts* and armies with critical reinforcements, and adjusting force boundaries and objectives based on these and other changes and the ongoing military situation. It was at these meetings that, exercising their discretion, Zhukov and Vasilevsky ordered the Southwestern Front and the Don Front's 65th Army to begin their assaults on 19 November and the Stalingrad Front to attack on 20 November—decisions that Stalin immediately approved.[50]

Since Stalin and the *Stavka* hoped that Operations Uranus and Mars would be only the first stage in a decisive counteroffensive and a much broader winter campaign, intelligence on the enemy would be crucial. Based on past experience, the Germans were known to be masters of the defense and capable of moving and regrouping forces effectively within the major strategic sectors of their eastern theater of military operation and even from the strategic depths and other major theaters. Therefore, on 16 November, deputy chief of the General Staff, Major General V. D. Ivanov, dispatched a directive to all Red Army *fronts* operating against Axis forces requesting immediate verification of the positions of all Axis forces (see appendix 2J in the *Companion*). Despite strong evidence of extensive German regrouping, Soviet intelligence organs at the front and army levels had lost track of 35 German divisions. To remedy this problem, Ivanov demanded that these organs undertake immediate measures to gather the necessary intelligence by 25 November, and he told them precisely how to do so.[51]

In addition to tightening up intelligence collection and analysis, the General Staff moved to eliminate deficiencies in the conduct of operations and, in particular, the accuracy of combat reports. To this end, and possibly as an example to the Red Army's *front* and army commanders, on 16 November, Ivanov singled out the Stalingrad Front's 28th Army for sharp criticism because its 52nd Rifle Brigade had been destroyed on 13 November while serving as a forward detachment. Since this was the third time in two weeks that the brigade had been destroyed performing the same function, Ivanov's directive asked "Why?" and demanded corrective action and punishment of those guilty of transgressions by 20 November (see appendix 2K in the *Companion*).[52]

During the final three days before the offensive began, the *Stavka* and the General Staff made last-minute adjustments to the force structures of the Southwestern, Don, and Stalingrad Fronts and continued to speed reinforcements to the Voronezh Front, whose forces would join the fray if Operation Uranus succeeded. On 16 November, for example, Bokov ordered 4th Reserve Army and the Volga Military District to push the headquarters of 4th and 6th Guards Rifle Corps forward so that they would be able to receive their subordinate combat forces and reinforce 1st Guards Army at the most opportune time.[53] Two days later, Bokov issued detailed movement orders to the two rifle corps' combat divisions, designating when and where they were to relocate behind 1st Guards Army's front.[54] Similarly, on 17 November, the General Staff directed the NKO's Main Auto-Armored Directorate to dispatch three rested and refitted tank brigades (173rd, 192nd, and 201st) to the Voronezh Front; they were scheduled to arrive between 17 and 25 November.[55] Ending this flurry of activity, on 18 November, Bokov ordered the commander of 4th Reserve Army to send 14th Rifle Corps to the Southwestern Front's 1st Guards Army, scheduled to arrive forward after 19 November.[56] This directive was the last one issued by the General Staff before Operation Uranus began.

Meanwhile, before leaving for the front the next day, Vasilevsky completed the *Stavka*'s preoffensive activities at 1415 hours on 18 November, establishing a new boundary between the Southwestern and Don Fronts. Passing directly through the town of Kletskaia, the new boundary extended from Atkarsk, 75 kilometers northwest of Saratov; southward 260 kilometers through Balanda and Motyshevo to Shurupovka, 7 kilometers southeast of Frolov; southwestward 65 kilometers and across the Don River to Kletskaia; and finally southward 45 kilometers from Kletskaia through Selivanov to Evseev, 42 kilometers northwest of Kalach-on-the-Don. All these towns except for Atkarsk, Motyshevo, and Shurupovka were the responsibility of the Southwestern Front.[57] Although seemingly mundane, the boundary established by this directive rationalized logistical support for the Southwestern and Don Fronts by leaving the railheads at Atkarsk, Krasnyi Iar, and Kamyshin in the latter's rear area. The issuance of this directive ended the planning for what would arguably become one of the most decisive struggles in the Soviet-German War, if not in World War II as a whole.

REFLECTIONS

Thus, for the better part of the period from 27 September through 18 November 1942, the *Stavka*, its representatives, and senior General Staff officers and commanders had to develop the concept of Operation Uranus and conduct preliminary planning for it, while simultaneously dealing with the deadly struggle in the city of Stalingrad. Their work was complicated not only by the ebb and flow of combat in and around the city and concern over the ultimate fate of Chuikov's 62nd Army but also by the demand for absolute secrecy. As a result, although *front* commanders were informed about the general nature of the offensive from 29 September through 2 October, even they did not learn the precise nature and timing of the offensive until 21–22 October. Vatutin certainly learned of the plan's existence on 21 October when he visited Moscow and received command of the new Southwestern Front during a meeting with Stalin. However, neither Rokossovsky nor Eremenko visited Moscow to attend any of Stalin's planning meetings before the offensive commenced. Instead, they received their orders and instructions from either Zhukov or Vasilevsky while in the field. Eremenko, whose proposals to the *Stavka* on 6 and 9 October contained the offensive's general outline, likely learned of its precise nature at roughly the same time as Vatutin. As for Rokossovsky, as he later explained:

> The long-awaited moment was approaching. Zhukov told Eremenko and me of the forthcoming offensive as early as October. He did not give us even an approximate date, but the knowledge enabled us to proceed, in utmost secrecy, with the preparation of certain measures. Much was done to mislead the enemy. To convince him that our intention was to attack in the sector between the Don and the Volga, we were especially active there and simulated intensive fortification work, digging of trenches, and so on, in other sectors. . . .
>
> On strict instructions from Zhukov, then representing GHQ, only a small group of staff workers was told of the impending offensive. All our preparations were made to look like attempts to strengthen the defenses.[58]

Although Stalin kept himself informed of their progress, he trusted his professional advisers far more than he had earlier in the year. Accordingly, while Stalin met with Vasilevsky and a host of senior branch experts in the

Kremlin on 1 and 2 October, Zhukov took the word of Uranus to the field, where he visited the Don and Stalingrad Fronts from late on 29 September to the evening of 3 October to acquaint Rokossovsky and Eremenko with the general plan and to identify problems and resolve them. Beginning on 1 November, a little more than a week before the originally scheduled start date for Operation Uranus, Zhukov presided over meetings of the commanders of all formations, from division through *front* (army group), involved in the offensive. As Rokossovsky recalled:

> On 4 November, I was summoned with a group of staff officers to a meeting in the sector of 21st Army, which was now part of the Southwestern Front. The meeting was presided over by G. K. Zhukov. It was attended by all army commanders and the commanders of divisions which were to attack along the axes of the main effort. Special attention was paid to the cooperation of neighboring units at the junctions of the *fronts* [the *fronts'* boundaries].
>
> Later we learned that a similar meeting was held in the Stalingrad Front as well. . . . Together with the army commanders, Batov, Galanin, Zhadov (who replaced Malinovsky, recalled by the *Stavka*), Rudenko, and the arms chiefs, I worked out the details of the campaign. By that time, the *Stavka* had defined our missions more precisely.[59]

Even at this late stage, the commanders themselves did most of the detailed planning, rather than informing their staff officers and thus increasing the security risk. In addition to uncertainty on the part of senior Soviet military leaders regarding the precise start of their new counteroffensives, the dense cloak of secrecy surrounding all correspondence and preparatory measures on the Soviet side justified Reinhard Gehlen's reluctance to predict when and where the counteroffensives would occur.

If the emergence of Uranus confounded German intelligence organs, it also perplexed some Red Army commanders when they learned of the *Stavka's* intent to implement such an ambitious plan. In an incident that one observer called "one of the most dramatic moments in the preparation for Uranus," Major General V. T. Vol'sky, commander of 4th Mechanized Corps, reportedly dispatched a letter directly to Stalin on 17 November, questioning the wisdom of proceeding with the counteroffensive and urging the dictator to postpone the operation to avoid suffering a catastrophic defeat. As described by Vasilevsky, based on an 18 November meeting with Stalin:

> A meeting of the State Defense Committee [GKO] occurred in Stalin's Kremlin office at 1800 hours. Stalin immediately greeted me and proposed that, while discussions went on over a series of important

economic questions, I familiarize myself with a letter he had received from the commander of the 4th Mechanized Corps, V. T. Vol'sky, who had been designated to fulfill a decisive role in the forthcoming operation in the Stalingrad Front's sector. The corps commander had written the GKO that, given the correlation of forces and weapons that existed at the beginning of the offensive, the planned offensive at Stalingrad would not only prevent us from counting on success but, in his opinion, would also undoubtedly doom it to failure with all the resulting consequences, and that he, as an honest Party member, knowing the opinions of other responsible participants in the offensive, was asking the GKO to verify the practicability of the decisions reached on the operation immediately and carefully, postpone it, and perhaps entirely renounce it.

Naturally, the GKO asked me to evaluate the letter. I expressed my astonishment concerning the letter: its author had participated actively in the preparation of the operation during recent weeks and had never expressed the least doubt over both the operation as a whole and the missions assigned to the forces of the corps entrusted to him. Furthermore, at the final meeting on 10 November, he assured the representative of the *Stavka* and the *front's* Military Council that his corps was ready to fulfill its mission and then reported about its complete combat readiness and about the excellence and the combat mood of the formation's personnel. In conclusion, I declared that, in my view, no basis whatsoever existed for not only postponing the prepared operation but also for reexamining its start date.

There and then, Stalin ordered he be put through to Vol'sky by telephone and after a short and by no means sharp conversation with him, recommended I pay no attention to the letter and leave the author of the letter in the corps since he just then gave his word that he would fulfill the mission assigned to the corps at all cost. This question, as well as the matter of the corps commander, would be definitively resolved based on the results of the corps' operations, about which Stalin ordered me to report to him in person during the initial days of the operation.[60]

Whether or not this exchange was apocryphal, it underscored one singularly unpleasant reality: the Red Army had been unable to mount a successful offensive against the Germans in 1942. Like most German commanders, many Red Army commanders remained convinced that their army was simply incapable of achieving victory over their German opponents. The fact that the attacking forces in Uranus would strike primarily Romanians indicated similar concerns within the *Stavka* itself. Only time would tell if these concerns were justified.

Iosif Vissarionovich Stalin – General Secretary of the Central Committee of the Communist Party of the Soviet Union, People's Commissar of Defense of the Soviet Union, Chairman of the State Defense Committee, Commander of the Soviet Armed Forces.

Colonel General Aleksandr Mikhailovich Vasilevsky, Chief of the Soviet Army's General Staff and the General Staff's Operations Deprtment, Deputy People's Commissar of Defense of the USSR, and Representative of the *Stavka*.

Colonel General Aleksei Innokent'evich Antonov, 1st Deputy Chief of the Soviet Army's General Staff and Chief of the General Staff's Operations Department (after 11 December 1942).

Major General Fedor Efimovich Bokov, Deputy Chief of the Soviet Army's General Staff.

Colonel General Nikolai Nikolaevich Voronov, Chief of the Soviet Army's Artillery, Deputy People's Commissar of Defense of the USSR, and Representative of the *Stavka*.

Colonel General Aleksandr Aleksandrovich Novikov, commander of the Soviet Army's Air Forces (VVS), Deputy People's Commissar of Defense for Aviation, and Representative of the *Stavka* for coordination of the Air Forces of multiple *fronts*.

CHAPTER THREE

Gathering the Troops:
Soviet Order of Battle and the Uranus Plan

REGROUPING FORCES FOR THE COUNTEROFFENSIVE

Strategic and Operational Deployment

After a period of roughly six weeks of painstaking planning and careful preparations, by 18 November, the *Stavka* managed to field an impressive array of forces with which to conduct its long-awaited counteroffensive in the Stalingrad region. When fully assembled, this force included 3 *fronts*, 10 field armies, 1 tank army, 4 air armies, 66 rifle divisions, 18 rifle and motorized rifle brigades, 1 destroyer brigade, 6 fortified regions, 5 tank corps, 1 mechanized corps, 3 cavalry corps with 8 cavalry divisions, 14 separate tank brigades, 4 tank regiments, and 124 RVGK artillery and mortar regiments, supported by tens of engineer, construction, and other types of specialized formations and units.[1] This force numbered more than 1 million soldiers and fielded more than 1,500 tanks, 22,000 artillery pieces, and 1,500 combat aircraft. Moreover, the *Stavka* accomplished the feat of assembling such a formidable force while heavy fighting raged in Stalingrad proper and while Red Army forces were launching continuous counterstrokes against German forces deployed northwest and south of Stalingrad. Most impressive of all, it amassed these forces without ceasing operations in the city proper and other front sectors, and it did so without being detected by German intelligence.

The force assembled to conduct Operation Uranus along the Stalingrad strategic axis consisted of the Southwestern, Don, and Stalingrad Fronts. These forces occupied the 850-kilometer-wide sector stretching from Verkhnyi Mamon on the Don River, 340 kilometers northwest of Stalingrad; southeastward to the Volga River, north of Stalingrad; and then southward roughly 420 kilometers along and west of the Volga River to the northern shore of the Caspian Sea, south of Astrakhan'. Arrayed from north to south in a single strategic echelon, backed up by modest strategic reserves, these three *fronts* were positioned as follows:

- The Southwestern Front, commanded by Lieutenant General N. F. Vatutin, occupied the 250-kilometer-wide sector extending from Verkhnyi Mamon to Kletskaia on the Don River, with 1st Guards, 5th Tank, and 21st Armies supported by 17th and 2nd Air Armies.

- The Don Front, led by Lieutenant General K. K. Rokossovsky, was deployed in the 150-kilometer-wide sector from Kletskaia on the Don River to Erzovka on the Volga River, with 24th, 65th, and 66th Armies supported by 16th Air Army.
- The Stalingrad Front, headed by Colonel General A. I. Eremenko, occupied the 450-kilometer-wide sector extending from Rynok on the Volga River north of Stalingrad to the northern shore of the Caspian Sea south of Astrakhan', with 62nd, 64th, 57th, 51st, and 28th Armies supported by 8th Air Army.

Like the three *fronts* operating along the Stalingrad axis as a whole, each individual *front* participating in Operation Uranus arrayed itself in a single-echelon operational formation with essentially no second echelon but with a small operational reserve. This was the case because, despite the large forces assembled for the offensive, the *fronts* lacked sufficient numbers to create a more deeply echeloned offensive formation. The correlation of opposing forces, though in the attackers' favor, was not overwhelming. This ratio, plus the nature of enemy defenses in the *fronts'* main attack sectors and the Soviets' desire to achieve both strategic and operational surprise, made it necessary to project as much force forward as possible in the initial stages. These factors impelled the *front* commanders to adopt single-echelon operational formations. As shown below, the tactical echeloning within each of the *fronts'* attacking or defending armies reflected the usual factors of mission, strength of opposing forces, terrain, and anticipated weather at the time of the attack.

Strategic and Operational Command and Control

As was the case during the development of Plan Uranus, the *Stavka VGK* (Headquarters of the Supreme High Command)—which, by definition and practice, was the highest organ of strategic leadership for the country's armed forces—played a leading role in coordinating and supervising the counteroffensive once it began.[2] In turn, while planning and conducting Operation Uranus, the *Stavka* received its strategic guidance from the USSR's State Defense Committee (GKO), which served as a virtual war cabinet for Josef Stalin, the first secretary of the Communist Party and, by 1942, the supreme high commander of the Soviet armed forces. Acting collectively, but with Stalin making the final decisions, the GKO directed, supervised, and supported the work of the people's commissars and their respective commissariats, the *Stavka*, and all other governmental and military organs and institutions involved in the war effort.

After receiving strategic guidance from Stalin, the Politburo of the Communist Party's Central Committee, and the GKO, as well as concrete proposals from its representatives in the field and the commanders of its operating *fronts*, the *Stavka* was responsible for making all decisions concerning the planning, preparation, conduct, and support of military campaigns and strategic operations and the creation and employment of strategic reserves. It was assisted in these tasks by a permanent "institute" of special advisers and the Red Army General Staff. The institute of advisers provided it with expertise in a wide variety of specialties, ranging from strictly military questions, such as the employment of artillery and armor, to other vital matters, such as state security and political control of the military. The Red Army General Staff, acting as the *Stavka's* principal working organ, was responsible for preparing all strategic and operational plans for the conduct of specific operations related to Uranus. However, throughout this entire process, the *Stavka* coordinated, amended, and approved these plans in close consultation with its representatives in the field and its operating *fronts*. Moreover, all this planning involved input from other people's commissariats (especially the People's Commissariat of Defense, or NKO) and required the approval of Stalin and the GKO. Once these plans were approved and operations commenced, the *Stavka*, its representatives, and its operating *fronts* coordinated, conducted, and provided material and logistical support for all military operations, under the constant direction of Stalin, the Communist Party, and the GKO.

The so-called representatives of the *Stavka* played a particularly vital role throughout the entire process of planning and conducting strategic operations for Uranus. These representatives were experienced senior marshals and generals handpicked by Stalin and dispatched to the *Stavka's* operating *fronts* in the field to ensure that its plans were properly developed, coordinated, and implemented once operations began. In the case of Operation Uranus, the most important representatives of the *Stavka* were Army General G. K. Zhukov, Colonel General A. M. Vasilevsky, and Colonel General of Artillery V. V. Voronov. These men supervised and coordinated all the planning for Operation Uranus, directed military operations during the critical planning phase in late September and early October, and organized command and control and cooperation within the Southwestern, Don, and Stalingrad Fronts. While doing so, they paid special attention to tank, mechanized, and cavalry corps operations; the preparation of directives, orders, and instructions; the achievement of operational security; strategic and operational communications; and close coordination among tanks, artillery, and infantry and between ground and air forces.

These representatives of the *Stavka*, in conjunction with the commanders of the *fronts* designated to conduct Operation Uranus, carried out their work at a complex network of headquarters, each of which was carefully positioned to facilitate more effective planning and conduct of the counteroffensive. In general, this network included *front* main command posts (CPs), which were located roughly 70 to 80 kilometers from the forward edge of battle, *front* forward CPs, situated 20 to 30 kilometers from the forward edge, and the CPs of the armies subordinate to these *fronts*. These army CPs were located 8 to 10 kilometers from the forward edge, in the case of armies operating along main attack axes, and at a slightly greater distance for armies operating along secondary axes.

SOVIET ORDER OF BATTLE

The Southwestern Front

In terms of Plan Uranus, the strongest and most important of the three attacking *fronts* was the Southwestern Front, first and foremost because it formed the plan's northern pincer, the stronger of the two pincers conducting the broad envelopment operation. The *front's* Military Council, which formulated its operational plan and directed, coordinated, and supervised the conduct of its military operations, consisted of Lieutenant General N. F. Vatutin, the *front* commander; Corps Commissar A. S. Zheltov; and Major General G. D. Stel'makh, the chief of staff.[3] Operating in the 250-kilometer sector extending along the Don River from Verkhnyi Mamon to Kletskaia, 115 kilometers northwest of Stalingrad, the *front's* task was to conduct one of the two main attacks from bridgeheads on the southern bank of the Don River in the Serafimovich and Kletskaia regions.

Vatutin's 5th Tank and 21st Armies constituted the nucleus of the shock group forming Uranus's northern pincer. Supporting these two armies was 1st Guards Army, which was tasked with protecting the right flank of the *front's* shock group while preparing to exploit the offensive toward the southwest, with the Southwestern Front's own 17th Air Army and most of the Voronezh's Front's 2nd Air Army for air support. The 5th Tank and 21st Armies fielded the infantry and supporting arms necessary to penetrate the enemy's defenses from bridgeheads on the southern bank of the Don River in the Serafimovich and Kletskaia regions, 110 to 180 kilometers northwest of Stalingrad, as well as the tank, mechanized, and cavalry forces to exploit the penetration into the operational depths and reach the *front's* intermediate and final objectives (see table 1).

Roughly half of Vatutin's forces, including all his mobile forces, came from the *Stavka* Reserve. Virtually all these men were veterans of previous combat; most had been blooded during the intense fighting in the Voronezh

Table 1. Composition and Senior Command Cadre of the Southwestern Front, 19 November 1942 (less artillery and engineer units)

Southwestern Front—Lieutenant General N. F. Vatutin
  1st Guards Army—Lieutenant General D. D. Leliushenko; Deputy Commander, Lieutenant General V. I. Kuznetsov
    1st, 153rd, 197th, 203rd, 266th, and 278th Rifle Divisions
    1st Guards Mechanized Corps—Major General I. N. Russianov
      1st, 2nd, and 3rd Guards Mechanized Brigades
      16th and 17th Guards Tank Regiments
    22nd Separate Motorized Rifle Brigade
  5th Tank Army—Major General P. L. Romanenko
    14th, 47th, and 50th Guards and 119th, 159th, and 346th Rifle Divisions
    1st Tank Corps—Major General of Tank Forces V. V. Butkov
      89th, 117th, and 159th Tank Brigades
      44th Motorized Rifle Brigade
    26th Tank Corps—Major General of Tank Forces A. G. Rodin
      19th, 157th, and 216th Tank Brigades
      14th Motorized Rifle Brigade
    8th Cavalry Corps—Major General M. D. Borisov
      21st, 55th, and 112th Cavalry Divisions
    8th Guards Tank Brigade
    8th Motorcycle Regiment
    510th and 511th Separate Tank Battalions
  21st Army—Lieutenant General I. M. Chistiakov
    63rd, 76th, 96th, 277th, 293rd, and 333rd Rifle Divisions
    4th Tank Corps—Major General of Tank Forces A. G. Kravchenko
      45th, 69th, and 102nd Tank Brigades
      4th Motorized Rifle Brigade
    3rd Guards Cavalry Corps—Major General I. A. Pliev
      5th and 6th Guards and 32nd Cavalry Divisions
    5th Separate Destroyer Brigade
    1st, 2nd, and 4th Guards Separate Tank Regiments
    1st, 21st, 60th, and 99th Separate Antitank Rifle Battalions
  17th Air Army—Lieutenant General of Aviation S. A. Krasovsky
    1st Mixed Aviation Corps—Major General of Aviation V. I. Shevchenko
      267th Assault Aviation Division
      288th Fighter Aviation Division
    221st Bomber Aviation Division
    262nd Night Bomber Aviation Division
    282nd Fighter Aviation Division
    208th and 637th Assault Aviation Divisions
    10th Long-Range Reconnaissance Aviation Squadron
    331st Separate Bomber Aviation Squadron
  2nd Air Army (from the Voronezh Front)—Major General of Aviation K. N. Smirnov
    205th and 207th Fighter Aviation Divisions
    208th Night Bomber Aviation Division
    227th Assault Aviation Division
    50th Reconnaissance Aviation Regiment
    324th Long-Range Reconnaissance Aviation Squadron
  Front **forces**: no rifle, tank, mechanized, or cavalry formations

Table 1. (continued)

Sources: A. M. Samsonov, *Stalingradskaia bitva* [The Battle of Stalingrad] (Moscow: Nauka, 1983), 569; V. A. Zolotarev, ed., *Velikaia Otechestvennaia, Deistvuiushchaia armiia 1941–1945 gg.* [The Great Patriotic (War), the operating army 1941–1945] (Moscow: Animi Fortitudo Kuchkovo pole, 2005); M. G. Vozhakin, ed., *Velikaia Otechestvennaia Komandarmy: Voennyi biograficheskii slovar'* [The Great Patriotic (War) army commanders: A military-biographical dictionary] (Moscow-Zhukovskii: Kuchkovo pole, 2005); M. G. Vozhakin, ed., *Velikaia Otechestvennaia Komkory: Voennyi biograficheskii slovar' v 2-kh tomakh*] [The Great Patriotic (War) corps commanders: A military-biographical dictionary] (Moscow-Zhukovskii: Kuchkovo pole, 2006); *Komandovanie korpusnogo i divizionnogo zvena Sovetskikh vooruzhennykh sil perioda Velikoi Otechestvennoi voiny 1941–1945 gg.* [The command cadre at the corps and divisional level of the Soviet armed forces during the Great Patriotic War 1941–1945] (Moscow: Frunze Academy, 1964), classified secret.

and eastern Donbas regions and along the approaches to Stalingrad during the summer and early fall. Now, after rest and refitting, and with experienced commanders leading them, they were returning to the front to conduct an operation the *Stavka* hoped would add luster to their hitherto less than distinguished combat records.

Pride of place among Vatutin's forces went to the refurbished 5th Tank Army, which was commanded by Lieutenant General Prokofii Logvinovich Romanenko, who had already learned the hard lessons of mechanized warfare while commanding 3rd Tank Army during the Western Front's offensive in the Kozel'sk region in August.[4] Romanenko was assisted by Major General of Tank Forces L. G. Tumanian, a member of his Military Council, and Major General A. I. Danilov, the army's chief of staff. With different corps under its command, the previous incarnation of 5th Tank Army had conducted the magnificently futile counterstrokes in the Voronezh region during July 1942. Precious few of the army's staff officers or command cadre remained with the army as it sought to recoup its damaged reputation in the Stalingrad region (see volume 2 of this trilogy).

After being withdrawn from the front in late July, 5th Tank Army rested and refitted at Plavsk, in the Briansk Front's rear area, and then secretly redeployed southward to the Southwestern Front's rear area, north of the Don River at Serafimovich. In the process, Romanenko's new command grew to an imposing force totaling 6 rifle divisions, 2 tank corps, 1 cavalry corps, 1 separate tank brigade, 2 separate tank battalions, 11 tank destroyer regiments, 9 artillery regiments (4 howitzer and 5 gun), 3 mortar regiments (plus a fourth in 8th Cavalry Corps), 3 guards-mortar [*Katiusha*] regiments, 10 heavy guards-mortar battalions (plus a twelfth in 1st Tank Corps), an entire division of antiaircraft guns with 4 regiments, 5 antiaircraft artillery regiments, 3 separate antiaircraft artillery battalions, a special designation engineer brigade, 2 separate engineer battalions, and 5 pontoon-bridge battalions.[5]

The 1st and 26th Tank Corps formed the armored nucleus of 5th Tank Army. The former, which was organized on 31 March 1942 and now commanded by General V. V. Butkov, had performed more creditably than most of its fellow corps when commanded by General Katukov during the July and August fighting in the Voronezh region. Butkov, who had been deputy commander of 5th Mechanized Corps during the fight at Lepel' and the Smolensk region in summer 1941 and then deputy chief to Fedorenko in the Main Armored Directorate in late 1941 and 1942, had taken command of the corps on 13 September.[6] By early November, Butkov's corps was at full strength, with 13,559 men and 171 tanks; however, this number fell by 18 November, after the corps was hit by German air strikes as it deployed forward.

The 26th Tank Corps, led by General A. G. Rodin since its formation in late July 1942, had missed the heavy fighting in the summer but would receive its baptism of fire in Operation Uranus. With roughly the same number of personnel as 1st Tank Corps, Rodin's corps had its full complement of 171 tanks, but some of the fighting vehicles were in disrepair.[7] Rodin had a distinguished record prior to 1942 and would ultimately rise to command 2nd Tank Army during the battle for Kursk.

The 8th Cavalry Corps was also a veteran, battle-hardened outfit. After being formed on 15 January 1942, it had fought under three commanders— Colonel P. P. Korzun, Major General A. S. Zhadov, and Colonel I. F. Lunev— and also participated in heavy fighting in the Voronezh region in July and August. Its latest commander was Major General M. D. Borisov, an artilleryman who had transferred to the cavalry in 1924. Borisov had led a cavalry regiment in the struggle against Basmachi insurgents in Central Asia in the late 1920s and commanded the Central and Briansk Front's 31st Separate Cavalry Division during the summer and fall of 1941 during Operation Barbarossa. His division then fought with distinction during the battle for Moscow, after which it was awarded the designation of 7th Guards. Following a short stint as deputy commander of 1st Guards Cavalry Corps, Borisov was given command of 8th Cavalry Corps in October 1942.[8] The two-division corps fielded just over 16,000 men on the eve of Operation Uranus.[9]

As of 20 November 1942, 5th Tank Army's ration strength was 104,196 men, of which 90,600 were assigned to combat formations and units. It fielded 2,538 guns and mortars and 359 tanks (60 heavy, 144 medium, and 155 light models).[10]

Deployed on the *front's* left wing, immediately to the east of 5th Tank Army, was Lieutenant General Ivan Mikhailovich Chistiakov's 21st Army, with Brigade Commissar P. I. Krainov as its member of the Military Council and Major General V. A. Pen'kovsky as its chief of staff. Chistiakov commanded six rifle divisions, plus 4th Tank Corps, 3rd Guards Cavalry Corps, one separate destroyer brigade, three separate tank regiments, four separate antitank rifle battalions, one full artillery division (with three howitzer, two gun, and three tank destroyer regiments), six tank destroyer regiments, two gun artillery regiments, three mortar regiments (plus a fourth in 3rd Guards Cavalry Corps), three guards-mortar regiments, and one separate guards-mortar battalion in 3rd Guards Cavalry Corps. The 21st Army also controlled an antiaircraft artillery division with four regiments, five antiaircraft regiments, one separate antiaircraft artillery battalion, and two separate engineer battalions.[11]

The mobile group of 21st Army consisted of 4th Tank and 3rd Guards Cavalry Corps, commanded by Major General of Tank Forces A. G. Kravchenko and Major General I. A. Pliev, respectively. Created on 31 March 1942, 4th Tank Corps had fought against German forces conducting Operation Blau since July, participating in the intense fighting west of Voronezh in July 1942 under the command of General Mishulin. After refitting, and under Mishulin's command once again, it moved to the Kotluban' region in late August, where it was decimated in a bitter fight against XIV Panzer Corps as part of Group Kovalenko (see volumes 1 and 2 of this trilogy). After General Kravchenko took command of the corps on 18 September, it participated in the two counterstrokes conducted by the Stalingrad and Don Fronts in the Kotluban' region, once again suffering immense casualties but impressing the *Stavka* and *front* command with its persistence and combat ardor.[12] Kravchenko had distinguished himself while leading 2nd Tank Corps in the fighting along the immediate approaches to Stalingrad in September, and his reward had been promotion to the rank of major general and command of 4th Tank Corps in the vital struggle with Sixth Army's XIV Panzer Corps northwest of Stalingrad. Despite the heavy losses suffered only weeks before, the *Stavka* and *front* command managed to provide Kravchenko's corps with 159 tanks by mid-November, 143 of which were operable when Uranus began.[13]

As indicated by its "guards" designation, 3rd Guards Cavalry Corps was one of the three most distinguished cavalry corps in the Red Army in the fall of 1942. Created on 14 March 1941 as 5th Cavalry Corps, it was one of the Red Army's three cavalry corps in existence when the war began. It had participated in the heavy fighting in the Kiev region of the Ukraine in the summer and fall of 1941 under the command of Generals Kamkov and Kriuchenkin and had spearheaded Group Kostenko in its signal victory over German Second Army at Elets in December 1941. The latter operation earned the corps its guards designation on 26 December 1941. Subsequently, Kriuchenkin's corps participated in the Briansk Front's abortive offensive toward Orel in January and February 1942 and formed the Southwestern Front's northern pincer in the failed Khar'kov offensive in May 1942. General Pliev took charge of the corps in early July 1942 and led it throughout the summer campaign. In mid-November, Pliev's corps fielded over 22,000 cavalrymen.

Arguably one of the two finest cavalry commanders the Red Army produced during the war, Pliev had commanded 50th Cavalry Division during Cavalry Group Dovator's dramatic raids into the Germans' rear at Smolensk in August and in the Moscow region in late October. After his division was renamed 3rd Guards Cavalry, Pliev led 2nd Guards Cavalry Corps during the battle for Moscow; he led the Southern Front's newly formed 5th Cavalry Corps during the Barvenkovo-Lozovaia offensive of January and February 1942 and during the defeat at Khar'kov in May 1942. After receiving command of 3rd Guards Cavalry during the initial stages of Operation Blau, he led its retreat eastward across the Don River in July and was in command when it spearheaded the Stalingrad Front's successful effort to seize the vital Serafimovich bridgehead in late August.[14]

By 20 November 1942, the ration strength of 21st Army was 103,270 men, with 92,056 in its combat elements. The army fielded 2,520 guns and mortars and 199 tanks (85 heavy, 57 medium, and 57 light models).[15]

Finally, the 1st Guards Army, the reinforced former 63rd Army, was commanded by Lieutenant General Dmitri Danilovich Leliushenko, with Brigade Commissar I. S. Kolesnichenko as its member of the Military Council and Major General I. P. Krupennikov as its chief of staff. It was deployed on the Southwestern Front's right wing on the basis of a 1 November *Stavka* directive and initially consisted of 4th and 6th Guards Rifle Corps, 1st Guards Mechanized Corps, and 1st, 153rd, and 197th Rifle Divisions. Leliushenko had earned fame leading the 1st Guards Rifle Corps in its successful delaying action at Orel and Mtsensk against Guderian's Second Panzer Group in October 1941. Later, he led the Western Front's 5th and 30th Armies during the Moscow defense and counteroffensive.[16]

Leliushenko's army was numerically stronger than Vatutin's other armies for two reasons. First, since it had not been involved in heavy fighting since late July, its rifle divisions were nearer full strength and relatively unscathed. Second, many of the army's rifle divisions were relatively fresh because the *Stavka* was relying on Kuznetsov's army to play a significant role in expanding the Uranus offensive (should it succeed) into the far more ambitious Operation Saturn. The *Stavka* hoped Saturn would propel Red Army forces to the Rostov region and, perhaps, even bag the better part of German Army Group A before it could escape from the Caucasus region. Third, as an indicator of its future intent, the *Stavka* added the new 1st Guards Mechanized Corps to 1st Guards Army before Uranus began, although with the specific instruction that it be withheld from combat until Uranus succeeded. Finally, although the *Stavka* initially reneged on assigning 4th and 6th Guards Rifle Corps to Leliushenko's army (allocating six separate rifle divisions instead), given its anticipated role in Operation Saturn, Stalin ultimately earmarked the newly formed guards rifle corps, as well as 14th Rifle Corps, for inclusion in Leliushenko's army shortly after Uranus began.[17]

On 20 November, 1st Guards Army consisted of six rifle divisions, all at nearly full strength; one mechanized corps; a separate motorized rifle brigade; one gun artillery regiment; three tank destroyer regiments; one guards-mortar regiment and one guards-mortar battalion (the latter part of 1st Guards Mechanized Corps); an antiaircraft artillery regiment; a separate engineer battalion; and two pontoon-bridge battalions.[18] The army's ration strength was 155,096 men, of which 142,869 were in combat formations. It fielded 3,308 guns and mortars and 163 tanks (113 medium and 50 light models), all of which were assigned to 1st Guards Mechanized Corps.[19]

With no combat formations in reserve, by the time Operation Uranus commenced, Vatutin's Southwestern Front consisted of 18 rifle divisions, 3 tank corps, 1 mechanized corps, 2 cavalry corps with 6 cavalry divisions, 1 separate tank brigade, 3 separate tank regiments, 2 separate tank battalions, 1 separate motorized rifle brigade, 1 separate destroyer brigade, 1 motor-cycle regiment, and 4 separate battalions of antitank rifles. This armada was supported by 1 artillery division, 12 artillery regiments, 20 tank destroyer artillery regiments, 8 mortar regiments, 7 guards-mortar regiments and 13 guards-mortar battalions, 2 antiaircraft artillery divisions, 12 separate antiaircraft artillery regiments, 6 separate antiaircraft artillery battalions, 1 special-designation engineer brigade, 1 sapper brigade, 5 engineer battalions, and 7 pontoon-bridge battalions. The *front*'s ration strength was 389,902 men, with a combat strength of 331,984 men, supported by 8,655 guns and mortars, 721 tanks (145 heavy, 314 medium, and 262 light models), and 359 combat aircraft, 311 of which were operational.[20] The average divisional strength in the Southwestern Front was 8,800 men. The *Stavka* was confident that the Southwestern Front's forces were sufficient to strike and decisively defeat the six weak divisions of Romanian Third Army opposite it.

The Stalingrad Front

Although in second place among the three attacking *fronts* in terms of combat strength, the Stalingrad Front's combat mission was just as important as the Southwestern Front's because it formed the southern pincer of the planned broad envelopment. The Stalingrad Front's Military Council consisted of Colonel General A. I. Eremenko, the *front*'s commander; Brigade

Commissar N. S. Khrushchev; and Major General I. S. Varennikov, the chief of staff.[21] Operating in the roughly 450-kilometer sector from Rynok in Stalingrad's northern suburbs, southward along and west of the Akhtuba and Volga Rivers, to the northern shore of the Caspian Sea, south of Astrakhan', the *front's* mission was to conduct the second of Operation Uranus's two main attacks from the Beketovka bridgehead and lake region, 5 to 70 kilometers south of Stalingrad.

To perform this task, the shock group of Eremenko's *front* consisted of 64th, 57th, and 51st Armies. These armies' rifle forces were supposed to penetrate Axis defenses in several sectors south of the city; their 13th Tank and 4th Mechanized Corps formed a mobile group that would constitute Uranus's southern pincer, while 4th Cavalry Corps pushed southward to protect the shock group's left flank. Deployed on the Stalingrad Front's right wing, the remnants of Chuikov's 62nd Army were still clinging to ever-shrinking footholds in Stalingrad; they were to put up an active defense and thus tie down the forces of German Sixth Army still fighting in the city. On the Stalingrad Front's distant left wing, the far smaller 28th Army, which was defending the approaches to Astrakhan' and the mouth of the Volga River, was to advance westward to protect Eremenko's *front* against any threats from the south and, if possible, establish communications with Soviet forces operating in the Caucasus region. The Stalingrad Front's five armies were supported by the combat aircraft subordinate to the 8th Air Army, the ships and boats of the Volga Military Flotilla, and, in the vicinity of Stalingrad proper, the antiaircraft guns and fighter-interceptors of the Stalingrad PVO (Anti-Air Defense) Corps Region.

In the *Stavka's* view, Eremenko's *front* fielded sufficient rifle forces and supporting arms to penetrate Axis defenses in two main sectors south of Stalingrad. It had enough tank and mechanized forces to exploit that penetration into the operational depths and reach the *front's* intermediate and final objectives (see table 2).

All five field armies of Eremenko's *front* were relatively small in terms of their assigned manpower and artillery strength. Their ration strength ranged from roughly 54,000 to just short of 67,000 men, and they fielded between 1,093 and 1,196 guns and mortars.[22] This was entirely understandable, given the strength of the forces they opposed: nine pathetically weak German divisions fighting in or defending Stalingrad city; two German and one Romanian infantry divisions in and south of Stalingrad's southern suburbs; and four more weak Romanian infantry divisions, part of a cavalry division, and a motorized detachment in the lake district farther south of the city. However, the armies differed from one another far more significantly in terms of the mobile forces they fielded—specifically, their tank, mechanized, and cavalry forces.

Table 2. Composition and Senior Command Cadre of the Stalingrad Front, 19 November 1942 (less artillery and engineer units)

Stalingrad Front—Colonel General A. I. Eremenko
  62nd Army—Lieutenant General V. I. Chuikov
    13th, 37th, and 39th Guards and 45th, 95th, 112th, 138th, 193rd, 284th, and 308th Rifle Divisions
    42nd, 92nd, 115th, 124th, 149th, and 160th Rifle Brigades
    84th Tank Brigade
    506th Separate Tank Battalion (235th Tank Brigade)
  64th Army—Lieutenant General M. S. Shumilov
    7th Rifle Corps—Major General S. G. Goriachev
      93rd, 96th, and 97th Rifle Brigades
    36th Guards and 29th, 38th, 157th, and 204th Rifle Divisions
    66th and 154th Naval Rifle Brigades
    20th Destroyer Brigade
    Composite Student Regiment of the Vinnitsa Infantry School
    118th Fortified Region
    13th and 56th Tank Brigades
    28th Separate Armored Train Battalion
  51st Army—Major General N. I. Trufanov
    15th Guards and 91st, 126th, and 302nd Rifle Divisions
    76th Fortified Region
    4th Mechanized Corps—Major General of Tank Forces V. T. Vol'sky
      36th, 59th, and 60th Mechanized Brigades (with 26th, 20th, and 21st Tank Regiments, respectively)
    55th and 158th Separate Tank Regiments
    4th Cavalry Corps—Lieutenant General T. T. Shapkin
      61st and 81st Cavalry Divisions
    38th Separate Motorized Rifle Brigade
    254th Tank Brigade
  57th Army—Lieutenant General F. I. Tolbukhin
    169th and 422nd Rifle Divisions
    143rd Rifle Brigade
    45th, 172nd, and 177th Separate Machine Gun–Artillery Battalions (76th Fortified Region)
    13th Tank Corps—Major General of Tank Forces T. I. Tanaschishin
      17th, 61st, and 62nd Mechanized Brigades (with 44th, 176th, and 163rd Tank Regiments, respectively)
    90th and 235th Tank Brigades
    156th Separate Motorcycle Battalion
  28th Army—Lieutenant General V. F. Gerasimenko
    34th Guards and 248th Rifle Divisions
    52nd, 152nd, and 159th Rifle Brigades
    78th and 116th Fortified Regions
    Separate cavalry regiment (battalion)
    6th Guards Tank Brigade
    565th Separate Tank Battalion
    35th Separate Armored Car Battalion
    30th, 33rd, and 46th Separate Armored Train Battalions
  8th Air Army—Major General of Aviation T. T. Khriukin
    2nd Mixed Aviation Corps—Major General of Aviation I. T. Eremenko
      201st and 235th Fighter Aviation Divisions
      214th Assault Aviation Division
    206th Assault Aviation Division

Table 2. (continued)

8th Air Army (continued)
226th and 289th Mixed Aviation Divisions
270th Bomber Aviation Division
272nd Night Bomber Aviation Division
268th and 287th Fighter Aviation Divisions
8th Reconnaissance Aviation Regiment
23rd, 282nd, 633rd, 655th, and 932nd Mixed Aviation Regiments
678th Transport Aviation Regiment
31st and 32nd Corrective Aviation Squadrons
459th Antiaircraft Artillery Regiment
Stalingrad PVO (Antiaircraft Defense) Corps Region—Colonel E. A. Rainin to
February 1943
73rd Guards and 748th, 1077th, 1079th, 1080th, 1082nd, and 1083rd Antiaircraft Artillery
Regiments
82nd, 106th, 188th, and 267th Antiaircraft Artillery Battalions
72nd, 122nd, 126th, 132nd, 137th, 141st, 142nd, and 181st Separate Armored Trains
(Antiaircraft)
102nd PVO Fighter Aviation Division
Volga Military Flotilla—Vice Admiral D. D. Rogachev to February 1943
1st and 2nd Brigades of River Ships
Separate Armored Trawlers
Front **forces**
300th Rifle Division
77th, 115th, and 156th Fortified Regions
85th Tank Brigade
35th and 166th Separate Tank Regiments

Sources: A. M. Samsonov, *Stalingradskaia bitva* [The battle of Stalingrad] (Moscow: Nauka, 1983), 569; V. A. Zolotarev, ed., *Velikaia Otechestvennaia, Deistvuiushchaia armiia 1941–1945 gg.* [The Great Patriotic (War), The operating army 1941–1945] (Moscow: Animi Fortitudo Kuchkovo pole, 2005); M. G. Vozhakin, ed., *Velikaia Otechestvennaia Komandarmy: Voennyi biograficheskii slovar'* [The Great Patriotic (War) army commanders: A military-biographical dictionary] (Moscow-Zhukovskii: Kuchkovo pole, 2005); M. G. Vozhakin, ed., *Velikaia Otechestvennaia Komkory: Voennyi biograficheskii slovar' v 2-kh tomakh*] [The Great Patriotic (War) corps commanders: A military-biographical dictionary] (Moscow-Zhukovskii: Kuchkovo pole, 2006); *Komandovanie korpusnogo i divizionnogo zvena Sovetskikh vooruzhennykh sil perioda Velikoi Otechestvennoi voiny 1941–1945 gg.* [The command cadre at the corps and divisional level of the Soviet armed forces during the Great Patriotic War 1941–1945] (Moscow: Frunze Academy, 1964), classified secret.

Unlike the Southwestern Front, which received much of its force from the *Stavka* Reserve, most of the Stalingrad Front's forces had been participating in heavy fighting in the region since September 1942. This was particularly true of the divisions and brigades assigned to 62nd and 64th Armies. The *Stavka* reinforced the Stalingrad Front with 13th Tank, 4th Mechanized, and 4th Cavalry Corps; 87th and 315th Rifle Divisions; six rifle, one motorized rifle, and three tank brigades; and six PVO artillery and two tank destroyer regiments. Yet 13th Tank Corps had been "through the mill," experiencing heavy fighting in the Great Bend of the Don in late July and August 1942; 87th Rifle Division had fought in Stalingrad's suburbs in September, before being withdrawn into the *Stavka* Reserve for rest and refitting; and 315th Rifle Division had fought in the Kotluban' region with 1st Guards Army as recently as September.

The strongest of Eremenko's armies were Lieutenant General Fedor Ivanovich Tolbukhin's 57th and Major General Nikolai Ivanovich Trufanov's 51st. Together, they constituted the *front*'s shock group, tasked with conducting the main attack in two sectors. As such, each fielded well over 200 tanks, far more than the other three armies subordinate to the *front*. Tolbukhin's army had been fighting, as part of the Southeastern Front, in the northern half of the lake region south of Stalingrad since early August 1942; it became subordinate to the Stalingrad Front after 30 September. By 18 November, 57th Army consisted of the powerful 13th Tank Corps, two rifle divisions, one rifle brigade, two tank brigades, three separate machine gun–artillery battalions, and one separate motorcycle battalion.[23] The army's Military Council consisted of Tolbukhin, Brigade Commissar N. E. Subbotin, and the chief of staff, Colonel N. Ia. Prikhid'ko.[24]

Despite its designation, the composition of Colonel T. I. Tanaschishin's 13th Tank Corps resembled that of a large mechanized corps. The 13th consisted of three mechanized brigades, each with a separate tank regiment; it fielded a total armored strength of 205 medium and light tanks. Formed on 23 May 1942, the tank corps had been commanded by Tanaschishin since 17 July and, under 1st Tank Army's control, had served with distinction in the bitter fighting at the Great Bend of the Don River during August 1942, although it was virtually destroyed in the effort. The corps' remnants then supported 64th Army in its fighting for the Beketovka bridgehead south of Stalingrad during September. Since the heavy fighting stripped the corps of its original tank brigades, a *Stavka* directive dated 1 November shipped three new mechanized brigades and tank regiments to the Stalingrad region, which ultimately ended up reconstituting 13th Tank Corps. By mid-November, Tanaschishin's corps was at full strength, with 205 tanks.[25]

As of 20 November, 57th Army's ration strength was 66,778 men, 56,026 of them assigned to combat forces. The army fielded 1,604 guns and mortars and 225 tanks (4 heavy, 122 medium, and 99 light models).[26]

General Trufanov had replaced Major General T. K. Kolomiets on 2 October 1942 as commander of 51st Army, which was only slightly smaller than 57th Army. It was augmented with the new 4th Mechanized Corps and 4th Cavalry Corps to increase its shock power. No newcomer to heavy fighting, the army had been formed in the Crimea in October 1941 and was directly subordinate to the *Stavka*. Its first action was an unsuccessful defense of the peninsula against Manstein's German Eleventh Army in October and November 1941. After being driven back to the Taman' Peninsula in the north Caucasus in November, it took part in the Trans-Caucasus Front's daring Kerch'-Feodosiia amphibious operation in late December 1941 and January 1942, which regained the Kerch' Peninsula on the eastern tip of the Crimea. From February to May, the 51st endured confused fighting in the Kerch' region, at the end of which it was again summarily expelled from the Crimea with heavy losses. During Operation Blau, Kolomiets's army conducted an unsuccessful defense of the Don River line east of Rostov, after which it withdrew to the lake region south of Stalingrad, where it defended on the Southeastern Front's and then the Stalingrad Front's left wing from September to November 1942.[27]

The army's new commander, Nikolai Ivanovich Trufanov, had served as chief of staff of 28th Mechanized Corps when the war began, only to become chief of staff of the Trans-Caucasus Front's 47th Army in August 1941. After serving as 47th Army's chief of the rear and deputy commander, he commanded 1st Separate Rifle Corps successfully enough to lead 51st Army briefly in July 1942 and again in October, after recovering from an extended illness.[28]

By 20 November 1942, the *Stavka* had beefed up Trufanov's army with 4th Mechanized Corps, 4th Cavalry Corps, and two rifle divisions, giving it the strength necessary to play a major role in the Uranus counteroffensive. As a result, by the time Uranus began, the army consisted of four rifle divisions, one fortified region, one mechanized corps, one cavalry corps, one tank brigade, one separate motorized rifle brigade, three artillery regiments (one army and two gun), three tank destroyer regiments (plus one more each in 4th Cavalry and 4th Mechanized Corps), one mortar regiment, two guards-mortar regiments, one antiaircraft artillery regiment (in 4th Mechanized Corps), three separate engineer battalions, and one pontoon-bridge battalion.[29] The army's Military Council consisted of Trufanov, Brigade Commissar A. E. Khalezov, and the chief of staff, Colonel A. I. Kuznetsov.

The armored fist of 51st Army was Major General of Tank Forces V. T. Vol'sky's 4th Mechanized Corps. One of the Red Army's newer formations, the corps was formed between 18 September and 10 October 1942 from the headquarters and remnants of 28th Tank Corps, which had been decimated in the fighting in the Great Bend of the Don and the approaches to Stalingrad in late July and August. Major General G. S. Rodin (distinct from A. G. Rodin, commander of 26th Tank Corps) led the corps during its formation, only to relinquish command to Vol'sky when that process was completed on 10 October. Although a largely "green" formation in November, most of the corps' command cadre and some of its personnel had combat experience. Once formed, the corps numbered roughly 20,000 men and had a paper strength of 220 tanks.[30]

The 4th Cavalry Corps, which consisted of two cavalry divisions, was commanded by Lieutenant General T. T. Shapkin. It was new to combat, despite being formed in the Central Asian Military District on 17 December 1941. There it remained, under Shapkin's leadership, until it was dispatched to reinforce the Stalingrad Front's 51st Army in mid-October 1942. Sixty percent of the 4th's cavalrymen were from ethnic Kazakh, Kirgiz, Uzbek, Tadzhik, and Turkmen. Shapkin was one of the few veterans of the Tsar's army and anti-Bolshevik "White" forces during the Civil War to rise to prominence in the Red Army.[31]

As of 20 November, 51st Army's ration strength was 55,184 men, with 44,720 in its combat formations. The army was equipped with 1,077 guns and mortars and 207 tanks, including 118 medium and 89 light models.[32]

The third strongest army in the Stalingrad Front was Lieutenant General Vasilii Filippovich Gerasimenko's 28th Army. It had been formed on 9 September 1942 from forces assigned to the Stalingrad Military District and the Southeastern Front and was tasked with defending the port city of Astrakhan' on the Caspian Sea's northern coast and the lower Volga River region. The army's Military Council consisted of Gerasimenko, Corps Commissar A. N. Mel'nikov, and the chief of staff, Major General S. M. Rogachevsky.

Originally under the direct control of the *Stavka*, Gerasimenko's army was assigned to the Stalingrad Front on 30 September as a part of the reorganization of forces in the Stalingrad region in anticipation of a counteroffensive. Before taking command of 28th Army, General Gerasimenko had commanded the Western Front's ill-fated 21st and 13th Armies in late June and July 1941; he then served as deputy commander of the Reserve Front's rear services in September, assistant chief of the Red Army Rear in October, and commander of the Stalingrad Military District in December.[33]

As of early November, the army's only opponent was German 16th Motorized Division, whose reinforced regiments covered the vast region east of Elista between the right wing of Army Group B and the left wing of Army Group A. By the time Uranus began, 28th Army consisted of two rifle divisions, three rifle brigades, two fortified regions, one tank brigade, one separate tank battalion, an armored train battalion, three separate armored trains, a weak artillery force of one guards-mortar regiment, two separate engineer battalions, and a pontoon-bridge battalion. Its strongest division, the 34th Guards Rifle, had been formed from the 7th Airborne Corps on 6 August 1942, one of nine guards airborne corps the *Stavka* had converted into guards airborne divisions to reinforce its beleaguered forces in southern Russia.[34] As of 19 November, 28th Army's ration strength was 64,265 men, with 47,891 men assigned to its combat forces. It fielded 1,196 guns and mortars and 80 tanks (10 heavy, 26 medium, and 44 light models).[35]

The two weakest armies in Eremenko's *front* were the 62nd and 64th, both of which had constantly been involved in intense fighting with heavy losses since late July. After surviving violent struggles in and south of the Great Bend of the Don River in July and early August and along the approaches to Stalingrad in August and early September, the two armies fought to hold on to bridgeheads on the Volga River's western bank, the 62nd in Stalingrad city and the 64th in the Beketovka region south of the city. By November, the attrition caused by this fighting had reduced the two armies' divisions and brigades to barely regimental and sometimes only battalion strength.

Under the command of Lieutenant General Vasilii Ivanovich Chuikov since 9 September, 62nd Army thereafter served as the "bait" to draw German Sixth Army into a costly attrition battle in the streets, factories, and other buildings in Stalingrad for more than two months (see volume 2 of this trilogy).[36] During this period, on the *Stavka's* instructions, the Southwestern Front and, after 30 September, the Stalingrad Front provided Chuikov with just enough forces and replacements to hold parts of Stalingrad and tie down and grind up Sixth Army, but not a man more. This kept 62nd Army's combat strength at roughly 50,000 men, but less than half of them were actually fighting in Stalingrad. Most artillery units, for example, remained on the eastern bank of the Volga during the battle. While 62nd Army's forces were decimated in the city fight, Stalin dispatched the bulk of Red Army replacements to the forces designated to conduct Operation Uranus. As a result, by the time Uranus began, 62nd Army defended the city with only a clutch of skeletal divisions and brigades.

When Uranus began, Chuikov's army consisted of ten rifle divisions, three of them guards formations; six rifle brigades; one tank brigade; one separate tank battalion; three gun artillery regiments; three tank destroyer regiments; one mortar regiment (less a battalion); five guards-mortar regiments; two antiaircraft artillery regiments; and two separate engineer battalions.[37] The army's Military Council consisted of Chuikov, Division Commissar K. A. Gurov, and the chief of staff, Major General N. I. Krylov.[38]

As of 20 November, belying the imposing number of divisions and brigades assigned to it, the army's ration strength was 54,199 men, with 41,667 assigned to combat formations. The army fielded 1,237 guns and mortars and 23 tanks (7 heavy, 15 medium, and 1 light model), all subordinate to its single tank brigade.[39] By this time, the strength of 62nd Army's ten rifle divisions ranged from a low of 659 men to a high of 5,201 men, for an average of roughly 2,744 men per division. Its brigades ranged in strength from 271 men to 3,637 men, for an average of roughly 1,590 men per brigade.[40]

The 64th Army, which had been formed in late July 1942 and had been commanded by Lieutenant General Mikhail Stepanovich Shumilov since 9 September, was the smallest of the Stalingrad Front's five field armies.[41] Although slightly larger than 62nd Army in terms of its assigned tanks, it was slightly smaller than Chuikov's army based on personnel strength and assigned artillery. Like its neighbor in Stalingrad city, Shumilov's army had been struggling to hold the Beketovka bridgehead on the Volga's western bank since early September. Since that time, it had also conducted three major counterstrokes and several lesser counterattacks south of the city, attacks that cost its subordinate divisions and brigades heavily. As of mid-November, the army consisted of one small rifle corps with three new rifle brigades; five rifle divisions, including one guards division; two naval infantry brigades; a separate destroyer brigade; one fortified region; two tank brigades; a composite student infantry regiment; one armored train battalion; four tank destroyer regiments; one heavy guards-mortar regiment (less two battalions); two guards-mortar regiments; two antiaircraft gun regiments; and three separate engineer battalions.[42] The army's Military Council consisted of Shumilov, Brigade Commissar Z. T. Serdiuk, and the chief of staff, Major General I. A. Laskin.[43]

The premier infantry formation in 64th Army was 36th Guards Rifle Division, which, like 28th Army's 34th Guards, had been formed from an airborne corps (the 9th) on 6 August 1942. Thereafter, it had fought under 57th Army in mid-August and 64th Army in late August against the advancing Fourth Panzer Army and helped 64th Army defend the Beketovka bridgehead throughout the fall by spearheading virtually all its counterstrokes and counterattacks.[44] Unlike its neighboring 62nd Army to the north, 64th Army received significant reinforcements from the *Stavka* during the first two weeks of November. These additions included the new 7th Rifle Corps, with its three rifle brigades sent from the *Stavka* Reserve, and 38th Rifle Division and 13th Tank Brigade from the Stalingrad Front's reserve. The 38th Division had already experienced heavy fighting under 64th Army in the fall but had been withdrawn from the front for rest and refitting in late September. The 13th Tank Brigade, which had belonged to 13th Tank Corps in September and early October, had been withdrawn into the *front*'s reserve by the end of October, only to return to 64th Army in early November as a separate tank brigade designated to provide infantry support.

With these reinforcements, the ration strength of 64th Army on 20 November was 53,742 men, with 40,490 assigned to its combat formations. Shumilov's army was supported by 1,093 guns and mortars and 40 tanks (1 heavy, 27 medium, and 12 light models), assigned to the army's 13th and 56th Tank Brigades.[45]

Overall, when Operation Uranus began, Eremenko's Stalingrad Front (including reserves) consisted of 1 rifle corps, 24 rifle divisions (1 in reserve), 15 rifle brigades, 7 fortified regions (3 in reserve), 1 tank corps, 1 mechanized corps, 1 cavalry corps with 2 cavalry divisions, 8 separate tank brigades (1 in reserve), 1 motorized rifle brigade, 1 separate destroyer brigade, 2 separate tank regiments (in reserve), and 1 separate tank battalion. This force was supported by 14 artillery regiments; 18 tank destroyer artillery regiments; 3 mortar regiments; 14 guards-mortar regiments and 1 guards-mortar battalion; 4 armored train battalions; 1 antiaircraft artillery division, 14 antiaircraft artillery regiments, and 5 antiaircraft artillery battalions; 1 special-designation engineer brigade; 2 sapper brigades; 14 engineer battalions; 6 pontoon-bridge battalions; 1 guards-miner battalion; and 1 separate sapper battalion.[46] The *front's* ration strength was 367,943 men, with a combat strength of 258,317 men, supported by 6,739 guns and mortars, 575 tanks (22 heavy, 308 medium, and 245 light models), and 782 combat aircraft, 637 of which were operational.[47] The average divisional strength in the Stalingrad Front was 4,000 to 5,000 men, with the weakest divisions in 62nd Army and, to a lesser extent, 64th Army. The *Stavka* was confident the Stalingrad Front possessed enough combat power to penetrate the defenses of the four weak Romanian divisions south of Stalingrad and project its forces into the region east and southeast of Kalach-on-the-Don.

The Don Front

The third and by far the weakest of the three *fronts* participating in Operation Uranus was the Don Front, whose Military Council consisted of Lieutenant General Konstantin Konstantinovich Rokossovsky, the *front's* commander; Brigade Commissar A. I. Kirichenko; and Major General M. S. Malinin, the *front's* chief of staff.[48] It was the weakest *front* because its armies, located on the Stalingrad Front's right wing until 28 September, had been conducting constant but unsuccessful offensive operations against German Sixth Army's left wing since 3 September. Therefore, the Don Front's rifle divisions and tank corps and brigades were woefully understrength when the *Stavka* began developing Plan Uranus. Rokossovsky's armies remained weak throughout the planning and preparation of the counteroffensive because available reinforcements quite naturally flowed to the Southwestern and Stalingrad Fronts, which would conduct the counteroffensive's main efforts. Thus, Plan Uranus clearly assigned a secondary role to Rokossovsky's *front*—specifically, to pin down German Sixth Army's left wing and protect and support the offensive by Vatutin's Southwestern Front.

To fulfill its assigned missions, the Don Front's three armies—65th, 24th, and 66th—operated in the 150-kilometer-wide sector extending from its bridgehead south of the Don River from Kletskaia to Sirotinskaia, further southeastward along the Don to Verkhnyi Gnilovskii, and eastward to the Volga River south of Erzovka. The final Uranus plan required 65th Army, which was operating on the Don Front's right wing, to support and protect the Southwestern Front's 21st Army as it advanced southward from the Kletskaia region. It required the Don Front's 24th and 66th Armies, which were deployed in the *front*'s center and on its left wing, to tie down German forces and conduct secondary attacks to facilitate the destruction of German Sixth Army. Finally, 16th Air Army provided Rokossovsky's *front* with air support. Additionally, if Operation Uranus proved successful and German Sixth Army was encircled, Rokossovsky's *front* was to assume primary responsibility for liquidating the encircled force, after being reinforced by the *Stavka*, of course. Despite the Don Front's weakness, the *Stavka* was convinced Rokossovsky had enough forces to accomplish his limited missions (see table 3).

The greatest challenge Rokossovsky's armies faced was that they were to attack German rather than Romanian forces. As previous combat indicated, this was no mean task. Compounding this difficulty, because so many of his *front*'s divisions had been decimated in the fighting during September and October, Rokossovsky ordered seven of his armies' rifle divisions disbanded by 2 November.[49] Their surviving soldiers were redistributed among other divisions within the two armies. This measure alone reduced the number of rifle divisions in his three armies from 31 to 24, albeit the remaining divisions were a bit stronger.

The strongest of the Don Front's three armies was 65th Army, commanded by Lieutenant General Pavel Ivanovich Batov. It occupied a place of honor in an 80-kilometer-wide sector on the *front*'s right wing because Batov's army was designated to deliver the *front*'s main attack in support of the Southwestern Front's 21st Army, which was to advance southward from the Kletskaia bridgehead on Batov's right. The 65th Army had been created on 22 October from 4th Tank Army, thus putting paid to the sarcastic and derisive comments that 4th Tank Army was really just an army with four tanks. Batov, an experienced army commander, had been assigned command of 4th Tank Army on 13 October, after which he busied himself converting it into a full-fledged field army.[50]

Table 3. Composition and Senior Command Cadre of the Don Front, 19 November 1942 (less artillery and engineer units)

Don Front—Colonel General K. K. Rokossovsky
  24th Army—Lieutenant General I. V. Galanin
    49th, 84th, 120th, 173rd, 214th, 233rd, 260th, 273rd, and 298th Rifle Divisions
    54th Fortified Region
    58th and 61st Separate Antitank Rifle Battalions
    16th Tank Corps—Major General of Tank Forces A. G. Maslov (assigned to the *front* after 19 November)
      107th, 109th, and 164th Tank Brigades
      16th Motorized Rifle Brigade
    10th Tank Brigade
    134th, 224th, and 229th Separate Armored Car Battalions
  65th Army—Lieutenant General P. I. Batov
    4th, 27th, and 40th Guards and 23rd, 24th, 252nd, 258th, 304th, and 321st Rifle Divisions
    59th and 64th Separate Antitank Rifle Battalions
    91st and 121st Tank Brigades
    59th Separate Armored Train Battalion
  66th Army—Lieutenant General A. S. Zhadov
    64th, 99th, 116th, 226th, 299th, and 343rd Rifle Divisions
    63rd Separate Antitank Rifle Battalion
    58th Tank Brigade
  16th Air Army—Major General of Aviation S. I. Rudenko
    220th and 283rd Fighter Aviation Divisions
    228th and 291st Assault Aviation Divisions
    271st Night Bomber Aviation Division
    10th Guards Bomber Aviation Regiment
    325th Reconnaissance Aviation Squadron
  ***Front* forces**
    159th Fortified Region
    65th, 66th, 97th, 98th, 99th, 100th, 101st, and 102nd Separate Antitank Rifle Battalions
    64th and 148th Tank Brigades
    39th, 40th, and 377th Antiaircraft Armored Train Battalions

Sources: A. M. Samsonov, *Stalingradskaia bitva* [The Battle of Stalingrad] (Moscow: Nauka, 1983), 569; V. A. Zolotarev, ed., *Velikaia Otechestvennaia, Deistvuiushchaia armiia 1941–1945 gg.* [The Great Patriotic (War), the operating army 1941–1945] (Moscow: Animi Fortitudo Kuchkovo pole, 2005); M. G. Vozhakin, ed., *Velikaia Otechestvennaia Komandarmy: Voennyi biograficheskii slovar'* [The Great Patriotic (War) army commanders: A military-biographical dictionary] (Moscow-Zhukovskii: Kuchkovo pole, 2005); M. G. Vozhakin, ed., *Velikaia Otechestvennaia Komkory: Voennyi biograficheskii slovar' v 2-kh tomakh*] [The Great Patriotic (War) corps commanders: A military-biographical dictionary] (Moscow-Zhukovskii: Kuchkovo pole, 2006); *Komandovanie korpusnogo i divizionnogo zvena Sovetskikh vooruzhennykh sil perioda Velikoi Otechestvennoi voiny 1941–1945 gg.* [The command cadre at the corps and divisional level of the Soviet armed forces during the Great Patriotic War 1941–1945] (Moscow: Frunze Academy, 1964), classified secret.

Batov's army originally consisted of three rifle divisions, a fortified region, one tank brigade, and one motorized rifle brigade, with four tank destroyer, one guards-mortar, and two antiaircraft artillery regiments in support. By 1 November, it had grown to six rifle divisions, with essentially the same tank and artillery support.[51] By the time Operation Uranus began, 65th Army had expanded further to field nine rifle divisions (three of them guards), two separate antitank rifle battalions, two tank brigades, one armored train battalion, four artillery regiments (three army and one howitzer), one tank destroyer regiment, five guards-mortar regiments (one heavy and four standard), three antiaircraft artillery regiments, one engineer battalion, and one pontoon-bridge battalion.[52]

Thankfully for 65th Army, many of its divisions had not taken part in the bloodletting at Kotluban' in late October, although the 24th, 258th, and 321st Rifle Divisions had suffered heavy casualties in previous fighting. By definition, the best of Batov's divisions were his guards formations—specifically, the 4th, 27th, and 40th. However, the 4th and 40th had participated in the fighting in the Kletskaia and Sirotinskaia regions in late August, and the 27th had resisted XIV Panzer Corps' dramatic advance to the Volga during the same period.

As of 20 November, 65th Army's ration strength was 74,709 men, with 63,187 of them assigned to combat formations and units. By this time, the army fielded 1,922 guns and mortars and 49 tanks (10 heavy, 22 medium, and 17 light models).[53]

The two remaining armies subordinate to the Don Front, 24th and 66th Armies, were substantially weaker than the 65th because both had conducted counterstrokes in the Kotluban' and Erzovka regions. Even though both armies had suffered mightily as Zhukov's "sacrificial lambs" in these counterstrokes, their nearly suicidal attacks contributed significantly to 62nd Army's successful defense of Stalingrad city. In addition, since they faced prepared defenses manned by the divisions of Sixth Army's VIII Army and XIV Panzer Corps, 24th and 66th Armies lacked the combat power to do anything more than harass and tie down the opposing Germans forces during Operation Uranus.

The stronger of these two forces was Major General Ivan Vasil'evich Galanin's 24th Army, deployed in the Kotluban' and Kuz'michi sector in the Don Front's center. It was a "fourth-formation" army created on the base of 9th Reserve Army on 1 September 1942. The 24th Army's three predecessors had been either destroyed in previous fighting or simply disbanded.[54] Galanin, who took over from his predecessor, Major General D. T. Kozlov, in mid-October, was an experienced commander who had led 18th Army in the Ukraine and 59th Army in the Tikhvin region in 1941 and had served as deputy commander of the Western Front's 33rd Army and deputy commander of the Voronezh Front in 1942.[55]

Fighting under Kozlov's and Galanin's command, 24th Army had spearheaded the counterstroke in the Kotluban' region from 3 to 12 September 1942; conducted supporting attacks during three more counterstrokes launched in the same region from 18 to 22 September, 23 September to 2 October, and 9 to 11 October; and once again formed the main shock group in a counterstroke in the same region from 20 to 26 October. As a result, the army's divisions had been decimated, to the extent that four of its divisions had to be disbanded in order to keep its other divisions combat ready. By the time Operation Uranus began, Galanin's army consisted of nine rifle divisions, one fortified region, one tank brigade, two separate antitank rifle battalions, three separate armored car battalions, six artillery regiments (one army, two howitzer, and three gun), two tank destroyer regiments, four guards-mortar regiments (one heavy and three standard), two antiaircraft artillery regiments, one engineer battalion, and four sapper battalions.[56]

Unlike the other armies of Rokossovsky's Don Front, 24th Army was allocated a tank corps, the veteran 16th, but only after the offensive began. This would enable the army to conduct a major supporting attack of its own—a thrust from the Kachalinskaia region toward Vertiachii to encircle the German corps defending along the Don River—but only if the Uranus offensive itself proved successful. Commanded by Major General of Tank Forces A. G. Maslov, 16th Tank Corps had served as an armored spearhead in the first three counterstrokes in the Kotluban' region, suffering heavy casualties in each.[57] Therefore, after being withdrawn briefly for rest and refitting, the corps fielded only 140 operable tanks when it rejoined 24th Army after 19 November—sufficient, in Rokossovsky's view, to fulfill its mission.

Although the Don Front and the Stalingrad Front before it had routinely shuffled divisions between its subordinate armies, all of 24th Army's divisions were severely understrength. Therefore, as of 20 November, the ration strength of Galanin's 24th Army was 68,489 men, with 56,409 in combat formations and units. At least in part, the army compensated for its manpower shortages by fielding 1,899 guns and mortars and 48 tanks (21 heavy, 14 medium, 9 light, and 4 special-purpose models, such as flamethrower tanks).[58]

By far the weakest of Rokossovsky's three armies was Major General A. S. Zhadov's 66th Army, which manned positions in the Orlovka and Erzovka sector on the Don Front's left wing. Formed on 27 August from the 8th Reserve Army in the *Stavka* Reserve, this army was one of the three formed by Zhukov in late August and early September to pound German Sixth Army's XIV Panzer Corps manning defenses between the Don and Volga Rivers north and northwest of Stalingrad.[59] An experienced cavalryman, Zhadov had commanded 4th Airborne Corps in the Ukraine in late June and July 1941, served as chief of staff of the Central Front's 3rd Army and the Briansk Front from August 1941 through the battle for Moscow, and commanded 8th Cavalry Corps from May 1942 to his appointment as 66th Army's commander in October 1942.[60] Despite his reputation as a tenacious combat leader—a reputation confirmed by his army's performance in the Erzovka region in late October—Zhadov's 66th Army lacked the combat power to make a dent in German XIV Panzer Corps' defenses. Like Galanin's army on his right, Zhadov had to disband four divisions in early November because they were simply too weak to fight.

When Operation Uranus began, 66th Army consisted of six rifle divisions, one tank brigade, one antitank rifle battalion, two artillery regiments (one army and one gun), one tank destroyer regiment, two mortar and two guards-mortar regiments, one antiaircraft artillery regiment, and two separate engineer battalions.[61] The smallest army in the entire Uranus force (including the decimated 62nd Army), its ration strength was only 51,738 men, with 39,457 in its combat formations and units. The army was supported by 1,568 guns and mortars and only 5 tanks (2 medium and 3 light) assigned to its single tank brigade.[62] Despite its woeful weakness, largely due to Zhadov's ferocity, his army would inflict a grievous wound on its opponent, the famed XIV Panzer Corps, shortly after Operation Uranus began.

Therefore, when Operation Uranus began, Rokossovsky's Don Front (including reserves) consisted of 24 rifle divisions, 2 fortified regions (1 in reserve), 1 tank corps, 6 separate tank brigades (2 in reserve), 3 separate armored car battalions (in reserve), 4 separate armored train battalions, and 13 separate antitank rifle battalions (8 in reserve). This combat force was supported by 13 artillery regiments, 4 tank destroyer regiments, 2 mortar regiments, 12 guards-mortar regiments, 9 antiaircraft artillery regiments, 4 separate antiaircraft artillery battalions, 1 special-designation engineer brigade, 1 sapper brigade, 8 engineer battalions, 5 pontoon-bridge battalions, and 4 sapper battalions.[63]

The *front*'s ration strength was 284,373 men, with a combat strength of 192,193 men, supported by 6,625 guns and mortars, 254 tanks (72 heavy, 90 medium, 88 light, and 4 specialized models), and 388 combat aircraft, 329 of which were operational.[64] The average divisional strength in the Don Front was 5,850 men, with 65th Army's divisions averaging over 7,000 men and 66th and 24th Armies well under 4,500 men each. Although the *Stavka* realized the Don Front lacked the combat power to penetrate German defenses, it hoped the *front* would be able to support and protect the Southwestern Front's attacking shock groups and perhaps encircle and destroy the German divisions isolated west of the Great Bend of the Don River.

Thus, by dint of its Herculean efforts, the *Stavka* managed to assemble a formidable force to conduct Operation Uranus. In combination, the ration strength of the three attacking *fronts* was 1,042,218 men, with 782,548 men serving in combat forces. The three *fronts* fielded 22,019 guns and mortars, 1,550 tanks (239 heavy, 712 medium, 595 light, and 4 special-purpose models), and 1,529 combat aircraft, 1,277 of which were operational.[65] The *Stavka*, its senior representatives Zhukov and Vasilevsky, the General Staff, and the commanders of the three participating *fronts* were convinced this force was sufficient to penetrate Romanian defenses and encircle and destroy German Sixth Army.

THE URANUS PLAN

Context: The Broader Strategic Plan

Although not understood until recently, Operation Uranus was actually part of a much larger complex—a solar system of plans that together constituted a Soviet strategic offensive at least as vast as that which evolved after the Red Army's victory at Moscow in early and mid-December 1941. In both cases, conditioned by their understanding of operational art, *Stavka* planners recognized that no single operation, however successful, would defeat the *Wehrmacht*. Therefore, they planned to use forces from their strategic reserve for offensive action along the entire German-Soviet front, creating so many ruptures that the Germans would be unable to restore the situation. As in the previous winter, however, this strategic concept showed that the Soviet command was not only thinking big; it was also biting off more than it could chew.

If the Uranus encirclement were successful, it would destroy the spearhead of German Army Group B. Building on this, the *Stavka* hoped to conduct Operation Saturn, which would involve a major thrust westward to Rostov to finish off the bulk of Army Group B and destroy Army Group A by cutting off its withdrawal from the Caucasus region. Leading Operation Saturn would be 2nd Guards Army, a massive force held in the *Stavka* Reserve. If it could seize this key transportation junction, it would cut off all supplies to German forces south of the Don and Volga Rivers and strangle Army Group A in the Caucasus.

The companion piece to Operation Uranus was code-named Operation Mars, a massive offensive planned against German Army Group Center's forces defending the Rzhev-Viaz'ma salient. Here, the German line bulged menacingly northeast toward Moscow, surrounded on three sides by the Red Army's Kalinin and Western Fronts. In August 1942, as described in volume 1 of this study, Zhukov had failed to pinch off this salient, which contained portions of Ninth and Third Panzer Armies. Undeterred, Zhukov proposed to attack again. At a late September meeting with Stalin and Vasilevsky, the stubborn commander had convinced the Soviet dictator that there were sufficient reserves to conduct two major offensives in the fall of 1942—one at Stalingrad, and the second at Rzhev.

Originally, in fact, the Rzhev-Viaz'ma offensive was scheduled for 12 October, probably in tandem with the Don and Stalingrad Fronts' offensive in the Stalingrad region. However, the *Stavka's* decision on 13 October to pursue a far broader envelopment of all German forces in the Stalingrad region—the "different solution"—prompted postponement of the Mars offensive, first to 28 October and ultimately, after repeated delays due to poor weather, to 25 November, six days after the Uranus counteroffensive began along the Don River.

In theory, these delays should have increased Zhukov's chances for success because the Uranus counteroffensive would have attracted German operational reserves southward from Army Group Center.[66] By the time Operation Mars began, its scope had been broadened to include attacks against German forces in the Velikie Luki region and as distant as Demiansk, 200 kilometers northwest of Rzhev. The Velikie Luki assault was scheduled to begin on 24 November, the day before the Kalinin and Western Fronts initiated their main efforts south and southwest of Rzhev. As described in the most recent Russian history of the war, "Along the western axis, the Kalinin and Western Fronts were ordered to conduct offensive operation 'Mars,' with the aim of destroying the German Ninth and Third Panzer Armies in the Rzhev, Sychevka, and Olenino regions and to capture Velikie Luki and Novosokol'niki with part of their force."[67]

As it finally developed, the Mars offensive was set to begin on 24 November, when the forward detachments of 3rd Shock Army of General Maksim Alekseevich Purkaev's Kalinin Front assaulted German Third Panzer Army's defenses protecting Velikie Luki from the east. A day later, the Kalinin and Western Fronts' main shock groups were to attack the Rzhev salient simultaneously from west and east: two new mechanized corps of the Kalinin Front would attack from the west and attempt to link up with a tank and cavalry corps of Colonel General Ivan Stepanovich Konev's Western Front, attacking from the east. Zhukov, who planned and would supervise the offensive, believed these mobile formations were strong enough to penetrate German defenses and link up midway across the bases of the salient. Once they came together, cutting off German forces in the Rzhev region, the combined force would turn southeast toward Viaz'ma, where it would meet General P. S. Rybalko's 3rd Tank Army (refurbished after its disastrous attack along the Zhizdra River in August), which was to attack westward. If successful, Operation Mars promised to create an encirclement pocket second in size only to Stalingrad, and it would tear a great hole in Army Group Center just as Army Groups A and B were disintegrating.[68]

Although not yet confirmed by Soviet or Russian sources, the final planet in the constellation of Soviet offensives was likely code-named either Jupiter or Neptune. Just as Saturn depended on the success of Uranus, so Jupiter or Neptune was designed to build on Mars. The Western Front would carry out new thrusts westward through Viaz'ma, while the reinforced Kalinin Front attacked southward. They would then link up with the victorious forces from the Rzhev salient to destroy all of German Army Group Center and seize Smolensk.

Thus, it is pointless to study Operation Uranus in isolation. To fully understand the *Stavka's* intent in conducting the Uranus counteroffensive, as well as the scope and intent of the ensuing strategic offensive and the entire winter campaign, it is necessary to consider the context that gave Operation Uranus its full meaning. As for Uranus's place in history, that was guaranteed when the counteroffensive proved successful.

Scope, Concept, and Strategic Missions

Within the context of this grand strategic venture, Stalin and his *Stavka* assigned the Red Army's three *fronts* operating along the Stalingrad axis—the Southwestern, Don, and Stalingrad Fronts—the task of conducting the Uranus counteroffensive.[69] In terms of its nature, the counteroffensive was a single strategic offensive operation aimed at encircling and destroying the entire Axis force in the Stalingrad region—specifically, the Romanian Third, German Sixth, and German Fourth Panzer Armies. The operation took the form of a massive and broad double envelopment carried out by pincers consisting of large mobile (tank, mechanized, and cavalry) forces subordinate to the Southwestern and Stalingrad Fronts. These *fronts'* mobile forces conducted the double envelopment from the north and south, respectively, while the armies of the Don Front performed the twin tasks of supporting and protecting the pincers and pinning down and containing the bulk of the Axis forces as they were enveloped (see map 4).

The three attacking *fronts* conducted the counteroffensive across a 400-kilometer-wide front by employing two major pincer forces. The Southwestern Front's northern pincer was to advance southward to depths of 120 to 140 kilometers, and the Stalingrad Front's southern pincer was to thrust northwestward 100 kilometers to link up deep in the Axis rear.

The *Stavka's* concept of operations for Uranus began with classic penetrations conducted by the armies of the Southwestern and Stalingrad Fronts. These attacks aimed to break through the defenses of Romanian Third Army, defending on German Sixth Army's left flank northwest of Stalingrad, and the defenses of Romanian and German forces on Fourth Panzer Army's right flank south of the city. After completing the twin penetrations, powerful tank,

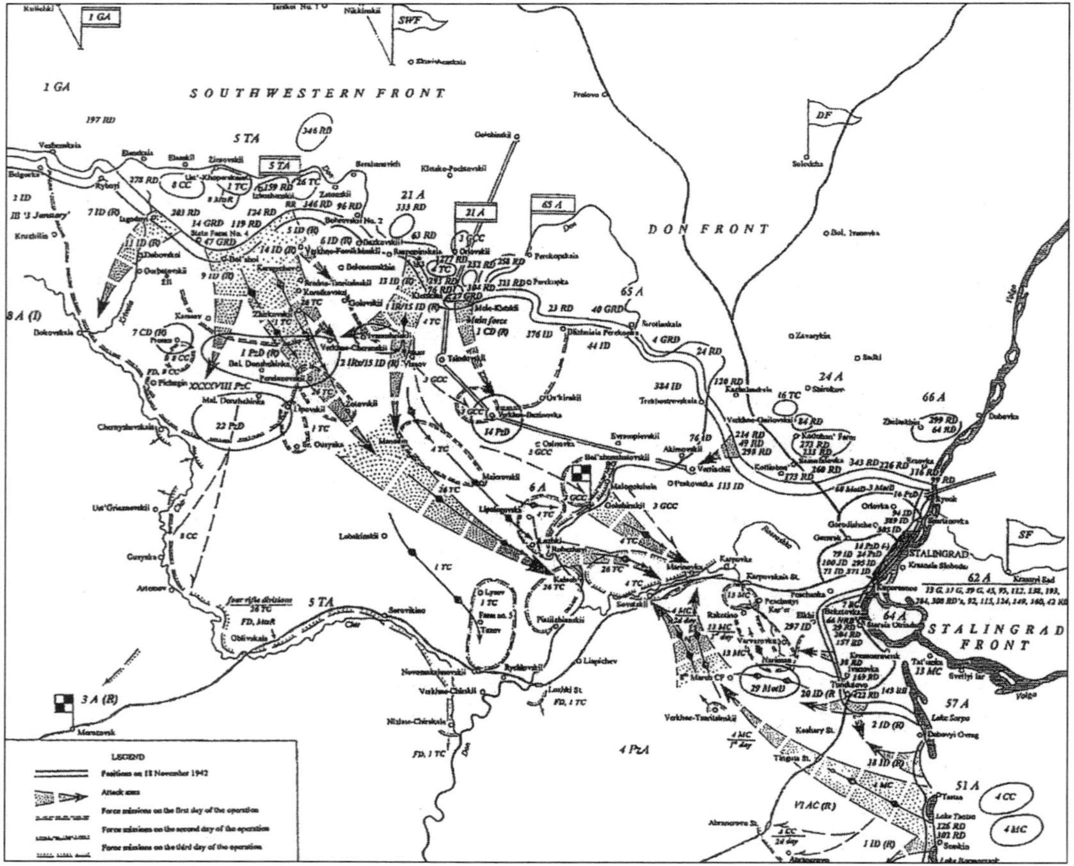

Map 4. Operation
Uranus: The Soviet plan

mechanized, and cavalry forces were to exploit deeply into the Germans' rear area and link up near Kalach-on-the-Don. The mobile forces of the Southwestern and Stalingrad Fronts were to complete the encirclement phase of the operation in three days.

After the linkup, these mobile forces were to form both inner and outer encirclement fronts (lines), with tank, mechanized, and infantry forces creating the inner encirclement front and cavalry and rifle forces forming the outer encirclement front. The combat positions forming the two fronts were to contain the two German armies in the Stalingrad region and prevent or contain any German attempt to rescue or reinforce their encircled Stalingrad grouping.

Once this massive encirclement operation proved successful, the armies of the Don Front, supported by the bulk of the Southwestern and Stalingrad Fronts' tank and mechanized forces, were to attack the encirclement pocket concentrically and destroy the two encircled German armies. Simultaneously, the cavalry and part of the rifle forces forming the outer encirclement front were to expand the offensive by attacking westward and southwestward to drive the remnants of Romanian and German forces away from Stalingrad.

Although Stalin and his *Stavka* planners originally hoped to begin Uranus (as well as Mars) in late October, planning, logistical, and regrouping problems forced them to alter the attack dates, first to 9 November for the Southwestern and Don Fronts and 10 November for the Stalingrad Front and, ultimately, to 19 and 20 November, respectively. The staggered attack dates for the two *fronts* were necessary because it would take three days for the Southwestern Front's northern pincer to traverse the 120 to 140 kilometers to the Kalach region, while it would take only two days for the Stalingrad Front's southern pincer to advance 100 kilometers to its objective.

Based on this concept of operations, Vatutin's Southwestern Front, whose three armies were deployed along and south of the Don River roughly 120 to 340 kilometers northwest of Stalingrad, was to conduct a main attack from bridgeheads on the Don's southern bank, southwest of Serafimovich and near Kletskaia, and penetrate Romanian Third Army's defenses. The *front's* mobile troops would then advance southward to capture Kalach-on-the-Don and link up with the mobile forces of the Stalingrad Front advancing to the Sovetskii region. Subsequently, the Southwestern Front was supposed to destroy the enemy's Stalingrad grouping in cooperation with the Don and Stalingrad Fronts and protect its main shock group by attacking southwestward with the forces on its right wing, reaching the line of the Krivaia and Chir Rivers and creating an "active" outer encirclement front. By "active," the *Stavka* meant a force capable of advancing even farther toward the southwest, specifically, toward the key German logistical and communications facilities at Tatsinskaia and Morozovsk [Morozovskii].

Attacking one day after the Southwestern Front, Eremenko's Stalingrad Front had five armies deployed across a broad front from Stalingrad's northern suburbs southward 450 kilometers along and west of the Akhtuba and Volga Rivers to the northern shore of the Caspian Sea, south of the city of Astrakhan'. Eremenko's *front* planned to conduct its main attack from the region north and south of Lake Sarpinskii. It was to penetrate the defenses of Romanian IV Army Corps, destroy the enemy force, expand the offensive northwestward with its mobile forces, and encircle the enemy's Stalingrad grouping by linking up with the Southwestern Front's mobile forces in the Sovetskii region, 10 to 15 kilometers southeast of Kalach. Subsequently, the *front's* forces were to destroy the enemy's Stalingrad grouping in cooperation with the Don and Southwestern Fronts and then attack southwest toward Abganerovo and Kotel'nikovo with part of those forces, organizing an outer encirclement front along this axis.

Completing this complex mosaic of offensive operations was Rokossovsky's Don Front, whose three armies were deployed in the 150-kilometer-wide sector extending from the western bank of the Volga River 20 kilometers north of the center of Stalingrad city and northwestward to Kletskaia on the Don River. The Don Front was to conduct supporting attacks southward from the Kletskaia bridgehead and the Kachalinskaia region along the Don. Rokossovsky's mission was to penetrate the defenses of German Sixth Army's XI and VIII Army Corps, destroy the opposing enemy, and advance southward to Vertiachii to encircle and destroy XI Army Corps' forces in the small bend of the Don River, in cooperation with the Southwestern Front's 21st Army. Subsequently, the *front's* forces were to destroy the enemy encircled in the Stalingrad pocket, in cooperation with part of the forces of the Southwestern and Stalingrad Fronts.

Regrouping, Reinforcement, Concentration, and Concealment of Forces in Jumping-off Positions

The First Stage: 27 September–12 October
The initial preparation stage for Operation Uranus took place from 27 September, when the *Stavka* made the decision to conduct Uranus, to 12 October, the day before Zhukov and Vasilevsky submitted their revised concept and draft plan for Uranus to Stalin for his approval. During this period, the *Stavka* began withdrawing the key forces required to conduct Operation Uranus from *fronts* and armies operating in other sectors. Prior to this period, the *Stavka* had already withdrawn 3rd and 5th Tank Armies into its strategic reserves and formed five new reserve armies and a large number of tank, mechanized, and cavalry corps; artillery penetration divisions; and separate tank brigades, regiments, and battalions.[70] On 22 and 23 September,

respectively, it assigned 5th Tank Army to Plavsk in the Briansk Front for further training and 3rd Tank Army to Kaluga in the Western Front for further training and possible employment in Operation Mars.[71]

Offensive preparations accelerated after Stalin met with his senior military advisers in the Kremlin on 27–29 September. On 28 September, the *Stavka* issued three directives aimed at reinforcing its *fronts* in the Stalingrad region and preparing other forces for future employment in the region. The first ordered the Ural Military District to dispatch its new 7th Rifle Corps, with its 93rd, 96th, and 97th Rifle Brigades, to the region east of Stalingrad; the second directed the chief of the Red Army's Main Armored Directorate to send 84th and 90th Tank Brigades to the Stalingrad region, although the former was used almost immediately to reinforce 62nd Army in Stalingrad city.[72] The third directive ordered the Voronezh Front to go over to the defense and send 17th and 24th Tank Corps to its reserve for rest and refitting.[73] Two more directives, issued by the *Stavka* on 29 and 30 September, dispatched 87th and 315th Rifle Divisions from Kamyshin to the 10th Reserve Army, where they were to prepare for Operation Uranus, and sent two rifle brigades to the Kalinin Front's 43rd Army, ostensibly in preparation for Operation Mars.[74]

Once the late September meetings adjourned, the *Stavka* prepared a new wave of directives associated with the buildup for Uranus. First, two directives issued on 1 October ordered the Voronezh Front to send its 17th and 18th Tank Corps to Tatishchevo Station in the Don Front's rear for rest and refitting and requested the Don Front to do the same with its 4th Tank Corps.[75] The second directive also assigned seven rifle divisions, the 277th, 62nd, 252nd, 212th, 226th, 333rd, and 293rd, which had just completed their refitting in 10th Reserve Army, to the Don Front.[76] The following day, two more *Stavka* directives dispatched 45th and 300th Rifle Divisions to 4th Reserve Army for future employment in the Stalingrad region, although the deteriorating situation in 62nd Army forced the early commitment of these forces to the fight in the city.[77] As that fight intensified, the *Stavka* continued the buildup of 5th Tank Army, assigning it the refurbished 117th and 159th Tank and 44th Motorized Rifle Brigades on 3 October.[78]

The *Stavka* issued yet another sheaf of preparatory orders shortly before Stalin approved the draft plan for Operation Uranus on 13 October. The most important of these ordered 4th Cavalry Corps to relocate "immediately" from the Central Asian Military District to the Stalingrad region (10 October), directed the Don Front to send its 1st Guards Army and 32nd and 41st Guards Rifle Divisions to the *Stavka* Reserve for rest and refitting (11 October), and directed 1st Reserve Army to dispatch its 18th Rifle Division to its reserve for refurbishing (11 October).[79] The next day, the *Stavka* completed this round of preparations by reinforcing the Stalingrad Front with substantial amounts of antitank weapons, artillery, and machine guns, along with the full 19th Sapper Brigade.[80]

The Second Stage: 13–31 October

In the wake of Stalin's approval of the draft plan code-named Uranus on 13 October, preparations moved forward on all *fronts*, in particular, those measures necessary for the Northwestern, Kalinin, and Western Fronts to conduct Operation Mars and the associated Demiansk offensive. The most important development during this period, however, was the formation of the Southwestern Front on 22 October. Before this date, the *Stavka* issued another spate of directives continuing the process it had begun a month earlier, along with several critical NKO orders. These reinforced the *fronts* participating in Uranus, created a strict security regime in forward forces and NKVD security zones in the rear area, and provided detailed instructions on the employment of tank and mechanized forces in penetration and exploitation operations (see appendix 3A in the *Companion* for the contents of these directives).

Simultaneous with its formation of the Southwestern Front under Vatutin's command, the *Stavka* issued several more directives that provided the Southwestern Front with the forces necessary to spearhead the Uranus offensive. The first two directives on 22 October formed the Southwestern Front by 31 October, assigned it 63rd and 21st Armies from the Don Front and 5th Tank Army from the *Stavka* Reserve, provided it with its commander and the other members of the Military Council, and designated the *front's* operational sector.[81] Associated directives added 17th Air Army to the structure of Vatutin's *front* and reinforced it with 8th Cavalry Corps, one rifle division, and five artillery regiments from the Voronezh Front.[82] Yet another order, this time issued by the NKO, mandated the formation of 1st Guards Mechanized Corps by 5 November, 2nd Guards Mechanized Corps by 25 November, and a total of eight mechanized corps by 1 December.[83] The latter also reorganized the majority of the Red Army's tank brigades and separate tank battalions into a new tank regiment for each of the mechanized corps' mechanized brigades and separate tank regiments for infantry support.

The following day, two *Stavka* orders directed the formation of 1st Guards Army from 4th Reserve Army by 10 November and 2nd Guards Army from 1st Reserve Army by 25 November, each with a full-blooded guards mechanized corps in its makeup.[84] These actions created the necessary strategic reserves to expand Operation Uranus into Operation Saturn once the former offensive succeeded.

On 25 and 26 October, three *Stavka* directives put the finishing touches on the forces required to conduct the Southwestern Front's penetration operations from the Serafimovich and Kletskaia bridgeheads and the subsequent exploitation by Uranus's northern pincer. The first directive reinforced the Southwestern Front and its subordinate armies with 4 rifle divisions (226th, 293rd, 333rd, and 277th), 4th Tank Corps, 3rd Guards Cavalry Corps, and 11 artillery and 5 antiaircraft regiments from the Don Front.[85] Vatutin then assigned the two mobile corps to Chistiakov's 21st Army. The second directive transferred 4th Mechanized and 4th Cavalry Corps, 143rd Rifle Brigade, and 235th Flamethrower Tank Brigade from the *Stavka* Reserve to the Stalingrad Front for employment as its deep exploitation force.[86] The third directive assigned the Southwestern Front's 21st Army 3 guards tank penetration regiments with 21 KV tanks each and 2 flamethrower tanks to support the infantry as it conducted the penetration near Kletskaia.[87]

These and other directives involving lesser forces and more minor issues effectively concluded the *Stavka*'s efforts to form the basic forces needed to conduct Operation Uranus. With its three attacking *fronts* essentially in place by the end of October, during the first ten days of November, it was up to the commanders of the Southwestern, Don, and Stalingrad Fronts to regroup their forces, shape them into attack configuration, and deploy them, first into forward assembly areas and ultimately into their final jumping-off positions for the attack.

The Final Stage: 1–18 November

As the final preparatory period began, Zhukov and Vasilevsky underscored the importance of final adjustments to the Uranus plan and associated force deployments. They flew to the respective headquarters within their purview to supervise each and every measure Vatutin, Eremenko, and Rokossovsky undertook, accompanied by a whole entourage of senior general officers who were specialists in virtually every aspect of military operations.[88] These included Generals Novikov and Golovanov for air operations, Voronov for the employment of artillery, and Fedorenko for armored operations. Their schedule was demanding. Vasilevsky traveled to the Stalingrad Front's headquarters on 1 November to finalize the attack plans of its 57th and 51st Armies. Zhukov did the same, spending the first three days of November at the Southwestern Front's headquarters, where he consulted with Vatutin and his key army commanders. He then moved on to the headquarters of 21st and 65th Armies on 4 and 5 November to meet with Chistiakov, Batov, and their staffs to refine their plans and missions. After a short visit to Moscow on 6 November to consult with Stalin, the deputy supreme commander returned to the front, where he spent 7, 8, and part of 9 November working at the headquarters of Rokossovsky's Don Front. Finally, he traveled to the Stalingrad Front's headquarters on 9 November to consult with Vasilevsky, Eremenko, and the *front*'s army commanders through 15 November. After hours of intensive work with virtually every commander whose force would play a vital role in Uranus, Zhukov returned to Moscow on 16 November to report to Stalin and the *Stavka*. He then sped off to the Kalinin and Western Fronts on 18 November to supervise Konev's and Purkaev's preparations for Operation Mars. There Zhukov remained until 6 December, supervising last-minute planning and then the initial attacks before returning to Moscow. Vasilevsky followed basically the same schedule in the Stalingrad Front, punctuated by occasional brief meetings with Zhukov to coordinate their plans. It was this personal attention to detail by the two *Stavka* representatives in the field that marked a watershed in how the Red Army planned and conducted major operations.

On Zhukov's and Vasilevsky's recommendation, the *Stavka* issued a new series of directives pertaining to Uranus and the three *fronts* taking part in it that altered or reinforced their force structures, coordinated various aspects of their operations, shuffled their command cadre so that the most qualified men were assigned to the most important posts, or simply postponed the counteroffensive because of unresolved problems (see appendix 3B in the *Companion*). The most important of these actions shuffled command in the attacking formations, generated new forces and reinforcements for the participating *fronts*, and postponed the counteroffensive, ultimately to 19 November.

As these many orders and directives indicated, refinements in Plan Uranus, as well as in the composition of the three *fronts* conducting the counteroffensive, went on until the last hour before the operation began. In addition, throughout this period, the *Stavka* kept its focus on those forces required for the anticipated follow-on operations, assigning forces to the Southwestern and Voronezh Fronts above and beyond those needed for Uranus.

Overall, the *Stavka* provided substantial reinforcements to its *fronts* operating along the Stalingrad axis during the fall. Specifically, during the six-week span from 1 October through 20 November, it sent the following to the Voronezh, Southwestern, Don, and Stalingrad Fronts:

- March (individual) replacements—105,211 men
- Guns and mortars—3,391
- Tanks—376
- Forces:
    - Rifle divisions—25
    - Cavalry divisions—9
    - Mechanized corps—3
    - Tank Corps—3[89]

Table 4. Reinforcement and Internal Regroupings of Ground Forces within and between the Southwestern, Stalingrad, and Don Fronts, 1–18 November 1942

Southwestern Front—moved and concentrated three tank, one mechanized, and two cavalry corps into forward assembly areas and final jumping-off positions and transferred five rifle divisions between its armies, including:

- **5th Tank Army**:
  - **1st and 26th Tank Corps and 8th Cavalry Corps** (the latter from the *front*)—moved into concentration regions 30–40 kilometers from the forward edge and then into jumping-off positions in the Serafimovich bridgehead, 10–15 kilometers from the forward edge (during which 1st Tank Corps failed to complete its movement in the Zimovskii region in daylight and was subjected to German bomber strikes on 9 November)
  - **203rd Rifle Division**—sent to 1st Guards Army
  - **14th Guards and 124th (50th Guards) Rifle Divisions**—received from 21st Army
- **21st Army**:
  - **4th Tank and 3rd Guards Cavalry Corps** (the latter from the *front*'s reserve)—moved into forward concentration regions north of the Don River and subsequently crossed into the Kletskaia bridgehead
  - **14th Guards and 124th (50th Guards) Rifle Divisions**—sent to 5th Tank Army
  - **278th Rifle Division**—sent to 1st Guards Army
- **1st Guards (former 63rd) Army**:
  - **1st Guards Mechanized Corps**—received from the Volga Military District
  - **203rd Rifle Division**—received from 5th Tank Army
  - **266th Rifle Division**—received from 4th Reserve Army
  - **278th Rifle Division**—received from 21st Army

Stalingrad Front—moved and concentrated one mechanized, one tank, and one cavalry corps; three rifle divisions; three tanks brigades; and nine artillery and mortar regiments, many across the Volga River, into forward assembly areas and jumping-off positions in combat conditions, including:

- **62nd Army**—no change
- **64th Army**:
  - **422nd Rifle Division and 90th Tank Brigade**—sent to 57th Army
  - **126th Rifle Division**—sent to 57th Army
  - **13th Tank Brigade**—received from the *front* (from 13th Tank Corps)
- **57th Army**:
  - **17th, 64th, and 62nd Mechanized Brigades** (with 44th, 176th, and 163rd Tank Regiments)—received from the Main Armored Directorate for 13th Tank Corps
  - **13th Tank Corps**—received from the *front* and deployed into the woods east of Krasnoarmeiskaia
  - **422nd Rifle Division and 90th Tank Brigade**—received from 64th Army
  - **235th Tank Brigade**—received from the *front*'s reserve
  - **15th Guards Rifle Division**—sent to 51st Army
  - **76th Fortified Region** (minus 172nd and 177th Machine Gun-Artillery Battalions)—sent to 51st Army
- **51st Army**:
  - **4th Mechanized and 4th Cavalry Corps**—received from the *front* and deployed forward into assembly areas 15–20 kilometers east of Tsatsa
  - **15th Guards Rifle Division**—received from 57th Army
  - **126th Rifle Division**—received from 64th Army
  - **76th Fortified Region** (minus 172nd and 177th Machine Gun–Artillery Battalions)—received from 57th Army
  - **302nd Rifle Division**—regrouped from the army's left wing to its right wing
- **28th Army**—no change

Table 4. (continued)

Don Front—moved and concentrated one tank corps, four rifle divisions, and two separate tank brigades into forward assembly areas and jumping-off positions, including:
- **24th Army**:
  - ○ **16th Tank Corps**—received from the *front*
  - ○ **49th, 84th, and 120th Rifle Divisions**—received from 66th Army
  - ○ **207th, 221st, 292nd, and 316th Rifle Divisions**—disbanded on 2 November and their forces distributed to other divisions
  - ○ **258th Rifle Division**—sent to 65th Army
- **65th Army**:
  - ○ **27th Guards and 252nd Rifle Divisions**—received from the *front's* reserve
  - ○ **258th Rifle Division**—received from 24th Army
  - ○ **91st and 121st Tank Brigades**—received from the *front's* reserve
- **66th Army**:
  - ○ **49th, 84th, and 120th Rifle Divisions**—sent to 24th Army
  - ○ **62nd, 212th, and 231st Rifle Divisions**—disbanded on 2 November and their soldiers distributed to other divisions

All *Fronts*—Deployed all infantry support tank regiments and battalions into forward concentration regions 4–6 kilometers from the forward edge two to three days before the counteroffensive began.

Sources: V. A. Zolotarev, ed., *Russkii arkhiv: Velikaia Otechestvennaia: Stavka VGK: Dokumenty i materialy 1942 god, T. 16 (5-2)* [The Russian archives: The Great Patriotic (War): *Stavka* VGK: Documents and Materials 1942, vol. 16 (5-2)] (Moscow: Terra, 1996); V. A. Zolotarev, ed., *Russkii arkhiv: Velikaia Otechestvennaia. General'nyi shtab v gody Velikoi Otechestvennoi voiny: Dokumenty i materialy. 1942 god. T. 23 (12-2)* [The Russian archives: The Great Patriotic (War). The General Staff in the years of the Great Patriotic War: Documents and materials. 1942. Vol. 23 (12-2)] (Moscow: Terra, 1999); K. K. Rokossovsky, ed., *Velikaia pobeda na Volge* [Great victory on the Volga] (Moscow: Voenizdat, 1965), 226.

In addition to these reinforcements, the *Stavka* sent three rifle divisions, two rifle brigades, and three tank brigades to the Voronezh Front during the same period and added 2nd Bomber Aviation Corps to the Don Front's 16th Air Army and 3rd Mixed Aviation Corps to the Southwestern Front's 8th Air Army after the Uranus counteroffensive began.[90] Table 4 illustrates the reinforcements and the massive scale of the internal regrouping that took place within and among the three *fronts* during the final 18 days before the counteroffensive began.

In summary, from 1 October to 18 November, the *Stavka* created an additional *front* in the Stalingrad region and reinforced the three *fronts* designated to conduct the Uranus counteroffensive with 5th Tank Army; 10 rifle divisions; 6 rifle brigades; 3 tank, 1 mechanized, and 2 cavalry corps; 4 tank brigades; 1 tank regiment; and about 20 artillery and mortar regiments. In addition to the forces listed in table 4, these included the following:

- Southwestern Front—5th Tank Army; 14th and 47th Guards and 119th, 159th, and 346th Rifle Divisions; 1st and 26th Tank and 8th Cavalry Corps; 8th Guards Tank Brigade; 3 tank, 13 artillery, 7 mortar, and 6 rocket artillery regiments; 1st Mixed Aviation Corps (to 17th Air Army), 2nd Air Army from the Voronezh Front, and long-range aviation forces
- Stalingrad Front—87th and 315th Rifle Divisions; six rifle brigades; 13th Tank, 4th Mechanized, and 4th Cavalry Corps; one motorized rifle and three tank brigades; six PVO artillery and two tank destroyer regiments; and 2nd Mixed Aviation Corps (to 8th Air Army)
- Don Front—27th Guards and 226th and 252nd Rifle Divisions[91]

Logistical Preparations

All these plans for a galaxy of offensive operations depended on the success of Uranus. Although the time allocated to prepare for Uranus was greater than that for any previous Soviet offensive, this preparation involved unprecedented logistical efforts. In that regard, the same rail and road networks that hampered German logistics also restricted Soviet operations. The chief problem associated with the transfer of such a massive quantity of forces into the region was the limited capacity of the transport network, including the limited number of locomotives and railcars—both boxcars for personnel, horses, and equipment and flat-bed cars for heavier equipment such as tanks and artillery pieces.

The *Stavka*, NKO, and logistical organs had no choice but to rely on existing rail and road networks in the region to reinforce, regroup, and support their attacking forces. This meant, first and foremost, the Rtishchevo-Balashov-Povorino-Frolov railroad line for the Southwestern and Don Fronts and the Urbakh, Baskunchak, and Akhtuba railroad line for the Stalingrad Front. During the buildup for Uranus, the Southwestern and Don Fronts shared a single main rail line running from Rtishchevo, midway between Tambov and Saratov on the Volga River and roughly 400 kilometers north of Stalingrad, southward through Balashov, Povorino, and Frolov to Ilovlia, north of the Don River and 70 kilometers north-northwest of Stalingrad. The Stalingrad Front had only one rail line. It extended from Urbakh (Pushkino), situated roughly 80 kilometers east of Saratov and 325 kilometers north-northeast of Stalingrad, due southward 340 kilometers to Baskunchak, 180 kilometers east-southeast of Stalingrad, and then west-northwestward 150 kilometers to the Akhtuba region, 20 to 25 kilometers east of Stalingrad.

Since the load capacity of both railroad lines proved inadequate to support the buildup of forces for Operation Uranus, the GKO facilitated troop movements during late October and the first half of November by constructing six branch lines totaling 1,160 kilometers of new rail lines, refurbishing 1,958 kilometers of existing rail lines, and building 293 railroad bridges. These measures increased the amount of cargo sent to the region from 22,292 wagonloads in September to 33,236 wagonloads in October and 41,461 in November.[92] A total of roughly 117,000 men were involved in this construction effort. By virtue of their labors, Major General P. A. Kabanov's railway troops were able to move 1,300 freight cars each day.

Despite these prodigious efforts, rail and road transport remained inadequate, and major bottlenecks existed. For example, when the counteroffensive began on 19 November, the 87th and 315th Rifle Divisions, which were supposed to be in Stalingrad by this time, were stranded at the railroad station at Borisoglebsk.[93] In addition, although the *Luftwaffe* tended to concentrate on battlefield support, it interdicted Soviet trains on a regular basis. Moreover, because Soviet commanders wished to conceal the extent of their preparations from German aerial observation, most trains moved only at night.[94]

Rail movement was only the first step in distributing troops and materiel to the front. From railheads, Red Army trucks transported men and supplies to their designated assembly areas, usually driving at night without headlights. The Stalingrad Front alone used 27,000 motor vehicles to supply Chuikov while preparing for the offensive. Despite this huge motor fleet, which for the first time included significant numbers of Lend-Lease vehicles, there was never sufficient motor transportation. This shortage had a dual effect on Uranus. First, fewer troops and supplies than were required were assembled at the line of departure prior to the counteroffensive. Second, once the counteroffensive began, the tank and mechanized formations conducting deep penetrations often ran short of supplies, especially fuel and ammunition.

In addition to rail and motor transport, water transport was a problem. Once in the Stalingrad region, most of the troops and supplies had to cross the Don or Volga River to reach their starting positions for the offensive. This problem was particularly acute south of Stalingrad, where the river level was two meters higher than normal, and tanks and other heavy equipment could not cross on the available floating bridges. With winter ice beginning to accumulate, Rear Admiral Dmitri Dmitrievich Rogachev's Volga River Flotilla had to ferry the heaviest loads across. Prior to 15 November, Rogachev conducted all water crossings at night to conceal the troop buildup from the Germans. Crossings that previously required 50 minutes now took as long as 5 hours because of drifting ice. Despite these difficulties, during the first 20 days of November, 160,000 soldiers, 10,000 horses, 427 tanks, 556 guns, 14,000 vehicles, and 7,000 tons of ammunition crossed the freezing Volga.[95]

Given these logistical challenges, shortfalls were inevitable. Rokossovsky's Don Front received only three of the seven rifle divisions earmarked from the *Stavka* Reserve, and his other armies were well below strength despite major efforts to identify replacements from hospitals and other areas in the rear.[96] The other two *fronts* had a higher priority for transportation and supply and therefore fared better than the Don Front. Nevertheless, the difficulty of assembling enough troops and supplies was the major reason the offensive was delayed from 9 to 19 November.

FRONT AND ARMY PLANS

Preparations

The *fronts*, armies, corps, and divisions designated to participate in the Uranus counteroffensive prepared their respective directives and orders in the last stage of the planning process, between 1 and 18 November 1942. The Southwestern, Stalingrad, and Don Fronts developed their respective concepts of operations from 1 through 6 November, when Zhukov, Vasilevsky, and their groups of experts met with each *front* commander, their subordinate army commanders, and a select group of corps and division commanders whose forces were expected to play particularly important roles in the counteroffensive. After these sessions ended, on either 5 or 6 November, Zhukov and Vasilevsky approved each *front's* completed concept of operations before returning to Moscow. Then, on 8 November, the *front* commanders issued directives to their subordinate armies that described their missions in the counteroffensive, as well as the precise combat formations and specific schemes of maneuver each was to employ. In the case of the Southwestern Front, for example, Vatutin issued his command directive to 5th Tank Army on 8 November (see appendixes 3C–3H in the *Companion* for representative planning documents).[97]

The armies, corps, and divisions subordinate to the *fronts* prepared their offensive plans and associated directives or orders between 9 and 11 November, being careful to coordinate each step with both higher headquarters and adjacent formations and units. For example, the Southwestern Front's 5th Tank Army issued its combat directive on 11 November; the same army's 26th Tank Corps and 47th Guards Rifle Division issued their combat orders on 9 November. In the few instances in which one force's plan depended heavily on the final plans of other forces, or when a major force was assigned to the *front* late in the planning process, they prepared their plans much later. For example, the Southwestern Front's 1st Mixed Aviation Corps issued its combat order on 17 November.[98]

This planning process produced an intricate matrix of *front*, army, corps, and division offensive and defensive operations—an elaborate series of interrelated actions unified under a single concept and designed to achieve one overarching strategic aim: the encirclement and destruction of the enemy's Stalingrad grouping. As such, from the company, battalion, and regimental levels up to the army and *front* levels, this matrix consisted of carefully integrated and coordinated actions aimed at achieving, in succession, tactical, operational, and the ultimate strategic objectives. If properly carried out, dozens of tactical penetration operations by rifle, tank, artillery, and engineer regiments, brigades, and divisions of the *fronts'* field armies would culminate in penetration and exploitation by numerous regiments, brigades, and divisions belonging to the Southwestern and Stalingrad Fronts' tank, mechanized, and cavalry corps. After the exploitation operations conducted by these mobile forces resulted in linkups at designated locations deep in the enemy's rear, and after the field armies, which were following in the mobile forces' wake, liquidated the encircled enemy, the Soviets would consider the entire operation a strategic success. Within this matrix, acting collectively, tactical units (battalions, regiments, and divisions) attacked to accomplish tactical objectives; mobile forces conducting operational maneuvers, together with follow-on armies, exploited deep into the enemy's rear to achieve operational (intermediate) objectives; and the three attacking *fronts*, operating in concert, advanced to accomplish the overall strategic objective (see map 4).

The Southwestern Front

Front Mission

Within the complex matrix of operations making up the Uranus counteroffensive, Vatutin's Southwestern Front formed the northern pincer of a broad double-envelopment operation (see map 5). The *front's* main attack force was subdivided into two distinct "fists": the first, consisting of 5th Tank Army's 1st and 26th Tank and 8th Cavalry Corps, in the bridgehead south of Serafimovich, and the second, consisting of 21st Army's 4th Tank and 3rd Guards Cavalry Corps, in the bridgehead near Kletskaia. Together with its supporting rifle forces and artillery, the shock group constituted half the *front's* rifle divisions and brigades, all its tank and cavalry corps, more than two-thirds of its RVGK artillery regiments, and all its air forces. Attacking southward from the twin bridgeheads, Vatutin's main attack force was to penetrate Romanian Third Army's defenses in sectors totaling 22 kilometers in width; exploit southeast toward Perelazovskii and Kalach-on-the-Don to destroy German operational reserves and strike the flank and rear of the enemy's Stalingrad grouping; and, while the Don Front protected its left flank, reach the Kalach and Sovetskii regions, where it was to link up with the Stalingrad Front's exploitation force by the end of the operation's third day and encircle the enemy's Stalingrad grouping. Subsequently, Vatutin's forces

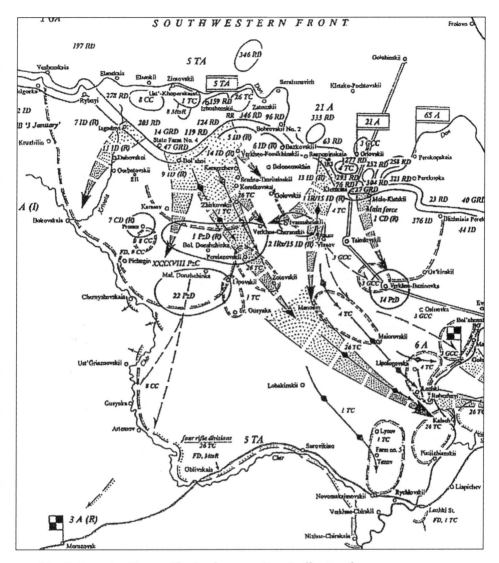

Map 5. Operation Uranus: The Southwestern Front's offensive plan

were to help the Don Front destroy the encircled enemy forces. Simultaneously, on the *front*'s right wing, 5th Tank Army's 8th Cavalry Corps and the other half of the army's rifle formations, together with most of 1st Guards Army's forces, were to attack southward and reach the Krivaia, Bokovskaia, and Chir Rivers, where they would create a firm outer encirclement front capable of protecting the *front*'s main shock group against enemy attacks from the west and southwest.[99]

Army Missions
The 5th Tank Army, commanded by General Romanenko, was to launch both main and secondary attacks. Its main attack would occur southward from the Serafimovich bridgehead in a 10-kilometer-wide sector in the army's center toward Perelazovskii, with a shock group made up of 4 of its 6 rifle divisions, 2 tank corps, and 1 cavalry corps supported by 1 tank brigade, 1 tank battalion, 16 RVGK artillery and mortar regiments, and 1st Mixed Aviation Corps. This main attack had the following objectives:

- Penetrate Romanian Third Army's tactical defenses;
- Exploit the penetration with its mobile group (technically, called an echelon for the development of success);
- Encircle and destroy Romanian Third Army's forces along the Bol'shoi and Kletskaia line with the rifle forces on its left wing in cooperation with the rifle forces of 21st Army's right wing; and
- Exploit southeastward with 1st and 26th Tank Corps to reach the Nizhne-Chirskaia and Kalach sector along the Don River and complete the encirclement of the enemy's Stalingrad grouping.

Simultaneous with the main attack, 5th Tank Army was to mount a secondary attack from the right flank of its main attack sector with a shock group consisting of one rifle division and 8th Cavalry Corps' 21st, 55th, and 112th Cavalry Divisions, with the following objectives:

- Penetrate Romanian Third Army's tactical defenses;
- Exploit the penetration with its cavalry corps toward the south and southwest;
- Erect an outer encirclement front in the Bokovskaia, Chernyshevskaia, and Nizhne-Chirskaia sector along the Chir River;
- Seize bridgeheads on the right (western) bank of the Chir River from Chernyshevskaia to Ust'-Griaznovskii; and
- Dispatch reconnaissance units farther southward from the Chir River toward Morozovsk.

The army's forces were to reach the following lines (positions) by the end of each day of the operation:

First Day
- 26th Tank Corps—Perelazovskii and Zotovskii region, with reinforced reconnaissance units operating toward Chernyshevskaia and Oblivskaia on the Chir River, to sever enemy rail and road communications in the region
- 1st Tank Corps—Lipovskii and Sredniaia Gusynka region
- 8th Cavalry Corps—Pronin region, with forward detachments in the Pichugin region
- Rifle formations—Marker 211, Karasev, and the Verkhne-Cherenskii line

Second Day
- 26th Tank Corps—Kalach and Piatiizbianskii region
- 1st Tank Corps—Lysov, Novomaksimovskii, and Farm No. 5, with its forward units seizing crossings over the Don River in the Nizhne-Chirskaia and Lozhki region and cutting railroad lines in the Surovikino region on the Chir River
- 8th Cavalry Corps—Ust'-Griaznovskii, Gusynka, and Artemov
- Rifle formations—Chir River line from Bokovskaia to Chernyshevskaia and eastward to Kalach-Kurtlak and Perelazovskii

Third Day
- 1st and 26th Tank Corps—establish communications with the Stalingrad Front's mobile group in the Kalach and Sovetskii region and encircle and begin destroying the enemy's Stalingrad grouping[100]

General Chistiakov's 21st Army would also be conducting main and secondary attacks. It was to launch its main attack southward from the Kletskaia bridgehead in a 12-kilometer-wide sector from Marker 163 eastward to Kletskaia on the army's left wing, with a shock group consisting of 5 of its 6 rifle divisions, 1 tank corps, and 1 cavalry corps supported by 3 tank regiments and 11 artillery, 3 mortar, and 3 multiple rocket launcher regiments, to accomplish the following objectives:

- Penetrate Romanian Third Army's tactical defenses;
- Exploit the penetration south toward the Manoilin and Maiorovskii region with its tank and cavalry corps;
- Reach the enemy's rear and the Don River in cooperation with 5th Tank Army's main shock group; and

- Dispatch a rifle division mounted on trucks to follow and facilitate 4th Tank Corps' exploitation.

Simultaneous with the main attack, 21st Army was to conduct a secondary attack in the army's center and on its left wing with a shock group consisting of four rifle divisions, to achieve the following objectives:

- Penetrate Romanian Third Army's tactical defenses;
- Exploit the penetration southward and southwestward; and
- Wheel the shock group westward to encircle and destroy Romanian Third Army, in cooperation with the rifle forces on 5th Tank Army's left wing.

The army's forces were to reach the following lines (positions) by the end of each day of the operation:

First Day
- 4th Tank Corps—Manoilin and Maiorovskii region, to prevent Romanian Third Army from withdrawing southward and to block approaching enemy reserves, with forward units reaching the Don River
- 3rd Guards Cavalry Corps—Verkhne-Buzinovka region, to prevent Romanian Third Army from withdrawing southward and to block approaching enemy reserves, with forward units reaching the Don River
- Rifle formations—Golovskii and Vlasov region, to link up with forces on 5th Tank Army's left wing and encircle and destroy Romanian Third Army

Second Day
- 4th Tank Corps—Rubezhnyi and Lipo-Logovskii region on the western bank of the Don River, accompanied by one truck-mounted rifle division
- 3rd Guards Cavalry Corps—Golubinskii and Bol'shenabatovskii region, with forward detachments seizing bridgeheads over the Don River
- Rifle formations—liquidate encircled Romanian Third Army and follow and support the mobile corps

Third Day
- 4th Tank and 3rd Guards Cavalry Corps—force the Don River in cooperation with 5th Tank Army's mobile corps, capture Kalach, support the linkup with the Stalingrad Front, and begin destroying the encircled Stalingrad grouping
- Rifle formations (four rifle divisions)—follow and support the mobile forces; reach the Rubezhnyi, Golubinskii, and Evlampievskii line; and prepare to destroy the enemy's encircled Stalingrad grouping[101]

The 1st Guards Army, commanded by General Kuznetsov, was to conduct a supporting attack and defend along the remainder of its front. Its supporting attack would be launched in the 10-kilometer-wide sector extending from Iagodnyi eastward to Farm No. 4 in the western part of the Serafimovich bridgehead. Its 278th and 203rd Rifle Divisions and one regiment of 197th Rifle Division would be supported by three RVGK artillery regiments advancing south toward Gorbatovskii and Bokovskaia to assist 5th Tank Army's main shock group, which was advancing on its left. The objectives were as follows:

- Penetrate Romanian Third Army's tactical defenses;
- Destroy opposing Romanian forces in the sector;
- Exploit southwestward to reach positions extending from east of Belogorka southward to Vislogubov and Bokovskaia by the end of the second day of the operation; and
- Dig in and be prepared to repel enemy attacks against the *front*'s main shock group from the west.

In addition to defending along the remainder of its 165-kilometer front along the Don River, 1st Guards Army was to employ separate assault detachments to conduct local attacks to tie down enemy forces and prevent them from dispatching reinforcements to the east.[102]

Characteristics of the Offensive
OPERATIONAL INDICES

All military operations differ, sometimes significantly, in terms of their nature, form, structure, and ultimate conduct. In general, the nature and form of an operation depend on a wide range of factors, the most important of which are "mission," that is, the operation's intent; the correlation of opposing forces, meaning the strength and capabilities of one's own forces relative to those of the enemy; the terrain conditions in the area of operations; and the prevailing weather conditions. All these factors help determine how an attacking or defending force should structure its forces, as well as the appropriate pace or operational tempo of the attack or defense. Ultimately, all these facets of a military operation are measureable by so-called operational indices—precise spatial and temporal measurements of an operation that describe its scale, scope, form, and duration.

Before conducting any offense or defense, planners strive to determine and achieve the specific operational indices that will ensure success. They can exploit past experiences by comparing the operational indices and ultimate outcomes of completed operations to plan future operations more effectively.

Table 5. Operational Indices of the Southwestern Front's Offensive

| Operational Formation | Width of Sector (km) | | Depth (km) | Duration (days) | Movement | |
| | Overall | Penetration | | | Tempo (km/day) | |
					Rifle	Mobile
Southwestern Front	85	32	140	3	20–25	40–45
5th Tank Army	35	10	140	3	20–25	40–45
21st Army	40	12	100–110	3	20–25	30–35
1st Guards Army	10	10	30–35	3	15–17	—
Total	—	64	30–140	3	—	—

Source: K. K. Rokossovsky, ed., Velikaia pobeda na Volge [Great victory on the Volga] (Moscow: Voenizdat, 1965), 233.

Since the Red Army had conducted precious few successful offensive operations prior to November 1942, many of the operational indices characterizing Plan Uranus were little more than educated guesses or assumptions based on either Soviet or German experience. Thus, given the favorable outcome of Uranus, as well as the fact that Soviet planners would exploit their Stalingrad model as they devised future offensives, it is useful to examine the operational indices characterizing the role of each of the three attacking *fronts* in Operation Uranus. Needless to say, the sharply differing indices applicable to each *front* resulted from the radically different missions they performed. This is most apparent in the Southwestern Front, which played the most decisive role in the offensive (see table 5).

The most important operational indices applicable to the Southwestern Front's offensive included the following:

- Depth—140 kilometers
- Duration—three days
- Tempo of advance—40 to 45 kilometers per day
- Length of inner encirclement line (front)—variable
- Length of outer encirclement line (front)—200 to 250 kilometers
- Distance between inner and outer encirclement lines (fronts)—25 to 100 kilometers

The first three indices underscore the ambitious nature of the offensive in terms of its planned depth and speed. Since the Red Army had never achieved comparable rates of advance in the past, these anticipated indices resulted largely from a combination of confidence (or even overconfidence) and a thorough analysis of deep operations the German army had conducted in 1941 and 1942. Given past experience, it is not surprising that many Red Army commanders, especially those who had led mobile forces in previous operations, genuinely questioned the wisdom of attempting to do too much too soon.

OPERATIONAL AND TACTICAL FORMATIONS

The manner in which the Southwestern Front and its subordinate armies, corps, and divisions structured their forces for combat was also indicative of an inherent problem: a shortage of necessary forces. Ideally, if a *front* or army hoped to conduct a successful offensive, it would have to deploy its forces in two echelons with a small reserve. The second echelon added depth to the attacking force, thus permitting it to create initial offensive momentum and strengthen [*narashchivanie*] the offensive throughout its duration. However, because of a relative paucity of forces, the Southwestern Front had no choice but to deploy its attacking armies in a single-echelon formation with only a small reserve. Planners rationalized this method based on the limited depth of the operation, although the offensive itself would underscore the weakness of this formation.

At the army level, however, planners were able to adopt a two-echelon formation, at least in the two armies constituting the *front*'s main shock group (5th Tank and 21st Armies). They did so by deploying roughly one-third of the armies' forces in their second echelons and in echelons designated to exploit success (the tank, mechanized, and cavalry corps), and even then, they were able to form small reserves. Thus, 5th Tank Army's operational formation included:

- First echelon—four rifle divisions, two tank brigades, and two separate tank battalions
- Second echelon—two rifle divisions
- Echelon to exploit success (the official designation for exploitation forces; hereafter, termed exploitation echelon or simply mobile group)—two tank corps and one cavalry corps[103]
- Reserve—two rifle division performing alternative missions; for example, 21st Army's two rifle divisions could exploit westward into the enemy rear or southeastward to support the exploitation echelon

At the tactical level, corps, divisions, brigades, and regiments subordinate to the *front*'s three armies adopted a wide variety of tactical formations suited to the forces' condition and actual missions, as follows:

- Tank corps—two echelons of brigades, with two tank brigades in the first echelon and one tank and one motorized rifle brigade in the second echelon.
- Divisions and regiments—a single echelon of regiments and battalions.
- Separate tank brigades and regiments (one tank brigade, three tank regiments, and two tank battalions)—infantry support tanks organized in single-echelon formation with one-third of the force in reserve during the penetration, including 5th Tank Army's 8th Guards Tank Brigade and 510th and 511th Tank Battalions and 21st Army's 1st, 2nd, and 4th Guards Tank Regiments. Neither 1st Guards Army nor the *front* had tank units in reserve.[104]

ARTILLERY

The Southwestern Front organized and employed its artillery in accordance with the *Stavka*'s 10 January 1942 directive requiring centralized control over most of its artillery and guards-mortars (multiple rocket launchers) and the conduct of a full-fledged "artillery offensive" to accompany any offensive operation. The artillery offensive consisted of an artillery preparation fired before the attack; artillery, mortar, and rocket fire accompanying the attacking forces; supporting fire when the exploitation echelons were committed to the penetration; and extensive fire into the depths of the enemy's defenses to a distance commensurate with the forces' assigned missions of the day. Thus, artillery was to provide continuous support for infantry and tanks well into, if not entirely through, the tactical depth of the enemy's defenses.

Throughout the entire *front*, the artillery preparations fired by armies were supposed to last 80 minutes, and each preparation included, in succession, a 5-minute fire raid of sudden overwhelming shelling, 65 minutes of suppression and destruction fire, and a second fire raid lasting 10 minutes. Artillery below divisional level—in particular, 45mm antitank artillery battalions and 76mm regimental artillery battalions—conducted direct fire during the artillery preparation and direct fire support to rifle and tank forces as they advanced into the penetration.

To facilitate effective centralized employment of artillery, armies and divisions formed distinct artillery groups. These included infantry support groups (GPP) within divisions, which provided all first-echelon rifle regiments with direct support artillery, and long-range action groups (GDD) and rocket artillery groups within armies to provide general support artillery for the army as a whole.

In general, artillery, mortars, and rocket artillery employed various specialized methods or types of fire within each stage of the artillery offensive. These included preplanned concentrations and rolling barrages during the artillery preparation, preplanned and on-call concentrations and fires of successive concentrations to the depth of 2 kilometers in support of the actual troop assault, and fires from army long-range action groups, division artillery, and the two artillery regiments attached to each tank and cavalry corps to provide accompanying fire for advancing mobile corps.[105]

AVIATION

Centralized air support for the Southwestern Front throughout the offensive came from 17th Air Army, which was commanded by Major General of Aviation Stepan Akimovich Krasovsky and consisted of the army's own organic aircraft and planes from attached air regiments of the Voronezh Front's 2nd Air Army.[106] NKO and *Stavka* directives governing air operations required Krasovsky to organize and conduct an "air offensive," which consisted of two stages: first, an air preparation conducted throughout the *front's* entire sector by all available aircraft and second, air support of attacking forces while advancing into the operational depths, in which groups of echeloned assault and fighter aircraft provided direct support to the advancing tank and cavalry corps.[107]

Within the parameters of the air offensive, air forces performed specific missions in three distinct stages. First, prior to the offensive, aircraft were tasked with destroying enemy aircraft at their airfields, enemy reserves, and enemy headquarters and with protecting friendly forces while situated in their concentration areas. Second, during the infantry and tank (NPP) attack, aircraft were to destroy enemy personnel, artillery, mortars, and reserves. Third, during the exploitation phase of the operation, aircraft were required to support the commitment of mobile forces into the penetration and then protect their actions while in the operational depths.

In addition, Southwestern Front planners assigned two special missions to 17th Air Army. First, they ordered the air army to devote one bomber aviation division and four regiments of night bombers solely to the mission of combating enemy reserves. Second, they attached entire air formations and units to specific armies to provide maximum air support. For example, 1st Mixed Aviation Corps was attached to 5th Tank Army throughout the penetration and exploitation phases of the operation.

ENGINEERS

The Southwestern Front needed extensive engineer expertise and forces if it hoped to overcome the many challenges it faced. First, the *front* had to construct and conceal numerous crossings over the Don River and an extensive road and trail network within its two bridgeheads south of the river, in support of its forward concentration and concealment of troops and materiel. In addition, it had to surmount sometimes formidable enemy defensive fortifications, fieldworks, and obstacles and move forces across numerous water obstacles, such as large and small rivers and streams, during the offensive. These realities forced the *Stavka* to reinforce the *front*'s already extensive engineer force structure with specialized engineer forces from its reserve. As a result, by the time the offensive began, the Southwestern Front included engineer and sapper brigades, regiments, and battalions at the *front* and tank army levels and engineer, sapper, and pontoon-bridge battalions and companies at the army and division levels. In terms of their distribution, these engineer forces above division level included the following:

- 5th Tank Army
  - 44th Special-Designation [*Spetsnaz*] Engineer Brigade
  - 181st and 269th Separate Engineer Battalions
  - 26th, 100th, 101st, 102nd, and 130th Pontoon-Bridge Battalions
- 21st Army
  - 205th and 540th Separate Engineer Battalions
- 1st Guards Army
  - 350th Separate Engineer Battalion
  - 28th and 37th Pontoon-Bridge Battalions
- Subordinate to *front*
  - 12th Sapper Brigade[108]

These engineer and sapper forces, as well as the engineer and sapper battalions and companies at and below division level, performed a wide variety of offensive and defensive missions. Before the operation began, engineer forces at all combat levels conducted reconnaissance; helped the assaulting forces outfit their jumping-off positions; constructed march routes, ferry crossings, and bridges into concentration areas; camouflaged assembly areas and other positions, such as 12 frontal roads, 2 main and several auxiliary dirt roads, 17 bridges, 18 ferry crossings, and 20 kilometers of trenches and communication trenches; and paved the way for attacking forces by cutting routes through enemy minefields and barbed wire (6 to 10 routes per division and regiment) and removing mines and incendiary explosives.[109]

Once the offensive began, engineer forces echeloned in depth supported the attack throughout its duration by providing continuous engineer support for assault groups and first- and second-echelon infantry, in succession. As the attacking forces seized their designated objectives, engineer forces formed mobile obstacle detachments at the division and army levels to help repel enemy counterattacks and fortify captured positions.

The Stalingrad Front

Front Mission

Eremenko's Stalingrad Front was no less important than Vatutin's South-western Front because it formed the southern pincer of the double envelop-ment (see map 6). In addition to carrying out its offensive mission with three of its armies, the Stalingrad Front was to act defensively with 62nd Army to tie down German forces in the Stalingrad region and prevent them from reinforcing their defenses opposite the *front*'s main attack. Whereas Vatu-tin's Southwestern Front was to conduct its main attack with two armies, the Stalingrad Front planned a large shock group formed from the 64th, 57th, and 51st Armies, which occupied the sector extending from the Beketovka bridgehead south of Stalingrad southward through the lake region east of the Volga River to the northern shores of Lake Barmantsak. As in the South-western Front, Eremenko also subdivided his shock group into two armored "fists"—the first consisting of 57th Army's 13th Tank Corps in the southern extremity of the Beketovka bridgehead, southeast of Krasnoarmeiskaia, and the second consisting of 51st Army's 4th Mechanized and 4th Cavalry Corps in the region east of the gap between Lakes Tsatsa and Barmantsak. Together with its supporting rifle forces and artillery, the main shock group included 8 of the *front*'s 12 rifle divisions; 1 of its 8 rifle or naval rifle brigades; all 5 of its tank brigades; all 3 of its tank, mechanized, and cavalry corps; half its RVGK artillery and mortar regiments; and all its air forces.[110]

The 64th, 57th, and 51st Armies were to conduct Eremenko's main at-tack westward from the 65-kilometer-wide swath of territory stretching from the Beketovka bridgehead southward to the lake region, a sector manned primarily by Romanian forces subordinate to German IV and Romanian VI Army Corps. However, the armies concentrated their shock groups, together with the two armored fists, in three penetration sectors totaling more than 40 kilometers in width. At the end of the first day of the offensive, presumably after the penetration was complete, the *front* was to commit its two armored corps to an exploitation toward the northwest. The aim was to destroy enemy reserves and reach the Kalach and Sovetskii region by the end of the second day, where the armored corps would link up with the Southwestern Front's mobile group to complete the encirclement of the enemy's Stalingrad group-ing. Meanwhile, the *front*'s cavalry corps, reinforced by infantry, was to ad-vance southwest and south and erect an outer encirclement front to protect the *front*'s left wing against enemy counterattacks.

As the shock groups of Eremenko's *front* were savaging Axis defenses south of Stalingrad, 62nd Army was to conduct local attacks and raids de-signed to tie down the bulk of German Sixth Army in Stalingrad. As was the case before, this meant feeding just enough fresh replacement troops into the city to prevent Chuikov's army from perishing. Immediately after the Uranus encirclement was complete, the *front's* forces were to begin destroying the encircled enemy grouping in cooperation with the Don Front and, to a lesser degree, the Southwestern Front.

Army Missions

The 64th Army, commanded by General Shumilov and operating in the 36-kilometer-wide sector from Krasnaia Sloboda southward to Ivanovka, was to conduct a main attack in its center and on its left wing and defend on its right wing. Its main attack would be mounted northwestward from the Beketovka bridgehead in the 12-kilometer-wide sector from 5 kilometers south of Elkhi southward to Ivanovka. The shock group consisting of 204th, 157th, and 38th Rifle Divisions; 13th and 56th Tank Brigades; and reinforcing units was to achieve the following objectives:

- Penetrate the tactical defenses of Fourth Panzer Army's IV Army Corps (German 197th Infantry Division and Romanian 20th Infantry Division);
- Destroy the opposing enemy and reach the Iagodnyi and Nariman line by the end of the first day;
- Cooperate with 57th Army in enveloping and encircling the enemy grouping from the south and occupy the Elkhi and Varvarovka line; and
- Simultaneous with the main attack, defend on the army's right wing and support the attacking forces.

The army's forces were to reach the following positions by the end of each day of the operation:

- First day—Elkhi and Nariman line
- Second day—Elkhi and Varvarovka line[111]

General Tolbukhin's 57th Army, operating in the center of the *front's* 40-kilometer-wide penetration sector, was to conduct a main attack on its right wing and in its center and defend on its left wing. It was to launch its main attack westward from the region south of the Beketovka bridgehead in the 16-kilometer-wide sector from southwest of Tundutovo to south of Solianka with a shock group consisting of all its forces, less 76th Fortified Region, to achieve the following objectives:

- Penetrate the enemy's tactical defenses at the junction of Fourth Panzer Army's IV Army Corps (Romanian 20th Infantry Division) and Romanian VI Army Corps (Romanian 2nd Infantry Division);

Map 6. Operation Uranus: The Stalingrad Front's offensive plan

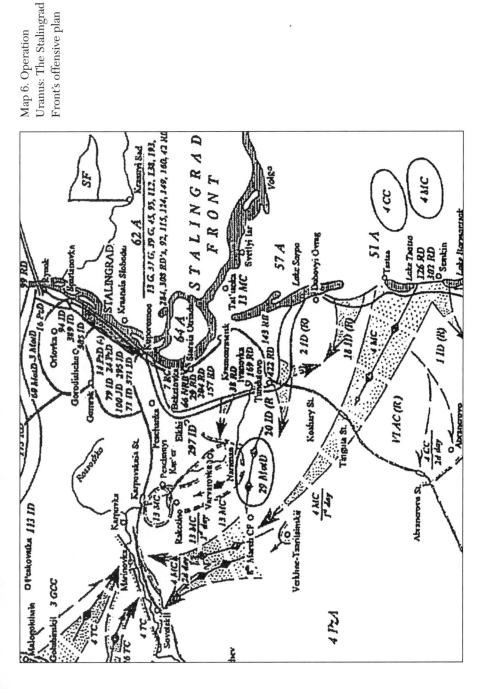

- While developing the attack toward the northwest, support the commitment of 13th Tank Corps (the *front's* exploitation echelon) into the penetration on the first day of the operation;
- 13th Tank Corps—exploit northwestward to capture Nariman, Varvarovka, and Rakotino by the end of the first day and also advance one brigade to the 8th of March State Farm; as the rifle forces start to reach these regions, advance northwestward and occupy the Peschanyi Kar'er and Karpovskaia line and farther along the eastern bank of the Chervlenaia River while facing northeast to cut off enemy withdrawal routes to the south and southwest;
- 169th Rifle Division with 90th Tank Brigade—advance to reach positions from Andreevka to south of Koshary Station;
- 422nd Rifle Division and 143rd Rifle and 235th Tank Brigades (the left wing)—attack southward from the region southeast of Solianka and encircle the Romanian 2nd Infantry Division operating in the Dubovoi *Ovrag* region in cooperation with 51st Army's 15th Guards Rifle Division, which is to attack westward from the defile between Lakes Sarpa and Tsatsa; and
- Simultaneous with the main attack, defend the remaining 19-kilometer sector on the army's left wing with three separate machine gun–artillery battalions (from 76th Fortified Region).[112]

The 51st Army, commanded by General Trufanov and operating in a 110-kilometer-wide sector, was to conduct both main and secondary attacks in its center and on its left wing and defend on its extreme right wing. Its main attack would be launched from the 12-kilometer-wide sector between Lakes Tsatsa and Barmantsak in its right-center with a shock group consisting of 302nd and 126th Rifle Divisions to accomplish the following objectives:

- Penetrate the enemy's tactical defenses at the junction between Romanian VI Army Corps' 18th and 1st Infantry Divisions and destroy the opposing enemy.
- Commit the exploitation echelons (4th Mechanized Corps and 4th Cavalry Corps) into the penetration at the end of the first day:
  - 4th Mechanized Corps—enter the penetration late on the first day, demoralize the enemy rear by a decisive advance, and, while avoiding heavy combat, reach the Karpovka and Sovetskii line by the end of the second day to link up with the Southwestern Front's mobile forces.
  - 4th Cavalry Corps (61st and 81st Cavalry Divisions)—enter the penetration late on the first day, reach the Abganerovo and Abganerovo

Station region by the next morning, and be prepared to repel any enemy counterattacks against the left flank of the army's main shock group.

- Subsequently, develop the offensive in cooperation with 57th Army to encircle the enemy west of the Volga River and protect the shock group's left flank against enemy counterattack from the south and southwest:
  - Flank protection by 302nd Rifle Division—attack southwestward and reach the Kirov State Farm region to repel any enemy counterattacks against the left flank of the army's main shock group.

Simultaneous with the main attack, 51st Army would conduct a secondary attack on the army's left wing with 15th Guards Rifle Division to achieve the following objectives:

- Penetrate the tactical defenses of Romanian VI Army Corps' 18th Infantry Division and destroy the opposing enemy; and
- Wheel northwestward and northward to encircle and destroy Romanian 2nd Infantry Division west of Lake Sarpa in cooperation with the forces on 57th Army's left wing.[113]

General Chuikov's 62nd Army was to keep a firm hold on the eastern part of Stalingrad city and, after the offensive began, conduct active local operations to tie down enemy forces.[114]

The 28th Army, commanded by General Gerasimenko, was to hold the Astrakhan' defensive line and be prepared to destroy the German 16th Motorized Division and capture the Elista region.[115]

Characteristics of the Offensive
OPERATIONAL INDICES
In general, because its role in Operation Uranus paralleled that of the Southwestern Front, the operational indices of the Stalingrad Front's offensive closely mirrored those pertaining to Vatutin's *front* (see table 6). The most important operational indices applicable to the Stalingrad Front's offensive included the following:

- Depth—up to 90 kilometers
- Duration—two days
- Tempo of advance—45 kilometers per day
- Inner encirclement line (front)—65 kilometers
- Outer encirclement line (front)—90 kilometers
- Distance between inner and outer lines (fronts)—up to 65 kilometers

Table 6. Operational Indices of the Stalingrad Front's Offensive

Operational Formation	Width of Sector (km)		Depth (km)	Duration (days)	Movement	
					Tempo (km/day)	
	Overall	Penetration			Rifle	Mobile
Stalingrad Front	180	40	90	2	10–15	45
64th Army	36	12	10–15	2	5–8	—
57th Army	35	16	45–50	2	8–12	20–25
51st Army	110	12	90	2	10–15	45
Total	—	80	10–90	2	—	—

Source: K. K. Rokossovsky, ed., *Velikaia pobeda na Volge* [Great victory on the Volga] (Moscow: Voenizdat, 1965), 240.

These goals were even more ambitious than the Southwestern Front's because the mobile forces available to Eremenko were weaker than those allocated to Vatutin. For example, 4th Cavalry Corps, with its two divisions, was far weaker than 3rd Guards Cavalry Corps, with its two guards and one standard divisions. In addition to operating along a much broader front (180 kilometers versus 85) and having a larger penetration sector (40 kilometers versus 32), Eremenko allocated far weaker forces to his outer encirclement front than did Vatutin. And because the front itself was a bit closer to the inner encirclement front, there was a greater likelihood the Germans would try to relieve or reinforce their encircled Sixth Army by going against the Stalingrad Front.

OPERATIONAL AND TACTICAL FORMATIONS

Eremenko faced the same constraints as Vatutin—in particular, an acute shortage of forces relative to the increased width of his front. Eremenko compensated for these problems by structuring his *front*'s forces for combat in a predominantly single-echelon fashion. Specifically, at the *front* level, he deployed his attacking 64th, 57th, and 51st Armies side by side in a single-echelon formation, but he retained his tank (mechanized) corps as an exploitation echelon and also formed a small reserve.

At army level, too, the paucity of forces compelled two of his armies to employ single-echelon formations; the third, primarily because it was the weakest, adopted a two-echelon configuration. As a result, 64th Army formed in two echelons; 57th Army employed a single-echelon formation, but with the *front*'s 13th Tank Corps serving as an exploitation echelon; and 51st Army also deployed in one echelon, but with its own exploitation echelon (4th Mechanized Corps and 4th Cavalry Corps) and a small mobile reserve (38th Separate Motorized Rifle Brigade). At the tactical level, subordinate corps, divisions, brigades, and regiments employed a wide variety of formations, depending on the precise nature of their objectives.

To compensate for the general weakness of his *front's* rifle forces, Eremenko had no choice but to rely almost entirely on skillful maneuver by his tank, mechanized, and cavalry forces if he hoped to achieve success, particularly when they began to operate in the operational depths. This meant the three mobile corps had the vital functions of establishing a reliable outer encirclement front and protecting the main shock group's left flank throughout the operation. The remainder of the tank and mechanized forces were to stiffen the infantry during the penetration operation and protect exploiting rifle and cavalry forces against attacks by enemy motor-mechanized forces. Accordingly, the *front* command allocated these forces carefully wherever they were required and assigned them missions well within their capabilities. Thus, all the mobile forces subordinate to the *front* received specific missions and echeloned their forces accordingly, as follows:

- 13th Tank Corps (the *front's* exploitation echelon organized into two echelons of brigades and deployed in 57th Army's sector) was to attack on the internal flank of the *front's* mobile forces and advance northwestward to the line of the Chervlenaia River to prevent the enemy from withdrawing to the south and southwest.
- 4th Mechanized Corps (the *front's* exploitation echelon organized in a single echelon and deployed in 51st Army's sector) was to advance decisively through a 6-kilometer-wide sector and exploit toward the northwest to link up with the Southwestern Front's mobile forces and encircle the enemy's Stalingrad grouping by the end of the second day.
- 4th Cavalry Corps (an exploitation echelon organized in columns of divisions deployed in 51st Army's sector) was to enter the penetration after 4th Mechanized Corps late on the first day, reach the Abganerovo and Abganerovo Station region by the next morning, and establish an outer encirclement front designed to repel any enemy counterattacks against the left flank of the army's main shock group.
- Separate tank brigades, regiments, and battalions (eight tank brigades, two tank regiments, and one tank battalion) were to provide infantry support (NPP) to advancing rifle divisions and brigades (with a density of three tanks per kilometer of penetration front), as follows:
  - 62nd Army—84th Tank Brigade and 506th Tank Battalion (235th Tank Brigade)
  - 64th Army—13th and 56th Tank Brigades
  - 57th Army—90th and 235th Tank Brigades
  - 51st Army—254th Tank Brigade

- ○ 28th Army—6th Guards Tank Brigade and 565th Tank Battalion
- ○ *Front*—85th Tank Brigade and 35th and 166th Tank Regiments[116]

FLANK PROTECTION

After the *front's* main shock group completed its penetration operation and while the exploitation echelons advanced into the operational depths, Eremenko and the commanders of 51st and 64th Armies were responsible for protecting the main shock group's flanks against enemy attacks from the southwest. Shumilov of 64th Army was to protect the shock group's right flank simply by constantly extending his army's left flank toward the west and northwest as the main forces of 57th Army moved toward Karpovka and Sovetskii. Although this would guarantee flank protection, it also deprived Shumilov of the forces necessary to effect a real penetration of enemy defenses in his sector.

Eremenko and Trufanov of 51st Army acted jointly to protect the shock group's left flank. For his part, Eremenko assigned the two-division 4th Cavalry Corps to advance smartly southwest toward the Aksai River and erect a flexible outer encirclement front along it. To assist 4th Cavalry Corps, Trufanov ordered his 302nd Rifle Division, once it completed its penetration, to wheel southward in tandem with 4th Cavalry Corps and extend the outer encirclement front farther west, where it would tie into the positions of 51st Army's 91st Rifle Division and 76th Fortified Region, which, by then, should have been slowly advancing their forces westward from the lake district. While these modest measures did indeed protect the *front's* left flank against any threat posed by Romanian forces, they proved quite inadequate when fresh German panzer and motorized forces appeared on the scene.

ARTILLERY

By the time Operation Uranus began, the Stalingrad Front lacked sufficient artillery and mortars to fire a preparation with the artillery densities required by Red Army regulations. There were a variety of reasons for this inadequacy, but primarily it was due to redeployment difficulties. Therefore, to achieve the requisite densities, Eremenko had no choice but to organize a staggered artillery preparation, first firing a preparation in support of 64th Army and then, after a pause to shift the artillery southward, firing a preparation in 57th Army's sector. Although this was clearly undesirable, it was made less so by the firepower weaknesses of the opposing Romanian forces. Otherwise, Eremenko's chief of artillery organized all fires in accordance with the precepts of the "artillery offensive," that is, firing in distinct phases throughout the operation.

Regardless of when the preparations were fired, the artillery employed the same techniques and methods used in the Southwestern and Don Fronts.

In terms of their duration, the preparations lasted from 40 to 75 minutes. As for the grouping of artillery, it varied somewhat between armies, depending on the breadth of their penetration sectors and the location of their artillery. For example, all three armies employed long-range artillery (DD) groups consisting of three to four gun artillery regiments per army, as well as infantry support artillery (NPP) groups. While 64th and 57th Armies formed NPP groups with 25 to 35 guns and mortars in each group in all their divisions and regiments, 51st Army formed and employed an army artillery group for long-range action, a multiple rocket launcher group, and several NPP subgroups at the army level and used only subgroups at the division level.[117]

AVIATION

Eremenko delegated the planning and conduct of air support for the Stalingrad Front to Major General of Aviation Timofei Timofeevich Khriukin, the commander of 8th Air Army.[118] Khriukin had at his disposal all the aircraft subordinate to his air army, plus the aircraft from the attached 2nd Mixed Aviation Corps. The 8th Air Army's staff and headquarters planned and organized air support and conducted a wide variety of air missions prior to and throughout the operation in the same fashion as Southwestern Front's air forces, essentially implementing the standard procedures of an "air offensive." In addition, the army provided special communications equipment to ensure immediate radio contact between its fighter aircraft and the ground units subordinate to 13th Tank, 4th Mechanized, and 4th Cavalry Corps. It also dispatched special air liaison officers to corps and perhaps brigade headquarters; these officers were responsible for ensuring timely and appropriate air support.

Indicative of the vastly increasing strength of the Red Army Air Force, Khriukin's staff planned aircraft sorties numbering 647 flights on the first day of operations, 520 on the second day, 448 on the third day, and 383 on the fourth day.[119]

ENGINEERS

Prior to the offensive, the Stalingrad Front's forces, and especially its main shock groups, were situated within the narrow confines of the Beketovka bridgehead west of the Volga River and south of Stalingrad and in the expansive lake region far south of the city. The *front's* area of operations was immense, and the road network in the lake region was sparse at best; in addition, the *front* had to move all newly arrived reinforcements and many of its internally regrouping forces back and forth across the Volga River. This posed a major challenge to engineers because they also had to manage a host of routine combat engineer functions prior to and during the offensive.

The *Stavka* responded to this challenge by assigning the Stalingrad Front massive engineer reinforcements—more than twice as many as it dispatched to the Southwestern Front. As a result, by the time the offensive began, Eremenko's *front* included a total of 38 battalions and 3 companies of various types of engineers and sappers. Twenty-three of these battalions were directly subordinate to the *front*, and the remaining battalions were assigned to armies. These forces above the division level were distributed as follows:

- 62nd Army
  - 326th and 327th Separate Engineer Battalions
- 64th Army
  - 328th, 329th, and 330th Separate Engineer Battalions
- 57th Army
  - 122nd and 175th Separate Engineer Battalions
- 51st Army
  - 205th, 275th, and 742nd Separate Engineer Battalions
  - 6th Pontoon-Bridge Battalion
- 28th Army
  - 57th and 130th Separate Engineer Battalions
  - 121st Pontoon-Bridge Battalion
- Subordinate to the *front*
  - 43rd Special-Designation Engineer Brigade
  - 19th and 21st Sapper Brigades
  - 17th Guards Battalion of Miners°
  - 44th, 47th, 103rd, and 107th Pontoon-Bridge Battalions
  - 119th and 240th Separate Engineer Battalions
  - 1504th Separate Sapper Battalion[120]

° Guards battalions of miners were responsible for conducting reconnaissance and diversionary operations for the *front* in the same fashion as the more modern *Spetsnaz* forces.

While performing the same missions as engineers and sappers assigned to the Southwestern Front, engineer forces in the Stalingrad Front constructed additional crossings over the Volga River at Tat'ianka, Svetlyi Iar, Solodniki, and Kamennyi Iar and supported the movement of more than 110,000 men, 427 tanks, 556 guns, and 6,561,500 tons of ammunition across the Volga River from 1 through 20 November. Despite these prodigious feats, because of the difficulty of crossing the broad Volga in often icy conditions and the continuous heavy fighting at the Beketovka bridgehead, some of the forces necessary to support the offensive were unable to cross the river by the time Uranus began.[121]

The Don Front

Front Mission

Although Rokossovsky's Don Front clearly played a secondary role in Operation Uranus, it was required to perform two vital functions—one offensive and the other defensive (see map 7). Offensively, when Uranus commenced, the Don Front was to conduct a secondary attack with 65th and 24th Armies on the right wing of the *front's* 150-kilometer-wide sector, aiming to penetrate German forces defending the small bend of the Don River southeast of Kletskaia and then exploit the penetration to encircle and destroy the entire enemy force. Rokossovsky designated two shock groups to conduct the attacks. The first shock group, consisting of four rifle divisions and two tank brigades from 65th Army's forces, was to conduct the main attack southward in the sector just east of Kletskaia through the defenses of German XI Army Corps. Farther to the east, the second shock group, consisting of six rifle divisions, one tank corps, and one tank brigade from 24th Army, was to attack southward on the eastern bank of the Don River south of Kachalinskaia and penetrate VIII Army Corps' defenses. After penetrating the Germans' defenses, the two shock groups were to destroy the opposing enemy forces and advance along converging axes to reach the Vertiachii region on the eastern bank of the Don River, 40 kilometers northeast of Kalach. The secondary attack by 65th and 24th Armies was to destroy German Sixth Army's XI Army Corps and drive its remnants back into the land bridge between the Don and Volga Rivers.

Defensively, the Don Front's 66th Army and the bulk of 24th Army were to conduct local actions to tie down German forces north and northwest of Stalingrad and prevent them from dispatching forces to close the anticipated breaches in the Romanian defense northwest and south of Stalingrad. The *front's* 65th Army, while conducting its secondary attack, was to protect the left flank of the Southwestern Front's mobile forces as they advanced toward Kalach. Once it fulfilled these tasks, the Don Front was to assume responsibility, together with forces from the Stalingrad Front, for reducing the pocket of German forces encircled in the Stalingrad region.[122]

The Don Front faced two daunting problems: the obvious weakness of its forces after months of continuous combat, and the fact that they would be attacking prepared defenses manned by German troops. These two factors alone made it highly unlikely that the secondary attack would succeed. Furthermore, both the *Stavka* and Rokossovsky realized that his *front* would require substantial reinforcement before it could hope to reduce the ensuing encirclement.

Map 7.
Operation
Uranus: The
Don Front's
offensive plan

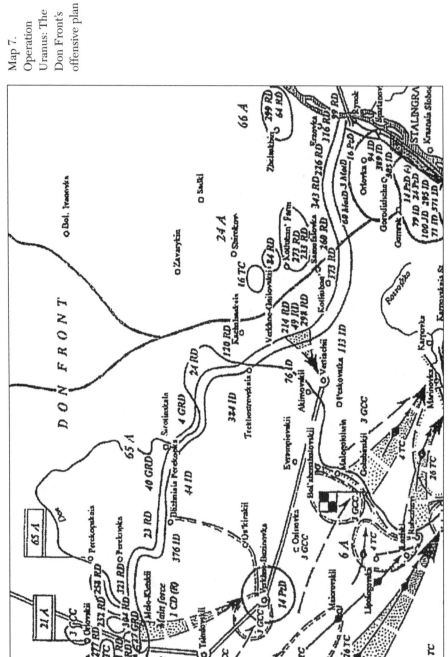

Army Missions
The 65th Army, commanded by General Batov and operating in the 80-kilometer-wide sector from Kletskaia, south of the Don River, eastward to the Kachalinskaia region on the eastern bank on the Don River, was to conduct a main attack on its right wing and defend in its center and on its left wing. The main attack was aimed southward and southwestward from the Kletskaia bridgehead in the 6-kilometer-wide sector south and east of Kletskaia. The shock group, made up of four rifle divisions and two tank brigades supported by nine artillery and mortar regiments, was to achieve the following objectives:

- Penetrate the tactical defenses on the right wing of Romanian Third Army (Romanian 1st Cavalry Division) and the left wing of German Sixth Army's XI Army Corps (376th Infantry Division);
- Develop the attack toward the south and southeast to capture the Verkhne-Buzinovka, Os'kinskii, and Blizhniaia Perekopka line by the end of the first day;
- Subsequently, while cooperating with 24th Army on the left, develop the attack toward Vertiachii to encircle and destroy the enemy's grouping in the northwestern portion of the Great Bend of the Don River; and
- Simultaneously, dispatch part of the force southward to block any enemy retreat to the west.

While 65th Army was conducting its main attack, the forces in its center and on its left were to conduct local operations to tie down the remainder of German XI Army Corps and prevent it from shifting its forces to the west. When the army's main shock group reached the Verkhne-Buzinovka and Blizhniaia Perekopka regions, the forces in the army's center and on its left wing were to attack south and southeast toward Vertiachii.[123]

General Galanin's 24th Army, operating in a 40-kilometer-wide sector in the *front*'s center, was to conduct a main attack on its right wing and defend in its center and on its left wing. It was to conduct the main attack southward in a 4.5-kilometer-wide sector south of Kachalinskaia and east of the Don River with a shock group consisting of six rifle divisions, one tank corps, and a tank brigade supported by seven artillery regiments and four multiple rocket launcher regiments. It had the following objectives:

- Penetrate the tactical defenses of German Sixth Army's VIII Army Corps (76th Infantry Division);
- Commit the exploitation echelon into combat and advance southward along the eastern bank of the Don River to capture Vertiachii and link

Table 7. Operational Indices of the Don Front's Offensive

Operational Formation	Width of Sector (km)		Depth (km)	Duration (days)	Movement	
					Tempo (km/day)	
	Overall	Penetration			Rifle	Mobile
Don Front	150	10.5	60	3	15–20	20
65th Army	80	6	60	3	15–20	20
24th Army	40	4.5	20	2	8–10	10
Total	—	—	20–60	2	—	—

Source: K. K. Rokossovsky, ed., *Velikaia pobeda na Volge* [Great victory on the Volga] (Moscow: Voenizdat, 1965), 245.

up with 65th Army's forces advancing from the northwest to encircle and destroy all German forces west of the Don River; and

- For the exploitation echelon (16th Tank Corps)—advance from the region south of Verkhne-Gnilovskii, develop the penetration, and advance to the Vertiachii region to encircle and destroy the enemy's grouping in the small bend of the Don River, cut off the enemy grouping south of the Don from its main forces to the east, and destroy that grouping in cooperation with 65th Army.

Simultaneous with the main attack, the forces in 24th Army's center and on its left wing were to conduct local attacks and raids along a 35-kilometer-wide front to destroy enemy strongpoints and tie down enemy forces.[124]

The 66th Army, commanded by General Zhadov and operating in the 30-kilometer-wide sector on the *front's* left wing from the Kotluban' region eastward to the Volga River south of Erzovka, was to tie down enemy forces by conducting local attacks and raids and preventing the enemy from shifting forces toward the west.[125]

Characteristics of the Offensive
OPERATIONAL INDICES
Since the Don Front performed only secondary missions during the initial stages of Operation Uranus, its operational indices were far more modest than those of its neighboring *fronts* (see table 7). The Don Front's most important operational indices included the following:

- Depth—60 kilometers
- Duration—three days
- Tempo of advance—10 to 20 kilometers per day

Even though these indices were far more modest than those for the Southwestern and Stalingrad Fronts, they were still wildly optimistic. It was unlikely that 65th Army's rifle forces could advance 60 kilometers in three days, 24th Army could advance 20 kilometers in two days, and 24th Army's 16th Tank Corps could thrust 10 kilometers deep in two days, especially considering that they would be attacking well-prepared German defenses with forces that had been severely worn down in previous fighting. In addition, 65th Army fielded a total force of 48 tanks, only about two-thirds of them in 16th Tank Corps. The *Stavka* and the *front* could take solace in the fact that, even if futile, these attacks would certainly tie down the bulk of two of Sixth Army's corps and at least four of its infantry divisions.

Operational and Tactical Formations

Commensurate with the limited scope of its missions, the Don Front deployed its three armies in a single-echelon formation, in essentially the same positions they had been in for the past two months. Within Rokossovsky's *front*, 65th and 24th Armies formed the shock groups designated to conduct their main attacks in two echelons, with a tank corps serving as an exploitation echelon in 24th Army. They defended the remainder of their fronts with divisions deployed in a single echelon, with each retaining small reserves. Since its mission was defensive throughout the operation, 66th Army organized its forces in two echelons, with four divisions in the first echelon (99th, 226th, 64th, and 116th) and two in the second (299th and 343rd). To conserve forces and project maximum strength forward, all the divisions and regiments in the three armies formed for combat in single echelons of regiments and battalions.

Since Rokossovsky's *front* had only secondary missions, the *Stavka* allocated it just enough armor to make its attacks credible, but not one tank more. Therefore, it assigned 16th Tank Corps to serve as 24th Army's exploitation echelon; once the army's rifle forces penetrated the Germans' tactical defenses, the 16th was supposed to lead it to the town of Vertiachii. Although General Maslov's corps arguably had sufficient tanks to accomplish this mission, it was certainly not strong enough to encircle and destroy German XI Army Corps. As for the remaining tank forces in the three armies, these amounted to six separate tank brigades, all of which were designated to serve as infantry support tanks (NPP) for the Don Front's three armies, as follows:

- 24th Army—10th Tank Brigade
- 65th Army—91st and 121st Tank Brigades
- 66th Army—58th Tank Brigade
- *Front*—64th and 148th Tank Brigades[126]

ARTILLERY AND AVIATION

The Don Front's chief of artillery attached the bulk of the *front*'s RVGK artillery and mortar regiments to the 65th and 24th Armies for use in their artillery offensives in support of their secondary attacks. In turn, the chiefs of artillery in 65th and 24th Armies formed army artillery groups and multiple rocket launcher groups tasked with providing preparatory fire and general support to each army prior to and during the attacks. The two armies' rifle divisions created infantry support (NPP) groups in all their first-echelon rifle regiments.

The artillery preparations for both 65th and 24th Armies were to last for 1 hour and 20 minutes. In 65th Army, the preparation consisted of five distinct fire raids, two false cessations of fire, and two longer periods of destruction fire. The 24th Army developed a different pattern: a 10-minute fire raid followed by 60 minutes of destruction fire and a final 10-minute fire raid. As subsequent action confirmed, the artillery preparations did not produce the damage anticipated by the armies' fire planners.[127]

Major General Sergei Ignat'evich Rudenko's 16th Air Army provided the Don Front with air support.[128] In this case, Rudenko allocated virtually all the *front*'s aircraft to protect and support 65th Army's shock group during and after its penetration operation. However, he was also careful to assign small groups of aircraft to support 16th Tank Corps during its exploitation. To that end, Rudenko dispatched air representatives to the tank corps' headquarters and perhaps to some of its subordinate brigades.[129]

ENGINEERS

The engineers assigned to the Don Front faced many of the same challenges as those in the Southwestern Front. These involved transporting large quantities of troops and material for 65th Army across the Don River and into the Kletskaia bridgehead, preparing the bridgehead itself in terms of defensive fortifications, concealing and camouflaging concentrations of troops and material, and performing other routine preparations before and during the offensive.

Aside from divisional and regimental engineer and sapper forces, the *front* distributed its own engineer assets as follows:

- 65th Army
  - 9th Pontoon-Bridge Battalion
  - 321st Separate Engineer Battalion
- 24th Army
  - 48th Separate Engineer Battalion
  - 530th, 532nd, 534th, and 1361st Separate Sapper Battalions

- 66th Army
  - ○ 1st and 432nd Separate Engineer Battalions
- Subordinate to the *front*
  - ○ 16th Special-Designation Engineer Brigade
  - ○ 20th Sapper Brigade
  - ○ 6th, 7th, 20th, and 104th Pontoon-Bridge Battalions
  - ○ 120th, 257th, 258th, and 741st Separate Engineer Battalions[130]

Overall, these forces facilitated the passage of 12,800 men, 396 guns, 1,684 vehicles, and 822 carts across the Don River in the Antonovka region between 8 and 17 November.[131]

Logistics

After the Herculean efforts of the *Stavka* and NKO to locate, generate, organize, deploy, and concentrate the more than 1 million soldiers fielded by the Southwestern, Don, and Stalingrad Fronts on 19 November, they faced the equally arduous task of supporting and sustaining this force logistically both prior to the counteroffensive and after it began. Since the subject of force generation and reinforcement and the associated transportation measures required to bring Plan Uranus to fruition was detailed above, a few words are warranted about the parallel logistical effort. This is particularly true because, since the beginning of the war, logistics had been one of the Red Army's most serious Achilles' heels, and Stalin knew it. Therefore, from the outset, supplying the force required to conduct Uranus had been at the center of Stalin's attentions. He ensured that it was also the focus of his senior commanders by centralizing all aspects of logistics, particularly with regard to fuel, ammunition, and food, at the highest level; he appointed a deputy commissar of defense to ensure that logistics was a priority and established a formidable hierarchy of logistical chiefs at all levels of command.

By November 1942, the chief of the Red Army Rear, Lieutenant General of the Quartermaster Service Andrei Vasil'evich Khrulev, was in charge of military logistics, along with a host of directorates (including fuel, ammunition, and food) under his direct supervision.[132] A frequent attendee at Stalin's Kremlin meetings, Khrulev (who was also a deputy commissar of defense) directed the army's logistical efforts through a hierarchy of deputy commanders for the rear (rear services), each with his own specific directorates, at the *front* and army levels and deputy commanders for the rear at the corps and division levels. By late 1942, Khrulev and his headquarters were responsible for virtually all logistical activities, including procurement, storage, and delivery of all troops and supplies to the *fronts*. By far, their highest-priority

Table 8. Growth of Soviet Production of Combat Equipment, Weapons, and Ammunition, 1942

| | Number of Items Produced | | |
Type of Equipment	1st Half of 1942	2nd Half of 1942	Rate of Growth
Combat Aircraft			
Fighters (total)	3,871	5,973	1.54-fold
Mig-3	12	36	3-fold
LaGG-3	1,766	970	—
La-5	—	1,129	—
Iak-1	1,578	1,895	1.2-fold
Iak-7 and Iak-9	515	1,943	3.77-fold
Assault (Il-2 Shturmovik)	2,629	5,596	2.13-fold
Bombers	1,641	1,867	1.1-fold
Total	**8,141**	**13,436**	**1.65-fold**
Tanks			
Heavy (KV)	1,663	890	—
Medium (T-34)	4,414	8,106	1.8-fold
Light (T-60)	5,100	4,272	—
Total	**11,177**	**13,268**	**1.19-fold**
Artillery Pieces			
Antitank guns (47mm and 57mm)	8,957	11,142	1.24-fold
Antiaircraft guns	2,368	4,120	1.7-fold
76mm field guns	11,052	12,257	1.1-fold
122mm guns	2,240	2,597	1.16-fold
152mm guns	1,008	766	—
Total	**25,625**	**30,882**	**1.2-fold**
Mortars			
50mm	66,802	36,511	—
82mm	45,485	55,378	1.2-fold
107mm and 120mm	10,183	15,164	1.5-fold
Total	**122,470**	**107,053**	**—**
Multiple Rocket Launchers (MRLs)			
BM-8 MRLs (*Katiushas*)	459	386	—
BM-13 MRLs (*Katiushas*)	1,087	1,305	1.2-fold
Total	**1,546**	**1,691**	**1.1-fold**
Rifle Weapons			
Rifles and carbines	1,943,400	2,100,509	1.08-fold
Automatic weapons (machine pistols)	524,473	952,332	1.8-fold
Submachine guns	71,923	100,183	1.4-fold
Heavy machine guns	16,011	40,544	2.5-fold
Machine guns (12.7mm)	1,864	5,478	3-fold
Antitank rifles	114,400	134,400	1.17-fold
Total	**614,271**	**1,098,537**	**1.78-fold**
Ammunition (in thousands of rounds)			
Rounds for rifle weapons	1,508,736	2,236,477	1.5-fold
Mortar bombs (shells) of all caliber	17,799	35,959	2-fold
Shells for guns of all caliber	31,827	44,678	1.4-fold
Rocket shells for MRLs	1,300	2,600	2-fold

Table 8. (continued)

Sources: K. K. Rokossovsky, ed., *Velikaia pobeda na Volge* [Great victory on the Volga] (Moscow: Voenizdat, 1965), 210–211; M. E. Morozov, ed., *Velikaia Otechestvennaia voina 1941–1945 gg. Kampanii i strategicheskie operatsii v tsifrakh v 2 tomakh. Tom 1* [The Great Patriotic War 1941–1945. Campaigns and strategic operations in numbers in 2 vols. Vol. 1] (Moscow: Ob'edinennaia redaktsiia MVD Rossii, 2010), 373, 478.

missions were to provide fuel, food, and forage for Red Army forces; procure and move reinforcements; and support the regrouping of forces prior to and during specific military operations.

Despite the catastrophic defeats the Red Army suffered in the spring and summer of 1942, Khrulev's organization coped well with its responsibilities. By November, it had eased severe transportation problems by repairing and expanding the rail and road networks in the southern Soviet Union; it had tapped the Soviet Union's new industrial base, now fully operational in and east of the Ural region, to procure weapons and other supplies; and it had organized an effective distribution of Lend-Lease materials, including military hardware, raw materials, and vital foodstuffs necessary to keep the Red Army operational. Although shortages occurred, Khrulev skillfully managed them, placing the right amount of supplies in the right place at the right time.

Without covering all classes of supplies, table 8 illustrates the growth of Red Army combat power during 1942, based on the production of the most important types of military weapons and equipment.[133] For the sake of comparison, table 9 illustrates German weapons production in 1942, which also increased, particularly in terms of guns, mortars, tanks, and armored troop carriers. Even with these increases, German production lagged well behind the Soviets' in all categories except armored troop carriers. For example, even though the Germans doubled their production to 4,759 tanks in 1942, the Soviets produced more than 24,400 tanks that year and would continue to increase production rates in 1943. However, because the Soviets were unable to develop and field an armored troop carrier, this remained a significant German advantage until the war's end.

Supplementing Soviet war production, Stalin's allies (the United States, Great Britain, and Canada) provided critical war materials to the Soviet Union and, in particular, to the Red Army through the Lend-Lease program. After the program was instituted in October 1941, these materials were shipped to the Soviet Union via convoys to Murmansk and Arkhangel'sk, through the so-called Persian corridor, and via an air route from Alaska to Siberia (the ALSIB highway). Under the provisions of the first Lend-Lease protocol signed in October 1941, the Allies shipped 267 bomber and 278 fighter aircraft, 363 medium and 420 light tanks, and 16,502 cargo trucks

Table 9. German Weapons Production, 1942

Types of Weapons	Estimated Army Stocks in January 1942	Number of Weapons Produced in 1942
Rifles and carbines	4,748,260	1,149,593
Submachine guns/assault rifles	211,940	152,683
Machine guns	208,130	81,199
Mortars	26,494	18,199
Antiaircraft guns		
Army	2,915	2,966
Luftwaffe	—	8,430
Total	—	**11,396**
Antitank guns		
Light	13,607	4,798
Medium	—	4,344
Total	**13,607**	**9,142**
	(2,018 [555 light and 1,463 medium] from 22 June to 31 December 1941)	
Artillery		
Infantry guns	4,684	1,687
Rocket launchers (*Werfer*)	12,615	3,864
Light	6,701	1,476
Heavy	3,419	935
Extra-heavy	469	33
Total	**27,888**	**7,975**
Armored fighting vehicles (AFVs)		
Tanks (Pz-II, Pz-III, Pz-IV, and 38[t])	3,365 (2,234 from 22 June to 31 December 1941)	4,759
Assault guns	625 (348 from 22 June to 31 December 1941)	—
Armored troop carriers	1,888 (other AFVs)	2,527
Total	**5,878** (5,138 produced in 1941)	**9,278**
Trucks	250,061	49,707
Staff cars	199,452	24,152
Motorcycles	215,009	34,017
Prime movers	—	7,627
Combat aircraft	—	15,109
Shells (75mm or greater)	—	58,070,000

Sources: Horst Boog, Jurgen Forster, Joachim Hoffmann, Ernst Klink, Rolf-Dieter Muller, and Gerd R. Ueberschar, *Germany and the Second World War*, vol. 4, *The Attack on the Soviet Union*, ed. Ewald Osers et al. (Oxford: Clarendon Press, 2001), 1122; Horst Boog, Werner Rahm, Reinhard Stumpf, and Bernd Wegner, *Germany and the Second World War*, vol. 6, *The Global War: Widening of the Conflict into a World War and the Shift of the Initiative 1941–1943*, trans. Ewald Osers et al. (Oxford: Clarendon Press, 2001), 613, 637–638, 668, 670–671, 678–679, 684, 687–688, 691, 700, 805.

Table 10. Supply of the Southwestern, Don, and Stalingrad Fronts' Armies with Ammunition and Fuel at the Beginning of Operation Uranus

Types of Supplies	Unit of Measure	Southwestern Front		Don Front		Stalingrad Front	
		5th Tank Army	21st Army	65th Army	24th Army	57th Army	51st Army
82mm shells	Combat load	2.0	1.82	1.65	1.0	1.0	1.9
120mm shells	Combat load	2.3	2.28	3.1	1.7	1.0	0.8
76mm shells (regimental artillery)	Combat load	1.4	1.83	2.6	1.5	2.65	4.1
76mm shells (divisional artillery)	Combat load	2.66	2.0	2.6	4.57	1.1	2.8
122mm shells	Combat load	1.9	3.2	1.7	1.4	1.0	1.0
Diesel fuel	Refill	3.8	4.8	2.2	3.3	3.8	6.3
Gasoline	Refill	1.4	2.6	1.57	1.08	1.9	9.0

Source: K. K. Rokossovsky, ed., *Velikaia pobeda na Volge* [Great victory on the Volga] (Moscow: Voenizdat, 1965), 248.

Note: Combat load means the amount of ammunition needed per gun to sustain operations for *x* number of days. At this stage of the war, one combat load was sufficient to sustain three days of fighting.

to the Soviet Union by June 1942.[134] A second protocol, which lasted from roughly June 1942 through June 1943, included another 3,816 aircraft, 1,206 tanks, 62,292 automatic weapons, and 93,713 trucks, along with other strategic materials and foodstuffs.[135] Although most of the tanks and trucks sent to the Soviet Union via the Persian corridor ended up with Red Army forces in the Trans-Caucasus and North Caucasus regions, some reached the forces fighting at Stalingrad.

In general, with a few notable exceptions, Lend-Lease shipments amounted to only a small fraction of Soviet war production. This fraction ranged from a low of 2 percent of artillery to a staggeringly high figure of about 70 percent of trucks and other vehicles. Lend-Lease deliveries amounted to roughly 12 percent of actual Soviet wartime tank production. However, during the difficult period of the battle for Stalingrad and the struggle for the Caucasus, this figure likely reached 15 percent or higher with regard to Soviet tank forces fighting in the Caucasus region.[136]

At the receiving end of Khrulev's logistical umbilical, the armies conducting Operation Uranus had just enough fuel and ammunition to fulfill their assigned combat missions (see table 10). Thus, at the outset of the counteroffensive, all the armies conducting the main attacks had sufficient ammunition to sustain their operations for at least 3 days and, in many cases, for well over 6 days. With between 3.8 and 9.0 refills of fuel, the mobile groups of 5th Tank and 21st, 57th, and 51st Armies could conduct operations for 11 to 18 days, but those of 65th and 24th Armies needed resupply to conduct operations for more than 7 and 10 days, respectively. In general, 24th, 51st, and 57th Armies had the greatest shortages of ammunition, and 5th Tank and 24th and 57th Armies were most deficient in fuel. This necessitated Herculean efforts to "top off" these armies' supplies of both commodities shortly after the offensive began if the three *fronts* were to sustain operations beyond the estimated 3 days required to achieve the encirclement.

CHAPTER FOUR

The Balance of Opposing Forces on 18 November

SOVIET FORCES

Composition

As described earlier, the force the *Stavka* mustered to conduct Operation Uranus consisted of the Southwestern, Don, and Stalingrad Fronts. Their units were deployed in the 850-kilometer-wide sector extending southeastward from Verkhnyi Mamon on the Don River to Stalingrad and then southward along the Volga River to the city of Astrakhan' near the northern coast of the Caspian Sea. Arrayed from north to south, these forces included the Southwestern Front, whose 1st Guards, 5th Tank, and 21st Armies, supported by 17th Air Army and part of 2nd Air Army, were deployed in the 250-kilometer sector from Verkhnyi Mamon to Kletskaia; the Don Front, with its 24th, 65th, and 66th Armies, supported by 16th Air Army, deployed in the 150-kilometer sector from Kletskaia to Erzovka on the Volga River; and the Stalingrad Front, whose 62nd, 64th, 57th, 51st, and 28th Armies, supported by 8th Air Army, occupied the 450-kilometer sector from Rynok on the Volga River southward through Stalingrad to Astrakhan'.

The ten field, one tank, and four air armies assigned to these three *fronts* were a formidable force, even though more than two-thirds of it had already survived two months of deadly combat in the Stalingrad region. By 18 November, this force consisted of the following:

- 1 rifle corps
- 2 mixed aviation corps
- 66 rifle divisions
- 25 aviation divisions (2 bomber aviation, 2 mixed aviation, 10 fighter aviation, 1 PVO fighter aviation, 6 assault aviation, and 4 night bomber aviation)
- 15 rifle, 2 motorized rifle, and 2 destroyer (infantry antitank) brigades
- 9 fortified regions
- 5 tank corps, 2 mechanized corps, and 3 cavalry corps with 8 cavalry divisions

- 15 separate tank brigades, 5 separate tank regiments, and 3 separate tank battalions
- 1 motorcycle regiment
- 3 separate armored car battalions
- 8 armored train battalions
- 17 separate antitank rifle battalions
- 1 artillery division
- 127 RVGK artillery and mortar regiments (42 tank destroyer, 39 artillery, 13 mortar, and 33 guards-mortar)
- 14 guards-mortar battalions
- 3 antiaircraft artillery divisions, 35 separate antiaircraft artillery regiments, and 15 separate antiaircraft artillery battalions
- 7 engineer brigades (3 special-designation engineer and 4 sapper)
- 51 engineer battalions (27 engineer, 18 pontoon-bridge, 5 sapper, and 1 guards-miner)
- 10 aviation regiments (1 bomber aviation, 2 assault aviation, 2 reconnaissance aviation, and 5 mixed aviation)[1]

Because the Southwestern and Stalingrad Fronts were to conduct the main attacks in the forthcoming operation, they received priority in terms of replacement personnel distributed among the four *fronts* in the Stalingrad region in October and November 1942 (see appendix 4A in the *Companion*).[2] They received 105,211 of the 327,239 personnel replacements the NKO sent to all the *fronts* operating in the West, or 32 percent; the 102,351 men sent to the Kalinin, Western, and Briansk Fronts amounted to another 31 percent of the whole. This is indicative of the importance of Operation Mars in comparison with Operation Uranus.

Despite these personnel replacements, the average strength of rifle divisions subordinate to the three Uranus *fronts* differed sharply, and there were also significant differences in strength based on the divisions' assigned missions. For example, the average personnel strength of rifle divisions subordinate to the Southwestern Front was 8,800 men, while divisions in the Stalingrad and Don Fronts averaged 4,000 to 5,000 men and 5,850 men, respectively. These averages were misleading, however, because the divisions participating in the main attacks of 57th and 51st Armies contained far more men than those assigned secondary roles in the operation.[3]

Once Soviet forces were in their jumping-off positions for the attack, each first-echelon rifle division operated along an average frontage of 9 kilometers. The artillery and tanks available to the three *fronts* enabled them to establish operational weapons densities of 16.7 guns and mortars per kilometer of front and more than 1 tank per kilometer of front. The concentration of these weapons in main attack sectors increased the tactical densities of artillery and tanks to astronomical proportions.[4]

Strength

Past attempts to quantify the actual strength of the Red Army *fronts* and armies participating in Operation Uranus engendered considerable controversy. While Soviet sources tend to understate the strength of their own forces and overstate the strength of opposing Axis forces, they also disagree about which forces should be counted. For example, when calculating the actual personnel strengths of the three *fronts* operating in the Stalingrad region, most sources fail to count personnel physically operating in the region but directly subordinate to the *Stavka*, other NKO directorates (such as railroad and construction troops and local PVO [air defense] organs), other people's commissariats (such as the NKVD), and the Stalingrad or other military districts. Many of these men and women provided administrative, logistical, or other support services. Furthermore, when calculating the strengths of the *fronts* and armies, some sources count only combat soldiers, while others include the entire ration strength of these organizations.

The same counting dilemmas apply to German forces. In addition, German sources often count only German personnel assigned to operating army groups and their subordinate armies, while Soviet estimates of German strength include all Axis personnel. Further compounding these problems is the fact that, by November 1942, many if not most German divisions included Russian auxiliary troops, called *Hiwis*, sometimes numbering in the thousands. For example, as shown in table 46 of volume 2, the number of *Hiwis* and attached [*Zugeteilte*] soldiers present in Sixth Army's divisions ranged from as low as 10 percent to well over 100 percent of the division's actual ration strength. German sources do not count these personnel, but Soviet sources do. For the sake of simplicity, the passages that follow include only the most recent, and presumably the most accurate, figures (see appendix 4B in the *Companion* for varying estimates of Soviet and German forces at the outset of the offensive).

Table 11 shows the latest Russian estimates of the strength of the three attacking *fronts*. The fact that the Southwestern Front was 1.7 and 2.8 times stronger than the Don Front in terms of combat personnel and tanks, respectively, and nearly 1.3 times stronger than the Stalingrad Front in both categories is indicative of the importance the *Stavka* placed on the operations assigned to Vatutin's *front*. Conversely, the excessive number of noncombat troops in the Don and Stalingrad Fronts—specifically, 92,180 men in the former and 109,626 men in the latter, as opposed to the 57,954 support troops in the Southwestern Front—indicates the necessity of augmenting the two weaker *fronts* with firepower and with engineer and other types of combat and combat service support.

Careful examination of the relative strengths of the armies participating in the operation demonstrates that this tailoring of forces to specific missions persisted at the army level and below (see table 12). Once again, and by design, the Southwestern Front's 5th Tank and 21st Armies, which were to conduct its main attack, were twice as strong in infantry as the Stalingrad Front's 57th and 51st Armies, which constituted its main shock group. In this case, however, the *Stavka* equipped the Stalingrad Front's mobile groups, which were to conduct their exploitation through 57th and 51st Armies, with 432 tanks; the mobile groups serving the Southwestern Front fielded a roughly equivalent strength of 450 tanks. The weakest army in the offensive was the Don Front's 66th Army, which, with a combat strength of less than 40,000 men, was roughly equivalent in strength to the Stalingrad Front's 62nd and 64th Armies. These armies were assigned solely defensive missions. At the other end of the spectrum, the Southwestern Front's massive 1st Guards Army, with ration and combat strengths of over 155,000 and 142,000, respectively, was twice as strong as the next strongest field army, Batov's 65th. This tailoring process would become a hallmark of Red Army force structuring for offensive operations throughout the remainder of the war.

The bulk of the armor assigned to the three attacking *fronts* belonged to the *fronts'* and armies' mobile groups (exploitation echelons), specifically, the tank and mechanized corps subordinate to 5th Tank and 21st, 24th, 51st, and 57th Armies. These were supplemented by separate tank brigades, regiments, and, in a few cases, battalions designated to provide tank support for infantry. Although the precise composition (i.e., types of tank) of some forces remains unclear, in most cases, the overall tank strength is known (see table 13).[5]

Finally, given the significant role they played in the counteroffensive, the three cavalry corps assigned to the Southwestern and Stalingrad Fronts must be mentioned. The primary difference between the *fronts* was that the Southwestern Front's 3rd Guards and 8th Cavalry Corps fielded three cavalry divisions each, while the Stalingrad Front's 4th Cavalry Corps fielded only two. In addition, while 3rd Guards Corps was overstrength in cavalrymen and understrength in horses, 8th and 4th Cavalry Corps were understrength in both. In fact, 8th and 4th Cavalry Corps were understrength in a wide range of weaponry (see table 14), making it very difficult for them to perform their primary missions of creating outer encirclement fronts and defending against German counterattacks.

Table 11. Strengths of the Southwestern, Don, and Stalingrad Fronts, 18 November 1942

Category	Southwestern Front	Don Front	Stalingrad Front	Total
Personnel	331,948/ **389,902**	192,193/ **284,373**	258,317/ **367,943**	782,548/ **1,042,218**
Guns and mortars (less antiaircraft guns and 50mm mortars)	**8,655**	**6,625**	**6,739**	**22,019**
Tanks	**721**	**254**	**575**	**1,550**
Combat aircraft	**359**/311	**388**/329	**782**/637	**1,529**/1,277

Sources: *Velikaia Otechestvennaia Deistvuiushchaia armiia 1941–1945 gg.* [The Great Patriotic (War) and the operating army 1941–1945] (Moscow: Animi Fortitudo Kuchkovo pole, 2005), 585, citing *Boevoi i chislennyi sostav Vooruzhennykh Sil SSSR v period Velikoi Otechestvennoi voiny (1941–1945 gg.)* [The combat and numerical composition of the armed forces of the USSR in the period of the Great Patriotic War (1941–1945)], No. 5, 1997 (its figures for artillery strength include 25mm and 37mm antiaircraft guns); Aleksei Isaev, *Stalingrad: Za Volgoi nas zemli net* [Stalingrad: There is no land for us beyond the Volga] (Moscow: Iauza Eksmo, 2008), 277, 281–282.

Notes: Total personnel and weapons strengths are shown in **bold**. The numerator of the fraction showing personnel strength indicates combat strength (infantry, engineer, artillery, and armored forces [*tankists*]); the denominator indicates ration (overall) strength. The numerator of the fraction showing aircraft strength indicates the total quantity of aircraft (in **bold**), and the denominator indicates the number of operable aircraft.

AXIS FORCES AND DEFENSES

General

As Army Group B prepared to face another winter in the East, it looked more like a patchwork international force than a powerful German field command. German Second Army still anchored the army group's northwestern flank, covering the railheads at Kursk and Khar'kov but barely retaining the disputed river bend at Voronezh. However, by November 1942, the three armies of Germany's Axis allies—Hungarian Second, Italian Eighth, and Romanian Third Armies—protected German Sixth Army's left flank on a 360-kilometer-wide front (as the crow flies) along the Don River from just south of Voronezh to the Kletskaia region. South of the sector extending from Kletskaia (on the Don) through Stalingrad (on the Volga) to the Beketovka bridgehead south of the city, where Sixth Army and a shrunken Fourth Panzer Army were fighting, two Romanian army corps (VI and VII, which were slated to become Romanian Fourth Army on 20 November) extended this brittle cordon southward through the lake region, where it faded out in the barren steppes north of Elista. Beyond the Romanians, the Axis defense

Table 12. Strengths of the Armies Subordinate to the Southwestern, Don, and Stalingrad Fronts, 18 November 1942

Force	Personnel Strength (Combat/Total)	Total Artillery (Guns/Mortars/Multiple Rocket Launchers)	Total Tanks (Heavy/Medium/Light)	Combat Aircraft
Southwestern Front				
1st Guards Army	142,869/**155,096**	**3,308** (973/2,293/14)	**163** (—/113/50)	
21st Army	92,056/**103,270**	**2,520** (803/1,554/40)	**199** (85/57/57)	
5th Tank Army	90,600/**104,196**	**2,538** (929/1,456/—)	**359** (60/144/155)	
Front forces (including 17th Air Army)	6,423/**27,340**	**289** (—/279/164)	—	**359**/311
Total	331,948/**389,902**	**8,655** (2,705/5,582/218)	**721** (145/314/262)	**359**/311
Don Front				
24th Army	56,409/**68,489**	**1,899** (722/1,123/—)	**48** (21/14/9/4 special)	
65th Army	63,187/**74,709**	**1,922** (638/1,230/—)	**49** (10/22/17)	
66th Army	39,457/**51,738**	**1,568** (515/1,230/—)	**5** (—/2/3)	
Front forces (including 16th Air Army)	33,140/**89,437**	**1,236** (263/786/194)	**152** (41/52/59)	**388**/329
Total	192,193/**284,373**	**6,625** (2,138/4,162/194)	**254** (72/90/88/4 special)	**388**/329
Stalingrad Front				
28th Army	47,891/**64,265**	**1,196** (369/816/8)	**80** (10/26/44)	
51st Army	44,720/**55,184**	**1,077** (318/698/45)	**207** (—/118/89)	
57th Army	56,026/**66,778**	**1,604** (539/962/—)	**225** (4/122/99)	
62nd Army	41,667/**54,199**	**1,237** (453/744/—)	**23** (7/15/1)	
64th Army	40,490/**53,742**	**1,093** (356/673/—)	**40** (1/27/12)	
Front forces (including 8th Air Army)	27,523/**73,775**	**532** (162/330/—)	—	**782**/637
Total	258,317/**367,943**	**6,739** (2,197/4,223/53)	**575** (22/308/245)	**782**/637
Grand total	782,548/**1,042,218**	**22,019** (7,040/13,967/465)	**1,550** (239/712/595/4 special)	**1,529**/1,277

Sources: *Velikaia Otechestvennaia Deistvuiushchaia armiia 1941–1945 gg.* [The Great Patriotic (War) and the operating army 1941–1945] (Moscow: Animi Fortitudo Kuchkovo pole, 2005), 584, citing *Boevoi i chislennyi sostav Vooruzhennykh Sil SSSR v period Velikoi Otechestvennoi voiny (1941–1945 gg.)* [The combat and numerical composition of the armed forces of the USSR in the period of the Great Patriotic War (1941–1945)], No. 5, 1997; *Velikaia Otechestvennaia voina 1941–1945 gg.: Kampanii i strategicheskie operatsii v tsifrakh, Tom I* [The Great Patriotic War 1941–1945: Campaigns and strategic operations in numbers, vol. 1] (Moscow: Ob'edinennaia redaktsiia MVD Rossii, 2010), 495.

Notes: The total figure for artillery strength includes 25mm–37mm antiaircraft guns. Total personnel and weapons strengths are shown in **bold**. The numerator of the fraction showing aircraft strength indicates the total quantity of aircraft, and the denominator indicates the number of operable aircraft.

Table 13. Armored Strength of the Southwestern, Don, and Stalingrad Fronts' Tank and Mechanized Formations and Units, 18 November 1942 (based on available data)

		Type of Tank		
Force	KV Heavy	T-34 Medium	T-60, T-70 Light	Total
SOUTHWESTERN FRONT				
1st Guards Army				
1st Guards Mechanized Corps	—	113	50	163
Total	**—**	**113**	**50**	**163**
5th Tank Army				
1st Tank Corps (authorized/ on hand)	—	101/—	70/—	171/136 (80% fill)
26th Tank Corps (authorized/ on hand)	—	101/—	70/—	171/157 (95% fill)
8th Guards Tank Brigade				
510th Separate Tank Battalion				
511th Separate Tank Battalion				
Total	**60**	**144**	**155**	**359**
21st Army				
4th Tank Corps (authorized/ on hand/operable)	—/—/29	—/—/57	—/—/57	171/159/143
1st Guards Separate Tank Regiment	Authorized 21 each, for a total of 63, but only 56 on hand			56
2nd Guards Separate Tank Regiment				
4th Guards Separate Tank Regiment				
Total	**85**	**57**	**57**	**199**
Front **subordinate**	—	—	—	—
Southwestern Front grand total	**145**	**314**	**262**	**721**
DON FRONT				
24th Army				
10th Tank Brigade	21	14	9 + 4 special	48
Total	**21**	**14**	**9 + 4 special**	**48**
65th Army				
91st Tank Brigade				
121st Tank Brigade				
Total	**10**	**22**	**17**	**49**
66th Army				
58th Tank Brigade	—	2	3	5
Total	**—**	**2**	**3**	**5**
Front **subordinate**				
16th Tank Corps (authorized/ on hand/operable)	—/40/35	—/47/37	—/53/33 (includes 10/5 T-60 models)	171/140/105
64th Tank Brigade				
148th Tank Brigade				
Total	**41**	**52**	**59**	**152**
Don Front grand total	**72**	**90**	**88 + 4 special**	**254**

Table 13. (continued)

Force	Type of Tank			
	KV Heavy	T-34 Medium	T-60, T-70 Light	Total
STALINGRAD FRONT				
62nd Army				
84th Tank Brigade				
506th Separate Tank Battalion (235th Tank Brigade)				
Total	**7**	**15**	**1**	**23**
64th Army				
13th Tank Brigade				
56th Tank Brigade				
Total	**1**	**27**	**12**	**40**
51st Army				
4th Mechanized Corps (on hand/present and operable)				220/179
254th Tank Brigade				28
Total	**—**	**118**	**89**	**207**
57th Army				
13th Tank Corps (on hand/ present and operable)				205/171
90th Tank Brigade	3	14	9	26
235th Tank Brigade	26	2		28
Total	**4**	**122**	**99**	**225**
28th Army				
6th Guards Tank Brigade				
565th Separate Tank Battalion				
Total	**10**	**26**	**44**	**80**
Front **subordinate**				
85th Tank Brigade				
35th Separate Tank Regiment				
166th Separate Tank Regiment				
Total	**—**	**—**	**—**	**—**
Stalingrad Front grand total	**22**	**308**	**245**	**575**
Grand total for all 3 *fronts*	**239**	**712**	**595 + 4 special**	**1,550**

Sources: *Velikaia Otechestvennaia Deistvuiushchaia armiia 1941–1945 gg.* [The Great Patriotic (War) and the operating army 1941–1945] (Moscow: Animi Fortitudo Kuchkovo pole, 2005), 584, citing *Boevoi i chislennyi sostav Vooruzhennykh Sil SSSR v period Velikoi Otechestvennoi voiny (1941–1945 gg.)* [The combat and numerical composition of the armed forces of the USSR in the period of the Great Patriotic War (1941–1945)], No. 5, 1997; Aleksei Isaev, *Stalingrad: Za Volgoi nas zemli net* [Stalingrad: There is no land for us beyond the Volga] (Moscow: Iauza Eksmo, 2008), 277, 281–282; V. T. Minov, *Nastupatel'naia operatsiia 5-i Tankovoi armii v kontrnastuplenii pod Stalingradom (19–25 noiabria 1942 goda)* [The offensive operation of 5th Tank Army in the counteroffensive at Stalingrad (19–25 November 1942)] (Moscow: Voroshilov Military Academy of the General Staff, 1979).

Note: Although totals for *fronts* are correct, the precise distribution of tank types in units is not available.

Table 14. Personnel and Weapons Strength of Cavalry Corps Subordinate to the Southwestern and Stalingrad Fronts, 18 November 1942

Category	5th Tank Army's 8th Cavalry Corps	21st Army's 3rd Guards Cavalry Corps	51st Army's 4th Cavalry Corps
Cavalrymen	22,512/+24	16,134/–1,874	10,284/–1,172
Horses	18,057/–3,752	14,908/–2,379	9,284/–988
Rifles and carbines	14,102/–1,388	10,974/–1,014	7,354/–1,777
Automatic weapons (PPSh)	2,153/+193	1,369/–607	566/–757
Submachine guns	374/–94	366/–32	264/–64
DShK machine guns	40/+5	33/+4	—/–61
Antitank rifles	388/+10	188/–146	140/–11
Guns			
76mm field	70	66/+4	32/–26
45mm antitank	55/+9	35/–3	24
37mm antiaircraft	21/–29	6/–12	8/–4
Mortars			
120mm	44	37/–7	16
82mm	108/+22	66/–8	45/+10
50mm	294/+96	123/–43	118/+10

Source: "Konnitsa v nastupatel'nykh operatsiiakh pod Stalingradom" [Cavalry in the offensive operations at Stalingrad], in *Sbornik materialov po izucheniiu opyta voiny, No. 6, aprel'-mai 1943 g.* [Collection of materials for the study of war experiences, no. 6, April–May 1943] (Moscow: Voenizdat, 1943), 88, classified secret.

Note: The minus (–) or plus (+) signs in the denominator of each fraction indicate the amount understrength or overstrength.

line became an immense hole in the wide-open Kalmyk steppes, punctuated by strongpoints erected by German 16th Motorized Division around and east of Elista, remote outposts manned by "Turkestan" battalions subordinate to this division, and roving German and "Turkestan" patrols between these strongpoints and ranging farther east toward distant Astrakhan'. (The term "Turkestan" refers to volunteer battalions raised in the Turkestan Autonomous Region that joined the German side.)

The soldiers of these three and three-quarters allied field armies were neither incompetent nor cowardly, but their units were generally understrength, lightly equipped infantry formations that could do little to defend against a modern, mechanized force. If Germany had experienced difficulties in reequipping for the 1942 campaign, its allies lacked the industrial capacity to even begin to prepare their troops to fight in modern combat conditions. Moreover, the different Axis armies had ongoing animosities with one another and with the sometimes overbearing Germans, all of which complicated their efforts to coordinate.[6] Many of the German soldiers had such contempt for their allies that their ethnically Russian opponents in

Stalingrad reported the Germans taunting them by asking, "Do you wanna swap an Uzbek for a Romanian?"[7]

A few German divisions were scattered at wide intervals along the front in an attempt to stiffen existing defenses. Such reinforcement was limited not only by the overall scarcity of German troops but also by the fact that no nationality wished to be commanded by another. Indeed, the national field armies were intended more to minimize political friction than to provide coherent operational or tactical defenses. To mend political fences, in August 1942, Hitler had even proposed grouping the two Romanian field armies along with Paulus's Sixth Army as an army group under Ion Antonescu, the Romanian dictator. Fortunately for the troops in the field, this deal did not reach fruition.[8] Instead, the Germans assigned small, radio-equipped liaison teams to the major headquarters of their allies, and German liaison officers performed minor miracles of diplomacy to hold the front together. By November 1942, these allied forces, which, in essence, formed an entire allied army group, defended the strategically vital Don River front.

Composition

By mid-November 1942, Army Group B's patchwork quilt of German and other Axis forces extended from the Livny region in south-central Russia southeastward roughly 840 kilometers (as the crow flies) along the Don and Volga Rivers to the vicinity of Elista in the Kalmyk steppes of the North Caucasus region. After four months of heavy fighting, the army group's strategic frontage had increased in width from about 400 kilometers in early June to 840 kilometers in mid-November. Since, in both theory and practice, a full army group was considered capable of operating in a sector 400 to 500 kilometers wide, Army Group B's Second and Sixth Field Armies and Fourth Panzer Army were patently unable to fight and survive along such a broad front.[9] Therefore, in August and September, Hitler tried to remedy the situation by inserting four allied armies into Army Group B's front lines. With a sector of about 360 kilometers under their control, these allied armies constituted a virtual allied army group—but in name only. It was therefore no coincidence that Stalin and his *Stavka* chose this ersatz allied army group as the target of the Red Army's fall counteroffensive.

Army Group B's force structure in mid-November consisted of six armies supported by an air fleet and a small operational reserve (see table 15). Roughly two-thirds of Army Group B's forces were deployed along the Stalingrad axis opposite the Red Army's Southwestern, Don, and Stalingrad Fronts. This force included roughly half of Italian Eighth Army and all of Romanian Third Army and German Sixth and Fourth Panzer Armies. Therefore, Army Group B fielded the following forces along the Stalingrad axis:

- 13 army corps headquarters: 5 German (XXIX, XI, VIII, LI, and IV), 6 Romanian (I, II, IV, V, VI, and VII), and 2 Italian (II and XXXV)
- 2 panzer corps headquarters: German (XIV and XXXXVIII)
- 49 divisions:
  ○ 34 infantry divisions: 16 German (298th, 62nd, 376th, 44th, 384th, 76th, 113th, 94th, 389th, 305th, 79th, 100th Jäger, 295th, 71st, 371st, and 297th), 5 Italian (3rd Ravenna, 9th Pasubio, 52nd Torino, 2nd Sforzesca, and 3rd Celere), and 13 Romanian (7th, 11th, 9th, 14th, 5th, 6th, 13th, 15th, 20th, 2nd, 18th, 1st, and 4th)
  ○ 5 panzer (armored) divisions: 4 German (14th, 16th, 22nd, and 24th Panzer) and 1 Romanian (1st Armored)
  ○ 4 motorized divisions: German 3rd, 60th, 29th, and 16th
  ○ 4 cavalry divisions: Romanian 1st, 5th, 7th, and 8th
  ○ 2 rear area security divisions: German 213th and 403rd
- 2 brigades: "23 March" and "3 January" Blackshirt (Italian)[10]

Operational and Tactical Formations

Because of its immense front and relative paucity of forces, Army Group B had no choice but to deploy all its subordinate armies forward, literally side by side in a single-echelon strategic formation. The army group was able to form a small operational reserve whose nucleus consisted of the headquarters of Fourth Panzer Army's XXXXVIII Panzer Corps. It attached this reserve to Romanian Third Army, with portions of German 22nd Panzer Division and Romanian 1st Armored Division subordinate to it.[11] The 14th Panzer Division, which Sixth Army decided to deploy in reserve positions in XI Army Corps' rear area on the army's extreme left wing shortly after the Soviet counteroffensive began, received orders to cooperate with XXXXVIII Panzer Corps' forces and back up Romanian Third Army's defenses.

Army Group B also maintained the headquarters of Romanian Fourth Army and German XVII Army Corps and 294th Infantry Division in its reserve. However, the Romanian army headquarters had no troops of its own and was never activated; the headquarters of General Hollidt's XXVII Corps received troops in an ad hoc fashion only after the counteroffensive began; and 294th Infantry Division, which was, in effect, in Italian Eighth Army's reserve, ended up assigned to XVII Army Corps soon after the Soviet counteroffensive commenced. In addition to this small reserve, Army Group B held on to two combat divisions, Hungarian 105th Light Division (with 46th Infantry Regiment) and Italian 156th Vicenza Infantry Division, in its Rear Area Command. Together with 213th and 403rd Security Divisions, the single Hungarian and Italian divisions were tasked with crushing Soviet partisan activity in the army group's rear and preparing to cope with crises at the

Table 15. Composition and Senior Command Cadre of German Army Group B, 18 November 1942 (from North to South)

Army Group B—Colonel General Maximilian Freiherr von Weichs
  Second Army (German)—Colonel General Hans von Salmuth
    LV Army Corps
      299th, 45th, 383rd, and 88th Infantry Divisions
    XIII Army Corps
      82nd, 68th, 340th, 385th, and 377th Infantry Divisions
    VI Army Corps
      387th, 57th, 75th, and 323rd Infantry Divisions
    27th Panzer Division
  Second Army (Hungarian)—Colonel General Gusztáv Jany
    III Army Corps (H)
      9th and 6th Light (Infantry) Divisions (H)
    XXIV Panzer Corps (G)
      168th and 336th Infantry Divisions (G) and 7th, 13th, and 30th Light Divisions (H)
    IV Army Corps (H)
      10th and 12th Light Divisions (H)
    VII Army Corps (H)
      19th and 23rd Light Divisions (H)
    1st Armored Division (H)
  Eighth Army (Italian)—Army General Italo Gariboldi
    Alpine Corps (I)
      2nd Tridentina, 3rd Julia, and 4th Cuneense Alpine Divisions
    II Army Corps (I)
      5th Cosseria and 3rd Ravenna Infantry Divisions (I)
      318th Infantry Regiment (213th Security Division) (G)
      "23 March" Blackshirt Brigade (I)
    XXXV Army Corps (I)
      9th Pasubio Motorized Division (I)
      298th Infantry Division (G)
      "3 January" Blackshirt Brigade (I)
    XXIX Army Corps (G & I) (activated after 19 November)
      52nd Torino Motorized Division (I)
      3rd Celere Mobile Division (I), with 57th *Bersaglieri* Tank Battalion, 2nd Sforzesca
        Infantry Division (I), and 62nd Infantry Division (G)
    71st Reconnaissance Air Group (I)
      38th and 116th Squadrons (15 reconnaissance and 17 bomber aircraft)
    22nd Fighter Air Group (I)
      356th, 361st, 382nd, and 386th Squadrons (43 aircraft)
  Third Army (Romanian)—Army General Petre Dumitrescu
    I Army Corps (R)
      7th and 11th Infantry Divisions (R)
    II Army Corps (R)
      9th and 14th Infantry Divisions (R)
    IV Army Corps (R)
      13th Infantry Division (R)
      1st Cavalry Division (R)
      "Colonel Voicu" Detachment (R), with 12th Infantry Regiment and 13th Light
        Infantry, 611th Panzer Jäger, and 54th Pioneer Battalions
    V Army Corps
      5th and 6th Infantry Divisions (R)
      15th Infantry Division (R)
      7th Cavalry Division (R)

Table 15. (continued)

XXXVIII Panzer Corps (attached)
   22nd Panzer Division (G)
   1st Armored Division (R)
1st Air Corps [*Corpul Aerian*]
   7th Fighter Group
      56th, 47th, and 58th Squadrons (36 fighter aircraft)
   8th Fighter Group
      41st, 42nd, and 60th Squadrons (36 fighter aircraft)
   6th Fighter-Bomber Group
      61st and 62nd Squadrons (22 aircraft)
   1st Bomber Group
      71st and 72nd Squadrons (15 bomber aircraft)
   3rd Bomber Group
      73rd, 74th, and 81st Squadrons (24 bomber aircraft)
   5th Bomber Group
      79th and 80th Squadrons (15 bomber aircraft)
Sixth Army (German)—General of Panzer Troops Friedrich von Paulus
   XI Army Corps (G)
   376th, 44th, and 384th Infantry Divisions
   VIII Army Corps (G)
   76th and 113th Infantry Divisions
   177th Assault Gun Battalion
   XIV Panzer Corps (G)
   60th and 3rd Motorized Divisions
   16th Panzer Division
   94th Infantry Division
   LI Army Corps (G)
   389th, 305th, and 79th Infantry; 100th Jäger; and 295th and 71st Infantry Divisions
   14th and 24th Panzer Divisions
   244th and 245th Assault Gun Battalions
Fourth Panzer Army (German)—Colonel General Hermann Hoth
   IV Army Corps (G)
   371st and 297th Infantry Divisions (G) and 20th Infantry Division (R)
   VI Army Corps (R)
   2nd, 18th, 1st, and 4th Infantry Divisions (R)
   6th *Rosiori* Regiment (Motorized) (5th Cavalry Division)
   VII Army Corps (R)
   5th and 8th Cavalry Divisions (R)
   16th and 29th Motorized Divisions (G)
Army Group B's Reserve
   Headquarters, Fourth Army (Romanian)—General of Artillery Constantin Constantinescu
      (supposed to be activated on 20 November with VI and VII Army Corps [R], but
      never activated)
   294th Infantry Division (G)
   Headquarters, XVII Army Corps (G)

Army Group B's Rear Area Command
   105th Light Division (H), with 46th Infantry Regiment (H)
   213th and 403rd Security Divisions (G)
   156th Vicenza Infantry Division (I)

Table 15. (continued)

Fourth Air Fleet
  Combat forces
   VIII Air Corps
      27th Bomber, 2nd Dive-Bomber, 1st Assault, 3rd Fighter, and 1st Heavy Fighter
      Wings°
   9th *Flak* (antiaircraft) Division
   91st *Flak* Regiment[†]
  Air transport forces
   1st (Staff), 5th, 50th, and 102nd Transport Wings—supplying VIII Air Corps
   172nd Transport Wing—supporting Air District Rostov [*Luftgau Rostov*] and providing
      logistical support for VIII Air Corps
   900th Special Purpose Bomber Wing—serving Fourth Air Fleet's command, with
      operational rates averaging 40 percent and as low as 30 percent[†]

Notes: G, German; I, Italian; R, Romanian.

° *Einsatz bereitschaft der fliegenden Verbände*, vol. 22, 20 Sept.–30 Nov. 1942, RL 2/v. 1751, states that on 10 November, VIII Air Corps had 330 aircraft, 137 of which were nonoperational, broken down as follows: 27th Bomber Wing (KG 27), 29 (13 operational and 16 nonoperational); 2nd Dive-Bomber Wing (St. G. 2), 55 (42 operational and 13 nonoperational); 1st Assault Wing (Schl. G. 1), 89 (49 operational and 40 nonoperational); 3rd Fighter Wing (JG 3), 86 (55 operational and 31 nonoperational); 1st Heavy Fighter Wing (ZG 1), 71 (34 operational and 37 nonoperational). The same source indicates that by 20 November, 1st Assault Wing decreased in strength to 47 aircraft (26 operational and 21 nonoperational), 3rd Fighter Wing to 78 aircraft (48 operational and 30 nonoperational), and 1st Heavy Fighter Wing to 57 aircraft (33 operational and 24 nonoperational). Unlike most previous Soviet and Russian sources, which inflate German aircraft strength, *Stalingrad: Tsena pobedy* [Stalingrad: The cost of victory] (Moscow: AST, 2005), 43, credits VIII Air Corps with 313 aircraft: 84 fighters, 57 two-engine and night bombers, 111 dive-bombers and assault aircraft, and 61 bombers.

[†] Joel S. A. Hayward, *Stopped at Stalingrad: The Luftwaffe and Hitler's Defeat in the East, 1942–1943* (Lawrence: University Press of Kansas, 1998), 247, asserts that on 9 November, 12 of 900th Wing's 41 Ju-52 aircraft were operational, and only 13 of 50th Wing's 35 Ju-52s were operational. Thus, only 25 of Fourth Air Fleet's 295 transports were functional on 25 November. By 8 December, all reinforcing transport aircraft sent to VIII Air Corps were centralized at Tatsinskaia under VIII Air Corps' commander, General Fiebig; these included 9 Ju-52 wings, 2 strong He-111 wings, 2 converted Ju-86 wings, 1 converted He-177 wing, and a long-range wing with FW 200, Condor, Ju-90, and Ju-290 aircraft. These wings were organized and subordinated by aircraft type to 1st Special Purposes Bomber Wing (Ju-52, under Colonel Hans Förster based at Tatsinskaia) and 55th Bomber Wing (He-111, under Colonel Kühl based at Morozovskaia). All converted long-range bomber and reconnaissance aircraft were based at Stalino under Major Willers.

front. In reality, however, the army group considered the two allied divisions backup for Hungarian Second and Italian Eighth Armies. As for the two security divisions, they were light infantry formations comprising two regiments each, with no appreciable fire support; therefore, they were considered unfit for front-line combat.[12]

All four of Army Group B's armies in the Stalingrad region deployed their forces in a single echelon of divisions backed up by only small reserves. The Italian Eighth Army maintained 3rd Celere Mobile Division as its reserve. Celere ultimately joined the joint German-Italian XXIX Army Corps headquarters well after the Red Army began its Uranus counteroffensive. If necessary, Eighth Army could also call on the German 294th Infantry Division, which, though in the army group's reserve, was positioned to the rear of the Alpine Corps, and 156th Vicenza Division, which was in the Kupiansk region, much farther to the rear. For its part, Romanian Third Army kept its 15th Infantry and 7th Cavalry Divisions in reserve. However, the former, which was positioned well forward on the army's right wing, was swept up in combat almost immediately after the Soviet attack, and the latter was subordinated to XXXXVIII Panzer Corps immediately after the Soviets began their assaults. In essence, therefore, XXXXVIII Panzer Corps, which was ostensibly Army Group B's principal operational reserve, ended up functioning as Romanian Third Army's second echelon and tactical reserve.

Since Fourth Panzer Army dispatched its XXXXVIII Panzer Corps to Romanian Third Army's rear shortly before the Soviets began Operation Uranus, German Sixth Army was left with essentially no reserve whatsoever. Nonetheless, it tried in vain to constitute a reserve just hours after the Soviet attack by dispatching a combat group [*kampfgruppe*] from the weak 14th Panzer Division to concentration areas in the Verkhne-Buzinovka region, 30 kilometers south-southeast of Kletskaia, in the rear of its left wing XI Army Corps.[13] The 14th Panzer's mission was to bolster XI Corps on Sixth Army's left flank and possibly cooperate with XXXXVIII Panzer Corps. Finally, the only credible reserve force left to the Germans in the immediate vicinity of Stalingrad on 18 November was Fourth Panzer Army's 29th Motorized Division. This division was fresh, rested, and full strength because it had deliberately been held out of combat for weeks so that it could spearhead Hitler's anticipated dash to Astrakhan'. It was positioned well to the rear of Fourth Panzer Army's IV Army Corps.

Reflecting its woefully overextended state, by 18 November, Army Group B's infantry divisions were operating on frontages averaging 17 kilometers wide, with the greatest concentration in the sector from Kletskaia to Beketovka, where division frontages averaged 9 kilometers, and in Stalingrad city, where they averaged 3 kilometers.[14] Of course, by this time, most of Sixth and Fourth Panzer Armies' divisions were operating at well under 50 percent of their required combat strength. With regard to operational densities of weaponry, Axis forces overall averaged roughly 12 guns and mortars and less than 1 tank or assault gun for each kilometer of front.[15]

Characteristics of the Defending Axis Armies

Italian Eighth Army

Headquartered at Voroshilovgrad, a major rail and road center on the Northern Donets River, this Italian army, under the command of Army General Italo Gariboldi, anchored the left wing of Army Group B's forces deployed along the Stalingrad axis (see map 8). Its defenses stretched along the Don River from Pavlovsk, 140 kilometers south of Voronezh, southward 40 kilometers to Novaia Kalitva and then southeastward roughly 120 kilometers along and south of the Don River to west of Baskovskaia. Gariboldi's army had its Alpine Corps on its left wing, backed up by German 294th Infantry Division in the Rossosh region to its rear, Italian II Corps covering its center from Novaia Kalitva eastward along the southern bank of the Don River west of Kazanskaia, and Italian XXXV Army Corps on its right wing, with German 62nd Infantry Division flanked by Italian divisions. The army's reserve, Italian 3rd Celere Mobile Division, was situated at Millerovo, a key road junction and supply depot more than 80 kilometers behind the front. Although labeled "mobile," this division was not fully motorized; rather, it was an odd combination of elite *Bersaglieri* motorized infantry supported by a few light tanks and self-propelled guns. The Germans rated only four of the Italian infantry divisions capable of performing independent missions.[16]

Romanian Third Army

Situated on Italian Eighth Army's right, this army, commanded by Army General Petre Dumitrescu, was in an even more difficult operational and tactical position than its neighbor to the left (see map 8). Headquartered at Morozovsk, a vital rail and road junction 140 kilometers south of the Don River, its four army corps—I, II, V, and IV—were spread out from northwest to southeast along a front of approximately 160 kilometers, extending from Baskovskaia to just east of Kletskaia, along and south of the Don River. Each corps headquarters controlled only two divisions, each of which, in turn, had only seven battalions. Thus, a typical Romanian infantry division defended across a frontage of 20 kilometers. One-half of Third Army's reserve, Romanian 15th Infantry Division, was located at Gromki, 10 kilometers west-southwest of Kletskaia, almost on the front line between the two right-hand corps. Romanian 7th Cavalry Division, largely without horses, was in the Pronin region, roughly 25 kilometers behind the western end of the army's forward defense line. Although the total ration strength of Romanian Third

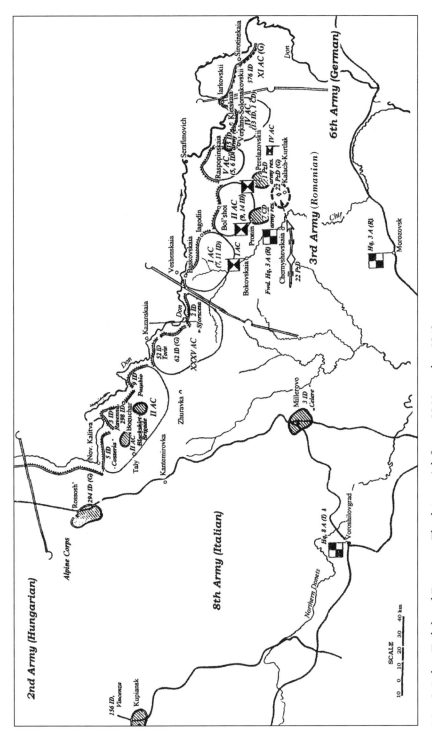

Map 8. Italian Eighth and Romanian Third Armies' defenses, 18 November 1942

Army on 18 November was just over 155,000 men, the actual combat forces available to its ten divisions and supporting artillery and engineers was approximately 100,000 men, well under one-third the size of the Southwestern Front alone (see the subsection Strength, below).[17]

In addition to its ten divisions, Romanian Third Army's headquarters controlled three motorized antitank companies, with 12 47mm guns each. Each of the Romanian divisions and regiments also had an antitank company armed with 47mm or obsolete 37mm guns. In mid-October, the Germans provided a single battery—6 guns—of the more effective 75mm antitank guns to each Romanian division. Third Army had a total of 60 such guns, or one for every 2.5 kilometers of front. Romanian field artillery batteries had no antitank ammunition, and the army possessed only about one-sixth of its requested antitank mines; it had little in the way of obstacle construction materials. Given the approaching winter on the open steppes, any construction efforts along this defensive front tended to focus on warm shelters rather than defensive fortifications.[18]

ROMANIAN THIRD ARMY'S DILEMMA: THE BRIDGEHEAD PROBLEM

The most serious problem facing Romanian Third Army was the fact that, unlike the Italians, whose defenses were on or very close to the southern bank of the Don River, the Romanians' defensive line dipped as much as 30 kilometers south and west of the river in the Serafimovich and Kletskaia sectors, allowing the Southwestern Front large bridgeheads where it could mass forces for the forthcoming attack. This problem, in turn, generated a serious discussion among the Romanian command, Army Group B, and Hitler himself over whether to attack and eliminate the threatening Soviet bridgehead or substantially reinforce Romanian Third Army. Ultimately, this debate resulted in the assignment of German XXXXVIII Panzer Corps to the Romanian Army to serve as its operational reserve or safety net.

General Dumitrescu, commander of the Romanian army, was no fool. From the moment he received the mission of defending this sector, he repeatedly insisted that the river line itself was the only effective defensive position for a force so deficient in antitank weapons. General Weichs's staff at Army Group B agreed with him in principle, but the struggle in Stalingrad monopolized the additional troops and fire support Dumitrescu needed to eliminate the Soviet bridgeheads. On 16 October, Dumitrescu raised the subject again, asking permission to make a minor attack near Blinov. Instead, Army Group B instructed him to extend his frontage to the west, taking over part of the Italian sector so that two Italian divisions could move into reserve positions! This provoked a formal protest from both Antonescu and General Ilie Şteflea, chief of the Romanian General Staff. Hitler had to intervene personally, agreeing that only one Italian division—the 3rd Celere—would be allowed to move into reserve.[19]

Dumitrescu's German counterparts were well aware of his exposed position. Yet the forces available to reinforce this position were laughably small because Army Groups B and A were already stretched taut by the vast distances and steady attrition of the campaign. On 9 November, the original start date for Operation Uranus, a German close support group (Group Simon) consisting of one motorized infantry battalion, one antitank company, and one section of self-propelled guns received orders to move into position behind Romanian Third Army. A day later, the Germans began to create a larger mobile reserve in this sector. The headquarters of XXXXVIII Panzer Corps, commanded by Lieutenant General Ferdinand Heim (former liaison officer to Third Army), was transferred from Fourth Panzer Army to Army Group B's reserve behind the Romanian sector. Unfortunately, this "panzer corps" was as flimsy as the units it was supposed to support. Its nucleus, 22nd Panzer Division (the victor in the fighting on the Kerch' Peninsula), had sent its panzer engineer battalion to fight for Paulus in Stalingrad, while its 140th Panzer-Grenadier Regiment was detached to German Second Army at Voronezh. For months, the remaining elements of 22nd Panzer Division had been sitting behind the Italian sector, immobilized by fuel shortages and camouflaged in straw. When the division's 204th Panzer Regiment finally attempted to start its engines in November, it found that field mice had chewed the insulation off much of the wiring! This, plus the long period of inactivity and temperatures of minus 20 degrees Celsius (minus 4 degrees Fahrenheit), produced numerous short-circuits and other malfunctions when the regiment finally moved into the Romanian sector. Only 42 tanks reached the assembly area, and on 18 November, only 24 were actually functional in the division. At the critical moment, the division's acting commander [*mit der Führung beauftragt*], Colonel Eberhard Rodt, could field only a reinforced battalion *kampfgruppe*. The 14th Panzer Division, again minus its infantry units, which had also moved into reserve positions farther east prior to the Soviet counteroffensive, was able to muster only 55 tanks on 18 November, 36 to 41 of them operational.[20]

In addition to the skeletal 22nd and 14th Panzer Divisions, XXXXVIII Panzer Corps controlled one German artillery battalion, a portion of an antitank battalion, and Romanian 1st Armored Division, which had been decimated in the fighting of 1941. Of the 108 tanks assigned to this division, at least 87 were the lightly armed and armored Czech 38-t, a model long considered obsolete. In short, General Heim's panzer corps appeared much more effective on paper than it was in reality.[21]

German Sixth Army

The composition, deployment, and combat state of German Sixth Army on 18 November 1942 are described in detail in volume 2 of this trilogy. Suffice it to say, by this time, General Friedrich Paulus's army had lost virtually all its offensive capability and was exhausted. The intense ten-week fight for possession of Stalingrad city had not only consumed the bulk of Sixth Army's combat power but also drawn in most of the combat engineer forces available to Army Group B as a whole. As a result, virtually the entire army was "on line," with some sectors defended by units directly subordinate to the army (separate machine gun battalion) or ad hoc units formed from supporting *Luftwaffe* air and *Flak* forces (Group Stahel).

Thus, at nightfall on 18 November, Sixth Army defended its roughly 120-kilometer-wide sector from just east of Kletskaia on the Don River to Stalingrad's southern suburb of Kuporosnoe on the Volga River with all four of its corps—XI and VIII Army, XIV Panzer, and LI Army—deployed abreast in a single-echelon formation. Sixth Army's only reserve corps, XXXXVIII Panzer, had been dispatched to back up Romanian Third Army beginning on 10 November. Thereafter, the only force the army possessed in any sort of reserve position was the weak armored portion of 14th Panzer Division (36th Panzer Regiment), which Paulus sent to the Verkhne-Buzinovka region on the army's left flank, 32 kilometers south-southeast of Kletskaia, late on 19 November in an attempt to shore up XI Army Corps' defenses.

More telling in terms of Sixth Army's combat readiness was a daily assessment its Ia (Operations Department) prepared on 16 November. Of the army's 96 infantry or panzer-grenadier battalions, 20 were rated strong or medium strong, 37 were rated weak or exhausted, and the remaining 39 were simply average. The same pattern existed in the army's 17 pioneer battalions, with 1 rated medium strong, 7 weak or exhausted, and 9 average. Only the army's 4 motorcycle battalions defied this trend, with 1 rated strong and 3 medium strong (see table 16).[22] If these figures were not depressing enough, the army's 17 divisions fielded only 96 infantry or panzer-grenadier battalions, whereas the divisions' tables of organization indicated they should have had 139 battalions. Thus, with regard to its fighting troops, Sixth Army's overall combat rating was somewhere between weak and exhausted.

Nor were the army's tank and motorized forces in much better shape (see the subsection Strength, below). As of 16–18 November, the army's three panzer divisions (14th, 16th, and 24th) and two motorized infantry divisions (3rd and 60th) were able to field a total of 218 tanks, 180 of them operable; its three assault gun battalions had 68 guns, 43 of them operable. While these totals seemed reasonable under the circumstances, 21 of these tanks were Pz-II or command models, leaving 144 Pz-III and 53 Pz-IV tanks, or the equivalent of one full-blooded panzer division.[23] Fuel was also a major problem.

In summary, Sixth Army was incapable of mounting any sort of offensive action. And it was doubtful whether it could withstand a major attack by numerically superior forces.

Table 16. Combat Ratings of Infantry (Panzer-Grenadier), Pioneer, and Motorcycle Battalions Subordinate to Sixth Army's Divisions, 16 November 1942

Unit	Combat Rating
XI ARMY CORPS	
384th Infantry Division	
6 infantry battalions	6 average
1 pioneer battalion	Average
44th Infantry Division	
7 infantry battalions	2 strong, 2 medium strong, 3 average
1 pioneer battalion	Average
376th Infantry Division	
7 infantry battalions	3 medium strong, 4 average
1 pioneer battalion	Average
VIII ARMY CORPS	
113th Infantry Division	
6 infantry battalions	2 medium strong, 4 average
1 pioneer battalion	Average
76th Infantry Division	
6 infantry battalions	2 medium strong, 4 average
1 pioneer battalion	Average
XIV PANZER CORPS	
3rd Motorized Division	
4 infantry battalions	3 medium strong, 1 average
1 pioneer battalion	Average
1 motorcycle battalion	Medium strong
60th Motorized Division	
6 infantry battalions	3 average, 2 weak, 1 exhausted
1 pioneer battalion	Weak
1 motorcycle battalion	Medium strong
16th Panzer Division	
4 panzer-grenadier battalions	1 medium strong, 1 average, 2 weak
1 pioneer battalion	Weak
1 motorcycle battalion	Strong
94th Infantry Division	
7 infantry battalions	2 weak, 5 exhausted
1 pioneer battalion	Average
LI ARMY CORPS	
24th Panzer Division	
4 panzer-grenadier battalions	1 medium strong, 3 average
1 pioneer battalion	Medium strong
1 motorcycle battalion	Medium strong
100th _Jäger_ Division	
5 infantry battalions	2 medium strong, 2 average, 1 weak
1 pioneer battalion	Average
305th Infantry Division	
6 infantry battalions	2 weak, 4 exhausted
1 pioneer battalion	Exhausted
295th Infantry Division	
7 infantry battalions	1 average, 5 weak, 1 exhausted
1 pioneer battalion	Weak
389th Infantry Division	
6 infantry battalions	2 average, 4 weak
1 pioneer battalion	Weak

Table 16. (continued)

Unit	Combat Rating
79th Infantry Division	
6 infantry battalions	6 weak
1 pioneer battalion	Exhausted
14th Panzer Division	
2 panzer-grenadier battalions	2 strong
1 pioneer battalion	Average
71st Infantry Division	
7 infantry battalions	5 average, 2 weak
1 pioneer battalion	Weak
TOTALS	
96 infantry battalions (including 10 panzer-grenadier)	4 strong, 16 medium strong, 39 average, 26 weak, 11 exhausted
17 pioneer battalions	1 medium strong, 9 average, 5 weak, 2 exhausted
4 motorcycle battalions	1 strong, 3 medium strong

Source: "Betr.: Zustand der Divisionen, Armee-Oberkommando 6, Abt.-Ia, A.H.Qu., 16. November 1942, 12.00 Uhr," in Florian Freiherr von und zu Aufsess, *Die Anlagenbänder zu den Kriegstagebüchern der 6. Armee vom 14.09.1942 bis 24.11.1942, Band I* (Schwabach: Januar, 2006), 285–290.

Fourth Panzer Army (with Romanian VI and VII Army Corps)

Anchoring Army Group B's long right flank south of Stalingrad was Colonel General Hermann Hoth's Fourth Panzer Army. Left with only a shell of a force after being deprived of its last panzer division (14th) more than a month earlier, on 18 November, Hoth's army consisted of three army corps—German IV and Romanian VI and VII—and two separate motorized divisions (German 16th and 29th). These forces were deployed in a single-echelon formation across a front extending almost 250 kilometers from Kuporosnoe in Stalingrad's southern suburbs southward to the Elista region in the Kalmyk steppes. However, Hoth kept the powerful 29th Motorized Division in army reserve and assigned 16th Motorized Division to protect the vast region around Elista, on the army's and Army Group B's distant left flank. The 29th Motorized Division had moved into an assembly area around Karpovka, 70 kilometers southwest of the city, at the beginning of October to refit after bleeding itself white in city fighting.[24] By mid-November, it was the fittest German formation in the Stalingrad region, with roughly 12,000 men and 59 tanks.[25] The 16th Motorized Division, which was reinforced by several battalions of volunteer auxiliaries from the Turkestan Autonomous Region, numbered 14,000 to 15,000 men and 43 tanks.[26]

Hoth concentrated the bulk of his army—German IV Army Corps and

Romanian VI Army Corps—in the roughly 70-kilometer-wide swath of territory from Kuporosnoe southward to the northern shore of Lake Barmantsak, deploying his forces abreast from left to right. However, this sector was far too wide to be defended effectively by the six divisions assigned to these two corps. While the relatively strong German 371st and 297th Infantry Divisions defended on IV Corps' left wing and center, four weak Romanian outfits—20th, 2nd, 18th, and 1st Infantry Divisions, reinforced by 6th *Rosiori* Regiment (Motorized) detached from VII Corps' 5th Cavalry Division—defended IV Corps' right wing and all of VI Corps' sector. The remainder of Hoth's army—Romanian VI Army Corps' 4th Infantry Division, Romanian VII Army Corps' 5th and 8th Cavalry Divisions (minus one regiment), and German 16th Motorized Division—was responsible for defending the 180-kilometer-wide front from Lake Barmantsak to Elista.

They had many problems, but the chief weakness of the Romanian divisions in the two Romanian army corps was that they were defending frontages 50 percent longer than those defended by their counterparts in Romanian Third Army. Worse still, because they opposed two Soviet mechanized corps, they were equipped with only 34 75mm antitank guns, or one for every 7.3 kilometers of front.

So configured, the two German divisions faced all of Soviet 64th Army, the Romanian 20th and 2nd Infantry Divisions opposed all of Soviet 57th Army, and the Romanian 18th and 1st Infantry Divisions confronted most of Soviet 51st Army. Farther south, the weak Romanian 5th and 8th Cavalry Divisions and German 16th Motorized Division had to contend with 51st Army's 91st Rifle Division and 76th Fortified Region, as well as the Stalingrad Front's entire 28th Army. Fourth Panzer Army thus found itself in a very precarious position.

Strength

The Problem with Determining Strength

The calculation of the personnel strength of Army Group B's four armies defending along the Stalingrad axis has been the subject of major discussions for many years, with no concrete resolution. There are primarily four reasons why it has been so difficult to determine the exact strength of German Sixth Army and Fourth Panzer Army, as well as the many divisions and other units subordinate to Army Group B but attached to or supporting the armies of Germany's Axis allies. The first reason is the absence of archival records, both German and Soviet, regarding the personnel and armored strength of German forces, particularly those of Sixth Army and Fourth Panzer Army. Sixth Army's records for September 1942 through 2 February 1943 were presumed lost or captured by the Soviets during the war, and until recently, the

Russians have been reluctant to release their archival records. The second reason is that German and Romanian forces were completely intermingled after the encirclement operation was complete.

Third, and perhaps most important, it is virtually impossible to distinguish between Sixth and Fourth Panzer Armies' forces and those subordinate to Army Group B and other *Wehrmacht, Heere* (army), or *Luftwaffe* (air force) support and auxiliary troops who were caught up in the encirclement pocket. These additional personnel, who were not carried on Sixth Army's strength roles, included men from German administrative services, *Luftwaffe Flak* (antiaircraft) forces, troops assigned to more than ten separate combat engineer battalions sent to Stalingrad from other army group divisions, medical units and troops, construction troops of the Todt organization, field police units, agents from German intelligence and counterintelligence services [*Abwehr*], special security forces, military police, and so on. For this reason, it is doubtful that Sixth Army ever knew the precise number of German and Romanian troops who ended up in the encirclement.

The fourth and final issue is whether to count or ignore *Hiwis* [*Hilfswilligen*], or Russian auxiliary troops, and attached [*Zugeteilte*] soldiers, as well as those special battalions and other detachments [*abteilungen*] consisting of troops from other ethnic nationalities in service to the German army or *Luftwaffe*. For example, virtually every German division included thousands of Russian *Hiwis* who performed hundreds of combat support and service support functions and, in a few instances, actually fought in combat. Although this number is surprisingly high, precious few accounts bothered to tally them, primarily because they presumably performed mostly noncombat functions. In addition, most if not all German divisions had other attached forces [*Zugeteilte*] that, rather than being labeled and quantified in their own right, were generally lumped together with the *Hiwis*.

Fortunately, many (but not all) of these problems have been solved. Although fragmentary, Sixth Army's newly discovered and published records permit a fairly clear assessment of its condition and actual strength. In addition, the Russians have released intelligence reports about Sixth Army's condition and strength, even though these indicate that the *Stavka* and its subordinate *fronts* seriously misestimated the size and capabilities of German forces. Resolution of these problems, however, still leaves the issue of the commingling of forces and whether to count *Hiwis* and *Zugeteilte* in overall strength figures.

It is equally difficult to determine the exact strength of Italian and Romanian forces, largely for the same reasons cited in the German case. Here, however, one other element makes such calculations difficult: the chaos of combat. The abrupt and total disintegration of Romanian Third Army, the two Romanian corps south of Stalingrad, and, later, Italian Eighth Army in the wake of the Soviet attacks makes a retrospective analysis of force strengths difficult. At the same time, it makes an accurate calculation of Romanian and Italian losses impossible because no one knows for sure how many of these troops perished in combat and how many simply went to ground and disappeared somewhere in the depths of eastern Ukraine. Nor have the Soviets released sufficiently accurate records to determine how many were taken captive during Operation Uranus. In any case, the following passages attempt to quantity the personnel and armored strength of German and Romanian forces on the eve of the Soviet offensive.

German Forces
Three recently identified or released German archival documents provide the most reliable basis for calculating the personnel and armor strength of German Sixth Army on the eve of Operation Uranus. The first two documents are reports Sixth Army prepared on 11 and 19 November that show the strengths of its major combat formations—specifically, its infantry, panzer, and motorized divisions—as well as the weapons strength of two of its three subordinate assault gun battalions. They indicate not only the ration, combat, and noncombat strengths of each division but also each division's manpower deficit, number of *Hiwis* and *Zugeteilte*, and number of antitank guns [*Panzerabwehrkanone*, or *Paks*] and tanks (see table 17).[27] The third document is a report Sixth Army's Ia (Operations Department) prepared on 12 November that identifies personnel shortages in all the army's infantry divisions as of 1 November.[28] Above and beyond these three documents, other more fragmentary reports in Sixth Army's rediscovered daily records fill in some of the gaps, providing the weapons strength of panzer and motorized divisions and all three assault gun battalions assigned to the army.

Supplementing these German materials are several useful Soviet documents that were recently released. The first is Intelligence Summary No. 033a, which was issued by the Stalingrad Front's Intelligence Directorate on 2 November 1942 and purports to show, on the basis of captured Sixth Army documents, the numerical strength of Sixth Army's infantry divisions fighting in Stalingrad city on 1 November. This document, together with the German sources, provides an interesting if sometimes confusing mosaic of Sixth Army's strength in early November. It lists the combat strengths of the six German infantry divisions fighting in Stalingrad: 94th Infantry Division, 1,700 men; 389th Infantry Division, 3,000 men; 305th Infantry Division, 1,800 men; 79th Infantry Division, 3,500 men; 76th Infantry Division, 2,000 men; and 100th Light Infantry [Jäger] Division, 2,200 men, for a total of 14,200 men.[29] Most likely, the figure for 76th Infantry Division actually refers to 71st Infantry Division, since the former was in the Kotluban' region and the latter was in Stalingrad (as indicated by 62nd Army's companion report that

Table 17. Personnel Strength and Weaponry of Sixth Army's Forces, Mid-November 1942

| | | Personnel Strengths | | | | | Weapons |
| | | | | | | | Tanks or Assault |
Force	Ration	Combat	Noncombat	*Hiwis*°	Deficit	*Paks*	Guns
XI Army Corps							
376th ID	8,187	5,269	2,918	4,105	6,464	33	
44th ID	10,601	6,748	3,865	2,365	4,238	28	
384th ID	8,821	5,025	3,796	1,804	5,937	30	
VIII Army Corps							
76th ID	8,023	4,740	3,283	8,033	6,981	24	
113th ID	9,461	5,064	4,397	5,564	5,854	24	
177th AGBn							11
XIV Panzer Corps							
94th ID	7,469	2,924	4,345	2,581	8,233	10	
16th PzD	11,051	4,855	6,196	1,843	7,673	21	28
60th MotD	8,933	4,812	4,121	2,071	5,848	13	27
3rd MotD	8,653	4,498	4,155	4,530	4,831	16	29
LI Army Corps							
71st ID	8,906	4,331	4,575	8,134	7,353	25	
295th ID	6,899	3,459	3,440	50	9,037	18	
100th JgD	8,675	4,688	3,987	2,132	7,739	15	
79th ID	7,980	4,304	3,676	2,018	8,294	49	
305th ID	6,683	2,915	3,768	1,562	8,520	17	
389th ID	7,540	4,021	3,519	2,379	7,852	21	
Gr. Seydel (14th PzD)	—	588	—	934	5,434	8	6
24th PzD	10,950	6,160	4,790	1,675	5,126	—	58
244th AGBn							20
245th AGBn							2

Source: Manfred Kehrig, *Stalingrad: Analyse und Dokumentation ener Schlacht* (Stuttgart: Deutsche Verlag-Anstalt, 1974), 662–663, citing reports dated 11 and 19 November 1942.

° Includes attached [*Zugeteilte*].

follows). Further, the summary estimates that German Sixth Army fielded a combat strength of 78,800 men equipped with 790 field guns, 430 antitank guns, and 540 tanks.

A second document is an excerpt from an intelligence summary prepared by Chuikov's 62nd Army on 2 November 1942 entitled "The Operations and Grouping of the Enemy during the Period from 20 October through 1 November 1942." It states that "7 infantry divisions, including the 71st, 79th, 94th, 100th, 295th, 305th, and 389th, 50th and 635th Sapper Battalions of the High Command Reserve, and three tank [panzer] divisions, including the 14th, 16th, and 24th," were operating before the army's front. This assessment, which is more accurate than the Stalingrad Front's intelligence report because it correctly identifies the German divisions fighting in the city, asserts that the opposing forces included 80 infantry battalions and 28 artillery battalions with a total combat strength of 23,000 men and 130 to 150 tanks.[30]

A comparison of these estimated and actual strengths leads to some interesting conclusions about the real condition of Sixth Army in early November (see table 18). The most obvious conclusion is that, as had been the case in September and October, the ration strength and, to an even greater extent, the combat strength of Sixth Army's 17 combat divisions dwindled significantly during the first half of November, two weeks before Operation Uranus commenced. As the ration and combat strengths of the divisions fell, their personnel deficits rose precipitously, explaining why Army Group B felt compelled to send 5 combat engineer battalions and an assault company, with a total of 2,500 men, to reinforce its divisions fighting in the city. The total personnel shortages in Sixth Army's combat divisions in mid-November amounted to 115,414 men. When added to the total ration strength of the 17 divisions (149,832 men), the total authorized strength of these divisions should have been 265,246 men.

Likewise, the manpower deficit among Sixth Army's army troops [Heerestruppen], that is, those forces directly subordinate to the army staff, was 6,486 men by mid-November. Assuming this figure amounted to about 20 percent of the authorized strength of army troops (significantly lower than in the combat divisions), the ration strength of Sixth Army's army troops should have been 25,944 men, and the authorized strength of Sixth Army's army troops should have totaled 32,430 men in mid-November.

Therefore, by mid-November, Sixth Army's manpower deficit included 115,414 men in its combat divisions plus 6,486 men in its army troops, for a total of 121,900 men. Its ration strength by this time equaled 149,832 men in its combat divisions plus 25,944 men in its army troops, for a total of 175,776 men. Adding the army's total personnel shortage of 121,900 men to its total ration strength of 175,776 men reveals that Sixth Army's authorized strength

Table 18. Personnel Strength of German Sixth Army Based on Its Daily Records, 11, 12, and 19 November 1942, and on Soviet Military Intelligence Reports, 2 November 1942

Division	Soviet Estimates of Sixth Army's Personnel Strength, 2 November		Sixth Army's Personnel Shortages, 12 November	Sixth Army's Strength Reports, 11 and 19 November
	Stalingrad Front	62nd Army		
44th Infantry			4,053 deficit 10,786 ration	4,238 deficit 10,601 ration 6,748 combat
71st Infantry	2,000	°	7,079 deficit 9,180 ration	7,353 deficit 8,906 ration 4,331 combat
113th Infantry			4,595 deficit 10,720 ration	5,854 deficit 9,461 ration 5,064 combat
295th Infantry		°	8,313 deficit 7,623 ration	9,037 deficit 6,899 ration 3,459 combat
376th Infantry			6,206 deficit 8,445 ration	6,464 deficit 8,187 ration 5,269 combat
384th Infantry			5,865 deficit 8,893 ration	5,937 deficit 8,821 ration 5,025 combat
94th Infantry	1,700	°	7,002 deficit 8,700 ration	8,233 deficit 7,469 ration 2,924 combat
389th Infantry	3,000	°	6,556 deficit 8,836 ration	7,852 deficit 7,540 ration 4,021 combat
305th Infantry	1,800	°	5,644 deficit 9,559 ration	8,520 deficit 6,683 ration 2,915 combat
79th Infantry	3,500	°	6,324 deficit 9,950 ration	8,294 deficit 7,980 ration 4,304 combat
76th Infantry			6,765 deficit 8,239 ration	6,981 deficit 8,023 ration 4,740 combat
100th Jäger	2,200	°	5,705 deficit 10,709 ration	7,739 deficit 8,675 ration 4,688 combat
3rd Motorized				4,831 deficit 8,653 ration 4,498 combat
60th Motorized				5,848 deficit 8,933 ration 4,812 combat
14th Panzer (Group Seydel)		°		5,434 deficit 11,000 ration (est.) 588 combat
16th Panzer		°		7,673 deficit 11,051 ration 4,855 combat

Table 18. (continued)

Division	Soviet Estimates of Sixth Army's Personnel Strength, 2 November		Sixth Army's Personnel Shortages, 12 November	Sixth Army's Strength Reports, 11 and 19 November
	Stalingrad Front	62nd Army		
24th Panzer		°		5,126 deficit
				10,950 ration
				6,160 combat
Army troops				6,486 deficit (20%)
[*Heerestruppen*]				25,944 ration
		Sixth Army Totals		
Battalions		80		81 (on 29 October)
				74 (on 9 November)
Personnel	14,200 infantry	23,000 infantry		**Division troops (17):**
	78,800 total			115,414 deficit (44%)
				265,246 authorized
				149,832 ration (57%)
				74,401 combat
				Army troops:
				6,486 deficit (20%)
				32,430 authorized
				25,944 ration (80%)
				Army strength, 18 November:
				121,900 deficit (41%)
				297,676 authorized
				175,776 ration (59%)
				74,401 combat
				Sixth Army after the encirclement:
				250,000–300,000 men (best estimate: 284,000), including Sixth Army, Fourth Panzer Army, and Romanian army group and auxiliary forces
Field guns	790	320		—
Antitank guns [*Paks*]	430			372
Tanks and assault guns	540	130–150		181 (16 November)
				225 (18 November)

Sources: "Intelligence summary No. 033a of the Stalingrad Front's headquarters, dated 2 November 1942," cited in Aleksei Isaev, *Stalingrad: Za Volgoi dlia nas zemli net* [Stalingrad: There is no land for us beyond the Volga] (Moscow: Iauza Eksmo, 2008), 289–290; archival document *TsAMO RF*, f. 38, op. 11360, d. 251, ll. 135–138; "Betreff.: Meldung über personellen Fehlbestand vom 01.11.42 getrennt, Anlage 1, Armee-Oberkommando 6, Abt.-Ia,

Table 18. (continued)

Nr. 4534/42 geh, A.H.Qu., 12. November 1942," in Florian Freiherr von und zu Aufsess, *Die Anlagenbänder zu den Kriegstagebüchern der 6. Armee vom 14.09.1942 bis 24.11.1942, Band I* (Schwabach: Januar, 2006), 284–296; Manfred Kehrig, *Stalingrad: Analyse und Dokumentation einer Schlacht* (Stuttgart: Deutsche Verlag-Anstalt, 1974), 662–663.

Notes: The ration strengths for 16 of the 17 combat divisions are from reports prepared by Sixth Army on 11 and 19 November. The figures for 14th Panzer Division show only the combat strength and deficit because only Group Seydel was fighting in Stalingrad; the bulk of the division was in rear assembly areas in the Kotel'nikovskii region, resting and refitting. Therefore, the ration strength of the division (11,000) is only an estimate. Sixth Army's actual tank strength of 225 is from a Sixth Army report issued on 18 November 1942.

° Divisions considered in the estimate.

was 297,676 men. Thus, the army's ration strength (175,776 men) amounted to about 59 percent of its authorized strength.[31]

Stated differently, the average combat division in German Sixth Army was operating at about 59 percent of its required strength. At the low end of the spectrum, 295th Infantry Division fielded 7,623 men, or roughly 43 percent of its authorized strength; 305th Infantry Division had 6,683 men, or 44 percent; 94th Infantry Division had a ration strength of 7,469 men, or 48 percent; and 79th Infantry Division fielded 7,980 men, or 49 percent. At the higher end of the spectrum, 44th Infantry Division, with a ration strength of 10,601 men, operated at 71 percent of its authorized strength; 113th Infantry Division, with 9,461 men, possessed 62 percent of its authorized strength; 3rd Motorized Division's 8,653 men represented 64 percent of its authorized strength; and 14th Panzer Division fielded 13,500 men, or 72 percent of its authorized strength.

Finally, the overall combat (fighting) strength of Sixth Army's 17 combat divisions (74,401 men) amounted to roughly half of their total ration strength (149,832 men). At the low end of this spectrum, 94th Infantry Division's combat strength of 2,924 men represented only 28 percent of its ration strength, 305th Infantry Division's combat strength of 2,915 men amounted to 30 percent of its total strength, and 16th Panzer Division's 4,855 combat troops constituted 31 percent of its overall strength. At the high end of the spectrum, 44th Infantry Division's combat strength of 6,748 represented 64 percent of its ration strength, 113th Infantry Division's 5,064 combat troops amounted to 54 percent of its ration strength, and 24th Panzer Division's 6,160 combat troops equaled 56 percent of its ration strength.

It is important to note, however, that the Germans defined combat strength as infantry (or panzer-grenadiers), combat engineers, artillery-men, reconnaissance and motorcycle troops, security elements, and antitank troops assigned to the divisions. This is significant because, as table 19 demonstrates, the Soviets defined combat strength differently; that is, they limited combat troops to combat infantrymen plus combat engineers or sappers. In this regard, a more careful analysis of the ration, combat, and infantry (infantry and combat engineer) strengths of Sixth Army's divisions fighting in Stalingrad city on 18 October and in mid-November 1942 tends to qualify if not contradict assertions that Soviet intelligence wildly overestimated the strength of the opposing German forces.

Table 19 compares German Sixth Army's assessments of its combat divisions fighting in and adjacent to Stalingrad city on 18 October and in mid-November 1942 with two estimates prepared by the Soviets' Stalingrad Front and 62nd Army on 2 November. Although the two German assessments include the ration and combat strengths of each division, the 24 October report (strengths as of 18 October) goes much further by breaking down combat troops by precise type and quantity (see table 36 in volume 2). For example, the entries for 295th Infantry and 14th Panzer Divisions are as follows:

295th Infantry Division
Ration strength: 10,865° with 2,553 Russians (*Hiwis*)
Combat strength:
    Infantry: 1,990 and attached (*Zugeteilte*)
    Artillery: 1,225
    Pioneer Bn: 230
    Antitank Bn: —
    Cyclist Bn: 187
    Signal Bn: 255
Total combat strength: 3,887
° Includes one march battalion with 912 men that is not included in combat strength.

14th Panzer Division
Ration strength: 12,070 with 523 Russians (*Hiwis*)
Combat strength:
    Panzer-grenadiers: 1,640 and attached (*Zugeteilte*) (4 battalions)
    Motorcycle Bn: 515
    Panzer Regiment: 829
    Artillery: 1,140
    Flak Abteilung (Bn): 435
    Pioneer Bn: 242
    Antitank Bn: 289
    Signal Bn: 328
Total combat strength: 5,418

Table 19. Accuracy of Soviet Intelligence Estimates of the Combat Strength of Sixth Army's Divisions Fighting in Stalingrad City, 1–2 November 1942

Division	Sixth Army's Strength Report, 28 October (as of 18 October)	Soviet Estimates of Sixth Army's Personnel Strength, 2 November		Sixth Army's Strength Reports, 11 and 19 November
		Stalingrad Front	62nd Army	
71st Infantry	12,277 ration 4,723 combat 2,453 infantry	2,000 combat infantry	°	8,906 ration 4,331 combat 2,150 infantry
295th Infantry	10,865 ration 2,887 combat 2,220 infantry		°	6,899 ration 3,459 combat 2,500 infantry
94th Infantry	11,438 ration 3,473 combat 1,495 infantry	1,700 combat infantry	°	7,469 ration 2,924 combat 1,600 infantry
389th Infantry	8,604 ration 2,736 combat 979 infantry	3,000 combat infantry	°	7,540 ration 4,021 combat 1,800 infantry
305th Infantry	10,578 ration 3,345 combat 1,352 infantry	1,800 combat infantry	°	6,683 ration 2,915 combat 1,300 infantry
79th Infantry (estimate for 18 October)	14,000 ration 6,500 combat 4,500 infantry	3,500 combat infantry	°	7,980 ration 4,304 combat 3,000 infantry
100th Jäger	11,700 ration 5,765 combat 3,171 infantry	2,200 combat infantry	°	8,675 ration 4,688 combat 2,200 infantry
14th Panzer (Group Seydel) (estimate for mid-November)	12,070 ration 5,462 combat 1,828 infantry		°	11,000 ration 588 combat 588 infantry
16th Panzer	13,126 ration 5,164 combat 1,810 infantry		°	11,051 ration 4,855 combat 1,700 infantry

		Sixth Army Totals (in Stalingrad City)	
24th Panzer	11,785 ration 5,387 combat 1,750 infantry		10,950 ration 6,160 combat 1,800 infantry
Six infantry divisions (71st, 94th, 389th, 305th, and 79th Infantry and 100th Jäger)	68,597 ration 26,542 combat 13,950 infantry	78,800 total 14,200 infantry	47,253 ration 23,183 combat 12,050 infantry
All ten divisions	114,443 ration 44,842 combat 21,558 infantry	23,000 infantry °	87,153 ration 38,245 combat 18,638 infantry

Sources: Sixth Army's 24 October report is in "Betreff.: Meldungen über Verpflegungs–und Gefechtsstärken der Division, Armee-Oberkommando 6, Ia, Nr. 3446/42 g, K., A.H.Qu., 24. Oktober 1942," in Florian Freiherr von und zu Aufsess, *Die Anlagenbänder zu den Kriegstagebüchern der 6. Armee vom 14.09.1942 bis 24.11.1942. Band I* (Schwabach: Januar, 2006), 201–205. Soviet reports are from Aleksei Isaev, *Stalingrad: Za Volgoi dlia nas zemli net* [Stalingrad: There is no land for us beyond the Volga] (Moscow: Iauza Eksmo, 2008), 289–290; and "Deistviia i gruppirovka protivnika za period s 20.10 po 1.11.42" [The operations and grouping of the enemy during the period from 20 October through 1 November 1942], in 62nd Army's Combat Journal.

Notes: Combat strength, by German definition, includes all combat personnel (infantry, artillery, pioneers [combat engineers], reconnaissance, motorcycle, etc.), while Soviet estimates include only infantrymen, combat engineers (pioneers), and sappers.

° Divisions considered in the estimate.

These examples indicate that, while the combat strengths of the two divisions by German definition amount to 3,887 and 5,418 men, respectively, the infantry strength by Soviet definition (infantry and combat engineers) is much lower: 2,220 and 1,828 men, respectively. As table 19 shows, one can calculate the exact infantry strength of all ten divisions as of 18 October (column 2) and then apply these rough percentages to determine the approximate infantry strength of these divisions in mid-November (column 5). Based on these figures, the Stalingrad Front's estimates of the combat (infantry) strength of six German infantry divisions (column 3) and 62nd Army's estimate of the combat (infantry) strength of all ten divisions (column 4) are quite accurate. For example, the Stalingrad Front's estimate of 71st Infantry Division's combat (infantry) strength of 2,000 men on 2 November approximates its actual infantry and combat engineer strengths of 2,453 on 18 October and 2,150 in mid-November. Likewise, its estimate of 79th Infantry Division's combat (infantry) strength of 3,500 on 2 November is roughly midway between its actual infantry and combat engineer strengths of 4,500 on 18 October and 3,000 in mid-November, and its estimate of 100th Jäger Division's combat (infantry) strength of 2,200 is exactly the number the division fielded in mid-November. In fact, rather than underestimating German combat (infantry) strength, this table shows that the Stalingrad Front's 2 November report overestimated the combat strength of 94th, 389th, and 305th Infantry Divisions.

Considering the six German infantry divisions as a whole, the Stalingrad Front placed their combat (infantry) strength at 14,200 men and their total (ration) strength at 78,000 men at a time when their actual combat (infantry) strength was 13,950 men and their overall ration strength was 68,597 men. Finally, considering the ten German divisions as a whole, 62nd Army estimated that they fielded 23,000 combat infantrymen, which is quite close to the figures of 21,558 infantrymen indicated on Sixth Army's 24 October report and 18,538 on its mid-November report.

Once again, all these data confirm the accuracy of Soviet estimates and refute, at least in part, the assertion that Soviet forces underestimated German combat strength. However, there are sound grounds for defending the widespread Soviet (and Russian) judgment that the *Stavka* and its *front* planners were surprised by the greater than anticipated number of troops they encircled and were not prepared to liquidate such a large force. Shortly after the encirclement ring closed, Vasilevsky and the commanders of the participating *fronts* estimated that they had encircled 85,000 to 90,000 German troops in the pocket. Ultimately, they realized they had encircled between 250,000 and 284,000 men. However, Soviet intelligence organs were assessing German Sixth Army's combat strength in terms of its infantry and sappers, and they were doing so fairly accurately. Thus, when the 15,000 to

20,000 men of Fourth Panzer Army were added to Sixth Army's actual combat (infantry) strength of 74,401 men, the resulting figure nearly matched Vasilevsky's and the *Stavka*'s initial estimate.

Ultimately, where the Soviets went wrong was their poor understanding of the "tooth to tail" relationships in the German army and their inability to count "extra" forces in Sixth and Fourth Panzer Armies' area of operations. If the combat strength of German forces (by the Germans' definition) was roughly 50 percent of the forces' ration strength, and the infantry strength (by the Soviet definition) was 40 to 60 percent of German combat strength, using infantry strength as the determining factor left up to two-thirds of the forces unaccounted for. Thus, if the infantry strength of Sixth and Fourth Panzer Armies was calculated at about 90,000 to 95,000 men, this represented a real force (on a ration basis) of about 240,000 to 250,000 men. Add another 40,000 to 60,000 "extra" or Romanian forces, and that leads to the actual estimate of 280,000 to 310,000 encircled forces.

In summary, based on all the available data concerning 14 of the 16 infantry divisions and all 8 of the panzer and motorized divisions operating along the Stalingrad axis, the average personnel strengths of these divisions were as follows:

- Infantry: ration, 8,676 men; combat, 4,571 men; *Hiwis* and attached, 3,394 men
- Panzer: ration, 10,862 men; combat, 5,391 men; *Hiwis* and attached, 1,739 men
- Motorized: ration, 9,897 men; combat, 5,703 men; *Hiwis* and attached, 3,300 men[32]

With regard to German armored strength along the Stalingrad axis on the eve of the Soviet counteroffensive, the four panzer and four motorized divisions available to Army Group B fielded a total of 360 tanks: 218 tanks in Sixth Army, 102 in Fourth Panzer Army, and 40 in 22nd Panzer Division in Army Group B's reserve XXXXVIII Panzer Corps. Added to the 68 assault guns and self-propelled infantry guns in the four assault gun battalions subordinate to Sixth and Fourth Panzer Armies, this brought the total available armor force to 428 armored fighting vehicles (see table 20).

Romanian Forces
Calculating the overall strength of Romanian forces participating in the defense against Operation Uranus is a bit easier than determining overall German strength. However, determining the ration and combat strengths of Romanian divisions compared with their authorized personnel strengths is just as difficult as calculating German strengths. This is the case because

Table 20. Armored Strength of Sixth Army and Fourth Panzer Army, 16–18 November 1942 (total tanks, including those nonoperational)

| | | | | Type of Tank | | | | |
Division	Pz-II	Pz-III (short)	Pz-III (long)	Pz-IV (75mm)	Pz-IV (short)	Pz-IV (long)	Command	Total
Sixth Army (18 Nov)								
14th Panzer	5	9	17	5	5	12	2	55
16th Panzer	—	—	38	—	2	10	—	50
24th Panzer (19 Nov)	5	13	18	5	5	12	2	60
3rd Motorized	3	—	22	3	—	4	—	32
60th Motorized	4	—	12	2	—	3	—	21
Total	**17**	**22**	**107**	**15**	**12**	**41**	**4**	**218**
Fourth Panzer Army (16 Nov)								
16th Motorized	8	—	16	7	—	11	1	43
29th Motorized	7	—	23	9	—	18	2	59
Total	**15**	**—**	**39**	**16**	**—**	**29**	**3**	**102**
Army Group B								
22nd Panzer	2	5 (Pz-38[t])	12	10	1	10	—	40
Grand total	**34**	**27**	**158**	**41**	**13**	**80**	**7**	**360**

Assault Gun Battalion (AGBn)	Stug III (long)	Type of Assault Gun Stug III (short)	SPIG	Total
177th AGBn	8/0/0	2/0/0	0	10/0/0
243rd AGBn	7/0/0	0	0	7/0/0
244th AGBn	7/1/0	7/5/0	5/2/0	19/8/0
245th AGBn	7/0/6	0/3/5	0/2/1	7/5/12
Total	**29/1/6**	**9/8/5**	**5/4/1**	**43/13/12**

Sources: Aleksei Isaev, *Stalingrad: Za Volgoi dlia nas zemli net* [Stalingrad: There is no land for us beyond the Volga] (Moscow: Iauza Eksmo, 2008), 295–297; "Betr.: Zustand der Divisionen, Armee-Oberkommando 6, Abt-Ia, A.H.Qu., 09. November 1942, 16.20 Uhr" and "Betr.: Zustand der Divisionen, Armee-Oberkommando 6, Abt.-Ia, A.H.Qu., 16. November 1942, 12.00 Uhr," in Florian Freiherr von und zu Aufsess, *Die Anlagenbänder zu den Kriegstagebüchern der 6. Armee vom 14.09.1942 bis 24.11.1942, Band I* (Schwabach: Januar, 2006), 284–296.

Note: Entries for assault guns indicate operable/short-term repair/long-term repair.

Romanian archival documents provide the daily strength returns of Romanian Third Army as a whole periodically, as well as the overall strength of Romanian forces fighting under Fourth Panzer Army control. However, historians have yet to reveal the strength returns of each and every Romanian division.

Based on existing sources, as of 18 November 1942, Romanian Third Army was organized into four army corps, eight infantry divisions, two cavalry divisions, one armored division, and one air corps, with the last including two fighter, one fighter-bomber, and three bomber groups. The army's ration (on-hand) strength was 155,492 men. Romanian forces fighting under Fourth Panzer Army's control south of Stalingrad included two army corps, five infantry divisions, and two cavalry divisions, for an overall ration strength of 75,380 men.[33]

However, sources disagree about the precise ration strength of each Romanian division. For example, the standard English-language source on Romanian forces in the war asserts that the combat strength of six of Third Army's eight infantry divisions (5th, 6th, 7th, 9th, 11th, and 15th) averaged 68 percent of their authorized strength of 16,097 men. According to this source, the combat strength of two other divisions (13th and 14th), both of which had suffered heavy casualties in October, were at roughly 50 and 60 percent strength by mid-November. With regard to the divisions fighting under Fourth Panzer Army's control, the same source claims that the personnel strengths of 1st, 2nd, 4th, 20th, and 18th Infantry Divisions and 5th and 8th Cavalry Divisions were at only 25, 30, 34, 48, 78, 57, and 64 percent, respectively, on 20 November, the day the Stalingrad Front began its offensive.[34] In addition, a formerly secret Soviet study on the operations of 5th Tank Army in Operation Uranus tends to substantiate this source by asserting that Romanian Third Army's infantry divisions averaged 70 percent of their authorized combat personnel strength (infantry and sappers) on the eve of the Soviet counteroffensive.[35]

Based on these sources, the ration strength of Romanian divisions defending against Uranus ranged from 8,049 to 10,946 men for infantry divisions and 7,400 to 7,500 for cavalry divisions. Factoring in the 70 percent figure postulated by Soviet intelligence for actual combat strength, the combat strength of these infantry divisions ranged from just under 5,000 to roughly 7,700 men, and the cavalry divisions ranged from 4,500 to 6,500 men (see table 21). Alternatively, Soviet classified studies place the average ration strength of Romanian infantry divisions at 10,000 to 11,000 men and the "bayonet" strength (infantrymen and sappers) at 5,500 to 7,500 men.[36]

With regard to Romanian Third Army's armored strength, Romanian 1st Armored Division fielded 12,196 men and 105 operable tanks on 18 November. These included 84 R-2 Romanian-produced light tanks, 19 German

Table 21. Personnel Strengths (Ration and Combat) of Romanian Divisions Defending in Operation Uranus

Division	Authorized	Ration (% Filled)	Soviet Estimate of Combat Strength (%)[*]	Estimated Combat Strength
		Personnel Strengths		
Romanian Third Army: total strength 155,492 men				
11th Infantry	16,097	10,946 (68)	70	7,500
9th Infantry	16,097	10,946 (68)	70	6,000
5th Infantry	16,097	10,946 (68)	70	7,600
6th Infantry	16,097	10,946 (68)	70	7,500
15th Infantry	16,097	10,946 (68)	70	6,500
13th Infantry	16,097	8,049 (50)	70	5,000
14th Infantry	16,097	9,658 (60)	70	5,230
1st Cavalry	7,600	7,500 (99)	?	6,500
7th Cavalry	7,600	7,400 (97)	?	6,400
1st Armored	13,000	12,196 (94)	?	9,000
Fourth Panzer Army (south of Stalingrad): total strength 75,380 men				
20th Infantry	16,097	Unknown	48	7,727
1st Infantry	16,097	Unknown	25	4,025
2nd Infantry	16,097	Unknown	30	4,829
4th Infantry	16,097	Unknown	34	5,480
18th Infantry	16,097	Unknown	78	12,555
5th Cavalry	7,600	Unknown	57	4,332
8th Cavalry	7,600	Unknown	64	4,864
6th *Rosiori* Motorized	—			1,074

[*] Soviet estimates of combat strength include infantry and sappers.

Pz-III and Pz-IV medium tanks, and 2 captured Soviet tanks. In addition, the division left up to 37 inoperable R-2 tanks and 3 German models back in its service areas along the Chir River.[37]

Italian Forces
Since Italian forces played virtually no role in the Uranus counteroffensive, a detailed assessment of the personnel and armor strength of Italian Eighth Army is relegated to the supplemental volume covering military operations tangential to the fighting in the immediate Stalingrad region. That volume contains a detailed analysis of all aspects of Operation Little Saturn, which took place in mid-December, well after the Soviets began their counteroffensive. Suffice it to say that, on 18 November 1942, Eighth Army fielded roughly 130,000 men, with the average ration strength of Italian infantry divisions ranging from 9,000 to 10,000 men and combat strength from 5,000 to 7,000 men.

Distribution of Forces

As the preceding passages indicate, past accounts of the Soviets' Uranus counteroffensive contain enormous discrepancies regarding the strength of opposing forces as a whole, as well as along the three major axes where the counteroffensive occurred. Nevertheless, based on previous Soviet (Russian) estimates and what I term "ground truth," that is, the actual or real balance of forces when the counteroffensive occurred, table 22 provides an "educated estimate" of the distribution of Axis forces, artillery, and armored vehicles deployed opposite the Soviet Southwestern, Don, and Stalingrad Fronts on the morning of 19 November 1942.

THE CORRELATION OF OPPOSING FORCES

Definition

One way to assess the capabilities of opposing forces is simply to quantify them and then compare their strength in terms of assigned personnel and major weapons systems. Westerners call this the "balance of forces" and consider it one of many indicators of a force's combat capabilities. The Soviets then and the Russians today have termed this the "correlation of forces and means," or, in short, the "correlation of forces." As proponents of the belief that war is a science and can therefore be studied and understood in scientific terms, the Soviets believed that the correlation of forces was a prime determinant of success or failure in the conduct of war at the tactical, operational, or strategic levels, which, in Russian parlance, means engagements, battles, military operations, campaigns, and wars as a whole. Further, as the clear losers in tens if not hundreds of clashes at every level, even though they fielded greater numbers of men and materials, they also understood that correlation of forces is not the only indicator of combat success. Specifically, they understood that training, the quality of both soldier and weapon, and troop morale—though difficult to quantify—certainly fit within the science of war, along with many other factors such as command skill and acumen, which is just one of the many ephemeral factors they include under the rubric of the art of war. However, all other things being equal, in the Soviet and Russian view, correlation of forces remains the single most important indicator of success in battle.

Regardless of how hard the Soviets worked to retain the scientific basis of their analysis, other factors intruded to pervert an unbiased and objective scientific approach. Nowhere is this more apparent than in the realm of correlation of forces. Over time, simple pride, often complicated by political factors such as the desire to protect the reputation of the communist state

Table 22. Distribution and Estimated Strength of Axis Forces Operating against the Southwestern, Don, and Stalingrad Fronts, 19 November 1942

Axis Forces Facing the Southwestern Front—Italian Eighth Army's XXXV Army Corps; Romanian Third Army's I, II, V, and IV Army Corps; and XXXXVIII Panzer Corps
- **Soviet estimate of Axis strength**—432,000 men, 4,360 guns and mortars, and 255 tanks, including five divisions of Italian Eighth Army's II and XXXV Army Corps; Romanian Third Army's I, II, V, and VI Army Corps; and Army Group B's XXXXVIII Panzer Corps
- **Actual Axis strength**—roughly 201,703 men (100,000 combat) and 145 tanks, including:
  ° **Italian Eighth Army** (II and XXXV Army Corps, with headquarters, XXIX Army Corps)—roughly 35,000 men
  ° **Romanian Third Army** (I, II, V, and VI Army Corps)—155,492 men, including 1st Armored Division with 12,196 men, and 105 tanks
  ° **German XXXXVIII Panzer Corps** (22nd Panzer Division)—11,211 men with 40 tanks, plus Group Simon (823 men), 611th Panzer *Jagd Abteilung*, and 104th *Flak* (antiaircraft) Regiment

Axis Forces Facing the Don Front—German Sixth Army's XI and VIII Army Corps and XIV Panzer Corps
- **Soviet estimate of Axis strength**—200,000 men, 1,980 guns and mortars, and 280 tanks in Sixth Army
- **Actual Axis strength**—roughly 100,000 men, with a division ration strength of 81,199 and a combat strength of 43,935, and 113 tanks and assault guns, including:
  ° **XI Army Corps**—ration strength, 27,609 men; combat strength, 17,042 men; 8,274 *Hiwis* and *Zugeteilte*; no tanks
  ° **VIII Army Corps**—ration strength, 17,484 men; combat strength, 9,804 men; 13,597 *Hiwis* and *Zugeteilte*; 10 assault guns
  ° **XIV Panzer Corps**—ration strength, 36,106 men; combat strength, 17,089 men; 11,025 *Hiwis* and *Zugeteilte*; 103 tanks and assault guns

Axis Forces Facing the Stalingrad Front—Sixth Army's LI Army Corps, Fourth Panzer Army's VI Army Corps and Romanian VI and VII Army Corps, and German 29th and 16th Motorized Divisions
- **Soviet estimate of Axis strength**—379,000 men, 3,950 guns and mortars, and 140 tanks
- **Actual Axis strength**—roughly 220,000 men, with a division ration strength of 192,548 (181,548 without 14th Panzer Division) and a combat strength of 90,317, and 250 tanks and assault guns, including:
  ° **Sixth Army** (LI Army Corps)—ration strength, 69,633 men°; combat strength, 30,466 men; 18,884 *Hiwis* and *Zugeteilte*; 141 tanks and assault guns
  ° **Fourth Panzer Army** (VI Army Corps)—ration strength, 33,315 men; combat strength, 16,788 men, including 20th Infantry Division (R); approximately 8,000 *Hiwis* and *Zugeteilte*; 7 assault guns
  ° **Romanian Fourth Army**[†] (VI and VII Army Corps)—roughly 75,380 men, including a ration strength of 67,600 and a combat strength of 31,063; no tanks
  ° **German 29th and 16th Motorized Divisions**—ration strength, about 22,000 men; combat strength, about 12,000 men; 102 tanks and assault guns

---

° Includes 14th Panzer Division's ration strength of 11,000 men, most of whom were in rest areas to the rear.

† Due to be activated on 20 November, but never realized.

and system, its Red Army, and the men who led it, influenced the scientific calculations. As a result, numbers were altered to provide a less embarrassing correlation of forces than actually existed. In the case of the Soviets, for the sake of maintaining some semblance of the scientific approach, this tinkering with the numbers usually took the form of overstating enemy strength rather than understating their own. Thus, in the case of Operation Uranus, the official correlation of forces has evolved to reflect political circumstances in the state a whole.

Comparative Strengths Based on Recent Assessments

Traditionally, analysts of the so-called Great Patriotic War—that is, the Soviet Union's struggle with Hitler's Germany—have employed the measurement of correlation of forces when assessing the strength of opposing forces in a battle or in an operation as a whole (e.g., Moscow, Stalingrad, Kursk, or hundreds of other major and minor operations) or when studying opposing forces employed in sectors where main attacks occurred in a specific battle or military operation (see appendix 4C in the *Companion* for the evolution of Soviet and Russian views on the correlation of opposing forces in Operation Uranus and specific estimates of opposing strengths over the past 50 years). However, new Soviet archival materials released since the fall of the Soviet Union in 1991, particularly those related to the actual ration and combat strengths of German Sixth Army, now make it possible to assess more accurately the correlation of Soviet and Axis forces at the beginning of Operation Uranus. These documents, along with the new German archival materials discussed earlier and extensive information on the strength of Romanian forces on the eve of the offensive, allow an assessment of the strength of opposing forces in the operation as a whole, as well as in the two main attack sectors of Operation Uranus: specifically, the Southwestern Front's 5th Tank and 21st Armies and the Stalingrad Front's 57th and 51st Armies (see tables 23 and 24). Because these figures are merely estimates based on the best available data, they are not flawless. The three most serious shortcomings involve the following elements:

1. The number of artillery pieces available to the opposing forces, in particular, the on-hand and serviceable artillery pieces fielded by Romanian Third Army and German Sixth and Fourth Panzer Armies.
2. The nature and strength of Army Group B's forces supporting German Sixth and Fourth Panzer Armies in the Stalingrad region, which are not included in the ration strength of these armies.
3. The nature and strength of German auxiliary and attached forces (*Luftwaffe*, construction troops, security service, police, etc.) in the Stalingrad region.

Table 23. Strategic Correlation of Opposing Soviet and Axis Forces in Operation Uranus, 19–20 November 1942

Category	Soviet	Axis	Ratio
Personnel	1,042,218 men	521,703 men	2 to 1
	(782,548 combat)	(234,252 combat)	(3.3 to 1)
Tanks and assault guns	1,550	508	3 to 1
Guns and mortars	22,019	Unknown, but well under 10,000 tubes	At least 3 to 1
Combat aircraft	1,529 total	732 total	2.1 to 1
	(1,277 operable)	(402 operable)	(3.2 to 1)

Sources: V. A. Zolotarev, ed., *Velikaia Otechestvennaia, Deistvuiushchaia armiia 1941–1945 gg.* [The Great Patriotic (War), the operating army] (Moscow: Animi Fortitudo Kuchkovo pole, 2005), 587; Manfred Kehrig, *Stalingrad: Analyse und Dokumentation einer Schlacht* (Stuttgart: Deutsche Verlag-Anstalt, 1974), 662–663, citing reports dated 11 and 19 November; Mark Axworthy, Cornel Scafeş, and Cristian Crauciunoiu, *Third Axis, Fourth Ally: The Romanian Armed Forces in the European War, 1941–1945* (London: Arms & Armour, 1995), 89–91, 109; Joel S. A. Hayward, *Stopped at Stalingrad: The Luftwaffe and Hitler's Defeat in the East, 1942–1943* (Lawrence: University Press of Kansas, 1998), 225, citing USAFHRA K113.106-153: *Zusammenstellung der 1st-Starken und der einsatzbereiten Flugzeuge an der Ostfront 1942.*

Regardless of these flaws in the correlations, it is clear that the Soviet forces were far superior to their Axis foes, at least numerically, than was previously thought. This applies to virtually every index of combat power, including personnel, artillery, tanks, and combat aircraft. Nor should this be surprising, since the Red Army held the numerical edge in every major operation conducted during 1941 and 1942. For the Germans, the problem this time was that the Soviet troops, as well as their commanders, proved far more capable than their predecessors. Compounding this reality, the Red Army's main attacks were about to savage Romanian forces, which the Red Army had handled roughly before.

German Misperceptions

This section on comparative force strengths would be incomplete without some mention of the Germans' perceptions—or, more appropriately, their striking misperceptions—on the eve of Uranus. This is necessary because, with a few tactical exceptions, what was about to happen to Paulus's Sixth Army was unprecedented.

If it is true that Hitler and many of his senior generals underestimated the Soviet threat, particularly with regard to their instinctive concern for the security of Army Group B's and Sixth Army's long left flank, they were also

Table 24. Operational Correlation of Opposing Soviet and Axis Forces in the Main Attack Sectors of the Red Army's Southwestern and Stalingrad Fronts, 19–20 November 1942

Forces and Weapons	Soviet	Axis	Ratio
Southwestern Front (5th Tank and 21st Armies—22 km)			
	207,466 total	166,703 total	1.24 to 1
Personnel	(182,656 combat)	(90,000 combat)	(2 to 1)
Guns and mortars	5,058	2,000 (estimate)	2.5 to 1
Tanks and assault guns	558	145	3.8 to 1
Stalingrad Front (57th and 51st Armies—28 km)			
	121,962 total	94,315 total	1.3 to 1
Personnel	(80,000 combat)	(44,788 combat)	(1.8 to 1)
Guns and mortars	2,104	400 (estimate)	5.3 to 1
Tanks and assault guns	432	59	7.3 to 1

Sources: V. A. Zolotarev, ed., *Velikaia Otechestvennaia, Deistvuiushchaia armiia 1941–1945 gg.* [The Great Patriotic (War), the operating army] (Moscow: Animi Fortitudo Kuchkovo pole, 2005), 587; Manfred Kehrig, *Stalingrad: Analyse und Dokumentation einer Schlacht* (Stuttgart: Deutsche Verlag-Anstalt, 1974), 662–663, citing reports dated 11 and 19 November; Mark Axworthy, Cornel Scafeș, and Cristian Crauciunoiu, *Third Axis, Fourth Ally: The Romanian Armed Forces in the European War, 1941–1945* (London: Arms & Armour, 1995), 89–91, 109.

poorly served by their professional military intelligence experts.[38] Colonel Reinhard Gehlen, head of the *Fremde Heere Ost* (FHO; Foreign Armies East), the army's (OKH's) military intelligence organ, consistently misunderstood the capabilities and intentions of his opponent. Like Hitler, Gehlen believed the Red Army had exhausted its reserves in the summer battles and was capable of conducting only limited attacks in November. In addition, the series of local Red Army offensives in the Rzhev and Viaz'ma regions west of Moscow during August and September 1942, together with preparations for Operation Mars in October, fueled the Soviets' deception and convinced Gehlen that Army Group Center was the most likely target for a major Soviet attack.[39]

Despite extreme efforts to maintain secrecy and operational security, preparations for the Uranus counteroffensive inevitably provided the Germans some clues. In mid-October, front-line units of Army Group B as well as aerial reconnaissance flights indicated considerable Soviet troop movements all along the Don River flank. Romanian Third Army, tortured by its own perceived weakness, reported a steady increase in night traffic in the Serafimovich bridgehead, where 5th Tank Army was massing. Initially, Army Group B's staff attributed this traffic to simple replenishment of supplies. By 3 November, however, the army group's headquarters became aware that some form of attack was likely in the region; the formation of the Southwestern Front's headquarters only reinforced this perception. Soviet prisoners indicated that an offensive would begin as early as 7 November, and when this attack failed to materialize, it reinforced German complacency. Such reports prompted the movement of limited German reserves to the area and led German liaison officers to urge the Romanians to move their reserves closer to the front line.[40]

Long after the battle, Gehlen claimed that Hitler and his generals had ignored FHO's clear warnings of an impending assault. In fact, however, such warnings were often diminished by various caveats, as well as by Gehlen's continuing belief in the likelihood of an offensive elsewhere. On 6 November, for example, FHO issued another assessment:

a) The point of main effort of the future Russian operations against the German Eastern Front looms with increasing distinctness in the sector of Army Group Center. However, it is still not clear whether, along with this, the Russians intend to conduct a major operation along the Don or they will limit their aims in the south due to the considerations that they cannot achieve success simultaneously along two axes because of insufficient forces. In any event, we can conclude that the offensive they are preparing in the south is not so far advanced that one must reckon with a major operation here in the near future simultaneously with the expected offensive against Army Group Center. Presently there is no information indicating that the Russians have given up the attack across the Don entirely, an idea which undoubtedly affected their previous intentions. The likely demarcation of this operation according to time will accord them the advantage of, for the time being, holding the forces designated for this attack back as a reserve to throw in against Army Group Center if the situation developing there warrants their use. . . .

b) The configuration of Army Group Center's front, with the presence of concentration areas suitable from the point of view of transport and advantageous jumping-off regions (the Sukhinichi-Toropets salient) for an operation against Smolensk, is very favorable for the development of a major operation. The Smolensk region ought to be viewed as the first objective of a decisive operation against Army Group Center. In distance, this objective fully corresponds to the resources and capabilities of the Russian command.

c) In the event of success, after destroying the forces in the center of the German front, the possibility will exist to exploit the success by continuing the operation to the west, into the Baltic countries, to cut off German forces on the northern wing.

    d) In contradistinction with this are the greater difficulties in control-
ling the forces and supplying them in an operation against Rostov.[41]

Despite such ambivalent guidance, General Paulus became increasingly concerned about his flank and made various representations to the army group
commander, Weichs, about the weakness of Axis units in that sector. Still, the
scope and goal of the coming offensive were not apparent to the Germans
until the last minute, if at all.[42]

    On 12 November, concerned by reports of Soviet preparations, Weichs
ordered Paulus to "squeeze 10,000 men out of his engineer and artillery units
to man a support line behind the Rumanians."[43] In reality, of course, Sixth
Army was so understrength as a result of the prolonged struggle for Stalingrad that there were few if any troops available to fulfill this order. To cite but
one example, Weichs and Paulus had already transferred five pioneer battalions into the city to bolster the depleted attack formations already there.[44]

    As was so often the case during the war, the Germans had a fairly accu-
rate picture of the Red Army's front-line dispositions but little knowledge of
troop concentrations or logistical movements behind enemy lines. As General Hoth ruefully remarked when Uranus began, "We have overestimated
the Russians at the front, but completely underestimated their reserves."[45]
For example, 5th Tank Army went undetected, while many of the bridges
attacked by German air strikes were dummies intended to distract attention from the real crossing sites. In addition, the Soviets put out false radio
signals and other indications to convince their opponents that they planned
to defend along the Don River while attacking Army Group Center. Such
deceptive measures succeeded in misleading Hitler and Gehlen, even if
lower-level Axis commanders became increasingly concerned by a vaguely
perceived threat.[46]

    More fundamentally, however, the Germans had beaten off so many pre-
vious Soviet counterattacks with ease that they were convinced they could
handle any future threat. Unlike all the frantic, premature attacks of summer
and fall, however, the coming blow would be launched with sufficient time
and resources to be decisive. Moreover, the new offensive was focused not
against the veteran German units of Fourth Panzer and Sixth Armies but
against the poorly equipped and badly positioned troops of Romanian Third
Army and the two Romanian corps defending south of Stalingrad.

Lieutenant General Nikolai
Fedorovich Vatutin, commander of
the Southwestern Front. He became
Colonel General on 7.12.42

Corps Commissar Aleksei Sergeevich Zheltov, Member of the Military Council
(Commissar) of the Southwestern Front (second from the left), with the
Southwestern Front's Military Council (N. F. Vatutin, A. S. Zheltov, S. A. Krasovsky,
V. I. Vozniuk, and S. P. Ivanov, from left to right). Zheltov became Lieutenant
General on 6.12.42.

Lieutenant General Vasilii Ivanovich
Kuznetsov, commander of 1st Guards Army

Major General Prokofii Logvinovich
Romanenko, commander of 5th Tank
Army

Lieutenant General Ivan Mikhailovich
Chistiakov, commander of 21st Army

Lieutenant General of Aviation Stepan
Akimovich Krasovsky, commander of 17th
Air Army

Major General of Tank Forces
Vasilii Vasil'evich Butkov, commander
of 1st Tank Corps

Major General of Tank Forces Aleksei
Grigor'evich Rodin, commander of 26th
(1st Guards) Tank

Lieutenant Colonel Georgii Nikolaevich
Filippov, commander of 26th Tank
Corps' 14th Motorized Rifle Brigade,
whose forces captured the bridge at
Kalach-on-the-Don.

Major General of Tank Forces Andrei
Grigor'evich Kravchenko, commander,
4th Tank Corps

Major General Issa Aleksandrovich Pliev, commander, 3rd Guards Cavalry Corps

Lieutenant General Konstantin Konstantinovich Rokossovsky, commander of the Don Front

Major General Konstantin Fedorovich Telegin, Member of the Military Council (Commissar) of the Don Front (after 20 December 1942) (second from the right), with the Don Front's Military Council (K. K. Rokossovsky, N. N. Voronov, K. F. Telegin, and M. S. Malanin from left to right)

Major General Dmitrii Timofeevich Kozlov, commander of 24th Army

Lieutenant General Pavel Ivanovich Batov, commander of 65th Army

Lieutenant General Aleksei Semenovich Zhadov, commander of 66th Army

Major General of Aviation Sergei Ignat'evich Rudenko, commander of 16th Air Army

Major General of Technical Forces
Aleksei Gavrilovich Maslov, commander
of 16th Tank Corps

Lieutenant General Andrei
Ivanovich Eremenko,
commander of the Stalingrad
Front

Nikita Sergeevich Khrushchev, Member of
the Military Council (Commissar) of the
Stalingrad Front

Lieutenant General Vasilii Ivanovich
Chuikov, commander of 62nd Army

Lieutenant General Mikhail Stepanovich
Shumilov, commander of 64th Army

Major General Nikolai Ivanovich
Trufanov, commander of 51st Army

Lieutenant General Fedor Ivanovich
Tolbukhin, commander of 57th Army

Lieutenant General Vasilii Filippovich Gerasimenko, commander of 28th Army

Major General of Aviation Timofei Timofeevich Khriukhin, commander of 8th Air Army

Major General of Tank Forces Vasilii Timofeevich Vol'sky, commander of 4th (3rd Guards) Mechanized Corps

Major General of Tank Forces Trofim Ivanovich Tanaschishin, commander of 13th Tank (later Mechanized) Corps

Lieutenant General Timofei
Timofeevich Shapkin, commander of
4th Cavalry Corps

Colonel General Maximilian
Freiherr von Weichs, commander-
in-chief of Army Group B

Colonel General Maximilian *Freiherr* von Weichs, commander-in-chief, Army
Group B, with Generals Paulus and Seydlitz (left to right)

Colonel General Hermann Hoth (center), commander of Fourth Panzer Army
(Army Group Hoth), giving an order

Colonel General Hermann
Hoth, commander of Fourth
Panzer Army (Army Group
Hoth)

General *der Flieger* Wolfgang von Richtofen (second from right), commander of
Fourth Air Fleet

General of Panzer Troops Hans-
Valentin von Hube, commander of
XIV Panzer Corps

PART II

The Uranus Counteroffensive

CHAPTER FIVE

The Penetration Battle, 19–20 November

Winter came to southern Russia. It snowed on the night of 18–19 November 1942, and the temperature fell to minus 7 degrees Celsius (20 degrees Fahrenheit). The snow, by now measuring several inches deep, combined with early-morning fog to reduce visibility to near zero and muffle the sounds of Soviet engineers clearing lanes through the minefields along the Don River front. To the delight of the *Stavka* and the commanders of the Southwestern and Don Fronts, and to the relief of the tens of thousands of Red Army troops anxiously awaiting the order to attack, the snow and fog also grounded enemy aircraft, depriving the defending Romanian and German troops of their most deadly defensive weapon.[1]

PRELIMINARIES

The Reconnaissance Phase, 14–18 November

Contrary to most accounts, the Soviet attack did not come out of the blue on the morning of 19 November. Following a tactic that had become standard in the Red Army, armies conducting main attacks in offensive operations were supposed to carry out reconnaissance in force with their first-echelon rifle divisions prior to H-hour to determine the location of the forward edge of the enemy's defenses and identify the enemy's main firing points. Prior to November 1942, attacking Soviet armies routinely conducted this reconnaissance the evening before H-hour, and only in the sectors where the main attack would occur. Thus, for the Germans, the reconnaissance in force had become a prime indicator of precisely when and where the Red Army intended to conduct offensive operations. Realizing this fact, the Soviet generals who planned Operation Uranus decided to exploit the Red Army's past predictable behavior to surprise the enemy. Instead of conducting the reconnaissance the evening before H-hour in the intended main attack sectors, they deliberately ordered the three *fronts'* armies to conduct more extensive reconnaissance in force over a period of several nights and across the entire front. By doing so, they hoped not only to determine the enemy's forward edge and firing system but also to confuse the enemy about when and where the main attacks would occur.

Pursuant to instructions received from General Staff planners, the commanders of the Southwestern, Don, and Stalingrad Fronts staggered the timing of their reconnaissance in force, conducting it over the course of six nights, on 14–19 November. In fact, some of the armies in the attacking *fronts* routinely conducted reconnaissance as early as 10 November and then, periodically, through the 14th.[2] The Southwestern Front's 21st Army and the Stalingrad Front's 51st and 57th Armies carried out their reconnaissance in force on the night of 14–15 November, the Southwestern Front's 5th Tank Army did so on the night of 17–18 November, and the Stalingrad Front's 51st Army conducted a second reconnaissance in force on the night of 19–20 November, just hours after the Southwestern and Don Fronts had already begun their offensive. Since the three *fronts* were required to carry out these actions across the entire width of their sectors, they employed reconnaissance forces ranging in size from reinforced rifle companies to reinforced rifle battalions from their first-echelon rifle divisions, with battalion-size forces operating along main attack axes and company-size forces along secondary axes.[3]

For example, in the Serafimovich bridgehead on the southern bank of the Don River, all four of 5th Tank Army's first-echelon rifle divisions conducted their reconnaissance in force with reinforced rifle battalions on the night of 17–18 November. Supported by dedicated artillery groups, reinforced battalions from 119th Rifle Division and 50th Guards, 47th Guards, and 14th Guards Rifle Divisions struck the forward security outposts of Romanian Third Army's 5th, 14th, and 9th Infantry Divisions across 5th Tank Army's entire planned offensive front. Overcoming Romanian forward security outposts and eliminating obstacles as they encountered them, the reinforced battalions advanced as deep as 1 to 2 kilometers to reach the following locations:

- 124th Rifle Division (designated 50th Guards on 17 November)— through Romanian 5th Infantry Division's forward security zone to 250 meters south of the burial mound at Marker +1.2 and Hill 222 (5 kilometers east-northeast of Kalmykovskii)
- 119th Rifle Division—through Romanian 14th Infantry Division's forward security zone to Hill 219.5 (10 kilometers southeast of Kalmykovskii)
- 47th Guards Rifle Division—through Romanian 14th Infantry Division's forward security zone to the gardens on the northern outskirts of Bol'shoi (6 kilometers south of Kotovskii) and the hill with the burial mound at Marker +1.8 (3.5 kilometers southeast of Kotovskii)
- 14th Guards Rifle Division—through Romanian 9th Infantry Division's forward security zone to the southern slope of Hill 220 (6 kilometers

southwest of State Farm No. 4) and the northern outskirts of State Farm No. 3 (7 kilometers south of State Farm No. 4)[4]

During the reconnaissance phase of the offensive, 5th Tank Army's reconnoitering forces determined the Romanians had constructed and occupied a combat security zone 2 to 3 kilometers in front of the forward edge of their main defenses. These forces eliminated many of the defenders' minefields and obstacles, identified many of the Romanians' main defensive works and firing positions, and detected the weakest spots in the main defensive belt. By the time this phase was over, 5th Tank Army's attacking battalions had succeeded in driving many if not most of the Romanians' forward security forces back to their main defensive positions. The attackers were in direct contact with the main forces of Third Army's defending divisions in well over half the tank army's main attack sector. This permitted Romanenko's army to adjust its artillery preparation and pound the enemy troops as they manned their forward defensive positions and to push the jumping-off positions of its attacking first-echelon divisions well forward of their original locations. Therefore, by the time the actual offensive began early on 19 November, most of the tank army's first-echelon rifle divisions were in direct contact with the forward edge of Romanian Third Army's defenses.

The 5th Tank Army's experience with its reconnaissance in force typified that of the other armies conducting similar operations. For example, as indicated earlier, on the Stalingrad Front's left, the Don Front's 65th Army succeeded in identifying German attempts to reinforce defenses in the Kletskaia region. Far to the south, in the main attack sector of the Stalingrad Front, reconnaissance forces of 51st Army detected the presence of elements of Romanian 5th Cavalry Division in defensive positions south of Malaia Derbety, at a time when Soviet intelligence believed the cavalry division was still operating in the northern Caucasus region.

Although the Soviet decision to stagger reconnaissance efforts over several days led to many positive results, it also generated some problems. For example, Soviet after-action critiques noted that 21st Army's and 5th Tank Army's reconnaissance on 14 and 17 November, respectively, also permitted the Romanians to adjust their force dispositions, emplace new minefields and obstacles, and bring more reinforcements forward.[5] The reconnaissance activity also increased apprehension about a possible Soviet offensive in Army Group B's headquarters and at the headquarters of Romanian Third and German Sixth Armies. Consequently, the army group urged General Paulus to reinforce XXXXVIII Panzer Corps and consider moving more of 14th Panzer Division to positions behind XI Army Corps, and it prompted Romanian Third Army to reposition its 1st Armored and 7th Cavalry Divisions farther forward. Ultimately, it was the panzer corps' 22nd Panzer Division and the Romanian armored division that would wreak havoc with 5th Tank Army's offensive timetable.

Based on its critiques of these reconnaissance efforts, the Red Army General Staff concluded that prolonging the reconnaissance phase for six nights was inexpedient because it permitted the enemy up to five days of warning, more than enough time to regroup forces and reinforce forward defenses. Moreover, the employment of reinforced battalions from first-echelon divisions to conduct the reconnaissance, coupled with the casualties these battalions suffered, ultimately weakened the initial assault by depriving the assaulting first-echelon rifle regiments of up to one-third of their combat strength. Therefore, the General Staff concluded, first, that it was better to conduct the reconnaissance immediately before the offensive, and second, that companies rather than battalions were the most effective reconnaissance force because they were smaller and less easily detected and engaged, and their losses affected their parent divisions less severely.[6]

The Fruits of Reconnaissance: Axis Dispositions Opposite the *Fronts'* Main Attack Sectors

The last-minute reconnaissance in force was just the final phase in an elaborate Soviet intelligence-collecting and -processing effort conducted over days, weeks, and even months before Operation Uranus began. This effort involved meticulous intelligence collection and analysis by specialists at every level of command. The intelligence data came from a multiplicity of sources and were gathered by raids, searches, and prisoner snatches conducted by reconnaissance units at company, battalion, and regimental levels; reconnaissance in force launched by divisions; insertions and raids by long-range reconnaissance patrols dispatched by armies; communications intercepts by *front* signal units; aerial reconnaissance (both photographic and direct observation); and agents operating under the auspices of armies, the General Staff's Main Intelligence Directorate (GRU), the NKVD, and even Communist Party underground cells operating deep in the German rear area. Ultimately, this collection and analysis effort produced a detailed and fairly accurate mosaic of the dispositions and strength of Axis forces defending in the Stalingrad region, particularly those forces opposite the main attack sectors of the three attacking *fronts*. These intelligence-based assessments, modified by calculations made after the offensive operation was completed, provide a detailed picture of the nature, composition, and effective combat strength of opposing Romanian and German forces in the sectors of each Soviet *front* as a whole and in the main attack sectors of the *fronts'* subordinate armies (see appendix 5A in the *Companion*).

After analyzing all these data, the three attacking Soviet *fronts* and their subordinate armies adjusted their operational and tactical formations to accommodate last-minute changes in the configuration of the Romanian and German defenses. Ultimately, these changes provided a basis for recalculating the correlation of opposing forces for each attacking *front* and army, with an emphasis at this stage on the balance of forces in terms of their "bayonet" strength—that is, the number of combat infantrymen and sappers each could employ (see table 25).

As table 25 and previous tables indicate, contrary to the correlations of opposing forces contained in most Soviet and Russian studies of the Uranus counteroffensive, Red Army forces outnumbered their Romanian and German foes strategically, operationally, and tactically along virtually every axis of advance in the Stalingrad region. Strategically, the three Soviet *fronts* outnumbered their foes by a ratio of two to one in manpower and more than three to one in tanks. Operationally, by concentrating their forces, the Southwestern and Stalingrad Fronts were able to maintain their two-to-one superiority in manpower while increasing their superiority in tanks to almost four to one in Vatutin's *front* and well over seven to one in Eremenko's *front*. Tactically, the same pattern prevailed. Through further concentration, the Southwestern Front's 5th Tank and 21st Armies increased their tactical superiority in "bayonets" to a ratio of almost two and a half to one and their superiority in tanks to better than three to one. Likewise, the Stalingrad Front improved its tactical superiority in manpower to almost three to one and pushed its advantage in tanks to roughly eight to one. Although far weaker than its two neighbors, by concentrating its forces, the Don Front was also able to create tactical superiority in its 65th Army: better than two to one in "bayonets" and nearly two to one in tanks.

Although the *Stavka*, the General Staff, and the three *fronts* operating in the Stalingrad region managed to achieve a modest superiority in both manpower and tanks over opposing Axis forces, these correlations still fell far short of the ratios called for by regulations and those actually achieved later in the war. Specifically, instead of a strategic advantage of roughly three to one, which, with concentration, would produce operational superiorities of about five to one and tactical superiorities of roughly seven or eight to one, the correlation of forces in Uranus failed to reach these ideals. However, Soviet leaders and planners took solace from the fact that the bulk of the forces they were attacking were Romanian, not German.

Table 25. Configuration and Estimated Tactical Correlations of "Bayonets" (Infantry and Sappers) in the Main Attack Sectors of the Southwestern, Don, and Stalingrad Fronts and the Armies Conducting Their Main Attacks

SOUTHWESTERN FRONT

5th Tank Army
- Main attack force:
  - 14th, 47th, and 50th (former 124th Rifle) Guards and 119th and 159th Rifle Divisions—average strength of 8,800 men (6,500 "bayonets")
  - 1st Tank Corps (89th, 117th, and 159th Tank and 44th Motorized Rifle Brigades)—about 13,500 men and 136 tanks
  - 26th Tank Corps (19th, 157th, and 216th Tank and 14th Motorized Rifle Brigades)—about 13,500 men and 157 tanks
  - 8th Cavalry Corps (21st, 55th, and 112th Cavalry Divisions)—16,134 men
  - 8th Guards Tank Brigade and 510th and 511th Separate Tank Battalions—66 tanks
  - 8th Guards Motorcycle Regiment
  - 16 RVGK artillery and mortar regiments
- Strength—80,000 men and 359 tanks
- Enemy forces:
  - 9th (½) and 14th Infantry Divisions (R) of Romanian Third Army's II Army Corps, with 8,230 men
  - 5th Infantry Division (R) (½) of Romanian Third Army's V Army Corps, with 3,800 men
  - 22nd Panzer Division (G) and 1st Armored and 7th Cavalry Divisions (R) of German XXXXVIII Panzer Corps, with about 28,000 men and 146 tanks
- Estimated correlation of forces ("bayonets"):

	5th Tank Army	Romanian/German	Ratio
Personnel	80,000	40,000	2:1
Tanks	359	146	2.5:1

21st Army
- Main attack force:
  - 76th, 293rd, 96th, 277th, and 333rd Rifle Divisions—average strength of 8,800 (6,500 "bayonets")
  - 4th Tank Corps (45th, 69th, and 102nd Tank and 4th Motorized Rifle Brigades)—about 12,500 and 143 tanks
  - 3rd Guards Cavalry Corps (5th and 6th Guards and 32nd Cavalry Divisions)—22,512 men
  - 1st, 2nd, and 4th Guards Tank Regiments—56 tanks
  - 17 RVGK artillery and mortar regiments
- Strength—70,000 men and 199 tanks
- Enemy forces:
  - 5th (½) and 6th Infantry Divisions (R) of Romanian Third Army's V Army Corps, with 11,300 men
  - 13th Infantry Division (R) of Romanian Third Army's IV Army Corps, with 5,000 men
  - 15th Infantry Division (R) of Romanian Third Army, with 6,500 men
- Estimated correlation of forces ("bayonets"):

	21st Army	Romanian	Ratio
Personnel	70,000	22,800	3.1:1
Tanks	199	27°	7.4:1

Table 25. (continued)

DON FRONT
65th Army
- Main attack force:
  - ° 27th Guards and 252nd, 304th, and 321st Rifle Divisions—average strength of 8,800 men (6,500 "bayonets")
  - ° 91st and 21st Tank Brigades—49 tanks
  - ° Nine RVGK artillery and mortar regiments
- Strength—50,000 men and 49 tanks
- Enemy forces:
  - ° 1st Cavalry Division (R) of Romanian Third Army's IV Army Corps, with 6,500 men
  - ° 376th Infantry Division (G) of Sixth Army's XI Army Corps, with 5,269 men
  - ° 14th Panzer Division (G) [*kampfgruppe*] of German Sixth Army, with 1,500 men and 55 tanks
- Estimated correlation of forces ("bayonets"):

	65th Army	German	Ratio
Personnel	28,000	13,300	2.1:1
Tanks	49	28°	1.8:1

STALINGRAD FRONT
64th Army
- Main attack force:
  - ° 204th, 157th, and 38th Rifle Divisions—average strength of 7,000 men (6,000 "bayonets")
  - ° 13th and 56th Tank Brigades—40 tanks
- Strength—20,000 men and 40 tanks
- Enemy forces:
  - ° 20th Infantry Division (R) of Fourth Panzer Army's IV Army Corps, with 7,727 men
- Estimated correlation of forces ("bayonets"):

	64th Army	Romanian	Ratio
Personnel	20,000	7,700	2.6:1
Tanks	40	—	Absolute

57th Army
- Main attack force:
  - ° 169th and 422nd Rifle Divisions—average strength of 7,000 men (6,000 "bayonets")
  - ° 143rd Rifle Brigade—4,000 "bayonets"
  - ° 13th Tank Corps (17th, 61st, and 62nd Mechanized Brigades, with 26th, 20th, and 21st Tank Regiments)—15,000 men and 171 tanks
  - ° 235th and 90th Tank Brigades—54 tanks
  - ° 10 RVGK artillery and mortar regiments
- Strength—35,000 men and 225 tanks
- Enemy forces:
  - ° 2nd Infantry Division (R) of Fourth Panzer Army's VI Army Corps (R), with 4,829 men
  - ° 29th Motorized Division (G) of Fourth Panzer Army, with 12,000 men and 59 tanks
- Estimated correlation of forces ("bayonets"):

	57th Army	German/Romanian	Ratio
Personnel	35,000	16,800	2.1:1
Tanks	225	59	3.8:1

51st Army
- Main attack force:
  - ° 302nd and 126th Rifle and 15th Guards Rifle Divisions—average strength of 7,000 men (6,000 "bayonets")

Table 25. (continued)

- ° 4th Mechanized Corps (36th, 59th, and 60th Mechanized Brigades, with 26th, 20th, and 21st Tank Regiments and 55th and 158th Separate Tank Regiments)—15,000 men and 179 tanks
- ° 4th Cavalry Corps (61st and 81st Cavalry Divisions)—10,284 men
- ° 254th Tank Brigade—28 tanks
- ° 8 RVGK artillery and mortar regiments
- • Strength—38,000 men and 207 tanks
- • Enemy forces:
  - ° 18th and 1st Infantry Divisions (R) of Fourth Panzer Army's VI Army Corps (R), with 16,580 men
  - ° 6th *Rosiori* Regiment (Mot.) (R) of 5th Cavalry Division (R), with 1,074 men
- • Estimated correlation of forces ("bayonets"):

	51st Army	**Romanian**	**Ratio**
Personnel	45,000	17,500	2.6:1
Tanks	207	—	Absolute

° Half of 14th Panzer Division's strength of 55 tanks.

THE SOUTHWESTERN AND DON FRONTS' OFFENSIVE, 19–20 NOVEMBER

19 November

> The Southwestern Front defended its previous positions on its right wing and fulfilled a mission in accordance with the plan in its center and on its left wing. The enemy undertook no active operations, and his aircraft conducted reconnaissance flights.
>
> The Don Front continued to defend its previous positions and conducted combat reconnaissance on its right wing.
>
> Red Army General Staff operational summary,
> 0800 hours on 20 November 1942[7]

These cryptic entries were the height of understatement. The General Staff, whether it was being cautious for security reasons or to avoid embarrassment if its forces suffered defeat, simply noted that Vatutin's Southwestern Front and Rokossovsky's Don Front had "fulfilled a mission in accordance with the plan." And indeed, that was true, but they had done so far more dramatically than the summary indicated.

5th Tank Army's Assault

Hours earlier, just before midnight on Wednesday, 18 November, Vatutin's *front* completed its preparations for the Uranus counteroffensive (see map 9). In the sector of 5th Tank Army, whose forces were designated to conduct the *front*'s main attack, riflemen from 14th Guards Rifle Division manned security positions in a 15-kilometer-wide sector along the army's forward edge, concealing the forward deployment of 47th Guards and 119th Rifle Divisions into their assigned jumping-off positions for the assault. Hidden by the 14th's screen, the riflemen, sappers, and artillerymen of the two reinforcing divisions' field guns moved forward stealthily in total blackout conditions, taking up their positions to provide supporting fire for the attack. Several kilometers behind, the heavier divisional artillery units occupied firing positions side by side with the army's supporting RVGK artillery.

As groups of sappers protected by submachine gunners from all four of 5th Tank Army's assault divisions began to clear the remaining minefields and obstacles to their front, infantry support tanks rolled into position in and behind the combat formations of the deploying infantry (see map 10). These included 64 tanks from the army's 8th Guards Tank Brigade and 511th Separate Tank Battalion, in support of 47th Guards Rifle Division, and 74 tanks from 26th Tank Corps' 216th Tank Brigade and the army's 510th Separate Tank Battalion, assigned to strengthen 124th (50th Guards) Rifle Division. With all the infantry support armor concentrated in the sectors of the two rifle divisions through which 1st and 26th Tank Corps were to advance, the army's two other main attack divisions, 14th Guards on the right and 119th Rifle on the left, relied on the antitank guns of attached tank destroyer regiments (four for the former and one for the latter) to support and protect their advance. In assembly areas several kilometers to the rear, the tank and motorized brigades of 1st and 26th Tank Corps, equipped with 137 and 157 operable tanks, respectively, formed into two columns of brigades and awaited the alert signal to advance. Echeloned to the left rear of the tank corps were the 8th Guards Motorcycle Regiment and the three cavalry divisions of 8th Cavalry Corps, all of them prepared to exploit deep once the advancing riflemen and accompanying tanks overcame the Romanian defenses.

Roughly 50 kilometers to the east, the soldiers of General Chistiakov's 21st Army were also moving into their assigned jumping-off positions late on 18 November (see map 11). Riflemen, sappers, and field gunners from the army's 76th, 293rd, and 63rd Rifle Divisions, accompanied by 56 tanks from the supporting 4th, 2nd, and 1st Guards Tank Regiments, respectively, occupied jumping-off positions in a 12-kilometer-wide sector in a narrow bridgehead extending northwestward from Kletskaia on the southern bank of the Don River. Because of the bridgehead's limited depth, however, the artillery of the army's three assault divisions remained in firing positions on the river's northern bank. Farther to the rear, the four brigades and 143 operable tanks belonging to 4th Tank Corps formed in two columns of brigades, with the three cavalry divisions of 3rd Guards Cavalry Corps several dozen kilometers behind them.

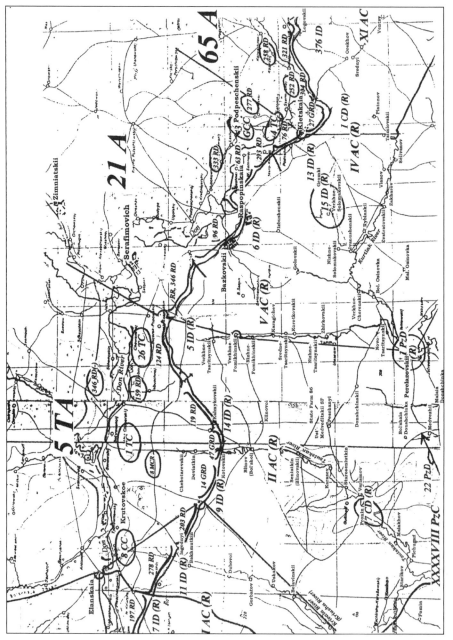

Map 9. Southwestern Front's offensive: situation in the Serafimovich and Kletskaia bridgeheads at 0500 hours, 19 November 1942

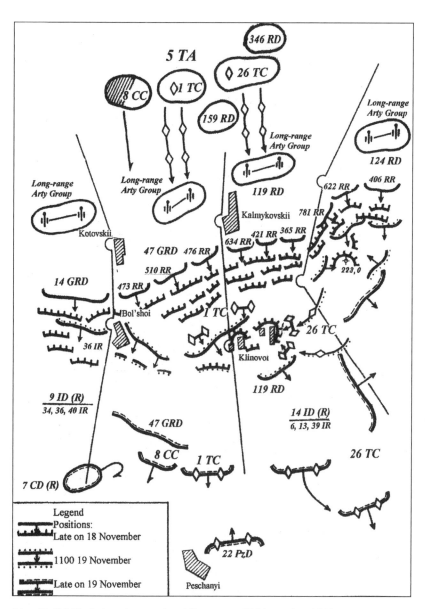

Map 10. 5th Tank Army's operational formation, 19 November 1942

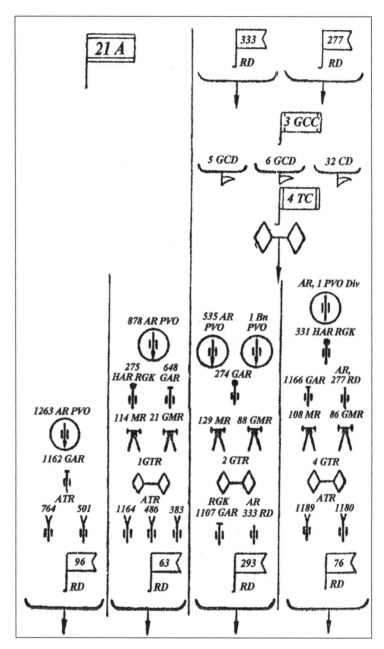

Map 11. 21st Army's operational formation, 19 November 1942

On 21st Army's left flank, the 304th Rifle and 27th Guards Rifle Divisions of General Batov's 65th Army moved into their jumping-off positions in the 6-kilometer-wide sector extending eastward from Kletskaia to the village of Melo-Kletskii on the Don's southern bank. On the 304th Division's left, the army's 321st Rifle Division concentrated its forces in a 4-kilometer sector extending from Melo-Kletskii eastward to Melo-Logovskii. Behind these three assault divisions, 252nd Rifle Division formed up in 304th Division's immediate rear, prepared to reinforce the assault at the right moment. Lacking a mobile exploitation echelon of its own, 65th Army relied on 49 tanks from 91st and 121st Tank Brigades to provide its advancing riflemen and sappers with direct armor support. However, the main attack sectors of 65th and 21st Armies were so close together that the latter's mobile group, 4th Tank and 3rd Guards Cavalry Corps, constituted the exploitation force of both armies.

Romanian forces defending opposite the Southwestern Front's two main attack sectors had every reason for genuine concern. Despite their senior officers' constant warnings to higher headquarters that their defenses were vulnerable, if not utterly untenable, Army Group B and Sixth Army had done precious little to assuage their concerns. If severe shortages of armor and antitank guns and the understrength condition of their divisions were not enough cause for concern, the positions they defended were atrocious, stretching in a 50-kilometer-wide arc up to 20 kilometers deep south of Serafimovich on the Don River and in a 15-kilometer-wide arc up to 10 kilometers deep south of the river at Kletskaia. When Army Group B's forces had advanced into this region in late August, German forces had established formidable defenses along the high ground overlooking the river in both the Serafimovich and Kletskaia sectors. Since the terrain south of the river rose precipitously to an elevation averaging more than 200 meters in both sectors, the river's southern bank was superbly defensible.

However, Italian Eighth Army had taken over defense of the Serafimovich sector on 15 August, leaving Sixth Army's XI Army Corps responsible only for the Kletskaia sector. Five days later, the Soviets had launched a surprise attack southward across the river (see volume 2 of this trilogy). This combined attack by Soviet 63rd and 21st Armies on 20 August had thrown Italian forces back from the river's southern bank; in the process, the Soviets seized the dominating heights and formed a sizable bridgehead on the southern bank by 28 August. Likewise, farther to the east, the Soviet 1st Guards Army had struck southward across the river in the Kletskaia region on 22 August, forcing the defending divisions of German Sixth Army's XI Corps to withdraw to new defenses up to 10 kilometers south of the river. Although the German command well understood the potential vulnerability of these sectors, it made no attempt to counterattack and liquidate the two Soviet bridgeheads because it was preoccupied with the ongoing struggle in

Stalingrad city. That was still the case when the troops of Romanian Third Army were assigned to defend the Serafimovich sector and the western part of the Kletskaia bridgeheads between 1 and 10 October 1942. From that time forward, Romanian political and military leaders constantly warned of dire consequences should the Soviets retain the bridgeheads.

Thus, the Romanian forces defending opposite the Southwestern Front's 5th Tank and 21st Armies found themselves in a perilous and frustrating position. First, since their main defensive line in the Serafimovich sector traversed a series of parallel ridges running from north to south, 3 to 20 kilometers south of the Don River, they were unable to observe and appreciate the full scope of the Soviet buildup of forces in the depths of the bridgeheads. Second, since rivers and streams in the region also ran from south to north, dissecting the Romanians' defensive positions, the terrain offered Soviet forces excellent avenues of approach through those defenses and into the operational depths. Third, the Romanian defenses were situated on open and virtually treeless ground, with few terrain features available to strengthen their positions. The same unfavorable conditions prevailed at Kletskaia, although the smaller size of the bridgehead there prevented the Soviets from packing such a dense force into the bridgehead without detection. Thus, on all counts, Romanian commanders and their troops had no grounds for confidence in the durability of their defenses.

At precisely 0720 hours (0520 hours Berlin time) on 19 November, the Southwestern Front's chief of artillery issued the alert order "Siren" [*Sirena*] by telephone to all of the *front*'s artillery groups. This signal meant they were to load their guns and mortars and commence firing their preplanned artillery preparation in 10 minutes. At 0730 hours, upon receiving the order "Fire" [*Ogon'*], the preparation began with an impressive volley of *Katiusha* rockets, announcing the beginning of the 80-minute preparation across the entire 28-kilometer-wide penetration sectors of the Southwestern and Don Fronts. More than 3,500 guns, mortars, and multiple rocket launchers took part in the preparation, firing primarily on targets identified by reconnaissance organs before the counteroffensive began.

The first 60 minutes of the preparation consisted of "destruction" fire designed to eliminate specific targets such as enemy firing points, command posts, communications centers, and troop concentration areas (see map 12). The final 20 minutes involved "suppression" fire aimed at damaging or otherwise silencing other targets not yet identified. This period culminated in 5 minutes of multiple volleys of often wildly inaccurate *Katiusha* rocket fire, designed, in part, to terrify the troops on whose heads the rockets rained down. Although the bulk of these fires fell on the first three tactical positions in the Romanians' first main defensive belt, long-range artillery groups fired at more distant targets in the second defensive belt or even deeper in the enemy rear. However, as frightening and destructive as this preparation was to the Romanians, poor visibility caused by snow and heavy ground fog significantly reduced its effectiveness and made it impossible for artillery observers to adjust the firing onto specific targets. More important, the fog and low ceiling also prevented aircraft from the *front*'s 17th and 2nd Air Armies from conducting the planned "air offensive." As a result, many Romanian firing points, command posts, and troop concentration areas on the flanks of the intended penetration sectors survived with enough strength to hinder the Soviet ground attack when it began.

The general din caused by the massive Soviet barrages certainly attracted the Romanians' attention. Even before the bombardment ended, Third Army's headquarters reported on its ferocity to Army Group B, no doubt also warning of an impending ground assault. Reacting quickly, General Weichs at Army Group B informed General Zeitzler, the army's chief of staff in the OKH, of "very heavy artillery bombardment of the entire Romanian front northwest of Stalingrad" and asked for permission to halt ongoing operations in Stalingrad. Just as in the famous case of the June 1944 Normandy invasion, German commanders required Hitler's permission to commit their armored reserves, in this instance, XXXXVIII Panzer Corps. When Weichs asked for authorization to do so, Zeitzler had to contact Hitler, who was aboard his personal train traveling from East Prussia to Berchtesgaden, and, with some difficulty, persuaded the Führer to release Heim's panzer corps to the control of Army Group B. Zeitzler then responded to Weichs with this order: "Panzer Corps Heim [XXXXVIII Panzer Corps] to be made ready for action immediately. Application has already been made to Hitler for its release from reserve."[8] Contrary to Hitler's expectations, this formation did not have the decisive effect he thought it would.

At 0840 hours, even before the artillery preparation ended, and at roughly the same time Romanian Third Army headquarters was reporting the terrible bombardment to Army Group B, forward rifle battalions from the shock groups belonging to the Southwestern Front's 5th Tank and 21st Armies, accompanied by sappers and a handful of infantry support tanks, pushed to within 200 to 300 meters of the forward edge of the Romanian and German defenses. Still exploiting the morning fog and gloom, the sappers ranged far ahead, painstakingly cutting passages through newly emplaced barbed wire and removing mines wherever they found them. Once the forward battalions were in position directly in front of the enemy's first line of trenches, Generals Romanenko and Chistiakov, commanders of 5th Tank and 21st Armies, respectively, ordered the ground assaults to begin. As the artillery preparation began its final five-minute crescendo of intense *Katiusha* fire and the armies' artillery groups began shifting their fires into the depths of the enemy's defenses, the infantry assault began.

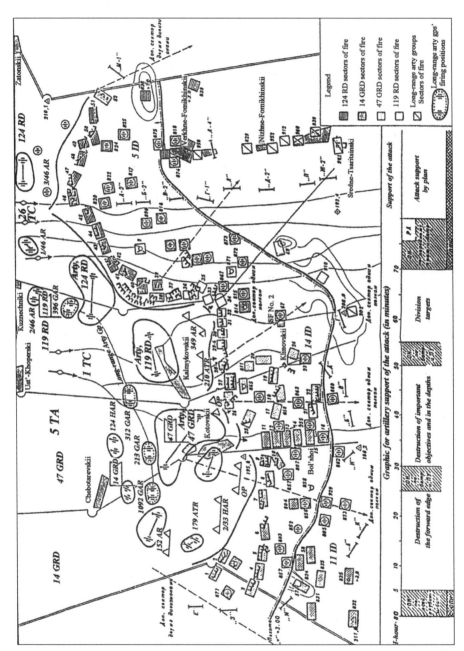

Map 12. Grouping and fire plans of 5th Tank Army's artillery, 19 November 1942

Between 0848 and 0850 hours Moscow time, riflemen and sappers from the first-echelon rifle divisions of the Southwestern Front's 5th Tank and 21st Armies and the Don Front's 65th Army commenced virtually simultaneous assaults against Romanian and German defenses from their bridgeheads on the southern bank of the Don River (see map 13). The assaulting troops were clad in white camouflage uniforms so as to blend in with the snow-covered terrain. On the right wing of Vatutin's Southwestern Front, arrayed from left to right in the Serafimovich bridgehead, the troops of 50th Guards, 119th, 47th Guards, and 14th Guards Rifle Divisions, supported by 138 tanks, struck the defenses of Romanian Third Army's 5th, 14th, and 9th Infantry Divisions in the roughly 15-kilometer-wide sector from just west of Verkhne-Fomikhinskii on the Tsaritsa River westward to State Farm No. 3, 5 kilometers west of the small village of Bol'shoi on the Tsutskan' River. Roughly 45 kilometers to the east, the soldiers of 63rd, 293rd, and 76th Rifle Divisions from the Southwestern Front's 21st Army, supported by 56 tanks and flanked on the left by infantrymen and sappers from 27th Guards and 304th and 321st Rifle Divisions of the Don Front's 65th Army, bolstered by 49 tanks, attacked southward from a roughly 20-kilometer-wide sector in the Kletskaia bridgehead. The forces collided with the defenses of German XI Army Corps' 376th Infantry Division and Romanian Third Army's 1st Cavalry and 13th Infantry Divisions and the right wing of 6th Infantry Division.[9] Since the defending Germans and Romanians had no tanks and the Romanians lacked adequate antitank guns, the struggle proved to be an unequal one.

During the first hour of the counteroffensive, the 5th Tank Army's four attacking rifle divisions overcame Romanian Third Army's first defensive positions with relative ease, not only because they attacked with all three of their regiments forward but also because two of the four divisions had significant numbers of supporting tanks. On the left wing of the tank army's main attack sector, riflemen from 781st, 622nd, and 406th Regiments of Colonel A. I. Belov's 50th Guards Rifle Division, accompanied by tanks from 26th Tank Corps' 216th Tank Brigade and 510th Separate Tank Battalion, attacked southward along the ridgeline midway between the villages of Kalmykovskii and Verkhne-Fomikhinskii. The intense assault tore a gaping hole through the defenses on Romanian 5th Infantry Division's left wing and captured the Romanian strongpoint on Hill 223 by 1100 hours. This forced 5th Division to withdraw the remnants of its left wing to new defensive positions protecting the western approaches to the Tsaritsa River and the villages of Verkhne- and Nizhne-Fomikhinskii.

On 50th Guards Division's right, even without supporting tanks, 634th, 421st, and 365th Regiments of Colonel I. Ia. Kulagin's 119th Rifle Division exploited their neighbor's success by thrusting due south from the

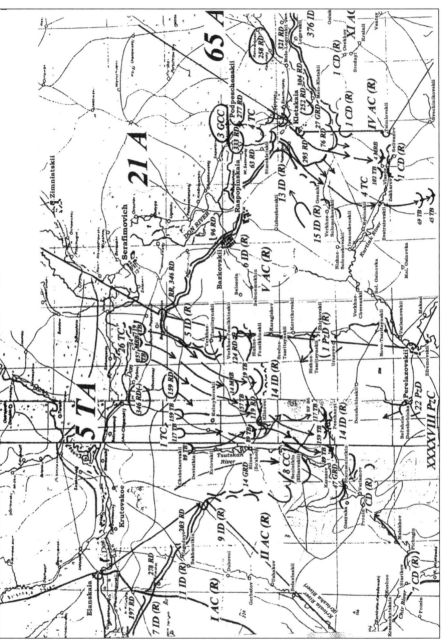

Map 13. Southwestern Front's offensive: situation in the Serafimovich and Kletskaia bridgeheads at 2200 hours, 19 November 1942

Kalmykovskii region against the defenses of Romanian 14th Infantry Division. The attacking riflemen smashed the Romanians' first defensive position and approached the village of Blinovskii by 1100 hours. In the Kotovskii sector farther to the west, 473rd, 510th, and 476th Regiments of Major General Fokanov's 47th Guards Rifle Division advanced southward along and east of the Tsutskan' River. With more than adequate armor support from 8th Guards Tank Brigade and 511th Separate Tank Battalion, Fokanov's troops shattered the defenses on the left wing of 14th Infantry Division, captured the Romanians' first defensive position as well as the village of Bol'shoi, and prepared to advance south toward Blinovskii. Hammered by the assaults of two full Soviet rifle divisions, Romanian 14th Infantry Division clung desperately to its second defensive position east of the Tsutskan' River.

Contrasting sharply with the modest successes achieved by its neighbors on the left, Major General A. S. Griaznov's 14th Guards Rifle Division found the going far more difficult. Attacking from jumping-off positions in a 4-kilometer-wide sector extending westward from the Tsutskan' River just south of Kotovskii to the northern outskirts of State Farm No. 3, Griaznov's troops barely dented the defenses of Romanian 9th Infantry Division. Lacking any supporting tanks, 14th Guards Division's multiple assaults were quickly broken up by intense flanking artillery, mortar, and machine gun fire from a Romanian strongpoint on Hill 228, 4 kilometers northwest of the state farm. By this time, stiffening Romanian resistance throughout 5th Tank Army's entire sector provided proof positive that the tank army's artillery preparation had been far less effective than planned.

Thus, by 1100 hours on 19 November, 5th Tank Army's 50th Guards, 119th, and 47th Guards Rifle Divisions had overcome Romanian Third Army's first defensive position with relative ease and were now beginning the struggle to surmount the Romanians' second defensive position. Despite these modest successes, however, the three rifle divisions managed to advance a distance of only 2 to 3 kilometers, far short of the 15 to 18 kilometers called for in the offensive plan. Compounding this harsh reality, the assault by the army's fourth main attack division, Griaznov's 14th Guards, ground to an abrupt halt after advancing several hundred meters when it encountered intense flanking fire from an undestroyed Romanian strongpoint on the shock group's right flank. With his tank army's attack clearly faltering, General Romanenko faced a crucial decision. First, he knew full well that his artillery preparation had failed to silence the Romanians' guns, the fog and poor visibility had prevented his aircraft from smashing Romanian defenses, and a slight rise in the temperature had allowed the advancing tanks and infantry to churn up the unfrozen ground, making the going far more difficult than anticipated for both man and tank. Second, a stouter than anticipated Romanian defense had significantly delayed his offensive timetable. Third, and most disturbing, he realized the Germans were bound to take advantage of his delayed advance by bringing up panzer forces from their reserves. Faced with these problems, Romanenko decided to unleash the full force of his two tank corps.

Confirming the worst of Romanenko's concerns, at 1000 hours (0900 Berlin time), Lieutenant General Ferdinand Heim, commander of XXXXVIII Panzer Corps, had requested permission from General Weichs, commander of Army Group B, to release his panzers so that he could attack northeastward from Peschanyi through Perelazovskii and toward the Kletskaia region to stave off any Soviet attempt to mount an armored thrust southward to split Romanian Third Army away from Sixth Army's defenses along the Don. Heim also requested that Romanian 1st Armored Division, then stationed at Perelazovskii, join his corps' advance toward the northeast. Major General Sodenstern, Army Group B's chief of staff, approved Heim's request. Weichs did so himself in an order issued at about 1010 hours.[10]

At the time, Heim's XXXVIII Panzer Corps consisted of Colonel Eberhard Rodt's 22nd Panzer Division and Major General Radu Gheorghe's Romanian 1st Armored Division. The former fielded 33 operable tanks—22 Pz-III and 11 Pz-IV short- and long-barreled tanks—complemented by 9 panzer jäger (assault guns), 5 with 76.2mm guns and 4 with 47mm guns. The latter had a personnel strength of 12,196 men and was equipped with 103 tanks—84 R-2 and 19 Pz-III and -IV models—plus 2 captured Soviet tanks.[11] In addition, Sixth Army apparently hoped to reinforce XXXXVIII Panzer Corps with a large *kampfgruppe* from 14th Panzer Division that supposedly fielded 55 tanks, 36 to 41 of which were operational.[12] However, this never occurred because General Bässler's panzer division was fully occupied with fending off 21st Army's offensive in the Kletskaia region.

With Weichs's authorization, Heim began moving his XXXXVIII Panzer Corps northeastward from the Peschanyi region at 1030 hours, with 35 to 40 tanks. His intent was to link up with Romanian 1st Armored Division north of Zhirkovskii and then conduct a three-pronged attack with it and Romanian 7th Cavalry Division to defeat the Soviet tank forces penetrating southward from Kletskaia. Heim's plan required the Romanian armored division to march northeastward from Perelazovskii through Verkhne-Cherenskii toward Kletskaia and 7th Cavalry Division to move northeast toward Pronin, in the Tsutskan' River valley, roughly 20 kilometers to the rear of Romanian Third Army's forward positions.

However, before Heim's panzer corps could implement the commander's plan, Hitler intervened with new orders. At 1150 hours, when the corps' headquarters and 22nd Panzer Division were approaching the village of Malaia Donshchinka, 10 kilometers southwest of Perelazovskii, Heim received a curt message from Hitler through General Zeitzler in the OKH.

The message ordered him to shift the direction of his panzer corps' attack: 22nd Panzer Division was instructed to wheel 90 degrees to the left and attack northwest through the Peschanyi region toward Blinov (Blinovskii, according to Soviet sources and maps), which was situated roughly 12 kilometers behind the original center of Romanian Third Army's front lines (HKL).[13] Of course, by this time, Soviet forces had already pushed the army's front as much as 3 kilometers to the rear. Hitler's order also required Romanian 1st Armored Division, which was nearing Verkhne-Cherenskii, 15 kilometers northeast of Perelazovskii, to pivot its axis of advance west toward Zhirkovskii. Romanian 7th Cavalry Division was to continue its attack northeastward from Pronin at dawn on 20 November to catch and cut off 5th Tank Army's spearheads. The order also subordinated Romanian II Army Corps, with its 7th, 9th, and 14th Infantry Divisions—that is, the entire center sector of Third Army—to XXXXVIII Panzer Corps' control. However, because it had already lost radio contact with the panzer headquarters, General Gheorghe's armored division failed to receive the message and continued its northeastward march.

21st Army's Assault
Meanwhile, 35 to 50 kilometers to the northeast, where the Southwestern Front's 21st Army and the Don Front's 65th Army were launching their well-coordinated offensive, an even worse crisis was brewing for Romanian Third Army and its neighbor to the right, German XI Army Corps. Like General Romanenko's 5th Tank Army, General Chistiakov's 21st Army had launched its ground assault at 0850 hours, following a massive artillery preparation (see map 13).[14] Supported by the army's three guards tank regiments, 76th, 293rd, and 63rd Rifle Divisions attacked in the 14-kilometer-wide sector from just west of Kletskaia to Hill 163.3, 5 kilometers east of Raspopinskaia. Still farther to their right, two regiments of the army's 96th Rifle Division assaulted Romanian defenses between Raspopinskaia and Bazkovskii to distract the defenders from the Soviet main attack developing to the east. As was the case in 5th Tank Army's sector, two of Chistiakov's attacking divisions recorded significant advances, while attacks by the third and fourth divisions faltered after only insignificant gains.

On the left wing of the army's main attack sector, Colonel N. T. Tavartkiladze's 76th Rifle Division struck as planned, attacking the Romanians' defenses precisely at the boundary between Romanian IV Army Corps' 13th Infantry and 1st Cavalry Divisions. Tavartkiladze's assault succeeded in driving a 3-kilometer-deep wedge between the two defending Romanian divisions by midday. Worse still for the defenders, on 76th Division's right, 293rd Rifle Division made even greater progress under its experienced commander Colonel P. F. Lagutin, who had led the division since its formation in July 1941. Exploiting the effects of 76th Division's assault, which had shattered Romanian 13th Infantry Division's entire right wing, Lagutin's riflemen surged forward up to 4 kilometers, overcoming the Romanians' first defensive positions and penetrating into their second position by 1200 hours.

However, on the right wing of 21st Army's penetration sector, Colonel N. D. Kozin's 63rd Rifle Division faced stronger resistance and managed to advance only a kilometer against Romanian 13th Infantry Division's stouter defenses east of Raspopinskaia before grinding to a halt under heavy enemy fire. Farther to the west, the assault by two regiments of Colonel G. P. Isakov's 96th Rifle Division in the sector on both sides of Bazkovskaia registered no gains whatsoever against the determined Romanian 6th Infantry Division, whose defending troops actually forced Isakov's riflemen to withdraw to their jumping-off positions. Nonetheless, Chistiakov ordered Isakov to continue his assaults, if only to tie down Romanian forces and prevent them from sending reinforcements to more threatened sectors. Faced with circumstances that replicated those of Romanenko's tank army, Chistiakov reached a similar conclusion. He decided it was the right moment to commit his powerful mobile forces to battle.

65th Army's Assault

On 21st Army's left, General Batov's 65th Army also launched its offensive at 0850 hours on 19 November (see map 13). The nucleus of Batov's shock group consisted of Colonel S. P. Merkulov's 304th Rifle and Colonel V. S. Glebov's 27th Guards Rifle Divisions, the former supported by 91st Tank Brigade; they were deployed in the 5-kilometer-wide sector extending from Melo-Kletskii westward to Kletskaia, directly opposite the defenses of Romanian 1st Cavalry Division. On the shock group's left, Major General I. A. Makarenko's 321st Rifle Division was to attack southward along both sides of the Mokryi Log *Balka*, which marked the boundary between Romanian Third Army's 1st Cavalry Division and 376th Infantry Division of German Sixth Army's XI Army Corps. Finally, Colonel Z. S. Shekhtman's 252nd Rifle Division, deployed in the army's second echelon behind 304th Rifle Division, was to reinforce the shock group's assault as it progressed. The mission of Batov's shock group as a whole was to smash the defenses of Romanian 1st Cavalry Division, which anchored the right flank of Romanian IV Army Corps south and east of Kletskaia, and then attack southeastward to turn the left flank of Sixth Army's XI Army Corps and protect the left flank of 21st Army's mobile group as it exploited southward into the depths. This meant that Batov's army had to assault German as well as Romanian defenses.

The commander of the Don Front, General Rokossovsky, had gone to General Batov's forward observation post in 65th Army's sector early in the morning to observe his *front*'s main attack and provided a vivid description of the scene:

> Air Force General S. I. Rudenko was extremely put out. The massive air strikes provided for by the plan were ruled out by the bad weather. . . .
>
> The battlefield was obscured in dense mist, and optical instruments were of no avail. All we could see were the flashes of explosions lighting up the milky shroud. The guns rumbled ceaselessly. . . . A mighty "Hurrah" mingled with the grinding roar of the tanks. The assault had begun. We exchanged glances. Would we succeed in penetrating the enemy's fortifications?. . .
>
> Gradually the mist cleared, and the battlefield came into sight. Through field glasses I watched our troops storm the precipitous chalk hills in the Kletskaia area. I could see men clinging to ledges and climbing stubbornly. Many lost their hold and slid down, only to get up and start climbing again, helping each other up the steep slopes and rushing the enemy positions. The Nazis resisted desperately, but our infantry overcame them and drove them off the heights. The enemy's main line of defense began to show signs of cracking. The 65th Army kept pounding it steadily and pushing forward—with difficulty on the left flank, more successfully at the boundary with 21st Army, on the right.[15]

General Batov too shared his impressions of his shock group's assault on the Romanian and German defenses:

> The first two trench lines on the high ground on the [Don River's southern] bank were taken immediately. Fighting then developed on the nearby heights. The enemy's defenses were made up of separate strong points linked together by full-profile trenches. Each height was a strongly fortified point. Ravines and depressions were mined, and the approaches to the heights were covered by coiled barbed wire.
>
> The guardsmen on the right [27th Guards], which were pressed up against the neighboring 76th Division, advanced well. In the center it was worse: Merkulov [304th Rifle Division] was forced to the ground in front of Melo-Kletskaia. What was happening with Makarenko [321st Rifle Division]?[16]

The answer to Batov's rhetorical question was, "Nothing positive." Although the guardsmen of Glebov's 27th Guards were able to exploit the successes of 21st Army's neighboring 76th Division on their left by advancing up to 3 kilometers deep, 304th and 321st Rifle Divisions encountered skillfully fortified strongpoints manned by German troops that they could not overcome. Worse still, they faced nearly constant counterattacks on their left by XI Army Corps' 376th Infantry Division, supported later in the day by elements of the newly arriving German 14th Panzer Division. This lack of success was not surprising, considering that the Southwestern Front's 21st Army was attacking Romanian defenses, while roughly half the shock group of the Don Front's 65th Army was attacking German defenses. The same held true on the Don Front's left wing and center, where supporting attacks conducted by the *front's* 66th and 24th Armies faltered after meeting strong resistance by divisions of Sixth Army's XIV Panzer and VIII Army Corps.

5th Tank Army's Exploitation
By midday on 19 November, General Romanenko at 5th Tanks Army's forward command post (CP) and General Chistiakov at 21st Army's forward CP reached identical conclusions. Both decided that if the counteroffensive was to succeed, it was time to unleash their armored fists—the roughly 300 tanks of 1st, 26th, and 4th Tank Corps. Thus, instead of committing the tank corps to exploit the penetration and conduct deep maneuvers into the operational depths, the two army commanders (with General Vatutin's approval) ordered their three tank corps to help the forward shock groups complete their tactical penetrations and then commence their exploitations from the march.

At 1200 hours on 19 November, 5th Tank Army's 47th Guards Rifle Division was fighting 2 to 3 kilometers deep in the center of Romanian Third Army's second defensive position south of Bol'shoi, and 119th Rifle and 50th Guards Rifle Divisions were still struggling in the Romanian's first defensive position north and northeast of Klinovoi. At that time, Romanenko ordered General Butkov's 1st and General Rodin's 26th Tank Corps to deploy forward into their jumping-off positions and prepare to join the attack. Marching in columns of brigades, the two tank corps moved southward over the next 60 minutes, taking their jumping-off positions for the attack. Butkov's corps deployed for combat just west of Kalmykovskii, in the rear of the advancing 47th Guards and 119th Rifle Divisions. Rodin's corps did so in positions northeast of Kalmykovskii and Hill 220, 5 kilometers to the northeast.

At 1250 hours, with the bulk of 1st and 26th Tank Corps' combat units in position, Vatutin ordered the two corps to enter the penetration to "strengthen the attacks by the rifle divisions, complete the penetration, and develop success into the depths" before German reinforcements could arrive.[17] Following Vatutin's orders, the two tank corps began their southward advance promptly at 1400 hours, with 1st Tank Corps deployed across an 8- to 9-kilometer-wide front and 26th Tank Corps on a 12- to 14-kilometer front (see map 14). Each corps initiated its attack by advancing southward along four march routes that had been selected in advance, and each led its advance with a full tank brigade advancing along two routes. Following Romanenko's guidance, the four advancing tank brigades surged forward in precombat march formation, with instructions to attack from the march and bypass any and all Romanian strongpoints they encountered.

Butkov's 1st Tank Corps advanced with Lieutenant Colonel S. P. Khaidukov's 159th Tank Brigade leading its left column, followed by the corps' headquarters and 44th Motorized Rifle Brigade. Lieutenant Colonel D. I. Fedorov's 117th Tank Brigade led the corps' right column, followed by 33rd Tank Destroyer Regiment and Lieutenant Colonel A. V. Zhukov's 89th Tank Brigade. On 1st Tank Corps' left, Rodin's 26th Tank Corps (which had already detached Lieutenant Colonel K. G. Kozhanov's 216th Tank Brigade to support 50th Guards Rifle Division's assault) advanced with Colonel N. M. Filippenko's 19th and Lieutenant Colonel I. I. Ivanov's 157th Tank Brigades leading its left and right columns, respectively, followed by its 14th Motorized Rifle Brigade in the second echelon.[18] In both instances, for defensive purposes, the corps scattered antitank and antiaircraft units throughout its march formations, the former in expectation of inevitable panzer counterattacks. But those counterattacks failed to materialize on the first day; nor did German aircraft interfere with their advance.

As the two tank corps advanced southward, their lead tank brigades formed a formidable wall of armor stretching across a 20- to 22-kilometer frontage of relatively open terrain—virtually the entire ridgeline extending from the village of Bol'shoi on the Tsutskan' River, northeastward past Hill 223.0, to the western bank of the Tsaritsa River near Verkhne-Fomikhinskii. As recorded in archival documents, "On the personal orders of the tank army's commander, the tank corps went forward, bypassing the infantry and finally penetrating the enemy's defenses in the center, between the Tsutskan' and Tsaritsa Rivers. While throwing away their weapons and surrendering en masse, the enemy began to withdraw rapidly toward the south."[19] The "tank fright" generated by the massed tank attack soon obliterated the regiment defending on the left wing of Romanian 14th Infantry Division. Soon after, the assault by 26th Tank Corps struck the 14th Division's two other regiments, completing its virtual destruction.

The lead tank brigades of General Butkov's 1st Tank Corps joined the penetration battle by advancing directly through the combat formations of Colonel Kulagin's 119th Rifle Division and General Fokanov's 47th Guards Rifle Division as the latter prepared to assault the defenses of Romanian 14th Infantry Division at the village of Klinovoi. At the last minute, Butkov ordered Lieutenant Colonel Zhukov's 89th Tank Brigade to deploy forward from the second echelon on 159th Tank Brigade's right. As a result, when they struck the Romanians' defenses, all three tank brigades did so simultaneously on line, with only 44th Motorized Rifle Brigade in the second

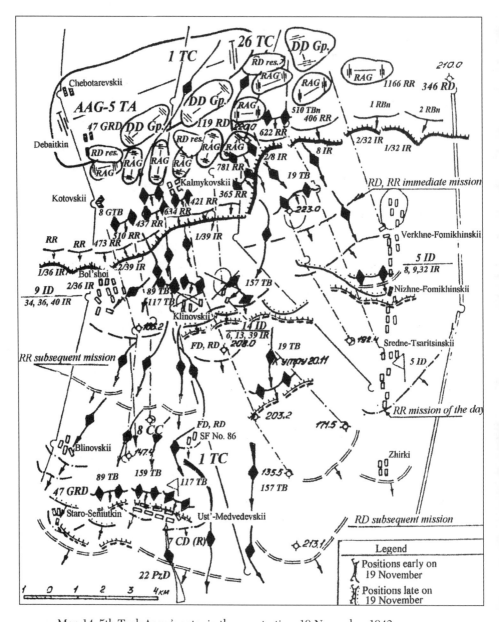

Map 14. 5th Tank Army's entry in the penetration, 19 November 1942

echelon. This violent armored assault struck Romanian II Army Corps (defending 14th Infantry Division) in the roughly 7-kilometer-wide sector extending from the eastern part of Frunze State Farm No. 1, along the western bank of the Tsutskan' River, and eastward across the river to the village of Klinovoi, 5 kilometers east-southeast of Bol'shoi. As Butkov drove home his attack, the right flank tank brigade of Rodin's 26th Tank Corps, Lieutenant Colonel Ivanov's 157th, joined the assault by attacking Romanian defenses east of Klinovoi.

The combined assault by four Soviet tank brigades fielding more than 180 tanks obliterated Romanian 14th Infantry Division's defenses. With tanks descending on them from all sides, the surviving Romanian troops caught "tank fright" and withdrew from the field of battle in utter disorder. In cooperation with 26th Tank Corps' 157th Tank Brigade, Butkov's three brigades smashed the Romanian defenses, bypassed and then destroyed the Romanian strongpoints at Klinovoi and on the eastern outskirts of Frunze State Farm No. 1, and lunged into the depths of the Romanians' defenses. The headlong advance, which lasted all afternoon, propelled Butkov's tanks forward a distance of roughly 18 kilometers.

During 1st Tank Corps' advance, 159th and 117th Tank Brigades seized other strongpoints on Hill 147.4 and at State Farm No. 86, 8 to 10 kilometers south of Klinovoi. On their left, 26th Tank Corps' 157th Tank Brigade also advanced southward and captured another Romanian strongpoint on Hill 208.0, 4 kilometers southeast of Klinovskii. On the right wing of Butkov's corps, 89th Tank Brigade, in cooperation with riflemen from 47th Guards Rifle Division, enveloped and seized the Romanian strongpoint at the village of Blinovskii in the Tsutskan' River valley, 12 kilometers south-southeast of Klinovoi.[20] Thus, by nightfall on the 19th, 1st Tank Corps' three tank brigades were approaching the northern outskirts of Ust'-Medveditskii State Farm, 1 kilometer northwest of Peschanovskii (Peschanyi) and 20 kilometers northwest of Perelazovskii. By now, they were already more than 10 kilometers behind the forward edge of Romanian Third Army. There, however, the corps' lead elements encountered stiffer resistance by the remnants of Romanian 14th Infantry Division and, supposedly, the lead elements of German 22nd Panzer Division, which reportedly cost the advancing tank corps 17 of its tanks destroyed or damaged.[21] At about the same time, the lead elements of Romanian 7th Cavalry Division also counterattacked north toward Blinovskii. This forced 47th Guards Rifle Division to halt its advance and temporarily go over to the defense.

Meanwhile, 5th Tank Army's 8th Motorcycle Regiment, commanded by Lieutenant Colonel P. A. Belik, followed Butkov's *tankists* through the now gaping penetration. Once through the Romanians' defenses, the motorcyclists sped southward in the wake of the advancing tanks to reach the region just northwest of Ust'-Medveditskii by late afternoon.[22] By nightfall, they too encountered elements of Romanian 14th Infantry Division and the forward elements of either Romanian 7th Cavalry Division or German 22nd Panzer Division.

Capping the day's frenetic action in 1st Tank Corps' sector, Major General M. D. Borisov's 8th Cavalry Corps was the last major force to capitalize on the tank corps' dramatic advance. Moving from its forward assembly areas 8 to 12 kilometers south of the Don River, the cavalry corps followed Butkov's tanks and Belik's motorcyclists through the penetration and galloped south toward Blinovskii, accompanied by the advancing riflemen of 47th Guards Rifle Division. The corps' 112th Cavalry Division, commanded by Major General M. M. Shaimuratov, cooperated with 47th Guards Division's 473rd Regiment and supporting tanks from Major V. G. Nikolov's 8th Guards Tank Brigade. This force conducted the assault that captured the Romanian strongpoint at Blinovskii. Marching southward in tandem with 112th Cavalry, Major General N. P. Iakunin's 21st Cavalry Division lunged farther to the southwest and captured the village of Karasev in the Tsutskan' River valley, 5 kilometers south of Blinovskii. By day's end, 112th and 21st Cavalry Divisions, together with elements of 8th Guards Tank Brigade and 473rd Regiment, also engaged elements of Romanian 7th Cavalry Division south of Karasev. In this encounter, General Heim claimed 7th Cavalry "fought gallantly until early on the 20th."[23]

Farther east, 8th Cavalry Corps' 55th Cavalry Division, commanded by Colonel I. T. Chalenko, in cooperation with the main body of General Fokanov's 47th Guards Rifle Division, left the fighting in the Ust'-Medveditskii region to 1st Tank Corps and 8th Motorcycle Regiment and moved westward about 8 kilometers to the vicinity of the village of Staro-Seniutkin in the Tsutskan' River valley, midway between Blinovskii and Pronin. There, the cavalry division's troopers also engaged elements of Romanian 7th Cavalry Division and, perhaps, some of the lead elements of German 22nd Panzer Division. In the fighting at Karasev and in the Staro-Seniutkin region, 7th Cavalry Division reportedly lost three of the six R-1 light tanks belonging to its 4th Mechanized Squadron.[24]

The engagement involving 1st Tank Corps' advancing tank brigades, 8th Motorcycle Regiment, the three cavalry divisions of 8th Cavalry Corps, and the lead elements of XXXXVIII Panzer Corps' 22nd Panzer and Romanian 7th Cavalry Divisions had been precipitated by orders received by Heim at 1150 hours on the 19th. According to these orders, 22nd Panzer Division was to move northeastward and concentrate in the Peschanyi region, Romanian 1st Armored Division was to move northwest toward Zhirkovskii, and Romanian 7th Cavalry Division was to advance northeastward from Pronin—all converging on the Blinovskii region. The resulting confused struggle that began late on 19 November and endured for several days ultimately threw a monkey wrench into 1st Tank Corps' ambitious offensive timetable.

While the tanks of Butkov's 1st Tank Corps were savaging the center of Romanian Third Army's defenses and generating a confused meeting in the Ust'-Medveditskii and Peschanyi region, those of Rodin's 26th Tank Corps were wreaking havoc on Romanian Third Army's defenses in a broad sector to the east. The two lead tank brigades of Rodin's tank corps (216th Tank Brigade was already providing 50th Guards Rifle Division with direct tank support) entered the fight on 1st Tank Corps' left in an attempt to pass through the advancing ranks of 119th Rifle and 50th Guards Rifle Divisions and complete the penetration. With Colonel Filippenko's 19th Tank Brigade and Lieutenant Colonel Ivanov's 157th Tank Brigade arrayed from left to right in the roughly 8-kilometer-wide sector southeast of Kalmykovskii, the advancing corps immediately encountered strong resistance by Romanian forces on the left wing of 5th Infantry Division and the right wing of 14th Infantry Division, which were dug into defenses protecting Hills 217 and 223, 10 to 12 kilometers southeast of Kalmykovskii. The stout Romanian defense halted the corps' forward progress in its tracks.

Faced with this unexpectedly strong resistance, Rodin decided to leave 19th and 216th Tank Brigades on his corps' left flank and center, opposite and just west of Hill 223, and dispatch Ivanov's 157th Tank Brigade southwestward to envelop the Romanians' strongpoints on the twin hills. Accordingly, Ivanov withdrew the roughly 45 tanks of his 157th Tank Brigade from their positions opposite Hill 217 and wheeled them southwestward through the village of Klinovoi, in 1st Tank Corps' sector. Cooperating with riflemen from 119th Rifle Division's 634th Regiment, Ivanov's tanks advanced through the defenses of Romanian II Army Corps' 14th Infantry Division east of Klinovoi and then dashed southward 22 kilometers, meeting only light resistance. In the process, Ivanov's armor captured Romanian strongpoints at State Farm No. 2, 4 kilometers east of Klinovoi; at State Farm No. 86, 5 kilometers east of Blinovskii; and at Separate Farm No. 3 and Ust'-Medveditskii by the end of the day.

Far to the rear, Colonel Filippenko's 19th Tank Brigade and Lieutenant Colonel Kozhanov's 216th Tank Brigade supported the riflemen of 50th Guards Rifle Division as they struggled to seize Hills 217 and 223. This fight lasted all afternoon. Supported by the two tank brigades, Colonel Belov's 50th Guards Rifle Division finally overcame Romanian resistance on the two hills by 1800 hours. Thereafter, 216th Tank Brigade and the left-wing regiment of 50th Guards Rifle Division wheeled eastward and were engaged in fighting along the western approaches to Verkhnyi and Nizhnyi Fomikhinskii, in the Tsaritsa River valley, by day's end. The 19th Tank Brigade, still cooperating with 50th Guards Rifle Division's main forces, advanced to positions east of

Hill 208, 5 to 7 kilometers southeast of Klinovoi, where it faced the remnants of Romanian 14th Infantry Division's right-wing regiment, which was now supported by a handful of tanks from the lead elements of General Gheorghe's Romanian 1st Armored Division. Gheorghe's armor was just beginning to deploy northwestward from the Perelazovskii region after spending the bulk of the day on a "wild goose chase" toward the Kletskaia region.

While 5th Tank Army's two tank corps and cavalry corps were conducting their headlong advance southward through the center of Romanian Third Army's defenses, the rifle divisions constituting its main shock group struggled to keep up with the exploiting tanks and cavalry. In the shock group's center, where the exploitation force's forward progress was greatest, General Fokanov's 47th Guards Rifle Division advanced southward in the wake of 1st Tank Corps' 89th and 159th Tank Brigades to reach positions extending roughly 8 kilometers westward from the northwestern and western outskirts of Ust'-Medveditskii, through Staro-Seniutkin, to the Karasev region in the Tsutskan' River valley. On 47th Guards Division's left, Colonel Kulagin's 119th Rifle Division, which was following 1st Tank Corps' 117th Tank Brigade, reached positions extending from Separate Farm No. 2, 4 kilometers east of Klinovoi; southward to west of Hill 208 and State Farm No. 86; and ultimately to the eastern outskirts of Ust'-Medveditskii. When it did, its left-wing 365th Regiment and its 421st Regiment in the center were facing east, and its right-wing 634th Regiment was facing south. Echeloned behind 119th Division's left flank, Colonel Belov's 50th Guards Rifle Division, along with 26th Tank Corps' 216th and 19th Tank Brigades, advanced to positions extending from the western approaches to Verkhne-Fomikhinskii on the Tsaritsa River southwestward to Hill 208, 5 kilometers southeast of Klinovoi, with its front facing east and southeast by day's end.

Finally, on the right (western) wing of 5th Tank Army's main shock group, General Griaznov's 14th Guards Rifle Division, whose forces were attacking in the 4-kilometer-wide sector westward from Bol'shoi to State Farm No. 3, recorded only limited progress against Romanian 9th Infantry Division's 36th Regiment. Although the two regiments on the right wing of Griaznov's division failed to advance more than several hundred meters against the Romanians' stout defense, its left-wing regiment managed to exploit the successes of 47th Guards Rifle Division and 8th Cavalry Corps in the Bol'shoi sector by advancing up to 2 kilometers and reaching positions roughly 15 kilometers southwest of Bol'shoi.

Thus, by the end of the first day of fighting in 5th Tank Army's main attack sector, 1st Tank Corps, 47th Guards Rifle Division, and 119th Rifle Division's 634th Regiment had thoroughly smashed Romanian 14th Infantry Division's defenses and those on the right wing of Romanian 9th Infantry Division. Thereafter, Butkov's tank corps advanced southward about 18 kilometers to the Ust'-Medveditskii region, where they encountered the lead elements of XXXXVIII Panzer Corps' 22nd Panzer Division, backed up by the remnants of 14th Infantry Division. Farther east, however, 26th Tank Corps' three tank brigades, operating with the remaining two regiments of 119th Rifle Division and 50th Guards Rifle Division, registered far slower progress against Romanian 14th Infantry Division's right-wing regiment and Romanian 5th Infantry Division's left-wing regiment. Rodin's tank corps advanced only 6 kilometers to the western approaches to Verkhne-Fomikhinskii on the left and 7 to 8 kilometers to the region east of Hill 208 on the right. Farther east in 5th Tank Army's sector, the defenses of Romanian 5th and 6th Infantry Divisions held firm, halting the advance by 50th Guards Rifle Division's left wing and the single attacking regiment of 346th Rifle Division astride the Tsaritsa River valley north and northeast of Verkhne-Fomikhinskii.

21st Army's Exploitation

If the offensive by General Romanenko's 5th Tank Army from the Serafimovich bridgehead failed to live up to Vatutin's expectations, the situation was far more encouraging in the Kletskaia sector, 40 to 50 kilometers to the east (see map 13). Despite its slow beginning, and thanks to quick action by General Chistiakov, the 21st Army's offensive recorded spectacular successes that, within hours, threatened to split the defenses of Romanian Third Army away from those on Sixth Army's left wing. By doing so, the successful Soviet attack also drew precious German reserves away from the Southwestern Front's main attack sector.

At about 1200 hours on 19 November, General Chistiakov decided to take advantage of the limited gains made by his army's 76th and 293rd Rifle Divisions by committing his exploitation echelon—first, 4th Tank Corps, then, hard on the *tankists'* heels, 3rd Guards Cavalry Corps—into the still incomplete penetration. Acting quickly, he ordered General Kravchenko to move his 4th Tank Corps forward across the Don River near the village of Nizhne-Zatonskii and, with two tank brigades leading the assault, enter the penetration formed by the two rifle divisions south of the villages of Podnizhnyi and Karazhenskii, 4 to 8 kilometers west of Kletskaia. Following Chistiakov's orders, Kravchenko organized his corps into two echelons of brigades and marched them southward along two parallel routes in precombat formation. The 102nd Tank Brigade, commanded by Colonel N. V. Koshelev, led the corps' left column, followed by 4th Motorized Rifle Brigade; 69th Tank Brigade, commanded by Colonel V. S. Agafonov, spearheaded its right column. Lieutenant Colonel P. K. Zhidkov's 45th Tank Brigade marched southward in 69th Brigade's wake.

The 4th Tank Corps' mission was, "in cooperation with the mobile units of 5th Tank Army and 3rd Guards Cavalry Corps, [to] attack [southeastward]

toward Evstratovskii and Manoilin to destroy the enemy's reserves, headquarters, and rear services, cut off the withdrawal routes of the Germans'
Perelazovskii grouping, and prevent enemy operational reserves from approaching the battlefield from the depths."[25] The main forces of Kravchenko's corps were supposed to reach the vicinity of Manoilin on the Krepkaia
River, 35 kilometers south of Kletskaia, and Farm No. 1 of Pervomaiskii
(First of May) State Farm, several kilometers south of Manoilin, by day's end
on 19 November. Ranging far ahead, the tank corps' forward detachments
were to race southeastward and reach the western bank of the Don River 10
to 15 kilometers north of Kalach and 5 to 10 kilometers south of the town of
Golubinskii, where Sixth Army supposedly had its headquarters. It was a very
ambitious mission to assign to a single tank corps.

The Southwestern Front's plan called for 3rd Guards Cavalry Corps,
commanded by General I. A. Pliev, an experienced cavalryman, to follow
Kravchenko's tank corps through the penetration and advance southeastward
parallel to but east of the advancing armor to protect the tank corps' left
flank. Pliev's cavalry had been waiting patiently in assembly areas well to
the rear of 4th Tank Corps from 10 through 18 November. The corps consisted of Colonel N. S. Chepurkin's 5th Guards Cavalry Division, Colonel
A. I. Belogorsky's 6th Guards Cavalry Division, and Colonel A. F. Chudesov's
32nd Cavalry Division, with more than 22,000 skilled and experienced cavalrymen from Central Asia. It had been Pliev's corps that spearheaded the
daring counterstroke in late August that seized the Serafimovich bridgehead.

On 16 November, General Chistiakov issued Pliev's corps new orders
that assigned it the following mission for the first day of the offensive:

> The 3rd Guards Cavalry Corps, with 5th Tank Destroyer Artillery Bri-
> gade, 1250th Tank Destroyer Artillery Regiment, 21st Guards-Mortar
> Regiment, 4th Guards Tank Regiment, and 3rd Antiaircraft Artillery Bat-
> talion, supported by one assault aviation regiment, while following 4th
> Tank Corps, will pass through the combat formations of 293rd and 76th
> Rifle Divisions' infantry and, by conducting its attack along the Seliva-
> novo and Verkhne-Buzinovka axis, in cooperation with 4th Tank Corps,
> will complete the defeat and destruction of enemy reserves, headquar-
> ters, and rear services, prevent enemy operational reserves from ap-
> proaching the battlefield from the depths, and reach the (inclusive) Erik,
> Verkhne-Buzinovka, and Svechinikovskii region [25 to 40 kilometers
> south-southeast of Kletskaia] by day's end, where it will dig in.[26]

The only flaw in this order was that the supporting tank destroyer brigade
and guards tank regiment would be attached to the cavalry corps just before its commitment to action, since those two units first had to support 21st

Army's 76th and 293rd Rifle Divisions during their penetration operation. Neither unit made it to the cavalry corps in time to support its attack (see appendix 5B in the *Companion* for Pliev's recollections of planning for Operation Uranus).

Shortly before Pliev's corps moved forward into its jumping-off position north of Kletskaia Station on the night of 18–19 November, Chistiakov assigned the cavalrymen their mission for the second day of the operation:

> With present reinforcing units, by attacking toward Osinovskii and Bol'shenabatovskii [15 to 30 kilometers southeast of Verkhne-Buzinovka], to continue to defeat enemy reserves and headquarters in cooperation with 4th Tank Corps and reach the Don River along the Golubinskii, Bol'shenabatovskii, Kalachkin, and Evlampievskii line [20 to 35 kilometers north-northeast of Kalach], and, after dispatching reinforced reconnaissance from Malonabatovskii toward the northeast, seize crossings over the Don River with your forward units.[27]

The two brigade columns of General Kravchenko's 4th Tank Corps began their advance into the penetration promptly at 1300 hours on the 19th. At the time, 76th and 293rd Rifle Divisions had already penetrated the first defensive position of Romanian 13th Infantry Division in the sector 4 to 8 kilometers west of Kletskaia and were advancing toward the second position, about 2 to 3 kilometers deep into the Romanians' defenses. By this time, 13th Division's right wing was situated on the high ground 3 kilometers south of the villages of Podnizhnyi and Karazhenskii and was nearing collapse. To the rear, however, the lead elements of General Ioan Sion's 15th Infantry Division, which had been in Romanian IV Army Corps' reserve in the Verkhne-Solomakovskii region, 15 kilometers southwest of Kletskaia, had moved forward into defensive positions on and east of Hill 186.0, 8 to 10 kilometers west of Kletskaia, to back up the beleaguered 13th Division. General Sion was an experienced commander who had previously led Romanian 1st Armored Division and knew how to engage tanks.[28]

The right column of Kravchenko's 4th Tank Corps, led by Colonel Agafonov's 69th Tank Brigade and followed by Colonel Zhidkov's 45th Tank Brigade, passed through the ranks of the advancing 293rd Rifle Division with little difficulty, crushing the second defensive line of Romanian 13th Infantry Division and then pushing rapidly toward the south and southwest. Bypassing strongpoints in their path, including the redeploying Romanian 15th Infantry Division, the two brigades passed through the town of Gromki, 10 kilometers west of Kletskaia, at 1400 hours. There, they captured or dispersed 13th Division's headquarters and then raced southward another 14 kilometers to seize crossings over the Kurtlak River at the village of Evstratovskii, 20 kilometers southwest of Kletskaia, at about 1600 hours. On the tank brigade's right wing, a battalion task force from 45th Tank Brigade tried to wheel westward and raid into the rear of Romanian 6th Infantry Division, only to encounter strong resistance and lose 8 of its 15 tanks.[29]

Without pausing at the Kurtlak River, 4th Tank Corps' right column pushed southward to its objectives of the day: the village of Manoilin and Farm No. 1 of the First of May State Farm. The two tank brigades captured these objectives at 0100 hours on 20 November. Farther to the east, 4th Tank Corps' left column, led by Colonel Koshelev's 102nd Tank Brigade, found the going much more difficult. After routing Romanian 13th Infantry Division's right-wing regiment, it encountered Romanian 15th Division's defenses east of Hill 186.0, 5 kilometers southwest of Kletskaia. Supported by the corps' 4th Motorized Rifle Brigade, Koshelev's tanks faced far stiffer resistance than their neighbor on the right. After several hours of fighting, and with help from riflemen from 76th Rifle Division and tanks and antitank guns from 4th Guards Tank Regiment and 5th Tank Destroyer Brigade, 102nd Tank and 4th Motorized Brigades eventually forced General Sion's troops to retire southeastward in the late afternoon. Following the loss of up to 25 tanks (by the Romanians' count) in the fighting, the two brigades finally captured the villages of Zakharov and Vlasov on the Kurtlak River, 15 to 18 kilometers south-southwest of Kletskaia, by nightfall. By this time, Koshelev's left column lagged about 20 kilometers behind the tank corps' right column. In 4th Tank Corps' wake, the riflemen of 76th and 293rd Rifle Divisions succeeded in advancing to positions 5 to 7 kilometers south of Kletskaia by day's end. Kravchenko's tank corps reportedly lost 27 tanks—5 KV, 19 T-34, and 3 T-70 models—on the first day of the offensive.[30]

Meanwhile, marching in 4th Tank Corps' wake, General Pliev's 3rd Guards Cavalry Corps prepared to cross the Don River and move south toward its objectives in the Verkhne-Buzinovka region. Although hindered by incessant bombing raids by groups of 9 to 15 German aircraft that destroyed 11 of the 12 pontoon bridges over the Don in the sector from Lastushinskii to Nizhne-Zatonskii, Pliev's cavalry used the one remaining bridge on the southwestern outskirts of the latter to conduct its crossing. However, it was a perilous effort because of extremely icy conditions on the bridge, and the river below permitted only cavalrymen and light weapons to cross the fragile pontoon bridge. Therefore, by the time Pliev received Chistiakov's order to advance through the penetration, only 5th and 6th Guards Cavalry Divisions had crossed the river; 32nd Cavalry Division was still in the process of crossing. Pliev credited his corps' sappers with Herculean work to arrange the crossing.

Compounding the cavalry corps' difficulties, 4th Guards Tank Regiment and 5th Tank Destroyer Brigade, which were supposed to support the corps during its commitment into the penetration, were still tied up with

76th and 293rd Rifle Divisions and could not provide the requisite support. After overcoming resistance by Romanian 13th Infantry Division in its first defensive position, 76th Rifle Division, together with its supporting armor, was abruptly halted by strong resistance from Romanian 15th Division upon reaching the villages of Platonov, Tsimlovskii, and Selivanovo, situated along the Kurtlak River 13 to 15 kilometers south of Kletskaia. This was less than 2 kilometers east of where 15th Infantry Division also halted the advance by 4th Tank Corps' 102nd Tank and 4th Motorized Rifle Brigades late in the afternoon. In addition, since no one had bothered to clear Romanian minefields from 3rd Guards Cavalry Corps' attack routes, this too slowed the cavalry corps' forward progress.[31]

Despite these problems, Pliev's cavalry finally bypassed the struggling infantry at 1700 hours and drove southward at a full gallop; 6th Guards and 32nd Cavalry Divisions were on the left, heading for Platonov and Tsimlovskii, and 5th Guards Cavalry Division was on the right, advancing toward Vlasov and Selivanovo. The 20th Guards Cavalry Regiment of Colonel Chepurkin's 5th Guards Cavalry Division, which was leading the right column, reached the vicinity of Marker 187.5, west of Tsimlovskii on the Kurtlak River, at 2330 hours, where it began an intense firefight with elements of Romanian 15th Infantry Division. Shortly before 20th Regiment made contact with the Romanian infantry, the division's main body swept westward in an attempt to envelop the Romanians' defenses by seizing Selivanovo and Vlasov in the river valley, 3 to 6 kilometers west of Tsimlovskii. This force reached the road southwest of Dubovaia *Balka*, within sight of its objectives, at 2300 hours.

While observing the action on his corps' left wing, Pliev noticed that Colonel Belogorsky, commander of 6th Guards Cavalry Division, was unable to organize his troops properly for the penetration and relieved him on the spot, appointing Colonel P. P. Brikel', the division's assistant commander, as his replacement.[32] With order restored in its ranks, 6th Guards surged forward toward its designated penetration sector and reached the approaches to Platonov at 2000 hours. There, it ran into heavy machine gun, mortar, and artillery fire from dug-in Romanian troops, apparently dismounted cavalry on the left wing of 1st Cavalry Division. After several unsuccessful assaults that lasted until 2300 hours, reportedly against infantry reinforced by several tanks, the division failed to capture either Tsimlovskii or Platonov.[33] During the fighting, 32nd Cavalry Division, which was following 6th Guards, joined the struggle at 2230 hours and attacked Platonov from the northeast. Together, the two cavalry divisions finally captured the two Romanian strongpoints in fierce overnight fighting. Several kilometers to the west, 5th Guards Cavalry Division finally enveloped and captured the strongpoints at Selivanov and Vlasov by 0700 hours the next morning.

Therefore, although roughly half of Kravchenko's 4th Tank Corps drove southward all the way to Manoilin on the Krepkaia River by nightfall on 19 November, the tank corps' left column, together with the bulk of Pliev's cavalry corps, remained locked in combat for the four Romanian strongpoints in the Kurtlak River valley, 20 kilometers to the rear, until shortly after dawn on 20 November. Soviet critiques of 21st Army's offensive found that 76th and 293rd Rifle Divisions, supported by 4th Tank Corps' left column and most of 3rd Guards Cavalry Corps, failed to encircle Romanian 15th Infantry Division's forces in the hills south of Kletskaia because the division attacking on 65th Army's left wing, 27th Guards Rifle, failed to overcome Romanian 1st Cavalry Division's defenses southeast of Kletskaia in time to support the planned encirclement maneuver.[34]

Although the offensive by the Southwestern Front's 21st Army and the forces on the right wing of the Don Front's 65th Army failed to encircle the Romanian forces defending the sector between Romanian Third Army and German Sixth Army's XI Army Corps, Soviet sources nonetheless assert that the spectacular exploitation by half of Kravchenko's 4th Tank Corps 35 kilometers deep into the Axis rear led the German command to mistakenly conclude that the Kletskaia sector was the focal point of the offensive's main effort:

> It is characteristic that, even in works written many years after the war, participants in the events on the German side continued to believe the attack by the Don Front was the main blow that led to the encirclement of Sixth and part of Fourth Panzer Armies. Thus, I. Vidor [Joachim Wieder] wrote, "The Russians went on the offensive and immediately struck a crippling blow at first against the Romanian formations that were situated on the left flank of our grouping. This occurred in the great band of the Don River south of Kremenskaia Station." . . . But it is well-known that 65th Army delivered its blow south of Kremenskaia Station, whereas the blow which led to the encirclement of the Stalingrad grouping was delivered from the region which lay to the west, at the town of Serafimovich.[35]

In fact, the initial German reaction to the offensive supports this contention. For example, the initial orders Army Group B sent to Heim's XXXXVIII Panzer Corps required German 22nd Panzer and Romanian 1st Armored Divisions to march northeast toward Kletskaia. Only at 1150 hours did the army group direct the two divisions to change course and head northwest toward Blinov to intercept Soviet 5th Tank Army's armor as it marched south.[36] Likewise, Sixth Army took measures to close the Kletskaia "gap" through which 4th Tank Corps and 3rd Guards Cavalry Corps were advancing. First, Paulus dispatched the rest of 14th Panzer Division to the Verkhne-Buzinovka region, expecting that it would be able to reinforce XI Corps' left wing and counterattack to eliminate or at least contain the Soviet offensive in the Klets-kaia sector. Second, during the morning of the 19th, he ordered XIV Panzer Corps to send the mobile elements of 16th and 24th Panzer Divisions west toward the region between Verkhne-Buzinovka and the Don River north of Kalach to cut off and halt the southeastward advance by 5th Tank and 21st Armies' mobile forces (see below).

Axis Reactions

Both XXXXVIII Panzer Corps and Sixth Army took measures to halt the Soviet advance on 19 November (see map 13). After receiving Army Group B's order to attack northwest toward Klinov [Klinovoi], from 1200 to 1600 hours, XXXXVIII Panzer Corps' 22nd Panzer Division moved northward along separate routes from the Bol'shaia Donshchinka region, 10 kilometers west of Perelazovskii, toward Ust'-Medvcditskii State Farm and Peschanyi [Peschanovskii]. To the east, Romanian 1st Armored Division, still en route to Kletskaia, finally turned back at Verkhne-Cherenskii, 15 kilometers north-east of Perelazovskii, and countermarched westward through Zhirkovskii, 17 kilometers north of Perelazovskii. Its lead elements reached the vicinity of Hill 208, 8 kilometers northwest of Zhirkovskii, just in time to reinforce Romanian 14th Infantry Division's right-wing regiment and face 26th Tank Corps' assault.

At roughly 1600 hours, the lead elements of Colonel Rodt's 22nd Panzer Division, including its reconnaissance battalion and some antitank guns, en-countered a strong force of Russian tanks near Peschanovskii, 2 kilometers south of Ust'-Medveditskii, but were unable to coordinate their actions with 1st Armored Division because German communications with Romanian forces fell silent shortly before nightfall. This occurred when lead elements of 5th Tank Army's 26th Corps conducted a surprise attack at the headquar-ters of Romanian 1st Armored Division near Zhirkovskii, destroying the li-aison officer's radio before the Soviet tank corps' assault was repulsed. By this time, 22nd Panzer Division's main body included roughly 30 operational tanks.[37]

A major fight ensued, which lasted from 1600 hours to well after 1800 hours. It took place in the roughly 20-kilometer-wide sector extending from Gusynka on the Tsutskan' River, 7 kilometers north of Pronin, across the same river at Karasev to the higher ground from Ust'-Medveditskii State Farm and Peschanyi (2 kilometers south of the farm), to the vicinity of Hill 208, 20 kilometers northwest of Zhirkovskii (from 33 kilometers northwest to 20 kilometers north of Perelazovskii). Deployed from west to east, the Axis forces included Romanian 7th Cavalry Division, which was attacking northward and northeastward from the Pronin region; German 22nd Panzer

Division, which was closing into the region from the south and southeast; and Romanian 1st Armored Division, which was advancing cautiously into the region from the east. These Axis forces engaged 5th Tank Army's forces advancing southward, which included (from west to east), riflemen from 47th Guards Rifle Division; 1st Tank Corps' 89th, 159th, and 117th Tank Brigades; 26th Tank Corps' 157th and 19th Tank Brigades; and 119th Rifle Division, reinforced later in the day by the three divisions of 8th Cavalry Corps. This struggle took the classic form of a meeting engagement, with forces intermingled and new units joining the battle from every point of the compass before and after nightfall.

Hitler was distraught over the failure of Heim's panzer corps to live up to his expectations. When it became clear that XXXXVIII Panzer Corps could not halt 5th Tank Army's exploitation, an incensed Führer reportedly ordered Keitel to "send for the corps commander at once, tear off his epaulets, and throw him into jail. It's all his fault!" General Heim was imprisoned without a trial. Parenthetically, more than two weeks later, on 5 December, Hitler took the time to issue an exhaustive critique of XXXXVIII Panzer Corps' performance designed to prove that it "was the complete failure of [Heim's panzer corps] alone that made it possible for the Russians to grip the Romanian Third Army on its flanks."[38] Although the urge to blame someone is quite human, the fact is that Heim's force was totally inadequate for this mission. Ironically, however, it was the mere presence of Heim's force blocking 5th Tank Army's advance that threw the Southwestern Front's mission so far off schedule.

At least for 24 hours, the presence of XXXXVIII Panzer Corps on its left wing bolstered Sixth Army's confidence in the soundness of its position. As of midday on 19 November, as one study based on German sources points out, Sixth Army left the problems outside the city to XXXXVIII Panzer Corps and focused on reconnaissance operations in Stalingrad proper, stating, "On that day [19 November], Sixth Army did not yet feel directly threatened, and therefore its command did not think it needed to undertake decisive measures. At 1800 hours the army command reported that on 20 November it intended to continue the actions of reconnaissance subunits in Stalingrad."[39]

Amidst the confusion of the meeting engagement developing in the Peschanyi region, an increasingly concerned Army Group B sent another order to Heim at 1830 hours, instructing the corps "to fight a delaying action and then, in view of the serious developments along the army's entire front, disengage and move [southward] toward the 'K' [Kurtlak River] line, east of Petrovka [15 to 20 kilometers southwest of Perelazovskii]."[40] Even though the Serafimovich axis was supposedly protected by the panzer corps, at 2130 hours, Army Group B dispatched an order to Sixth Army reiterating its alarm over the deteriorating situation in the region. This message strongly recommended that Sixth Army shift the focus of its fighting from Stalingrad city toward the west and immediately begin moving forces westward to counter the threat materializing in the Great Bend of the Don (see appendix 5C in the *Companion*). It specifically mentioned using 14th and 24th Panzer Divisions, one infantry division, and strong antitank forces to screen the left flank of Sixth Army and protect the army's supply routes to the west.[41]

Throughout the day on 19 November, even before receiving the army group's order, staff officers in Sixth Army's headquarters appeared to be troubled by the unusually violent Soviet offensive. As early as 0830 on the 19th, for example, Paulus began discussing the situation with General Arthur Schmidt, his chief of staff, and the Ia of XIV Panzer Corps. He asked their opinion about assembling mobile forces to head west and hold the main line of communications extending westward through Kalinovka and Kalach to the Chir River region. Although the panzer corps anticipated problems disengaging from Stalingrad city, it agreed to send 16th and 24th Panzer Divisions, Panzer *Jäg. Abteilungen* (Detachments) 295 and 389, and 244th Assault Gun Battalion westward on a schedule to be worked out later in the day. At the same time, they also alerted ARKO (Artillery Command) 129 and various supply and alarm units, plus *Flak* (antiaircraft) *Kampfgruppe* Selle (91st *Flak*) along the main supply route to the west. At 1100 hours, they ordered 403rd Security Division's 354th Grenadier Regiment to move northward from the Morozovskii region to the railroad line along the Chir River, paying particular attention to the Surovikino sector.[42]

At around 1700 hours, Colonel Wilhelm Adam, Paulus's adjutant, reported that he saw only one solution to the problem: a withdrawal of the army to the southwest.[43] However, Paulus refused to even consider violating Hitler's orders. During the early evening of 19 November, even more alarming reports arrived at Sixth Army's headquarters. First, 14th Panzer Division, whose lead elements were already heading into the Verkhne-Buzinovka region, reported that Russian tanks and cavalry had penetrated up to 30 kilometers deep into the rear of Sixth Army. This was confirmed by a report from XI Army Corps that Russian armor had struck Romanian forces south of Kletskaia, forcing them to give way, and that German rear service units in the region were beginning to panic.

Later in the evening, Paulus received an order from Weichs at Army Group B to halt all attacks in Stalingrad and dispatch XIV Panzer Corps, with four divisions, out of the city to protect the army's threatened left flank. The Sixth Army commander then met with key members of his staff to discuss how to handle the situation.[44] At this meeting, his chief of staff,

General Schmidt, presented Paulus with a set of proposals that had already been coordinated with other senior staff officers (see appendix 5D in the *Companion*). Among other things, Schmidt recommended sending XIV Panzer Corps, with the panzer regiments of 16th and 24th Panzer Divisions, to the Don River front "by forced march." Once in position, they were to join 14th Panzer Division in an attack northwestward from the heights west of Golubinskii against the flank of Red Army forces advancing to the south to destroy them. General Paulus reportedly approved these recommendations and issued the appropriate orders.[45] As the Russian historian Samsonov appropriately noted, "Witnesses familiar with these [proposals] confirmed our conclusions that if the command of Sixth Army had a notion about the counteroffensive prepared by Soviet forces, then it bore only a general nature; they were informed neither about the precise axes of the attack nor, especially, about its date."[46]

Ultimately, during the late evening of 19 November, on Army Group B's instructions, Sixth Army ordered 14th Panzer Division to concentrate on the left flank of XI Army Corps' 376th Infantry Division, in positions centered on Verkhne-Buzinovka, and to extend its control northward to southeast of Kletskaia. In addition, 177th Assault Gun Battalion was to move northward to support VIII Army Corps, and XIV Panzer Corps headquarters and 24th and 16th Panzer Divisions were to block any Soviet approach to the Don River at Kalach by deploying westward into the Great Bend of the Don on 14th Panzer Division's left (southern) flank. The 24th Panzer Division was to deploy into positions in the Suchanowskij [Sukhanovskii] and Jerusslanowskij [Eruslanovskii] regions, and 16th Panzer Division was to position itself in the Lipo-Losowskij [Lipo-Logovskii] region. All these forces were to deploy westward in three increments according to a precise schedule from 0800 hours on 20 November through 21 November (see appendix 5E in the *Companion*).[47]

This series of decisions meant there was no possibility of continuing Operation Schwerin, the assault by LI Corps' 79th Infantry Division and supporting engineer battalions against the Krasnyi Oktiabr' Factory in Stalingrad city. Recognizing this reality, at 2205 hours, Sixth Army's LI Army Corps issued Corps Order [*Korpsbefehl*] No. 116, which ended the operation, dispatched forces to the west, and reorganized the corps' forces (see appendix 5F in the *Companion*).[48]

General Seydlitz at LI Army Corps reported back to Sixth Army at 2245 hours: "The assault actions in Stalingrad—apart from the storm troop operations east of the gun factory—are suspended with immediate effect. LI Army Corps will immediately withdraw 14th and 24th Panzer Divisions and 244th Assault Gun *Abteilung* and set them in march in the direction of the Don River bridge at Luchinskoi."[49]

However, by the time Army Group B and Sixth Army changed their minds and shifted their attention to the crisis on Sixth Army's left flank, it was too late. As Major General Hans Dörr correctly noted, "After 19 November the weak attempts to launch counterattacks were stopped by the enemy and the path to distant objectives was opened."[50] This reality was confirmed when the Stalingrad Front began its offensive on the morning of 20 November.

Conclusions

Virtually all Soviet critiques of Uranus acknowledge that Vatutin's Southwestern Front failed to accomplish its assigned missions on 19 November and, in fact, fell well short of fulfilling the demanding requirements of the *Stavka's* plan. Although 5th Tank and 21st Armies managed to tear large holes through Romanian Third Army's forward defenses, only 21st Army was able to project mobile forces into the operational depths. These exploitation forces amounted to just two of 4th Tank Corps' three tank brigades. Based on past experience, this force would have become cannon fodder for the Germans if they could have generated panzer reserves of their own. The problem for German Sixth Army was that it lacked serious panzer forces in reserve and, in fact, lacked credible operational reserves of any size. Thus, the Soviets were able to take advantage of the time necessary for Sixth Army to locate and redeploy panzer and mechanized forces from the vicinity of Stalingrad city to develop their exploitation.

Despite the conflicting orders it received, Romanian Third Army's reserve, Heim's XXXXVIII Panzer Corps, placed sufficient forces in the path of 5th Tank Army's two tank corps to disrupt the tempo of their advance. Coupled with stubborn resistance by outgunned Romanian infantry, XXXXVIII Panzer Corp's three divisions were able to halt the two tank corps in the shallow operational depths, thereby turning a clean exploitation into a complex and time-consuming meeting engagement. Likewise, in the Kletskaia region, a stout forward defense by Romanian infantry and cavalry, coupled with the timely commitment of Romanian 15th Infantry Division in reserve, contained 21st and 65th Armies' rifle forces and cavalry in the tactical depths. Therefore, the Red Army General Staff obscured actual developments by recording in its daily summaries that this or that force was only "operating in accordance with the plan."

Based on what occurred on 19 November, the die was now cast for the series of complex battles that took place on 20 and 21 November in the broad belt of territory between the southern edges of the former Serafimovich and Kletskaia bridgeheads southward to the Chir and Don Rivers between the towns of Oblivskaia on the former and Kalach-on-the-Don on the latter. This fight pitted the assembling troops of XXXXVIII Panzer Corps, together with the remnants of Romanian Third Army, against 5th Tank Army's advancing riflemen, 8th Cavalry Corps, and 1st Tank Corps in the region west of Perelazovskii and the exploiting forces of 5th Tank Army's 26th Tank Corps and 21st Army's 4th Tank Corps and 3rd Guards Cavalry Corps in the broad corridor from the Manoilin and Verkhne-Buzinovka region southward to the Don River at and north of Kalach.

At stake in this series of swirling battles was the fate of German Sixth Army, which would face encirclement if the attacking Soviet tank and cavalry forces managed to punch sufficient mobile forces forward to the Don River at Kalach and beyond.

20 November

> The Southwestern Front and the Don Front's right wing began their attack on 19 November, and the Stalingrad Front went over to the attack on 20 November.
>
> In two days of fighting, the shock groups of the Southwestern and Don Fronts, attacking southward from Serafimovich and Kletskaia, destroyed three enemy infantry divisions and advanced 20–22 kilometers and up to 30 kilometers along individual axes, while doing so seizing more than 2,000 prisoners, 205 guns, and a significant amount of other military equipment.
>
> Southwestern Front defended its right-wing positions and fulfilled missions in accordance with the plan in its center and its left wing.
>
> Don Front, on 20 November, fulfilled missions in accordance with the plan with its right wing and defended its positions and conducted combat reconnaissance in its center and on its left wing.
>
> The enemy displayed no activity, [although] his aircraft conducted reconnaissance flights.
>
> Red Army General Staff Operational Summary,
> 0800 hours on 21 November 1942[51]

As indicated by the Red Army General Staff's daily operational summary, Stalin and the *Stavka* had lingering doubts about the ultimate outcome of Operation Uranus. Consequently, the General Staff limited itself to simply mentioning the Southwestern and Don Fronts' initial success and the fact that the Stalingrad Front had joined the counteroffensive. It left the details to the reader's imagination.

The Southwestern and Don Fronts' Missions

Overnight on 19–20 November, Vatutin and Rokossovsky, after consulting with the commanders of their subordinate armies, formulated new missions for them to accomplish on 20 November. Given that the attacking forces' progress on 19 November fell well short of what the Uranus plan required, these missions were quite straightforward. In essence, they required 5th

Tank and 21st Armies, supported on the left by the Don Front's 65th Army, to persevere in pursuit of their previously assigned missions (see appendix 5G in the *Companion*).

In brief, these missions required the rifle forces of 5th Tank and 21st Armies to encircle the bulk of Romanian Third Army's IV and V Army Corps in the region southwest of Raspopinskaia and clear Third Army's remnants and the forces of German XXXXVIII Panzer Corps out of the Karasev, Ust'-Medveditskii, and Peschanyi regions, the Tsaritsa River valley north of Perelazovskii, and the region from Kletskaia southward to the Kurtlak River. Thereafter, these forces were to advance westward to the Krivaia River and southward to the Kurtlak River line from the Chernyshevskaia region eastward to Platonov. At the same time, the mobile forces of the two armies were to conduct their exploitation southeastward to encircle German Sixth Army. In 5th Tank Army's sector, Borisov's and Butkov's 8th Cavalry and 1st Tank Corps were to assist the army's rifle divisions as they pushed XXXX-VIII Panzer Corps south toward the Chernyshevskaia region and the lower Kurtlak River, while Rodin's 26th Tank Corps, after demolishing the Romanian strongpoints blocking its advance southeast of Klinovoi, was to advance southward to capture Perelazovskii. In 21st Army's sector, Kravchenko's 4th Tank Corps was to thrust forward to the Don River north of Kalach, while Pliev's 3rd Guards Cavalry Corps and follow-on rifle divisions were to assault German XI Army Corps in the Verkhne-Buzinovka region and protect 4th Tank Corps' ever-lengthening left flank.

German Defensive Measures
As Vatutin and Rokossovsky formulated their plans, Axis commanders struggled frantically first to comprehend and then to stabilize the situation. At 0055 hours, Sixth Army continued to shift its forces when the army's Ia notified XI Army Corps, "*Sturmgeschutz Abteilung* [Assault Gun Battalion] 177 is going to XI AC via Werchnjaja-Businowka [Verkhniaia Buzinovka]."[52] At 0200 hours, the German liaison staff at Romanian V Army Corps sent a radio transmission to 14th Panzer Division, whose forces were closing into the rear of XI Army Corps, stating, "14th PzD and all are east of the Jewstaratowskij-Kletskaja line, with the mass of the group subordinate to AOK 6 immediately."[53] Fifteen minutes later, the German liaison staff with V Army Corps sent another brief message to Sixth Army, notifying it that "the Russians are in Gromki. Tanks have broken through to Kalmykoff [Kalmykovskii, 11 kilometers west of Manoilin]. The front of Romanian V AC is holding."[54] During this period, Army Group B attached Romanian 9th Infantry Division to Romanian I Army Corps and assigned Romanian I and II Army Corps to German XVII Army Corps, commanded by General Karl Hollidt, which was just then advancing eastward from Italian Eighth Army's rear to join the battle.[55]

As dawn broke on the morning of the 20th, Sixth Army began receiving situation reports from its corps that clarified the situation a bit. For example, at 0600 hours, XI Army Corps reported that the usual disruptive artillery fire had occurred opposite 384th and 44th Infantry Division's fronts, and it had scheduled the relief of 44th Infantry Division's 132nd Grenadier Regiment so that it could be transferred westward to reinforce 14th Panzer Division's forces in the Verkhne-Buzinovka region later in the day.[56] On the corps' threatened left wing, Romanian 1st Cavalry Division's 12th Regiment was holding on to its positions southwest of Logovskii, but groups of enemy cavalry with 15 tanks were noted west of Selivanov in the Kurtlak valley, and other groups were seen heading southward across the open country toward Manoilin.[57]

Meanwhile, 14th Panzer Division's lead forces had reached Verkhne-Buzinovka and were trying to hold that sector northward to Romanian 12th Cavalry Regiment's defenses southwest of Logovskii, in the hope that 44th Infantry's 132nd Regiment could reach and stabilize the defenses on the corps' left flank. Coincidentally, 376th Infantry Division reported that it had suffered 30 casualties. In addition, at 0715 hours, the German liaison team with Romanian IV Army Corps reported that Russian tanks in the Kalmykovskii region, along the Krepkaia River, had advanced to within 15 kilometers of Perelazovskii.[58] This most likely referred to one of 4th Tank Corps' two forward tank brigades.

Finally, at 0750 hours, Sixth Army dispatched a report to Army Group B summarizing the situation as of that time. It reported strong artillery fire and infantry assaults against 376th Infantry Division's left wing southeast of Kletskaia and heavy attacks by Russian tanks and cavalry in the Logovskii and Platonov line, with large Russian forces heading southward across the Kurtlak River region toward Manoilin. The report identified a combat group with one cavalry regiment, an artillery battery, and tanks west of Verkhne-Buzinovka and other Russian detachments west of a security line established by XI Army Corps along the Jerik (Erik) and Roshko line southwest of Verkhne-Buzinovka. After describing the weather as 0 degrees with light snowfall and icy conditions, it informed the army group that, in accordance with orders it had issued the night before, additional forces were en route from Stalingrad to the threatened region (see appendix 5H in the *Companion*).[59] These forces included elements of 14th and 24th Panzer Divisions, plus 295th and 389th Antitank [*Pz. Jäg. Abt.*] and 244th Assault Gun Battalions.

As the report indicated, Sixth Army, which had only fragmentary information at its disposal, was not yet fully aware of the size of the Soviet force heading into its rear area. Nor were the measures it took to move forces westward commensurate with the scale of the Soviet threat. As the morning progressed, new and more frightening information arrived at Sixth Army's headquarters, prompting it to take further actions to shore up its sagging left flank. At 0945 hours, for example, on Paulus's instructions, Seydlitz at LI Army Corps notified its subordinate Group Schwerin (79th Infantry Division):

> While firmly holding the previous front-line, the following will be withdrawn as quickly as possible and set in march:
> 1) From Group Schwerin: a) Group Seydel of 14th Panzer Division. The previously withdrawn elements will move off on 20 November. b) Group Scheele of 24th Panzer Division. With that, Group Schwerin is disbanded.
> 2) From 305th Infantry Division: the heavy infantry guns of 14th Panzer Division will be sent to 14th Panzer Division without delay.
> 3) From 389th Infantry Division: 244th Assault Gun *Abteilung* to Luchinskoi during the course of 20 November. The assault company of 24th Panzer Division is to be speedily supplied to Group Scheel.[60]

5th Tank Army's Advance
If the *Stavka* hoped the Southwestern Front's 5th Tank and 21st Armies could finally overwhelm Romanian Third Army's defenses and push its forces, as well as those of XXXXVIII Panzer Corps, southward to the Chir and Don Rivers, it was badly mistaken (see map 15). Since 5th Tank Army's immediate aim was to reach the rivers as quickly as possible, its exploitation echelon (mobile group)—specifically, 1st and 26th Tank Corps and 8th Cavalry Corps—would play the most important role in the fighting on 20 November. Here, however, Romanenko's mobile forces achieved only mixed results at best. While Butkov's 1st Tank Corps and Borisov's 8th Cavalry Corps remained tied down in a messy meeting engagement in the Peschanyi and Ust'-Medveditskii region that would endure through 24 November, Rodin's 26th Tank Corps broke through the remainder of Romanian Third Army's defenses, only to spend the entire day in a prolonged effort to seize the key road junction at Perelazovskii.

Beginning at dawn, 1st Tank Corps, now fighting alongside 8th Cavalry Corps' 55th and 112th Cavalry Divisions and the dismounted 8th Motorcycle Regiment, fought with the remnants of Romanian 14th Infantry Division and tanks and motorized infantry of XXXXVIII Panzer Corps' 22nd Panzer Division in the Ust'-Medveditskii State Farm and Peschanyi region, 18 to 22 kilometers northwest of Perelazovskii. This fight still took the form of a meeting engagement, because 22nd Panzer's forces continued to filter into the region from the south and southeast. By this time, the division's armor, still amounting to about 30 tanks in 204th Panzer Regiment, was formed in a single *kampfgruppe* led by Colonel von Oppeln-Bronowski.[61] Oppeln's group

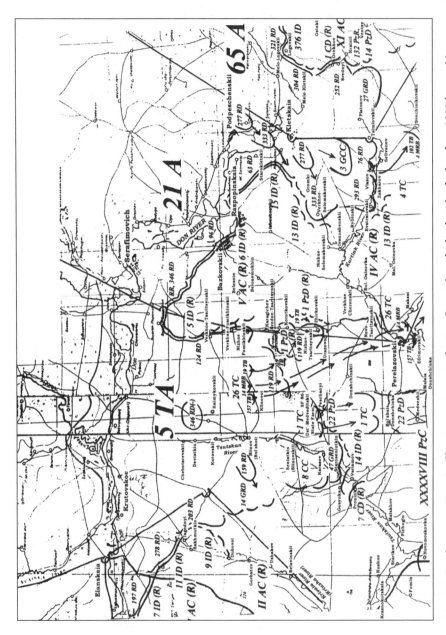

Map 15. Southwestern Front's offensive: situation in the Serafimovich and Kletskaia bridgeheads at 2200 hours, 20 November 1942

was supported by the division's antitank *Abteilung*, 1st Battalion, 129th Panzer Grenadier Regiment, and a few batteries of artillery.

During the first half of the day on 20 November, Butkov's tank corps, which was cooperating with 8th Cavalry Corps' 55th and 112th Cavalry Divisions operating in the Staro-Seniutkin and Karasev region on the tank corps' right flank, attacked southward with its 89th, 159th, and 117th Tank Brigades. The corps managed to advance 2 kilometers and captured most of Ust'-Medveditskii Farm by noon. However, Butkov's tanks were abruptly halted by new defenses thrown up by elements of 22nd Panzer Division several kilometers south of the state farm. Impatient with the forward progress of 1st Tank Corps, at 1300 hours, General Romanenko ordered Butkov to turn his sector over to 55th and 112th Cavalry Divisions of Borisov's 8th Cavalry Corps, bypass Peschanyi by marching southward to its east, and then thrust southward to reach its objectives along and south of the Kurtlak River, 30 kilometers south of Peschanyi. In spite of the problems it experienced trying to disengage from 22nd Panzer Division's hedgehog defense, the tank corps succeeded in turning its positions over to 8th Cavalry Corps' two divisions by 1800 hours. It then refueled its tanks and moved southward in a single column of brigades, reaching Separate Ust'-Medveditskii State Farm No. 3 and the villages of Malaia Donshchinka and Bol'shaia Donshchinka, 10 kilometers west and 10 kilometers southwest of Perelazovskii, respectively, by 2130 hours. Even so, the forces on the corps' right wing failed to break contact with 22nd Panzer Division.[62] At nightfall, 22nd Panzer Division reported it was still defending against Soviet armored forces along "a line from Bol. Donschtschinka–Hill 191.2."[63]

The final element of 5th Tank Army's mobile exploitation force was 8th Motorcycle Regiment, which Romanenko had subordinated to 1st Tank Corps' control for the first 24 hours of the counteroffensive. Although this regiment fought dismounted in the Peschanyi region during the first half of 20 November, in the afternoon, Romanenko ordered Butkov to dispatch it eastward because of the threat posed by a possible breakout by Romanian forces encircled in the Raspopinskaia region. Butkov responded by directing the motorcycle regiment to concentrate its main forces in the Separate Farm No. 3 and Ust'-Medveditskii State Farm region and to send one motorcycle and one armored car company, three tanks, and an antitank battery eastward to the Zhirkovskii region to support the army's rifle divisions as they encircled Romanian forces south of Raspopinskaia.[64]

While 1st Tank Corps was trying in vain to bypass the dug-in 22nd Panzer Division, General Rodin's 26th Tank Corps was achieving far greater success in its sector. Rodin's orders from 5th Tank Army required his corps' 157th Tank Brigade and several battalions of 14th Motorized Rifle Brigade, supported by riflemen from 119th Rifle Division, to overcome or bypass

Romanian strongpoints and other obstacles to his front and on his left flank, attack into the depths to strike the enemy's flanks and rear, and capture the towns of Zhirkovskii and Perelazovskii. At the time, 216th and 19th Tank Brigades of Rodin's tank corps were occupied supporting 5th Tank Army's 50th Guards Rifle Division and the left-wing regiment of 119th Rifle Division as they fought to contain Romanian forces (5th Infantry and 1st Armored Divisions) being encircled east of the Tsaritsa River, on 5th Tank Army's left wing.

After capturing State Farm No. 86, Separate Farm No. 3, and Ust'-Medveditskii State Farm overnight on 19–20 November, 26th Tank Corps' 157th Tank Brigade, now commanded by Major P. S. Makhur, was joined by two battalions of the corps approaching 14th Motorized Rifle Brigade at 0200 hours on 20 November. The third battalion of 14th Motorized Brigade was still supporting the corps' 19th Tank Brigade to the north. With infantry now available to protect it, Makhur's tank brigade raced southeastward, destroying small bands of Romanian forces as it advanced. The brigade task force captured the town of Novo-Tsaritsynskii, 7 kilometers north of Perelazovskii, at dawn by attacking it from the march. Leaving one of 14th Motorized Brigade's battalions to defend the town, Makhur's tanks and remaining motorized riflemen surged southward and attacked Perelazovskii later in the morning, with the tanks assaulting the town from the north and west and the attached motorized riflemen doing so from the east. In the process, the Soviet task force destroyed the headquarters of Romanian V Army Corps and captured most of its staff along with "mountains" of documents. The Soviet attack was so sudden that a German liaison officer who was supposed to report to the headquarters of Romanian V Army Corps showed up and was captured at the headquarters of 26th Tank Corps, which had set up operations in the town at about noon on the 20th.[65] During the fight for Perelazovskii, in addition to capturing V Army Corps' headquarters, the Soviets claimed they destroyed 8 Romanian tanks, captured more than 1,270 Romanian troops and 155 horses, seized 3 inoperable Romanian aircraft (destroying 2) at a nearby airstrip, and captured 8 warehouses with a considerable amount of ammunition and other military equipment.[66]

With Perelazovskii in Soviet hands, Makhur's tank brigade moved 3 kilometers south, approaching the town of Efremovskii on the Kurtlak River at 1600 hours and capturing it two hours later from its Romanian defenders. The brigade then formed an all-round defense at the town while awaiting the arrival of 26th Tank Corps' remaining brigades. The successful capture of Novo-Tsaritsynskii and Perelazovskii also destroyed the rear services of Romanian 1st Armored Division and left General Gheorghe's division isolated in the region northwest of Zhirkovskii and east of the Tsaritsa River.

Meanwhile, north along the Tsaritsa River from Perelazovskii, Colonel Filippenko's 19th Tank Brigade, with one battalion of 14th Motorized Rifle

Brigade, supported 119th Rifle Division's fight for Hill 208.0 (6 kilometers west of Korotkovskii). After seizing the hill, it pushed eastward to reach the west bank of the Tsaritsa River in the sector encompassing Zhirkovskii northward to Korotkovskii, 17 to 23 kilometers north of Perelazovskii. After repulsing attempts by Romanian 1st Armored Division and the remnants of Romanian 14th Infantry Division to attack northwestward from Hill 208.0 toward Blinovskii (supposedly to link up with 22nd Panzer Division's forces advancing toward the north), the Soviet *tankists* and riflemen pushed farther eastward, isolating part of the Romanian armored division in the region northwest of Zhirkovskii and reaching the western bank of the Tsaritsa River. Of course, because they were pinned down in the Peschanyi region, 22nd Panzer Division's forces could not carry out their part of the plan. As a result, General Gheorghe withdrew eastward, consolidated his remaining armor, and drew up plans to escape toward the southwest. After clearing Romanian forces from the region west of the Tsaritsa River, Filippenko's tank brigade and supporting battalion of 14th Motorized Rifle Brigade wheeled southward to link up with 26th Tank Corps' headquarters and main forces at Perelazovskii on the morning of 21 November.

As 157th Tank and 14th Motorized Rifle Brigades of Rodin's 26th Tank Corps were capturing Perelazovskii, the corps' 216th Tank Brigade and 50th Guards Rifle Division, operating on 5th Tank Army's extreme left wing, continued to attack Romanian Third Army's forces defending along the Tsaritsa River line. Their intent was to drive these forces back from the river into the group of Romanian forces forming south of Raspopinskaia. Ultimately, they sought to encircle this entire force by linking up with 21st Army's 277th and 333rd Rifle Divisions, which were advancing westward along and north of the Kurtlak River from the Kletskaia region.

Since 5th Tank Army's forces had overrun and destroyed the headquarters of Romanian 13th and 14th Infantry Divisions on 19 November and then either cut off or scattered the headquarters of Romanian II, IV, and V Army Corps by the morning of the 20th, only one major command and control element in Romanian Third Army remained intact: the headquarters of Romanian I Corps, situated in the town of Bokovskaia on the Chir River, 55 kilometers west of Perelazovskii. Early on 20 November, General Mihail Lascar, commander of Romanian 6th Infantry Division, took the initiative and assumed control over all the Romanian forces that had become increasingly isolated in the region south of Raspopinskaia. Lascar's group consisted of Romanian 5th, 6th, and 15th Infantry Divisions, a composite group formed from the remnants of 13th and 14th Infantry Divisions, and the remains of Group Voicu.[67] The newly formed Group Lascar controlled the region bounded on the west by the Tsaritsa River from Verkhne-Fomikhinskii southward to Novo-Tsaritsynskii, 10 kilometers south of Zhirkovskii; on the north and northeast by the high ground south of the Don River from south of Serafimovich southeastward through Raspopinskaia to the region west of Gromki, 15 kilometers west of Kletskaia; and on the southeast and south by the Kurtlak River from Verkhne- and Nizhne-Solomakovskii and west to the Tsaritsa River near Zhirkovskii.

The brief but heated fight along and west of the Tsaritsa River reportedly cost Gheorghe's 1st Armored Division 25 of its tanks, including 5 R-2s due to mechanical failure and at least 4 German tanks and 14 R-2s knocked out. Romanian forces claimed they destroyed 62 Soviet tanks and 61 motor vehicles and captured 332 Soviet troops, but these figures seem excessive, given the size of the attacking Soviet force.[68] As for 22nd Panzer Division, although its losses are unknown, its tank strength must have dwindled to fewer than 20 tanks, forcing the division to rely on its infantrymen, artillery, and remaining troop carriers. By this time, its stout defense, together with the remnants of Romanian 14th Infantry Division, had probably destroyed or disabled up to 50 of 1st Tank Corps' tanks.

Romanian critiques of the fighting take solace in the fact that XXXXVIII Panzer Corps' forces tied down three of the six brigades subordinate to 5th Tank Army's two tank corps, and Romanian 1st Armored Division, together with the remains of 14th and 5th Infantry Divisions, tied down two more. Actually, the Germans and Romanians disabled six of seven tank brigades, since 8th Guards Tank Brigade was also involved in the battle for the Peschanyi region. This left just 26th Tank Corps' 157th Tank and 14th Motorized Brigades to conduct the "deep operations" Romanenko assigned his mobile forces on the morning of 20 November.[69]

Soviet critiques were even harsher than Romanian assessments of the day's action. First, they chastised Butkov's 1st Tank Corps for becoming decisively engaged in the Peschanyi region:

> The main reason for 1st Tank Corps' lack of success on 20 November was that, instead of enveloping it, it became engaged in a prolonged battle with the German 22nd Panzer Division in the Ust'-Medveditskii region. In order to have information about the enemy at one's disposal and, first and foremost, about the presence of open flanks and unprotected gaps in his defense, it is necessary to conduct constant reconnaissance, maintain communications with one's neighbors, and know their positions. Weak reconnaissance, the absence of communications of 1st Tank Corps with 26th Tank Corps' 157th Tank Brigade, and the lack of knowledge about its success were the chief reasons why 1st Tank Corps became decisively engaged in the Ust'-Medveditskii region instead of enveloping it.[70]

Nor did 26th Tank Corps escape criticism. In the words of another Soviet after-action critique, "The 26th Tank Corps spent the entire day clearing the enemy out of the Perelazovskii region and fighting with the Romanian 1st Armored Division, in spite of the fact that, by exploiting the delay in the movement of our forces, the Romanian divisions could have escaped from under the blows of 21st Army by moving south."[71]

As 5th Tank Army's mobile forces struggled to free themselves from the stubbornly defending Romanian and German forces west of Perelazovskii and begin their exploitation into the operational depths, Vatutin goaded the tank army's rifle and cavalry forces to move quickly to encircle and liquidate bypassed Romanian forces and push forward to the Krivaia and Chir Rivers. On the army's left wing, 119th Rifle Division, flanked on the left by 50th Guards Rifle Division with 26th Tank Corps' 216th and 19th Tank Brigades in support, wheeled eastward and reached the Tsaritsa River from Novo-Tsaritsynskii, 10 kilometers south of Zhirkovskii, to Verkhne-Fomikhinskii, 12 kilometers north of Korotkovskii, by 1200 hours on 20 November. They pressed the right-wing regiment of Romanian 14th Infantry Division, now supported by Gheorghe's 1st Armored Division and all of Romanian 5th Infantry Division, eastward across the Tsaritsa River and into an emerging encirclement sack. Continuing their assaults eastward and southeastward in the afternoon, the two rifle divisions faced near-constant counterattacks and probes by Romanian 1st Armored and a composite regiment made up of remnants of 6th and 13th Infantry Divisions, as the encircled Romanians tried in vain to find an escape route to the southwest. About 35 kilometers to the east, 21st Army's 63rd, 333rd, and reinforcing 277th Rifle Divisions exploited 4th Tank Corps' success by wheeling westward and advancing 2 to 12 kilometers toward Izbushenskii and Nizhne-Solomakovskii. The twin pincers of 5th Tank Army's rifle divisions pushing from the west and 21st Army's rifle divisions driving from the east threatened Group Lascar with encirclement and destruction.

Meanwhile, in 5th Tank Army's center, 47th Guards Rifle Division, supported by 8th Guards Tank Brigade, advanced slowly southwestward along the Tsutskan' River from the village of Karasev, surprised the lead regiment of Romanian 7th Cavalry Division, and captured the villages of Varlamov and Pronin No. 2, 6 and 9 kilometers south-southwest of Karasev, respectively. The riflemen and tanks struck the Romanian cavalry in the early afternoon, just as they were deploying for an advance northeast toward the Staro-Seniutkin region. Caught flatfooted by an assault by the tank brigade's heavy tanks, the Romanians broke and ran. According to 47th Guards Rifle Division, the Romanian cavalry left up to 3,000 dead on the battlefield and lost up to 700 prisoners and 12 guns. Thoroughly worn out by the fighting, 7th Cavalry Division fell back toward Staryi Pronin at the end of the day and then to

Chernyshevskaia on the Chir River on 21 November. The 47th Guards' advance also forced Romanian II Army Corps to abandon its headquarters near Pronin.

While 47th Guards Division was seizing Pronin and advancing southwest toward Chernyshevskaia, the divisions on 5th Tank Army's right wing ended the stalemate on their front by forcing the remnants of Romanian 14th Infantry Division's left wing and Romanian I Army Corps' relatively fresh 9th Infantry Division to grudgingly withdraw southwest toward the Krivaia River. Reinforced at midday by 159th Rifle Division from the tank army's second echelon, 14th Guards Rifle, with 8th Cavalry Corps' 21st Cavalry Division on its left, forced Romanian 9th Infantry Division and a reinforcing regiment from 7th Cavalry Division to withdraw to a new defensive line extending from Hill 212, 14 kilometers southwest of Bol'shoi; through Frunze State Farm No. 2, 10 kilometers west of Blinovskii; to the village of Gusynka, 5 kilometers west of Karasev. Early the next morning, pursued by Soviet tanks and infantry, the remnants of the Romanian force withdrew behind the Chir River west of Illarionov.

21st Army's Advance
When his 21st Army resumed operations early on 20 November, General Chistiakov's principal concern was to eliminate the obvious imbalances in his army's progress the previous day (see map 15). Half of Kravchenko's 4th Tank Corps was overextended in the Manoilin region, 35 kilometers south of Kletskaia, and the other half, along with Pliev's 3rd Guards Cavalry Corps and most of 21st Army's supporting rifle divisions, was still in the Evstratovskii and Platonov sector along the Kurtlak River, lagging far behind. If his army's mobile forces were to fulfill their mission of reaching the Don River, they somehow had to break the logjam south of Kletskaia before the Germans mounted some sort of counterstroke to pinch off his army's penetration. Chistiakov realized that the lead elements of German 14th Panzer Division were already in the Verkhne-Buzinovka region. He also knew from experience that even though Sixth Army's other panzer divisions, 16th and 24th, were in Stalingrad, they might suddenly appear in the Kletskaia sector. Therefore, Chistiakov goaded and cajoled his subordinates to finish the job correctly and fast.

As a seasoned veteran of many tank battles, General Kravchenko of 4th Tank Corps shared Chistiakov's fears. Therefore, he sought to consolidate his tank corps' brigades as far forward as possible and then launch them on a precipitous march toward the Don River north of Kalach. On the morning on 20 November, 4th Tank Corps' 69th and 45th Tank Brigades were reconnoitering southward from Manoilin and the First of May State Farm on the Krepkaia River. However, 25 kilometers to the rear, the corps' 102nd Tank and 4th Motorized Rifle Brigades were fighting alongside 21st Army's 76th and 293rd Rifle Divisions, still trying to dislodge Romanian IV Army Corps' 15th Infantry and 1st Cavalry Divisions from their defenses at Gromki and along the Kurtlak River from Evstratovskii eastward to Platonov. Thus, minus those two brigades of 4th Tank Corps, 21st Army's entire shock group was boxed in along and north of the Kurtlak River. In addition to 293rd and 76th Rifle Divisions, this included 277th and 333rd Rifle Divisions, moving forward from the second echelon to reinforce 293rd Rifle Division, and Pliev's 3rd Guards Cavalry Corps, already fighting in support of 76th Rifle Division.[72]

During the day, 76th Rifle Division—supported by 4th Tank Corps' 4th Motorized Rifle Brigade and 3rd Guards Cavalry Corps' three divisions, and with 65th Army's 27th Guards Rifle Division on its left—assaulted Romanian 1st Cavalry Division's defenses south of Platonov, which by now had been reinforced by a small *kampfgruppe* from German 14th Panzer Division. After hours of intense fighting, the attackers finally dislodged the defenders, forcing them to withdraw to new defensive positions to the southeast. Farther west, in the sector from Evstratovskii on the Kurtlak River northward to Gromki, 293rd Rifle Division—supported by 4th Tank Corps' 102nd Tank Brigade and the reinforcing 333rd Rifle Division, and with 63rd Rifle Division on its right—attacked Romanian 15th Infantry Division's defenses with two battalions of infantry and 35 to 40 T-34 tanks. After repelling several Soviet attacks, during which it reported destroying 5 tanks and capturing 45 Soviet prisoners, 15th Division had no choice but to abandon Gromki and withdraw westward to new defenses on the right flank of Group Lascar.[73]

Immediately after penetrating the Romanians' defenses, Colonel Koshelev's 102nd Tank Brigade raced southward to the vicinity of Maiorovskii Farm on the Krepkaia River, 30 kilometers south of Kletskaia, where it linked up with detachments from 69th and 45th Tank Brigades, whose main forces were still in the Manoilin region, 8 kilometers to the southwest. As Kravchenko consolidated 4th Tank Corps for its exploitation to the Don, Lieutenant Colonel Zhidkov's 45th Tank Brigade marched west and overran Romanian IV Army Corps' headquarters at Kalmykovskii (Kalmykov), 10 kilometers west of Manoilin. Later in the day, 4th Motorized Rifle Brigade also broke loose from the stalemate south of the Kurtlak River and rejoined its parent corps in the Maiorovskii region.

Roughly 30 kilometers to 4th Tank Corps' rear, Romanian 1st Cavalry Division, reinforced by the Voicu Detachment, conducted a mounted sortie southwestward between the Kurtlak and Krepkaia Rivers in an attempt to reestablish links with Romanian Third Army. However, this effort failed when the attackers were repulsed by Soviet cavalry, supposedly from 3rd Guards Cavalry Corps' 5th Guards Cavalry Division. Thereafter, the Romanian cavalry "fell back in confusion," burning the four remaining R-1 tanks belonging to the attached 1st Mechanized Squadron as it retired eastward. The Romanian Voicu Detachment, with a regiment from 15th Infantry Division, the remnants of 13th Infantry Division, and motorized 100mm howitzers from 1st Armored Division, also withdrew eastward to occupy defenses on the left flank of German XI Army Corps' 376th Infantry Division.[74]

During 21st Army's assault on the Romanian defenses along and south of the Kurtlak River, Pliev's 3rd Guards Cavalry Corps finally joined the exploitation. At 0700 hours, Colonel Chepurkin's 5th Guards Cavalry Division attacked and seized the Romanian strongpoints along the river at Selivanov and Vlasov and began its southward exploitation. At about 0800 hours, 5th Division's cavalrymen encountered and defeated a force of Romanian infantry, cavalry, and 30 tanks that attacked its left flank and center from positions 1.5 kilometers south of Vlasov to Farm No. 1 of State Farm No. 20, about 5 kilometers southeast of Selivanov. Romanian sources identified this force as cavalrymen from Romanian 1st Cavalry Division and infantry and R-1 tanks belonging to the Voicu Detachment and confirmed that it was smashed by 5th Guards Cavalry Division and sent reeling back to the southeast.

Thereafter, as 4th Tank Corps' two lagging brigades raced to rejoin their parent corps, Pliev's 3rd Guards Cavalry Corps turned the Vlasov and Selivanov sector over to 76th Rifle Division and moved southeastward to join 4th Tank Corps' exploitation and protect the tank corps' long left flank. The 5th Guards Cavalry Division resumed its march at 0900 hours, scattering small groups of enemy soldiers as it advanced. After reaching Maiorovskii at 1430 hours, it continued east toward Verkhne-Buzinovka, where it was struck by a counterattacking Romanian cavalry regiment near Checherov *Balka*, 7 kilometers northeast of Maiorovskii. The division's 20th Guards Regiment defeated this small force, reportedly killing 150 Romanians and capturing up to 800 horses.[75] As the cavalry division continued its advance, it was attacked again by an enemy force of 18 tanks from the vicinity of Hill 190.3 and 13 tanks from Hill 207.2, which had apparently been dispatched westward from Verkhne-Buzinovka by German 14th Panzer Division. After repelling both attacks, supposedly "with heavy losses" to the enemy, Chepurkin's division withdrew into Checherov *Balka* to rest and reorganize its forces.

Meanwhile, Colonel Belogorsky's 6th Guards Cavalry Division, cooperating with 76th Rifle Division, captured the Romanian strongpoint at Platonov Farm on the Kurtlak River, just northeast of Platonov, seizing 180 prisoners. Belogorsky's division then joined the corps' 32nd Cavalry Division in a slow but steady advance toward the southeast. Their mission, which Pliev assigned at 1200 hours, was to seize Svechinikovskii, 10 kilometers northwest of Verkhne-Buzinovka, and then join 5th Guards Cavalry Division in an assault on German defenses at Verkhne-Buzinovka proper. Led by forward detachments, the two cavalry divisions pursued enemy forces southeastward and captured Svechinikovskii at 2300 hours. Overnight on 20–21 November, Pliev's three cavalry divisions prepared to attack and seize the German strongpoint at Verkhne-Buzinovka, hoping that doing so would turn German XI Army Corps' left flank and collapse its defenses.

While Kravchenko's 4th Tank Corps and Pliev's 3rd Guards Cavalry Corps were advancing toward Verkhne-Buzinovka en route to the Don River, 21st Army's rifle forces consolidated their hold on the army's penetration sector south of Kletskaia. After clearing Romanian forces from the Kurtlak River valley, 293rd Rifle Division captured Gromki from Romanian 15th Infantry Division, turned its sector over to the reinforcing 333rd Rifle Division, and advanced into the region west of Evstratovskii on the Kurtlak River, 10 kilometers west of Vlasov, by 1600 hours. After joining the battle on 293rd Division's right, 333rd Rifle Division advanced southwestward into the Verkhne-Solomakovskii region, 15 kilometers west-southwest of Kletskaia, by 1600 hours. Together with 63rd Rifle Division on their right, which had pushed forward north of Gromki, 293rd and 333rd Rifle Divisions now represented the eastern pincer encircling Romanian Third Army's Group Lascar.[76]

65th Army's Advance

Though Chistiakov's 21st Army proved successful in expanding its penetration and unleashing its mobile forces on a deep exploitation, General Batov's 65th Army, attacking on the Don Front's right wing and Chistiakov's left, found the going much more troublesome (see map 16). Overnight on 19–20 November, the front lines of Batov's army extended westward 30 kilometers from the southern bank of the Don River just north of Sirotinskaia to the northern approaches to Logovskii, 15 kilometers east of Kletskaia, and then southward 14 kilometers to the western outskirts of Orekhovskii, 15 kilometers southeast of Kletskaia. The defenses in this sector were manned by Sixth Army's XI Army Corps and anchored on the fortified towns of Sirotinskaia, Blizhniaia Perekopka, Osinki, Logovskii, and Orekhovskii. Batov's forces would have to capture one or more of these strongpoints to penetrate XI Corps' tactical defenses.

The 65th Army's attacks on 19 November only managed to dent the German defenses at Logovskii and Orekhovskii, both of which were heavily fortified. Orekhovskii was a particularly "hard nut to crack" because it was protected by high ground dominating its approaches from the north to the southwest. By day's end on the 19th, 21st Army's 76th Rifle Division had captured Hill 207.8, 16 kilometers southwest of Orekhovskii, and Colonel Glebov's 27th Guards Rifle Division, attacking on 65th Army's extreme right wing, had seized Hills 219.3 and 232.2, 12 kilometers southwest and

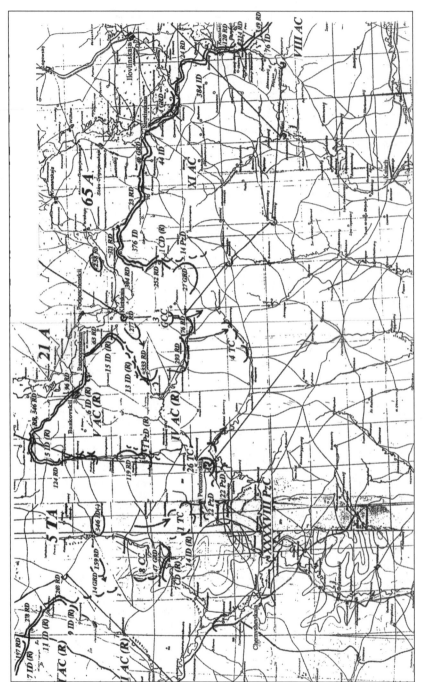

Map 16. Southwestern and Don Fronts' advance at 2200 hours, 20 November 1942

7 kilometers south of Orekhovskii, respectively. On the left of 27th Guards Division, Colonel Merkulov's 304th Rifle Division, supported by Colonel I. I. Iakubovsky's 91st Tank Brigade, had repeatedly attacked Orekhovskii from the northwest and northeast, with only minimal success. However, a single battalion of 304th Division's 807th Regiment, commanded by Major Chebotaev, managed to capture Marker 202.2, situated on the high ground just 2 kilometers west of the town's center.[77]

Overnight on 19–20 November, Batov and his staff worked out a new plan to exploit 807th Regiment's limited success. After a lengthy discussion, they decided to form a mobile group for 65th Army to exploit 304th Division's foothold in Orekhovskii's outer defenses. This group consisted of T-34 and heavy KV tanks from Iakubovsky's 91st Tank Brigade, with submachine gunners riding on their decks, accompanied by four battalions of riflemen loaded in trucks and towed artillery pieces to provide immediate artillery support. To command this group, Batov chose Colonel G. I. Anisimov, a former division commander who had distinguished himself in the fighting for the Erzovka sector. Anisimov's mobile group was to follow the rifle forces developing 807th Regiment's penetration of Orekhovskii's defenses and then exploit as deeply as possible into the Germans' rear area. The group was to advance and first seize Verkhne-Golubaia, 30 kilometers southeast of Orekhovskii, and then seize Akimovskii on the northern bank of the Don River, to the rear of XI Army Corps' forces defending the region due south of Sirotinskaia. The most formidable problem Batov faced in forming this group was withdrawing the necessary tanks from their infantry support role. He did so on the morning of 20 November, and Anisimov's group was prepared for action by early afternoon. By this time, the mobile group also had dedicated support from 16th Air Army and multiple rocket launchers from the army's artillery.

Batov's attack plan required 40th Guards and 23rd Rifle Divisions, deployed in the army's center and on its right wing, to assault Hill 145.0, midway between Blizhniaia Perekopka and Sirotinskaia, and the strongpoint of Osinki, respectively, to draw German attention and reserves away from the army's point of main attack. Simultaneously, Merkulov's 304th Rifle Division was to assault Logovskii and Orekhovskii, with Chebotaev's 807th Regiment spearheading the advance into the latter; Glebov's 27th Guards Rifle Division was to advance eastward from Hills 219 and 232, southwest of Orekhovskii. Batov ordered Colonel Shekhtman's fresh 252nd Rifle Division, which had crossed the Don River into the bridgehead the night before, to enter combat at the boundary between 304th and 27th Guards Divisions when the fighting reached its crescendo. The 252nd Division was to advance along and south of the attack axis of Major Chebotaev's 807th Regiment through Orekhovskii. Anisimov's mobile group, which now numbered about 45 tanks, was to advance through the center of the 252nd's combat formation, quickly penetrate the Romanians' defenses, and begin its exploitation. By this time, the Orekhovskii sector was defended by Romanian 1st Cavalry Division's 1st and 2nd Regiments, stiffened by reinforcements from XI Army Corps' 376th Infantry Division and possibly a few tanks from 14th Panzer Division.

The 65th Army's 304th Rifle and 27th Guards Divisions began their assault shortly after dawn on 20 November and pushed deeply into the Romanians' defenses during several hours of heavy fighting. At about 1000 hours, Colonel Shekhtman's 252nd Rifle Division attacked at the boundary between the two divisions and penetrated the Romanians' first two defensive positions. Anisimov's mobile group went into action shortly after 1200 hours, passed through the advancing infantry, and began its exploitation. Benefiting from shock action and surprise, Anisimov's tanks and infantry advanced 23 kilometers into XI Army Corps' left rear by nightfall on 20 November. Dispersing or destroying small groups of Romanian and German rear service units, Iakubovsky's tanks seized a small enemy airstrip near Os'kinskii, reportedly destroying 42 German aircraft (a woeful exaggeration). Anisimov's accompanying truck-mounted infantry raided into the town of Golubinskaia, near the headquarters of German 44th Infantry Division, sowing panic in the rear area and reportedly capturing a German field hospital. Although the raid produced only short-lived results, together with 4th Tank and 3rd Guards Cavalry Corps' deeper thrust, it helped convince XI Army Corps that its position in the Great Bend of the Don was becoming untenable.[78]

While Colonel Anisimov's mobile group was conducting its deep raid into XI Army Corps' left rear, 65th Army's 252nd Rifle, 27th Guards, and 304th Rifle Divisions advanced southeastward 2 to 4 kilometers against stiffening resistance by Romanian IV Army Corps' 1st Cavalry Division and German XI Army Corps' 376th Infantry Division. By this time, Colonel General Karl Strecker, commander of XI Army Corps, was reinforcing his corps' threatened left flank with 44th Infantry Division's 132nd Regiment and tanks from 14th Panzer Division's stronghold at Verkhne-Buzinovka, 20 kilometers south of Orekhovskii. The divisions of Batov's shock group capitalized on Anisimov's raid the next day by capturing Logovskii, the remainder of Orekhovskii, and Osinki.

1st Guards Army's Attack

The forces of Romanenko's 5th Tank Army and Chistiakov's 21st Army did most of the "heavy lifting" for Vatutin's Southwestern Front on 20 November and received credible support from the Don Front's 65th Army. However, the same could not be said of Leliushenko's 1st Guards Army, whose mission was to secure and protect 5th Tank Army's right flank as Romanenko's army carried out its deep exploitation. On 19 November, after the attack by

5th Tank Army's 14th Guards Rifle Division stalled in front of the defenses of Romanian II Army Corps' 9th Infantry Division, 1st Guards Army tried to assist its neighbor by mounting an assault with 203rd Rifle Division in the sector from Iagodnyi on the Krivaia River eastward to State Farm No. 3. This assault failed, however, in the face of determined resistance by Romanian I Army Corps' 11th Infantry Division. The setback on 19 November was so serious that Leliushenko's forces declined to attack on the 20th, instead relying on 5th Tank Army's attack to weaken the Romanians' defenses. Although some sources claim this failure occurred because of Leliushenko's inability to deploy his army's 1st Guards Mechanized Corps quickly enough, he was actually following Vatutin's order to withhold the powerful mechanized corps until it was needed to expand Operation Uranus into Operation Saturn.

Axis Reactions
Romanian Third Army suffered serious damage during the first two days of the Uranus counteroffensive. By midday on the 20th, three of its four corps headquarters had been either destroyed or dispersed, and south of Serafimovich, its 6th, 5th, and 15th Infantry Divisions had been combined into Group Lascar. General Lascar had already earned a reputation as a superb and tenacious fighter, based on his division's stellar performance during the siege of Sevastopol' in June and early July 1942. When it was formed, Lascar's group was supposedly subordinate to its presumed rescuer, XXXXVIII Panzer Corps, with which it had no communications. Although it might have escaped encirclement by a concerted attempt to break out to the southwest, as suggested by General Steflea at Rostov (when Soviet 26th Tank Corps was occupying the Perelazovskii region), Hitler categorically forbade such a move.[79] Thus, when 26th Tank Corps broke free into the operational depths on the evening of 20 November and began its dash toward Kalach-on-the-Don, this opportunity was lost, and Lascar's group was condemned to ultimate destruction.

On Romanian Third Army's right wing, south of the Kletskaia bridgehead, the concentric assaults into Group Lascar's rear by four rifle divisions of Soviet 21st and 65th Armies (76th and 293rd of the former, and 27th Guards and 304th of the latter) had smashed the right wing of Romanian IV Army Corps' 13th Infantry Division and the left wing and center of its 1st Cavalry Division. However, after half of 21st Army's 4th Tank Corps plunged through the gap into the Romanians' deep rear, Romanian 15th Infantry Division (whose headquarters was at Golovskii, 25 kilometers west of Kletskaia) raced forward from its reserve position and took over the task of defending the Kletskaia gap, along with 1st Cavalry Division's forces that had escaped destruction in the initial Soviet assault and the small but mobile Voicu Detachment. After performing credibly in the defense of the Kurtlak River line,

15th Infantry gave way under heavy Soviet pressure and, together with the remnants of 13th Division and Group Voicu, swung its front southwestward to the western bank of Solomakovskaia *Balka* to protect Group Lascar's right flank and rear and await possible relief by XXXXVIII Panzer Corps.

Farther east, on Romanian Third Army's extreme right wing, 1st Cavalry Division and Group Voicu finally gave way to pressure from 21st Army's 3rd Guards Cavalry Corps and 65th Army's advancing rifle divisions and swung their defenses eastward to protect the approaches to Orekhovskii. As they did, they were subordinated to Sixth Army's XI Army Corps and, within days, ended up trapped in the Stalingrad pocket.

In Romanian Third Army's most vital sector south of Serafimovich, its reserve 1st Armored and 7th Cavalry Divisions were already subordinate to XXXXVIII Panzer Corps. However, by day's end on 20 November, the panzer corps' Romanian 7th Cavalry and German 22nd Panzer Divisions became locked in combat in the region from Karasev eastward to Malaia and Bol'shaia Donshchinka, while Gheorghe's 1st Armored Division ended up fighting in the Zhirkovskii region along the Tsaritsa River, in the southern portion of Group Lascar's encirclement pocket south of Raspopinskaia. Thereafter, XXXXVIII Panzer Corps directed 1st Armored Division to break out southwestward and rejoin it in the Donshchinka region. However, it could not do so because its path was blocked by 5th Tank Army's 119th and 50th Guards Rifle Divisions and 26th Tank Corps' 19th and 216th Tank Brigades, reinforced by a 76mm tank destroyer regiment and one of the army's two flamethrower tank battalions. Although Gheorghe's forces managed to seize a 4-kilometer-wide bridgehead on the western bank of the Tsaritsa River at Sredne-Tsaritsynskii, they failed to break through to 22nd Panzer Division and lost 25 tanks in the process.

Meanwhile, in Romanian Third Army's center, XXXXVIII Panzer Corps' 22nd Panzer Division and the remnants of Romanian 14th Infantry Division tried to disengage from 5th Tank Army's forces in the Peschanyi and Ust'-Medveditskii region and march southward to safety. However, the combination of rough terrain and a determined Soviet pursuit thwarted the panzer division's attempts to escape. Unable to break contact entirely, the beleaguered panzer division succeeded in withdrawing only 10 to 15 kilometers into the Bol'shaia and Malaia Donshchinka regions, 10 to 15 kilometers west of Perelazovskii. The best that can be said of its performance is that it tied down two divisions of Borisov's 8th Cavalry Corps and most of Butkov's 1st Tank Corps, preventing them from beginning their operational exploitation. In the process, however, the Germans lost contact with Romanian 1st Armored Division, leaving it cut off and facing destruction in an encirclement pocket in and north of Zhirkovskii.

Romanian I Army Corps, whose 7th and 11th Infantry Divisions were deployed on Third Army's left wing, took pride of place with regard to its combat performance on 20 November. Together with the remnants of 9th Infantry Division on its right flank, it gave ground only grudgingly in its struggle with 1st Guards Army's forces and 5th Tank Army's 14th Guards Division. In fact, the Romanians' resistance was so stout that Romanenko had no choice but to commit his reserve 159th Rifle Division to the fight. In addition, a desperate counterattack by Romanian 9th Infantry Division and elements of 11th Division, which was designed to push Soviet forces back to the Tsutskan' River north of Pronin, compelled 5th Tank Army to reinforce its rifle divisions fighting west and northwest of Pronin with 8th Cavalry Corps' 21st Cavalry Division. In the end, however, a concerted attack by this reinforced Soviet grouping, supported by a handful of tanks from 1st Tank Corps, forced Romanian 7th Cavalry Division to give way, uncovering Romanian I Army Corps' right flank and forcing its 9th and 11th Divisions to withdraw.

As for Sixth Army, since its left-wing XI Army Corps was facing potential envelopment, its principal concerns on 20 November were to reinforce its threatened corps and, more important, identify and assemble panzer forces that could deploy westward to thwart any attempts by Soviet mobile forces to exploit southward from either the Kletskaia or the Serafimovich bridgehead to the Don River in its deep rear, with clear priority assigned to Kletskaia. Therefore, Sixth Army continued to withdraw forces from the fighting in Stalingrad proper and dispatched them to the west.

The most important of these forces was 14th Panzer Division, whose panzer elements had already been moved to the Verkhne-Buzinovka region on 19 November to back up German XI Army Corps. However, as described by the division's biographer, in the wake of its costly struggle in the rubble of Stalingrad, on 19 November, 14th Panzer Division was but a shell of its former self. Although its 36th Panzer Regiment had been withdrawn to rest and refit and fielded about 30 tanks, its two panzer-grenadier regiments consisted of only a battalion each, and its motorcycle battalion was at company strength (see appendix 5I in the *Companion*).[80]

The most important decision General Paulus reached on 20 November was to dispatch a sizable force westward to block the Soviets' northern pincer before it reached the Don River. Paulus revealed this plan in a message he sent to his subordinate corps at 1445 hours on 20 November (see appendix 5J in the *Companion*). After briefly sketching out the situation at the time, in particular, stating where Soviet forces had already penetrated Romanian Third Army's defenses, the order directed the army to cease its attacks in Stalingrad and transfer forces westward, first "to organize a defensive line" and later to launch "an offensive . . . from that line toward the west." Specifically, LI Army Corps was to take over and defend XIV Panzer Corps' sector in the city, and VIII and XI Army Corps were to hold their positions, as defined in the order, and prepare reserves for dispatch to XIV Panzer Corps. More important, XIV Panzer Corps, with its headquarters in Sukhanov, 35 kilometers northwest of Kalach, was to defend the army's western flank southward from XI Army Corps' left flank and also secure the railroad line from Parchin, west of Oblivskaia, eastward to Chir Station, with 403rd Security Division's 354th Grenadier Regiment. Finally, Paulus subordinated 16th and 24th Panzer Divisions, 295th and 389th Antitank Battalions, 244th Assault Gun Battalion, and 129th Artillery Command to General Hube's XIV Panzer Corps.[81]

Thus, Paulus's plan called for a line of panzer divisions stretching from Logovskii southward to the Liska River at Skvorin, with security forces protecting the main rail line north of the Chir River. All he needed to do was move sufficient forces westward fast enough to halt the Southwestern Front's juggernaut. Given the effects of attrition on these once proud panzer divisions during the two mouths of fighting in Stalingrad city, this was no mean task.

German operational maps of the situation at 2000 hours on 20 November show XI Army Corps' 376th Infantry Division clinging doggedly to its defenses in the sector from Logovskii eastward to Blizhniaia Perekopka, with its 673rd, 672nd, and 767th Regiments online. However, it had no choice but to dispatch reinforcements, including at least one battalion from 767th Regiment, to bolster Romanian 1st Cavalry Division's defenses to the west. At the time, the cavalry division's 12th, 1st, and 2nd Regiments were straining to withstand 65th Army's assaults and hold on to the sector from Logovskii southward to Orekhovskii. In addition, on the order of Colonel General Strecker, commander of XI Army Corps, 44th Infantry Division's 132nd Regiment and 384th Infantry Division's 534th Regiment were en route to reinforce 14th Panzer Division's *kampfgruppe* in the Verkhne-Buzinovka region, 32 kilometers south-southeast of Kletskaia.

Farther to the south, XIV Panzer Corps' newly assigned forces were moving westward from Stalingrad and were expected to arrive sometime overnight on 20–21 November. These forces included the following:

- 24th Panzer Division—marching toward a goose-egg position drawn on the map in the Sukhanovskii region, 33 kilometers northwest of Kalach;
- 16th Panzer Division—moving through Bol'shenabatovskii and Malo-Golubinskii en route to the Lipo-Logovskii region, 18 to 25 kilometers north of Kalach (possibly reinforced by Romanian 1st Cavalry Division upon its relief from the fighting in the Orekhovskii region); and
- 3rd Motorized Division—moving westward via Bol'shaia Rossoshka toward Kalach to seize bridges across the Don by 21–22 November.

Fighting under XIV Panzer Corps' control were 14th Panzer Division (reinforced by 44th Infantry Division's 132nd Regiment and 384th Infantry Division's 534th Regiment), 24th and 16th Panzer Divisions, and 3rd Motorized Division—all tasked with halting the Southwestern Front's armored juggernaut. However imposing this array of division symbols looked on Sixth Army's operational maps as they reached and crossed the Don River, in reality, these divisions were mere shadows of their former selves, nothing more than hastily assembled battalion or multibattalion *kampfgruppen* with 30 to 35 tanks apiece.

Meanwhile, inside Stalingrad, Seydlitz's LI Army Corps issued its Corps Order No. 117 at 2250 hours. Though recognizing the emerging crisis to the west, it stubbornly continued to stoke the combat fires still blazing in the city:

> Strong enemy forces have achieved a deep penetration against the neighboring army to the west. It must be reckoned that the enemy will attempt to extend his penetration with armoured forces. Countermeasures have been initiated by the army under cessation of the attack in Stalingrad. LI Army Corps will discontinue its attack in Stalingrad, organize itself for defence, and hold the entire front-line that has been won in heavy fighting.
>
> 305th Infantry Division [supported by 245th Assault Gun *Abteilung*] will continue storm group operations until the final destruction of the enemy group in the tightly compressed area east of the gun factory. . . .
>
> 389th Infantry Division will prepare for the attack to capture the "Rote Haus" and carry it out in agreement with 305th Infantry Division. In addition, the division must reconnoiter so that it can take over the southern sector of 94th Infantry Division up to the Orlovka mouth, which must be reckoned on after the destruction of the enemy group east of the gun factory.[82]

Conclusions

As had been the case the day before, on 20 November, the forces of Vatutin's Southwestern Front once again fell well short of achieving their assigned missions. In the Serafimovich sector, the exploitation by 5th Tank Army's 1st Tank Corps was utterly thwarted by the intervention of XXXXVIII Panzer Corps' 22nd Panzer Division. By skillfully employing its armored personnel carriers and a handful of tanks, Rodt's division fought far more effectively than its actual strength warranted. In addition to limiting the advance by Butkov's 1st Tank Corps to less than 20 kilometers, Romanian infantry, in conjunction with tanks from Romanian 1st Armored Division, restricted the advance by Rodin's 26th Tank Corps to roughly 25 kilometers. When 1st Tank Corps finally managed to begin maneuvering around 22nd Panzer

Division's right flank, it was halted short of its objective (the lower Kurtlak River), and two-thirds of Borisov's 8th Cavalry Corps was sucked into the fighting in the Ust'-Medveditskii and Peschanyi regions. Worse still, by the end of the day, only 26th Tank Corps' 157th Tank and 4th Motorized Rifle Brigades had succeeded in fulfilling their assigned missions by capturing the Perelazovskii region. However, after doing so, Rodin's tank corps spent an excessive amount of time assembling its forces and consolidating its positions around the town.

Meanwhile, to the west, the ragtag Romanian 7th Cavalry Division put up enough of a fight to tie down 5th Tank Army's 47th Guards Rifle Division and 8th Cavalry Corps' 21st Cavalry Division well short of their objectives. Nevertheless, heavy attrition and sheer exhaustion finally compelled the Romanian cavalry to abandon the battlefield and withdraw southwestward to the Chir River.

Farther east, in 21st and 65th Armies' sectors in the Kletskaia region (on the Southwestern Front's left wing and the Don Front's right), Kravchenko's 4th Tank Corps and Pliev's 3rd Guards Cavalry Corps finally succeeded in projecting their forces into the operational depths. Coupled with the dramatic raid by 65th Army's ad hoc mobile group, the successes achieved by 4th Tank and 3rd Guards Cavalry Corps in the Kletskaia sector had two positive consequences. First, they kept German attention riveted on this sector, and second, they prompted discussions within Sixth Army about the feasibility of withdrawing XI Army Corps back to more defensible lines.

Despite these successes, Soviet critiques of the counteroffensive as a whole noted one major shortcoming. Because the Southwestern and Don Fronts' 17th and 16th Air Armies failed to provide the necessary air support to advancing forces, enemy aircraft seemed to operate with impunity against 5th Tank Army's and 21st Army's mobile groups.

THE STALINGRAD FRONT'S OFFENSIVE, 20 NOVEMBER

If Hitler, Weichs at Army Group B, and Dumitrescu and Paulus at Romanian Third and German Sixth Armies were thrown completely off balance by the Southwestern and Don Fronts' offensives, the attack by Eremenko's Stalingrad Front on 20 November made a bad situation catastrophic. First and foremost, this catastrophe occurred because, while Romanian Third Army had a reserve panzer corps at its disposal, General Hoth's Fourth Panzer Army counted only one German motorized division, the 29th, in its reserve. This, together with the weakness of Fourth Panzer Army's two subordinate Romanian army corps, made Hoth's defense essentially untenable from the start.

As indicated by table 25 and appendix 5A in the *Companion*, Fourth Panzer Army was responsible for defending the roughly 300-kilometer-wide sector extending southward from Stalingrad city's southern suburbs through the lake region west of the Volga River to the Elista region west of Astrakhan'. To defend this immense sector, Hoth had roughly 110,000 soldiers and officers assigned to the veteran German IV Army Corps (German 371st and 297th and Romanian 20th Infantry Divisions), Romanian VI Army Corps (Romanian 2nd, 18th, 1st, and 4th Infantry Divisions), Romanian VII Army Corps (Romanian 5th and 8th Cavalry Divisions), German 16th Motorized Division (protecting the panzer army's long left flank), and German 29th Motorized Division (situated in reserve southwest of Stalingrad). Since his army was far too weak to defend such a broad front, Hoth concentrated two of his army's three corps and about half his total forces in the sector he considered most threatened—the 90-kilometer-wide sector from Stalingrad's southern suburb of Kuporosnoe southward to the middle of Lake Barmantsak. Even so, only the divisions of German IV Army Corps, which were deployed in the 32-kilometer sector opposite the Soviet bridgehead at Beketovka, manned continuous defenses in adequate depth. This left the divisions of Romanian VI Army Corps with no choice but to man strongpoint defenses, with sizeble gaps between each strongpoint, although these were supposedly covered by fires.

The offensive plan of Eremenko's Stalingrad Front required the shock groups of 64th, 57th, and 51st Armies to strike directly at Fourth Panzer Army's defenses in the 65-kilometer-wide sector from Elkhi, west of Beketovka, southward to the northern shore of Lake Barmantsak. Thus, Eremenko's attacking forces outnumbered their Axis foes by ratios of well over two to one in infantry and roughly eight to one in tanks. By any measure, the Stalingrad Front's offensive would be an unequal fight.

19 November: Preliminaries

In the Stalingrad Front, on 19 November our units repelled enemy attacks in the vicinity of the "Barrikady" Factory. . . .

62nd Army. The Northern Group (124th and 149th RBs) exchanged fire with the enemy from their previous positions.

138th RD repelled several attacks by up to a battalion of enemy infantry and 3 tanks and held on to their previous positions. The division fought in difficult conditions. Re-supply of ammunition and food across the Volga River is impossible due to heavy ice flows. Transport of ammunition and food is being carried out by aircraft. The division received 10,000 rifle bullets and boxes of food on 19 November. 250 active bayonets remain in the division.

95th RD repelled an attack by a battalion of enemy infantry from the Tuvinsk region at 1630 hours on 19 November and fought in the vicinity of the gasoline tanks (southeast of the Barrikady Factory).

The army's remaining units exchanged fire with the enemy from their previous positions.

64th, 57th, 51st, and 28th Armies occupied and fortified their previous positions.

Red Army General Staff Operational Summary,
0800 hours on 20 November 1942[83]

While Vatutin's Southwestern Front and Rokossovsky's Don Front were unleashing their armies against Romanian Third Army's defenses on 19 November, the armies of Eremenko's Stalingrad Front struggled to complete their offensive preparations. The only fighting in this region took place in Stalingrad proper, where Chuikov's 62nd Army and Shumilov's 64th Army continued their determined defense, coupled with reconnoitering and raiding aimed at keeping German Sixth Army and Fourth Panzer Army tied down in the fighting. To this end, 62nd Army's 138th Rifle Division continued to tenaciously defend its isolated positions on so-called Liudnikov's Island, east of the Barrikady Factory. Meanwhile, 95th Rifle Division struggled mightily to reestablish contact between Chuikov's forces, defending the Krasnyi Oktiabr' Factory and the narrow strip of land northward along the western bank of the Volga River, and Liudnikov's imperiled forces (see appendix 19A in the *Companion*).

Elsewhere in the Stalingrad Front's sector, the commanders of 64th, 57th, and 51st Armies continued to concentrate their forces for the offensive and, in the case of 57th Army, conducted a final reconnaissance in force overnight on 19–20 November. As indicated in chapter 3, Eremenko's armies experienced serious delays in crossing the Volga, primarily due to deteriorating weather conditions but also because of transport shortages (trains, barges, and trucks). As a result, roughly one-third of 13th Tank Corps, including many of its trucks, failed to cross the river by the appointed time, a fact that seriously hindered the corps' actions once it encountered German 29th Motorized Division late on the first day of operations. Likewise, similar delays prevented some of the rifle forces from going into combat with their full "combat kit" and slowed the transport of ammunition and fuel across the river into the Beketovka bridgehead. At this stage, however, these were minor inconveniences, given the *front*'s imposing numerical superiority over Fourth Panzer Army.

20 November

The Stalingrad Front, after penetrating the enemy's defenses south of Stalingrad city on 20 November, destroyed 2 enemy infantry divisions and advanced 7–9 kilometers. Prisoners and trophies were seized. . . .

Stalingrad Front occupied its positions and conducted fighting of local importance in individual sectors.

62nd Army, remaining in its previous positions, repulsed attacks by small groups of enemy with part of its forces and conducted fire fights on 20 November.

138th RD repelled attacks by an enemy force of up to a company and held its positions firmly. The division has no ammunition and food.

The army's remaining units exchanged fire with the enemy and defended their positions.

64th, 57th, 51st, and 28th Armies operated in accordance with the command's plan.

Red Army General Staff Operational Summary,
0800 hours on 21 November 1942[84]

This operational summary indicates that, even on the second day of Operation Uranus, Stalin and his senior military leaders remained reluctant to expose what was going on in the Stalingrad Front's sector, just as they had been the previous day with regard to developments in the Southwestern and Don Fronts' sectors. In short, early on 21 November, no one in the Soviet military hierarchy was prepared to claim any sort of success until its forces had accomplished something important, obvious, and irreversible.

Despite this lingering lack of confidence among the Soviet High Command, the Stalingrad Front began its offensive on 20 November (see map 17). However, the deteriorating weather delayed H-hour for two hours. Shortly before dawn on the 20th, a cold front approaching from the north produced showers, cloudy conditions, and dense ground fog in Stalingrad and in the lake region to the south. Soon after, these rain showers turned into a snowfall. As had been the case in the Southwestern and Don Fronts the day before, the heavy fog and low ceilings, which limited visibility to about 200 meters, prevented aircraft flights and made it impossible for the Stalingrad Front's artillery to fire and adjust its artillery preparation at 0800 hours, as planned.[85] Therefore, General Eremenko, who was located at the forward observation post of General Tolbukhin's 57th Army on Hill 114.3, about 5 kilometers southeast of Tundutovo Station, contacted the *Stavka* and received permission to delay the preparations and assaults until the fog lifted. After twice delaying for an hour, at 0930 hours, Eremenko alerted 57th Army to begin its artillery preparations at 1000 hours. Beset by the same problems as Tolbukhin's army, General Shumilov's 64th Army commenced its artillery bombardment at 1420 hours. Since the weather was better in the sector containing General Trufanov's 51st Army, it adhered to Eremenko's original guidance and began its preparations at 0730 hours.

The preparations themselves ranged from 40 to 75 minutes in duration and were fired only against preplanned targets because the rain and fog prevented observation. This lack of observation and adjustment seriously limited the preparations' effectiveness. The weather also prevented 8th Air Army from participating in the preparation and flying in support of the advancing ground troops. The presence of aircraft would be sorely missed by 13th Tank Corps in the afternoon.

Despite the lack of effective artillery and air support, the initial infantry attacks succeeded everywhere except in 64th Army's sector. Therefore, 57th and 51st Armies were able to commit their mobile groups at about midday, as planned.

64th Army's Assault

General Shumilov's army began its 75-minute artillery preparation at 1420 hours and launched its ground assault at about 1535 hours.[86] Supported by about 40 infantry support tanks from 13th and 56th Tank Brigades, 157th, 38th, and 204th Rifle Divisions attacked westward in the 12-kilometer-wide sector from the northern bank of the Chervlenaia River, west of Ivanovka, and northward to just east of Elkhi. As they did, they cooperated closely with 57th Army's shock group—169th and 422nd Rifle Divisions, which were attacking westward south of the Chervlenaia River. The three attacking divisions of 64th Army struck the defenses of German 297th Infantry Division's 523rd Regiment, which manned defenses in and around the fortified town of Elkhi, and Romanian 20th Infantry Division, which had two regiments defending the sector from Elkhi southward to the northern bank of the Chervlenaia River and a third regiment in the 3-kilometer wide sector stretching from the river's southern bank to Khara-Uson and Tundutovo Station, on the extreme right wing of Fourth Panzer Army's IV Army Corps.

Shumilov's attacking forces achieved almost instant success everywhere except in the Elkhi sector. On the shock group's left wing and in its center, 157th and 38th Rifle Divisions surged forward 4 to 5 kilometers, overcoming the forward tactical positions on Romanian 20th Infantry Division's left wing and in its center with relative ease. After 38th Division captured Andreevka on the northern bank of the Chervlenaia River, 4 kilometers west of Ivanovka, 157th and 38th Divisions pushed westward and northwestward to the approaches to Nariman and Iagodnyi, 10 to 18 kilometers southwest of Beketovka. However, on the shock group's right wing, 204th Rifle Division faltered against determined resistance by 297th Infantry's 523rd Regiment at and north of Elkhi, recording only a minimal advance despite launching multiple assaults during the afternoon and early evening.

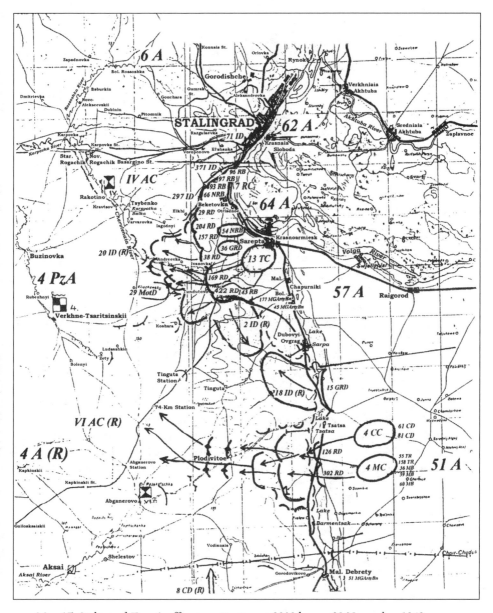

Map 17. Stalingrad Front's offensive: situation at 2200 hours, 20 November 1942

57th Army's Assault

The most dramatic developments of the day took place in the offensive sector of General Tolbukhin's 57th Army.[87] The army fired its 75-minute artillery preparation from 1000 to 1115 hours, ending with 5 minutes of massed *Katiusha* rocket fire. The shock group began its assault at precisely 1115 hours, as the army's longer-range artillery began shifting its fire into the depths.[88] Deployed from left to right, the shock group's 143rd Rifle Brigade and 422nd and 169th Rifle Divisions attacked in the 8-kilometer-wide sector extending from Kul'turnyi northward through Khara-Uson to Erdeshkin on the Chervlenaia River's southern bank. This sector was defended by Romanian 2nd Infantry Division, a woefully understrength formation that consisted of four infantry battalions and a single company, and the right-wing regiment of Romanian 20th Infantry Division.[89] Attacking in the shock group's center and on its right wing, 422nd and 169th Rifle Divisions were supported by 54 infantry support tanks from 235th and 90th Tank Brigades, respectively. In addition, on the day of the attack, either Eremenko or Tolbukhin decided to reinforce 422nd Rifle Division's assault with 28 tanks from 13th Tank Corps' 176th Separate Tank Regiment. Interestingly, this use of Colonel Tanaschishin's tank regiments violated regulations for the employment of mechanized and tank corps, which required that tank units be committed intact rather than dispersed in penny-packet fashion in an infantry support role.[90]

With substantial armor in support, the two rifle divisions easily penetrated Romanian 2nd Infantry Division's defenses by 1200 hours, reportedly producing "tank fright" among the defenders that led to a virtual rout. The two Soviet divisions advanced 6 to 8 kilometers by midafternoon. The 422nd Rifle Division, cooperating with 235th Tank Brigade and 176th Tank Regiment, captured 54-km Station, on the railroad line 10 kilometers north of Tinguta Station, and reached the eastern outskirts of Koshary by day's end. Likewise, 169th Rifle Division and its supporting 90th Tank Brigade captured Khara-Uson, Erdeshkin, and Nariman and reached the eastern approaches to the Shosha *Balka*, 3 to 5 kilometers west of the railroad line, by midafternoon.

Meanwhile, on the left wing of 57th Army's shock group, 143rd Rifle Brigade attacked and penetrated Romanian VI Army Corps' defenses near the boundary between its 2nd and 18th Infantry Divisions and then wheeled southward to seize the villages of Morozov and Khomiakov, 10 to 12 kilometers west of Lake Sarpa. Its mission was to link up with 51st Army's 15th Guards Rifle Division, which was attacking northwestward from the Shalimovo region south of Lake Sarpa, near the village of Kamenskii, 10 to 15 kilometers northeast of Tinguta. Eremenko hoped this pincer operation on the adjoining flanks of 57th and 51st Armies would encircle most of Romanian 2nd Infantry Division and the regiment on 18th Infantry Division's left wing. Just as Eremenko anticipated, the two attacking forces effected their linkup and accepted the surrender of the Romanian forces isolated in this pocket west of Lake Sarpa overnight on 20–21 November. The success of 57th Army's initial assault left the remnants of Romanian 2nd and 18th Infantry Divisions in shambles.

According to General Tolbukhin's offensive plan, if the ground assault by the shock group's two rifle divisions was successful, at about midday on 20 November, Colonel Tanaschishin's 13th Tank Corps was to exploit through a 5-kilometer-wide penetration sector between Khara-Uson and Kul'turnyi, at the boundary between the advancing 422nd and 169th Rifle Divisions. After crossing the Volga River from the Tat'ianka and Svetlyi Iar region on 10–19 November, the corps was to advance into combat in a two-echelon formation of two columns of brigades, with 62nd and 61st Mechanized Brigades deployed from left to right in the first echelon and 17th Mechanized Brigade in the second echelon behind 62nd Brigade. Each of the three mechanized brigades contained a tank regiment—numbered 44th, 176th, and 163rd in 17th, 61st, and 62nd Brigades, respectively—with as many as 41 medium and light tanks each. In addition, the corps had two separate tank regiments, 166th and 35th, with about 39 tanks each. The two brigade columns were to be 3 to 4 kilometers apart when they advanced into combat.[91]

However, delays in the regrouping process, caused primarily by poor weather, left one-third of Tanaschishin's corps, including 35th and 166th Separate Tank Regiments, on the Volga's eastern bank on the morning of the 20th. Eremenko therefore postponed the corps' commitment into combat until later in the day. In addition, Tolbukhin had detached 176th Tank Regiment from the corps' 61st Mechanized Brigade, as well as most of the corps' auto transport, and assigned it to 422nd Rifle Division to support its infantry. This meant that when the corps advanced into the penetration, it had roughly 78 tanks and only one-third of its infantry riding on the tanks.

On Tolbukhin's order, Tanaschishin's 13th Tank Corps began its advance at 1620 hours, but it was so late in the day that the smoke of battle and the approaching darkness made it difficult to maneuver across the snow-covered terrain and the numerous *balkas* and *ovrags* (ravines and gulches) punctuating the monotonous flatness.[92] Since the corps lacked most of its trucks, the motorized riflemen of 61st and 62nd Mechanized Brigades advanced on foot. However, the two brigades spearheaded their advance with riflemen from their respective 1st Motorized Rifle Battalions riding on the decks of the 30 operational tanks available to their organic 176th and 163rd Tank Regiments. The two tank regiments, with 6 to 10 riflemen on board each tank, advanced into combat in columns of companies and at maximum speed, while soldiers from the other two motorized rifle battalions of each brigade followed on foot.

In this somewhat awkward formation, 62nd and 61st Mechanized Brigades' 163rd and 176th Tank Regiments, along with 169th and 422nd Rifle Divisions, overran the withdrawing remnants of Romanian 2nd Infantry Division and advanced into the operational depths. However, with much of its infantry on foot, the corps' lead tank regiments advanced only 10 to 15 kilometers northwestward and reached the eastern approaches to Nariman by nightfall, instead of achieving the planned 30- to 40-kilometer advance along the Nariman, Varvarovka, and Rakotino axis. By the time Tanaschishin's lead tank regiments approached Nariman, his infantry lagged far behind the tanks, and the entire corps became extremely overextended. With their radios operating poorly or their crews using them ineffectively, various sections of the advancing columns lost communication with one another, disrupting smooth command and control.

In addition, overnight on 20–21 November, 62nd Mechanized Brigade's 2nd Motorized Rifle Battalion lost its bearings in the darkness and wandered off its attack route. Instead of following 163rd Tank Regiment, with the brigade's 1st Battalion riding on the decks of the tanks, it advanced west toward the village of Zety, which was in 4th Mechanized Corps' sector. Thus, 62nd Mechanized Brigade would be denied additional support at a point when it was most needed. Exploiting 13th Tank Corps' delayed advance and overextended march columns, Fourth Panzer Army was able to throw its reserve 29th Motorized Division into its path, precipitating one of the most dramatic fights and sudden setbacks in the Stalingrad Front's otherwise successful offensive. The fortuitous arrival of 29th Motorized Division in the midst of a spectacular Soviet advance was the one bright spot in an otherwise dismal day, offering a flash of promise before ending in abject disappointment and retreat.

Overnight on 19–20 November, Lieutenant General Hans-Georg Leyser's 29th Motorized Division was in an assembly area south of Karpovka and west of the Chervlenaia River. This relatively fresh division was equipped with 59 tanks (7 Pz-II, 32 Pz-III, 18 Pz-IV, and 2 command tanks), most of them in its 129th Panzer Battalion. The division had been resting in anticipation of its advance on Astrakhan', but fortuitously, it was conducting a field exercise when it was ordered into battle. It is not clear whether General Hoth was able to reach Army Group B by telephone after the Stalingrad Front began its offensive or whether he took the initiative on his own, but at 1030 hours, Hoth ordered Leyser's division to strike the advancing Soviet mobile forces on their left flank as they approached Nariman from the south.

The attacking 29th Motorized Division engaged, in succession, the lead elements of 57th Army's 169th Rifle Division and 90th Tank Brigade as they advanced northwestward from Nariman and, later, 13th Tank Corps' 62nd Mechanized Brigade and accompanying 163rd Tank Regiment. In addition to surprising these forces, the 29th began its counterattack at a time when Tanaschishin's 13th Tank Corps was most vulnerable, before its tank companies could deploy from column into proper combat formation (see appendix 5K in the *Companion* for exaggerated and competing German and Soviet descriptions of this meeting engagement).[93] Leyser's counterattacking panzer-grenadiers and tanks first struck Colonel Ia. F. Eremenko's 169th Rifle Division and forced it to withdraw. Only the quick reaction of Lieutenant Colonel M. I. Malyshev's 90th Tank Brigade saved the day by engaging 29th Motorized Division's armor and destroying several of its tanks. However, the unequal contest resulted in the temporary loss of Nariman and cost Malyshev 8 tanks (2 T-34s burned, 3 KVs and 1 T-34 knocked out, and 1 T-34 and 1 T-70 lost to mines). Eremenko's rifle division lost 93 killed and 257 wounded.[94]

While Colonel Eremenko's infantry and Lieutenant Colonel Malyshev's tanks were seizing Nariman and then colliding with 29th Motorized Division, Colonel I. K. Morozov's 422nd Rifle Division and its supporting 176th Tank Regiment encountered problems of their own during their advance from 54-km Station toward Koshary. After beginning its exploitation in midafternoon, 176th Regiment stumbled into minefields laid by Romanian forces and lost 24 of the 28 tanks it had at the beginning of its advance: 19 T-34 and 3 T-70 tanks were taken out by mines, and antitank fire destroyed another T-34 and T-70.[95]

After 29th Motorized Division defeated 169th Rifle Division and 90th Tank Brigade near Nariman, Leyser's panzers and panzer-grenadiers also surprised 163rd Tank Regiment of 13th Tank Corps' 62nd Mechanized Brigade. The 29th decimated the regiment and the brigade's accompanying 1st Motorized Rifle Battalion, as well as some of the supporting infantry of 169th and 422nd Rifle Divisions. The most recent Russian history of the war grudgingly underscores the ferocity of 29th Motorized Division's counterattack, while still concealing the damage it did:

> The counterstroke delivered on the evening of 20 November [by 29th Motorized Division] happened to Colonel I. K. Morozov's 422nd Rifle Division, which, at that time, had captured Nariman. After a fierce battle with superior enemy forces, the soldier-Far Easterners were forced to abandon that town. Intense fighting also developed in the vicinity of the 8th of March State Farm. By order of the army commander, 13th Tank Corps moved to repel the counterstroke. All night on 20–21 November, its brigades, in cooperation with the rifle formations, repelled the savage enemy onslaught. The participants in the repulse of the counterstroke and also the remaining motorized infantry did not permit the [German] "tankers" to fulfill their assigned missions.[96]

The ensuing seesaw fight between 29th Motorized Division and 13th Tank Corps continued overnight on 20–21 November until Leyser received orders to return north and join Sixth Army. Even then, most of his 29th Motorized Division, with all its tanks, launched a counterattack north of the Chervlenaia River early on 21 November (see below) to support and rescue the beleaguered Romanian 20th Infantry Division and protect the right wing of 297th Infantry Division as it fended off renewed assaults by Soviet 64th Army. Finally, 13th Tank Corps' approaching 17th Mechanized Brigade and 44th Tank Regiment, together with infantry from 422nd and 169th Rifle Divisions, managed to stabilize the situation south of the Chervlenaia. Before Leyser's division could strike southward against 4th Mechanized Corps, Weichs recalled the division to the Stalingrad pocket late on 21 November. By this time, 13th Tank Corps was able to concentrate its remaining elements forward and resume its advance, albeit at a much reduced pace.

As a result of the fighting on 20 November, Tolbukhin's 57th Army smashed and largely destroyed Romanian 2nd Infantry Division and seriously damaged one regiment of Romanian 20th Infantry Division. As one history of the battle notes, "Fourth Panzer Army recorded that the Romanian corps disintegrated so rapidly that all measures to stop the fleeing troops became useless before they could be put into execution. At nightfall, the army concluded that by morning the Romanian VI Corps would have no combat value worth mentioning."[97] Supporting this judgment, Colonel Fangohr, General Hoth's chief of staff, remarked that "the work of weeks had been 'ruined in a day;' in many places, the Romanians had offered no resistance at all—they had fallen victim to 'an indescribable tank panic.'"[98]

Subsequently, 51st Army's 15th Guards Rifle Division and 57th Army's 143rd Rifle Brigade encircled and destroyed Romanian 2nd Infantry Division west of Lake Sarpa. After being rescued by the tanks of 29th Motorized Division, a few remnants of this division withdrew northward to the new defenses of Romanian 20th Infantry Division on the eastern bank of the Chervlenaia River at Varvarovka.

51st Army's Assault

The Stalingrad Front's 51st Army, whose visibility was not as limited as elsewhere, began its artillery preparation at 0730 hours, as planned. However, the weather was still too poor for aircraft to join in the bombardment, and the light fog prevented its artillery fire from being observed or adjusted. Prior to the attack, General Trufanov, the army's commander, was joined at his observation post by Nikita Sergeyevich Khrushchev, member of the Stalingrad Front's Military Council; Lieutenant General M. M. Popov, deputy *front* commander; and Generals Vasilii Timofeevich Vol'sky and T. T. Shapkin, commanders of 4th Mechanized and 4th Cavalry Corps, respectively.

When preparing his offensive plan, Trufanov had deliberately staggered the timing of his army's two ground assaults to confuse the Romanians with regard to the location of his main attack. Hence, he planned to attack at 0830 hours from the sector between Lakes Sarpa and Tsatsa on the army's right wing and at 0845 hours in the sector between Lakes Tsatsa and Barmantsak on the army's left wing. On the right (northern) wing, Major General K. I. Vasilenko's 15th Guards Rifle Division, cooperating with 125th Separate Tank Battalion, was to attack from positions in the vicinity of the villages of Semkin and Shalimovo and penetrate the defenses of 1st and 2nd Battalions of Romanian VI Army Corps' 18th Infantry Division. On the left (southern) wing, Colonel E. F. Makarchuk's 302nd Rifle Division and Colonel D. S. Kuropatenko's 126th Rifle Division, supported by 254th Tank Brigade, were to break through the defenses of 1st Battalion, 93rd Regiment, and 1st and 2nd Battalions, 75th Regiment, of VI Army Corps' 1st Infantry Division. At the last minute, Trufanov also ordered General Vol'sky's 4th Mechanized Corps to support 302nd Division's assault with its 55th Separate Tank Regiment and 126th Division's attack with its 158th Tank Regiment—another clear violation of the regulations governing the employment of tank and mechanized corps.[99]

The 51st Army's northern shock group, Vasilenko's 15th Guards Rifle Division and supporting tanks, began its attack promptly at 0830 hours and easily penetrated the defenses of Romanian 18th Infantry Division's two defending battalions, sending the survivors scurrying westward and northwestward. Wheeling northwestward, Vasilenko's guardsmen and supporting tanks advanced up to 11 kilometers by 1800 hours against virtually no opposition and linked up with the riflemen of 57th Army's 143rd Rifle Brigade near the village of Kamenskii. Having encircled much of the Romanian 2nd Infantry Division and about half of 18th Infantry Division, 15th Guards Division reported capturing 2,500 enemy soldiers and 550 rifles, 50 machine guns, 15 guns, 13 mortars, and other equipment by day's end.[100]

The offensive on 51st Army's left wing developed just as successfully as the one on its right, even though the attacking force faced much stronger resistance from several Romanian strongpoints. Here, 302nd and 126th Rifle Divisions, each supported by roughly half of 254th Tank Brigade's 28 tanks, attacked at 0845 hours. Shortly after the initial assault, 4th Mechanized Corps sent its 55th and 158th Tank Regiments, with about 40 tanks apiece, to reinforce the two attacking rifle divisions, accelerate their advance, and lead the subsequent exploitation by their parent mechanized corps. Lieutenant Colonel A. A. Aslanov's 55th Separate Tank Regiment followed in the path of 302nd Division, and Lieutenant Colonel F. V. Chernyi's 158th Separate Tank Regiment advanced through 302nd Division's combat formation. The initial assault propelled the advancing riflemen through Romanian 1st

Infantry Division's defenses in the 6-kilometer-wide front between Lakes Tsatsa and Barmantsak with relative ease. After penetrating the loose and noncontiguous Romanian defenses, which were only 4 to 5 kilometers deep, the attacking forces advanced westward up to 10 kilometers by 1300 hours.

The only substantial resistance the attacking forces encountered was on Hill 87.0, 7 kilometers west of the forward edge of the Romanians' defenses. The hill was defended by 1st Infantry Division's reserve 2nd Battalion, 85th Regiment, and, reportedly, two batteries of 88mm antiaircraft guns manned by German crews. Since Hill 87.0 sat squarely at the boundary between 126th and 302nd Rifle Divisions, elements of both divisions and their supporting tanks tried to capture the hilltop by both frontal assault and envelopment. Although the light fog finally lifted at 1000 hours, the Romanian strongpoint managed to hold out until the supporting 55th and 158th Separate Tank Regiments arrived at about 1100 hours. Then, after a 20-minute fight, the defenders gave up the hill and withdrew, reportedly westward in disorder.[101] Observing the fight from 57th Army's observation post, General Popov, the deputy *front* commander, contacted Eremenko by phone, reported on the army's success, and received permission to order Vol'sky's 4th Mechanized Corps and Shapkin's 4th Cavalry Corps to commence their advance through the penetration. After seizing Hill 87.0, 126th Division and its supporting tanks thrust westward, and the main body of 302nd Division reached the outskirts of Zakharov Farm, 10 kilometers west of its jumping-off position.[102]

Although they received their attack order at 1120 hours, the two lead mechanized brigades of Vol'sky's 4th Mechanized Corps were unable to cross their lines of departure until about 1300 hours. Soviet critiques credited this delay to several factors: the inexperience of the corps' senior command cadre, who had not practiced the march to contact enough; traffic jams on the few roads running east to west, caused by supply trucks and vehicles removing the wounded and prisoners from the battlefield; and, in the case of 59th Mechanized Brigade, the need to clear Romanian minefields in its path.

In addition, 4th Mechanized Corps had transferred 150 of its trucks to 51st Army's rifle divisions to hasten their advance. This left many of the corps' motorized riflemen with no choice but to advance on foot or on the decks of the attacking tanks. The delay was so bothersome and disruptive that Khrushchev, the *front*'s commissar, personally visited Lieutenant Colonel A. G. Karapetian's 60th Mechanized Brigade (in 4th Mechanized Corps' right column) to identify and fix the problem, dumping "harsh words and reproaches" on the brigade commander.[103] During this almost two-hour delay, 302nd and 126th Rifle Divisions continued their advance, with the latter capturing Bessilov, 12 kilometers west of its jumping-off position, and the former reaching the approaches to Kazuveev on the western shore of Lake Barmantsak.

General Vol'sky's mechanized corps finally began its advance at 1300 hours, with Karapetian's 60th Brigade on the right, Colonel V. F. Sten'shinsky's 59th Brigade on the left, and Lieutenant Colonel M. I. Rodionov's 36th Brigade behind 59th Brigade. The corps' mission was to penetrate deeply to the vicinity of the village of Sovetskii, 18 kilometers southeast of Kalach-on-the-Don, where it was to link up with the Southwestern Front's mobile forces. The remainder of 51st Army was to erect an outer encirclement front extending along the Don and Aksai Rivers to prevent German forces from mounting counterattacks toward Stalingrad from the southwest.

Even after Vol'sky's corps finally got under way, its advance proved painfully slow because of minefields emplaced by the Romanians, a lack of decent roads toward the west, and the difficulty of negotiating the generally flat but *balka*- and *ovrag*-ridden terrain. Once it reached the operational depths, 4th Mechanized Corps exploited west toward Plodovitoe, 20 kilometers west of its forward assembly area, essentially traveling along one march route with 36th Mechanized Brigade in the lead. As this brigade approached Plodovitoe, Colonel Rodionov dispatched Major N. A. Doroshkevich's 26th Tank Regiment to capture the town from the march. However, the town's defenders included elements of Romanian 18th Infantry Division's reconnaissance and engineer battalions, supported by at least a battery of German 88mm guns, and they offered strong resistance. After an intense fight between 36th Mechanized Brigade and 26th Tank Regiment and the town's determined defenders, 4th Mechanized Corps' forces finally captured Plodovitoe by envelopment in the early-morning hours of 21 November. The corps' main force brigades closed into the Plodovitoe region by 2000 hours. However, this was well short of the assigned objective of Verkhne-Tsaritsynskii, 48 kilometers to the northwest.

Overnight on 20–21 November, even before the fighting in Plodovitoe ended, Trufanov, 51st Army's commander, ordered Vol'sky to move 60th Mechanized Brigade and 21st Tank Regiment northwestward to Tinguta Station, 20 kilometers away, and to move 59th Mechanized Brigade and 20th Tank Regiment, along with 55th Separate Tank Regiment, westward to 74-km Station and Abganerovo Station, 20 kilometers distant. They were supposed to capture the two railroad stations and cut the rail line running from Sal'sk northward to Stalingrad. Trufanov insisted that Vol'sky's forces start moving immediately and capture their objectives by a night march. Doing as ordered, 59th and 60th Brigades bypassed Plodovitoe from the north and south and marched forward in the darkness, destroying or capturing scattered Romanian forces along the roads and seizing their twin objectives by dawn on 21 November. During the corps' thrust to Tinguta Station, it enveloped and destroyed a regiment of Romanian 2nd Infantry Division as it tried to withdraw westward from the Lake Sarpa region and seized a considerable amount of Romanian equipment and weapons. By day's end, Vol'sky's corps had lost 50 of its 200 tanks, about 20 to enemy fire and the others to mechanical breakdowns.[104]

Because of the delayed commitment of 4th Mechanized Corps into 51st Army's penetration, 61st and 81st Cavalry Divisions of Shapkin's 4th Cavalry Corps were unable to join the exploitation until 2200 hours on 20 November. Once they did, the two cavalry divisions followed in the wake of 4th Mechanized Corps to Plodovitoe. As 81st Cavalry Division galloped westward to cut the Sal'sk-Stalingrad railroad line at Abganerovo Station, 61st Cavalry Division proceeded to capture the town of Abganerovo, 18 kilometers southwest of Plodovitoe. The corps' overall mission was to protect 4th Mechanized Corps' left flank, block the approach of enemy reserves, and eventually reach the Don River on the army's left wing.

Despite the difficulties experienced by Vol'sky's 4th Mechanized Corps, 51st Army's offensive proved to be a resounding success. The army's assaults decimated Romanian 1st and 18th Infantry Divisions, surrounding and capturing many of their soldiers, and then cut off and captured the bulk of the survivors of 2nd Infantry Division as they attempted to flee 57th Army's attack northwest of Lake Sarpa. Although Romanian VI Army Corps' reserve—6th *Rosiori*'s 2nd Mechanized Squadron, supported by a motorized 105mm artillery battery—tried to counterattack, the effort failed, and part of 6th *Rosiori* was encircled and annihilated. By day's end on 20 November, Romanian VI Army Corps no longer existed as a viable military formation. The path was now wide open for 51st Army's mobile forces to reach their objectives utterly unimpeded.

28th Army

Rounding out the military operations conducted by the Stalingrad Front on the first day of its offensive, Lieutenant General V. F. Gerasimenko's small 28th Army had the mission of anchoring the *front*'s left flank in the Astrakhan' region and Kalmyk steppes and maintaining loose contact with Soviet forces in the Caucasus region (see map 18). Eleven days before, on 9 November, Gerasimenko's army had received orders to operate against the forward elements of German 16th Motorized Division in and around Khulkhuta (Kal'kutta), a town situated 40 kilometers east of Utta and 175 kilometers east of the German division's main base at Elista.[105]

Pursuant to this order, Gerasimenko had issued Order No. 9 on 13 November, directing his army to advance westward and clear German forces from the Khulkhuta, Utta, and Elista road. Major General I. I. Gubarevich's 34th Guards Rifle Division, supported by 565th Separate Tank Battalion, a "flying" battalion mounted on trucks from 248th Rifle Division's 905th Regiment, and 76th Guards-Mortar Regiment, was to conduct the army's main

Map 18. 28th
Army's area of
operations

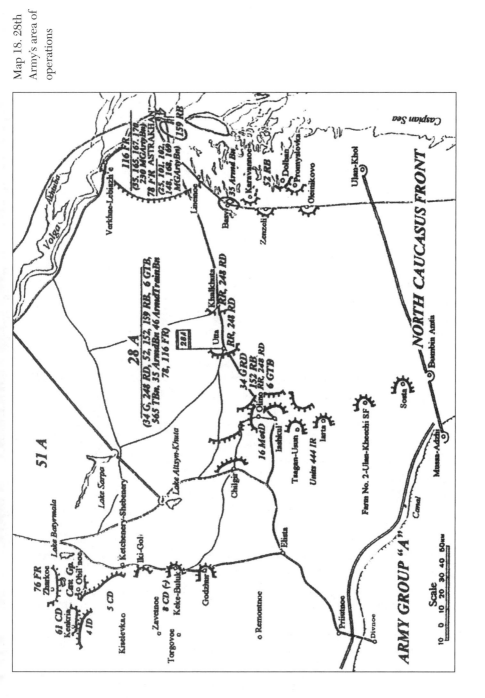

attack westward along the Utta road and capture Khulkhuta. Advancing parallel to but slightly south of 34th Guards Division, 152nd Separate Rifle Brigade was to seize the village of Siantsik and dispatch a reinforced company to race forward and capture the German airfield at Utta. Farther north, 248th Rifle Division's 899th Regiment was to attack south toward Utta from the Sarpa region, 100 kilometers away.

The 28th Army's initial advance ended in misfortune when a motorized group from 2nd Battalion of 16th Motorized Division's 60th Regiment and 116th Panzer Battalion [*Abteilung*] intercepted and destroyed 152nd Rifle Brigade's forward detachment, its reinforced 4th Battalion, on a road south of the main road to Utta. Only four Red Army soldiers survived this fight, prompting the Red Army General Staff to issue a blistering rebuke to Gerasimenko.[106] Otherwise, 28th Army's mini-offensive continued with only minimal gains as German motorized troops exploited their mobility to check the army's advances short of their objectives.

Based on new guidance from the Stalingrad Front, at 0200 hours on 19 November, Gerasimenko issued Order No. 52 to his subordinate forces for the initial stage of the Uranus offensive:

1. Begin operations on the night of 19–20 November in accordance with combat order No. 52.
2. Attack the enemy:
    a. 34th Gds. RD at 0300 hours on 20 November 1942.
    b. 6th Gds. TB, with its motorized rifle battalion and a battalion of 152nd Sep. RB, at 0300 hours on 20 November 1942, and reach Siantsik at 0600 hours on 20 November 1942 with the remainder.
    c. 152nd Sep. RB (without its motorized rifle battalion), reinforced by a motorized rifle company, occupy the airfield at Utta at 0300 hours on 20 November, and reach Siantsik with the remainder of the forces at 0600 hours on 20 November 1942.[107]

Following this order, 28th Army's combined force attacked Khulkhuta. The town was defended by 16th Motorized Division's 60th Motorized Regiment, which had just relieved the division's 156th Motorized Regiment on 17 November. Gubarevich's 34th Guards Division was to strike German defenses at the town from the front, while the tank and rifle brigades were to bypass the town and strike the village of Siantsik, on the road west of Khulkhuta, from the north and south, respectively. In addition, the "flying" company from the rifle brigade was to complete its raid on the Utta airfield, and 248th Rifle Division's 899th Regiment was to push toward Utta from the north. At the time, one battalion of German 156th Motorized Regiment defended Siantsik; another battalion, reinforced by 30 to 40 tanks of 116th Panzer

Battalion, occupied defenses at Iashkul'; and 60th Motorized Regiment, with 15 to 20 tanks, defended Khulkhuta.[108]

After an air preparation, 28th Army's forces advanced to contact from 1600 to 2000 hours on 19 November and reached their attack positions at 0330 to 0400 hours on 20 November. After a day-long fight during which 34th Guards Division captured the eastern outskirts of Khulkhuta, a relief column from 16th Motorized Division's 156th Motorized Regiment rescued the German defenders of the town. Overnight on 20–21 November, Gerasimenko ordered his forces to resume their assaults in the morning, but before they could do so, General Schwerin ordered 60th Motorized Regiment to withdraw, leaving the strongpoint in 28th Army's hands.

Army Group A's combat journal entry for 21 November claimed that 156th Motorized Regiment was almost entirely encircled in Khulkhuta but was ultimately rescued by 60th Motorized Regiment:

> At 1600 hours the commander of the 16th ID (Mot.), Generalmajor Graf von Schwerin, reported that the regiment located near Khalkhuta would have been encircled yesterday. The encirclement was avoided during the night with the support of a second regiment (60th Panzergrenadier Regiment). Three companies were destroyed (including equipment). The Russians did not pursue. He (von Schwerin) intended to leave a rear guard in Utta, where he was located, and withdraw the main body of the division into prepared positions near Yashkul.[109]

In the wake of its assaults, 28th Army's forces occupied Khulkhuta on 21 November, forcing 16th Motorized Division to withdraw all the way back to more strongly fortified defenses around Iashkul'. As it did, it left a small rear guard to defend the town of Utta.

The 28th Army's victory at Khulkhuta was a costly one: 34th Guards Division reported 680 dead and 800 wounded, 152nd Rifle Brigade suffered 91 dead and 82 wounded, and 6th Guards Tank Brigade lost 9 tanks—5 to mechanical failure and 4 burned.[110] German casualties in the operation are unknown. Whatever the cost of its victory, however, 28th Army was on its way toward Elista, with German 16th Motorized Division beginning what would become a long retreat westward across the barren Kalmyk steppes.

Conclusions

The Stalingrad Front's offensive on 20 November was nothing short of catastrophic for German Fourth Panzer Army, if not for Army Group B as a whole. Eremenko's assault essentially vaporized Romanian VI and VII Army Corps, destroying much of Army Group B's right wing in the process.

Although 29th Motorized Division's surprise appearance threw a fright into the advancing 57th Army as well as the *front* command, the effects of its intervention proved transitory. German insistence that, if permitted to continue its counterattack, Leyser's motorized division could have wrecked 57th Army's 13th Tank Corps and 51st Army's 4th Mechanized Corps and, by doing so, thwarted the Stalingrad Front's offensive as a whole rings hollow for several reasons.

First, Leyser's division achieved its signal victory by exploiting 13th Tank Corps' inability to bring its full force to bear during the first day of the Stalingrad Front's offensive. Instead of routing all of Tanaschishin's tank corps, the German panzers and motorized infantry engaged less than half of 13th Tank Corps on the first day—that is, two of its three mechanized brigades and two of its five tank regiments, or about 90 tanks. The remainder of Tanaschishin's forces, a mechanized brigade and three more tank regiments with well over 100 tanks, reached the battlefield either late on 20 November or early on the 21st, in time to reinforce and reinvigorate the corps' advance. Nonetheless, Tanaschishin's advance thereafter was far slower than Eremenko and Tolbukhin wished.

Second, the context in which 29th Motorized Division's counterattack occurred negated its dramatic successes and rendered its effects short-lived. By the end of the first day of fighting, 57th and 51st Armies' offensives had wrecked Romanian VI and VII Army Corps, leaving Leyser's panzergrenadiers virtually isolated on the battlefield. In turn, the Romanian collapse left Hoth no choice but to withdraw Leyser's division to the northwest to protect the withdrawal of Romanian 20th Infantry Division, thereby securing German IV Army Corps' vulnerable right flank. The only direction German 29th Motorized Division and Romanian 20th Infantry Division could safely withdraw was to the northwest, into what would soon become the Stalingrad pocket.

As for Romanian VI Army Corps, the bulk of the soldiers in its 2nd and 18th Infantry Divisions were killed or captured within 24 hours after the Soviet offensive began. Whatever remnants survived the Soviet onslaught fled southwestward, along with the shattered remains of Romanian 1st Infantry Division. To save what it could of the situation, Romanian VII Army Corps then pushed parts of its 5th and 8th Cavalry Divisions (4th *Rosiori*, 3rd Motorized *Călăraşi*, and one battalion of 2nd Horse Artillery Regiment, along with four of its motorized guns) into the Aksai region as a mobile reserve. This slim force, together with the remnants of 2nd and 18th Infantry Divisions, were the only forces available to defend the 70-kilometer-wide sector from the Don River eastward to the Aksai region.

Farther to the southeast, Romanian VII Army Corps' 4th Infantry and 5th Cavalry Divisions ended up defending the 55-kilometer-wide sector from Malaia Derbety and Sadovoe southward to Obil'noe, and 2nd *Călăraşi* Regiment had to defend the more than 80-kilometer-wide swath between Obil'noe and 16th Motorized Division's forces protecting the approaches to Iashkul' and Elista. In short, the defenses of German Fourth Panzer Army south of the Stalingrad region were tenuous at best, meaning the Aksai and Kotel'nikovo regions would soon become a major bone of contention between Army Group B—what little was left of Hoth's panzer army—and the Stalingrad Front.

CHAPTER SIX

The Encirclement Closes, 21–23 November

GERMAN DILEMMAS ON 21 NOVEMBER

For the German command, the Stalingrad Front's offensive on 20 November had made a bad situation worse. In addition to contending with the reality of Romanian Third Army's collapse on 19 and 20 November and the Soviets' apparent intent to push large tank and cavalry mobile forces south toward the Don River west of Stalingrad, the Germans' now had clear evidence that the Russians were actually trying to achieve a double envelopment of all German forces in the Stalingrad region. It was bad enough that the Soviet command was operating so audaciously. Even worse, by day's end on 20 November, this daring plan appeared to be working.

Paulus, the commander of Sixth Army, aptly summed up the distressing situation to his adjutant, Colonel Adam:

> Early this morning [20 November], after a strong artillery preparation, the enemy attacked the positions of Fourth Panzer Army and Fourth Rumanian Army. At this moment the situation there is still not clear. The Red Army has continued to attack from the north. Its left wing is advancing southeastward toward Verkhne-Buzinovka. We must reckon with the fact that XI Army Corps will be cut off from the road to the south within several hours. A most serious threat has been created for the Morozovskaia and Chir Station railroad line.[1]

After pondering whether XIV and XXXXVIII Panzer Corps could cope with these threats and what would happen if they could not, Colonel Adam described the crux of the dilemma faced by the German command (see appendix 5L in the *Companion*). "We lived through some harrowing days," Adam recalled, describing the confused situation as rumors filled the air and no one was certain of the Soviets' objective or what should be done to counter their offensive. "Slowly," he said, "with our nerves . . . strained to the limits," the Germans learned of the situation. But with the enemy "penetrating our front" and "no reserves whatsoever to stave off the deadly threat," it became clear to the adjutant that "we would be awaiting a terrible catastrophe if the German Command did not act quickly and effectively."[2]

General Krylov, the Stalingrad Front's chief of staff, later added a fillip to Paulus's and Adam's remarks, writing, "It was only proven on the night of 20–21 November that the enemy had decided to give up any further attempts to take Stalingrad completely. He suspended the attacks in the city (apart from Liudnikov's sector, where he continued to attack throughout the day of 21 and even 22 November) and began to withdraw certain troops, especially panzer units."[3] That alone indicated just how seriously the German command took the situation.

On the ground, the rapidly developing Soviet counteroffensive was also pressuring Axis forces in the Stalingrad region to shift their headquarters, further complicating command and control, which was vital in responding effectively to the growing crisis. For example, because Fourth Panzer Army's forward command post at Verkhne-Tsaritsynskii and its headquarters at Buzinovka were in the direct path of 51st Army's advance, Hoth would have to evacuate precipitously to Nizhne-Chirskaia. Similarly, Sixth Army's headquarters at Golubinskii, on the western bank of the Don 20 kilometers north of Kalach, was endangered by Soviet 21st Army's advance. Therefore, on the morning of 21 November, Paulus had no choice but to order his headquarters staff to move to Nizhne-Chirskaia on the western bank of the Don River, just south of the confluence of the Don and the Chir and 65 kilometers southwest of Golubinskii. Paulus chose Nizhne-Chirskaia as his headquarters because it had excellent communications facilities and had already been selected as the site for the army's winter headquarters.

Hitler himself, who was now totally immersed in operational matters on the Eastern Front, had to make or at least approve decisions that affected the very survival of Army Group B. Indeed, some observers have argued that Hitler's centralization of authority encouraged a sense of passivity among his military subordinates, a subconscious feeling that they had no responsibility for events.[4] This was particularly dangerous when the dictator stayed away from his headquarters, which, during his absence, had moved back from Vinnitsa [*Wehrwolf*] in the Ukraine to Rastenburg [*Wolfsschanze*] in East Prussia for the winter. As a result, Jodl and Keitel, the senior staff officers of OKW, were advising Hitler on his special train in the absence of Zeitzler and the OKH staff. For two months, Hitler had deliberately cut OKW out of eastern operations, which meant that Jodl and Keitel had no real sense of the weakness of Army Group B or the gravity of the Soviet threat. For example, when the Uranus storm broke, their first suggestion was to move a single panzer division from Army Group North to create a reserve in the south.[5] During this period, the Germans sent a significant number of troops and aircraft to Tunisia after the Allied landings in North Africa. Field Marshal Erwin Rommel was against these reinforcements, and Hitler was sending troops to North Africa when the Eastern Front needed them most.

Hitler was directly involved with command and control of forces in the field when he commanded Army Group A for two months. Three days before Operation Uranus began, on 16 November, Hitler had assigned Field Marshal von Manstein's Eleventh Army to Army Group Center. Then, on the 20th, the dictator reacted intelligently to the crisis, placing Manstein in command of a newly created Army Group Don formed from his army's staff, which Hitler and the OKH had created to control all forces in the threatened sector—German Sixth Army and Fourth Panzer Army, Romanian Third Army, and, if it had formed, Romanian Fourth Army (see appendix 5M in the *Companion*). As a result of these changes in command, Kleist, the commander of First Panzer Army, assumed command of Army Group A, while Weichs at Army Group B retained command of German Second, Hungarian Second, and Italian Eighth Armies northwest of the Soviet breakthrough. Given the situation, Manstein had to make bricks without straw. At Army Group B, Weichs had already directed IV Army Corps and 29th Motorized Division to withdraw toward Stalingrad and protect the southern flank of the emerging Stalingrad pocket. Thus, virtually all the German elements of Fourth Panzer Army came under Paulus's control and ended up in the encirclement. Manstein did not even have a full headquarters and communications staff with which to operate, and he had to use vastly inadequate forces to limit the Soviet penetration.[6]

To facilitate Manstein's task, General of Infantry Karl Hollidt soon assumed control of the ad hoc battle groups gathering to form a thin cordon to defend the Chir River southwest of Stalingrad. This Army Detachment [*Armee Abteilung*] Hollidt—built around its commander's XVII Corps headquarters and 62nd and 294th Infantry Divisions, which had been supporting Axis forces along the Don River—was essential if Army Group Don was to hold the river line as a takeoff point for the relief of Sixth Army.[7]

Manstein's task was made even more difficult because Hitler insisted on making basic decisions himself. On 20 November, General Hans Jeschonnek, chief of staff of the *Luftwaffe*, arrived at Berchtesgaden to discuss the air force's role in future breakout or relief operations. Reichsmarshal [*Reichsmarschall*] Hermann Göring, the titular head of the *Luftwaffe*, was chairing a petroleum conference at his country estate, Karinhall. Foreseeing an encirclement, Hitler asked Jeschonnek whether the *Luftwaffe* could supply Sixth Army by air for the (supposedly) short time before Manstein could relieve the siege. Jeschonnek replied that such an airlift was possible, assuming that the *Luftwaffe* retained control of forward airfields. The *Luftwaffe* general cited an example from the previous winter: 100,000 men of II Army Corps had survived when surrounded at Demiansk. This example was poorly chosen, however; the *Luftwaffe* had barely been able to supply this much smaller group of soldiers during a period when the Red Air Force was virtually neutralized. Supplying Sixth Army, a force three times the size of II Corps, would require far more supplies, and the unarmed German transports would be subject to intense Soviet air and antiaircraft attack. In fairness, one must recognize that neither the dictator nor the *Luftwaffe* chief of staff imagined that the airlift would have to continue for long.

Within a few hours of their first conversation, Jeschonnek had his staff make a rough estimate of the airlift requirements, and he discussed the situation by telephone with his friend General Wolfram von Richthofen. The outspoken commander of Fourth Air Fleet soon convinced the chief of staff that an airlift was impossible. Yet when Jeschonnek attempted to dissuade Hitler, the Führer brushed him aside. Predictably, Hitler based all his future decisions on Jeschonnek's ill-considered initial agreement that the airlift could be accomplished. When Göring arrived at Berchtesgaden on 22 November, he felt compelled to pledge that the *Luftwaffe* could accomplish the mission, even though there had been no opportunity to calculate the tonnages involved.[8]

The next day, when Paulus and Weichs asked permission to withdraw from the Volga River to avoid encirclement, they were met with blank refusal. Hitler bypassed Army Group B and the embryonic Army Group Don to reply directly: "Radio Message No. 1352—Urgent—To headquarters Sixth Army—Führer Decision: Sixth Army will hold rail line open as long as possible in spite of danger of temporary encirclement. Orders for supply by air will follow."[9] Paulus and his subordinates at Sixth Army were stunned by this decision. Zeitzler spoke at length with Hitler by telephone on the evening of 21 November, arguing that if Sixth Army withdrew immediately to the lower Don and Chir Rivers, it could outmaneuver and then defeat the Soviet spearheads. Yet the dictator insisted that abandoning Stalingrad was out of the question. Virtually every German commander in southern Russia believed that only an immediate breakout would save Sixth Army. Meanwhile, Paulus, a loyal and successful officer of the Third Reich, hesitated to disagree with Hitler. He had been under enormous nervous strain since the Khar'kov offensive in May. Now, faced with the crisis of encirclement, he seemed too much in control of himself, too passive, as if he were unwilling to give vent to his concerns.[10]

THE SOUTHWESTERN AND DON FRONTS' OFFENSIVE, 21 NOVEMBER

The Southwestern Front and the right wings of the Don and Stalingrad Fronts continued to develop their offensive successfully in their previous positions.

Southwestern Front continued to defend its positions on its right wing and fulfilled missions in accordance with the plan in its center and on its left wing.

Don Front, on 21 November, fulfilled missions in accordance with the plan on its right wing and defended its positions, conducted combat reconnaissance, and exchanged rifle and machine gun fire with the enemy in its center and on its left wing.

From 0900 to 1300 hours on 21 November, observation detected the movement of up to 1,000 enemy vehicles, 14 tanks, and a regiment of artillery southwestward through Kuz'michi and up to 720 vehicles and 50 tanks from the vicinity of Sukhaia Mechetka Balka (6 kilometers southwest of Erzovka) toward Dereviannyi Val Platform [Station] (8 kilometers northwest of Gorodishche).

Red Army General Staff Operational Summary,
0800 hours on 22 November 1942[11]

Despite the continued reticence of the *Stavka* and the Red Army General Staff to speak too openly about events in the Stalingrad region, the latter's daily operational summary about German troop movements was indicative of Sixth Army's reaction to the looming threats it faced. It was indeed pulling some of its mobile units and tanks from Stalingrad proper and moving them toward the west. But the most burning questions were: How many? Why? And to where?

The Southwestern and Don Fronts' Missions

As they had the night before, Vatutin and Rokossovsky met with their senior commanders overnight on 20–21 November to determine what missions the two *fronts'* subordinate armies would perform the next day. Obviously, the most urgent task was to push the *fronts'* mobile groups (exploitation echelons) forward, since they were only one-third of the way to their objective at and north of Kalach-on-the-Don. With the offensive already at least 36 hours behind schedule, Stalin and the *Stavka* were looking intently over their shoulders, demanding that everything possible be done to propel the *fronts'* mobile forces to and beyond Kalach before the Germans could concoct a plan to thwart the Soviets' high expectations, as they had done so often before. Not surprisingly, once formulated, the missions echoed those of the day before (see appendix 5N in the *Companion*).

Responding to fresh orders based on these missions, the Southwestern Front's 5th Tank and 21st Armies, spearheaded by their mobile corps, continued their offensive toward the southwest, south, and southeast, reaching to within 15 to 20 kilometers of the Don River by day's end. Far to the rear, the combined rifle forces of 5th Tank and 21st Armies encircled the remnants of Romanian Third Army's Group Lascar in the region southwest of Raspopinskaia.

The Southwestern Front's Offensive

5th Tank Army

Given the importance of their exploitation operations to the success of Operation Uranus, all Soviet eyes at the *Stavka* in Moscow and in the *fronts* operating in the Stalingrad region were firmly affixed to the progress of 5th Tank and 21st Armies' mobile groups. First and foremost, this meant the progress of 1st Tank Corps, since this corps' entanglement with German XXXXVIII Panzer Corps had most disrupted the fulfillment of Plan Uranus's objectives.

Responding to General Romanenko's demand that the tank corps disengage from the time-consuming fighting in the Ust'-Medveditskii State Farm and Peschanyi regions, Butkov's 1st Tank Corps had marched southward from the state farm overnight on 20–21 November, with all its brigades in a single column (see map 19). Its lead tank brigade, Lieutenant Colonel Zhukov's 89th, reached the Bol'shaia Donshchinka region at 0430 hours. However, rather than breaking contact with German forces, Zhukov's tanks once again encountered elements of 22nd Panzer Division and reported soon after, "All attempts to take Bol'shaia Donshchinka from the march have failed."[12] Several hours before, early on the morning of 21 November, XXXXVIII Panzer Corps had ordered Colonel Rodt's 22nd Panzer Division to disengage and withdraw southward to form a fortress [*Stellung*] position on the Kurtlak River to avoid being encircled.[13] However, by the time the division's withdrawing right wing reached the village of Medvezhyi, 12 kilometers south of Peschanyi and only 10 kilometers north of the Kurtlak River, it had received a new mission: advance northeastward to rescue the encircled Romanian Third Army's Group Lascar. As it attempted to do so, it ran into 1st Tank Corps' advancing columns near Bol'shaia Donshchinka and went over to the defense again, precipitating renewed fighting. When 1st Tank Corps' lead brigades failed to dislodge 22nd Panzer Division from its new defenses after several hours of futile fighting, Romanenko once again insisted that Butkov disengage his corps' main forces from XXXXVIII Panzer Corps and fulfill his mission. Leaving Zhukov's 89th Tank Brigade to cover its movements, Butkov decided to bypass 22nd Panzer Division from the east with 117th and 159th Tank Brigades and 4th Motorized Rifle Brigade.

The 1st Tank Corps' three brigades began withdrawing northward from the Malaia Donshchinka region toward the Ust'-Medveditskii State Farm No. 3 region at 1100 hours.[14] Then, after breaking contact with 22nd Panzer Division's forces, they wheeled northeastward and then eastward through State Farm No. 86 and Novo-Tsaritsynskii to end up at Perelazovskii, which was still occupied by elements of Rodin's 26th Tank Corps, at about 1300 hours. During the remainder of the afternoon, Butkov's forces wheeled

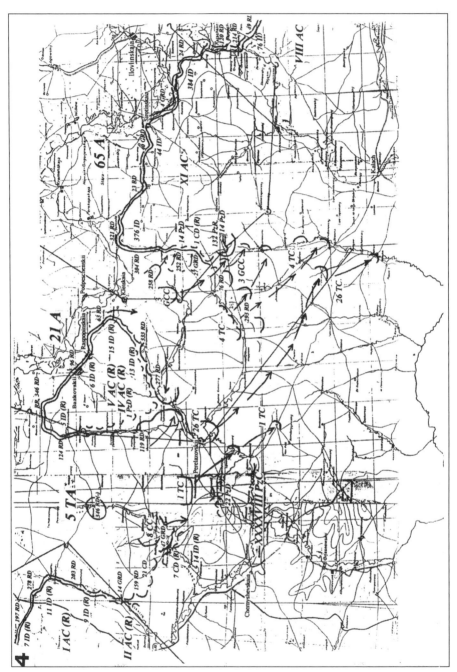

Map 19. Southwestern and Don Fronts' advance at 2200 hours, 21 November 1942

sharply toward the south and captured Sector 4 of State Farm No. 88 on the Kurtlak River, about 5 kilometers south of Perelazovskii. At the same time, its forward detachments slid farther south and concentrated in the Lipovskii and Sredniaia Gusynka regions, 10 and 18 kilometers south of Perelazovskii, respectively, by day's end. Later in the evening, the corps' 89th Tank Brigade, which had been relieved at Malaia Donshchinka by 8th Cavalry Corps' 55th and 112th Cavalry Divisions, rejoined its parent corps south of Perelazovskii. In turn, the two cavalry divisions of Borisov's cavalry corps assumed the task of destroying 22nd Panzer Division, whose forces were by now virtually encircled in and south of Malaia Donshchinka. Thus, by day's end on the 21st, although Butkov's 1st Tank Corps had advanced 66 kilometers in three days of often heavy fighting, it still had 70 to 80 kilometers to traverse before reaching its objectives west and southwest of Kalach-on-the-Don.

While Butkov's tank corps was finally breaking contact with 22nd Panzer Division's forces blocking its advance, the headquarters and 157th Tank Brigade of General Rodin's 26th Tank Corps remained in the Perelazovskii and Efremovskii regions all morning long, resting the troops, replenishing ammunition, and refueling vehicles. At the time, the corps' 216th Tank Brigade was still supporting 50th Guards Rifle Division along and west of the Tsaritsa River far to the north; its 19th Tank Brigade, together with three infantry battalions of 14th Motorized Rifle Brigade, was blocking Romanian forces encircled to the north from proceeding southward along the Tsaritsa River valley. However, 19th Tank and 14th Motorized Rifle Brigades rejoined the corps in midmorning.

After being bombarded all morning with orders from Romanenko to move, Rodin's tank corps resumed its advance at 1300 hours, rapidly pushing southward into the Kurtlak River valley, 10 to 15 kilometers west of Ma noilin, the town Kravchenko's 4th Tank Corps had captured several days before. The corps' *tankists* seized Kotovskii, Kalmykov, and Rozhki Farm in the Kurtlak valley; pushed southward across the river; and then wheeled southeast toward the Don River in an attempt to seize its objectives—river crossings at and north of Kalach.

Brushing aside only light resistance and marching through the seemingly endless detritus of the defeated Romanian Third Army, 26th Tank Corps' brigades advanced 60 to 70 kilometers during the day, reaching positions along the Liska River well after darkness fell. During this advance, Major Makhur's 157th Tank Brigade dispersed already scattered elements of Romanian 5th and 6th Infantry Divisions that had escaped from the Raspopinskaia pocket and then pushed southeastward to capture the town of Ostrov, together with a crossing over the Liska River, just 25 kilometers west-northwest of Kalach. Farther north, Colonel Filippenko's 19th Tank Brigade destroyed two battalions of infantry from Romanian 15th Infantry Division and captured the

village of Plesistovskii, 13 kilometers northwest of Ostrov. Advancing in between the two tank brigades, 14th Motorized Brigade seized the village of
Kachalinskaia, 3 kilometers north of Ostrov.

That evening, Rodin's tank corps reported, "The road from the Efremovskii line to Dobrinka was completely littered with enemy transports
[carts] loaded with ammunitions, foodstuffs, and military equipment, enemy
bodies, and processions of Romanian prisoners."[15] Rodin also informed 5th
Tank Army that Filippenko's 19th Brigade had seized Plesistovskii so quickly
that the Romanians fled in utter panic, leaving behind 300 Red Army prisoners, many of whom insisted on joining the brigade's ranks. In addition, the
brigade captured intact a maintenance workshop, two warehouses with food
and clothing, more than 400 vehicles, and about 300 motorcycles.[16]

However, unbeknownst to Rodin, by this time, his corps' lead elements
were roughly 12 kilometers southwest of the small *kampfgruppe* of XIV
Panzer Corps' 24th Panzer Division, which was just closing in on the town
of Sukhanov on the Liska River. This was about 35 kilometers west of the
town of Malo-Golubinskii on the Don River's northern bank, through which
the *kampfgruppe* of XIV Panzer Corps' 16th Panzer Division was marching en route to Lipo-Logovskii, 20 kilometers north-northwest of Kalach.
Therefore, it was virtually certain that Rodin's 26th Tank Corps, as well as
Kravchenko's 4th Tank Corps, advancing on Rodin's left, would encounter the
kampfgruppen of XIV Panzer Corps' 24th and 16th Panzer Divisions, which
General Paulus had dispatched westward from Stalingrad to halt the Soviet
onslaught. Late on 21 November, the most important unanswered questions
were: When and where would these forces collide? And how would this col-
lision affect the Southwestern Front's advancing mobile groups?

While 5th Tank Army's 26th Tank Corps was finally beginning its exploitation toward Kalach-on-the-Don, 8th Cavalry Corps' 55th and 112th Cavalry Divisions (after relieving 1st Tank Corps' 89th Tank Brigade) began the
task of dealing with XXXXVIIII Panzer Corps' increasingly isolated 22nd
Panzer Division. Although ordered to bypass the division from the east by
attacking southward to capture the town of Petrovka in the Kurtlak River
valley, Borisov's two cavalry divisions, by now reinforced by 511th Separate
Tank Battalion, instead collided with Colonel Rodt's almost tankless panzer
division northwest of Bol'shaia Donshchinka. The two cavalry divisions and
their supporting tanks spent the remainder of the day and the entire evening bogged down in desultory fighting with the remnants of Rodt's hapless
division. Although this virtual stalemate defeated 22nd Panzer's attempts to
withdraw south into the relative safety of the Kurtlak valley, it also prevented
Borisov's cavalry corps from completing its priority mission—to advance
south and clear Axis forces from the Chir River's northern bank.

As 5th Tank Army's tank and cavalry corps struggled to reach their deep objectives, the army's rifle forces consolidated their gains, completing the encirclement of the remnants of Romanian Third Army south of Raspopinskaia or advancing southward to support and assist the advancing mobile forces. On the tank army's left wing, Colonel Belov's 50th Guards Rifle Division, supported by 26th Tank Corps' 216th Tank Brigade, deployed its forces in a 12-kilometer-wide sector along the western bank of the Tsaritsa River from Verkhne-Fomikhinskii southward to Sredne-Tsaritsynskii. Facing eastward, Belov's forces confronted encircled Group Lascar's Romanian 5th Infantry Division. After repelling several Romanian counterattacks in the morning, 50th Guards assaulted eastward in the afternoon, crossing the Tsaritsa River with two regiments, penetrating Romanian defenses, and pushing eastward 6 kilometers, roughly halfway to its objective—the town of Golovskii. Situated 15 kilometers south-southwest of Raspopinskaia, Golovskii was also the objective of 21st Army's 333rd Rifle Division, which was attacking westward from the Kletskaia region. A linkup by 50th Guards and 333rd Rifle Divisions would complete the encirclement of Group Lascar.

While Belov's guardsmen were driving into the center of Group Lascar's positions, on their left, Colonel Danilov's 119th Rifle Division castled its forces southward along the Tsaritsa River to the Korotkovskii, Zhirkovskii, and Perelazovskii sector; attacked eastward; and advanced up to 5 kilometers against the remnants of Romanian 1st Armored Division. By this time, General Gheorghe's armor was cooperating with infantry in the southern part of Group Lascar's area of operations. The 119th Division's mission was to advance eastward from the Zhirkovskii region, 16 to 18 kilometers north of Perelazovskii, and link up with 21st Army's 277th Rifle Division, attacking westward from the town of Verkhne-Cherenskii on the Golaia River.

During the day, while part of Gheorghe's 1st Armored Division stayed behind to contend with 119th Division's attack, its main force crossed to the west bank of the Tsaritsa River and moved southward in an attempt to link up with 22nd Panzer Division, which it mistakenly thought was advancing northeastward through Bol'shaia Donshchinka.[17] Instead, the Romanian force encountered and was blocked by elements of 8th Cavalry Corps' 55th Cavalry Division. This fight cost the armored division 20 more of its R-2 tanks, although it reported destroying 21 Soviet tanks. Farther north, other elements of 1st Armored fought with 119th Rifle Division southeast of Zhirkovskii, as well as forces on the right wing of 50th Guards Division and 216th Tank Brigade roughly 8 kilometers west of Korotkovskii. More important, the southward dash by 1st Armored Division's main force opened a yawning gap between it and Romanian 5th Infantry Division, which was defending along the Tsaritsa River at and south of Verkhne-Fomikhinskii. Exploiting this gap, Colonel Belov's guardsmen promptly captured Verkhne-Fomikhinskii by enveloping it from the south. In the process, they advanced eastward several kilometers, overrunning and seizing most of Romanian 6th and 13th Infantry Divisions' logistical trains. This catastrophe forced General Lascar to order his forces to fall back to new defenses east of the Tsaritsa River.

Capping the obviously deteriorating situation for the Romanians, at 2000 hours the lead elements of 5th Tank Army's 119th Rifle Division and 21st Army's 277th Rifle Division linked up west of Verkhne-Cherenskii, slamming the trap shut around Group Lascar and the remnants of Romanian Third Army. Lascar's group, which now included the surviving forces of Romanian 5th, 6th, 13th, 14th, and 15th Infantry Divisions, plus elements of 1st Armored Division, was now completely surrounded in the region south of Raspopinskaia. It was confined to a 30-kilometer–by–30-kilometer sack southwest of Raspopinskaia by 5th Tank Army's 50th Guards and 119th Rifle Divisions to the west, by a regiment of 5th Tank Army's 346th Rifle Division and 21st Army's 96th and 63rd Rifle Divisions to the northeast, and by 21st Army's 333rd and 277th Rifle Divisions to the southeast. The situation was most critical at Golovskii, 11 kilometers east of Korotkovskii and 10 kilometers north of Verkhne-Cherenskii, where Group Lascar was assembling its wagons and wounded. However, Romanian 6th Infantry Division came to its rescue by sending a battalion of 15th *Dorobanţi* Regiment and some guns to defend the town. To the east, Romanian 13th and 15th Infantry Divisions fended off renewed assaults by 21st Army's 333rd Rifle Division in the afternoon.

Once 5th Tank Army's tank corps transferred the tedious task of contending with the remnants of 22nd Panzer Division to the two divisions of 8th Cavalry Corps and began exploiting south toward the Don River, the tank army's 47th Guards Rifle Division began clearing Romanian forces from the Tsutskan' River valley west of Peschanyi. At dawn, General Fokanov's guardsmen penetrated the security screen of Romanian 7th Cavalry Division south of Pronin, pursued the retreating cavalrymen southwestward 10 to 15 kilometers, and captured the villages of Malakhov, Khokhlachev, and Pichugin in the Tsutskan' River valley. By day's end, 47th Guards was only 3 kilometers from the junction of the Tsutskan' and Chir Rivers and less than 10 kilometers north of the cavalry division's headquarters at Chistiakovskaia.

On 47th Guards Division's right, 8th Cavalry Corps' 21st Cavalry Division, the newly committed 159th Rifle Division, and 14th Guards Rifle Division were deployed from left to right, with 8th Guards Tank Brigade in support. They slowly pushed the remnants of Romanian I Army Corps' 9th Infantry Division west and southwest toward the Krivaia River. General Iakunin's 21st Cavalry, with tanks from Major Chalenko's 8th Guards Tank Brigade in support, attacked and overcame the defenses on the left wing of Romanian 9th Infantry and advanced about 18 kilometers to capture the village of Belavinskii on the Krivaia River, 15 kilometers northeast of its junction with the Chir. The attacking cavalrymen, many of them mounted on tanks rather than horses, overran 9th Division's headquarters before it could relocate, capturing many of its troops and forcing the rest to flee southwestward in disorder.

On the cavalry division's right, Colonel N. I. Fedotov's fresh 159th Rifle Division penetrated 9th Infantry Division's center, pursued the withdrawing Romanians up to 16 kilometers, and captured the village of Nizhnegorskii on the Krivaia River, 10 kilometers south of Verkhnyi Gorbatovskii, by day's end. Farther to the right, General Griaznov's 14th Guards Division atoned for its embarrassing performance on the operation's first day by crushing 9th Infantry's right wing 12 to 14 kilometers east of Verkhnyi Gorbatovskii. Griaznov's riflemen encircled and captured most of a Romanian regiment 11 kilometers east of Gorbatovskii and pursued the remnants westward to the Krivaia River, capturing the town by day's end. The 14th Guards' forceful advance outflanked I Army Corps' 11th Infantry Division, forcing the corps to withdraw its right wing back to the Krivaia River. Overnight, 5th Tank Army's three right-wing divisions extended their frontages southeastward to connect with 47th Guards Division's right flank near the confluence of the Krivaia and Chir Rivers.

Although he was later criticized for maintaining too large a reserve, Romanenko kept 346th Rifle Division, less one regiment, in the Kalmykovskii region to protect the army's rear west of Raspopinskaia. The tank army commander also sent his reserve 8th Motorcycle Regiment to occupy blocking positions in the northern part of Ust'-Medveditskii State Farm's Sector 3 to prevent Group Lascar's troops from escaping southwestward from the region south of Raspopinskaia.

Even though Romanenko's forces made far better progress than they had the day before, particularly his mobile groups, the army as a whole was still well behind schedule in fulfilling its assigned missions. By day's end on 21 November—the third day of the offensive—Butkov's 1st Tank Corps had finally fulfilled its mission for the first day, and Rodin's 26th Tank Corps was close to fulfilling its mission for the second day. All Soviet critiques of the offensive blamed these delays on the hapless 22nd Panzer Division and Romanian forces, which refused to surrender:

> The stubborn defense by German 22nd Panzer Division and the desire of the Raspopinskaia grouping of Rumanian forces to escape destruction and penetrate to the southwest at any cost prevented the army's forces from fulfilling its assigned missions. By day's end on 21 November, that is, the third day of the offensive, 1st Tank Corps had fulfilled only its mission for the first day and 26th Tank Corps was close to fulfilling its mission for the second day.[18]

21st Army

Like the Southwestern Front's 5th Tank Army, 21st Army concentrated most of its efforts on 21 November on pushing its mobile group forward toward its initial objective—the Don River at and north of Kalach. Egged on by *front* commander Vatutin, as well as by Stalin and the *Stavka* in Moscow, Chistiakov urged Kravchenko's 4th Tank Corps and Pliev's 3rd Guards Cavalry Corps to brush aside any obstacles the Germans placed in their path and reach the river as rapidly as possible. The most important of these obstacles was General Bässler's 14th Panzer Division, whose panzer *kampfgruppe* was defending the Verkhne-Buzinovka region but had other smaller detachments supporting XI Corps' 376th Infantry Division in the Logovskii and Orekhovskii regions to the north. Still under XI Army Corps' control, Bässler's panzers would revert to XIV Panzer Corps' control within hours.

At the time, General Hube's XIV Panzer Corps was still in the process of deploying its divisions westward from Stalingrad, with the mission to block any Soviet advance toward the Don. Hube's corps controlled 24th Panzer Division's *Kampfgruppe* Don, which had 49 tanks and was already in the Sukhanov and Skvorin region along the Liska River, as well as a *kampfgruppe* from 16th Panzer Division with 34 tanks. The 16th Panzer's force had crossed the Don River and was heading westward, north of the river, through Luchinskii, 8 kilometers west of Vertiachii and 10 kilometers east of Malonabatovskii (see appendix 5O in the *Companion*).[19] If XIV Panzer Corps could concentrate all three of its panzer divisions successfully, it would control a force of more than 110 tanks. At this point, however, the corps' tanks were scattered across a 70- to 80-kilometer front, with scarcely more than 30 tanks in a single location. Thus, the corps faced the virtually impossible task of defeating three Soviet tank corps, with upward of 100 tanks each, advancing southeastward in tandem toward the Don River.

In addition to its deep operations, 21st Army had another important mission—to assist 5th Tank Army in destroying Group Lascar encircled south of Raspopinskaia. To fulfill this mission, Chistiakov's army initially allocated four (96th, 63rd, 277th, and 333rd) of his army's six rifle divisions to form the eastern half of the encirclement ring around Group Lascar, while the other two divisions (76th and 293rd) supported his mobile forces as they exploited southeastward. Later, Chistiakov retained three of these divisions (96th, 63rd, and 333rd) to liquidate Lascar's group, while 277th Rifle Division joined his mobile forces marching toward the southeast.

Fulfilling 21st Army's priority mission, which was to race to the Don River, Kravchenko's 4th Tank Corps began its thrust southeastward from the Manoilin and Maiorovskii regions early in the morning. Brushing aside small groups of primarily Romanian rear service troops, Kravchenko's four mobile brigades captured two towns on the Liska River: Eruslanovskii, 25 kilometers northwest of Kalach, and Sukhanov (Sukhanovskii), 10 kilometers to the north. Faced with this onslaught, *Kampfgruppe* Don of XIV Panzer Corps' 24th Panzer Division had no choice but to abandon Sukhanov and move eastward to the vicinity of Krasnyi Skotovod Farm, 10 kilometers northeast of Eruslanovskii, which it reached at 0800 hours.[20] Thereafter, the *kampfgruppe* tried but failed to slow or halt 4th Tank Corps' advance. Overpowering all resistance, the tank brigades of Kravchenko's corps lunged forward, and the corps' forward detachment captured the town of Lipo-Logovskii, 8 kilometers west of the Don River and 20 kilometers north-northwest of Kalach, by 1600 hours. During the advance, patrols from Kravchenko's corps reached to within 15 kilometers of Sixth Army's headquarters at Golubinskii, on the west bank of the Don River 20 kilometers north of Kalach. Kravchenko's losses on the 21st were negligible, amounting to only 16 tanks (3 KV, 3 T-34, and 10 T-70 models), while his corps reported capturing 550 enemy vehicles, an airfield with 25 aircraft, and several warehouses, including one with 150 heavy Maxim machine guns.[21]

Sixth Army's records contain only two reports concerning 24th Panzer Division's fight. The first, from *Korück* 593 [*Kommandeur rückwärtiges Armeegebeit*, or rear area command] at 0530 hours, stated that enemy tanks were advancing en masse from the Kiselev region toward Dobrinskaia (Dobrinka), probably a reference to 5th Tank Army's 26th Tank Corps. A second report at 0740 hours said that a detachment from 24th Panzer Division had engaged advancing enemy forces (3rd Guards Cavalry Corps' 5th Cavalry Division) near Nizhnaia Buzinovka, 9 kilometers north of Sukhanov. Early the next day, Sixth Army mentioned the engagement at Krasnyi Skotovod but provided no details and noted that 20 enemy tanks had reached the Popov 1 Farm and Ostrov region, probably also a reference to the lead elements of General Rodin's 26th Tank Corps.[22]

Meanwhile, on 4th Tank Corps' right, General Pliev's 3rd Guards Cavalry Corps fended off spoiling attacks by 14th Panzer Division's forces in the Verkhne-Buzinovka region and south of the town. It bypassed the panzer division's strongpoint from the southeast, with its cavalry divisions echeloned behind 4th Tank Corps' right flank. At dawn on the 21st, Colonel Chepurkin's 5th Guards Cavalry Division advanced southeastward from the Svechinikovskii region, 10 kilometers west-northwest of Verkhne-Buzinovka, toward the town of Nizhnaia Buzinovka, but it was attacked by German aircraft as it approached its objective. Despite the losses it suffered from the air strikes, the division managed to capture the town at about 0830 hours after a short fight, reportedly dispersing two companies of Romanian infantry and capturing 7 tanks, 17 vehicles, and several warehouses. However, at 1130 hours the division was struck by a strong counterattack, with enemy infantry and 12 tanks coming from the north and infantry and 15 tanks coming from

Sukhanov to the south—both groups apparently subordinate to 24th Panzer Division. After repelling these attacks, Chepurkin's cavalry advanced southward 9 kilometers and captured Sukhanov at 1800 hours, only to be attacked overnight by a battalion of infantry and 8 tanks, also from 24th Panzer Division. As before, the division repulsed this attack.[23]

As 5th Guards Cavalry Division was bypassing Verkhne-Buzinovka to the south, the cavalry corps' 6th Guards and 32nd Divisions advanced southward 40 kilometers from the Kurtlak River and assaulted Verkhne-Buzinovka all day on 21 November. After failing to overcome 14th Panzer Division's defenses in a prolonged and bloody fight during the morning that produced heavy losses on both sides, Pliev decided to leave a screening force at the town until 21st Army's supporting 76th and 293rd Rifle Divisions reached the region. In the meantime, he dispatched his two cavalry divisions on a raid deeper into the Germans' rear. Shortly after midday, despite heavy enemy artillery fire, 6th Guards and 32nd Cavalry Divisions marched southward, bypassing Verkhne-Buzinovka and Grishina *Balka* south of the town. They then wheeled eastward through Nizhnaia Buzinovka to the town of Osinovskii, 10 kilometers to the east, which Colonel Chudesov's 32nd Cavalry seized after a sharp fight. At the same time, Colonel Belogorsky's 6th Guards Division supported Chudesov's assault and then moved east toward Evlampievskii, 20 kilometers east of Osinovskii and only 9 kilometers north of the Don River at Bol'shenabatovskii.[24]

By this time, Pliev's cavalry had traversed more than 100 kilometers in three days of fighting and had seized both Nizhnaia Buzinovka and Osinovskii. In the process, his corps had turned the left flank of Sixth Army's XI Army Corps and was seriously threatening the corps', if not Sixth Army's, deep rear area. In fact, by capturing Nizhnaia Buzinovka, Sukhanov, Eruslanovskii, and Lipo-Logovskii by nightfall on 21 November, Kravchenko's 4th Tank Corps and Pliev's 3rd Guards Cavalry Corps had torn a gaping hole in XIV Panzer Corps' anticipated deployment line, extending from Verkhne-Buzinovka in the north, southward along the Liska River through Sukhanov and Skvorin, to the Kachalinskaia region, 25 kilometers west of Kalach. This was the line from which Paulus and Army Group B hoped XIV Panzer Corps could launch its concerted attack to foil the anticipated Soviet envelopment operation. The inability of XIV Panzer Corps to hold on to this line was a new disaster.

Sixth Army observed these developments but was utterly incapable of dealing effectively with the looming crisis on its left flank. Before dawn, the army recorded that 14th and 24th Panzer Divisions were fighting in their assigned positions northwest of Kalach, but 16th Panzer Division was lagging seriously behind.[25] At 1725 hours it reported that 16th Panzer was still en route across the Don River bridge at Luchinskii as of 1710, and at 2030 hours, it reported that both 14th and 24th Panzer Divisions were en route westward.[26] The latter report added that LI Army Corps was dispatching elements of 3rd and 60th Motorized Divisions (Group von Hanstein) to the Karpovka region east of Kalach, heavy fighting was under way at Verkhne-Buzinovka, and Osinovskii had already fallen to the Soviet cavalry. Finally, the report confirmed that portions of 44th and 384th Infantry Divisions were being sent to bolster XI Army Corps' left wing and XIV Panzer Corps' supposed position along the Liska River.[27] By this time, however, it was apparent that the Liska line was a phantom position.

If 21st Army's mobile forces were making life miserable for Paulus's Sixth Army, Chistiakov's rifle divisions were not being passive. On the army's right wing, Colonel V. G. Chernov's 277th Rifle Division, committed from the army's second echelon late the day before, advanced westward from the Nizhne-Solomakovskii and Ivanushenskii region to capture Verkhne-Cherenskii, only 7 kilometers east of the Tsaritsa River. There, it linked up overnight with 5th Tank Army's 119th Rifle Division, which was advancing east toward Novo-Tsaritsynskii and northeast from Perelazovskii. This completed the encirclement of Romanian Third Army's Group Lascar in the region south of Raspopinskaia.

Once Group Lascar was encircled, 21st Army's 96th, 63rd, and 333rd Rifle Divisions formed the northeastern and southeastern cordon around the encircled Romanians, while Chernov's 277th Division joined 76th and 293rd Rifle Divisions as they advanced southeastward to reinforce 4th Tank and 3rd Guards Cavalry Corps' advance. Although the bulk of these three divisions lagged well behind because they were advancing on foot, Chistiakov was able to provide trucks for one-third of 76th and 293rd Rifle Divisions' riflemen, which facilitated their advance.

Completing the mosaic of the Southwestern Front's operations on 21 November, 1st Guards Army, which was deployed on 5th Tank Army's right wing, continued to play a secondary role. But this was intentional. Vatutin, in accordance with the *Stavka*'s guidance, was retaining General Leliushenko's army for far greater purposes—to spearhead the expanded offensive once Operation Uranus succeeded. Therefore, throughout the day, Leliushenko's forces concentrated on tying down Romanian I Army Corps' 7th and 11th Infantry Divisions by conducting reconnaissance in force, raids, and probes with 203rd, 278th, and 197th Rifle Divisions along the lower Krivaia River and south of Elanskaia on the Don River.

The Don Front's Offensive

65th Army
Unlike the Southwestern Front's 5th Tank and 21st Armies, which were finally registering significant advances on the third day of Uranus, Batov's 65th

Army continued to play a largely sacrificial role in the operation, protecting the advance of Chistiakov's 21st Army on its right (see map 19). By striking the defenses of Sixth Army's XI Army Corps frontally, its divisions suffered heavy losses trying to penetrate German-built defenses, with only minimal gains. During the day, Batov spent virtually all his time at division level with an operational group of officers from his army's staff. He had to admit, however, that "the army's leadership became only observers of events."[28] With Batov looking on, the army's 321st, 304th, and 252nd Rifle and 27th Guards Rifle Divisions, reinforced later in the day by Colonel I. Ia. Fursin's 258th Rifle Division from the second echelon, ground their way forward against fierce resistance offered by 376th Infantry Division of General Strecker's XI Army Corps.

Although now reinforced by 177th Assault Gun Battalion from 44th Infantry Division's 131st Regiment and by most of Romanian 1st Cavalry Division, General von Daniels's 376th Division was still hard pressed. Flanked on the left by 14th Panzer Division and now reinforced by 44th Infantry Division's 132nd Regiment, von Daniels's division occupied defenses extending westward from Blizhniaia Perekopka to Logovskii and then due southward past Orekhovskii to 14th Panzer's Division's right flank, somewhere north of Verkhne-Buzinovka. The ambiguous term "somewhere" meant that, by day's end on 20 November, a distinct gap existed between 376th Division's left and 14th Panzer Division's right, through which Colonel Anisimov's small ad hoc mobile group had passed the night before. On 21 November, Anisimov's detachment was supposedly somewhere between Orekhovskii and Verkhniaia Golubaia, 25 kilometers southwest of Orekhovskii. However, Russian sources remain mysteriously quiet about its actual location and fate.

In any case, throughout the day on 21 November, 65th Army's five divisions recorded advances of between 1 and 10 kilometers, reaching positions extending from Svechinikovskii, 17 kilometers southwest of Orekhovskii, northward to the Logovskii region by day's end. Most important, largely because of Anisimov's raid, 376th Division had no choice but to withdraw its forces from the town to a new defensive line just to the east overnight on 21–22 November. Farther to the east, even though XI Corps' 44th and 384th Infantry Divisions had dispatched more than half their forces to reinforce German units fighting elsewhere, 65th Army's 4th and 40th Guards and 23rd Rifle Divisions waited patiently for orders to join the attack.[29]

Sixth Army's records substantiate Soviet accounts of the fighting in 65th Army's sector. In fact, Strecker's XI Army Corps bombarded Paulus's headquarters with periodic accounts of the situation. Attesting to the ferocity of the fighting, in the "morning report" it submitted to Sixth Army at 0522 hours, XI Corps admitted that 376th Infantry Division suffered at least 25 dead and 66 wounded.[30] In its morning report the next day, XI Corps claimed that Russian forces had reached the high ground between Orekhovskii and Srednyi, 1.5 kilometers east of Orekhovskii, meaning that Romanian 1st Cavalry Division had abandoned the town.[31]

Axis Reactions

The successes achieved by the Southwestern Front's mobile groups on 21 November had a serious impact on both Romanian Third and German Sixth Armies. By totally collapsing the defenses in Third Army's center and left wing and encircling the remainder of the army in the region south of Raspopinskaia, it was clear that all the territory north of the Chir River and east of the Krivaia River would soon fall to 5th Tank Army. Therefore, at 1600 hours, the increased Soviet pressure forced General Dumitrescu to move his army's headquarters from Chernyshevskaia on the upper Chir River back to a safer location in the larger town of Morozovsk (Morozovskii), a key communications hub on the railroad line 55 kilometers southwest of Oblivskaia on the Chir River. In and of itself, this was an open admission that the army no longer existed.[32]

At the same time, General Steflea, chief of the Royal Romanian Army's General Staff, and General Dumitrescu, commander of Third Army, consulted each other and requested permission for Group Lascar to break out of its encirclement. However, in accordance with Hitler's order the previous day, Weichs repeated that Group Lascar must stand fast. Determined to save what they could of Third Army, at 2200 hours, Steflea and Dumitrescu secretly ordered General Lascar to make preparations to break out to the southwest. However, early the next day, General Arthur Hauffe, chief of the German Military Mission, claimed that this undermined the Romanians' determination to hold out in the pocket and argued that Group Lascar should sacrifice itself for the good of the whole. Reportedly, Army Group B also relented and ordered XXXXVIII Panzer Corps to fight its way southwest toward Chernyshevskaia.[33]

If catastrophe was in the air in Romanian circles, a sense of impending doom began to grip Sixth Army's headquarters late on 21 November. Given the day's disturbing events, there was no denying the perils facing the army at this juncture. As described by General Dörr:

A serious crisis began on Sixth Army's front on 21 November. Both enemy armies turned 90° in relation to their previous axis and, united, now moved to the Don in the Kalach region and to the north, that is, in the rear of the Germans' Stalingrad front.

In the morning about 40 Russian tanks attacked the bridgehead at Kalach. When these attacks were repulsed, they turned to the northeast and by midday appeared on the high western bank of the Don several kilometers southeast of Golubinskii, where Sixth Army's command post was located.[34]

Colonel Adam later shared his view of the mood in Paulus's command post and also vividly described the ensuing movement of Sixth Army's headquarters from Golubinskii to the relative safety of Nizhne-Chirskaia on the western bank of the Don River, 50 kilometers southwest of Kalach (see appendix 5P in the *Companion*). Adam noted the threats to Sixth Army from all points of the compass, particularly that posed by Kravchenko's 4th Tank Corps. He went on to refer to what he termed the "flight" of Fourth Panzer Army's headquarters to its new location, and he underscored the absolute necessity of moving Paulus's headquarters out of harm's way.[35] Finally, Adam described the actual movement of Sixth Army's headquarters to its new location and the chaos and confusion associated with its transfer.

Later in the morning and just prior to this move, General Hube, commander of XIV Panzer Corps, reached Golubinskii with his headquarters staff (see map 20). He informed Paulus that the panzer elements of 24th and 16th Panzer Divisions had left Stalingrad and would reach their designated positions along the Liska River during the afternoon or early evening. Paulus then assigned Hube's corps the mission of attacking the flanks of the advancing Soviet mobile groups with 14th, 24th, and 16th Panzer Divisions' panzer regiments to eliminate the threat to Sixth Army's rear.[36]

General Paulus and General Schmidt, his chief of staff, along with their personal aides, traveled to Sixth Army's new forward command post at Nizhne-Chirskaia by air. The remainder of the headquarters staff headed to the town by a circuitous route in ground vehicles. Organized in five columns, the headquarters first moved from Golubinskii across the Don River at Perepol'nyi and assembled at the headquarters of VIII Army Corps in Peskovatka. The five columns then merged into one, heading southwestward to Nizhne-Chirskaia.

During the night of 21–22 November, Sixth Army's headquarters column met up with the moving columns of 16th Panzer Division, which were crossing the Don from east to west to occupy their concentration areas in the Lipo-Logovskii region; from there, they were to join 14th and 24th Panzer Divisions' attacks against the Southwestern Front's advancing mobile groups. Little did 16th Panzer Division know that the forward elements of both its sister divisions were already engaged and had been forced to give ground, and that the forward detachments of Soviet 4th Tank Corps had already seized Lipo-Logovskii. Thereafter, Sixth Army's headquarters column headed to Kalach early on 22 November and then proceeded to Nizhne-Chirskaia, where it arrived late that day.[37] They were greeted by Paulus and

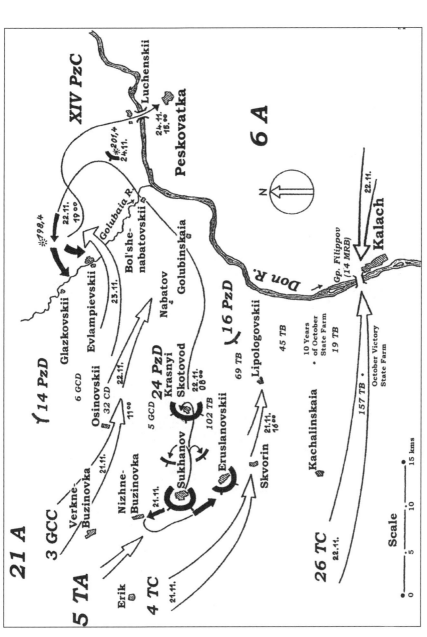

Map 20. XIV Panzer Corps' counterattack along the Don River, 21–24 November 1942

Schmidt and also by General Hoth, commander of Fourth Panzer Army, who, rather than fleeing, as Colonel Adam described, had been forced to move his headquarters to the town late on 21 November.

With Army Group B's command structure in the Stalingrad region in total chaos, General Weichs's only hope of restoring the situation north of the Don River rested with Hube's XIV Panzer Corps. Everything now depended on whether Hube's threadbare panzer division could muster enough skill, strength, and determination to thwart what was now recognized by friend and foe alike as a successful deep exploitation operation. Of course, the future viability of the army group's defenses also depended on the fate of Hoth's Fourth Panzer Army, which on 21 November was decisively engaged with the armies of Eremenko's Stalingrad Front in the steppes south of the city. And the news from south of Stalingrad was by no means encouraging.

THE STALINGRAD FRONT'S OFFENSIVE, 21 NOVEMBER

The Southwestern Front and the right wings of the Don and Stalingrad Fronts continued to develop their offensive successfully in their previous positions. . . .
  Stalingrad Front.
  62nd Army. 138th RD repelled several attacks by up to a battalion of enemy infantry with tanks and held on to its previous positions.
  284th RD and 92nd RB attacked toward Mamaev Kurgan and captured the crest of Hill 102.0 by day's end.
  The army's remaining units exchanged fire with the enemy and defended their positions.
  64th, 57th, 51st, and 28th Armies operated in accordance with the command's plan.

Red Army General Staff Operational Summary,
0800 hours on 22 November 1942[38]

Similar to the Southwestern and Don Fronts north and northwest of Stalingrad, the Red Army General Staff was not certain enough of the Stalingrad Front's victory south of the city to announce it to the Red Army as a whole. Therefore, as Eremenko's mobile groups continued their headlong dash to the northwest and their anticipated linkup with Vatutin's mobile groups, the General Staff once again limited itself to informing those who needed to know that the Stalingrad Front's armies were operating in accordance with the *Stavka*'s plan. And indeed, they were.

The three armies of Eremenko's Stalingrad Front participating in the main attack on Fourth Panzer Army resumed operations early on 21 November. Their missions were essentially the same as the day before, with an emphasis on projecting 57th Army's 13th Tank Corps and 51st Army's 4th Mechanized and 4th Cavalry Corps toward their deep objectives (see map 21).

Opposite Eremenko's forces, the defenses of Hoth's Fourth Panzer Army were already in shambles. Soviet forces had torn a huge gap between German IV and Romanian VI Army Corps; virtually destroyed the bulk of the latter's 1st, 2nd, and 18th Infantry Divisions; and savaged IV Corps' Romanian 20th Infantry Division by overrunning its regiment south of the Chervlenaia River and forcing its two regiments north of the river to withdraw precipitously. The commitment of 29th Motorized Division had been the only bright spot in an otherwise dismal day. It had halted the westward thrust by 57th Army's 13th Tank Corps and bloodied two of its mechanized brigades. However, with the collapse of 20th Infantry Division and the resulting threat to IV Corps' defenses as a whole, overnight on 20–21 November, Army Group B ordered 29th Motorized to withdraw northward and support IV Corps' right flank as it too wheeled northwestward to occupy defenses on Sixth Army's right flank. At the same time, Hoth moved his headquarters from Verkhne-Tsaritsynskii back to Buzinovka.

Hoth's decision was a wise one, given the catastrophic situation to the south and the fact that Leyser's division had defeated less than half of 13th Tank Corps. Furthermore, if 29th Motorized Division had charged off southward in search of new prey, IV Corps' defenses would have completely collapsed, leaving no forces to protect Sixth Army's now open right flank. Therefore, as dawn approached on 21 November, Leyser left the bulk of his panzer-grenadiers to withdraw south of the Chervlenaia River, while most of his panzers moved northward across the river to bolster IV Army Corps' defenses. A most interesting day was about to begin.

64th Army

General Shumilov's 64th Army resumed its offensive shortly after dawn, in the wake of a short artillery preparation and with the same shock group as the day before—38th, 157th, and 204th Rifle Divisions attacking in the sector from the Chervlenaia River, 4 kilometers west of Andreevka, northeastward to the southern outskirts of the German strongpoint at Elkhi. Once again, the assault struck the two regiments of Romanian 20th Infantry Division north of the Chervlenaia River and the right wing of 297th Infantry Division at Elkhi, both of which anchored the right wing of German IV Army Corps. Army Group B had subordinated 29th Motorized Division to Sixth Army the night before, a fact Paulus did not know until many hours later. Even so, Leyser had reinforced IV Corps' defenses with much of his division's armor.

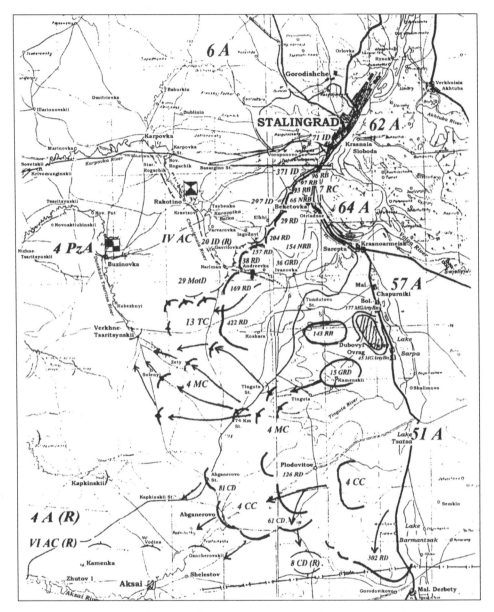

Map 21. Stalingrad Front's offensive: situation at 2200 hours, 21 November 1942

Therefore, soon after 64th Army's shock group began its attack, it encountered intense counterattacks against its center and right wing by up to two regiments of 297th Infantry Division, reportedly supported by 50 to 70 tanks. Although the provenance of these tanks remains unclear and their numbers were clearly exaggerated, the most likely source was 29th Motorized Division, whose orders on 21 November were to support Romanian 20th Infantry Division.[39] This counterattack not only halted the advance by 157th and 204th Rifle Divisions in the Iagodniki region but also compelled Colonel G. B. Safiulin's 38th Rifle Division to fall back a short distance north of the Chervlenaia River at Nariman after suffering heavy losses.

57th Army

In the sector of General Tolbukhin's 57th Army, most Soviet accounts assert that Tanaschishin's 13th Tank Corps continued its intense fight with 29th Motorized Division all day long on 21 November. However, most of the action actually took place during the afternoon and evening of the 20th. It is clear, however, that after the losses they incurred against Leyser's division the night before, 13th Tank Corps' 62nd Mechanized Brigade and 163rd Tank Regiment were barely combat effective on the morning of the 21st. As a result, the defeated Soviet force manned defenses south of Nariman, along with 422nd and 169th Rifle Divisions' infantry, in the morning. Later in the day, after 29th Motorized began withdrawing northward, Tanaschishin's tank corps committed its 17th and 61st Mechanized Brigades (with their 44th and 176th Tank Regiments), parts of the corps' fresh 35th and 166th Separate Tank Regiments, and elements of the army's 90th and 235th Tank Brigades to the fight.

Throughout the remainder of the day, the remnants of 13th Tank Corps' 62nd Mechanized Brigade and 163rd Tank Regiment, supported by elements of 422nd and 169th Rifle Divisions, fought to recapture Nariman from the rear guards of 29th Motorized Division's panzer-grenadiers. Farther to the west, as Leyser's division conducted its delaying action northward, 13th Tank Corps' 17th Mechanized Brigade and 44th Tank Regiment slowly pushed forward toward the vicinity of 8th of March State Farm, 13 kilometers west of Nariman.[40] Still licking its wounds from the previous day, Colonel I. K. Morozov's 422nd Rifle Division closely followed 17th Mechanized Brigade, reaching the region east of 8th of March State Farm by nightfall. By day's end, the advance by 57th Army's left wing threatened to outflank 29th Motorized Division's position stretching westward from Nariman, prompting German IV Army Corps to order Leyser's forces to start withdrawing to more secure defenses south of Karpovka beginning at midnight on 21 November.

When Sixth Army calculated the damage done to Soviet forces opposite IV Army Corps' defenses at day's end on 23 November, it claimed that the corps had destroyed 69 enemy tanks and captured 871 prisoners during the three days of fighting. It is likely that most of IV Corps' victims came from 13th Tank Corps and its two cooperating rifle divisions.[41]

51st Army

General Trufanov's 51st Army also resumed its offensive at dawn on the 21st, with 4th Mechanized and 4th Cavalry Corps leading its advance. To their rear, General Vasilenko's 15th Guards Rifle Division, with 57th Army's 143rd Rifle Brigade, cleared the remnants of Romanian 2nd Infantry Division from the Dubovoi *Ovrag* region west of Lake Sarpa. Vasilenko's division then reassembled in the Kamenka region, 12 kilometers southwest of the lake, and wheeled westward in the track of Vol'sky's armor and motorized troops. Farther south, Colonel Kuropatenko's 126th Rifle Division marched into the Plodovitoe region, which had recently been vacated by 4th Mechanized Corps; southeast of Plodovitoe, Colonel Makarchuk's 302nd Rifle Division swung its regiment southwest and south toward Tundutovo, 12 kilometers southwest of Lake Barmantsak. Thus, in combination with 4th Cavalry Corps, 126th and 302nd Divisions began constructing an outer encirclement front stretching from the Aksai region eastward 60 kilometers to Malye Derbety, 4 kilometers south of Lake Barmantsak.[42]

The honor of recording the greatest forward progress on 21 November fell to General Vol'sky's 4th Mechanized Corps. After a shaky start on the 20th, Vol'sky made by far the most spectacular progress on the 21st. After capturing Plodovitoe the day before, Vol'sky split his corps into three groups and dispatched them along three widely separate axes: north to Tinguta Station, northwest toward the railroad at 74-km Station, and west toward Privol'nyi and Iurkino State Farm. The corps' northern prong, consisting of 60th Mechanized Brigade and 21st Tank Regiment, captured Tinguta Station and Farm No. 3, 28 to 32 kilometers west of Lake Sarpa, by 1600 hours. In the process, they captured an entire regiment of Romanian 2nd Infantry Division and an immense store of supplies. Farther south, encountering little resistance, 59th Mechanized Brigade and 20th Tank Regiment seized 74-km Station and then pushed northwestward 14 kilometers to capture Zety, 40 kilometers due west of Lake Sarpa and about 15 kilometers southeast of Fourth Panzer Army's forward command post at Verkhne-Tsaritsynskii, by 1700 hours. There, it captured another 500 Romanians and was joined later by the corps' 158th Tank Regiment. Finally, by 1600 hours, the corps' 36th Mechanized Brigade and 55th Tank Regiment crossed the railroad running from Kotel'nikovo to Stalingrad about 3 kilometers north of Abganerovo Station;

helped 4th Cavalry Corps seize Abganerovo Station; captured Iurkino State Farm, roughly 40 kilometers west of Lake Tsatsa; and bivouacked at Farm No. 2, 10 kilometers north of Iurkino.[43]

By this time, having forced General Hoth to move his headquarters the night before, Vol'sky's mechanized corps now posed a definite threat to Fourth Panzer Army's new headquarters at Buzinovka, only 20 kilometers away from Vol'sky's tanks. This prompted Hoth to move his headquarters again on the night of 21–22 November, back to Nizhne-Chirskaia on the western bank of the Don, so as to take advantage of the protection of the broad river.

Farther to the south, General Shapkin's 4th Cavalry Corps, still under the watchful eye of General M. M. Popov, Eremenko's deputy, also resumed its advance at dawn on 21 November. After seizing Abganerovo and Abganerovo Station in the morning and reportedly capturing 5,000 Romanian troops, the corps' 81st and 61st Cavalry Divisions resumed their advance. But this time, General Popov ordered Shapkin's corps to advance its divisions along slightly diverging axes because of the weak enemy resistance. Accordingly, Colonel V. G. Baumshtein's 81st Cavalry Division galloped southwest toward the town of Aksai, and Colonel A. V. Stavenko's 61st Cavalry Division pushed southward west of Lake Barmantsak to reach the rear area of Romanian VII Army Corps' 4th Infantry Division. The 61st Cavalry did so because 4th Division's defenses west of Malye Derbety were holding up the advance by Major General M. V. Kalinin's 91st Rifle Division, which was deployed on 51st Army's left wing. As the two cavalry divisions advanced toward their objectives, they anxiously awaited the arrival of 126th Rifle Division, which had planned to catch up with and reinforce the cavalry the next day. The infantry would certainly be needed if the outer encirclement front was to be sufficiently durable to hold off any attempt by Fourth Panzer Army to counterattack and restore communications with its IV Army Corps.

62nd Army

While the three armies conducting the Stalingrad Front's main attack pushed toward their final objectives, Chuikov's 62nd Army continued to defend what little of its territory remained in Stalingrad city, as well as conducting local attacks to prevent Sixth Army's LI Army Corps from sending forces westward to help contain the Southwestern and Stalingrad Fronts' converging pincers (see map 22 and appendix 19A in the *Companion*). Chuikov's forces defended in the vicinity of the Barrikady and Krasnyi Oktiabr' Factories on their right wing but launched heavy assaults in the Mamaev Kurgan region in their center. Still isolated on "Liudnikov's Island," the narrow strip between the Barrikady Factory and the Volga River, the decimated 138th Rifle

Division repelled three attacks by up to a battalion of German infantry reportedly supported by seven assault guns (probably from LI Army Corps'
305th Infantry Division), as well as a fourth assault at nightfall. Colonel Liudnikov's division suffered heavy losses, including 180 men wounded, but in a
more positive vein, it finally received some ammunition and food. The ships
delivering the supplies also managed to evacuate 150 of the wounded. Similarly, 45th Rifle and 39th Guards Rifle Divisions repelled several battalion-
size assaults launched by LI Corps' 79th Infantry Division against their positions in the Krasnyi Oktiabr' Factory.[44]

In line with its assigned mission, 62nd Army's 284th Rifle Division, supported by part of 92nd Rifle Brigade, assaulted the defenses of 100th Jäger
Division on Mamaev Kurgan with its 1047th and 1045th Regiments at 1400
hours. Although it captured part of the crest of Hill 102.0 by day's end, the
General Staff credited Batiuk's division with only "limited gains." At nightfall, General Chuikov issued fresh orders to his threadbare forces, requiring
them to "hold on to your positions, attack locally to improve your positions,
and sharply increase your combat actions to support the *front*'s offensive and
tie down enemy forces."[45]

28th Army

On the Stalingrad Front's distant left wing west of Astrakhan', General Gerasimenko's 28th Army fully expected to conduct an all-out assault to seize
Khulkhuta on the morning of 21 November. It issued orders to that effect
to 34th Guards Rifle Division in the wee hours of the morning. However,
overnight, German 16th Motorized Division's 60th Panzer-Grenadier Regiment gathered up its wounded, its weapons, and its operable transport and
began evacuating the strongpoint, destroying all the equipment and supplies
it could not carry. During the evacuation, 16th Division's 156th Regiment
had the task of defending the corridor through which 60th Regiment had to
pass, as well as providing cover against attacks by 28th Army's forces from
the north and south.

At 0100 hours on 21 November, 60th Regiment's 2nd Battalion began the
evacuation, and the division's main forces concentrated for their breakout at
0300 hours. As dawn broke at 0500 hours, 156th Regiment launched spoiling attacks against Soviet forces threatening its flanks and 60th Regiment's
escape corridor. Not realizing their superiority, the Soviets, "conducted wild
and unceasing fire over the entire area, but could not understand that the
garrison was leaving Khulkhuta."[46] Later, in the after-action report he prepared on 14 December, General Gubarevich, commander of 34th Guards
Rifle Division, admitted, "During the offensive against Khulkhuta, the withdrawal of the enemy was noticed 12 hours late, which permitted the enemy

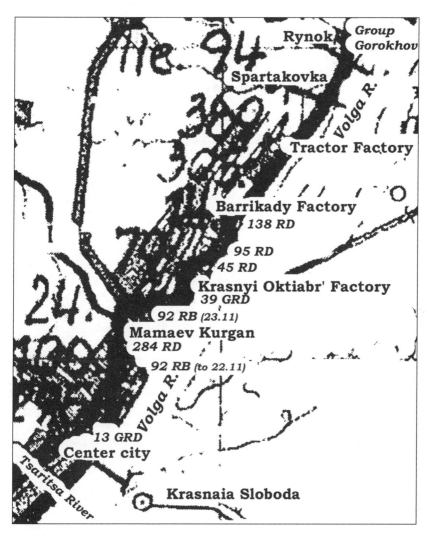

Map 22. Situation in Stalingrad, 19 November 1942

to separate themselves from our forces. On the morning of 21 November, the division reported about continuing stubborn enemy resistance, when, at that moment, there were already no enemy in the Khulkhuta region."[47] The division's chief of artillery seconded Gubarevich's judgment, adding that the Germans bypassed 152nd Separate Rifle Brigade's positions at Siantsik from the north; the division finally determined that the Germans had evacuated at 1000 hours.[48]

The first combat in the region took place after 1000 hours. Two infantry battalions from 156th Grenadier Regiment, supported by 15 tanks, attacked 152nd Separate Rifle Brigade's defenses at Siantsik to cover the withdrawal of 60th Regiment's covering forces from Khulkhuta, which had begun at 0800 hours. By 1000 hours, a forward detachment of Colonel Alekseenko's 152nd Separate Rifle Brigade, followed by 34th Guards Rifle Division's 105th Regiment, occupied the town, losing two tanks and 20 soldiers in the process.[49]

Summing up the two days of fighting in the Khulkhuta region, 28th Army's forces reported inflicting more than 1,100 casualties on 16th Motorized Division and destroying or capturing about 40 tanks and a significant amount of other weapons and equipment (see appendix 5Q in the *Companion*). The cost to 28th Army was about 1,300 killed, at least 1,100 wounded, and 14 tanks destroyed, which left the army with about 40 tanks.[50] In addition, during the initial pursuit from Khulkhuta to Iashkul', 28th Army recorded capturing 10 tanks, 5 76mm guns, 4 45mm guns, 6 37mm guns, 1 120mm mortar, 2 antiaircraft guns, 32 inoperable vehicles, 7 vehicles being repaired, 9 motorcycles, and 15 kilometers of telephone cable. However, these numbers seem inflated because 16th Motorized had 52 tanks initially—4 Pz-III and 48 Pz-IV models—and fielded 43 tanks on the 20th. The losses claimed by 28th Army would have reduced the motorized division's strength to about 18. Army Group A's combat journal entry for 22 November admitted that 16th Motorized Division "lost three companies and suffered heavy losses in material" in the fighting for Khulkhuta.[51] Overall, the division lost roughly 300 to 350 men killed or captured and about 700 men wounded.[52]

Soon after Khulkhuta fell, General Gerasimenko ordered a pursuit. The 34th Guards Division relieved 152nd Brigade in Siantsik, while the rifle brigade began to march west toward Utta. Soon after, 28th Army's 248th Rifle Division reached Khulkhuta, where it linked up with 34th Guards Division's 905th Regiment.

As far as 16th Motorized Division was concerned, the entry in Army Group A's combat journal on 22 November read:

Information from the 16th ID (Mot.): the main body of the division is located in a half-circle east and south of Yashkul [Iashkul']. The positions are good. The division command post is in Ulan Erge. The rear guard was forced out of Utta; the enemy has established himself 20 kilometers west of Utta. Apparently, he is operating with the 28th Guards Rifle Division, the 152nd Motorized Rifle Brigade and the 6th Heavy Tank Brigade. After defending against these forces, he (von Schwerin) wants to deploy as many forces as possible in order to attack the enemy in the north. —1700 hours: a message arrived: the 16th ID (Mot.) will be subordinated to the 4th Panzer Army. It and the 4th Rumanian will be subordinated to Generaloberst Hoth as Gruppe Hoth with the mission of holding line Yashkul-Tundutovo while covering the northern flank in the Aksai area.[53]

This order essentially ended 16th Motorized Division's relative independence. Henceforth, although still defending a broad front east of Elista, Schwerin's division was closely tied to Fourth Panzer Army's attempts to establish a reliable, coherent front southwest of Stalingrad and then mount an effort to relieve Sixth Army's forces isolated in the Stalingrad pocket.

Axis Reactions

The defeats suffered by Romanian VI and VII Army Corps during the first two days of the Stalingrad Front's offensive were so crippling that Fourth Romanian Army was never able to form and take control of operations south of Stalingrad. Instead, on 21 November, Army Group B assigned all of Romanian VI and VII Army Corps' forces not encircled in Stalingrad to Fourth Panzer Army's control. At the same time, General Hoth assumed control of 16th Motorized Division. Given the appalling losses suffered by most Romanian divisions, as well as their dismal combat performance, this was of little consolation to Hoth.

By day's end on 21 November, the dramatic thrust to Zety by 51st Army's 4th Mechanized Corps surrounded the remnants of Romanian 2nd and 18th Infantry Divisions; as they wandered individually and in small groups, the Romanians were policed by 57th Army's 143rd Rifle Brigade and 51st Army's 15th Guards Rifle Division as they marched westward in the mechanized corps' wake. The rapid Soviet advance, which overran most Romanian logistical installations north of the Aksai River, left the headquarters of Romanian VI Army Corps short of both fuel and ammunition. Nonetheless, it made every effort to assemble the remains of 6th *Rosiori* Regiment and 1st, 2nd, and 18th Infantry Divisions in the vicinity of the town of Aksai and employed them to erect a loose defensive cordon extending along the Aksai River from Shelestov, 15 kilometers south of Abganerovo; westward through Vodinski (Vodina), 15 kilometers southwest of Abganerovo; to Gniloaksaiskaia, 25 kilometers west-southwest of Abganerovo and 12 kilometers northeast of Aksai. Fourth Panzer Army soon reinforced these forces with a handful of tanks and assault guns from its workshops. However, the remnants of this Romanian corps, as well as Fourth Panzer Army, were now bereft of most of their heavy weapons and equipment and woefully short of both fuel and ammunition.

Nor was Romanian VII Army Corps in much better condition. Its combat force now consisted of the southernmost regiment of Romanian 1st Infantry Division (VI Corps' only unit that managed to avoid encirclement), which was protecting the approaches to Tundutovo from the north, and the as yet unscathed Romanian 4th Infantry Division, which was still defending in the sector from the middle of the western shore of Lake Barmantsak southward to Ar-Manutch, north of Lake Batyr-Mala. In addition, VII Corps shifted its 5th Cavalry Division into defenses south of Abganerovo and 8th Cavalry Division's 2nd *Călărasi* Regiment into defensive positions midway between 5th Cavalry and Tundutovo. This left the remainder of 8th Cavalry Division to defend the immense sector from Ar-Manutch southward to 25 kilometers north of Chilgir.[54]

Conclusions

By day's end on 21 November, the third day of the offensive, the Southwestern Front's 4th and 26th Tank Corps and 3rd Guards Cavalry Corps had developed the offensive toward Kalach to depths of 110 to 120 kilometers, reaching the Ostrov, Eruslanovskii, and Os'kinskii line. Their forward detachments were just 20 kilometers from the Don River north of Kalach and 35 kilometers west of the Don at Kalach. To the south, the Stalingrad Front's mobile groups had advanced northwestward 40 to 60 kilometers and occupied positions extending from State Farm No. 8 eastward through Zety to just north of Nariman on the Chervlenaia River. The gap between the forward elements of the two *fronts'* mobile groups was just 80 kilometers. However, as close as they were to fulfilling the *Stavka's* ultimate mission—to link up and encircle German Sixth Army—everyone in the *Stavka* and the two *front* headquarters realized that one question remained to be answered before victory would be assured: could Sixth Army's XIV Panzer Corps bring enough of its panzer forces to bear to halt the mobile group's headlong advance? They would learn the answer to that question by day's end on 22 November.

THE SOUTHWESTERN AND DON FRONTS' OFFENSIVE, 22 NOVEMBER

The Southwestern Front, during the course of 22 November, attacked westward and southwestward toward Gorbatovskii and Chernyshevskaia with part of its forces and fought to destroy the encircled forces of Rumanian V Army Corps in the Raspopinskaia, Bazkovskii, and Golovskii region; and its main forces, together with the right-wing units of the Don Front, attacked energetically southeastward in the general direction of Kalach to reach the flank and rear of the main grouping of German forces along the Stalingrad axis. The attacking forces captured the Kalach and Mostovskii region and reached the right bank of the Don River in the Malogolubaia and Bol'shenabatovskii region by day's end.

Red Army General Staff Operational Summary,
0800 hours on 23 November 1942[55]

The Southwestern and Don Fronts' Missions

Once their mobile groups reached Romanian Third and German Sixth Armies' operational rear areas overnight on 21–22 November, well within striking distance of the Don River at Kalach and to the north, Vatutin and Rokossovsky gave their armies missions that they hoped would finally achieve the primary objective of Operation Uranus—the encirclement of Paulus's Sixth Army. In close coordination with the commanders of their subordinate armies, they also assigned new missions to the other forces in the two attacking *fronts* (see appendix 5R in the *Companion*). The Southwestern Front was to reach and force the Don River with the mobile corps of 5th Tank and 21st Armies, capture the town of Kalach, and advance southeastward to the Sovetskii region, where it would link up with the Stalingrad Front's mobile groups to encircle German Sixth Army. Vatutin's cavalry and rifle forces were to advance across the Chir River and capture the enemy strongpoints of Bokovskaia, Chernyshevskaia, Oblivskaia, and Surovikino. The Don Front was to exploit its offensive southeastward with 65th Army and begin an offensive toward Vertiachii, 20 kilometers south-southwest of Kachalinskaia, while 24th Army encircled and destroyed Sixth Army's XI Army Corps in the northeastern extremity of the Great Bend of the Don.

Attesting to Stalin's and the *Stavka's* increasing confidence that the Southwestern and Don Fronts' armies could accomplish these missions, beginning at 0800 hours on 23 November, they finally permitted the General Staff to include in its daily operational summaries precise details regarding the accomplishments of their attacking forces down to the division and separate brigade levels.

The Southwestern Front's Advance

5th Tank Army

Pride of place in 5th Tank Army's 22 November advance went to its mobile groups, 1st and 26th Tank Corps, which finally reached Kalach-on-the-Don and the region to the southwest. General Rodin, commander of 26th Tank Corps (whose 216th Tank Brigade was still supporting 50th Guards Rifle Division far to the north), decided to resume his advance early in the morning with 19th and 157th Tank and 14th Motorized Rifle Brigades (see map 23 and appendix 5S in the *Companion* for the Southwestern Front's accomplishments on 22 November). At the time, the three brigades occupied positions extending from Plesistovskii, 35 kilometers northwest of Kalach, southward to Kachalinskaia and Ostrov on the Liska River, 23 to 25 kilometers west-northwest of Kalach. When Rodin reached Ostrov, he summoned the commander of 14th Motorized Rifle Brigade, Lieutenant Colonel G. N. Filippov, to his command post and ordered him to organize his brigade to "operate as a forward detachment and seize a crossing [in the Kalach region] from the march and hold on to it until the corps' main forces arrived."[56]

As context for Filippov's raid, a classified Soviet account of 26th Tank Corps' operations on 22 November recorded the following: "The corps resumed its offensive on the night of 21–22 November and encountered stubborn resistance along the line of the Liska River from subunits of the German 3rd Motorized Division, which had arrived from behind the Don with the mission of preventing Soviet forces from penetrating to the river."[57] Regardless of the resistance encountered by 26th Corps, Rodin created Filippov's forward detachment before the corps began its advance. The detachment consisted of two motorized rifle companies from his own motorized rifle brigade and armored cars from 26th Corps' 15th Separate Reconnaissance Battalion.[58]

Filippov's detachment left the Ostrov region, 23 kilometers northwest of Kalach, at 0300 hours. It skillfully maneuvered along the Kalach road at maximum speed, with the headlights on its armored cars shining, and reached the western bank of the Don River opposite Kalach, where the bridge was supposed to be, at 0600 hours. With regard to German defenses protecting Kalach, Colonel Wilhelm Adam, General Paulus's adjutant, later wrote, "A military-engineer school and a pilots' school, reinforced by all types of rear service subunits, under the command of Colonel Hans Mikosch, occupied a bridgehead on the western bank of the Don, which could not be bypassed. The officers' school in Suvorovskii was [also] being brought to combat readiness."[59] Adam noted that Mikosch had organized his defenses on the high ground (Hill 161.0) on the Don River's eastern bank, opposite Kalach and just south of the village of Berezovskii, and had prepared the bridge for destruction.

Map 23. Southwestern and Don Fronts' advance at 2200 hours, 22 November 1942

When Filippov's forward detachment found no intact bridge, it dismounted, assaulted on foot, and succeeded in penetrating the Germans' defenses with five armored cars and 50 motorized riflemen. Soon after, his small force was reinforced by a tank company with six tanks from Major Makhur's 157th Tank Brigade, which had also managed to filter through the Germans' defenses unscathed. Although one of Makhur's tanks turned back to catch the Germans from the rear and was never heard from again, Filippov's detachment pushed forward undeterred until it met a local inhabitant, who informed the commander that the Germans had blown the bridge at Kalach. The local then led the detachment northward 3 kilometers to a new bridge the Germans had just erected at Berezovskii, 4 kilometers west-northwest of the center of Kalach. The Don River at this location was 600 meters wide, with a small island in the middle, so there were actually two bridges connecting the island to the two banks of the river. On Filippov's orders, one tank, with a group of infantry on board, crossed the ice and captured the island, while the remainder of the detachment moved along the road to the crossing. It was between 0800 and 0900 hours, and the German sentries on the bridge initially displayed no real concern about the column because the Germans often used captured Russian T-34s. Only when the column reached the riverbank and approached the bridge did the sentries open fire, but by then, it was too late. Filippov's detachment seized the bridge after a brief exchange of fire and immediately dismantled the explosive charges on the bridge itself and the mines on its approaches.

Explaining what had happened from the Germans' perspective, Hans Dörr later wrote, "The Russians' tank unit approached the bridge and seized it without a fight, since the sentries on the bridge mistook it for a German training unit equipped with captured Russian tanks, which frequently used the bridge."[60] The failure of German engineers to blow up this bridge contributed mightily to the ultimate German defeat. If the bridge had been destroyed, it could have caused a one- to three-day delay in the linkup and may have influenced the decisions of the German High Command.

At 0619 hours on 22 November, XIV Panzer Corps sent a cryptic message to Sixth Army reporting that 24th Panzer Division had identified enemy forces in Ostrov; that the division's headquarters was in Krasnyi Skotovod, 23 kilometers to the north-northeast; that the situation regarding Soviet dispositions was unclear; and that communications had been interrupted. The report also announced: "Bridgehead Kalatsch [Kalach]: a breakthrough by 8–9 enemy tanks at [Reference or *Bezugspunkt* Point] 966 [Hill 162.9, 12 kilometers northwest of Kalach]. Supposedly, they want to drive over the bridge at Kalatsch. The security forces are in combat with enemy infantry at 966. At 0115 hours, 20 enemy tanks from the north are on the northern outskirts of Popow [Popov] 1. Ostrow [Ostrov] was occupied by enemy forces during the course of the night."[61]

At 1900 hours that evening, Sixth Army acknowledged to Army Group B, "Despite heroic sacrificial resistance, the entire Zarizatal [Tsaritsa valley], the railroad from Sowjetskij [Sovetskii] to Kalatsch [Kalach], the Don bridge at that location, and the heights on the west bank of the Don as far as Golubinskaja [Golubinskaia], Oskinskij [Oskinskii] and Krainij [Krainii] are in Russian hands."[62]

Interestingly, Filippov's detachment took the bridge in utter isolation and without the knowledge of the corps or his neighboring brigades because, at the time, he lacked radio communications with anyone. Filippov himself credited his good fortune to a combination of luck and surprise. In any case, Filippov's detachment remained encircled in an all-round defense but in possession of the vital bridge for 11 hours, during which time he repelled several German counterattacks before being relieved. For his detachment's gallant action in seizing the bridge, Filippov was later awarded the title Hero of the Soviet Union.

As for the remainder of 26th Tank Corps, it moved southeastward from its positions in the Liska River valley shortly after dawn. It traversed 15 to 18 kilometers during the day, engaging and defeating Romanian and German forces en route along a line extending from *Pobeda Oktiabriia* (October Victory) and *10 Let Oktiabriia* (10 Years of October) State Farms, 15 to 17 kilometers west of Kalach; northeastward through Hills 162.9 and 159.2, 15 kilometers west-northwest of Kalach; to the town of Lozhki, 12 kilometers northwest of Kalach.[63] The corps' three brigades reached the Don River at and north of Kalach late in the day, and 19th Brigade secured passage over the river by day's end.

Colonel Filippenko's 19th Tank Brigade, supported by 1241st Tank Destroyer Artillery Regiment, reached the Liska River early in the morning and then engaged and defeated an infantry battalion, reportedly from Romanian 15th Infantry Division, with its motorized rifle battalion by midmorning. During the fighting at the river, Filippenko ordered his lead tank battalion to engage the Romanians with its guns, while the rifle battalion and 1241st Tank Destroyer Regiment attacked the Romanians' defensive positions, forcing them to break and run.[64] After capturing numerous prisoners, the brigade's riflemen advanced eastward 12 kilometers to the approaches to Lozhki, where it linked up at midday with the brigade's tanks and wheeled vehicles, which had crossed the Liska River at Ostrov. After defeating lead elements of 16th Panzer Division at Lozhki, the brigade advanced another 12 kilometers southeastward, crossed the Don River at Berezovskii at 1700 hours, relieved Filippov's forward detachment, and then occupied positions in a grove of trees northwest of Kalach by 2000 hours.[65]

Meanwhile, Major Makhur's 157th Tank Brigade found the going a bit tougher. After advancing eastward from Ostrov at dawn, the brigade encountered its first serious resistance at *Pobeda Oktiabriia* and *10 Let Oktiabriia* State Farms, where a German force, reportedly equipped with about 50 captured and refurbished Russian tanks, occupied defensive positions left over from the fighting in July and August 1942. Major Makhur was killed early in the action, leaving the brigade under the temporary command of its political officer, Major V. Ia. Kudriashev. The brigade left a holding force on its front and maneuvered southward to find a weak point in the Germans' defenses. By 1400 hours, 157th Brigade attacked and overcame a force reportedly consisting of part of Romanian 6th Infantry Division and German rear service units (from Group Mikosch); it then raced northward to defeat Mikosch's forces on Hills 162.9 and 159.2, 2 to 3 kilometers west of the river, and pushed on toward Kalach, reaching the river's western bank opposite the southern part of the town by evening. Advancing in between 19th and 157th Tank Brigades, the remainder of 14th Motorized Rifle Brigade got tied up by enemy defenses on Hill 159.2 but overcame the resistance in the evening. Then it too closed into the Berezovskii region north of Kalach, where it reinforced 19th Tank Brigade early the next morning.

After being overrun by 5th Tank Army, the German forces defending west of Kalach either fell back into the town or withdrew southward under Colonel Mikosch's command to occupy defenses at Rychkovskii and Chir Station, key communications centers on the western bank of the Don along the railroad line stretching eastward to Stalingrad.

Late on 22 November, General Rodin arrived on the scene and set up his headquarters at *Pobeda Oktiabriia* State Farm. He then ordered 19th Tank and 14th Motorized Brigades, operating under the overall control of Lieutenant Colonel Filippenko, to seize Kalach early the next day. The remainder of the corps concentrated north of Kalach and in the Mostovskii region, awaiting orders to advance toward Sovetskii and Marinovka, 10 to 12 kilometers southeast of Kalach, and link up with the Stalingrad Front's 4th Mechanized Corps, which had just secured Sovetskii. Still later on the night of 22–23 November, one tank brigade of General Kravchenko's 4th Tank Corps also crossed the river at Berezovskii, while the corps' main forces reached the Don River at and north of Lipo-Lebedevskii, 12 to 16 kilometers north of Kalach.

While Rodin's corps was descending on Kalach-on-the-Don, General Butkov's 1st Tank Corps, far to the west, began its advance from the Lipovskii and Golubinka regions, 10 to 15 kilometers south of Perelazovskii, at 0350 hours. It moved southwestward into the Kurtlak River valley and overran Romanian 1st Armored Division's rear service elements east of Kalach-Kurtlak, 18 kilometers southwest of Perelazovskii, reportedly capturing 260 Romanians and considerable equipment. It also scattered a larger enemy garrison at Kalach-Kurtlak, 2 kilometers to the west, where 22nd Panzer

Division's rear services were based. At about midmorning, Butkov's entire corps wheeled 180 degrees and sped rapidly southeastward across the open steppes for up to 80 kilometers, capturing a series of towns and villages in its path and destroying or scattering their garrisons. By the end of the day, the corps' brigades were concentrated in the vicinity of the towns of Lysov, Zrianinskii (Zrianin), Tuzov, and Pogodinskii on the lower Liska River. By this time, Butkov's forces were positioned 25 kilometers west to 35 kilometers southwest of Kalach and 10 to 20 kilometers north of Chir Station and the town of Rychkovskii, 8 kilometers east of the station. From north to south, 159th Tank Brigade laagered in Lysov, 89th Tank Brigade in Zrianinskii, 117th Tank Brigade in Tuzov, and 44th Motorized Rifle Brigade in Pogodinskii.[66] Therefore, by the end of the fourth day of the offensive, Butkov's corps had finally accomplished the missions it should have completed by the end of the second day.

As 1st Tank Corps raced southeastward, it dispatched a motorized rifle battalion from its lead 44th Motorized Rifle Brigade to reconnoiter westward into the region north and northeast of Surovikino, 25 kilometers northwest of Chir Station, and protect its right flank as it advanced. When the corps completed its operations at nightfall, only 24 of its original 136 tanks remained operational. Of the remainder, roughly 40 had been destroyed or damaged in the fight with 22nd Panzer Division days before, another 30 to 40 had been destroyed by German air strikes during its long exploitation toward the Chir River, and the remaining 30 to 40 had fallen victim to mechanical difficulties.[67] Soviet critiques of the corps' performance lamented that, despite the lingering dense fog, small groups of enemy aircraft still managed to strike the tank columns as they advanced. Losses due to mechanical difficulties would become a standard feature of tank corps operations during the winter of 1942–1943. In this instance, the paucity of armor left in Butkov's corps made it exceedingly difficult for it to accomplish its missions along the Chir River. However, in early December, the Southwestern Front would provide the corps with more than 100 new tanks, allowing it to operate across the Chir.

Far to the rear of 5th Tank Army's two tank corps, 55th and 112th Cavalry Divisions of General Borisov's 8th Cavalry Corps had been left with the unpleasant task of dealing with XXXXVIII Panzer Corps' German 22nd Panzer and Romanian 1st Armored Divisions. The former was still fighting in the Bol'shaia Donshchinka region, and the latter was in the southern portion of Group Lascar's pocket east of the Tsaritsa River. The primary mission of Borisov's cavalry was to prevent the German panzer division from linking up with and rescuing any of the Romanian forces encircled south and southwest of Raspopinskaia, in particular, the Romanian armored division. The night before, both General Dumitrescu, commander of Romanian Third Army, and General Ilia Steflea, chief of the Royal Romanian Army's General Staff,

had secretly authorized Group Lascar and 1st Armored to break out of the
encirclement. This was in direct violation of Hitler's order to stand fast and,
if necessary, die.

As 55th and 112th Cavalry Divisions carefully contained the German
panzer division in the region between Bol'shaia and Malaia Donshchinka,
General Gheorghe's 1st Armored Division tried to break out once again.
Early in the morning on the 22nd, Gheorghe's division attacked southwest
toward the Tsaritsa River, between Novo-Tsaritsynskii and Zhirkovskii, with
a force of roughly 20 R-2 tanks and 220 trucks and other vehicles. The division's objective was to link up with 22nd Panzer Division somewhere in
the vicinity of Bol'shaia and Malaia Donshchinka. Catching 5th Tank Army's
119th Rifle Division by surprise, the assault quickly penetrated the rifle division's positions along and east of the river and propelled Gheorghe's armor
into 8th Cavalry Corps' rear, roughly 8 kilometers east of Peschanyi.[68]

Borisov reacted by ordering Colonel Chalenko's 55th Cavalry to engage
and block the Romanian armored force. Meanwhile, in accordance with
General Romanenko's orders, General Shaimuratov's 112th Cavalry moved
southwestward and then southward around 22nd Panzer Division's left flank
to reach Krasnoiarovka on the Chir River, 8 kilometers east of Chernyshevskaia. Once he arrived, Shaimuratov was to send part of his division east
toward Petrovka on the Kurtlak River to intercept the Romanian division
before it reached the Chir River; another part of the division was to move
southward to Arzhanovskii on the Chir, 17 kilometers southeast of Chernyshevskaia, to erect blocking positions along the Chir's western bank.

After penetrating 119th Rifle Division's defenses, Gheorghe's 1st Armored
thrust south toward Medvezhyi, generating a running fight with 55th Cavalry
Division, its supporting 511th Separate Tank Battalion, and perhaps part of
8th Guards Tank Brigade, whose main forces were still supporting the advance by 159th Rifle and 21st Cavalry Divisions farther to the west. From
this point on, Soviet and Romanian accounts vary sharply. The Soviets assert
that 55th Cavalry Division and its supporting armor repelled 1st Armored
Division's attack, destroying 27 tanks and 60 trucks, killing about 600 Romanian soldiers, and capturing another 150 men.[69] In contrast, Romanian
accounts claim that Gheorghe's division repulsed a Soviet attack and, in the
process, captured 256 prisoners and destroyed 65 tanks, 10 antitank guns,
129 motor vehicles, and 108 motorcycles at a cost of only 10 Romanian tanks
destroyed but extremely heavy losses in the division's antitank and reconnaissance battalions.[70] Given the size of the forces engaged, both accounts seem
to exaggerate their opponent's strengths and losses.

In any event, the bulk of Gheorghe's forces succeeded in penetrating
55th Cavalry Division's blocking positions and worked their way south. After
failing to link up with 22nd Panzer Division, which spent the day fencing

with Soviet cavalry and infantry in the region between Bol'shaia and Malaia Donshchinka and Medvezhyi, the remnants of 1st Armored Division made their way southward into the Kurtlak River valley east of Petrovka and, according to Romanian accounts, seized the town. However, Soviet accounts assert that, after completing its march around 22nd Panzer Division's left flank, Shaimuratov's 112th Cavalry Division captured Petrovo and reached the Kurtlak River by day's end. Then, in accordance with its orders, the division set up blocking positions at Krasnoiarovka on the Chir to prevent the remnants of the Romanian armored division from moving westward along the Kurtlak River.[71]

While Gheorghe's forces were making their escape, Colonel Rodt's 22nd Panzer Division remained essentially encircled in a loose pocket encompassing the region from Medvezhyi northeastward 8 kilometers to Bol'shaia Donshchinka on the Donshchinka River, southward 5 kilometers along the river to Malaia Donshchinka, and then westward 5 kilometers across a ridge to Medvezhyi. This pocket contained the division's *Kampfgruppe* Oppeln, with 204th Panzer Regiment, 2nd Battalion of 129th Panzer-Grenadier Regiment, and 24th Motorcycle Battalion, with 140th Panzer *Jagd Abteilung*, along the northern periphery of the ring and 1st Battalion, 129th Grenadier Regiment, and 3rd Battalion, 140th Panzer Artillery Regiment, along the southern circumference of the ring. Of course, all these units were significantly understrength and supported by only a handful of tanks.[72]

The final component of 5th Tank Army's mobile forces, 8th Motorcycle Regiment, embarked on a deep but short-lived and ultimately superfluous raid on 22 November. The evening before, Romanenko had ordered the regiment to move southward quickly and capture the town of Oblivskaia on the Chir River. By seizing this key terrain, the motorcycle troops would cut the Germans' rail communication to Stalingrad from their base area at Morozovsk and disrupt Romanian Third Army's deeper defenses along the Chir, the next major natural obstacle to 5th Tank Army's advance.

The motorcycle regiment began its southward advance at 0700 hours, initially following in the tracks of 1st Tank Corps. After passing through Perelazovskii and the town of Sredniaia Gusynka, 18 kilometers south of Perelazovskii, the regiment advanced southward 20 kilometers against only light resistance, passing through the village of Bokachevka, 30 kilometers north of Oblivskaia, and capturing the village of Krasnoe Selo at 1700 hours. However, after exploiting the heavy fog and dirt roads to traverse 90 to 95 kilometers in nine and a half hours, instead of marching directly on Oblivskaia, 8th Motorcycle formed five separate detachments and ordered them to conduct diversionary operations in and north of the Oblivskaia region.[73]

Subsequently, the five detachments conducted separate diversionary raids into Romanian Third Army's rear area (see appendix 5T in the

Companion for details). Although these failed to accomplish anything of major importance, the detachments created chaos in Third Army's rear area. A secret Soviet critique of 5th Tank Army's operations quoted a captured German officer from 22nd Panzer Division, who believed these raids had been conducted by "a special young Stalinist spy-diversionary division . . . , which always showed up unexpectedly and conducted sudden attacks on German and Romanian forces from the rear." However, the study concluded that, "having subdivided itself into detachments, the 8th MtrcR did not fulfill its main mission—[which was] to capture Oblivskaia and cut the Stalingrad-Likhaia railroad."[74]

With 5th Tank Army's mobile corps finally accomplishing their deep missions with a certain degree of aplomb, its rifle forces steadily pushed the survivors of Romanian Third Army back toward the Krivaia and Chir Rivers and fought to liquidate Romanian Group Lascar's encirclement pocket south and southwest of Raspopinskaia. During the day, the divisions on the right wing and right center of Romanenko's army reached positions extending from Belavinskii on the Krivaia River, 35 kilometers north of Chernyshevskaia, southward to the Krivaia's junction with the Chir River, and southeastward along the Chir River past Pichugin and Demin to the Chernyshevskaia region. Before doing so, however, General Vatutin directed Romanenko to transfer 14th Guards Rifle Division and its reinforcing artillery regiments, which were situated on the army's extreme right wing, to General Leliushenko's 1st Guards Army. This transfer left 159th Rifle Division anchoring the tank army's right wing.

Immediately after this transfer, Colonel M. B. Anashkin's 159th Division, supported by Major Nikolov's 8th Guards Tank Brigade, attacked southwestward at dawn, slowly pushing the remnants of Romanian I Army Corps' 9th and 11th Infantry Divisions back toward the Krivaia and Chir Rivers. As it advanced, Anashkin's division was supported on its right by 1st Guards Army's 14th Guards and 203rd and 278th Rifle Divisions, which conducted local attacks and raids northward east of the Krivaia. The 159th captured the villages of Kamenka, Astakhov, and Belavinskii, 20 to 32 kilometers north of Chernyshevskaia, by day's end, thus clearing Romanian forces from most of the eastern bank of the Krivaia River from Belavinskii southward to its junction with the Chir River and from the northern bank of the Chir southeastward to Illarionov, 18 kilometers northwest of Chernyshevskaia.

By this time, both of Romanian I Corps' divisions were thoroughly exhausted and completely disorganized. However, early the next day, as ordered by Army Group B, General of Infantry Karl Hollidt's XVII Army Corps, which had been in reserve, reinforced Romanian Third Army's defenses along the Krivaia River north of Bokovskaia with its 62nd and 294th Infantry Divisions. The arrival of the two relatively fresh German infantry divisions revitalized the defenses on the Romanian army's left wing and likely prevented the subsequent encirclement of Romanian I Army Corps. The appearance of General Hollidt's corps began a long period during which the name "Hollidt" would resound throughout southern Russia, first as a corps group and ultimately as a full-fledged army detachment [*Armee Abteilung*]. In addition, the timely commitment of Hollidt's corps not only prevented Soviet forces from collapsing Romanian Third Army's left wing but also forestalled a potential immediate threat to Italian Eighth Army.[75]

South of this region of intensified fighting along and east of the Krivaia and upper Chir Rivers, Colonel Iakunin's 21st Cavalry Division, which had been detached from Borisov's cavalry corps to reinforce the offensive by the rifle divisions on 5th Tank Army's right wing, attacked southwestward from the Kamenka region. Overcoming the defenses on Romanian 9th Infantry Division's right wing, 21st Cavalry reached the Chir River in the sector from Illarionov southward to Pichugin, 13 to 18 kilometers northwest of Chernyshevskaia, by the end of the day. On the cavalry's left, General Fokanov's 47th Guards Rifle Division drove what was left of the already withdrawing Romanian 7th Cavalry Division, now fighting alongside the remnants of Romanian 14th Infantry Division, back to the Chir's western bank from Pichugin southward to Chernyshevskaia by day's end.

Other than the exploitation by Rodin's 26th Tank Corps across the Don River at Kalach and by Butkov's 1st Tank Corps to the region southwest of Kalach, the most dramatic developments of 22 November occurred on 5th Tank Army's left wing. There, along and east of the Tsaritsa River, the rifle forces on the army's left wing struggled to liquidate encircled Romanian Group Lascar. Beginning before dawn, General Belov's 50th Guards Rifle Division, along with 26th Tank Corps' 216th Tank Brigade, and Colonel Kulagin's 119th Rifle Division, together with a regiment of 346th Rifle Division protecting its left flank, attacked Group Lascar's defenses along and east of the Tsaritsa River. Simultaneously, 21st Army's 96th, 63rd, and 333rd Rifle Divisions advanced from the east and southeast to link up with 5th Tank Army's divisions and destroy Romanian forces encircled in the region between Raspopinskaia and the towns of Verkhne-Fomikhinskii and Golovskii.

Belov's 50th Guards Division and 216th Tank Brigade's armor struck Group Lascar's 6th Infantry Division, drove the Romanians southeastward, and captured the remainder of Verkhne-Fomikhinskii and the village of Belosoin, 7 kilometers to the southeast. Simultaneously, Kulagin's 119th Division attacked eastward and northeastward from the Tsaritsa River valley, captured Korotkovskii, and fought to capture Zhirkovskii against strong resistance. It was at this juncture that Gheorghe's 1st Armored Division broke out westward across the Tsaritsa River in the early morning and moved southwestward in an attempt to reach 22nd Panzer Division's positions in the Bol'shaia Donshchinka region. Ignoring the Romanian breakout, 50th Guards and 119th Divisions lunged east toward the town of Golovskii, the site of Group Lascar's headquarters, 10 kilometers east of Korotkovskii.

Much earlier, at 0230 hours, 5th Tank Army had radioed a message to Group Lascar's beleaguered troops, demanding that they surrender immediately and unconditionally. Once they received this ultimatum, Generals Mihail Lascar, Nicolae Mazarini, and Iaon Sion, the commanders of 6th, 5th, and 15th Divisions, respectively, answered defiantly, "We will continue to fight without thought of surrender." This response was reportedly "received with uncharacteristic emotion by their German liaison officers."[76]

In reaction to this Romanian defiance, 50th Guards Division exploited southeast toward Belonemukhin in the morning, reaching the rear of Romanian 5th Infantry Division's left wing and forcing General Mazarini to withdraw his forces to new defensive positions stretching from Belonemukhin to Bazkovskaia. This left the northern third of Group Lascar's pocket in Soviet hands. By now, 5th Division was beginning to disintegrate. Throughout the morning, General Lascar sent a series of increasingly desperate messages to Romanian Third Army, asking for help. These, in turn, generated sharp recriminations between the Romanians and their German liaison officers. From the Romanian perspective, things were quite grim:

> Artillery ammunition was down to 40 rounds per gun, mortar ammunition was also short, many men had not eaten for days, the wounded could no longer be adequately tended and even the recently supplied German 75mm AT guns had proved of limited effect. The Germans later suggested that the shortage of ammunition and food, and the lack of medical evacuation, were the result of faulty Romanian administration, but the Romanians attributed it to the German domination of the railroads and their own lack of motor transport.[77]

The Romanian divisions did lack adequate antitank weapons, especially antitank guns [*Panzerabwehrgeschütze—Pak*], despite repeated promises by the Germans and by Hitler himself to provide these weapons. In general, despite comments by Colonel Adam and others about the Romanians' propensity to flee, the Romanians actually fought far better than many Germans gave them credit for. Nevertheless, many Germans were accustomed to blaming others for their own deficiencies.

Given the desperate circumstances faced by Group Lascar, Romanian Third Army once again asked for Hitler's permission to allow the group to break out; however, that permission was denied. Shortly thereafter, the Soviets radioed a second surrender ultimatum to Lascar, which the group's commanders rejected at 1000 hours. In the meantime, beginning at 0900 hours,

German aircraft began attempting to supply the group by air. After a single German light aircraft landed at Golovskii at 0900 hours, 10 He-111 aircraft dropped supplies to the beleaguered Romanians at 1100 hours, and another 5 Romanian Ju-52 aircraft landed food, fuel, and ammunition and evacuated 60 wounded officers at 1300 hours.[78] Frustrated by the lack of support, at 1600 hours, Generals Lascar, Mazarini, and Sion once again met at Golovskii and decided to begin a concerted attempt to break out at 2200 hours. According to Lascar's breakout plan, his own 6th Infantry Division was to head southwest toward Peschanyi, and Sion's 15th Infantry Division was to march parallel to but south of Lascar's column toward Bol'shaia Donshchinka. To protect the withdrawal, one battalion of 6th Division's 15th *Dorobanţi* Regiment and divisional troops were to replace the already departed 1st Armored Division in the Zhirkovskii region and serve as flank guards during the breakout.[79]

Despite Group Lascar's carefully orchestrated escape plan, Soviet attacks preempted its actions and radically changed the situation for the worse. After resuming their assaults eastward and southeastward at midday, 5th Tank Army's 119th Rifle and 50th Guards Rifle Divisions engaged the defending Romanian 6th Infantry Division west and northwest of Golovskii at about 1600 hours, precipitating a fight that lasted until 2100 hours, when Kulagin's and Belov's riflemen reached the town. Simultaneously, Colonel G. P. Isakov's 96th Rifle Division of 21st Army attacked southward from its positions west of Bazkovskaia, collapsed Romanian 5th Infantry Division's defenses, and advanced 20 kilometers to the vicinity of the village of Izbushenskii, 10 kilometers northeast of Golovskii. There, it linked up with a regiment of the same army's 63rd Rifle Division, which was advancing on the village from the east. Being assaulted from three sides by rifle forces from 5th Tank and 21st Armies, Golovskii fell to 50th Guards Rifle Division at 2100 hours on 22 November.[80]

The Soviets' final assault on the town knocked out Group Lascar's communications and forced the Romanian defenders to withdraw either to the north, to join 6th Infantry Division, or to the south, to join the remnants of 15th Infantry Division. This left Group Lascar divided into two parts. General Lascar's deputy, Brigade General Trojan Stanescu, escaped northward to lead the forces in 6th Infantry Division's pocket encircled west of Raspopinskaia, and General Sion escaped southward to rejoin the remnants of his 15th Infantry Division in a pocket south of Golovskii. As for General Lascar, after trying to escape northward, he was captured by Soviet troops, and his subsequent fate is unknown.[81] The German government later recognized his gallantry by the award of oak leaves to the Knight's Cross, a rarity for a foreign officer. Regardless, the entire Lascar "affair" left a bitter taste in Romanian circles. At the highest level, Marshal Antonescu, the Romanian head of state, had tried to intervene personally, sending a message requesting that the Führer permit Group Lascar to break out and fight another day. Hitler responded that he had done so, but it was clearly too late (see appendixes 5U and 5V in the *Companion* for this exchange of messages).

21st Army

On the left wing of the Southwestern Front's pincer threatening German Sixth Army's left flank and rear, the mobile group of General Chistiakov's 21st Army matched the spectacular advance by the mobile group of Romanenko's 5th Tank Army. At the same time, the rifle forces on 21st Army's right wing joined with 5th Tank Army's rifle formations in fracturing and liquidating Romanian Group Lascar. All in all, the 22nd proved to be a good day for Chistiakov's forces (see map 23 and appendix 5S in the *Companion*).

Spearheading 21st Army's advance to the Don River, the brigades of General Kravchenko's 4th Tank Corps began operations shortly before dawn with a force of roughly 90 tanks. Advancing without a pause and with all three of its tank brigades forward, the corps' main body traversed 30 to 45 kilometers, passed through Lozhki, and reached the Don River in the Golubinskii, Lipo-Lebedevskii, and Rubezhnyi regions, 6 to 15 kilometers north and northeast of Kalach, by the end of the day. Before reaching Lipo-Lebedevskii, Colonel Koshelev's 102nd Tank Brigade, which was advancing on the corps' left wing in tandem with 3rd Guards Cavalry Corps' 5th Guards Cavalry Division, struck 24th Panzer Division's defenses near Krasnyi Skotovod (Red Cattle-Breeder) State Farm shortly after 0800 hours. Taking fire from nearby Hill 189.2, the *tankists* and cavalrymen overcame 24th Panzer Division's defenses and captured the state farm by 1700 hours. Meanwhile, in 4th Tank Corps' center, Colonel Agafonov's 69th Tank Brigade struck 16th Panzer Division's *kampfgruppe*, most of which was still moving westward along the high road north of the Don River, northeast of Lipo-Logovskii, about an hour later.[82]

After a brief engagement, during which it lost several tanks, 24th Panzer Division's force of roughly 35 tanks withdrew eastward through Golubinskii to Bol'shenabatovskii on the Golubaia River, crossed the river, and moved northward to occupy defensive positions between Glazkov (Glazkovskii) and Evlampievskii on the same river, 19 to 24 kilometers north of Golubinskii-on-the-Don.[83] On 24th Panzer's left, after fencing with 4th Tank Corps' 69th Brigade west of Golubinskii, 16th Panzer Division's *kampfgruppe* withdrew eastward along the high road north of the Don River to Malonabatovskii, where it occupied defenses along the Golubaia River from its confluence with the Don northward to Evlampievskii. By this time, 16th Panzer's *kampfgruppe* probably numbered less than 25 tanks.[84]

From Lipo-Lebedevskii, 4th Tank Corps dispatched reconnaissance units toward Golubinskii, on the northern bank of the Don less than 10 kilometers to the east, from which Sixth Army had just evacuated its headquarters. At the same time, Kravchenko summoned Lieutenant Colonel Zhidkov, commander of 45th Tank Brigade, to his command post and ordered him to configure his brigade as a forward detachment and then push southward to seize a bridge near Kalach. Once formed, the brigade's forward detachment pushed past weak German resistance; crossed the Don River using an undestroyed bridge at Rubezhnyi, 8 kilometers north of Kalach; and established contact with 26th Tank Corps' 157th Tank Brigade on the river's eastern bank.[85] Once across the river, Zhidkov's brigade laagered at Kamyshi, a small village 5 kilometers north of Kalach, and fortified it for the night in expectation of the arrival of the corps' main forces the next morning.

As 4th Tank Corps' lead brigade was crossing the Don River north of Kalach, Pliev's 3rd Guards Cavalry Corps kept pace with Kravchenko's armor and protected its lengthening left flank. After capturing Krasnyi Skotovod State Farm with 4th Tank Corps' 102nd Tank Brigade, Colonel Chepurkin's 5th Guards Cavalry Division rested for two hours and then resumed its advance eastward, once again striking 16th Panzer Division's *kampfgruppe* north of Golubinskii and reportedly destroying 8 tanks, 20 vehicles, and 6 guns and capturing many carts filled with ammunition.[86] On the cavalry corps' right wing and in its center, Colonel Belogorsky's 6th Guards Cavalry Division and Colonel Chudesov's 32nd Cavalry Division captured Hills 151.9, 112.6, and 188.9 west of the Golubaia River; however, they received heavy surprise fire from 16th Panzer Division's *kampfgruppe*, which had withdrawn into defenses stretching from Evlampievskii southward along the Golubaia River to Bol'shenabatovskii on the Don River's northern bank. The two cavalry divisions organized and conducted several assaults on 16th Panzer's defenses, but according to Pliev, "Their efforts were not crowned with success." As Pliev put it:

> Then 6th and 32nd Cavalry Divisions' cavalrymen hurriedly began a planned attack on Evlampievskii. The enemy repeatedly launched decisive counterattacks, while committing 30–45 tanks to combat. But the enemy was thrown back toward the east.
>
> As a result of the furious encounter, more than 200 enemy soldiers and officers were destroyed and up to 300 vehicles, 20 aircraft at enemy airfields, a large amount of ammunition, foodstuffs and clothing warehouses, and a significant amount of guns and equipment were captured. All of this the enemy had designated for the supply of the German grouping bogged down in Stalingrad.
>
> Frightened by the blows of 21st Army's attacking forces, especially its mobile forces—4th Tank and 3rd Guards Cavalry Corps—the enemy

tried to halt our successful advance in the Bol'shenabatovskii region. But the tempo of the offensive increased.[87]

Despite Pliev's exaggerations, his 3rd Guards Cavalry Corps had reached the right bank of the Don River in the Malogolubaia and Bol'shenabatovskii region, 22 to 28 kilometers north of Kalach, by the end of the day on 22 November. Like Kravchenko's 4th Tank Corps, the cavalrymen had advanced more than 30 kilometers during the day.

Therefore, the successful exploitation by 5th Tank Army's 26th Tank Corps and 21st Army's 4th Tank and 3rd Guards Cavalry Corps frustrated General Paulus's plan to employ XIV Panzer Corps' 24th and 16th Panzer Divisions to block the Southwestern Front's northern pincer from reaching and crossing the Don River at and north of Kalach. Neither panzer division had sufficient strength to slow, much less defeat, the exploiting mobile corps. With 26th Tank Corps firmly ensconced in the Kalach region and 4th Tank and 3rd Guards Cavalry Corps now along the western bank of the Don River from Kalach northward to Golubinskii, Paulus's plan was in shambles. To make matters worse for Sixth Army's commander, farther north along the Don, the Don Front's 24th Army joined the Soviet offensive on the morning of the 22nd, creating another crisis that threatened the survival of Sixth Army's XI Army Corps.

As was the case in 5th Tank Army, while 21st Army's mobile corps raced southeastward to the Don River, the rifle forces on the army's right wing engaged Romanian forces isolated far to the rear. Cooperating with 5th Tank Army's 50th Guards and 119th Rifle Divisions and a regiment from 346th Rifle Division advancing from the west, 21st Army's 96th, 63rd, and 333rd Rifle Divisions compressed the defenses of encircled Romanian Group Lascar from the east and southeast. As described earlier, the attacks by these three divisions from the Bazkovskii, Raspopinskaia, Izbushenskii, and Verkhne-Cherenskii regions chopped Group Lascar's pocket in two by the end of the day on the 22nd. At the same time, 21st Army's 277th Rifle Division, which had been participating in the attacks against Group Lascar, wheeled southeastward to join the army's 76th and 293rd Divisions, then marching in the wake of the exploiting cavalry and tank corps. At day's end, 76th and 293rd Divisions reached the Osinovka, Nizhne-Buzinovka, and Sukhanovskii line, 10 to 18 kilometers behind the mobile forces, with 277th Division bivouacking roughly 20 kilometers to their rear. As they advanced, these divisions policed Romanian troops that had been bypassed by the mobile corps.

1st Guards Army

On 22 November, General Leliushenko's 1st Guards Army continued to play a secondary role in the offensive. However, on the army's left wing,

203rd and 278th Rifle Divisions, in conjunction with 5th Tank Army's 14th Guards Division (which was slated to be transferred to Leliushenko's army on the 23rd), attacked during the afternoon to exploit the morning successes achieved by 5th Tank Army's 159th Rifle Division and 8th Guards Tank Brigade. The three divisions attacked and penetrated the defenses of Romanian I Army Corps' 9th and 11th Infantry Divisions, drove westward, and seized the towns of Dubovoi (Dubovskoi), Rubashkin, Bakhmutkin, and Iagodnyi on the Krivaia River, 50 to 55 kilometers west-southwest of Serafimovich and 25 to 45 kilometers north-northeast of Bokovskaia (see appendix 5S in the *Companion*).

This advance was significant because Bokovskaia, situated due west of the junction of the Krivaia and Chir Rivers, was a vital objective in three important respects. First, it was a Romanian strongpoint in its own right. Second, it stood astride an important road junction dominating Romanian Third Army's communications south of the Don. Third and most important, it had just been designated the base of operations for General Hollidt's XVII Army Corps, whose German 62nd and 294th Infantry Divisions were about to reinforce Romanian I Army Corps to the north and II Army Corps to the south. At the time, II Corps was assembling its shattered formations, including Romanian 7th Cavalry and 14th Infantry Divisions, near Chernyshevskaia on the Chir River and awaiting the arrival of the remnants of XXXXVIII Panzer Corps, whose two divisions were still half encircled east of the river.

Meanwhile, on 1st Guards Army's right wing and center, along and south of the Don, 1st, 153rd, and 197th Rifle Divisions, together with the army's 1st Guards Mechanized Corps in the rear, waited patiently in the wings as they prepared for their role in Operation Saturn.

Axis Reactions

In the wake of the first two days of the Southwestern Front's offensive, the shattered Romanian Third Army, with German advice and counsel, worked frantically to erect new defenses along the western bank of the Krivaia River and upper reaches of the Chir River and along the southern bank of the lower Chir. By the evening of 22 November, Third Army was anchoring its left wing along the Krivaia River with I Army Corps' relatively intact 11th and 9th Infantry Divisions. Farther south, the remnants of Romanian II Army Corps' 14th Infantry and 7th Cavalry Divisions were attempting to defend the Chir River line from Bokovskaia southward to Chernyshevskaia and hoping to be reinforced by whatever forces of XXXXVIII Panzer Corps' 22nd Panzer and Romanian 1st Armored Divisions that managed to escape west across the Chir. Still farther south, the pitiful remnants of V Army Corps, primarily rear service units reinforced by German security forces and a steady stream of hastily assembled alarm units, manned defenses on the

Chir River's western bank from Chernyshevskaia southward to the eastward bend in the river west of Oblivskaia.

Late on 22 November, Army Group B bolstered Third Army's defenses by forming temporary Group Hollidt, consisting of the headquarters of German XVII Army Corps and 62nd and 294th Infantry Divisions, and it ordered the group to reinforce Third Army's left wing. Ultimately, General Hollidt's group also assumed control of Romanian I and II Army Corps' divisions, as well as XXXXVIII Panzer Corps' forces after they fought their way back across the Chir. General Weichs ordered Group Hollidt to hold at all costs defenses along the western banks of the Krivaia and Chir Rivers from the Don River southward to just south of Chernyshevskaia. He also directed Third Army to employ the remnants of its decimated IV and V Army Corps and Sixth Army's rear service units, reinforced by a wide variety of German security and alarm units and *Luftwaffe Flak* (antiaircraft) forces in the region, to defend its left wing. This meant manning defenses in the sector along the Chir River from west of Oblivskaia eastward to the Don River at Rychkovskii, with particular emphasis on fortifying and holding the towns of Oblivskaia and Surovikino on the river's northern bank, Chir Station and Rychkovskii between the Chir and the Don, and the vital bridgehead on the eastern bank of the Don opposite Rychkovskii. The Rychkovskii bridgehead was especially key terrain because it was the only base of operations from which the Germans could reinforce or rescue Sixth Army from the west.[88]

At the same time, Army Group B forwarded to Sixth Army Hitler's order that it defend its positions west of Kalach as long as possible, particularly the sector extending from Verkhne-Buzinovka southward to Dobrinskaia (Dobrinka) and to the security line being erected by Sixth Army's rear area command [*Korück*] east of Kalach.[89] Of course, this order was pointless, since all three of the Southwestern Front's tank corps were now east and southeast of this line.

Conclusions

The Southwestern Front's operations on 22 November were distinguished, first and foremost, by the rapid and deep advances achieved by 5th Tank and 21st Armies' mobile groups. These included the decisive thrusts by 5th Tank Army's 26th Tank Corps and 21st Army's 4th Tank Corps and 3rd Guards Cavalry Corps to the Don River from Kalach, northward to Malo-Golubinskii, and to the Golubaia River from Evlampievskii, northward to Glazkovskii; the advance by 5th Tank Army's 1st Tank Corps into the region north of Chir Station and Rychkovskii; and the spectacular raid by 5th Tank Army's 8th Motorcycle Regiment toward Oblivskaia on the Chir River. Notwithstanding this impressive armored juggernaut, the plaudits require careful qualification. Despite its dramatic advance, 1st Tank Corps failed to capture its ultimate objectives—Surovikino, Chirskaia Station, and Rychkovskii on the Chir and Don Rivers—primarily because its strength had dwindled to about 24 tanks. This was not enough to cause serious harm to the German security and rear service forces throwing up hasty defenses in the towns and villages along the railroad line following the northern bank of the Chir River. Likewise, 8th Motorcycle Regiment failed to seize its objective—Oblivskaia.

Ultimately, the failure of 5th Tank Army's mobile forces to seize these important objectives, as well as bridgeheads across the Chir River, would compel Generals Vatutin and Romanenko to mount yet another offensive to penetrate that river line in early December. It would also delay the tank army's advance by almost a full month, when the Germans' defenses along the Chir finally collapsed. Worse still, 1st Tank Corps' failure to capture Chir Station and Rychkovskii from the march meant that German forces continued to hold a bridgehead on the Don River's eastern bank from which they could mount an operation to relieve their forces encircled in Stalingrad. Ultimately, it would take until 14–15 December for the Soviets to liquidate the Germans' threatening bridgehead near Rychkovskii. By then, its capture required the Soviets to form and deploy an entirely new army—5th Shock.

Finally, despite reaching the Don River at and north of Kalach, thus rendering Paulus's defensive plan utterly irrelevant, 26th and 4th Tank Corps accomplished this feat on the fourth day of the offensive instead of the second day, as planned. This granted the Germans sufficient time to regroup and create the defenses necessary to prevent the rapid collapse of the emerging Stalingrad pocket as a whole.

These shortcomings aside, the Southwestern Front's rifle formations were able to encircle, contain, and ultimately destroy Romanian Third Army's forces south and southwest of Raspopinskaia and push forward as far south as the Chir River and as far west as the Krivaia River. This advance, combined with the savaging of XXXXVIII Panzer Corps, Romanian Third Army's only reserve, compelled the largely shattered army to establish threadbare defenses along the Chir River, defenses that were destined to collapse in the not-so-distant future. By itself, this placed severe time constraints on the Germans if they were to rescue their beleaguered Sixth Army—time constraints they could not satisfy.

The Don Front's Advance

For the first time since Operation Uranus began, a second army subordinate to Rokossovsky's Don Front—General Galanin's 24th—joined the Uranus offensive on the morning of 22 November (see map 23). The 24th Army, with Major General A. G. Maslov's experienced but bloodied 16th Tank Corps acting as its mobile group, was to attack southward from the Panshino region east of the Don River; capture the town of Vertiachii, 40 kilometers north-east of Kalach; and link up with 21st Army's 3rd Guards Cavalry and 4th Tank Corps, which were attacking from the west, in the vicinity of Vertiachii and Peskovatka. If this attack was successful, Galanin's and Chistiakov's armies, in cooperation with Batov's 65th, which was already attacking from the north-west and north, were to encircle and destroy Sixth Army's XI Army Corps before its forces could escape eastward from the already bloodied ground in the northwestern extremity of the Great Bend of the Don.

65th Army

At dawn on 22 November, just as peals of artillery fire to the east announced the beginning of 24th Army's offensive, the divisions on the right wing of General Batov's 65th Army resumed their attacks against General Strecker's stubbornly defending XI Army Corps. By this time, XI Army Corps' 376th Infantry Division, supported by the bulk of 14th Panzer Division in the Verkhne-Buzinovka region to XI Corps' left rear, had already withdrawn from its strongpoint at Orekhovskii, 12 kilometers south of Logovskii. Infantry from the 376th and tanks from 14th Panzer were now defending a salient jutting northwestward from Nizhnaia Perekopka through Osinki to Logovskii and then sharply southward past Orekhovskii to the Verkhne-Buzinovka region. It was becoming increasingly difficult for Strecker's corps to hold this ground because 21st Army's 3rd Guards Cavalry Corps had already captured Osinovskii in the corps' deep rear and was rapidly approaching the western bank of the Golubaia River north of Bol'shenabotovskii on the Don.

To protect his corps' increasingly vulnerable left flank and rear, Strecker had already transferred most of 44th Infantry Division's 132nd Regiment and part of its 131st Regiment from their sectors south of Sirotinskaia in the corps' center to bolster 14th Panzer Division's defenses at Verkhne-Buzinovka. Strecker had also dispatched 384th Infantry Division's 534th Regiment from its sector on the corps' right wing to reinforce 14th Panzer or erect new defenses facing southwest along the Golubaia River to protect the corps' rear. This left XI Corps' center and right wing defended by the seriously weakened 44th and 384th Infantry Divisions, which had already been considerably understrength when the Soviet offensive began. Therefore, despite Hitler's demand that Strecker's corps hold its ground at all costs, the renewed assaults by Batov's 65th Army, coupled with the offensive by Soviet 24th Army farther east, rendered XI Corps' defenses untenable.

Attacking shortly after dawn on 22 November, the right wing of Batov's 65th Army, which now included 321st and 258th Rifle, 27th Guards Rifle, and 252nd Rifle Divisions arrayed from left to right, struck the defenses of XI Army Corps' 376th Infantry and 14th Panzer Divisions in the sector extending from Logovskii southward to Verkhne-Buzinovka.[90] On the left wing of this shock group, General Makarenko's 321st Rifle Division—supported on the left by Colonel I. P. Sivakov's 23rd Rifle Division, which was assaulting 376th Infantry Division's right wing in the Osinki region—pounded the division's defenses at Logovskii and along the Mokryi Log *Balka* to the south. On 321st Division's right, Colonel I. Ia. Fursin's 258th Rifle Division launched heavy assaults against 376th Division's defenses just east of Orekhovskii, which by now had been reinforced by a small *kampfgruppe* of up to 20 tanks from 14th Panzer Division. Still farther to the south, Colonel Glebov's 27th Guards Rifle Division and Colonel Shekhtman's 252nd Rifle Division attacked 14th Panzer Division's defenses stretching from the northeastern extremity of Krepkaia *Balka*, 10 kilometers south of Orekhovskii, southward to the northeastern approaches to Verkhne-Buzinovka.

After hours of heavy fighting, at about 1000 hours, General Strecker ordered 376th Infantry Division to abandon Logovskii and conduct a fighting withdrawal eastward about 5 kilometers to a new defensive line extending from north to south along a ridgeline 3 kilometers west of Osinki and the town of Ventsy, 10 kilometers to the south. Batov's forces pursued, and heavy combat continued into the afternoon. Finally, shortly before nightfall, the heavy pressure exerted by Batov's forces, coupled with new threats posed by 24th Army's offensive to the east and the arrival of 21st Army's 3rd Guards Cavalry Corps on the western bank of the Golubaia River to the south, forced Strecker to order yet another withdrawal, this time by both 376th Infantry and 14th Panzer Divisions. Accordingly, 376th Infantry Division abandoned Osinki and Ventsy and pulled back to a ridgeline extending from roughly 2 kilometers west of Nizhnaia Perekopka southward to about 2 kilometers west of Os'kinskii.

At the same time, General Bässler's 14th Panzer Division, along with its reinforcing 132nd Infantry Regiment, abandoned the Verkhne-Buzinovka region and Os'kinskii, 14 kilometers to the east, and retreated to new defensive positions anchored on the high ground extending 2 kilometers west of Os'kinskii southeastward to the village of Teplyi, 5 kilometers west of the Golubaia River at Glazkovskii. By midnight on 22 November, 14th Panzer Division occupied defenses loosely tied in with those of XIV Panzer Corps' 24th and 16th Panzer Divisions along the eastern bank of the Golubaia River from Glazkovskii southward to the Don River near Bol'shenabatovskii (see map 20). Finally, reflecting his corps' increasingly perilous position, in the late afternoon or early evening, Strecker ordered 384th Infantry Division to send its 536th Regiment southward to defend the vital bridge over the Don River north of Vertiachii, and he ordered 44th Infantry Division to send its 134th Regiment to replace 384th Infantry Division's departed regiment.

Meanwhile, after encountering strong German resistance all day long, at nightfall, General Batov reported what his forces had done and precisely where they were located as of 1400 hours on 22 November (see appendix 5W in the *Companion*). After submitting his report, Batov's forces occupied Logovskii, Osinki, Ventsy, Verkhne-Buzinovka, and Os'kinskii and closed on XI Army Corps' new defensive line by 2400 hours.

The withdrawals conducted by XI Army Corps' 376th Infantry and 14th Panzer Divisions, together with the retreat by XIV Panzer Corps' 24th and 16th Panzer Divisions, left a 30-kilometer-wide gap along the Don River between the left flank of XIV Panzer Corps' 16th Panzer Division at Bol'shenabatovskii and the right flank of General Heitz's VIII Army Corps at Verkhne-Gnilovskii. If Galanin's 24th Army could close this gap by seizing Vertiachii, Strecker's entire XI Army Corps, along with two-thirds of General Hube's XIV Panzer Corps (24th and 16th Panzer Divisions), would indeed be encircled and threatened with destruction on the west bank of the Don. It all depended on the performance of Galanin's 24th Army.

24th Army
General Galanin's army began its assault from jumping-off positions at and east of the town of Panshino on the eastern bank of the Don River, 4 kilometers northeast of Verkhne-Gnilovskii. His plan required a shock group consisting of 49th and 214th Rifle Divisions, supported on the left by one regiment of 298th Rifle Division and on the right by two regiments of 120th Rifle Division, to attack from jumping-off positions in the roughly 8-kilometer-wide sector from the field station [*Polevaia Stantsiia*] 12 kilometers southeast of Verkhne-Gnilovskii, northwestward to Marker 44.2, 3 kilometers north of Verkhne-Gnilovskii. The 49th and 214th Divisions concentrated their forces in a 4.5-kilometer-wide sector in the shock group's center. Attacking concentrically toward the southwest and south, this force of three divisions was to penetrate the defenses of 76th Infantry Division, which occupied positions on the left wing of German Sixth Army's VIII Army Corps. Once they got through these defenses, the attacking divisions, reinforced by 84th Rifle Division and 10th Tank Brigade from the second echelon, were to seize Verkhne-Gnilovskii and Gerasimovka *Balka*, which extended southeast from Nizhne-Gnilovskii, and then pave the way for the commitment of General Maslov's 16th Tank Corps into the penetration. Maslov's corps, with the rifle divisions advancing in its wake, was to exploit southward with its 105 operational tanks, capture Vertiachii, and link up with 65th Army's forces advancing from the southwest somewhere in the Vertiachii or Peskovatka region.[91] The army's mission was to prevent XI Army Corps from withdrawing from the Sirotinskaia region and to encircle and destroy Strecker's corps.

The 24th Army began its offensive on the morning of 22 November after firing an artillery preparation. However, the army's ground assault faltered almost instantly as it encountered blistering German artillery, mortar, and machine gun fire. Galanin's report at day's end noted, "The army recorded only minimal gains in the face of stiff German resistance"; then it listed the location and status of each of his divisions (see appendix 5W in the *Companion*).

Rokossovsky later commented on 24th Army's failure to even dent the Germans' defenses:

> The 24th Army's offensive designed to cut off the withdrawal to the eastern bank of the Don by enemy formations under attack by 65th and 21st Armies was unsuccessful. Here, the Hitlerites held firmly to a well-organized defensive line and repulsed all of the attacks by Galanin's units. Now we regretted that the forces and weapons used to strengthen 24th Army had not been transferred to the forces that were advancing successfully.
>
> Certainly the 24th Army assisted the overall operation to some degree by pinning down and attracting to itself considerable enemy forces. Nor can the army commander, Galanin, be blamed entirely for the failure. No doubt he made some mistakes, but the fact of the matter is that the army simply lacked the strength to overcome so strong an enemy defense.[92]

Rokossovsky was correct about the impact of 24th Army's failed assault on the Germans' defenses. Fearful of what would happen if 24th Army's attacks succeeded, at day's end, Paulus ordered Strecker's XI Army Corps to shift 384th Infantry Division's 536th Regiment southward across the Don River to bolster 76th Division's defenses and guarantee that the bridges across the river at and north of Vertiachii remained open. Since this left 384th Division with only one regiment (535th) with which to defend its sector, Strecker ordered 44th Infantry Division to castle its 134th Regiment to the east to back up 384th Division or to assist 76th Division, should it need help. Galanin's assault was also instrumental in a decision Paulus made later in the day, when he ordered Strecker to withdraw his entire XI Army Corps from its exposed position southward across the Don as soon as possible.

Elsewhere on the Don Front's right wing, General Zhadov's 66th Army simply bided its time, awaiting the propitious moment to join the fray north of Stalingrad city.

Axis Reactions
Throughout the day on 22 November, Sixth Army continued to implement the orders issued by General Paulus on the afternoon on 20 November, particularly those requiring 24th and 16th Panzer Divisions of Hube's XIV Panzer Corps to move into positions from which they could block the advance by the Southwestern Front's mobile groups (see map 20). Since most of Hube's

forces had reached their designated positions by midday, Paulus and Hube now had to make adjustments to suit the rapidly altering situation. First and foremost, this meant bolstering the sagging defenses of XI Army Corps on the army's left wing and protecting XI Corps' rear as the menacing Soviet mobile groups brushed past the combat groups of XIV Panzer Corps and headed straight for the Don at and north of Kalach.

The most delicate of these adjustments involved coordinating the movements of XI Army Corps' 14th Panzer Division with those of XIV Panzer Corps' 24th and 16th Panzer Divisions, all of which had no choice but to give ground under intense Soviet pressure. Ultimately, Bässler's 14th Panzer Division, reinforced by a battalion *kampfgruppe* from 44th Infantry Division's 132nd Regiment and, later, by 384th Infantry Division's 534th Regiment, was able to withdraw eastward to new but clearly temporary defenses west of Verkhne- and Nizhne-Golubaia on the upper Golubaia River. These defenses ultimately tied in nicely with those along the lower Golubaia River into which 24th and 16th Panzer Divisions retreated late in the evening.

In addition to responding to the steady advance of Soviet mobile groups toward the Don and the impending loss of Kalach, Paulus had to react to the new threat posed by 24th Army's offensive, even though it failed badly on 22 November. Paulus thus ordered Strecker to send 384th Infantry Division's 536th Regiment southeast toward Vertiachii, and he replaced 384th Division's missing regiment with 44th Infantry Division's 134th Regiment. But these moves were just stopgap measures; by now, it had become fairly clear that XI Army Corps' survival would require abandoning its salient and moving southeastward across the Don River. In anticipation of this move, XIV Panzer Corps pulled its headquarters back across the Don to positions east of Golubinskaia, expecting its two panzer divisions to join it in a matter of days.

Despite these measures, Sixth Army was not optimistic. In a message dispatched to Army Group B at 1900 hours, it admitted, "It is doubtful whether we can succeed in building a thin line to Karpowka through Marinowka-Golubinka by weakening the strong North Front. The Don is frozen solid and can be crossed on foot. Supplies will soon be used up, and the tanks and heavy weapons will be immobile. The ammunition situation is strained, and there are enough foodstuffs for 6 days."[93]

Finally, to shore up Sixth Army's defenses at and east of Kalach, which was about to fall to the Soviets, Paulus ordered part of 113th Infantry Division, previously defending in VIII Army Corps' center (and on 76th Division's right) south of Kotluban', to move southwestward to the Sokarevka and Illarionovskii regions, east and northeast of Kalach, along with additional elements of 3rd Motorized Division. These forces were to reinforce 3rd Motorized Division's *Kampfgruppe* von Hanstein, which was already fighting in the Kalach region and erecting defenses near Marinovka, east of Kalach.

For Sixth Army, the sad fact was that the massive advances by Soviet mobile forces through its defenses and deep into its operational rear were necessitating a wholesale shuffling and regrouping, a process that would only accelerate in the coming days as Paulus's forces had to contend with the unthinkable: they were about to be encircled.

Conclusions

The Don Front's operations on 22 November were not characterized by the same kind of deep, dramatic advances achieved by the Southwestern Front's three mobile corps on 22 November. Instead, Batov's 65th Army continued its methodical but costly assaults against XI Army Corps' defenses, exerting just enough pressure to force General Strecker to constantly reshuffle his defending forces and eventually give way to the unrelenting pressure by ordering a phased fighting withdrawal back toward the Don River and the supposed safety of its eastern bank.

Although Rokossovsky tried to encircle Strecker's corps with a carefully planned double envelopment by 65th and 24th Armies, General Galanin's offensive failed from the start, well before it could bring its 16th Tank Corps to bear. In the end, as was the case with 65th Army, stout resistance by 76th Infantry Division of General Heitz's VIII Army Corps transformed 24th Army's bold advance into a costly slugfest that propelled its forces forward only hundreds of meters rather than entire kilometers. Despite the sacrificial bloodletting in 24th Army, however, Rokossovsky insisted that Galanin continue his attacks, if only to prevent the Germans from shifting forces to sectors that were even more threatened to the west and southwest.

The results were predictable. Although Galanin never achieved his anticipated penetration, the tremendous pressure on VIII Army Corps' left wing forced Paulus to weaken Strecker's XI Corps west of the Don by dispatching even more troops eastward to solidify Heitz's defenses. Ultimately, however, it was the collapse of the defenses of XIV Panzer Corps' 24th and 16th Panzer Divisions west of the Don River and the advance by the Southwestern Front's 26th and 4th Tank Corps across the Don the next day that forced Sixth Army to pull XI Army Corps back across the Don before it too became encircled.

THE STALINGRAD FRONT'S OFFENSIVE, 22 NOVEMBER

The forces of the Stalingrad Front continued to develop an offensive in the general direction of Krivomuzginskaia Station (Sovetskii) and captured these points.

The forces of the Southwestern and Stalingrad Fronts, after capturing the

Kalach and the Krivomuzginskaia Station (Sovetskii) region, interrupted all enemy supply routes, by doing so completing the operational encirclement of German Fourth Panzer and Sixth Armies on the Stalingrad axis.

Red Army General Staff Operational Summary,
0800 hours on 23 November 1942[94]

The Stalingrad Front's Missions

Since the armies of General Eremenko's Stalingrad Front had essentially routed the two Romanian army corps on Fourth Panzer Army's right wing the day before, on 22 November, Eremenko concentrated on pushing the *front*'s mobile forces northwestward as rapidly as possible to achieve Operation Uranus's prime objective—the encirclement of German Fourth Panzer and Sixth Armies. To that end, after consulting with his army commanders, Eremenko ordered his *front*'s 64th and 57th Armies, together with 51st Army's 4th Mechanized Corps, to continue their offensives northwestward, link up with the Southwestern Front's mobile group, and form an inner encirclement front around the Germans' Stalingrad grouping. At the same time, the remainder of 51st Army was to advance southwestward to establish an outer encirclement front along the Aksai River and block German operational reserves from rescuing Sixth Army (see appendix 5X in the *Companion*).

64th Army

General Shumilov's 64th Army resumed offensive operations early on 22 November with the intent to regain the territory it had lost on its left wing to German 297th Infantry Division's counterattack the previous day (see map 24 and appendix 5Y in the *Companion*). Therefore, Shumilov concentrated the attacks on his army's left wing, while the forces in the army's center and on its right wing remained on the defense. During the morning, Shumilov withdrew Colonel Safiulin's 38th Rifle Division from combat because of the excessive losses it had suffered the previous day and replaced it with Colonel M. I. Denisenko's relatively fresh 36th Guards Rifle Division. In addition, he reinforced 36th Guards Division with 56th Tank Brigade, 1104th Artillery Regiment, and a battalion of 4th Guards-Mortar Regiment.[95] Once in position, 36th Guards, flanked on the right by 157th and 204th Rifle Divisions, began its assault at 1300 hours. As had been the case the previous day, the shock group of three rifle divisions, supported by tanks from 13th and 56th Tank Brigades, assaulted the defenses of Romanian 20th Infantry Division in the sector extending from the Chervlenaia River northward to 297th Division's strongpoint at Elkhi. By now, however, the Romanians were supported by several battalion groups from their neighbor on the left, German 297th Infantry Division.[96]

In 64th Army's center and on its right wing, 29th Rifle Division and 7th Rifle Corps' 93rd, 97th, and 96th Rifle Brigades manned positions opposite IV Army Corps' 297th and 371st Infantry Divisions and remained on the defense. Finally, Shumilov retained 66th and 154th Naval Rifle Brigades in reserve, with instructions to reinforce the army's shock group if it achieved success.

On the left wing of the army's shock group, 36th Guards Division thrust westward at 1300 hours in an attempt to capture Karavatka *Balka*, 10 to 12 kilometers west of Beketovka. After a day of extremely intense fighting, the guardsmen advanced roughly 5 kilometers and reached positions extending from the eastern slope of Hill 110.9 to the ford, 3 kilometers east of Nariman and about 8 kilometers south of Varvarovka and Karavatka *Balka*, by 1730 hours. On 36th Guards Division's right, 157th Rifle Division attacked toward a group of burial mounds at Height Marker 1.7, 6 kilometers north of Nariman, and advanced roughly 3 kilometers by 1730 hours. Still farther to the right, 204th Rifle Division assaulted westward, south of Elkhi, and managed to advance about 4 kilometers and capture the Romanian strongpoint at Iagodnyi by 1730 hours.[97]

Under heavy pressure, at 2000 hours, General Jänecke, commander of IV Army Corps (which had been subordinated to Sixth Army early the previous day), ordered German 297th and Romanian 20th Infantry Divisions, whose forces were now thoroughly intermixed, to abandon Varvarovka on the eastern bank of the Chervlenaia River, 8 kilometers north of Nariman, and withdraw to a new defensive line anchored on the town of Tsybenko, at the mouth of Karavatka *Balka*, 10 kilometers north of Nariman. IV Corps' new defensive line extended from Tsybenko eastward along Karavatka *Balka* for 10 kilometers to the strongpoint at Elkhi, which was still under 297th Division's control.

Thus, by nightfall on the 22nd, Shumilov's army had pushed Sixth Army's IV Army Corps back to Karavatka *Balka*, superbly defensible terrain tied closely to the strongpoint at Elkhi. This would enable Jänecke's corps to defend effectively for many weeks before being forced to withdraw further. Henceforth, any Soviet advance south of Stalingrad would have to occur west of the Chervlenaia River, where 57th Army, 64th Army's neighbor on the left, was already beginning a spectacular advance.

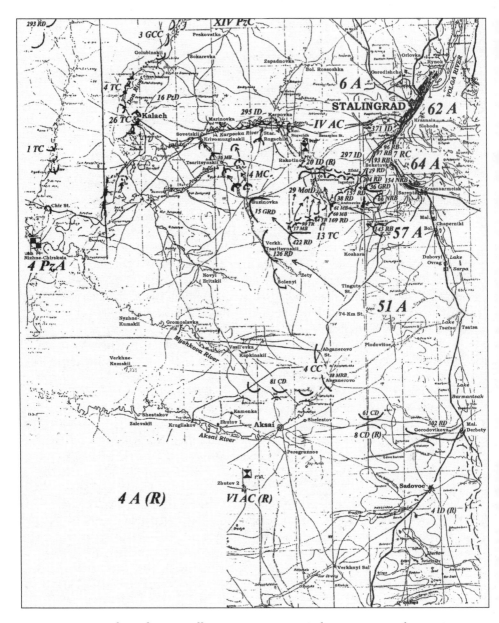

Map 24. Stalingrad Front's offensive: situation at 2200 hours, 22 November 1942

57th Army

General Tolbukhin's 57th Army, which had experienced several setbacks at the hands of German 29th Motorized Division roughly 36 hours before, finally resumed its exploitation along previously designated axes early on 22 November (see appendix 5Y in the *Companion*). Hours earlier, Leyser's 29th Motorized Division had already begun withdrawing northward from its positions west of Nariman to a new defensive line along the Chervlenaia River. The new line extended from the vital road and rail junction at Karpovka, 35 kilometers northwest of Beketovka and the same distance east of Kalach, southward to Rakotino, 5 kilometers northwest of Tsybenko. Now well fortified, the town of Tsybenko anchored the right flank of German IV Army Corps' defenses after it withdrew its forces northward late on 22 November.

With the Germans withdrawing northward, west of the Chervlenaia River, 57th Army advanced with relative ease on 22 November. The army's 422nd and 169th Rifle Divisions began their attack at dawn, dispersed German rear guards, and captured Nariman and the village of Gavrilovka, 4 kilometers north of Nariman. Although Soviet reports asserted this advance was against "strong enemy resistance," this was simply not the case.[98]

Meanwhile, 57th Army's mobile force, Colonel Tanaschishin's 13th Tank Corps, also advanced northwestward on 22 November. Its assigned objectives were crossing sites over the Chervlenaia River in the Varvarovka, Tsybenko, and Rakotino region, 15 to 20 kilometers west of Beketovka. On the tank corps' right wing, 61st and 62nd Mechanized Brigades, supported once again by 176th Tank Regiment and the remnants of 163rd Tank Regiment, marched north toward Tsybenko and Varvarovka against only light resistance. On the corps' left wing, 17th Mechanized Brigade and 44th Tank Regiment, which had reached 8th of March State Farm in the wee hours of the morning, were relieved by Colonel Morozov's 422nd Rifle Division shortly after dawn and wheeled east toward Rakotino and Varvarovka.[99] This, in turn, facilitated the advance by 61st and 62nd Mechanized Brigades and forced 29th Motorized Division's rear guards and the remainder of Romanian 20th Infantry Division to abandon the region northwest of Nariman and Gavrilovka and withdraw to IV Army Corps' new defenses along the Karpovka, Bereslavskii (Bereslavka), and Rakotino line by 2400 hours. Therefore, the main forces of Tolbukhin's army advanced 12 to 15 kilometers on 22 November and drove German IV Army Corps' 29th Motorized Division and Romanian 20th Infantry Division back into solid defenses that would contain any further Soviet advances for weeks.

Much farther to the east, 57th Army's 143rd Rifle Brigade, which had been busy for two days destroying or policing the remnants of Romanian forces isolated west of Lake Sarpa, moved westward and began assembling in the Chervleny and Tinguta region in Tolbukhin's reserve.

51st Army

Pride of place in the Stalingrad Front's offensive on 22 November went to General Trufanov's 51st Army (see appendix 5Y in the *Companion*). Its mobile group, General Vol'sky's 4th Mechanized Corps, strove mightily and with great success to link up with the Southwestern Front's mobile forces and encircle German Sixth Army.[100] No less spectacular was the army's southward advance, spearheaded by General Shapkin's 4th Cavalry Corps against diminished Romanian resistance, with the mission of erecting the outer encirclement front. The army's history simply notes, "On 22 November the enemy offered no organized resistance and only fought in small groups in separate sectors."[101]

As easy as 4th Mechanized Corps' advance seemed to be, it was actually beset by numerous problems that had to be resolved if it was to continue its exploitation. Uneasy about the corps' previous performance, Eremenko sent a messenger by light aircraft to Vol'sky's headquarters in Zety overnight on 21–22 November. As the *front* commander recalled:

> The 4th Mechanized Corps, after destroying 18th and 20th Rumanian Infantry Divisions, which were withdrawing under our blows, reached the Zety region before nightfall and . . . halted there without any reason for doing so. Considering this delay to indicate uncertainty on the part of Comrade Vol'sky, the corps commander, I sent a message to him by aircraft early on the morning of 22 November in which I categorically demanded he accelerate his movement in order to reach the Krivomuzginskaia [Sovetskii] and Karpovka line no later than 1200 hours this day. The mission was fulfilled precisely.[102]

The official history of 4th Mechanized Corps highlights the same problems:

> One should mention that the situation of the corps in Zety overnight on 21–22 November provoked extreme challenges: it required bringing the rear forward and concentrating the units, refueling the vehicles with fuel, and replacing exhausted reserves of ammunition in the tank and other subunits. Army General M. M. Popov, characterized the situation as follows: "The morning of 22 November began with a sharp warning from the *front* commander to General Vol'sky, cautioning the lagging mechanized corps with fulfilling his mission on time. But as it was already known before the receipt of this warning, the forces of this corps

were already aimed at Sovetskii and were developing their offensive at first light. Enemy resistance continued to grow. The overcoming of his defense occurred in the absence of sufficient ammunition and fuel."[103]

With Eremenko's warning ringing in his ears, Vol'sky pondered the various ways his corps could sustain operations as it traversed the 50 kilometers along the single road leading to Sovetskii. This was no mean task, considering that German air strikes had severely hindered the corps' advance the day before. Ultimately, the corps commander decided to lead his advance with Lieutenant Colonel Rodionov's 36th Mechanized Brigade, which was instructed to seize Sovetskii Farm as quickly as possible. Major Doroshkevich's experienced 26th Tank Regiment would lead 36th Brigade's advance. To both, Vol'sky reportedly said, "You must ram your way forward so as to be in Sovetskii by midday on 22 November. The honor of not only the brigade but also the entire corps depends on you."[104] Vol'sky's final orders directed Colonel Sten'shinsky's 59th Mechanized Brigade, with its organic 20th Tank Regiment, to follow 36th Mechanized Brigade and Lieutenant Colonel Karapetian's 60th Mechanized Brigade, with Colonel Brizhinev's 21st Tank Regiment, to bring up the rear and protect the corps' main forces should any threat materialize from either flank.[105]

Vol'sky's corps moved out well before dawn and reached the village of Verkhne-Tsaritsynskii, 12 kilometers north of Zety, before daybreak. Just before reaching the village, he received a new message from Eremenko, delivered by aircraft, that ordered his corps to seize Staryi and Novyi Rogachik, Karpovskaia, and Karpovka. This essentially altered his corps' mission by sending it northeastward into Sixth Army's rear instead of northward to Sovetskii. About 90 minutes later, however, he received yet another message, this time from Colonel Iudin, 51st Army's deputy commander. Iudin soon arrived by vehicle to confirm his order requiring Vol'sky's corps to seize Sovetskii and also reach the Karpovka and Marinovka line—that is, the line of the Stalingrad-Kalach railroad east and west of Sovetskii. Armed with conflicting orders requiring his corps to capture two objectives, Vol'sky "compromised," ordering 36th Brigade to continue its advance on Sovetskii and, once they reached Buzinovka, directing 59th and 60th Brigades to march northeast toward Karpovka.[106]

The 4th Mechanized Corps closed into Buzinovka after daybreak on the 22nd, shortly after its reconnaissance detachments confirmed that the Germans had abandoned the town hours before. However, the corps received no help whatsoever from air reconnaissance; poor flying condition grounded all aircraft, Soviet as well as German. Before his corps resumed its advance, Vol'sky sent out flank detachments to provide security along its two planned march routes and succeeded in establishing communications with 13th Tank

Corps on his right by using small patrols mounted in armored cars and other vehicles. After his corps passed through Buzinovka, Vol'sky split it into two separate columns and reinforced each so that it would have sufficient forces to accomplish its assigned mission. He allocated 59th Brigade's 20th Tank Regiment to Rodionov's 36th Brigade and 26th Tank Regiment for their advance toward Sovetskii and returned 21st Tank Regiment to Karapetian's 60th Brigade, which, with Sten'shinsky's 59th Brigade, was to advance on Karpovka.

Along 4th Mechanized Corps' main axis of advance to Sovetskii, tanks from Doroshkevich's 26th Regiment first encountered resistance at Krivomuzginskaia Station, on the railroad line less than a kilometer south of Sovetskii Farm. The three tank companies of 26th Regiment, supported by motorized infantry from Rodionov's 36th Brigade, overcame this resistance in about three hours of fighting. The defenders, apparently consisting of local German security and rear service units, then broke into small groups and disappeared east or west along the railroad line. Both Krivomuzginskaia Station and the nearby village at Sovetskii were in 36th Brigade's hands by 1220 hours on the 22nd. Rodionov and Doroshkevich immediately established all-around defenses. The brigade claimed that it killed and wounded several hundred Germans in the fight for Sovetskii and its nearby railroad station, captured many prisoners, and appropriated a significant amount of equipment, including about 1,000 vehicles of all types, maintenance shops, many enemy guns of various calibers, and warehouses containing food, ammunition, and fuel.[107] Most important, the fall of Krivomuzginskaia Station and Sovetskii Farm severed all of German Sixth Army's surface communications with the west.

Meanwhile, after separating from Vol'sky's 36th Mechanized Brigade, 59th and 60th Brigades headed northeast toward Karpovka but encountered far stronger resistance than Rodionov's brigade at Sovetskii. Worried that Soviet forces were penetrating so deep in its rear, Sixth Army had dispatched *Kampfgruppe* von Hanstein, consisting of battalion groups from 3rd and 60th Motorized Divisions and another battalion-size *kampfgruppe* from 295th Infantry Division, to man defenses in the 11-kilometer-wide sector extending from Karpovka westward through Voroshilov Camp to Marinovka. Farther east, Leyser's 29th Motorized Division had already completed its withdrawal northward to positions along the Karpovka and Chervlenaia Rivers from Karpovskaia southeastward to Rakotino. It defended this sector with a series of battalion-size *kampfgruppen* and defended the approaches to the key towns of Karpovskaia and Novyi Rogachik with its *Kampfgruppe* Woltz.[108]

At nightfall on 22 November, 59th Mechanized Brigade's 1st Battalion passed northward through Prudboi Station on the railroad line and reached positions south of Voroshilov Camp, midway between Marinovka and Karpovka, where it established defensive positions. After conducting a reconnaissance and determining that the camp was defended by two companies of German troops supported by some tanks and artillery, the battalion attacked the German positions at 0400 hours. After three failed attempts, the attacking troops finally seized a foothold in the camp, only to be driven back once again by counterattacking Germans. However, Colonel Sten'shinsky committed another battalion from his 59th Brigade and finally cleared German forces from the camp. Soon after, Lieutenant Colonel Karapetian's 60th Mechanized Brigade reinforced Sten'shinsky's forces at Voroshilov Camp, enabling it to fend off enemy counterattacks overnight on 22–23 November.

Meanwhile, farther to the east, 59th Mechanized Brigade's 3rd Battalion attacked and seized Karpovka Station; however, it lost the station to a counterattack by 29th Motorized Division early on 23 November.[109] Although heavy fighting continued in the Voroshilov Camp and Karpovka regions well into 23 November, Vol'sky's forces accomplished their primary mission by holding firmly to Sovetskii. As a result, by nightfall on 22 November, 4th Mechanized Corps' 36th Mechanized Brigade was situated less than 20 kilometers from the lead elements of the Southwestern Front's 26th Tank Corps on the northern outskirts of Kalach. Whatever German forces were defending the region between the two corps were thoroughly outgunned, if not utterly demoralized, by Soviet armor operating deep in Sixth Army's rear.

By virtue of its dramatic dash from Plodovitoe to Sovetskii, Vol'sky's mechanized corps reportedly killed more than 14,000 Axis troops and captured another 13,000 in three days of fighting, along with 360 guns of various calibers and significant amounts of other weapons and equipment.[110] Although most of this booty came from the destroyed or seriously damaged Romanian VI Army Corps and IV Corps' Romanian 20th Infantry Division, some of it came from forces defending Sixth Army's supply bases and warehouses situated along the stretch of railroad line extending from Sovetskii eastward to Karpovka.

While Vol'sky's mechanized corps was advancing 35 kilometers to reach Sixth Army's deep rear area and create consternation and carnage in German Fourth Panzer Army's ranks, General Shapkin's 4th Cavalry Corps, which was protecting the left flank of the *front's* shock group, also accomplished its mission with aplomb. Advancing through Plodovitoe to the Abganerovo region in 4th Mechanized Corps' wake, both of Shapkin's cavalry divisions surged south toward their objectives along, north, and southeast of the Aksai River. En route to its objective—the village of Korobkin, located in Lesnaia *Balka*, 10 kilometers northwest of Sadovoe—Colonel Stavenko's 61st Cavalry Division engaged elements of Romanian 8th Cavalry Division, which had just regrouped northward from Romanian VII Corps' area of operations. In a battle near Kitov State Farm, 20 kilometers north of Korobkin, Stavenko's cavalrymen drove the Romanian cavalry back roughly 4 kilometers to the vicinity of the village of Vodianaia. Simultaneously, to the northwest, Colonel Baumshtein's 81st Cavalry Division reached the northern approaches to the town of Aksai and captured the nearby villages of Gniloaksaiskaia, Vodinskii, and Shelestov from the remnants of Romanian VI Army Corps' shattered 1st and 18th Infantry Divisions.

Farther south, on 51st Army's extreme left wing, Colonel Makarchuk's 302nd Rifle Division cleared Romanian forces from the western shore of Lake Barmantsak and then marched south toward the Tundutovo region, which was defended by Romanian VI Army Corps' 4th Infantry Division. The lead elements of Makarchuk's division reached the outskirts of the town at midday, just as 76th Fortified Region's 51st Machine Gun–Artillery Battalion also began probing westward from its positions at Malye Derbety, on the southwestern shore of Lake Sarpa. The fortified region's remaining machine gun–artillery battalions stayed in their positions around Malye Derbety, awaiting a significant change in the situation.[111]

Still farther south, Major General N. V. Kalinin's 91st Rifle Division, which occupied positions south of Lake Sarpa and roughly 15 kilometers east of Sadovoe, remained on the defense. It was preparing for an attack against Romanian 4th Infantry Division's defenses in and around Sadovoe, in cooperation with a planned assault on the town from the north by 4th Cavalry Corps' 61st Cavalry Division.

As the bulk of 51st Army's forces advanced northwest or south toward their deep objectives, the rifle divisions that had done so much damage to Romanian defenses two days earlier reverted to the army's second echelon and moved forward slowly to support their exploiting colleagues. In the northern half of the army's sector, General Vasilenko's 15th Guards Division completed clearing Romanian forces from the region west of Lake Sarpa and then advanced into the Buzinovka region in the wake of Vol'sky's 4th Mechanized Corps. On its left, Colonel Kuropatenko's 126th Rifle Division finished policing Romanian stragglers southwest of Lake Sarpa and then advanced westward into the Verkhne-Tsaritsynskii region, 40 kilometers southwest of Beketovka. There, it relieved 4th Mechanized Corps' 60th Mechanized Brigade, which then marched northeastward to reinforce its sister 59th Mechanized Brigade at Voroshilov Camp. Finally, the army's 38th Separate Motorized Rifle Brigade, its only mobile reserve, advanced into the Abganerovo region to provide backup for 4th Cavalry Corps.

62nd Army

As the three armies constituting the Stalingrad Front's main shock group accomplished their primary missions, the skeletal remains of Chuikov's 62nd

Army performed secondary but nonetheless important tasks. Fighting as hard as it could, it tried to keep the divisions of Sixth Army's LI Army Corps virtually paralyzed in the fight for ruined factories and buildings in Stalingrad's factory district (see appendix 19A in the *Companion*).

As usual, LI Army Corps' 305th and 389th Infantry Divisions attacked Colonel Liudnikov's 138th Rifle Division as it defended so-called Liudnikov's Island, the narrow strip of ground between the Barrikady Factory and the Volga River. Liudnikov's forces, however, repelled the attacks. Similarly, 62nd Army's 95th Rifle Division repulsed battalion-size probes by 305th Infantry Division in and around the infamous Fuel Tank Farm southeast of Barrikady.

The most important actions in Stalingrad took place in the villages of Rynok and Spartanovka in the city's northern suburbs, in the Krasnyi Oktiabr' Factory, and on Mamaev Kurgan (Hill 102.0). There, in accordance with Eremenko's orders, Chuikov's forces launched heavy attacks designed to pin down German forces in the city. In the northern suburbs, 124th Rifle Brigade attacked at 1100 hours in an attempt to seize the western part of Spartanovka village, capturing several buildings from LI Corps' 94th Infantry Division but otherwise achieving only minimal success. At the same time, in the factory district to the south, 95th Rifle Division tried in vain to link up with 138th Rifle Division but was only able to capture a few buildings on Mashinnaia Street by 1800 hours. On 95th's left, assault groups from 45th Rifle and 39th Guards Rifle Divisions attacked 79th Infantry Division's strongpoints in the Krasnyi Oktiabr' Factory at 1200 hours, with little success. Other assault groups from 45th Division retook Hall No. 3 in the Krasnyi Oktiabr' Factory at 1700 hours, capturing several prisoners from 79th Infantry Division's 226th Regiment. Finally, on bloody Mamaev Kurgan (Hill 102.0), 284th Rifle Division, with 92nd Rifle Brigade now on its right, launched futile attacks on 100th Jäger Division's defenses near the Water Tower.

Although 62nd Army reported killing or wounding 700 Germans on the 22nd, it made little progress in any sector, prompting Chuikov to report that "German defenses were as strong as ever."[112] The army commander also reported to the General Staff that 138th Rifle Division fielded a total of 300 men fighting on Liudnikov's Island, and 95th Rifle Division had 547 combat soldiers. Even though replacements were arriving, the nearly continuous attacks quickly consumed these new arrivals.

Despite 62nd Army's travails, and amidst this fierce fighting, General Bokov of the Red Army's General Staff heaped criticism on Chuikov's army for failing to support Colonel Liudnikov's 138th Rifle Division, which was still fighting in isolation east of the Barrikady Factory:

The General Staff has information at its disposal that the provision of replacement, ammunition, and foodstuffs for 138th RD, which is cut off

on the right bank of the Volga River and has been fighting in encirclement, is not being ensured by appropriate floating means, ice cutters,
and icebreakers. As a result, the division has not received replacements,
ammunition has not been provided to it, food has not reached it, and the
wounded from the deployed division have not been evacuated from the
rear to the left bank over the past several days.

In addition, the General Staff knows that the commands of 39th Gds,
45th, and 95th Rifle Divisions have not organized the removal and burial
of the bodies of dead soldiers and commanders on the battlefield, which
produces negative morale among the personnel.

I request you correct this and report your measures to the General
Staff.[113]

28th Army

In the region west of Astrakhan', on the Stalingrad Front's distant left flank,
General Gerasimenko's 28th Army continued to press German 16th Motorized Division west toward Elista (see map 18 and appendix 5Y in the *Companion*). After General Schwerin's motorized division abandoned Khulkhuta
on 21 November, 28th Army's 152nd Separate Rifle Brigade, supported by
at least a company of tanks from 6th Guards Tank Brigade, pursued the Germans toward their base at Utta. Advancing rapidly westward, with its 1st
Battalion north of the road, its 3rd Battalion and supporting tanks on the
road, and its 2nd Battalion south of the road, the brigade traversed 7 kilometers and reached the outskirts of Utta late in the morning. Once there, it
immediately attacked and drove off an enemy force of two infantry platoons
and several tanks, destroying two tanks but suffering no losses of its own. As
the German rear guards abandoned the town and withdrew westward, 248th
Rifle Division's 899th Regiment arrived in Utta at 1900 hours, after a two-
day-long forced march.[114]

With 16th Motorized Division in full retreat, Gerasimenko ordered 34th
Guards Rifle Division, whose forces were still in Siantsik, 35 kilometers
east of Utta, to load the riflemen from its 103rd Regiment in trucks, head
westward through Utta toward Iashkul', and concentrate along the eastern
approaches to Iashkul' by 0200 hours on the morning of 24 November. The
army commander left 248th Division's 905th Regiment in Khulkhuta. The 103rd
Guards Regiment departed from Siantsik at 1800 hours along the Iashkul' road.

Gerasimenko's plan for the capture of Iashkul' required a motorized rifle
battalion from 152nd Separate Rifle Brigade, supported by the remainder of
6th Guards Tank Brigade, to advance westward, north of the Iashkul' road;
at the same time, 34th Guards Rifle Division and 248th Rifle Division's 899th
Regiment would be advancing along the Iashkul' road in the wake of 103rd

Guards Regiment. The army commander's intent was to engage the German motorized division along the Oling and Iashkul' front. Although the size of his attacking force was severely limited by a shortage of trucks, Gerasimenko assured Eremenko that it was strong enough to cope with 16th Motorized Division. However, to ensure that the offensive succeeded, Gerasimenko asked Eremenko to order Trufanov's 51st Army to form a small combat group consisting of a reinforced battalion mounted on trucks and dispatch it south toward Elista. Eremenko refused, asserting that 51st Army had enough to do without sending part of its forces that far south.

Thus, by day's end on 22 November, Schwerin's 16th Motorized Division occupied new defensive positions extending from 15 kilometers north of Chilgir southward to about 15 kilometers south of Iashkul'. Its mission was to protect the eastern approaches to Elista. Schwerin employed 811th Turkestan Volunteer Infantry Battalion [*Turkestanisches Infanteriebatallion*] to defend Chilgir, 782nd Turkestan Battalion to protect the region north of Chilgir, and his division's main forces, including 60th and 156th Grenadier Regiments and 165th Motorcycle Battalion, to occupy his new main defensive line around Iashkul'.[115] Often referred to incorrectly as "Turkish" because of the designation "Turk" on German operational maps, these battalions (450th, 782nd, and 811th) actually consisted of volunteers from the former Turkestan Autonomous Soviet Socialist Republic.

Axis Reactions

With Romanian VI Army Corps essentially hors de combat, the Stalingrad Front had free rein to accomplish its principal objectives on 22 November. Goaded by *front* commander Eremenko's entreaties and warnings, his subordinate armies moved quickly to exploit the huge gaps left by the Romanian corps' demise; these gaps extended from the Chervlenaia River southward to just northwest of Aksai and from Shelestov eastward to Tundutovo. In the north, Tanaschishin's 13th Tank Corps of Tolbukhin's 57th Army thrust northwestward and then wheeled northward and northeastward to press German IV Army Corps' 29th Motorized, Romanian 20th Infantry, and 297th Infantry Divisions back to defenses along the Karpovka and Chervlenaia Rivers. On 57th Army's left, almost unopposed, General Vol'sky's 4th Mechanized Corps of Trufanov's 51st Army advanced about 35 kilometers to reach the Morozovsk-Stalingrad railroad line on a broad front stretching from Sovetskii eastward to Karpovka Station. Most important, it secured jumping-off positions near Sovetskii for its final lunge northward to link up with the Southwestern Front's 26th Tank Corps.

In the south, while 81st Cavalry Division of General Shapkin's 4th Cavalry Corps contended with the remnants of Romanian VI Army Corps in the

Aksai region, 61st Cavalry Division began a headlong advance toward the region northwest and west of Sadovoe. Simultaneously, 51st Army's 302nd and 91st Rifle Divisions, supported by the heavy firepower of 76th Fortified Region's two machine gun–artillery battalions, prepared to advance on Sadovoe from north and east of the town.

Romanian VI Army Corps, now assisted by small detachments from Fourth Panzer Army, struggled to erect viable defenses along the Aksai River. However, it was now crystal clear that, to do so successfully, Fourth Panzer Army would have to be reinforced significantly and quickly. With the German part of Hoth's panzer army about to be encircled in the Stalingrad region, there was only one source available to provide these reinforcements—Army Group A.

Conclusions

If the Stalingrad Front made substantial progress in its center and on its left wing, the same could not be said of its right wing. Due partly to Eremenko's initial offensive plan, which concentrated the bulk of his *front's* forces in 57th and 51st Armies, and partly to 29th Motorized Division's dramatic counterattack on the first day of the offensive, which inflicted severe and unanticipated damage on 13th Tank Corps, the Stalingrad Front's right wing could do little more than press Fourth Panzer Army's IV Army Corps back to the southern approaches to Stalingrad. Worse still for Eremenko, the limited successes on his right wing drove IV Army Corps into superb defensive positions anchored on the Karpovka and Chervlenaia Rivers and Karavatka *Balka* to the east. This guaranteed that any offensive actions the Stalingrad Front conducted on it right wing would become nothing more than costly siege operations.

Accepting this reality, Eremenko now turned his attention to the completion of two equally important tasks: first, ensuring that the pincers around German Sixth Army quickly closed, and second, ensuring that 51st Army's forces on his *front's* left wing were strong enough to deal with any German efforts to mount a relief operation toward Stalingrad from the west or southwest. Since any German relief effort was still days, if not weeks, away, the narrow strip of territory separating Eremenko's 4th Mechanized Corps from 26th Tank Corps of Vatutin's *front* took priority.

As for Sixth Army, in his message to Army Group B at 1900 hours, General Paulus informed Weichs, "Army intends to hold remaining area as far as both sides of the Don and has initiated all steps to achieve it. Presupposition, successful closing of the South Front and continuously adequate airlift of supplies."[116] Then, for the first of what would be many times, Paulus requested "freedom of action in case hedgehog position does not succeed in the South. Situation can force giving up Stalingrad and North Front in order to hit enemy with full force on South Front between Don and Wolga [Volga] and connect with 4th Rumanian Army there."[117] The "freedom of action" Paulus desired was permission to escape from what would become the infamous Stalingrad pocket, and from the very beginning, Hitler categorically denied Paulus's request. There is no doubt that every general officer in Sixth Army shared his commander's opinion, but in Hitler's grand scheme of things, this was irrelevant.

THE SOUTHWESTERN AND DON FRONTS' OFFENSIVE, 23 NOVEMBER

On 23 November the Southwestern Front continued to attack toward the west and southwest with part of its forces against Rumanian-Italian units defending the Baskovskaia and Bokovskaia region, and other part of the forces crushed the resistance of Rumanian forces encircled in the Raspopinskaia and Golovskii region, completely capturing 5th and 6th IDs, two regiments of 15th ID, and the remnants of Rumanian V Army Corps' 13th ID; and, together with units on the Don Front's right wing, conducted an offensive against German VIII Army Corps' units defending the Sirotinskaia, Kamyshinka, Malonabatovskii, and Trekhostrovskaia region with its remaining forces, while pressing the encirclement ring around German 4th Panzer and 6th Army toward Stalingrad from the west.

Red Army General Staff Operational Summary,
0800 hours on 24 November 1942[118]

The Southwestern and Don Fronts' Missions

Despite Rokossovsky's travails on 22 November, Vatutin was both elated and energized by the armies' performance the day before. Even though his three tank corps were days behind schedule, two of the three were either across or nearly across the Don River in the Kalach region, and the third was approaching Rychkovskii on the Don. Furthermore, it was now clear that the wall of armor Paulus had tried to erect west and northwest of the Don River at Kalach was made of paper rather than steel. By day's end on 22 November, XIV Panzer Corps' 24th and 16th Panzer Divisions were already reconnoitering routes back east across the Don, and 14th Panzer Division was beginning a painstaking withdrawal under intense enemy pressure, along with the infantry divisions of Sixth Army's XI Army Corps. As XI Corps withdrew eastward, its already weakened divisions were detaching regimental and battalion groups for dispatch south across the Don to shore up Sixth Army's sagging or nonexistent defenses from Peskovatka southwestward to Kalach and from Kalach eastward along the main railroad line to Karpovka. If present circumstances were nightmarish for Paulus, they were nothing short of exhilarating for Vatutin (see map 25).

Therefore, overnight on 22–23 November, with victory in their sights, Vatutin, Rokossovsky, and their subordinate army commanders discussed their forces' missions for the next day. Within the context of the *Stavka's* clear instructions to complete the encirclement operation at all costs, Vatutin and Rokossovsky formulated tasks for their subordinate formations that, if achieved, would satisfy the initial objectives of Plan Uranus—that is, the complete encirclement of German forces in Stalingrad and the formation of an outer encirclement front along and across the Krivaia and Chir Rivers (see appendix 5Z in the *Companion*).

The Southwestern Front's Advance

5th Tank Army

As had been the case the day before, the performance of 5th Tank Army's two tank corps, together with 21st Army's 4th Tank Corps, most impressed *front* commander Vatutin and did the greatest damage to German defenses (see map 26). Capitalizing on the gains made the day before and the weak German defenses, on 23 November, 26th Tank Corps from the Southwestern Front and 4th Mechanized Corps from the Stalingrad Front linked up at the village of Sovetskii, 18 kilometers southeast of Kalach, completing the encirclement of German Sixth Army. In a broader context, by day's end on the 23rd, 1st and 26th Tank Corps of the Southwestern Front's 5th Tank Army, 4th Tank Corps of the same *front's* 21st Army, and 4th Mechanized Corps of the Stalingrad Front's 51st Army had captured Kalach and Sovetskii, 15 to 20 kilometers to the south, and spread out across a wide swath of territory extending westward 30 kilometers to the northern outskirts of Rychkovskii and eastward 5 kilometers to the western approaches to Marinovka. While doing so, the four Soviet mobile corps seized more than 15 kilometers of the vital railroad line extending from 12 kilometers southeast of Kalach eastward to the western outskirts of Marinovka. This severed all German rail and road communications between Sixth Army and Romanian Third Army's forces west of the Don River, as well as the German army's extensive base and rear service network along and south of the Chir River (see appendix 5AA in the *Companion*).

The mission of General Butkov's 1st Tank Corps, the westernmost of the four mobile corps, was to capture Surovikino, Rychkovskii, and Chir Station. The corps spent all of 23 November resting and refitting its three tank brigades in the Liska River valley. It had no choice because, at the time, its 89th,

Map 25. German XI Army Corps' defense, 22 November 1942

117th, and 159th Tank Brigades fielded only 24 operational tanks.[119] Despite this forced inactivity, Butkov sent detachments from 44th Motorized Rifle Brigade toward Novo-Maksimovskii, Rychkovskii, and Chir Station, key locations along the Morozovsk-Stalingrad railroad line 10 to 15 kilometers to the south. At the time, small ad hoc detachments of German security and rear service troops, commanded by Colonels Adam and Tzschöckel, defended these points with whatever manpower and weapons they could assemble. After short but intense fights, 44th Motorized Rifle Brigade's detachments managed to capture Chir Station, 2 kilometers northeast of the German strongpoint at Verkhne-Chirskii, and the village of Blizhne-Osinovskii, 15 kilometers southeast of Surovikino and 13 kilometers west of Chir Station. The seizure of these two points on the Morozovsk-Stalingrad railroad line

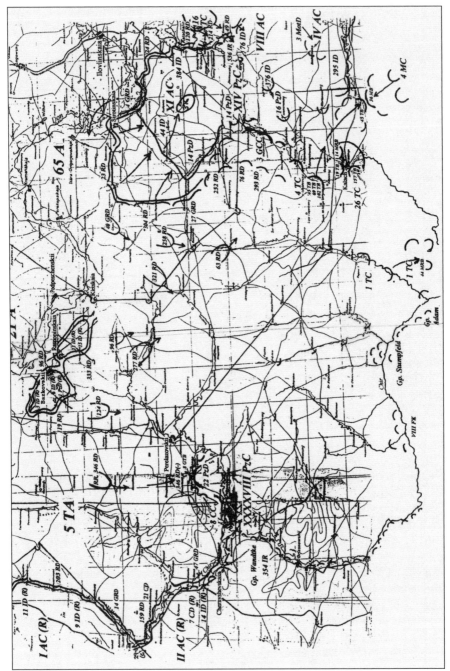

Map 26. Southwestern and Don Fronts' advance at 2200 hours, 23 November 1942

severed Sixth Army's communications with its rear services along the Chir River. The Soviet brigade reportedly seized 200 vehicles, 20 guns, and railroad cars filled with sugar, horses, and aircraft and killed up to 350 Axis troops in the fighting.

Despite losing Chir Station, Group Tzschöckel, which was now fighting under Romanian Third Army's control, continued to occupy and stoutly defend the village of Rychkovskii on the Don River's northern bank, 7 kilometers east of Chir Station, as well as a small bridgehead on the river's eastern bank south of Rychkovskii. It was absolutely vital that German forces continue to hold this minute piece of terrain because, once Sixth Army was encircled, this bridgehead would be the only territory under German control on the eastern bank of the Don River. As such, it was the only place from which the Germans could mount a relief operation toward Stalingrad from the west. Quite naturally, as the Germans fought desperately to retain this bridgehead, it became a prime target for Soviet offensive operations.

Whereas Butkov's 1st Tank Corps was virtually incapacitated by its shortage of operational tanks, General Rodin's 26th Tank Corps had between 30 and 40 tanks but was still without its 216th Tank Brigade, which was operating in support of 50th Guards Rifle Division much farther north. Rodin ordered his corps' 19th and 157th Tank and 44th Motorized Rifle Brigades to complete the twin tasks of capturing Kalach and advancing southward to link up with the Stalingrad's Front's 4th Mechanized Corps at or north of Sovetskii. At dawn on 23 November, Colonel Filippenko's 19th Tank Brigade concentrated in the woods northeast of Kalach, with 14th Motorized Rifle Brigade laagered nearby. Major Kudriashev's 157th Tank Brigade formed up on the western bank of the Don River, opposite the southern half of Kalach. On 26th Tank Corps' left, Lieutenant Colonel Zhidkov's 45th Tank Brigade of 21st Army's 4th Tank Corps was also on the eastern bank of the Don River, northeast of Kalach. The remainder of Kravchenko's 4th Tank Corps was marching south along the river's western bank to reinforce its forward brigade, join 26th Tank Corps' attack on Kalach, and advance southeast toward Sovetskii.

Opposing 26th and 4th Tank Corps' brigades were forces dispatched westward by Sixth Army to defend the Kalach region. These included XIV Panzer Corps' newly arrived 295th and 389th Panzer Antitank [*Jagd Abteilung*] and 244th Assault Gun Battalions, reinforced by lead elements of the army's 16th Panzer Division, manning defenses stretching from Peskovatka, 35 kilometers northeast of Kalach, southward to roughly 12 kilometers northeast of the town; the remains of Group Mikosch defending Kalach proper; and bits and pieces of 3rd Motorized Division and rear service units of Sixth Army and 71st Infantry Division occupying positions east and southeast of the town. In addition, police units, an antitank battalion, and a *Luftwaffe* antiaircraft battery, also under 3rd Motorized Division's control, helped defended Kalach proper. Considering the ad hoc and fragmented nature of these defenses and the strange mix of defending soldiers, Kalach was not a hard nut to crack. The 26th Tank Corps' history described the defenders as "security and antiaircraft artillery units, repair and rear service subunits, and also soldiers sent forward from hospitals but capable of employing weapons. All of these were combined under the commandant of the town and sent against our units."[120] Despite their disparate composition, the town's defenders supposedly resisted strongly, and one group even tried to break through to the Don River crossing before being driven back.

Colonel Filippenko's 19th Tank Brigade, supported by riflemen from 14th Motorized Rifle Brigade and 85th Guards-Mortar and 1241st Tank Destroyer Regiments, began their assault into the northern outskirts of Kalach at 0730 hours on 23 November, preceded by a 15-miinute artillery preparation and two volleys of *Katiusha* rocket fire. However, after several hours of fighting, intense German fire halted the assault before the Soviet troops reached the town. While Filippenko's forces were advancing on Kalach from the north, General Rodin ordered Major Kudriashev's 157th Tank Brigade to occupy firing positions on the western bank of the Don River and prepare to shell German positions in the southern half of the town. After 19th Tank Brigade's attacks stalled, at about 1300 hours, the motorized rifle battalion from Kudriashev's tank brigade assaulted across the river on the ice and seized a foothold on the eastern bank, in the southwestern part of Kalach. Even though Kudriashev's tanks could not follow the infantry because the ice on the river was too thin to support their weight, the German defenders appreciated the new threat, abandoned Kalach, and withdrew east toward Marinovka.

By 1400 hours, 26th Tank Corps' two tank brigades occupied all of Kalach. The next day, Rodin reported that his corps had killed up to 600 enemy troops in the fighting for Kalach; captured 25 tanks, 600 vehicles, 150 motorcycles, 150 horses, and 5 warehouses; and liberated as many as 3,000 Red Army prisoners of war from captivity.[121] While Rodin's forces were capturing Kalach, the tank brigades of Kravchenko's 4th Tank Corps bypassed the town from the east and wheeled southeast toward Sovetskii, where they linked up with the lead elements of the Stalingrad Front's 4th Mechanized Corps (see below).

As the two tank corps of Romanenko's 5th Tank Army played their vital role in encircling German Sixth Army, the tank army's rifle and cavalry forces strove to complete their own important missions: reaching the Krivaia and Chir Rivers and liquidating the remnants of German and Romanian forces that had delayed the army's advance for almost three days. These "obstacles to victory" included the remnants of XXXXVIII Panzer Corps' 22nd Panzer

Division, still half encircled in the Malaia and Bol'shaia Donshchinka region north of the Kurtlak River; Romanian Group Lascar, still holding out in the region southwest of Raspopinskaia; and Romanian 1st Armored Division, whose remnants had made their way southward into the Kurtlak River valley.

On 5th Tank Army's right wing, Colonel Anashkin's 159th Rifle Division relieved 21st Cavalry Division, with which it had been cooperating, and cleared the remnants of Romanian 9th and 14th Infantry Divisions from the eastern bank of the Chir River. It did so in the sector extending from the junction of the Krivaia and Chir Rivers east of Bokovskaia, southward to Pichugin, where the Tsutskan' River flowed westward into the Chir, 14 kilometers northwest of Chernyshevskaia. Anashkin's riflemen then fortified this sector and reconnoitered westward across the Chir River toward Bokovskaia. General Romanenko ordered this reconnaissance because 5th Tank Army's intelligence organ expected that General Hollidt's XVII Army Corps, whose 294th and 62nd Infantry Divisions were just reaching the town of Bokovskaia to reinforce Romanian I Army Corps' defenses, might launch counterattacks across the river.

After being relieved by 159th Rifle Division, the main body of General Iakunin's 21st Cavalry Division rested and refitted briefly in the rear area and prepared to rejoin its parent corps in an advance southward from the Kurtlak River region to clear German troops north of the Chir River. Although ignored in German records, 5th Tank Army reported that a regiment of Iakunin's cavalry conducted a raid across the Krivaia River, 25 kilometers north of Bokovskaia, and briefly seized the villages of Verkhnyi and Nizhnyi Maksai in the Romanians' rear area, killing 400 troops and seizing 100 prisoners, all from Romanian 9th Infantry Division.[122] If the raid occurred, its likely purpose was to test the strength of Romanian defenses in this region and confirm the arrival of German reinforcements. Whatever the case, all of 21st Cavalry Division marched southeastward to rejoin 8th Cavalry Corps late in the day.

On 159th Rifle Division's left, General Fokanov's 47th Guards Rifle Division finally ended its prolonged struggle with Romanian 7th Cavalry Division in the Tsutskan' River valley, forcing the cavalry division's remnants to retreat westward across the Chir River north of Chernyshevskaia overnight on 22–23 November. Thereafter, 47th Guards reached and fortified the Chir River's eastern bank from Pichugin southward to Chernyshevskaia. Along the river line, Fokanov's guardsmen faced the remnants of Romanian 14th Infantry and 7th Cavalry Divisions, which Romanian II Army Corps hastily reassembled to defend the river's western bank.

Farther east in 5th Tank Army's center, in the Kurtlak River valley and the Malaia and Bol'shaia Donshchinka region to the north, bitter fighting continued between 55th and 112th Cavalry Divisions of Borisov's 8th Cavalry

Corps and the remnants of German 22nd Panzer and Romanian 1st Armored Divisions. This fighting was so confused that, at day's end on the 23rd, 5th Tank Army and the Red Army General Staff could only state that "8th CC's positions are being verified."[123] Other sources, however, confirmed that the two cavalry divisions were simultaneously trying to destroy the two Axis forces and block their withdrawal westward across the Chir. In addition, an impatient General Romanenko, who was determined to settle the issue in his army's center, dispatched 346th Rifle Division and 8th Guards Tank Brigade from his reserve to eradicate this vexing obstacle to his army's advance.

In the chaotic battle, the remnants of General Gheorghe's Romanian 1st Armored Division pushed southward into the Kurtlak River valley east of Petrovka, but General Shaimuratov's 112th Cavalry Division, which had captured Petrovka the night before, blocked 1st Armored Division's escape route west to the Chir. Farther north, after Gheorghe's armored division broke through its cordon and marched south into the Kurtlak River valley, Colonel Chalenko's 55th Cavalry Division galloped southward and engaged the southern portion of 22nd Panzer Division's forces at the village of Medvezhyi, 5 kilometers west of Malaia Donshchinka. At about the same time, the survivors of General Sion's Romanian 15th Infantry Division, which had escaped from Group Lascar's encirclement the night before by penetrating the defenses of 5th Tank Army's 119th Rifle Division, drove southward and also broke through 55th Cavalry Division's defensive screen to rejoin the northern portion of 22nd Panzer Division near Bol'shaia Donshchinka (see below). Sion brought with him 3,680 men, 18 trucks, 1,045 horses, and 2 field guns.[124]

The northern portion of 22nd Panzer Division then left General Sion's small force to clear the remaining Soviet cavalrymen from Bol'shaia Donshchinka and moved southward to support the division's southern elements fighting at Medvezhyi.[125] Later, Chalenko's 55th Cavalry Division escaped the entire melee by turning its positions over to the newly arrived 346th Rifle Division and 8th Guards Tank Brigade. Chalenko's cavalrymen then galloped southeastward and southward, enveloping all of 22nd Panzer Division from the east, and reached the villages of Petrovskaia and Ozery, 15 kilometers east and southeast of Chernyshevskaia and 25 to 35 kilometers north of Oblivskaia. By virtue of this bold maneuver, at least one of Borisov's divisions succeeded in breaking free from the logjam of thoroughly intermingled Soviet, German, and Romanian forces east and northeast of Chernyshevskaia.

Meanwhile, the other division of Borisov's cavalry corps, Shaimuratov's 112th, repelled repeated attempts by Gheorghe's armored division to fight its way westward along the Kurtlak valley to the relative safety of the Chir's western bank. With less than half its initial combat strength and almost out of fuel, Gheorghe's division first attacked westward to break through 112th Cavalry Division's defenses. However, with help from 179th Tank Destroyer

Regiment and 511th Flamethrower Tank Battalion, Shaimuratov's cavalry defeated Gheorghe's assault, reportedly destroying a Romanian R-2 tank but losing 61 cavalrymen who were taken prisoner. Rebuffed by 112th Cavalry Division, Gheorghe's division reportedly destroyed 19 R-2 tanks that had run out of fuel and 9 inoperable R-2s before withdrawing southward across the Kurtlak River to the Oserski (Ozery) region, 8 kilometers south-southwest of Petrovka. There, it reassembled its troops and 11 remaining Pz-IIIs and Pz-IVs and 19 R-2 tanks, the latter towed by German armored vehicles.[126] Although Gheorghe's bloodied division managed to reestablish communications with Romanian Third Army after nightfall, it would have to wait another day before making good on its escape.

As 1st Romanian Armored Division struggled to escape, farther north, fresh Soviet forces joined the fight against 22nd Panzer Division. After relieving 55th Cavalry Division in the Bol'shaia Donshchinka region, Colonel A. I. Tolstov's 346th Rifle Division (from 5th Tank Army's reserve) and Major Nikolov's 8th Guards Tank Brigade (transferred east from 159th Rifle and 21st Cavalry Divisions' sector) assaulted the defenses of Sion's detachment in Bol'shaia Donshchinka and 22nd Panzer Division's forces in the Medvezhyi region. However, according to the General Staff, the afternoon attack failed due to "inadequate time to prepare the attack, poor reconnaissance of the enemy's defenses, inadequate artillery support, and the piecemeal commitment of tank brigade's battalions into combat."[127]

This failure permitted 22nd Panzer Division to withdraw its forces southward into the Kurtlak River, 20 kilometers east of Chernyshevskaia, relatively intact. Once there, however, the remnants of Colonel Rodt's division found themselves trapped between 112th Cavalry Division, which blocked the western exit from the valley, and 55th Cavalry Division, which was conducting its envelopment around the valley's eastern extremity. What was left of the panzer division was saved when, in accordance with 5th Tank Army's orders, Colonel Chalenko's 55th Cavalry broke contact with 22nd Panzer and pushed farther south after nightfall. As a result, the fighting in and north of the Kurtlak valley would endure another day before 5th Tank Army could finally rid itself of the "vexing obstacle" posed by the remnants of XXXXVIII Panzer Corps.

South of the Kurtlak River, after completing its raids toward the Oblivskaia region, 8th Motorcycle Regiment received an order from army headquarters at 0200 hours to immediately reassemble in the Perelazovskii region, ostensibly to help block Romanian forces from escaping from the Raspopinskaia pocket. However, when it turned out that Romanenko had issued the order by mistake, 5th Tank Army sent the regiment on another deep raid into the enemy's rear along the Oblivskaia and Morozovsk axis in the afternoon. In an obvious exaggeration, the regiment reported that it killed more than

1,000 enemy soldiers and officers and seized 25 aircraft and 70 vehicles at an airfield near Oblivskaia. It also supposedly captured a 5,000-head herd of livestock, which it turned over to the population, and blew up several warehouses, including a large one filled with ammunition.[128]

Finally, on 23 November, the rifle forces on 5th Tank Army's left wing fulfilled the army's second important mission—destroying the surrounded Romanian forces southwest of Raspopinskaia. Soviet forces had cut encircled Group Lascar in half and captured its commander the day before, so in the morning, Romanenko ordered General Belov's 50th Guards Rifle Division and supporting 216th Tank Brigade to disengage from the fight in the Fomikhinskii region and redeploy south toward the Chir River. This left Colonel Kulagin's 119th Rifle Division with the task of destroying the encircled Romanians, in cooperation with 21st Army's forces. The Soviets' final plan required Kulagin's division to attack the Romanian pocket from the west and 21st Army's 96th, 63rd, and 333rd Rifle Divisions to do so from the northeast, east, and southeast. By this time, the 50-square-kilometer encirclement pocket west and southwest of Raspopinskaia contained the remains of Romanian 5th, 6th, 13th, 14th, and 15th Infantry Divisions, all under the command of General Traian Stanescu, who had replaced General Lascar as commander of 6th Infantry Division.[129]

Kulagin's 119th Division captured the Romanian strongpoint at Zhirkovskii early in the morning. It then dispatched one of its regiments southward to prevent General Sion's column from escaping southwestward across the Tsaritsa River; it sent the remainder of its forces eastward into the center of the Romanians' shrinking pocket. Although this single regiment failed to block the escape by Sion's force, the division's main body captured Verkhne-Cherenskii at 1400 hours and linked up with 21st Army's 333rd Rifle Division. While parts of these two divisions liquidated the encircled Romanian force south of Izbushenskii, 119th Rifle Division's left-wing regiment and 21st Army's 96th and 63rd Rifle Divisions did the same to the Romanian grouping encircled north of Izbushenskii. Many Romanians were captured in both pockets overnight on 22–23 November, including Generals Lascar and Mazarini, the commanders of 6th and 5th Infantry Divisions; Lieutenant Colonel Nicolae Cambrea, 6th Infantry's chief of staff; and Colonel Anatescu, commander of one of 9th Infantry Division's regiments.[130]

As for the formal Romanian surrender, General Stanescu sent a representative under a white flag to meet his Soviet counterpart at day's end on 23 November. The delegation met at the headquarters of 63rd Rifle Division's 291st Regiment. After discussions in the evening, the Romanian group ceased fighting at 2320 hours, and General Stanescu and his staff gave themselves up at 0230 hours the next morning. All the Romanians surrendered over the next 12 hours, and the tally came to 27,000 officers and men.[131]

To complete the tale of Romanian Third Army's demise, the remnants of 15th Infantry Division and other units led by General Sion simply refused to surrender. Instead, with about 8,000 men, Sion's column broke out of the encirclement before dawn on 23 November and headed southwest toward the Tsaritsa River. This group was led by an advance guard consisting of an antitank battalion, two artillery batteries, and a mounted reconnaissance platoon, followed by two regiments and hundreds of stragglers from other units. On the march, this column was reportedly more than 12 kilometers long. Although Sion's troops managed to break contact with Soviet forces, when they tried to cross the Tsaritsa River with their heavy equipment, the ice on the river broke. At that point, the regiment of 119th Rifle Division that had just captured Zhirkovskii attacked the column's rear at midday, forcing all but its advance guard to flee southward and surrender that evening. Soviet sources reported that about 5,000 of Sion's troops were killed or captured in this fighting. Sion's advance guard, however, pressed on, made it across the Tsaritsa River, and reached Bol'shaia Donshchinka late in the morning, where its surviving force of more than 3,000 men joined 22nd Panzer Division and took over defense of the town.

Therefore, by day's end on 23 November, General Romanenko's 5th Tank Army had fulfilled its primary mission of projecting its two tank corps forward to the Kalach region and lower Chir River, as well as one of its two secondary missions: liquidating encircled Group Lascar. However, its third mission, to push Axis forces back beyond the Krivaia and Chir Rivers, remained only partially fulfilled. Due to the stubborn and prolonged resistance by XXXXVIII Panzer Corps, the forces in the tank army's center failed to reach the Chir and capture the three key towns on or near its northern bank. Instead, the rifle divisions and cavalry corps in the army's center were still tied up in fighting along the Kurtlak River. Exploiting this delay, makeshift German and Romanian forces threw up hasty but effective defenses around the two most important towns on the Chir River's northern bank, Oblivskaia and Surovikino, and at Rychkovskii on the Don. Although Romanenko released 50th Guards and 119th Rifle Divisions from the encirclement battle southwest of Raspopinskaia by nightfall on the 23rd, it would be days before they could join the tank army's struggle along the Chir and weeks before these three vital German strongpoints would finally fall into Soviet hands.

21st Army

If General Romanenko's 5th Tank Army had a good day on 23 November, General Chistiakov's 21st Army had an even better one (see appendix 5AA in the *Companion*). While the former's 26th Tank Corps was capturing Kalach, the latter's 4th Tank Corps was linking up with the Stalingrad Front's 4th Mechanized Corps at Sovetskii, thereby completing the encirclement of

German Sixth Army. Of course, Kravchenko's *tankists* must share credit with tens of thousands of other Red Army soldiers who tied down Sixth Army's forces in other sectors, preventing Paulus from freeing up enough forces to effectively defend his long lines of communication in the army's rear.

General Kravchenko's 4th Tank Corps, which had started crossing the Don River at Berezovskii with its 45th Tank Brigade late on 22 November, finished concentrating its four brigades on the river's eastern bank by 1000 hours on 23 November. Kravchenko formed his corps into two march columns of brigades, with the brigades configured in precombat formation so that they could deploy quickly to fight, if necessary. His corps' left column consisted of Lieutenant Colonel Zhidkov's 45th Tank Brigade, which was already on the eastern bank of the Don River north of Kalach, followed by Colonel Agafonov's 69th and Colonel Koshelev's 102nd Tank Brigades, which crossed the river west of Kamyshi, 6 kilometers north of Kalach. With Zhidkov's brigade in the lead, this column's mission was to bypass Kalach to the east and advance southeast toward the Morozovsk-Stalingrad railroad line to link up with the Stalingrad Front's forces that had captured Sovetskii on 22 November. The 4th Motorized Rifle Brigade, advancing on foot, was to swing eastward to Illarionovskii, near Vaniukova *Balka*, 10 kilometers northwest of Marinovka, and then turn south toward Platonov (Platonovskii), 4 kilometers west-southwest of Marinovka.[132] Kravchenko sent 4th Brigade on its wide sweep to the east to protect the corps' left flank against surprise attack as it advanced southeastward.

The 4th Tank Corps' lead tank brigade, Zhidkov's 45th, was specially tailored with attached artillery and engineer subunits to conduct independent missions as a forward detachment. It began its advance shortly after 1000 hours and moved eastward rapidly, capturing the village of Kamyshi, 5 kilometers north of Kalach, by midday. It then wheeled southward and advanced 12 kilometers, capturing several isolated German strongpoints en route before linking up at 1600 hours with Lieutenant Colonel Rodionov's 36th Mechanized Brigade of 51st Army's 4th Mechanized Corps in the northern section of Sovetskii State Farm. When it did, German Sixth Army was officially encircled. Shortly thereafter, Colonel I. N. Plotnikov, Kravchenko's deputy for political affairs, sent a message to Colonel P. N. Sokolov, the chief of 21st Army's Political Department, which Sokolov forwarded to *front* headquarters. The message, written in pencil on Plotnikov's notepad, read: "At 1600 hours on 23 November 1942, units of the 4th Tank Corps fought their way across the Don River and linked up in the Sovetskii region with units of the Stalingrad Front's 4th Mechanized Corps."[133]

The remainder of 45th Brigade, as well as portions of the right column's 69th and 102nd Tank Brigades, advanced southward and helped 26th Tank Corps capture Kalach. They too closed on their objectives by the end of the day. Specifically, Colonel Agafonov's 69th Brigade reached Sovetskii at 1900 hours, and Colonel Koshelev's 102nd Brigade seized Platonov Farm, 3 kilometers north of Sovetskii. There, it was joined later in the evening by elements of 4th Motorized Rifle Brigade, which had been delayed by a skirmish with German forces at Illarionovskii. The advance by Kravchenko's armor into the Sovetskii region was materially assisted by Vol'sky's 4th Mechanized Corps, whose 59th and 60th Motorized Brigades tied down German forces manning security outposts from Karpovka westward to Marinovka with constant, if futile, attacks.

Weeks later, Kravchenko's headquarters reported the results of his corps' advance from Kletskaia to Sovetskii, significantly exaggerating the number of German tanks destroyed: "The corps seized or destroyed 580 tanks, 276 guns, 4,130 vehicles, 38 warehouses, and significant amounts of other weapons and equipment. A total of 6,600 enemy soldiers and officers were destroyed and up to 16,000 enemy soldiers and officers were taken prisoner."[134] As later Russian sources indicated, the figure for destroyed German tanks was incredibly high because it included the hulks of tanks destroyed in the region during August 1942.

As Kravchenko's tanks were rolling eastward past Kalach toward Sovetskii, Pliev's 3rd Guards Cavalry Corps was galloping east toward Golubinskii and Bol'shenabatovskii on the Don River's western bank, 20 to 35 kilometers north of Kalach. After capturing Evlampievskii late on 22 November, General Pliev assigned new missions to his three cavalry divisions designed to advance them to the western bank of the Don River (see appendix 5AB in the *Companion*). In short, the corps' divisions were responsible for advancing east and southeast across the Don River, if possible, to threaten German XI Army Corps' withdrawal routes back across the river and seize the town of Vertiachii, in cooperation with 24th Army's 16th Tank Corps, which was advancing from the north (see the Don's Front's operations below). At a minimum, Pliev was supposed to force 16th Panzer Division of Hube's XIV Panzer Corps to withdraw from its defenses along the lower Golubaia River and back across the Don River south of Vertiachii. Thus, the cavalry corps' primary task boiled down to separating XIV Panzer Corps from XI Army Corps to pave the way for the destruction of both.

Beginning its advance before dawn on 23 November, Chepurkin's 5th Guards Division lunged eastward into the Golubinskii and Malo-Golubinskii region, seizing crossing sites over the Don in both places. Its bag of trophies by day's end reportedly included 36 aircraft the Germans left behind at an airfield, 55 abandoned tanks or tanks under repair, 12 armored personnel carriers, more than 700 trucks and 100 light vehicles, 25 guns, 1,500 rifles, and, most important for the cavalrymen, more than 600 horses. In addition, the division "liberated" many warehouses containing uniforms and ammunition and a German maintenance and repair base.[135] These figures are also inflated by the inclusion of German weapons and equipment lost during the fighting in August 1942, and the aircraft count is wildly exaggerated as well.

The advance by 3rd Guards Cavalry Corps' 32nd Cavalry Division toward Bol'shenabatovskii proved far more difficult because it ran into 16th Panzer Division's defenses at the town. According to the cavalry corps' intelligence section, the panzer division was defending the town with a battalion of motorized infantry, artillery, and more than 30 tanks—numbers that track well with 16th Panzer's actual strength at the time.[136] Colonel Chudesov's 32nd Cavalry assaulted German defenses at the town several times during the day and repulsed numerous counterattacks. By day's end, the cavalrymen had captured the northern and northwestern outskirts of the town, but nothing more. In fact, the heavy fighting continued overnight on 23–24 November and into the next morning before Bol'shenabatovskii fell into the cavalry division's hands.

While Chudesov's 32nd Cavalry was fighting for Bol'shenabatovskii, Colonel Belogorsky's 6th Guards Division bypassed the town to the north and advanced eastward to capture Markers 160.2 and 201.4, 3 to 9 kilometers northeast of Malonabatovskii. This attack penetrated 16th Panzer Division's defenses and cut the road running northeastward from the town. The panzer division reacted quickly, however, and succeeded in halting Belogorsky's thrust 3 to 4 kilometers short of Luchinskii Farm and Kalachkin, the cavalry's objectives on the Don River's western bank.

Pliev's advancing cavalry threatened XI Army Corps' rear area and XIV Panzer Corps' defenses along the Golubaia River, prompting the panzer corps to concentrate most, if not all, of 24th and 16th Panzer Divisions' remaining tanks and motorized infantry east of the Golubaia River. General Hube's intent was to strike the right flank of Belogorsky's 6th Cavalry Division and force it to fall back westward across the Golubaia River (see appendix 5AB in the *Companion* for General Pliev's description of the action on 23 November).

Parenthetically, the Red Army General Staff's daily operational summary for the 23rd stated, "3rd Gds. CC—repelled heavy attacks by elements of 16th and 14th PzDs (reportedly with 180 tanks) and, together with 76th RD, reached the Don River in the northern outskirts of Bol'shenabatovskii."[137] Since the combined strength of 14th, 24th, and 16th Panzer Divisions was no more than 80 to 90 tanks by this time, this report was also an exaggeration.

As for 21st Army's rifle forces, at midday on 23 November, Colonel Tavartkiladze's 76th Rifle Division caught up with the left wing of Pliev's 3rd Guards Cavalry Corps and took up positions along the western bank of the Golubaia. During the day, Tavartkiladze's riflemen protected the left flank of the cavalry corps as it advanced eastward. It accomplished this mission by forcing 14th Panzer Division's *kampfgruppe* and its reinforcing infantry from 44th Infantry Division's 132nd Regiment and 384th Infantry Division's 534th Regiment to withdraw from their defensive lines just east of Os'kinskii. Thereafter, as 14th Panzer continued its planned fighting withdrawal eastward, 76th Division pursued. The division advanced 5 to 7 kilometers, passing through Evlampievskii in the afternoon and reaching the western bank of the Golubaia River in the Verkhne-Golubinskii and Malo-Golubinskii regions by day's end. For its performance since 19 November, the *Stavka* awarded the division the new designation 51st Guards Rifle Division on 23 November.

Farther to the south, Colonel Lagutin's 293rd Rifle Division continued its steady advance in the wake of 3rd Guards Cavalry Corps' right wing. It ended the day in the Malo-Golubinskii and Golubinskii regions along the western bank of the Don River. Well to its rear, Colonel Chernov's 277th Rifle Division, which had been relieved from its fight on the army's right wing, hastened southeastward to reinforce 21st Army's forces along the western bank of the Don. Finally, 96th, 63rd, and 333rd Rifle Divisions, which were operating on the extreme right wing of Chistiakov's army, spent the day attacking and either destroying or capturing the remnants of Romanian Group Lascar encircled in the Bazkovskii and Raspopinskaia regions. After 63rd Rifle Division finally accepted the group's surrender in the early hours of 24 November, it, along with 96th Rifle Division, prepared to march southeastward to join the army's main forces on the Don.

1st Guards Army
Set against the backdrop of the major victories achieved by the Southwestern Front's 5th Tank and 21st Armies on 23 November, General Leliushenko's 1st Guards Army had little to boast of. As it had on previous days, the army limited itself to local firefights with Romanian forces from the positions it had occupied the day before. The only combat actions taking place in the army's sector were conducted by 278th and 203rd Rifle Divisions on the army's left wing, which launched probes and reconnaissance raids across the Krivaia River from Verkhne-Krivskaia southward to Gorbatovskii. These were designed simply to determine the actual positions and strength of Romanian I Army Corps' 9th and 11th Infantry Divisions and to identify any units from XVII Army Corps' 62nd and 294th Infantry Divisions that might have been inserted into the Romanians' forward lines. As before, 1st Guards Army was anxiously awaiting an opportunity to participate in the grander Saturn offensive once Uranus succeeded.

Conclusions

The forces of Vatutin's Southwestern Front acquitted themselves well on 23 November. In addition to helping to encircle Sixth Army's main forces in the Stalingrad region, they eliminated most of the Romanian forces that had been surrounded days before in the *front's* rear area. Although the stubborn remnants of XXXXVIII Panzer Corps still represented an obstacle for Vatutin's forces, that obstacle was now relatively minor and would disappear in a matter of hours.

With Romanian Third Army eliminated from the Axis order of battle in the region west of the Don River, Vatutin shifted his attention to the future. In this regard, he was most concerned with 5th Tank Army's failure to reach and capture the Chir River line. Romanenko's failure to do so not only complicated the planning and conduct of future offensives such as Operation Saturn but also left the door open for the Germans to attempt to rescue their encircled Sixth Army from the west. Specifically, the failure by Butkov's 1st Tank Corps to capture Rychkovskii, and with it the Germans' last bridgehead on the east bank of the Don, made a German relief operation from that location far more likely. Therefore, until Rychkovskii fell into Soviet hands, Vatutin and the *Stavka* kept that small but vital piece of terrain foremost in their minds. In short, Rychkovskii now replaced Sovetskii as the primary objective for Soviet forces in the Stalingrad region.

Ending the day on a positive note, late in the evening on 23 November, but before the surrender of the bulk of encircled Romanian Third Army, General Vatutin's chief of staff, Major General G. D. Stel'makh, reported to the General Staff about the damage his Southwestern Front had inflicted on Romanian and German forces during the first five days of the operation. Based on what Stel'makh described as incomplete data, he announced that "the *front's* forces captured over 25,000 troops, 158 tanks, 32 aircraft, 630 guns, 124 mortars, 820 machine guns, 1,700 vehicles, 180 motorcycles, 2,780 horses, around 3,000,000 shells, 15,000,000 rounds, and a great quantity of fuel, food, and forage warehouses and destroyed about 35,000 enemy troops, 67 aircraft, 90 tanks, 142 guns, and 400 automatic weapons from 19–23 November."[138] Although some of these figures are credible, the total of 248 tanks destroyed or captured is not: it exceeded the entire armored strength of German Sixth and Romanian Third Armies.

The Don Front's Advance

65th Army

As it had on previous days, Rokossovsky's relatively weak Don Front continued to do the "dirty work" of the Uranus offensive, while the armies of Vatutin's Southwestern Front and Eremenko's Stalingrad Front enjoyed the fame and glory associated with encircling German Sixth Army (see map 26 and appendix 5AC in the *Companion*). Throughout the day on 23 November, General Batov's 65th Army continued to pound the depleted divisions of General Strecker's XI Army Corps, compelling the Germans to conduct a harrowing but nevertheless effective withdrawal eastward out of their tenuous and perilous salient on the western bank of the Don south of Sirotinskaia (see map 27). Closely pursuing the withdrawing German 14th Panzer Division and 376th, 44th, and 384th Infantry Divisions toward the southeast, the rifle divisions on 65th Army's right wing reached positions extending from Kamyshinskii, 10 kilometers southwest of Sirotinskaia, southward to Golubaia, 5 kilometers northeast of Os'kinskii, by 1400 hours. Thereafter, XI Army Corps carried out yet another 5- to 10-kilometer "jump to the rear" in the evening, ending up in defensive positions stretching from Khmelevskii, 8 kilometers southeast of Sirotinskaia, southwestward to Verkhniaia Golubaia, 7 kilometers east of Os'kinskii. All the while, the divisions in 65th Army's center and on its left wing repeatedly attacked XI Corps' center and right wing along and south of the Don River, but with only limited success.

On 65th Army's extreme right and the right wing of the army's shock group, Colonel Shekhtman's 252nd Rifle Division advanced roughly 5 kilometers southeastward from the Perekopskii region during the day, pushing the defending 14th Panzer Division and supporting infantry from 132nd and 534th Infantry Regiments back to defenses between Verkhniaia Golubaia and Nizhnaia Golubaia by 2400 hours. On 252nd Division's left, Colonel Glebov's 27th Guards Division advanced roughly 4 kilometers against 14th Panzer Division's right wing and 376th Infantry Division's left-wing 767th Regiment. Glebov's guardsmen captured Hill 231.3 by 1200 hours and reached Hill 235.0, 6 kilometers northeast of Golubaia, by midnight.

Farther to the north, Colonel Fursin's 258th Rifle Division captured Ventsy and Perekopskii, 15 kilometers northeast of Verkhne-Buzinovka, from 376th Infantry Division's 673rd Regiment and then advanced to end the day roughly 8 kilometers north-northeast of Golubaia. Finally, on the left wing of 65th Army's shock group, Colonel Sivakov's 23rd Rifle Division, supported by a regiment from the neighboring 321st Rifle Division on its left, assaulted the defenses of 672nd Regiment on 376th Infantry Division's right wing in the region north and west of Blizhniaia Perekopka. After intense fighting, Sivakov's troops reached a position extending from the southwestern slopes of Hill 184.1 to the western outskirts of Blizhniaia Perekopka line by 1600 hours. Thereafter, the division employed a forward detachment to pursue the Germans as they withdrew to new defenses on the high ground roughly 3 to 8 kilometers northeast of Golubaia.

While the divisions on 65th Army's right wing managed to advance up to 10 kilometers on 23 November, those in the army's center and on its left wing

Map 27. German XI Army Corps' defense, 23 November 1942

faced far stronger resistance. In part, this was because the German defenses they attacked were well developed and situated on the high southern bank of the Don River. Nonetheless, Major General A. I. Pastrevich's 40th Guards Rifle Division, which attacked in the sector from Blizhniaia Perekopka east to the village of Khokhlachev, 8 kilometers west of Sirotinskaia, was able to exploit the successful advance by 65th Army's right wing. Assaulting the defenses of 44th Infantry Division's 131st Infantry Regiment (without its 3rd Battalion, which was still supporting 376th Infantry Division), Pastrevich's riflemen fought for and captured Hills 145.0, 180.2, and 172.4, 1.5 to 5.5

kilometers east of Blizhniaia Perekopka, in the morning. In the afternoon, the division captured Kamyshinskii and then drove across two large *balkas* to reach the western approaches to Hill 243.0, roughly 9 kilometers southwest of Khmelevskii.

On 65th Army's right wing, at 0600 hours, 4th Guards and 24th Rifle Divisions assaulted the defenses on 44th Infantry Division's right wing at and south of Sirotinskaia and the defenses of 384th Infantry Division's 535th Regiment in the 13-kilometer-wide front extending from the Podgorskii region, 12 kilometers southeast of Sirotinskaia, southeastward to 3 kilometers north of Trekhostrovskaia. Here, the fighting was very intense, even though XI Army Corps' 44th and 384th Divisions defended the entire sector with a force of only four reinforced infantry battalions. Given the weakness of the German defenses, Major General G. P. Lilenkov's 4th Guards Division managed to capture Hills 180.9 and 146.6, 2 to 3 kilometers west of Sirotinskaia, and reach the northern outskirts of Sirotinskaia; the eastern outskirts of Zimovskii, 5 kilometers to the south; and the eastern outskirts of Khmelevskii by the end of the day. At this point, with Lilenkov's riflemen enveloping Khmelevskii from the west, General Batov ordered General Makarenko's 321st Rifle Division, which had been withdrawn from combat several days earlier to rest and refit, to reinforce 4th Guards Division and seize Khmelevskii early the next day. Meanwhile, on 4th Guards' left, Colonel F. A. Prokhorov's 24th Rifle Division captured Hill 169.8 on the Don River's southern bank, 4 kilometers east of Podgornyi, as well as Hill 110.2, 1 kilometer north of Trekhostrovskaia on the Don, by day's end.[139] Prokhorov's "Iron" Division stormed and captured Trekhostrovskaia overnight on 23–24 November.

At this point, a heated dispute erupted between 65th and 24th Armies over exactly which one was at fault for failing to break through German defenses, capture Vertiachii, and thus encircle German XI Army Corps before it could withdraw eastward across the Don to the safety of Sixth Army's main defensive lines. The 24th Army began the dispute late on 23 November, after it became clear that its forces would fail to reach their objective of Vertiachii (see the description of 24th Army's operations below).

If the going was difficult for Batov's 65th Army, it was equally frustrating for Strecker's XI Army Corps. Despite a skillful and determined defense, XI Corps had no choice but to give ground because Sixth Army had no reinforcements to send it. Even Rokossovsky recognized why XI Army Corps had to give way, and he attributed the same problem to Sixth Army as a whole: "All of the enemy's attempts to impede the advance by our forces turned out to be too late. The tank and motorized formations, which were transferred from the Stalingrad region to the places where penetrations had formed, entered combat in piecemeal fashion and, coming under attack by our superior forces, suffered defeat."[140]

Consequently, as he had done the day before, General Strecker reluctantly ordered his corps to conduct a fighting withdrawal all day long, while he constantly shifted forces back and forth between his defending divisions and even dispatched some units out of his sector, at Sixth Army's behest. Thus, Strecker's corps began the day with 14th Panzer Division (reinforced by 44th Infantry Division's 132nd Regiment and 384th Infantry Division's 534th Regiment) and 376th Infantry Division's 767th Regiment defending on its left wing, 376th Infantry Division's 672nd and 673rd Regiments (reinforced by 3rd Battalion, 131st Regiment) and 44th Infantry Division's 131st Regiment (less its 3rd Battalion) deployed in its center, and one battalion of 44th Infantry Division's 131st Regiment and 384th Infantry Division's 535th Regiment defending on its right wing. However, after withdrawing to intermediate defenses at 1400 hours and to final defenses by midnight, Strecker's corps ended the day with 14th Panzer Division and its two reinforcing regiments defending on its left wing, 44th Infantry Division's 131st Regiment (reinforced by 376th Infantry Division's 767th Regiment) deployed in its center, and 384th Infantry Division's 535th Regiment defending on its right wing. By this time, because it was able to shorten its front, the corps placed 376th Infantry Division's 672nd and 673rd Regiments in reserve.

This frenetic reshuffling of XI Corps' forces occurred because Sixth Army directed Strecker to dispatch 384th Division's 536th Regiment southward across the Don to bolster its defenses east of Kalach, just as the army had done with 44th Infantry Division's 134th Regiment days before. Although this castling of regiments strengthened the army's defenses along the Don, it did little to help Strecker's beleaguered XI Army Corps. Despite these measures, XI Army Corps' fate rested firmly in the hands of Galanin's 24th Army, whose forces were supposed to seize the key town of Vertiachii by day's end on the 23rd. Fortunately for XI Corps, 24th Army did not.

24th Army

After 24th Army failed to crack German 76th Infantry Division's defenses on 22 November, its commander, General Galanin, resolved to do better on the 23rd. Overnight, he ordered his shock group to resume its assaults early on 23 November but altered the mission of General Maslov's 16th Tank Corps. Instead of entering combat as a single entity, with all three of its tank brigades serving as the army's mobile group, Maslov was to provide direct tank support to the infantry of the shock group's rifle divisions with two of his brigades. Accordingly, the shock group's 120th, 214th, 49th, and 233rd Rifle Divisions launched converging attacks southward through Verkhne- and Nizhne-Gnilovskii toward Vertiachii (see appendix 5AC in the *Companion*). During the attack, however, 16th Tank Corps' two brigades encountered both Soviet and German minefields that had not been cleared by sappers and lost 14 tanks to Soviet mines and 12 more to German mines. If this was not bad enough, German antitank guns destroyed another 7 tanks (3 KVs, 2 T-34s, and 2 T-60s), increasing the corps' tank losses to 55 by day's end.[141] In the daily summary it issued at 0800 hours the next day, the General Staff recorded, "24th Army tried to resume its offensive toward Vertiachii with its right-wing units (120th, 214th, 49th, and 233rd Rifle Divisions) but, after encountering strong and well-organized enemy fires, achieved no success and was fighting in its previous positions."[142]

The obvious failure of 24th Army's offensive generated harsh recriminations between its commander and senior officers and those of neighboring 65th Army, who felt that Galanin's army ultimately permitted German XI Army Corps to escape destruction north of the Don River (see appendix 5AD in the *Companion* for General Batov's comments). As events the next day would indicate, this exchange would not end the unpleasantness between Galanin, his neighbors, and his superiors.

66th Army

As had been the case during the first four days of Operation Uranus, General Zhadov's 66th Army, still deployed on the Don Front's left wing, simply occupied its previous positions and exchanged artillery and mortar fire with the enemy on 23 November. Denied even the smallest taste of glory during the encirclement of German Sixth Army, Zhadov's forces would finally begin contributing to victory in a matter of hours.

Conclusions

Although the Don Front's armies clearly played second fiddle to those of the Southwestern and Stalingrad Fronts during the dramatic first stage of Operation Uranus, the *front* was earmarked to perform a vital mission in the future—the destruction of German Sixth Army. And because this mission proved to be beyond its capabilities, Rokossovsky's *front* would inexorably grow in size, ability, and importance. Ultimately, Rokossovsky would put his *front*'s performance in a broader context and, at the same time, let Galanin off the hook by absolving him of blame for his army's defeat. Instead, he emphasized the importance of his 24th Army and Batov's 65th Army in tying down German forces that otherwise might have inhibited the Southwestern and Stalingrad Fronts' far more dramatic offensives to Kalach and Sovetskii.

Axis Reactions

For Paulus and Sixth Army, the most disturbing aspect of its fight with the Don Front's 65th and 24th Armies on 23 November was that by day's end, it was clear that Strecker's XI Army Corps and Hube's XIV Panzer Corps would not be able to retain any ground west of the Don River. Strecker's corps had already been withdrawing for two days, first to the Os'kinskii, Blizhniaia Perekopka, and Sirotinskaia line and then to the Verkhne-Golubinskii and Khmelevskii line. Likewise, Hube's XIV Panzer Corps moved back, first to the Teplyi, Os'kinskii, and Krasnyi Skotovod line and later to the Bol'shenabatovskii and Glazkovskii line along the Golubaia River. While the two corps were doing so, Paulus withdrew 384th Infantry Division's 534th Regiment and 44th Infantry Division's 134th Regiment southward across the Don and moved the bulk of 113th Infantry and the remainder of 3rd Motorized Divisions from the northern rim of Sixth Army's defenses southwest toward Sokarevka and Illarionovskii, northeast and east of Kalach.

What began as a reinforcement of Sixth Army's western front at the expense of the northern front would accelerate in the next few hours and ultimately result in the formation of a relatively coherent and viable western front for the army over the next few days. In and of itself, this reshuffling of forces, during which the army's motorized and panzer divisions gravitated southward and southwestward, clearly indicated that Paulus was thinking about the possibility of breaking out of the pocket. It was this possibility, in turn, that ignited lengthy discussions among Paulus, Weichs at Army Group B in Starobel'sk, the Army High Command (OKH), and Hitler and his Armed Forces High Command (OKW) in Berlin. Although these discussions initially involved Sixth Army's possible escape, within days they focused on the necessity of supplying and relieving the army from the outside. Escape or relief notwithstanding, in reality, they concerned the ultimate survival of Paulus's army.

THE STALINGRAD FRONT'S OFFENSIVE, 23 NOVEMBER

> The Stalingrad Front occupied the Aksai and Zhutov 1 region with part of its shock group's forces and, overcoming stubborn resistance, attacked from the Elkhi, Iagodnyi, Varvarovka, and Nariman region toward the northwest with its main forces, while pressing the German encirclement ring southwest of Stalingrad.
>
> Red Army General Staff Operational Summary,
> 0800 hours on 24 November 1942[143]

If 65th and 21st Armies of Vatutin's Southwestern Front recorded spectacular successes on 23 November, the accomplishments of the Stalingrad Front's 51st Army matched those of their sister armies to the north. In fact, in addition to achieving a physical linkup with the Southwestern Front's mobile forces at Sovetskii, Eremenko's *front* succeeded in destroying the equivalent of a full Romanian army south of Stalingrad in two days of fighting, whereas it had taken Vatutin's *front* slightly more than five days of combat to do the same to Romanian Third Army.

The Stalingrad Front's Missions

After accomplishing his main mission on 22 November by capturing Krivo-muzginskaia Station on the Morozovsk-Stalingrad railroad and the Sovetskii region slightly to the north, Eremenko assigned fresh missions to his subordinate armies overnight on 22–23 November (see appendix 5AE in the *Companion*). First and foremost among the many tasks the *Stavka* assigned to his *front* was completing the encirclement of German Sixth Army. This meant not only holding on to the Sovetskii region but also assisting the Southwestern Front's mobile groups as they advanced southward to their anticipated linkup point. Closely related to this mission was the task of expanding the *front's* grip on the Morozovsk-Stalingrad railroad line and nearby roads running east to west by advancing its forces along the railroad line. This, in turn, implied broadening the roughly 5-kilometer-wide corridor east and west of Sovetskii into a more substantial gap between Sixth Army's forces in the Stalingrad region and the rear services and security forces of both German Sixth Army and Romanian Third Army west toward the Don and Chir Rivers. In practical terms, this meant beginning the reduction of encircled German Sixth Army by attacking German defenses along and north of the railroad line and the roads running from Sovetskii eastward through Marinovka, Prudboi Station, and Karpovka to Karpovskaia Station, a distance of roughly 25 kilometers.

At the same time, the Stalingrad Front was still responsible for erecting an outer encirclement front along and south of the Aksai River to protect the *front's* left flank and prevent German forces from mounting an effort to reinforce or relieve its encircled Sixth Army from the south or southwest. This also implied dispatching forces westward to secure the eastern bank of the Don River from the mouth of the Aksai River north to Kolpachki, 12 kilometers south of Kalach. As for the *front's* remaining armies, 62nd Army and, for all practical purposes, 64th Army would simply tie down as many German forces as possible in and south of Stalingrad by conducting local attacks, raids, and feints. On the *front's* distant left wing, 28th Army was to continue its operations toward Elista to tie up German 16th Motorized Division.

The Stalingrad Front's Advance

64th Army
General Shumilov's army continued to attack with its left wing west of Beke-tovka but remained on the defense on its right wing at and southwest of

Stalingrad's southern suburb of Kuporosnoe (see map 28 and appendix 5AF in the *Companion* for the Stalingrad Front's accomplishments on 23 November). As it had the day before, the army's shock group consisted of 36th Guards and 157th, 204th, and 29th Rifle Divisions, supported by all the army's tanks and most of its artillery. The shock group's four divisions were deployed from left to right (west to east) in the sector extending from south of Tsybenko, on the northern bank of the western end of Karavatka *Balka*, eastward roughly 12 kilometers to the German strongpoint at Elkhi. When the four divisions resumed their assaults, they encountered strong resistance by German IV Army Corps' 297th Infantry Division, reinforced by Romanian 20th Infantry Division's 82nd Regiment and 371st Infantry Division's 670th Regiment and 1st Battalion, 671st Regiment. Nevertheless, the shock group advanced up to 8 kilometers during the day, capturing the strongpoint at Iagodnyi, 11 kilometers southeast of Beketovka, and the southern approaches to Tsybenko, 18 kilometers west of Beketovka.

Advancing on the shock group's left wing, Colonel Denisenko's 36th Guards Rifle Division, still supported by 56th Tank Brigade, pursued the withdrawing German and Romanian troops about 8 kilometers and breached 297th Division's defenses at the western end of Karavatka *Balka*, 2 kilometers east of Tsybenko, by 1600 hours. Although strong counterattacks, probably launched by 371st Infantry Division's 670th Regiment, contained 36th Guards' advance on the southern outskirts of Tsybenko, Denisenko's forces clung to a foothold they gained on the southern slope of Hill 111.6 on the *balka*'s northern bank.[144]

On the right of 36th Guards Division, Colonel A. V. Kirsanov's 157th Rifle Division, supported by 13th Tank Brigade, conducted an effective pursuit during the day, advancing about 4 kilometers and capturing the enemy strongpoint of Iagodnyi (Iagodniki), 4 kilometers southwest of Elkhi and 8.5 kilometers north of Nariman, from Romanian 20th Infantry Division's 82nd Regiment by 1600 hours. Kirsanov's division continued its advance and reached the southern approaches to the small village of Popov, 2 kilometers north of Iagodnyi, by the end of the day.[145]

Attacking on the right wing of 64th Army's shock group, Colonel A. V. Skvortsov's and A. I. Losev's 204th and 29th Rifle Divisions launched converging attacks against the Elkhi strongpoint and the hills to the west. Although 204th Division managed a short advance and seized Hill 116.3, 2 kilometers west of Elkhi, by 1600 hours, 29th Division's attack faltered under intense artillery, mortar, and machine gun fire and strong and skillful resistance by 1st and 3rd Battalions of 297th Infantry Division's 523rd Regiment.

These attacks, which proved costly to the four divisions in terms of personnel losses, propelled 64th Army's shock group forward to a formidable

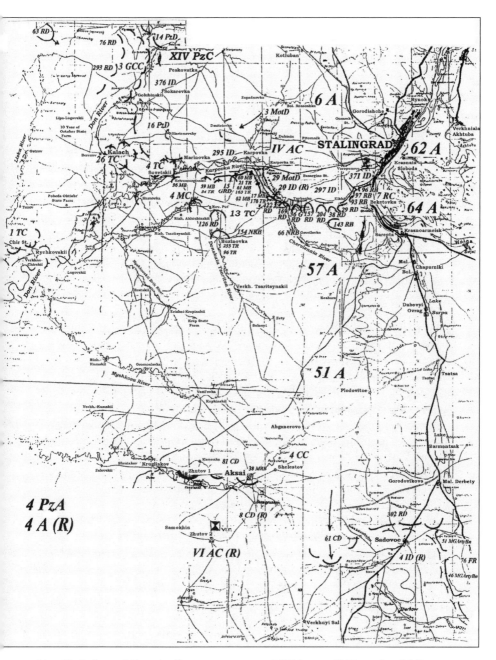

Map 28. Stalingrad Front's offensive: situation at 2200 hours, 23 November 1942

defensive line erected by German IV Army Corps along the northern bank of Karavatka *Balka* from the Chervlenaia River eastward to the western approaches to Elkhi and around the Elkhi strongpoint itself. It would take more than six weeks of bloody combat before Shumilov's forces could overcome these defenses.

While 64th Army's shock group was advancing westward to Karavatka *Balka* and Elkhi, on its right wing, 7th Rifle Corps' 97th, 93rd, and 96th Rifle Brigades and 66th and 154th Naval Rifle, and 20th Destroyer Brigades simply defended their current positions and occasionally raided and reconnoitered the strong German defenses opposite their front. Based on previous experience, Shumilov wisely chose to avoid attacking across this already blood-soaked ground.

Despite recording only negligible gains on the ground, 64th Army accomplished its principal mission of applying pressure to the southern front of Sixth Army's Stalingrad pocket to prevent IV Army Corps from dispatching forces westward to help fill in the yawning gaps on Sixth Army's western front along and east of the Don River.

57th Army

On 64th Army's left, west of the Chervlenaia River, General Tolbukhin's 57th Army resumed its northwestward advance past German defensive positions on the western bank of the Chervlenaia River and toward the German strongpoints at Karpovka and nearby Karpovka Station on the morning of the 23rd (see appendix 5AF in the *Companion*).[146] The fighting in this sector was especially intense because, after withdrawing northward the day before, General Leyser's 29th Motorized Division manned strong prepared defensive positions 1 to 2 kilometers west of the river. The division's position extended from the railroad line, 2.5 kilometers south of Karpovka, southeastward past of the towns of Rogachik, Bereslavskii, and Rakotino on the Chervlenaia River; it then turned eastward across the river south of Kravtsov to tie in with the western edge of 297th Infantry Division's defenses at Tsybenko. Thus, before crossing the Chervlenaia, which was beginning to freeze, Tolbukhin's army first had to overcome German defenses on the river's western bank. When the army did so on the 23rd, its troops advanced straight into the teeth of 29th Motorized Division's defenses. Even if 57th Army managed to push the Germans back to the river, it would then face the challenge of assaulting 29th Motorized Division's second defensive line along the river's eastern bank. Accomplishing this feat against Sixth Army's most combat-capable division was no mean task, especially since the army's premier tank force, 13th Tank Corps, had been moderately damaged during previous fighting.

As had been the case during the first three days of the Stalingrad Front's offensive, Colonel Tanaschishin's 13th Tank Corps spearheaded 57th Army's advance. However, because of the damage inflicted on 61st Mechanized Brigade and 163rd Tank Regiment by 29th Motorized Division's counterattacks on 20 and 21 November, the corps' strength on the 23rd had fallen to about 120 tanks. Nonetheless, Tanaschishin's forces assaulted 29th Motorized Division's defenses, primarily in the 8-kilometer-wide sector from Kravtsov south to Varvarovka, with 62nd and 17th Mechanized Brigades, their organic 176th and 44th Tank Regiments, and infantry from 422nd and 169th Rifle Divisions. Tolbukhin's attack plan sought to breach enemy defenses in this sector, cross the Chervlenaia River, and attack German 297th Infantry Division's stronghold at Tsybenko from the west and southwest. At the same time, 64th Army's 36th Guards Division was to attack Tsybenko from the south and southeast. Needless to say, Tolbukhin's assaults failed.

Thus, by day's end on the 23rd, Tolbukhin's army had scarcely dented 29th Motorized Division's defenses but had suffered heavy losses in men and tanks. However, other elements of Tolbukhin's force managed to connect the army's left flank to 51st Army's right flank north of Rakotino, several kilometers north of Kravtsov. Hereafter, his army would essentially conduct siege operations along the southern front of Sixth Army's newly created *Kessel* (pocket).

51st Army
In addition to building an outer encirclement front along the Aksai River, 51st Army's most important mission on 23 November was to move Vol'sky's 4th Mechanized Corps northwestward into the Sovetskii region so that it could link up with the Southwestern Front's mobile groups. However, Vol'sky's corps was also tasked with seizing as much of the vital Morozovsk-Stalingrad railroad line as possible in the 16-kilometer-sector from Platonovskii eastward through Marinovka to Karpovka. As a result, like Tolbukhin's 13th Tank Corps along the Karpovka and Chervlenaia Rivers, two-thirds of 51st Army's 4th Mechanized Corps became enmeshed in especially heavy and costly fighting along the railroad from Voroshilov Camp to Karpovka (see appendixes 5AF and 5AG in the *Companion*).

This struggle involved 1st Motorized Rifle Battalion of 4th Corps' 59th Mechanized Brigade at Voroshilov Camp and the same brigade's 3rd Battalion in equally heavy fighting on the outskirts of Karpovka, 6 to 8 kilometers to the east. The encounter near Karpovka finally ended in the evening, when 51st Army's 15th Guards Rifle Division arrived on the scene. As 15th Guards Division's history later recorded with a bit of braggadocio: "At first light on 23 November, 15th Guards Rifle Division received the mission—to cut the Stalingrad-Sovetskii railroad line, capture Karpovskaia Station and the villages of Karpovka and Novyi Rogachik, occupy a defense along the line of these points, and prevent an enemy penetration toward the south and southwest. The division fulfilled there missions brilliantly. Not a single Hit-lerite penetrated through its combat formations."[147]

German Sixth Army's report to Army Group B at about midafternoon confirmed the Soviet attacks in the Voroshilov Camp and Karpovka sectors amidst what was obviously a deteriorating situation: "The enemy break-through in the morning at Marinowka and Woroschilow Camp has been cleared up," and "a strong attack with tanks from the south and southeast against Marinowka (2 regiments with tanks) . . . was repelled at midday in bitter fighting" (see appendix 5AH in the *Companion*).[148] Further, Sixth Ar-my's situation map for 23 November indicates that 3rd Motorized Division's *Kampfgruppe* von Hanstein defended the Voroshilov Camp sector and that a *kampfgruppe* from 29th Motorized Division was fighting and launching counterattacks in the Karpovka and Novyi Rogachik sector.[149]

According to Soviet sources, although 59th Brigade's 1st Battalion suc-ceeded in holding on to its foothold along the railroad at Prudboi Station and on the southern outskirts of Voroshilov Camp, strong German counterattacks forced the brigade's 3rd Battalion and 15th Guards Rifle Division to abandon Karpovka and Karpovskaia Station by the evening of 23 November and with-draw to positions south of the railroad line by nightfall on the 24th. However, the same source correctly concluded, "These actions by 59th Mechanized Brigade's subunits prevented the enemy from advancing against the flank and rear of the corps' main force [36th Mechanized Brigade], thus ensuring fulfillment of its main mission [the linkup at Sovetskii]."[150]

The 51st Army's greatest success of the day took place at 1600 hours, when motorized riflemen from 4th Mechanized Corps' 36th Mechanized Brigade, commanded by Colonel Rodionov, and *tankists* of Major Dorosh-kevich's supporting 20th Tank Regiment linked up with a forward detach-ment leading the advance of 45th Tank Brigade of 21st Army's 4th Tank Corps on the northern outskirts of Sovetskii (see appendix 5AI in the *Com-panion* for a description of this dramatic meeting).[151] The officers and men of 51st and 21st Armies who took part in the celebrations marking this signal event understood just how unprecedented it was: for the first time in the war, they had encircled an entire German army.

Early that evening, Nikita Sergeyevich Khrushchev, the member of the Stalingrad Front's Military Council (commissar), and General M. M. Popov, Eremenko's deputy, arrived at 4th Mechanized Corps' headquarters to con-gratulate General Vol'sky and consult with him on future operations. After exchanging greetings, Vol'sky not only described his corps' accomplishment but also highlighted its problems. With Sovetskii in his hands, the corps com-mander informed Khrushchev that 59th Brigade was fighting for Voroshi-lov Camp and that 36th Brigade, which had seized Sovetskii, had crossed the Karpovka River and was marching on Platonovskii, just 4 kilometers southwest of Marinovka. Although he still had 60th Brigade in reserve, the corps was running short of ammunition at a time when the Germans were bringing up fresh forces from Stalingrad, placing them in the old fortifications along the railroad line, and offering ever-strengthening resistance.

When Khrushchev asked him whether he had met with Kravchenko, Vol'sky said he had not. He admitted, however, that the encounter between their two corps was not uneventful, stating, "It is true that . . . we failed to recognize one another, and we damaged several of Kravchenko's tanks." But, Vol'sky added, although Kravchenko's *tankists* "were responsible because they did not stop and send up a green signal, ours were also guilty because they failed to identify our own T-34s."[152]

Later in the evening, the two generals and Khrushchev met with Kravchenko in a house on the western edge of Sovetskii. However, the commissar said nothing about the inadvertent exchange of fire. After Kravchenko reported on his corps' actions, all three generals agreed that Paulus's army would probably try to escape southward, and Hitler would likely assemble a relief force and send it northward to support the escape. Unbothered by this prospect, Kravchenko noted, "In the small region of Kalach and Sovetskii alone, two tank corps and one mechanized corps have assembled. General T. I. Tanaschishin's 13th Mechanized Corps is located nearby. If, after being relieved by rifle divisions, we send these corps to Kotel'nikovo to reinforce 51st Army's forces, there can be no speaking about any sort of enemy penetration [relief] from the south."[153]

Of course, as dramatic as this linkup was, it was not the only thing happening in 51st Army on this red-letter day. To the south, General Shapkin's 4th Cavalry Corps, now reinforced by 38th Motorized Rifle Brigade, continued its southward march to erect an outer encirclement front along the Aksai River. Encountering only negligible resistance by a single regiment of Romanian 8th Cavalry Division, Colonel Baumshtein's 81st Cavalry Division, with 38th Motorized Rifle Brigade attached, captured the key town of Aksai on the river of the same name, 12 kilometers southwest of Abganerovo, as well as the village of Zhutov 1, 15 kilometers west of Aksai. This gave the cavalry corps firm control over a roughly 20-kilometer-wide sector along the Aksai, an ideal position to protect the *front's* southern flank against any German attack from the southwest.

Farther east, Colonel Stavenko's 61st Cavalry Division, which was cooperating with 302nd and 91st Rifle Divisions and 76th Fortified Region in a drive to capture the town of Sadovoe, outflanked the defenses of Romanian 4th Infantry Division from the west by capturing the Umantsevo region, 10 kilometers southwest of Sadovoe. At the same time, Colonel Makarchuk's 302nd Rifle Division captured the Tundutovo region, 18 to 20 kilometers north of Sadovoe; pursued the withdrawing Romanian 4th Infantry Division, plus part of 5th Cavalry Division, southward; and captured Hills 102.6 and 78.0, 15 kilometers west-southwest to 5 kilometers south of Tundutovo. The coordinated attacks by 61st Cavalry and 302nd Rifle Divisions outflanked Romanian forces south of Aksai and forced the regiment of Romanian 8th Cavalry Division to withdraw to Zhutov 2, 18 kilometers south of Aksai, leaving the bulk of its artillery behind.

Simultaneous with the attacks against Romanian defenses at Sadovoe from the northwest and north, 76th Fortified Region's 51st and 45th Machine Gun–Artillery Battalions attacked westward from the region south of Malye Derbety and reached the northeastern and eastern approaches to Sadovoe. Finally, on 76th Fortified Region's left, General Kalinin's 91st Rifle Division attacked west toward Obil'noe, 30 kilometers south of Sadovoe, and also toward Sadovoe from the southeast, reaching the eastern approaches to Obil'noe by day's end. The combined advances of four different Soviet formations against Sadovoe from the northwest, north, east, and southeast rendered the defenses of Romanian 4th Infantry and 5th Cavalry Divisions untenable, leaving them no choice but to abandon the town early the next day. Rounding out 51st Army's operations on 23 November, Colonel Kuropatenko's 126th Rifle Division hurried forward through Aksai to reinforce 4th Cavalry Corps' 81st Cavalry Division and strengthen 51st Army's outer encirclement front.

That evening, General Trufanov radioed General Eremenko at the Stalingrad Front's headquarters and reported, "The main mission is accomplished. The army's units are fighting with the enemy along the Karpovka, Sovetskii, Aksai, Umantsevo, and Sadovoe line."[154]

62nd Army

Throughout the day on 23 November, in accordance with Eremenko's instructions, General Chuikov's ragged 62nd Army maintained maximum pressure on Sixth Army's LI Army Corps in Stalingrad to prevent Paulus from transferring forces from the city to other threatened regions around the periphery of the Stalingrad pocket (see appendix 19A in the *Companion*). At day's end, 62nd Army reported that it had "repelled attacks by small groups of enemy, held on to its positions, and attacked to improve its own positions," adding that "the enemy was generally inactive but resisted strongly and conducted counterattacks in the Krasnyi Oktiabr' Factory. Three enemy transport aircraft landed west of Mamaev Kurgan and one landed at the Aviagorodok airfield."[155] By now, it was usual procedure to report the arrival of German aircraft in the pocket, primarily to assess how successful the Germans were in delivering supplies to their trapped army. It was already apparent that Paulus's army was not receiving enough supplies to sustain operations for very long.

In the only fighting of any consequence during the day, Chuikov reported that Colonel Batiuk's 284th Rifle Division and 92nd Rifle Brigade had attacked toward Hill 102.0 (Mamaev Kurgan) and the Krasnyi Oktiabr' Factory but managed to advance only 150 to 200 meters at each location. Attesting to the reduced strength of Chuikov's forces, the army's 95th Rifle Division claimed that the combat strength of its 241st Regiment was 230 men, and its 161st Regiment had 303 men. This was typical for the army's divisions and brigades fighting in the city, but it meant there was little these formations could do other than harass LI Army Corps' forces. As he did each evening, Chuikov ordered his forces to "attack along the army's entire front at dawn to destroy the enemy" and, in this case, reach the western outskirts of Stalingradskaia Street.[156]

In an interesting side note to the day's operations, General Seydlitz, commander of LI Army Corps, was anxious for Sixth Army to attempt a breakout from the pocket, and he issued an order that he thought would encourage General Paulus to make that decision. LI Corps' Order No. 118 directed its subordinate divisions to prepare for a breakout attempt, and it instructed the divisions located in the extreme northeastern part of the pocket to pull back to new positions around Orlovka and destroy all equipment not needed for the breakout.[157] When it was carried out overnight on 23–24 November, this order had extremely adverse consequences for German 94th Infantry Division (see below).

28th Army
Rounding out the Stalingrad Front's military operations on 23 November, in the Kalmyk steppes on the *front*'s extreme left wing, General Gerasimenko's 28th Army continued a westward advance with its main shock group and attacked Iashkul' with its forward detachments. This began a prolonged fight for Iashkul' that would last until the army finally captured the town on 29 December. As far as action on 23 November was concerned, 28th Army reported, and the General Staff duly recorded, the following:

- 6th Gds. TB, with subunits from 152nd RB—fought with a regiment of 16th MotD's infantry and 40 tanks 5–6 kilometers north and northeast of Iashkul'.
- 152nd RB—fortified the Utta region.
- Remaining units—occupied their existing positions.[158]

By this time, Schwerin's 16th Motorized Division had established formidable defenses around the town and a defensive line that extended from 25 kilometers north of Chilgir, 40 kilometers north-northwest of Iashkul', southward to Iashkul', and then southward another 15 kilometers to Zagan-Uban.

This extended line was designed to protect all approaches to Elista from the east. The 16th Motorized Division defended with its attached 811th Turkestan Volunteer Battalion at Chilgir; 782nd Turkestan Battalion midway between Chilgir and Iashkul', flanked on the right by 3rd Battalion, 156th Motorized Regiment, north of the Iashkul'–Ulan-Erge road; and all of 60th Motorized Regiment and 1st and 2nd Battalions of 156th Motorized Regiment occupying a defensive ring around Iashkul' proper. Schwerin retained the division's 165th Motorcycle Battalion in reserve midway between Iashkul' and Ulan-Erge. It was a powerful position, as subsequent events would indicate.

Axis Reactions

By late evening on 23 November, the rump formations of Fourth Panzer Army—including German 371st and 297th Infantry and 29th Motorized Divisions, together with the remnants of Romanian 20th Infantry Division—completed their withdrawal to the Elkhi, Popov, Tsybenko, Bereslavskii, and Karpovka region and finally halted their Soviet tormentors along the line of Karavatka *Balka* and the Chervlenaia River. There, these forces became Sixth Army's IV Army Corps, commanded by General Erwin Jänecke. IV Corps' left flank was anchored firmly on Stalingrad's southern suburb of Kuporosnoe, and its right flank was anchored on twin strongpoints at Karpovskaia Station and Staryi Rogachik. On the corps' right, west of Karpovskaia Station, was *Kampfgruppe* Korfes, consisting of a nucleus of several infantry battalions together with service support elements of 295th Infantry Division; it manned defenses extending from Karpovka west to the strongpoint at Marinovka. Deployed from east to west, *Kampfgruppe* Korfes consisted of the following:

- *Kampfgruppe* Seidel (one battalion of 103rd Motorized Regiment, 64th Motorcycle Battalion, and one fusilier company of 36th Panzer Regiment from 14th Panzer Division led by Lieutenant Colonel Seidel)—deployed from Karpovka to Prudboi Station.
- *Kampfgruppe* von Hanstein (one motorized battalion from 3rd Motorized Division under Colonel *Freiherr* von Hanstein)—deployed from Prudboi Station to Matiuchin Kurgan.
- *Kampfgruppe* Willig (one motorized battalion from 60th Motorized Division commanded by Major Karl Willig)—from Matiuchin Kurgan to Marinovka.[159]

As for the Romanian forces in the area, the northernmost regiment of 8th Cavalry Division had no choice but to abandon the Aksai region and withdraw to new defenses at Zhutov 2, 10 kilometers south of Aksai. The 4th Infantry Division abandoned Tundutovo and withdrew to the Sadovoe region, only to find itself once again under attack from three sides. In the region west of Aksai, the remnants of 1st, 2nd, and 18th Infantry Divisions withdrew to a weak defensive line along the Aksai River west of Aksai but were not heavily attacked.

General Constantin Constantinescu, commander of Romanian VI Army Corps, strongly advocated withdrawing all his forces to Kotel'nikovo, but he was overruled by General Hoth at Fourth Panzer Army, who demanded that Constantinescu hold his forward positions until the army could mount a relief attempt toward Stalingrad. However, at this point, a relief operation was but a distant hope.[160]

Conclusions

As it turned out, 23 November was a very good day for General Eremenko. After being badly embarrassed at the hands of his namesake in the fall of 1941, the so-called Soviet Guderian finally had his revenge. Penetrating deep into the Germans' operational rear, his *front*'s 4th Mechanized Corps linked up with the Southwestern Front's mobile groups on schedule and captured a segment of the main railroad and highway connecting Stalingrad with the Don River to the west. By doing so, it obliterated at least three Romanian divisions and encircled hundreds of thousands of German troops in the Stalingrad region—a feat the Red Army had never before come close to accomplishing. At the same time, the *front*'s 4th Cavalry Corps, now reinforced by motorized troops and several divisions worth of riflemen, succeeded in pushing southward to the Aksai River and beyond, making it extremely difficult for the Germans to relieve or support Sixth Army.

In four days of operations, Eremenko's forces completed the task they had begun on 20 November, essentially defeating Fourth Panzer Army and destroying the bulk of Romanian VI and VII Army Corps, thus preventing the creation of Romanian Fourth Army. Although the Germans would resurrect Fourth Panzer Army within days, it would never match the imposing force that had shattered Soviet defenses and two Soviet armies about five months before.

THE SITUATION LATE ON 23 NOVEMBER

Axis Losses

The count of German and Romanian forces killed, wounded, or captured during the Soviet counteroffensive, as well as the quantity of weapons destroyed, damaged, or captured, remains controversial for a variety of good reasons. First, the chaos produced by the counteroffensive resulted in the near total loss of command and control on the part of Romanian Third Army and Romanian VI Army Corps. Second, it was impossible to keep accurate records of losses, given the wholesale regrouping and shifting of forces that occurred within Sixth Army. Third, we will never know the precise number of Axis troops that perished in this and subsequent operations or the number that actually marched off into captivity once the encirclement was liquidated in early February.

Both German and Soviet sources assert that the Southwestern Front's forces destroyed the bulk of Romanian Third Army, including its three corps, five infantry divisions, and one armored division, and severely damaged two infantry divisions and one cavalry division. They also agree that the Stalingrad Front severely damaged Romanian VI and VII Army Corps, including three infantry divisions and one cavalry division. Since Romanian Third Army numbered 155,492 men before the Soviet counteroffensive began, and Romanian forces south of Stalingrad totaled 75,380 men, the combined Romanian force in the Stalingrad region on 18 November was about 230,000 men. According to their strength returns on 8 December, Romanian Third Army numbered 83,000 men, and the Romanian forces constituting Romanian Fourth Army numbered 39,000 men (most of whom had survived the earlier fighting), for an overall strength of 122,000 men.[161] Since roughly 20,000 Romanian troops ended up encircled in Stalingrad, this meant that total Romanian losses during the period from 19 to 23 November amounted to about 90,000 men, including the 37,000 men the Soviets claimed to have captured.

Recent Russian reassessments of the fighting from 19 to 23 November assert that the Germans lost about 34,000 men killed or captured, while another 39,000 escaped encirclement.[162] When added to Romanian losses, this would bring total Axis losses in the four-day period to about 124,000 men. These and other sources claim that Axis forces lost 457 tanks, 370 guns, 1,100 mortars, 1,000 machine guns, 1,266 antitank guns, 2,500 submachine guns, 35,000 rifles, 1 million shells, 5 million small-arms rounds, and 200 vehicles in the fighting.[163] Although, for the most part, these totals closely track with the "trophy" reports by the three attacking Soviet *fronts*, the tank count is far too high. For example, when the counteroffensive began, German forces in the Stalingrad region possessed about 340 tanks and 44 assault and infantry guns, for a total of 384 armored vehicles. Romanian forces fielded just over 140 tanks, including those in disrepair. This places total Axis armored strength at about 520, in addition to vehicles in repair and T-34 tanks employed by the Germans and Romanians (see table 20 in chapter 4). By day's end on 23 November, German armored strength had fallen to about 140 tanks and 30 assault guns, meaning that the Germans and Romanian Third Army lost a maximum of 350 armored vehicles.

The Stalingrad Pocket

By 2100 hours on 23 November, the combined forces of the Southwestern, Don, and Stalingrad Fronts formed a fairly continuous encirclement ring around German Sixth Army and the portion of Fourth Panzer Army that was trapped in the Stalingrad pocket [*Kessel*]. To the west and southwest, the Southwestern and Stalingrad Fronts created outer encirclement fronts (lines), although roughly half of the outer front south of the Don River was only partially occupied and consisted of rifle and cavalry forces manning non-contiguous positions (see table 26).

The forces trapped in the Stalingrad pocket included virtually all the combat formations of German Sixth Army and Fourth Panzer Army's IV Army Corps; various army group, security, and police forces; Romanian 20th Infantry and 1st Cavalry Divisions; and Romanian Group Voicu. This amounted to a total of 5 corps, 22 divisions, 1 *Flak* division, and a host of smaller combat support and combat service support units and subunits (see table 27).

GERMAN DILEMMAS ON 23 NOVEMBER

The dramatic events of 23 November confirmed Paulus's worse fears. After hours of shock and doubt, followed by days of hastily conceived and implemented countermeasures, disaster had indeed occurred. Large Soviet tank forces stood firmly astride Sixth Army's lines of communications. As this reality sank in, Paulus in his new command post at Nizhne-Chirskaia, Weichs at Army Group B, and Hitler in Berlin pondered what to do next.

From Hitler's perspective, there was nothing Sixth Army could do but stand its ground and fight. Recalling how he had saved the day at the gates of Moscow in December 1941 by ordering Army Group Center to stand firm, Hitler resolved to do the same at Stalingrad. Furthermore, since Sixth Army had come within a hair's breadth of seizing all of Stalin's namesake city, there was more than just a little face to be saved. In contrast, as an experienced military leader, Weichs instinctively understood the immensity of the crisis Sixth Army faced. So did Paulus and his corps commanders, although a gnawing desire to please their Führer probably undermined their better judgment. Therefore, at least initially, senior military commanders in the region chose escape as the best option.

The clash between Weichs's and Paulus's instinctive desire to break out and Hitler's insistence on rejecting that option had already begun early on

Table 26. Scope of the Stalingrad Pocket's Inner and Outer Encirclement Fronts, 23 November 1942

INNER ENCIRCLEMENT FRONT
- **Southwestern Front** (40 kilometers)—from Sovetskii, 17 kilometers east-southeast of Kalach; northward roughly 40 kilometers past Illarionovskii, 16 kilometers east-northeast of Kalach, and Bol'shenabatovskii, 30 kilometers north-northeast of Kalach; to Golubaia [Golubinskii], 37 kilometers north-northeast of Kalach
- **Don Front** (131 kilometers)—from Golubaia [Golubinskii], 37 kilometers north-northeast of Kalach; north-northwestward 30 kilometers to Blizhniaia Perekopka; eastward 16 kilometers to Sirotinskaia; southeastward 32 kilometers along and south of the Don River to Panshino; and east-southeastward 53 kilometers south of Samofalovka to the Volga River, south of Erzovka
- **Stalingrad Front** (71 kilometers)—15 kilometers in Stalingrad city, from the Volga River's western bank south of Kuporosnoe southwestward and westward 23 kilometers through Elkhi and Popov to Tsybenko; northwestward 17 kilometers past Rakotino and Staryi Rogachik to 5 kilometers south of Karpovka; and westward 16 kilometers past the southern outskirts of Marinovka to Sovetskii, 17 kilometers east-southeast of Kalach
- **Total distance**—242 kilometers

OUTER ENCIRCLEMENT FRONT
- **Southwestern Front** (165 kilometers)—along the Krivaia River from Verkhne-Krivskaia to Gorbatovskii and Bokovskaia, along the Chir River from Bokovskaia to Chernyshevskaia and, after a noncontinuous sector from Chernyshevskaia to Surovikino, from Bol'shaia Osinovka to Chir Station and north of Rychkovskii
- **Stalingrad Front** (111 kilometers)—from Buzinovka to Zety, Abganerovo, Aksai, and Umantsevo to southeast of Sadovoe
- **Total distance**—450 kilometers, 276 of which were covered by forces

DISTANCES BETWEEN THE INNER AND OUTER FRONTS
- **Southwestern Front**—maximum of 100 kilometers and minimum of 15 to 20 kilometers in the Sovetskii and Nizhne-Chirskaia axes
- **Stalingrad Front**—maximum of 75 to 80 kilometers and minimum of 15 to 20 kilometers along the Sovetskii and Nizhne-Chirskaia axes

Sources: K. K. Rokossovsky, ed., *Velikaia bitva na Volge* [Great victory on the Volga] (Moscow: Voenizdat, 1965), 283–284; A. M. Samsonov, *Stalingradskaia bitva* [The battle for Stalingrad] (Moscow: Nauka, 1983), 398–399.

Table 27. Axis Forces Encircled at Stalingrad

- **Armies**—2 (German Sixth and Fourth Panzer)
- **Corps**—5 (German IV, VIII, XI, and LI Army Corps and XIV Panzer Corps)
- **Divisions**—23 (21 German and 2 Romanian):
  - 15 infantry (German 44th, 71st, 76th, 79th, 94th, 113th, 295th, 297th, 305th, 371st, 376th, 384th, and 389th Infantry; 100th Jäger; and Romanian 20th)
  - 3 panzer (German 14th, 16th, and 24th)
  - 3 motorized (German 3rd, 29th, and 60th)
  - 1 cavalry (Romanian 1st)
  - 1 *Flak* (antiaircraft) division (9th), with 37th, 91st, and 104th *Flak* Regiments (11 heavy and 19 light antiaircraft batteries)
- **Separate regiments and battalions [*abteilung*]**—160 by Soviet count and 149 by German count, including:
  - 1 artillery command (310th ARKO)
  - 5 artillery regiments (4th, 46th, 64th, 50th, and 70th)
  - 1 antiaircraft regiment (91st)
  - 1 signal regiment (248th)
  - 1 fortress regiment (16th)
  - 2 engineer regiments (413th and 604th)
  - 3 heavy *Werfer* (engineer–mortar/rocket) regiments (2nd, 51st, and 53rd)
  - 4 assault gun battalions [*abteilung*] (177th, 243rd, 244th, and 245th)
  - 14 artillery battalions (II/46th, II/53rd, II/65th, II/72nd, 101st, 430th, 501st, 616th, 631st, 733rd, 800th, 849th, 851st, and 855th)
  - 3 separate antiaircraft battalions (602nd, 608th, and 614th)
  - 3 separate antitank battalions (521st, 611th, and 670th)
  - 15 separate engineer (pioneer) battalions (6th, 41st, 45th, 50th Motorized, 294th, 336th, 501st, 605th, 652nd, 672nd, 685th, 912th, 921st, 925th, and one unnumbered)
  - 3 separate bridge battalions (255th, 522nd, and 655th)
  - 2 construction battalions (110th and 540th)
  - 3 road construction battalions (521st, 540th, and 245th)
- **Men**—Estimates ranged from 250,000 to 330,000 men, with the most likely figure, being 284,000, including 264,000 Germans (175,000 assigned to Sixth Army, 50,000 to Fourth Panzer Army, 24,000 to 27,000 to various auxiliary forces, and 12,000 to 15,000 *Luftwaffe* troops) and about 20,000 Romanians. Roughly 60,000 *Hiwis* (Russian auxiliaries) and other troops attached to German divisions [*Zugeteilte*] increased this figure to 310,000 to 360,000 men, close to the earlier Soviet estimate of 330,000 men.
- Tanks—139
- Assault guns—31
- Antitank guns [*Paks*]—322
- Artillery (light and heavy)—535
- Rocket launchers/projectors [*Werfer*]—270
- Antiaircraft guns—238
- Vehicles—about 10,000

Sources: Florian Freiherr von und zu Aufsess, *Die Anlagenbänder zu den Kriegstagebüchern der 6. Armee vom 14.09.1942 bis 24.11.1942, Band I* (Schwabach: Januar, 2006), 330–336, and *Die Anlagenbänder zu den Kriegstagebüchern der 6. Armee vom 24.11.1942 bis 24.12.1942, Band II*, (Schwabach: Januar, 2006), 4–25; Hans Dörr, *Pokhod na Stalingrad* [March to Stalingrad] (Moscow: Voenizdat, 1957), 79–80; *Stalingrad: Tsena pobedy* [Stalingrad: The cost of victory] (Moscow: AST, 2005), 66–67; V. E. Tarrant, *Stalingrad: Anatomy of an Agony* (London: Leo Cooper), 123; Red Army General Staff daily operational summaries for the period 19–25 November 1942.

21 November, as Paulus realized that his plan to halt the Soviet juggernaut might come to naught. Accordingly, after he moved his headquarters to Nizhne-Chirskaia, discussions between General Martin Fiebig, commander of VIII Air Corps [*Fliegerkorps*], and General Schmidt, Paulus's chief of staff, made it crystal clear that the *Luftwaffe* could not sustain Sixth Army in Stalingrad by aerial resupply. General Wolfgang Pickert, commander of 9th *Flak* Division, which was supporting Sixth Army, confirmed Fiebig's opinion an hour later. Within this context, on the morning on 22 November, Hitler ordered Paulus to move his headquarters to Gumrak airfield, much closer to the front, obviously to discourage any lingering thoughts Paulus might harbor about ordering a withdrawal.

However, with evidence mounting that the creation of an air bridge to Stalingrad would be futile, Paulus once again indicated his preference for a breakout in a wireless message he sent to Army Group B at 1900 hours on 22 November (see appendix 5AJ in the *Companion* for the full text). Acknowledging that his army was "completely encircled" and that enemy forces were "advancing from the southeast through Businovka [Buzinovka] northwards and also in great strength from the west toward Malyj [Malyi]," he nonetheless hoped "to be able to construct a West Front east of the Don along the Golubaja [Golubaia] line."[164] Although the South Front east of the Don was "still open," he asserted that his army intended "to hold the area still in its possession between Stalingrad and the Don," although this was "conditional on closing the South Front and on receiving ample airborne supplies." Finally, Paulus asked for "freedom of action in the event the hedgehog position does not succeed in the south." Specifically, if the situation compelled the abandonment of Stalingrad and the North Front, then he recommended an attack in "full force on the South Front between the Don and Volga with the objective [of] the re-establishment of contact with Fourth Rumanian Army."[165]

Hitler responded to Paulus's message at 2200 hours in a clumsy but intimate message of his own. Received by Sixth Army at 2215 hours, the message read: "The 6th Army is momentarily encircled. I know the 6th Army and her commander, and I am aware that the Army will gallantly hold while being in this difficult situation. The Army should know that I will do everything to help her and to relieve her. I shall give new orders in due time."[166]

About 24 hours after Paulus sent his message, at 1845 hours on 23 November, Weichs at Army Group B radioed his own appreciation of the deteriorating situation and recommended a course of action to the Army High Command (see appendix 5AK in the *Companion*). Weichs began by recognizing the necessity of accepting "General Paulus' proposal for the withdrawal of Sixth Army."[167] He did so because he questioned whether the army could be supplied by air and rescued by a force from the outside before its ammunition and food ran out. Therefore, he believed that "a breakout by

Sixth Army in a south-westerly direction will result in favorable developments in the situation as a whole," first, because Sixth Army was "the only
fighting formation capable of inflicting damage on the enemy," and second,
despite suffering heavy losses in the breakout, the army would "provide an
essential reinforcement for the new defensive front that must now be built,
and for the preparation of our counter-attack."[168]

Before receiving Weichs's message, Hitler relocated from Berchtesgaden
to his forward command post in the *Wolfsschanze* at Rastenburg in East
Prussia. He was accompanied by Keitel, Jodl, and General Hans Jeschonnek,
the *Luftwaffe*'s chief of staff. During the 24-hour trip, made by rail instead of
air because of bad weather, General Zeitzler, the army's chief of staff in Berlin, contacted the Führer about withdrawing Sixth Army but was told to put
off all further discussions until the next morning, 23 November.[169] However,
by that time, Soviet tanks were well on their way to the linkup at Sovetskii.

On the evening of 22 November, well before Soviet forces met in the
Sovetskii region late on the afternoon of the 23rd, Paulus and his staff (probably after discussions with some of his subordinate commanders) began making plans for a breakout toward the southwest in an operation code-named
Umbau (Conversion). At this time, it is likely that the army staff also prepared associated plans for a phased withdrawal of Sixth Army's forces southward to positions from which they could initiate a breakout. Of course, all
this took place without Hitler's approval.

It was during this period that General Seydlitz, commander of LI Army
Corps, issued his infamous Order No. 118, requiring his corps' 3rd Motorized and 94th Infantry Divisions to withdraw from the northeastern corner
of the pocket south of Erzovka overnight on 23–24 November. Since Seydlitz
knew about Sixth Army's plans, he undoubtedly hoped this order would hasten Paulus's decision to orchestrate the breakout from the pocket toward the
southwest.[170] However, Seydlitz was mistaken, and the corps commander's
precipitous action would cost Sixth Army the better part of a full infantry
division.

On the evening of 23 November, after further meetings with his corps
commanders, Paulus sent yet another message to Hitler at 2345 hours, once
again requesting freedom of action to withdraw Sixth Army (see appendix
5AL in the *Companion*). Stressing the rapidly deteriorating situation, Sixth
Army's commander told the Führer that the army had failed "to close the
gaps in the west and southwest," "enemy breakthroughs in these sectors
were imminent," and "ammunition and fuel are almost exhausted." Therefore, Paulus insisted that although a breakout would be costly, it was the only
option if the bulk of Sixth Army was to be saved for future fights.[171]

Hitler received Paulus's message when he reached the *Wolfsschanze* at
about midnight on 23 November. By this time, Zeitzler had also flown to

Hitler's field headquarters. Mustering all his powers of reasoning, Zeitzler tried to persuade the Führer of the wisdom of withdrawing Sixth Army back to safety, but to no avail. After Hitler retired for the evening without reaching a decision, Zeitzler phoned General von Sodenstern, Army Group B's chief of staff, at about 0200 hours and reported—incorrectly, as it turned out—that Hitler would authorize a withdrawal between 0700 and 0800 hours the next morning. Weichs, still wedded to the idea of a withdrawal, actually drafted such an order and forwarded it to Paulus for implementation once Hitler gave his authorization.[172]

Completing this exchange, OKH sent a radio message to Army Group B at 0140 hours on 24 November. The army group forwarded the message to Sixth Army at 0540 hours, and it was received by the army at 0830 hours. This message, under the rubric of a Führer decision [*Führerentscheid*], specified Hitler's desire that Sixth Army defend its current Volga and North Fronts and the general line of Reference Point [*Bezugspunkt*] 564—Karpovka-Marinovka—while holding the sector behind the Don River from Nizhnyi Gerassimov to Marinovka and evacuating as much heavy weaponry and equipment as possible south of the river. The "decision" also mentioned a relief effort by two panzer divisions from the Kotel'nikovo region and an aerial supply effort with as many as 100 Ju aircraft.[173] A subsequent message from OKH to Army Group B at 1830 hours on the 24th, which was also forwarded to Sixth Army, announced that Hitler categorically forbade anyone from violating the parameters of his previous order—that is, there were to be no unauthorized withdrawals from Sixth Army's designated front sector.[174]

These messages, and the Führer's decision they contained, put to rest any further discussions or even thoughts of withdrawing Sixth Army. Henceforth, all discussions would focus solely on the matter of relief. As if to introduce this new theme, Field Marshal von Manstein, commander of the newly created Army Group Don, sent his own message to Paulus at 1338 hours on 23 November, shortly after being informed by Weichs that Sixth Army's position was untenable: "[I] assume command of Army Group Don on 26.11. We will do all we can to get you out. In the meantime, it is imperative that [Sixth] Army, while holding firm on the Volga and North fronts in accordance with the Führer's orders, stands by with strong forces as soon as possible, in order to force a supply route toward the southwest if necessary, at least temporarily."[175] This message from Manstein, who was not yet fully aware of Sixth Army's predicament, distanced the field marshal from the views of Weichs, Paulus, and Sixth Army's entire senior command cadre, who clearly advocated an immediate breakout. Unwittingly or by default, Army Group Don's new commander now found himself in Hitler's and Göring's camp.

In the wake of the "Seydlitz affair," on the morning of 23 November, Hitler decreed that there be no more talk of retreats, and he demanded a complete report on how and why Seydlitz had issued his order. But he also placed Seydlitz in command of the northern part of the pocket. Once he heard this, Paulus criticized Seydlitz's decision and reportedly told the corps commander, "Now that you have your own command, you can break out."[176] Soon after, at 1115 hours, Paulus issued an order to his corps explaining Hitler's order. Seydlitz did the same at 1445 hours. As a postscript to this affair, on 25 November, Seydlitz sent a formal written memorandum to Paulus, explaining his objections:

> In receipt of the army order of 24 November 1942 for the continuation of the fighting, and fully aware of the seriousness of the situation, I feel obliged to resubmit—in writing—my opinion, which has been further strengthened by events during the past 24 hours.
> The army is faced with a clear either/or situation.
> Either break out to the south-west in the general direction of Kotelnikovo or face destruction in a few days.
> This assessment is based on a sober evaluation of the actual conditions. . . .
> The OKH order to hold out in hedgehog positions until help arrives is obviously based on false assumptions. It is therefore not feasible and would inevitably lead the army to disaster. If the army is to be saved, then another order must be immediately issued, or another decision immediately taken. . . .
> Unless the OKH promptly rescinds the order to hold out in the hedgehog position, then my own conscience and responsibility to the army and the German people imposes the imperative duty to seize the freedom of action prevented by the previous order and to use what little time is left to avoid utter disaster by launching our own attack. The complete destruction of 200,000 soldiers and all of their equipment is at stake.
> There is no other choice.[177]

Thus, the cascading series of disasters that befell Sixth Army on 22 and 23 November created increasingly urgent problems for its commander, General Paulus. The most serious question Paulus faced late on the 22nd was whether the tanks of General Hube's XIV Panzer Corps could halt the Soviet armored juggernaut before it encircled all or part of Sixth Army. Soviet forces answered this question with a resounding "No" on the 23rd. Then, overnight on 23–24 November, Paulus confronted two new and more serious issues: whether XI Army and XIV Panzer Corps could escape eastward across the Don River before being destroyed, and whether his army as a whole could escape the Soviet trap. Twelve hours later, given Hitler's 24 November order forbidding any breakout attempt, Paulus's dilemmas fused into a single question: whether his army could survive long enough to be rescued. And this question would take far longer than 24 hours to answer.

Conclusions

The first stage of Operation Uranus proved to be a resounding success for Stalin, his *Stavka*, the three participating *fronts*, and the Red Army as a whole. From 19 through 23 November, the army's Southwestern, Don, and Stalingrad Fronts penetrated the defenses of Romanian Third and German Fourth Panzer Armies; inserted large tank, mechanized, and cavalry forces into the penetration; exploited up to 100 kilometers deep into German Sixth Army's operational rear; and linked these forces in the Kalach and Sovetskii region, encircling virtually all of Paulus's army. In the process, Soviet forces destroyed more than three-quarters of Romanian Third Army, severely damaged two-thirds of German Fourth Panzer Army, and inflicted a resounding defeat on XIV Panzer Corps, the most combat-capable element of Sixth Army. By accomplishing these feats, Vatutin's, Rokossovsky's, and Eremenko's *fronts* fulfilled most of the missions assigned to them by the *Stavka*. The only exception was 5th Tank Army of Vatutin's Southwestern Front, which failed to capture Oblivskaia, Surovikino, and Rychkovskii and seize bridgeheads across the Chir River.

The three *fronts* achieved many "firsts" during the initial stage of Operation Uranus. First, and most important from the *Stavka*'s perspective, this was the first time Soviet forces had been able to surround an entire Axis army. Prior to 23 November 1942, the Red Army's best effort had been to encircle German Sixteenth Army's II Army Corps in the Demiansk region, although in that instance, the Germans were able to form a land bridge between their corps and Army Group North's main lines. Thus, if the Soviets could prevent a German rescue at Stalingrad, it would be their first encirclement and destruction of any sizable German force.

Second, the first stage of Operation Uranus marked the first time in the war that Red Army forces had been able to penetrate Axis tactical defenses to their entire depth, develop the penetration into the operational depths, and create seemingly viable inner and outer encirclement fronts around an encircled German force. Although Red Army forces had managed to penetrate German defenses at the gates of Moscow in December 1941 and in several other locations during the ensuing winter campaign of 1941–1942, these penetrations had been tenuous at best, and the Soviet forces had been unable to form either viable inner and outer encirclement fronts or contiguous new front lines deep in the German rear.

Third, Operation Uranus marked the first time in the war that exploiting Soviet mobile forces were able to defeat Axis operational reserves in the operational depths, even though, by any definition, the Germans' weak XXXXVIII Panzer Corps barely constituted a genuinely viable operational reserve. Fourth, during the initial stage of Uranus, the Red Army's logistical structure was able to sustain mobile operations to far greater depths than before, particularly with regard to the resupply of vital fuel and ammunition. Fifth, for the first time in the war, exploiting Soviet tank and mechanized forces were able to defend themselves against and actually defeat counterattacking German panzer forces in the operational depths—in this case, the three panzer divisions of XIV Panzer Corps. The only similar experience had been in the Smolensk region in August 1941, when General Konev's 19th Army resoundingly defeated a counterattack by German 7th Panzer Division. However, the feat in the Smolensk region occurred on a tactical rather than an operational scale.

Although the Red Army managed to pull off many important "firsts" during the initial stage of its Uranus counteroffensive, it also experienced some outright disappointments, and some of its most notable successes require serious qualification. First, although the three Soviet *fronts* encircled German Sixth Army by 23 November, for weeks it remained to be seen whether they could actually destroy the forces they had encircled. Second, rather than the three days envisioned by the Uranus plan, the penetration and linkup stage of the operation took five days to complete. Third, although it was the Red Army's first successful penetration operation, both north and south of Stalingrad these penetrations took place against Romanian rather than German defenses. In fact, when Soviet forces attempted to penetrate German defenses, such as in the sectors of 65th, 24th, and 64th Armies, the attacks either failed outright or succeeded only because of the defeat of Romanian forces defending adjacent sectors.

Fourth, although the Southwestern Front's 5th Tank Army ultimately defeated Axis operational reserves, these reserves were far weaker than usual, and it took the better part of five days to do so. In fact, the stout resistance by XXXXVIII Panzer Corps tied up one Soviet tank corps for three days and seriously disrupted the *front*'s and the army's offensive timetables. Likewise, the three panzer divisions of XIV Panzer Corps that Soviet tank and cavalry corps engaged and defeated were mere shadows of genuine panzer divisions, since they had already been bloodied in the fighting in Stalingrad city. Finally, although the exploiting Soviet tank, mechanized, and cavalry corps sustained operations to far greater depths than ever before and ultimately fulfilled their missions, they also suffered severe attrition in tanks, largely due to enemy air strikes and serious maintenance problems. As Soviet General Staff after-action critiques noted, the advancing mobile corps lost up to 80 percent of their tanks in five days of field operations. Against a stronger foe, this problem could have proved fatal.

Yet, when all was said and done, the successful encirclement operation was as inspiring as it was unprecedented. By doing the unthinkable, the Red Army's three *fronts* conducting Operation Uranus not only dealt a strategic defeat to Axis forces but also inspired an army and a nation that desperately needed it. It was indeed a remarkable beginning for such an ambitious offensive. But its full promise still remained to be realized.

Generals Rokossovsky and Batov at 65th Army's observation post during the Uranus counteroffensive

Soviet *Katiusha* [Stalin organs] multiple-rocket launchers firing in the preparation for Operation Uranus

Soviet artillery firing the preparation for Operation Uranus

Soviet tanks entering the penetration in operation Uranus

Soviet infantry beginning their assault in operation Uranus

Soviet infantry advancing under a smoke screen

Soviet troops and tanks assaulting Kalach-on-the-Don

Troops of the Southwestern and Stalingrad Fronts linking up at the village of Sovetskii

Reducing the Stalingrad Pocket and Forming the Outer Encirclement Front, 24–27 November

When the Southwestern and Stalingrad Fronts' mobile corps linked up in the Kalach and Sovetskii regions, the nature of the Soviet counteroffensive changed. With German Sixth Army's encirclement in the Stalingrad region a reality, the *Stavka* began simultaneously orchestrating three separate but interrelated offensives along different operational axes, each of which had a profound impact on the outcome of the other two. The first and most important of these took place along the periphery of the Stalingrad pocket proper, where elements of all three Soviet *fronts* fought to liquidate encircled Sixth Army. The initial objective of this operation was to isolate and destroy Sixth Army's XI Army Corps and XIV Panzer Corps, which were still fighting in the northwestern corner of the Great Bend of the Don River, south of Sirotinskaia. The first stage of this operation was completed at day's end on 27 November, when the Don Front's 65th Army, together with the same *front's* 24th Army on its left and the Southwestern Front's 21st Army on its right, forced Sixth Army to withdraw these two corps southward across the Don into what soon became the infamous Stalingrad pocket [*Kessel*].

Simultaneous with this struggle, the Southwestern and Stalingrad Fronts conducted twin offensives along the external front of the Stalingrad encirclement as they strove to push German forces farther west and southwest. During this offensive, General Vatutin's Southwestern Front (less its 21st Army) advanced southwest and south toward the Chir River to seize key Axis strongpoints on its northern bank, force its way across the river, and sever vital Axis communication routes south of the Chir. Vatutin's principal objectives were the towns of Oblivskaia and Surovikino on the Chir's northern bank and Rychkovskii on the Don, along with the small German bridgehead on the river's eastern bank opposite Rychkovskii and Tormosin, 48 kilometers south of the Chir. Seizure of the first two towns would ensure Soviet control of the Chir, and the capture of Rychkovskii, Tormosin, or both would deny the Germans a launching pad from which to conduct a relief operation toward Stalingrad from the west.

As Vatutin's forces attacked south toward the Chir, 51st Army of General Eremenko's Stalingrad Front advanced simultaneously along two separate axes: westward from the Buzinovka region toward the Don River at

Verkhne-Chirskii and Nizhne-Chirskaia, and southwestward across the Aksai River toward Kotel'nikovo. The 51st Army's principal objectives were the Don River's eastern bank opposite Nizhne-Chirskaia and Kotel'nikovo, an important rail and road center whose seizure would complicate German plans for the conduct of relief operations toward Stalingrad from the southwest.

The Germans, still struggling to regain their balance after the disastrous encirclement of Sixth Army, resisted the Soviet offensives with whatever forces they had at hand. For starters, the OKH and General Weichs's Army Group B sent all the reserves they could spare to the Stalingrad region, while Field Marshal von Manstein's newly formed Army Group Don prepared to incorporate these reserves into Romanian Third and German Fourth Panzer Armies so that both could stabilize their fronts and reinforce or rescue Sixth Army.

The headquarters of Romanian Third Army, under strict German supervision, conducted defensive operations along the Chir River west of the Don River with a motley collection of ad hoc German army, security, police, and *Luftwaffe* units. It was soon reinforced by XXXXVIII Panzer Corps after it escaped westward across the Chir River. The Third Army was supported on its left by newly formed Army (Attack) Group Hollidt, formed from two German infantry divisions fighting under General Hollidt's XVII Army Corps, together with the remnants of Romanian I and II Army Corps.

East of the Don, General Hoth's Fourth Panzer Army, whose German forces were now fighting under Sixth Army's control in the Stalingrad pocket, conducted defensive operations along the Aksai and Kotel'nikovo axis with the remnants of Romanian VI and VII Army Corps, in the hope of slowing or halting the Stalingrad Front's southward advance. Meanwhile, Hoth anxiously awaited reinforcements so that he could mount relief operations toward Stalingrad, an important subject of discussion within the German Armed Forces High Command and Army High Command (OKW and OKH) and the army groups in and adjacent to the Stalingrad region. Ultimately, Hitler's decision to reinforce Hoth's army with divisions from Army Group A and the West would produce a genuine German relief attempt and fresh fighting along both the Chir River and the Kotel'nikovo axis in early and mid-December.[1]

Finally, while fighting raged along the outer front of the Stalingrad encirclement, General Paulus's Sixth Army fought in the Stalingrad pocket itself, offering far stronger resistance than anticipated, despite its increasingly desperate supply situation. By early December, however, its survival clearly depended on the *Luftwaffe*'s promises of adequate material support and assurances of relief from German Army Group Don. This army group, formed by Hitler's belated decision on 21 November to unify operations in the region outside the Stalingrad pocket, would become operational on 26

November when its commander, von Manstein, reached his new headquarters in Novocherkassk. Given Hitler's decision to refuse Sixth Army's request for "freedom of action," the first order of business was to find a way to relieve Paulus's beleaguered army.

SOVIET PLANS

After its three *fronts* in the Stalingrad region encircled German Sixth Army, the *Stavka's* principal concern on the evening of 23–24 November was the possibility of the Germans attempting to either reinforce or relieve Paulus's army. Given the configuration of the front, terrain considerations, and the state of Axis defenses, the most likely axes along which to mount such an effort were from a bridgehead on the Don River's eastern bank in the Rychkovskii and Nizhne-Chirskaia regions east toward Marinovka, or into the Stalingrad region from the Kotel'nikovo region to the southwest, where the Soviet's external encirclement front was the weakest.

Ironically, the success of the Uranus counteroffensive complicated Soviet decision making by creating an entirely new factor for the *Stavka* and its *front* commanders to consider: the Southwestern and Stalingrad Fronts had torn an immense 300-kilometer-wide gap in Axis strategic defenses west and southwest of Stalingrad. This gap extended from the right flank of German XVII Army Corps in the Bokovskaia region on the upper Chir River, southeastward along the Chir to Rychkovskii on the Don River, across the Don and southeastward to the left flank of Romanian VII Army Corps south of Aksai and west of Lake Sarpa. By nightfall on 23 November, the only Axis forces defending this gap were the skeletal remnants of the divisions and rear services of Romanian Third Army and its II and V Army Corps, plus a multitude of small German forces consisting of security and police units, logistical units from Sixth Army's rear services, and several *Luftwaffe Flak* (antiaircraft) and airfield support units. Quite naturally, these forces gravitated to major towns located along important rail and road routes, where they formed ad hoc *kampfgruppen*.

Instinctively, the Soviet commanders realized that, somewhere behind the southern half of this gap, but most likely in the Kotel'nikovo region and to the south, the German High Command was busy reconstituting Hoth's Fourth Panzer Army to reinforce or rescue Sixth Army. The questions they asked were: When and where would this force appear? And when it did, how strong would the force be? Therefore, from the *Stavka's* perspective, it was vital to liquidate the encircled German force quickly and, if possible, before any German relief attempt materialized. Since the *Stavka* estimated that its *fronts* had encircled 80,000 to 90,000 Germans in the Stalingrad region, it seemed reasonable to believe that the Don Front, if reinforced by several armies from its sister *fronts*, would be able to accomplish this task with relative ease. It was equally important to protect this liquidation operation by pushing the Southwestern and Stalingrad Fronts' outer encirclement fronts as far westward and southwestward from Stalingrad as possible to completely isolate the encircled grouping. However, since this was the Red Army's first major encirclement operation of the war, the *Stavka* and the General Staff remained uncertain about the quantity and mix of forces they should include in the outer encirclement front. For the time being, they decided to rely primarily on cavalry corps—the 8th in the north and the 4th in the south—reinforced by rifle divisions and, whenever possible, tank and mechanized corps.

Within this context, Stalin and his *Stavka* entrusted their representative, General Vasilevsky, chief of the Red Army General Staff, with the mission of developing a plan to accomplish both tasks. He did so, coordinating closely with the commanders of the Don and Stalingrad Fronts by telephone from the Southwestern Front's headquarters. Vasilevsky's primary assumption on which he based his plan was that the Germans would do everything in their power to assist Sixth Army. Thus, it was necessary to eliminate the pocket quickly, but the Red Army also had to isolate the encircled grouping by creating an outer encirclement front backed up by as many mobile formations as possible. Therefore, the three victorious *fronts* would begin liquidating the encircled grouping immediately, beginning on the morning of 24 November. The *Stavka* approved Vasilevsky's plan and issued directives to its three *fronts* overnight on 23–24 November, assigning them the following missions:

- Overall mission—dismember the encircled enemy Stalingrad grouping by launching converging blows toward Gumrak, and destroy it in piecemeal fashion.
- Missions of subordinates with regard to the encircled Stalingrad grouping:
  - Southwestern Front—attack from west to east along the Sokarevka, Bol'shaia Rossoshka, and Gumrak axis with 21st Army, reinforced by 26th and 4th Tank Corps, to throw enemy forces back from the Don to the Volga River and reach the Vertiachii and Dmitrievka line with 26th and 4th Tank Corps by day's end on 24 November and with rifle forces no later than 25 November.
  - Don Front—attack from the north with 65th, 24th, and 66th Armies, with 65th Army to liquidate the enemy grouping on the right bank of the Don River by day's end on 24 November, 24th Army to capture Vertiachii and isolate German forces west of the Don River by day's end and then attack east toward Podsobnoe Farm with 21st Army, and 66th Army to attack from the Erzovka region toward Orlovka to

penetrate German defenses and link up with the Stalingrad Front's 62nd Army near Rynok.

- ○ Stalingrad Front—attack from the east and south with 62nd, 64th, and 57th Armies, with 51st Army's main forces reaching the Dmitrievka and Karpovka region and 57th Army clearing the enemy from the line of the Chervlenaia River by 24 November; subsequently, 51st, 57th, and 64th Armies attack from the Kuporosnoe, Karpovka, and Dmitrievka line toward Gumrak in cooperation with 62nd Army, attacking from the east.

- Missions of subordinates with regard to the outer encirclement front:
  - ○ Southwestern Front—dig in and defend positions along the Krivaia River with 1st Guards Army; conduct converging attacks against Axis forces west of the Krivaia River with 1st Guards Army's left wing and center; capture and fortify the Oblivskaia, Surovikino, and Rychkovskii sector along the railroad on the northern bank of the Chir River with 5th Tank Army; and block any enemy advance from the southwest.
  - ○ Stalingrad Front—protect the operation from the south by capturing crossings over the Don River at Liapichev, 25 kilometers south of Kalach, with part of 51st Army's 4th Mechanized Corps; and defend the sector from Gromoslavka (on the Myshkovo River 27 kilometers north of Aksai) to Ivanovka (6 kilometers east of Gromoslavka) with 4th Cavalry Corps and Abganerovo and Umantsevo with the rifle divisions of 51st Army.[2]

THE SOUTHWESTERN AND DON FRONTS' OFFENSIVE, 24 NOVEMBER

On 24 November, the forces of the Southwestern Front continued their offensive toward Bokovskaia, Oblivskaia, and Surovikino and, together with the forces on the Don Front's right wing, attacked German 11th [XI] AC's forces and drove them to the southern bank of the Don River.

The forces on the Don Front's right wing, together with forces on the Southwestern Front's left wing, continued their offensive against German 11th [XI] AC's forces, crushed their resistance, and occupied the Sirotinskaia, Kamyshinka, and Trekhostrovskaia region; the forces in the center attacked toward Vertiachii; and the forces on the left wing attacked north of Stalingrad, overcame stubborn enemy resistance, and advanced to link up with the forces of Stalingrad Front's 62nd Army in the Rynok region.

Red Army General Staff Operational Summary, 0800 hours on 25 November 1942[3]

The Southwestern and Don Fronts' Missions

As on previous nights, Vatutin and Rokossovsky received Vasilevsky's directives and formulated missions for their subordinate armies—this time, looking in two directions. They did so with a mixture of relief and anxiety—relief that their forces had finally accomplished a significant strategic mission, but anxiety lest the Germans once again snatch victory from their grasp. However, this time they acted with determination born of obvious success. In general, the Southwestern Front's 5th Tank Army, protected on the right by 1st Guards Army along the Krivaia River, was to capture Oblivskaia, Surovikino, and Rychkovskii and secure the line of the Chir River from Bokovskaia southeastward to the confluence of the Chir and Don Rivers. Simultaneously, 21st Army was to begin crushing Sixth Army's Stalingrad pocket by advancing eastward along the Sokarevka, Bol'shaia Rossoshka, and Gumrak axis. Farther east, the Don Front's 65th and 24th Armies were to envelop and destroy German XI Army Corps north of the Don River by capturing Vertiachii, while 66th Army launched a supporting attack from the Erzovka region toward Orlovka (see appendix 6A in the *Companion* for specific missions).

As sound as these plans seemed, there were two potential flaws. First, Soviet intelligence organs placed Axis strength within the encirclement at about 80,000 to 90,000 men. If this estimate was too low, the correlation of forces might not favor the attackers. Second, the plan called for the Southwestern and Stalingrad Fronts to divide their attention and forces in two directions—in the pocket itself and along the outer encirclement fronts. It remained to be seen whether Vatutin and Eremenko could do so effectively.

The Southwestern Front

The most difficult tasks facing Vatutin's Southwestern Front on 24 November were to clear Axis forces from the region north of the Chir River and capture the key towns of Oblivskaia and Surovikino on the Chir River and Rychkovskii on the Don River (see map 29). These were also the most vexing tasks, for two reasons. First, despite four days of intense combat, the remnants of XXXXVIII Panzer Corps' 22nd Panzer Division and Romanian 1st Armored Division were still rooted to the region between Bol'shaia Donshchinka and the Kurtlak River valley to the south; therefore, they were still disrupting the orderly development of the *front's* offensive. Second, because of the panzer corps' obstinacy, together with the stubborn resistance offered by Group Lascar in its pocket southwest of Raspopinskaia, 5th Tank Army was still well behind schedule, especially with regard to seizing the three key objectives on the Chir and Don Rivers. Therefore, Vatutin bombarded his army commanders with a combination of encouragement and threats, lest they fail to accomplish their missions and thereby permit the Germans to mount a relief effort toward Stalingrad from the Rychkovskii bridgehead.

5th Tank Army

As in previous days, General Romanenko's 5th Tank Army faced the most daunting tasks in this phase of the offensive. While committing most of its armor to the fight for the Stalingrad pocket, it still had to deal with XXXXVIII Panzer Corps and capture the Chir River line, especially Rychkovskii. But now Romanenko had to do this with only one tank corps, since Vatutin had ordered him to rest General Rodin's 26th Tank Corps on 24 November and then transfer it to Chistiakov's 21st Army early the next day for use in reducing the Stalingrad pocket. This left Romanenko with General Butkov's 1st Tank Corps, whose strength had eroded to roughly 20 tanks. Regardless of 1st Corps' armor strength, its mission was still the army's most important—to capture Surovikino and Rychkovskii by day's end—and Butkov had to do so while maintaining contact with 21st Army in the Kalach region to the east. This forced Romanenko to spread his forces over an expanse exceeding 35 kilometers and concentrate all his tanks in a single brigade group.

Regardless of its weakness, Butkov's corps attacked south toward Verkhne-Chirskii and Rychkovskii, supposedly "in pursuit of the withdrawing enemy" (see appendix 6B in the *Companion* for the Southwestern Front's accomplishments on 24 November). At nightfall the corps reported that it had "reached the Dmitrievka (11 kilometers southeast of Surovikino) and Rychkovskii line, where it captured the railroad" and was "fighting for Surovikino with part of its forces."[4] It also noted that it had to repel numerous enemy counterattacks and was being pounded by groups of 20 to 30 German aircraft.[5] What the corps and the General Staff did not report was that Butkov's corps had failed to seize any of its objectives. To the east, Rodin's 26th Tank Corps completed its operations in the Kalach region, reassembled its forces, and, after receiving orders transferring it to 21st Army, began regrouping eastward to join 4th Tank Corps in assaults against German defenses at and north of Marinovka.

Meanwhile, in 5th Tank Army's center, Romanenko continued to feed fresh forces into the Bol'shaia Donshchinka and Kurtlak River regions in an attempt to liquidate the remnants of 22nd Panzer and Romanian 1st Armored Divisions once and for all. By this time, 22nd Panzer's forces had split into company- and battalion-size *kampfgruppen* that were defending the roughly triangular region extending from Bol'shaia Donshchinka southwestward 7 kilometers to Medvezhyi and southward the same distance to Malaia Donshchinka. The day before, Colonel Sion's small group from Romanian 15th Infantry Division, which had escaped from the Raspopinskaia pocket

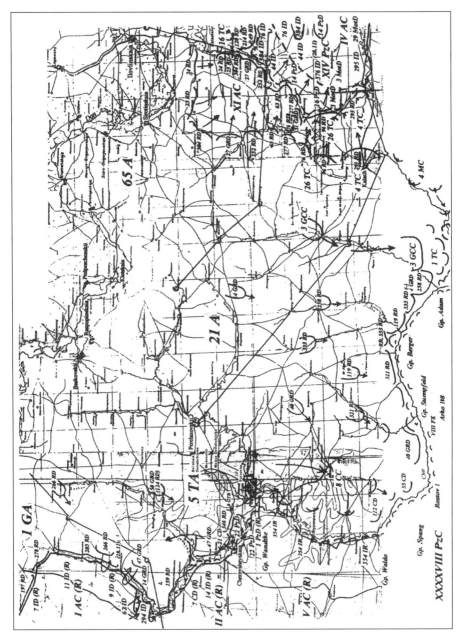

Map 29. Southwestern and Don Fronts' advance, 25–28 November 1942

with about 3,500 men, occupied defenses in Bol'shaia Donshchinka proper, supported by antitank guns from 22nd Panzer. To the south, the remnants of Romanian 1st Armored Division, with perhaps 1,500 men and a handful of tanks, were assembled south of the Kurtlak River, where they were still fencing with 8th Cavalry Corps' 55th and 21st Cavalry Divisions.[6]

Romanenko employed 346th, 50th Guards, and 119th Rifle Divisions; 8th Guards and 216th Tank Brigades; and 8th Motorcycle Regiment to contend with 22nd Panzer Division's pocket north of the Kurtlak River. Meanwhile, 8th Cavalry Corps' 21st and 55th Cavalry Divisions continued the fight against 1st Armored Division along and south of the Kurtlak River. Still under Colonel Tolstov's command, 346th Rifle Division, supported by 8th Guards and 216th Tank Brigades and 8th Motorcycle Regiment, assaulted 22nd Panzer Division's defenses at Bol'shaia Donshchinka from the west, north, and east at about 0700 hours. According to Romanian sources, Colonel Rodt withdrew his antitank guns from the town shortly before that time, leaving Sion's Romanian infantry to fend for itself. After the attacking Soviets encircled his forces, Sion pleaded in vain for 22nd Panzer's assistance; soon thereafter, he perished in an attempt to escape southward from the town.

As the fighting intensified, 119th Rifle and 50th Guards Rifle Divisions joined the fray, attacking the Romanian forces encircled in Bol'shaia Donshchinka. The 346th Rifle Division and its supporting armor bypassed the town and pursued 22nd Panzer's forces southwest toward the Chir River during the afternoon and early evening. By day's end, 50th Guards Division reassembled at Perelazovskii and prepared to march south toward the Chir River, leaving the 119th to finish off Sion's now leaderless group. According to Romanian accounts, although a detachment from 22nd Panzer Division managed to rescue about 800 of Sion's men before nightfall, the remainder perished or disappeared into captivity.[7]

In the meantime, while 22nd Panzer moved southward into the Kurtlak River valley and then west toward the Chir River, 21st and 55th Cavalry Divisions attacked eastward along and south of the Kurtlak River to block the panzer division's withdrawal toward the south and west. By this time, part of Romanian 1st Armored Division had joined 22nd Panzer Division's column. A sharp but confused fight ensued, during which the cavalrymen of General Borisov's corps ran short of ammunition, forcing them to halt their attack and take up positions to block the Germans' escape. General Iakunin's 21st Cavalry Division occupied defenses in the Novoriabukhin region, 12 kilometers east of Chernyshevskaia, and Colonel Chalenko's 55th Cavalry Division manned defenses to block any German advance between Novoriabukhin and Petrovka. During this period, 8th Cavalry Corps' third division, General Shaimuratov's 112th Cavalry, managed to break free from this struggle and move southward into the Ozery and Arzhanovskii region, 12 to 15 kilometers southeast of Chernyshevskaia.

After Borisov's cavalry failed to destroy 22nd Panzer's column in and south of the Kurtlak River valley, the remnants of XXXXVIII Panzer Corps reorganized into two march groups: one comprising 22nd Panzer's main body (*Kampfgruppe* Oppeln), with the corps' headquarters under General Heim, and the other comprising the rest of 22nd Panzer and the remnants of Romanian 1st Armored under Colonel Rodt.[8] Advancing westward on the night of 24–25 November, these two groups finally reached the safety of the western bank of the Chir River west of the village of Rusakov, just north of Chernyshevskaia. After its westward movement was blocked by cavalrymen from 55th and 112th Cavalry Divisions, another part of 1st Armored Division withdraw southward to Osinovskii, 12 kilometers south of the Kurtlak River, where it escaped westward across the Chir River on the night of 24–25 November.[9] Immediately after reaching the relative safety of the river's western bank, XXXXVIII Panzer Corps and its two shattered divisions received orders from Romanian Third Army to defend the river line north and south of Chernyshevskaia. There was indeed no rest for the wicked.

With the battle against XXXXVIII Panzer Corps nearing an end, Romanenko took measures to crack Axis defenses along the Chir River. Late on the evening of 24 November, he ordered Borisov's 8th Cavalry Corps, once it completed its operations east of Chernyshevskaia, to employ its three divisions to seize Oblivskaia and bridgeheads across the Chir north and south of Chernyshevskaia. Toward this end, Borisov dispatched 55th and 112th Cavalry Divisions southward, east of the Chir River, toward Oblivskaia and 21st Cavalry Division to the Chir River north of Chernyshevskaia, with the following missions:

- 55th Cavalry Division (Colonel Chalenko)—capture Oblivskaia and cut the railroad and roads running east to west north of the Chir River.
- 21st Cavalry Division (General Iakunin)—seize a bridgehead on the western bank of the Chir River north of Chernyshevskaia in cooperation with 47th Guards Rifle Division.
- 112th Cavalry Division (General Shaimuratov)—capture a bridgehead on the western bank of the Chir River south of Chernyshevskaia.[10]

Apparently, Romanenko intended to support the cavalry divisions with rifle divisions once they disengaged from the fight against XXXXVIII Panzer Corps. Tentatively, he earmarked 50th Guards for the region north of Chernyshevskaia, 346th Rifle for south of Chernyshevskaia, and 119th Rifle for the Oblivskaia region. In addition, Vatutin had already informed Romanenko that his tank army would receive additional divisions from 21st and 65th

Armies once the operations to encircle and destroy German XI Army Corps and XIV Panzer Corps west of the Don River were completed.

While most of 5th Tank Army's cavalry and a sizable portion of its infantry and tanks were finally eliminating the obstacle of XXXXVIII Panzer Corps in its center, the rifle divisions on the army's right wing solidified their positions on the Chir River's right (western) bank from Chernyshevskaia northwestward to its junction with the Krivaia River. Specifically, General Fokanov's 47th Guards Rifle Division fortified its sector from Chernyshevskaia northward to Pichugin at the mouth of the Tsutskan' River while it waited for 8th Cavalry Corps' 21st Cavalry Division to disengage from the fight against XXXXVIII Panzer Corps east of Chernyshevskaia and join it for a westward thrust across the Chir. On 47th Guards' right, Colonel Anashkin's 159th Rifle Division fortified its sector along the Chir River from Khokhlachev, across the Tsutskan' River from Pichugin, northwestward to Dulenskii, 6 kilometers east-northeast of Bokovskaia, and it conducted probing attacks toward Bokovskaia with the units on its right wing.

1st Guards Army

On 5th Tank Army's right and the Southwestern Front's extreme right wing, General Leliushenko's 1st Guards Army began concentric attacks at dawn on 24 November, designed to encircle and crush 7th and 11th Infantry Divisions of Romanian I Army Corps, which defended the wedge of territory forming a salient at a 90-degree angle between the Don and Krivaia Rivers (see appendix 6B in the *Companion*). Along the army's extended right wing, 1st and 153rd Rifle Divisions and one regiment of 197th Rifle Division remained on the defense in the sector along the Don River's northern bank from Nizhnyi Mamon eastward to the Eritskii sector, 10 kilometers southeast of Veshenskaia. In the army's center, two regiments from 197th Division and all of 278th Rifle Division attacked southward against the defenses of Romanian 7th Infantry Division in the sector from Rybnyi eastward to Iagodnyi on the Krivaia River. Simultaneously, on the army's left wing, 203rd Rifle and 14th Guards Rifle Divisions attacked westward across the Krivaia River in the 6-kilometer-wide sector from Gorbatovskaia southward to Ushakov against defenses manned by Romanian 11th Infantry Division. Leliushenko's plan required his attacking forces to link up along the Chernaia River, Verkhnyi Luchki, and Vislogubov line (across the base of the salient) and destroy the two Romanian divisions. Fearful of German intervention, at about midday, Leliushenko reinforced the attacks by committing his reserve 266th Rifle Division at the boundary between 203rd and 14th Guards Rifle Divisions. Its mission was to fend off any counterattacks that might materialize.[11]

However, the ensuing battle did not develop as Leliushenko intended. Instead, the assaults by 197th and 278th Rifle Divisions in the north faltered in the face of intense Romanian artillery, mortar, and machine gun fire. Likewise, 203rd Rifle Division's attack across the Krivaia River faltered after capturing a 2-kilometer-deep bridgehead on the western bank.[12] Only General Griaznov's 14th Guards Rifle Division, reinforced during the day by Major General L. V. Vetoshnikov's 266th Rifle Division on its right, achieved any significant gains. After a full day of heavy fighting, the two divisions penetrated Romanian 11th Infantry Division's defenses and drove westward up to 16 kilometers, reaching positions extending from Kon'kov, 5 kilometers north of Bokovskaia, northward to Bakhmutkin Farm, 4 kilometers west of the Krivaia River and 30 kilometers north-northeast of Bokovskaia. By nightfall, Griaznov reported that his 14th Guards had "attacked the enemy along the 2nd Section State Farm (10 kilometers southwest of Gorbatovskaia)–Il'in–Dulenskii line and advanced from 5–16 kilometers, reaching the Kon'kov, Vislogubov, and Nizhnyi Luchki line before being halted."[13] Within hours, however, General Hollidt, commander of XVII Army Corps and Army Group Hollidt, dispatched 62nd and 294th Infantry Divisions from the Kruzhilin and Bokovskaia regions with orders to reinforce the Romanians and counterattack to drive the Soviet forces back across the Krivaia River.[14]

Thus, Romanenko's tank army accomplished one significant mission on 24 November: it eliminated XXXXVIII Panzer Corps' long-standing blocking positions in the army's center. However, the army failed to accomplish its most important mission—seizing Oblivskaia and Rychkovskii and projecting its forces southward to the lower Chir River. By this time, *front* commander Vatutin was no doubt beginning to question Romanenko's ability to lead 5th Tank Army effectively, even though the army's failures could be explained, at least in part, by the weakness of its 1st Tank Corps.

21st Army
While 5th Tank Army was striving to accomplish critical missions along Stalingrad's outer encirclement front, the Southwestern Front's 21st Army was performing an equally significant role in the fight to destroy Sixth Army in its Stalingrad pocket (see appendix 6B in the *Companion*). To accomplish this task in the shortest possible time, General Chistiakov relied almost exclusively on his army's mobile corps, three of which were to strike Sixth Army's defenses from the west. He directed General Kravchenko's 4th Tank Corps, once it regrouped northeastward from the Sovetskii region, to advance northeastward along the Don River's southern bank and seize Sokarevka, 22 kilometers northeast of Kalach. On Kravchenko's left, General Pliev's 3rd Guards Cavalry Corps was to attack eastward along the Don's northern bank to capture Trekhostrovskaia, 55 kilometers northeast of Kalach. On Kravchenko's right, once 26th Tank Corps (transferred from 5th Tank Army) joined 21st Army's advance the next day, it was to move eastward and capture

Dmitrievka, 30 kilometers east-northeast of Kalach. To support Chistiakov's juggernaut, General Vol'sky's 4th Mechanized Corps from the Stalingrad Front's 51st Army was to advance northeastward from the Sovetskii region toward Marinovka, with its 36th Brigade operating toward Dmitrievka along with 4th Tank Corps' 102nd Tank Brigade, which would be operating on Kravchenko's extreme right wing until 26th Tank Corps arrived.

The chief weaknesses in Chistiakov's plan were that, before 26th Tank Corps reached the scene, 4th Tank Corps would have to operate across a 15-kilometer front, far too wide to be effective under normal circumstances. Furthermore, Pliev's three cavalry divisions, reinforced by infantry from at least one rifle division, would have to engage and defeat XIV Panzer Corps' 16th Panzer Division in its defenses along and east of the Golubaia River. Vatutin apparently believed these missions were reasonable because the opposing German forces were so weak. As for 21st Army's rifle forces, 76th, 293rd, 96th, and 333rd Rifle Divisions were to follow and support the mobile corps' advance, while 277th and 63rd Rifle Divisions were to approach the Don River by forced march from their fight against Group Lascar in the Raspopinskaia region.

Overnight on 23–24 November, Kravchenko moved Colonel Zhidkov's 45th Tank Brigade and Colonel Agafonov's 69th Tank Brigade northward from the Sovetskii region, and he moved 4th Motorized Rifle Brigade northward from Platonov State Farm. The brigades then spent the morning assembling and refitting their forces east and northeast of Kalach before beginning their northeastward advance in the afternoon. When they did, Zhidkov's and Agafonov's brigades rolled slowly northeast toward Sokarevka on the corps' left, and Colonel Koshelev's 102nd Brigade drove eastward, north of Marinovka, on the corps' right, in tandem with 4th Mechanized Corps' 36th Brigade. Slowed by the time required to reorganize, refit, and rearm in the morning and by increasing German resistance in the afternoon, 45th and 69th Brigades reached the Il'menskii and Riumino-Krasnoiarskii region, 17 kilometers northeast of Kalach, by day's end. Farther south, 102nd Brigade pushed eastward, reaching positions just northeast of Platonov State Farm.[15]

By this time, Kravchenko's brigades faced elements of 3rd Motorized Division's 29th and 8th Motorized Regiments, which had erected a weak defensive line extending from Sokarevka southward through Illarionovskii to Marinovka, with a light security screen deployed several kilometers to the west.[16] The 3rd Motorized was soon reinforced by elements of 14th Panzer Division, which withdrew westward from XI Corps' bridgehead west of the Don and then marched through Peskovatka to take up positions blocking the high road south of the Don on 3rd Motorized's right. Simultaneously, 24th Panzer Division's *kampfgruppe* also withdrew from the bridgehead and reached Peskovatka at 1500 hours.[17] General Hube, commander of XIV

Panzer Corps, had orders to withdraw 24th and 16th Panzer Divisions in stages from XI Corps' bridgehead and man defenses on the western front of Sixth Army's pocket east of the Don by late on 26 November. Hube planned to employ the two panzer divisions to reinforce the western face of the pocket, while 14th Panzer, transferred to his control, would ultimately revert to XIV Panzer Corps' reserve. However, it would take time for the three divisions to disengage and occupy their new positions.

Meanwhile, north of the Don on 4th Tank Corps' left, the three divisions of General Pliev's 3rd Guards Cavalry Corps, which were to strike at XI Army Corps' left, received a revised mission from Chistiakov overnight on 23–24 November:

> 3rd Guards Cavalry Corps, with 76th Rifle Division and reinforcing units, will destroy the enemy in the vicinity of Hills 138.0 and 118.4 [3 kilometers east to 4 kilometer southeast of Evlampievskii] and the road junction two kilometers north of Kartuli [5 kilometers east-northeast of Malonabatovskii] and advance in the sector with the Don River on the right and Malonabatovskii [should read Evlampievskii] and Kisliakov [15 kilometers northeast of Evlampievskii] on the left. After destroying the enemy grouping, reach the Trekhostrovskaia region [25 kilometers northeast of Evlampievskii].[18]

This order required Pliev's forces to penetrate the defenses of XIV Panzer Corps' 16th Panzer Division east of the Golubaia River and advance roughly 25 kilometers to the northeast to sever the withdrawal routes of both Hube's XIV Panzer Corps and Strecker's XI Army Corps. However, this mission was far too challenging for three cavalry divisions and one rifle division to accomplish. Pliev's daily report to the General Staff overnight on 24–25 November described the results: "3rd Gds. CC pursued the withdrawing enemy, repelled occasional counterattacks, and reached the Evlampievskii-Os'kinskii line (35–45 kilometers north of Kalach and 28 kilometers southwest to 28 kilometers south of Sirotinskaia), with its front facing northeast."[19] Plotted on a map, this entry indicates that, on 24 November, the cavalry corps' advance stalled abruptly in front of 16th Panzer Division's defenses, a reality Pliev later confirmed: "[On 25 November] the corps' units, together with 76th Rifle Division's units, continued intense fighting to take Kartuli, which the enemy had turned in to a strong point."[20] This meant that the cavalry corps registered no gains whatsoever against 16th Panzer Division's defenses on 24 November.

By nightfall on 24 November, the rifle divisions still in 21st Army's rear began closing up to the Don and prepared to lend critical support to the army's struggling mobile corps. On the army's left wing, 76th Rifle Division (now redesignated 51st Guards) was already cooperating with 3rd Guards Cavalry Corps' divisions in the Evlampievskii region on the Don's northern bank; it was reinforced by 277th Division, which concentrated near the crossroads 7 kilometers west of Bol'shenabatovskii and then wheeled northeastward to support the cavalry corps' forces fighting in the sector from Bol'shenabatovski to Evlampievskii. Farther south, in the army's center and on its right wing, 333rd Division reached Malogolubaia, 24 kilometers north of Kalach; 96th Division marched into Golubinskii, 20 kilometers north of Kalach; and 293rd Division closed into the Berezovskii and Kamenskii sector, 5 to 15 kilometers north of Kalach. Finally, the army's last rifle division, the 63rd (which became 52nd Guards Rifle Division on 27 November), concentrated in the Raspopinskaia region in the army's deeper rear, where it took several days off to rest and refit.[21]

If the mobile corps of the Southwestern Front's 21st Army served as the southern pincer in the planned envelopment and destruction of German XI Army Corps and XIV Panzer Corps, the Don Front's 65th and 24th Armies shouldered responsibility for forming the northern pincer and destroying the German forces once they were encircled. Galanin's 24th Army was to drive southward, east of the Don River, to capture Vertiachii, and Batov's 65th Army was to continue to assault XI Army Corps' defenses frontally to liquidate the encircled grouping. But this was easier said than done.

The Don Front

65th Army
General Batov's army continued to apply unrelenting pressure against XI Army Corps' shrinking perimeter west of the Don River on 24 November (see maps 29 and 30 and appendix 6C in the *Companion* for the Don Front's accomplishments on 24 November). Still smarting over General Galanin's accusation the day before that 65th Army was not fighting with the requisite vigor, Batov urged his troops on. During the day, his main shock group's 252nd, 27th Guards, and 258th Rifle Divisions forced the defending German 14th Panzer and 44th Infantry Divisions to withdraw eastward from positions extending diagonally from Verkhniaia Golubinskaia on the Golubaia River northeastward across the bridgehead to the Don River's southern bank between Zimovskii and Khmelevskii. Simultaneously, the army's 4th Guards Rifle Division attacked southeastward west of Khmelevskii, and 24th Rifle Division assaulted southward from the army's bridgehead on the Don's southern bank east of Khmelevskii. As General Strecker's XI Corps conducted a fighting withdrawal to new defensive positions, 65th Army's

divisions advanced 7 to 15 kilometers during the day. The intense fighting was costly for both sides, but especially for 65th Army, which had no choice but to attack frontally.

At nightfall, Batov's 252nd, 27th Guards, and 258th Divisions reached positions overlooking Sukhaia Golubaia *Balka*, a largely dry riverbed extending northward about 20 kilometers from the Golubaia River near Evlampievskii to just south of Khmelevskii. On their left, 4th Guards Rifle Division reached the western approaches to Khmelevski, and farther left, Colonel Prokhorov's 24th "Iron" Division fought its way southward to positions extending westward from just south of Trekhostrovskaia on the Don River's western bank. However, although XI Army Corps' bridgehead was shrinking, it was not being encircled. Across the Don on Batov's left, Galanin's 24th Army had recorded no success whatsoever in its advance on Vertiachii. As General Batov later lamented, "The 24th Army did not advance on Vertiachii. The crossings [over the Don], as before, remained in enemy hands."[22]

24th Army
Batov was indeed correct. After failing to advance on 22 and 23 November, Galanin's 24th Army resumed its assaults at dawn on the 24th. As on the previous day, instead of employing the 59 surviving tanks of Maslov's 16th Tank Corps as a battering ram to smash through to Vertiachii, Galanin once again used the tank corps' 109th, 107th, and 164th Tank Brigades to provide infantry support for the attacking 49th, 214th, and 120th Rifle Divisions. Galanin did, however, commit the fresh 84th Rifle Division into combat between 49th and 214th Rifle Divisions, but to no avail. In heavy fighting throughout the day, which cost the tank corps another 33 tanks (including 3 KVs and 4 T-34s burned and 7 KVs, 3 T-34s, and 2 T-60s destroyed in minefields), the attacking divisions advanced no more than 4 kilometers (see appendix 6C in the *Companion*).[23]

Although the General Staff made no comment about 24th Army's lack of success on 24 November, the next day it registered its displeasure in an after-action report, stating, "The infantry of the rifle formations did not attack [rise up] and remained lying down in front of the barbed wire."[24] Without infantry support, Maslov's tanks were simply "sitting ducks" for the German gunners.

66th Army
Although 24th Army made no progress in its offensive, General Zhadov's 66th Army did, but only by exploiting a problem created by German Sixth Army's LI Army Corps. As described earlier, the mission General Rokossovsky assigned to 66th Army overnight on 23–24 November was to attack southward from the Erzovka region toward Orlovka at dawn on the 24th, penetrate German defenses, and link up with the Stalingrad Front's 62nd

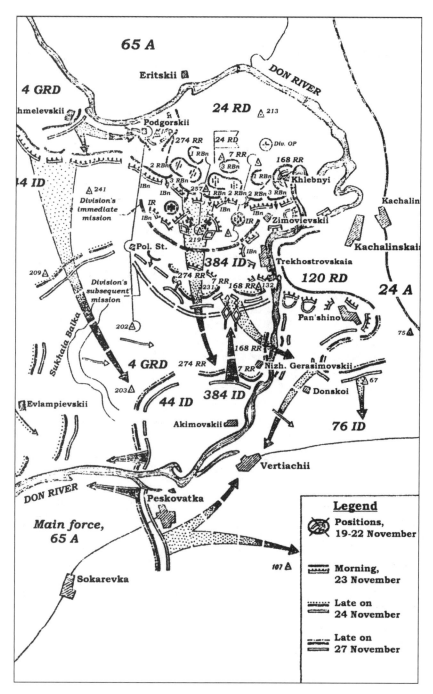

Map 30. Advance by the Don Front's 65th and 24th Armies toward Vertiachii, 19–27 November 1942

Army in the Orlovka and Rynok region. However, at 2240 hours the evening before, General Seydlitz, LI Army Corps' commander, issued Order No. 118. This order, designed in part to persuade Paulus to withdraw Sixth Army from the Stalingrad pocket, directed his forces occupying the sector north of Orlovka and Rynok to destroy all unneeded weapons and equipment and withdraw to new defenses near Orlovka overnight on 23–24 November.[25]

In addition to provoking a strong rebuke from Hitler, Seydlitz's order placed 94th Infantry Division in a perilous position that 66th Army was quick to exploit. At 0800 hours the next day, the General Staff described 66th Army's surprising success, noting, "66th Army went over to an offensive toward the Orlovka region early on the morning of 24 November and, overcoming stubborn enemy resistance, advanced 2–8 kilometers in the center and on the left wing." It then specified the exact objectives seized by the army's six attacking divisions and single tank brigade (see appendix 6C in the *Companion* for the General Staff's entry and appendix 6D for a description of the attack in 66th Army's history).[26]

German Sixth Army's records confirm that 94th Division's withdrawal was chaotic; as a result, the division lost several officers and roughly 200 men, which was a heavy blow to the already weakened force. The division lost about 50 more men on 25 November and another 200 on the 26th. Thus, by month's end, its 274th Regiment was reduced to two weak battalions, 267th Regiment to three weak battalions, and 276th Regiment to one exhausted battalion. By then, Sixth Army had rushed 24th Panzer Division back to the Orlovka region, assigning it both 94th Division's sector and the division's remnants.[27]

Conclusions

The first day of the Southwestern and Don Fronts' resumed offensive to exploit the encirclement of Sixth Army failed to develop as planned. Although Vatutin's *front* finally forced XXXXVIII Panzer Corps to withdraw westward across the Chir River, neither 5th Tank Army nor 21st Army achieved anything more substantial. Romanenko's army failed to capture any of its objectives along the Chir, and Chistiakov's army expanded its bridgehead on the Don's eastern bank only slightly. Both armies failed because the missions Vasilevsky assigned to them were too ambitious. After five days of constant movement and intense combat, 5th Tank and 21st Armies needed time to rest and refit their forces; Vasilevsky failed to give them that time. Nevertheless, 21st Army's 4th Tank Corps spent most of 24 November resting, and 26th Tank Corps sat out the action while preparing to join Chistiakov's army. As for the army's 3rd Guards Cavalry Corps, without rest, it too proved unable to dent XIV Panzer Corps' defenses west of the Don, even with infantry support.

Rokossovsky's Don Front fared no better. Despite 66th Army's signal success southwest of Erzovka, that success was local, and Zhadov's army was too weak to accomplish much more because it lacked a large tank force. As historian Samsonov later wrote, "66th Army was not able to accomplish its assigned main mission. The enemy dug in on the heights north and northeast of Orlovka. To reinforce his positions north of Stalingrad, [by 27 November] the German command returned 16th and 24th Panzer Divisions there from the Marinovka region."[28] Harsher still, Rokossovsky concluded, "The forces of 66th Army advanced slowly and, therefore, gave the enemy an opportunity to withdraw his forces to more tactically favorable positions along the heights (north and northeast of Orlovka) and organize a defense along a new line."[29]

At nightfall, Vatutin's and Rokossovsky's only consolation was the knowledge that Eremenko's Stalingrad Front had also accomplished very little on 24 November.

THE STALINGRAD FRONT'S OFFENSIVE, 24 NOVEMBER

On 24 November, the Stalingrad Front attacked in the region west of Beketovka with part of its shock group's forces and advanced forward insignificantly, while it continued developing its offensive toward the Kotel'nikovo region with the other part of its forces, occupying several populated points, including Sadovoe.

Red Army General Staff Operational Summary,
0800 hours on 25 November 1942[30]

The Stalingrad Front's Missions

As he formulated missions for his subordinate armies overnight on 23–24 November, General Eremenko, like Vatutin, had to look in two directions. The two missions Vasilevsky had assigned to his Stalingrad Front seemed equally important—to assist in the liquidation of the Stalingrad pocket, and to erect a reliable outer encirclement front along the Don River and somewhere along or south of the Aksai River. Based on Vasilevsky's guidance, Eremenko ordered 62nd, 64th, and 57th Armies and part of 51st Army to participate in the "pocket fight"; the remainder of 51st Army to erect the outer encirclement front; and 28th Army to secure the *front*'s extreme left wing (see appendix 6E in the *Companion* for specific missions).

In terms of the quantity of forces it committed to the struggle to liquidate the Stalingrad pocket, Eremenko's Stalingrad Front was a close second

to Rokossovsky's Don Front. While Rokossovsky employed three armies—
the 65th, 24th, and 66th—Eremenko employed the 62nd, 64th, 57th, and
part of a fourth, the 51st. As subsequent events would indicate, Eremenko's
forces encountered the same problems as Rokossovsky's; that is, despite intense fighting, they recorded only negligible gains. In fact, the Stalingrad
Front's only positive contributions to Vasilevsky's plan on 24 November were
to enlarge the gap separating German Sixth Army from Axis forces west of
the Don River and to push the *front's* outer encirclement south of the Aksai River. Otherwise, the *front's* offensive against Sixth Army's heavily fortified defenses east along the railroad line from Marinovka to Karpovka, along
the Karpovka and Chervlenaia Rivers to Karavatka *Balka*, and east and then
northeast from the *balka* to Stalingrad's southern suburb of Kuporosnoe essentially stalled (see map 31).

64th Army

General Shumilov's army resumed its assaults against the defenses of Sixth
Army's IV Army Corps early on 24 November (see appendix 6F in the *Companion* for the Stalingrad Front's accomplishments on 24 November). Once
again, the army's main shock group, consisting of 36th Guards and 157th,
204th, and 29th Rifle Divisions, launched its assault in the sector from the
Chervlenaia River eastward along Karavatka *Balka* to Elkhi on the army's left
wing and in its center. On the army's right, the three brigades of 7th Rifle
Corps defended the sector extending from north of Elkhi northeastward to
the southern edge of Kuporosnoe in Stalingrad's southern suburbs.

On the shock group's left wing, Colonel Denisenko's 36th Guards Rifle
Division repeatedly attacked toward the crest of Hill 111.6, in an attempt
to penetrate the German strongpoint at Tsybenko from the east. Although
these assaults failed against the stout defenses manned by 1st and 2nd Battalions of 371st Infantry Division's 670th Regiment (which was now subordinate to IV Corps' 297th Infantry Division), Denisenko's troops succeeded in
clinging to a small bridgehead on the northern bank of Karavatka *Balka*. Farther east, 157th and 204th Rifle Divisions' assaults along the line of the *balka*
faltered because of strong resistance by Romanian 82nd Infantry Regiment
and 297th Infantry Division's 523rd Regiment. Likewise, 29th Rifle Division's assaults against the fortified town of Elkhi, which was defended by 1st
and 3rd Battalions of 523rd Regiment, collapsed after the division suffered
heavy losses. To solidify his army's positions and protect against possible German counterattacks, General Shumilov committed his 20th Tank Destroyer
Brigade to defend the northern approaches to Iagodnyi, several kilometers
south of the *balka*.[31]

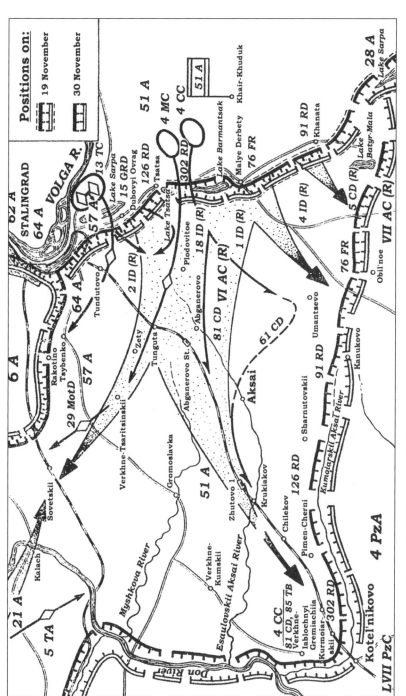

Map 31. 51st Army's advance, 19–30 November 1942

The frustrations Shumilov experienced on 24 November would continue unabated through the end of the month against the strong defenses erected by Sixth Army's IV Army Corps.

57th Army

Like 64th Army, the offensive by General Tolbukhin's 57th Army on Shumilov's left faltered soon after it began, in part because of 29th Motorized Division's strong defenses and in part due to immediate and incessant German counterattacks (see appendix 6F in the *Companion*). The army began the day with the mechanized brigades and tank regiments of General Tanaschishin's 13th Tank Corps and 422nd and 169th Rifle Divisions arrayed from left to right in the roughly 30-kilometer-wide sector west of and parallel to the Chervlenaia River from Staryi Rogachik southeastward to the southern approaches to Tsybenko. On the army's right wing, Colonel Eremenko's 169th Rifle Division, cooperating with 64th Army's 36th Guards Division east of the river, conducted repeated assaults against 297th Infantry Division's strongpoint at Tsybenko. Eremenko's troops actually penetrated into the strongpoint several times during the day before being expelled once and for all by nightfall. Meanwhile, on 169th Division's left, Colonel Morozov's 422nd Rifle Division also pounded the defenses of 1st and 2nd Battalions of 29th Motorized Division's 71st Panzer-Grenadier Regiment at and northwest of Kravtsov, but despite heavy fighting and significant losses, Morozov's riflemen could not penetrate the Germans' defenses.

Farther northwestward along the Chervlenaia, repeated assaults by 13th Tank Corps' 62nd and 61st Mechanized Brigades against 29th Motorized Division's 15th Panzer-Grenadier Regiment in the sector from Hill 100.5 to Bereslavskii and Staryi Rogachik also failed due to frequent German counterattacks with motorized infantry, reportedly supported by up to 45 tanks. These counterattacks likely involved 29th Motorized Division's 129th Panzer Battalion [*Abteilung*], although it fielded only about 30 tanks during this period.[32]

Thus, Tolbukhin's forces were unable to crack open the defenses on the southern front of Sixth Army's pocket. However, by day's end, the forces on 13th Tank Corps' extreme left wing (probably 17th Mechanized Brigade) succeeded in establishing firm connections with the right wing of 51st Army's 4th Mechanized Corps south of Voroshilov Camp, roughly midway between Karpovka and Marinovka.

51st Army

General Trufanov's 51st Army, which was fighting on the Stalingrad Front's left wing in the Stalingrad region, had the dubious distinction of being the only army conducting operations along both the inner and outer encircle-ment fronts. General Vol'sky's 4th Mechanized Corps and General Vasilenko's 15th Guards Rifle Division fought for the Marinovka and Voroshilov Camp regions of Sixth Army's Stalingrad pocket. The remainder of Trufanov's army operated against the remnants of Romanian VI and VII Army Corps along and south of the Myshkovo and Aksai Rivers and in the sector extending southeastward to Umantsevo and the approaches to Sadovaia (see appendix 6F in the *Companion*).

On the southwestern front of Sixth Army's pocket, General Vol'sky's 4th Mechanized Corps tried hard to encircle and destroy the forces of 3rd Motorized Division's *Kampfgruppe* Willig, which was defending the well-fortified strongpoint at Marinovka and several points along the railroad line to the east. Vol'sky ordered Colonel Sten'shinsky's 59th Mechanized Brigade, with Lieutenant Colonel Litvinov's 20th Tank Regiment, to assault German strongpoints from Platonovskii (Platonov) to the west and Lieutenant Colo-nel Rodionov's 36th Mechanized Brigade, with Major Doroshkevich's 26th Tank Regiment, to advance on the strongpoint from the northwest. During this attack, Doroshkevich's tanks were supposed to cooperate closely with 102nd Tank Brigade, which was deployed on 4th Tank Corps' right wing.

The joint attack against Marinovka began with a reconnaissance in force before dawn on 24 November and expanded into a full-scale assault against the strongpoint during the morning. Litvinov was severely wounded during the ensuing fight, which continued for two days. The 15th Guards Division joined the battle by attacking the sector between Marinovka and Voroshilov Camp. Despite the repeated assaults, Vol'sky's corps and Vasilenko's riflemen were unable to pry the Germans out of their fortified positions. While the two mechanized brigades assaulted Marinovka, 4th Mechanized Corps' 60th Brigade and 21st Tank Regiment continued their futile attempts to capture Karpovskaia Station, 14 kilometers to the east. At day's end, Vol'skys corps reported that "4th MC's 59th MRB is fighting for the Karpovka–Voroshilov Camp region, 36th MRB is fighting in the Marinovka-Sovetskii region, 60th MRB is fighting in the Karpovskaia Station region, and 55th Separate Tank Regiment is located in the Novo-Akhtubinskii region (10 kilometers south of Sovetskii)," but there was no mention of any real progress.[33] Sixth Army's morning report noted, "The enemy are at the moment attacking Marinovka from the west and southwest with tanks," but it later confirmed that the at-tacks did little damage.[34]

The Stalingrad Front recorded its best progress along its outer encir-clement front, where the forces in 51st Army's center and on its left wing advanced southward from the Aksai River and westward from the south-ern half of the lake region, 65 to 75 kilometers south of Stalingrad. General Shapkin, whose 4th Cavalry Corps was positioned on 51st Army's left wing, ordered 81st and 61st Cavalry Divisions to push southward into the broad region between the towns of Aksai and Sadovaia, which were 45 kilometers apart. Trufanov hoped this would compel Romanian VI Army Corps to abandon its defenses along the Aksai River and VII Army Corps to do the same in the Sadovaia region. During the day, Colonel Baumshtein's 81st Division captured Aksai and Peregruznyi, 8 kilometers to the south, and Colonel Stavenko's 61st Division captured the town of Umantsevo, 18 kilometers west-southwest of Sadovaia, from Romanian 4th Infantry Division. Between the two cavalry divisions, Colonel Kuropatenko's 126th Rifle Division marched southward to Abganerovo and dispatched forward detachments to Tebektenerovo, Kapkinskii Station, Shelestov, and Solianoi burial mound, 17 kilometers southeast of Aksai. On 126th Division's left, Colonel Makarchuk's 302nd Rifle Division concentrated two of its regiments in the vicinity of Plodovitoe, 40 kilometers northeast of Aksai, and sent the third regiment to the vicinity of Kalmytskie burial mound, 6 kilometers northwest of Sadovoe.

With its lines of communication cut by advancing Soviet cavalry and Soviet infantry pressing in from the north and east, Romanian 4th Infantry Division withdrew southwestward from Sadovoe. Hard on its heels, soldiers from 51st Army's 76th Fortified Region occupied the town at 0800 hours on 24 November. Simultaneously, General Kalinin's 91st Rifle Division advanced on Sadovoe from the east and northeast, capturing and occupying dominant heights 10 kilometers northeast of the town. Far to the rear, on Trufanov's orders, 38th Motorized Rifle Brigade (the army's reserve) moved forward into assembly areas around Zety, prepared to reinforce in either direction should the need arise. By now, despite German Fourth Panzer Army's demand that they hold their ground, Romanian 8th Cavalry and 4th Infantry Divisions had fallen back, the former southward to the vicinity of Zhutov 2, 20 kilometers south-southwest of Aksai, and the latter toward Obil'noe, 30 kilometers south of Sadovoe.

By nightfall on 24 November, Fourth Panzer Army's defenses south of Stalingrad were in shambles. The fall of Aksai ended any hope Romanian VI Army Corps had of holding on to the Aksai River line, leaving it no recourse but to withdraw 8th Cavalry and the remnants of other shattered infantry divisions along the Aksai, southward to the Kotel'nikovo region, and to withdraw 4th Infantry Division westward through Obil'noe to Kotel'nikovo. However, the winds of change were beginning to blow. The next day, the advance guards of German *Kampfgruppe* Pannwitz began reaching Kotel'nikovo. This ad hoc unit was commanded by Colonel Helmuth von Pannwitz, a German officer with a flair for the dramatic. He had been working to raise Russian volunteers (especially Cossacks) to serve in the German army. Pannwitz's *kampfgruppe*, which numbered several thousand men, consisted of a volunteer Cossack cavalry brigade, rear service and replacement personnel from Fourth Panzer Army, 18 tanks liberated from one of the panzer army's repair facilities, and a motorized Romanian artillery battalion.[35] Two days later, this group, together with Romanian 8th Cavalry Division, would inflict the first setback on Shapkin's cavalry. But it was still just a pale reflection of a force capable of defeating all the forces on 51st Army's left wing.

62nd Army

Although General Chuikov's threadbare and understrength 62nd Army had been harassing the forces of German Sixth Army's LI Army Corps for days with raids, sorties, and reconnaissances in force, Vasilevsky's 23 November directive required it to launch something close to a real offensive on 24 November. Chuikov reacted in characteristic fashion by ordering his army to "attack along its entire front at dawn on 24 November to destroy the enemy and reach the western outskirts of Stalingradskaia Street." The assault was to begin at 1000 hours.

Attacking promptly at that time, Chuikov later reported to the Stalingrad Front's headquarters and General Staff, "62nd Army attacked along its entire front at 1000 hours and, while overcoming strong enemy fire resistance, advanced forward insignificantly" (see appendixes 6G and 19B in the *Companion*). Reacting as if the day's bloody fighting on 24 November had been "just another day in the office," in the evening, Chuikov ordered his subordinate formations "to continue the offensive and reach the western edge of the city" the next day.

By this time, German soldiers fighting in Stalingrad and its northern factory district had become defenders rather than attackers. Although General Seydlitz rescinded the withdrawal order he had issued the day before at 1445 hours, Hitler, who learned about the order at 0845 the next morning, was irate over the corps commander's peremptory decision. The Führer immediately reiterated his stand-fast order, directing Paulus to convert his positions into "Fortress Stalingrad." Paulus, in turn, seconded Hitler's order, forcing a frustrated Seydlitz to rescind his order.[36] Paulus had already stripped the city of all its mobile troops, tanks, and assault guns and even some of its infantry, which were desperately needed to reinforce his pocket's western front. These included the bulk of 14th, 16th, and 24th Panzer Divisions; most of 3rd and part of 60th Motorized Divisions; and the army's three assault gun battalions. Nonetheless, the weakened condition of 62nd Army's formations made it impossible to mount any sort of genuine offensive capable of recapturing major chunks of the city.

28th Army

While the fighting raged in the vast expanse of territory from the Volga River westward to the Krivaia, Chir, and Aksai Rivers, General Gerasimenko's 28th Army on the Stalingrad Front's distant left wing continued to advance west toward Iashkul' and Elista (see map 32). However, the army's march was interrupted when its shock group halted abruptly less than 10 kilometers east of Iashkul', its first objective, which the Germans had converted into a veritable fortress bolstered by formidable outpost defenses north and south of the town. By day's end on the 24th, the army's shock group, now consisting of 34th Guards Rifle Division, 6th Guards Tank Brigade, and 248th Rifle Division's 899th Regiment, reported it had reached the Marker 1.2, Atskha-Khor-Tolga, and Marker 8.0 line, 6 to 8 kilometers northwest, east, and southeast of the fortified town. Gerasimenko's initial report to the Stalingrad Front asserted, "The enemy is defending previously-prepared centers of resistance in the Oling and Iashkul' region with a force of up to a regiment of infantry and artillery and tanks."[37] However, the defending force turned out to be far larger than a single regiment.

General Schwerin's 16th Motorized Division, which was now operating under Fourth Panzer Army's control, was supposed to make a stand in Iashkul' while the situation to the north developed further. This meant his division was to hold its positions and protect the panzer army's right flank as Hoth assembled the forces necessary to conduct a relief operation to reinforce or rescue Sixth Army in its Stalingrad pocket. Accordingly, his motorized division constructed the so-called Tobruk Line to defend Iashkul' and Elista to the west. This line extended from 25 kilometers north of Chilgir, southward 40 kilometers to Iashkul', and then 15 kilometers south of the town. On 16th Motorized Division's left wing, 811th Turkestan Volunteer Battalion occupied defenses at Chilgir, with a company at the village of Niukiun, 10 kilometers to the southeast. Farther south, 782nd Turkestan Volunteer Battalion manned defenses from the dry Lake [Il'men'] Ded-Khulsun southward about 6 kilometers to the terrain feature Oling, situated on the northern bank of dry Lake Dort-Khulsun, 19 to 25 kilometers northwest of Iashkul'. The 782nd Battalion was backed up by 60th Motorized Regiment's 3rd Battalion. The sector in front of 782nd Turkestan Battalion was protected by minefields, German antitank guns positioned on the burial mounds [kurgans] east of dry Lake Dort-Khulsun, and a series of outposts several hundred meters out in the steppes.

Iashkul' itself was protected by a semicircular ring of defensive positions, manned by 16th Motorized Division's 60th and 156th Motorized Regiments, that stretched 10 kilometers north, 6 kilometers east, and about 15 kilometers south of the town. The 60th Motorized Regiment's 2nd, 1st, and 3rd

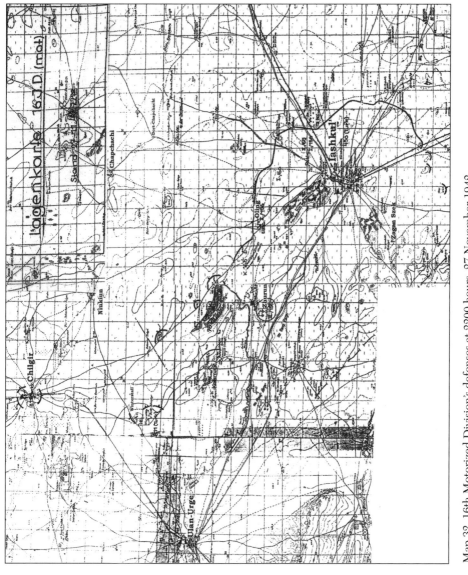

Map 32. 16th Motorized Division's defenses at 2200 hours, 27 November 1942

Battalions defended a ring of hills north and northeast of the town and were backed up by 1st Battalion, 156th Regiment, in reserve, and 2nd Battalion, 156th Regiment, occupying defenses east and southeast of the town. The 450th Turkestan Volunteer Battalion and 16th Motorized's 160th Panzer Battalion [*Abteilung*] were in reserve just west of the town. Finally, the division's 165th Motorcycle Battalion (K 165) manned reserve positions at the village of Chuduk, midway between Iashkul' and Ulan-Erge, 40 kilometers to the west.[38]

The formidable defenses erected by 16th Motorized around Iashkul' explain why it would take more than a month for 28th Army to capture the town. In fact, in microcosm, 16th Motorized Division's defense of Iashkul' resembled Soviet efforts to reduce Sixth Army's encirclement pocket at Stalingrad.

Conclusions

As was the case with the Southwestern and Don Fronts (with one notable exception), Eremenko's Stalingrad Front was unable to fulfill the ambitious objectives set forth in Vasilevsky's plan. Nor would his armies be able to do so over the next two days. The assaults by 62nd, 64th, 57th, and 51st Armies against the eastern, southern, and southwestern fronts of Sixth Army's Stalingrad pocket failed to achieve any significant gains and exacted a high cost in terms of personnel casualties. They failed because the attacking forces were worn out from previous offensive fighting and lacked sufficient armored strength to penetrate prepared German defenses. Credit for the successful defense goes, first and foremost, to German divisions that, despite the shock of previous catastrophic defeats, retained their composure and shifted their forces to and fro to erect credible defenses around the periphery of the Stalingrad pocket. To an even greater degree, however, credit must go to the numerous small *kampfgruppen* that, though hastily formed and made up of cooks, mechanics, supply clerks, and other rear service personnel, with a leavening of convalescent soldiers, replacements, and leave returnees, somehow managed to repel attacks by experienced but tired Red Army riflemen, *tankists*, and sappers. In short, whether through desperation or effective training, after surviving five days of cascading debacles, the encircled German soldiers were somehow able to convert the Stalingrad pocket into a genuine fortress.

The only saving grace for Vasilevsky was the knowledge that desperation had its limits, and the forces along the Stalingrad Front's outer encirclement front were still advancing southwestward, seemingly without hindrance. Therefore, he continued his offensive in the hope that German desperation would lead to inevitable collapse.

THE SOUTHWESTERN, DON, AND STALINGRAD FRONTS' OFFENSIVES, 25–27 NOVEMBER

On 25 November the Southwestern, Don, and Stalingrad Fronts' forces continued their offensive, overcame stubborn enemy resistance, and tightened the encirclement ring around German forces in Stalingrad. Simultaneously, the Southwestern Front's forces attacked toward Oblivskaia and Surovikino and Stalingrad Front's force attacked toward Kotel'nikovskii and occupied a number of populated points.

Our units liquidated the previously encircled enemy forces in the Bol'shaia Donshchinka region.

Red Army General Staff Operational Summary,
0800 hours on 26 November 1942[39]

On 26 November the Southwestern Front contained enemy counterattacks east of Bokovskaia with part of its forces, attacked toward and encircled Oblivskaia with its mobile units, and continued its offensive on the eastern bank of the Don River in the region northeast of Kalach, pressing the encirclement ring around the Germans at Stalingrad from the west.

The Don Front's forces continued their offensives in the Vertiachii and Orlovka regions but encountered stubborn enemy resistance and advanced insignificantly in individual sectors, essentially achieving no results.

The Stalingrad Front's forces continued their offensive toward Kotel'nikovo with part of their forces.

Red Army General Staff Operational Summary,
0800 hours on 27 November 1942[40]

On 27 November, the Southwestern Front fended off enemy counterattacks in the region northeast of Bokovskaia and Chernyshevskaia and fought to seize Oblivskaia with part of its forces, while other parts of its forces fought with encircled enemy units in the region northeast of Kalach.

The Don Front continued its offensive in the Verkhne-Gnilovskii and Nizhne-Gnilovskii regions on the eastern bank of the Don River with part of its forces and, after smashing enemy resistance, captured these points.

The Stalingrad Front fought to capture Karpovka (17 kilometers northeast of Sovetskii) with part of its force and continued its offensive toward Kotel'nikovo.

Red Army General Staff Operational Summary,
0800 hours on 28 November 1942[41]

The fighting on 24 November set the tone for operations taking place over the next three days. Call it stubbornness or perseverance, but with the *Stavka*'s backing, Vasilevsky resolved to do everything in his power to liquidate Sixth Army's Stalingrad pocket as quickly as possible. What drove him to that decision was the awful specter of a successful German operation to reinforce or relieve Sixth Army. Conditioned by 18 months of often frustrating experiences, no one in the Soviet High Command was willing to leave anything to chance. This time, the Soviet military leadership resolved, the Germans would not deny them their victory. Therefore, the costly struggle around the Stalingrad pocket went on unabated, just as it did along the Chir River and south of the Aksai River.

The *Fronts'* Missions

Based on recommendations from Stalin and the *Stavka* that he persist in his efforts, Vasilevsky issued a new set of orders to Vatutin, Rokossovsky, and Eremenko overnight on 24–25 November, instructing them to continue their offensives. If these orders sounded similar to those he had issued the night before, this is because the three *fronts'* missions were basically unchanged (see appendix 6H in the *Companion*). The Southwestern Front's 1st Guards and 5th Tank Armies were to secure positions along the Krivaia and Chir Rivers and capture Oblivskaia, Surovikino, and Rychkovskii. The *front's* 21st Army, cooperating with the Don Front's 65th and 24th Armies, was to destroy Sixth Army's XI Army Corps before it escaped southward across the Don River. Other armies, including the Don Front's 66th Army and the Stalingrad Front's 64th and 57th Armies, together with the smaller 62nd Army inside Stalingrad, were to support the main effort by pounding the defenses around the circumference of Sixth Army's pocket. Finally, southwest of Stalingrad, the Stalingrad Front's 51st Army was to continue its advance to seize Kotel'nikovo.

The only alteration in Vasilevsky's new orders pertained to the transfer of 4th Mechanized Corps from 51st to 57th Army and the employment of part of Vol'sky's mechanized corps to seize the eastern bank of the Don River south of Rychkovskii and opposite Nizhne-Chirskaia. This was necessary for two reasons: first, to protect the bulk of 51st Army as it began its southward drive toward Kotel'nikovo, and second, to position forces east of the Don that could eliminate the Germans' bridgehead on the river's eastern bank opposite Rychkovskii. Otherwise, all the armies subordinate to the three *fronts* were to do as they had done the day before, only more effectively. Most important, Vasilevsky did not alter his arrangements for the command and control of these forces. As before, both Vatutin and Rokossovsky had to manage battles occurring simultaneously along both the inner and outer encirclement fronts.

The Southwestern Front

As had been the case in previous days, two armies in Vatutin's Southwestern Front continued to do the "heavy lifting" in this phase of the offensive, and they continued to do so in opposite directions (see map 29 and appendix 6I in the *Companion* for the Southwestern Front's accomplishments on 25–27 November). Romanenko's 5th Tank Army focused its efforts along the Chir River, while Chistiakov's 21st Army fought along the western front of Sixth Army's Stalingrad pocket. For commanders who were accustomed to observing and directing ongoing fighting from observation posts well forward, this was an awkward arrangement indeed.

21st Army

When General Chistiakov's 21st Army resumed operations on 25 November, it should have been in far better shape to accomplish its assigned missions than it had been the day before. The army had been reinforced by General Rodin's 26th Tank Corps (transferred from 5th Tank Army), which had spent the previous day resting and refitting. However, as events would indicate, Rodin's corps needed far more than 24 hours to recoup its strength after five days of intense operations. First of all, it was still without its 216th Tank Brigade, which, after the fight for Bol'shaia Donshchinka, was so weak that it had to be placed in 5th Tank Army's reserve to rest and refit. In addition, by 25 November, Rodin's two tank brigades likely fielded fewer than 30 operable tanks, which prompted the corps' future commander, General M. F. Panov, to conclude, "At the time, the corps' units, considerably weakened in previous fighting, could not develop an offensive at high tempo."[42] In essence, the corps was capable of little more than providing infantry support.

Nonetheless, Chistiakov ordered Rodin's corps, supported by 293rd Rifle Division, to capture the towns of Sokarevka and Peskovatka by day's end on 25 November. This meant advancing up to 20 kilometers—a challenging task for even a full-strength tank corps. Rodin's corps was to advance in tandem with Kravchenko's 4th Tank Corps on its right, which was supposed to advance from the Sovetskii and Platonovskii regions eastward through Illarionovskii to Dmitrievka, also a distance of about 20 kilometers. This mission far exceeded the capabilities of a corps fielding no more than 40 tanks. At the time, Chistiakov's two mobile corps faced 3rd Motorized Division of Sixth Army's XIV Panzer Corps, whose forces occupied noncontiguous defenses stretching from Sokarevka southward through Illarionovskii to Marinovka. Soon, however, 3rd Motorized was reinforced by 14th Panzer Division, whose forces had been supporting XI Corps' defense of the Sirotinskaia bridgehead west of the Don for five days. On 25 November, 14th Panzer withdrew eastward over the river near Peskovatka in the morning and occupied defensive positions in the Sokarevka sector on 3rd Motorized Division's right in the afternoon. By this time, Bässler's division had only 24 operational tanks remaining from the 50+ it had possessed on 19 November.

On 21st Army's left wing north of the Don River, General Pliev's 3rd Guards Cavalry Corps received orders to continue its advance from the Evlampievskii and Malonabatovskii regions east toward Trekhostrovskaia—essentially, the same mission as the day before. It was to cooperate with Colonel Tavartkiladze's 76th Rifle Division, which had been given the honorific of 51st Guards the day before. However, at about midnight, Pliev received new orders from Chistiakov that read, "Once alerted, dispatch one cavalry division to the 'Pobeda Oktiabriia' [October Victory] State Farm, Kumovka, and Berezovskii region, with the mission to protect the axis from Nizhne-Chirskaia. The division will arrive in the designated region no later than 1600 hours on 25 November."[43] Pliev, in turn, ordered his 6th Guards Cavalry Division to ride southward and occupy perimeter positions roughly 6 kilometers northwest, west, and southwest of Kalach to protect against a surprise German advance from the lower Chir River. This change in mission left Pliev's corps with two weakened cavalry divisions, 76th Rifle Division, and the approaching 277th Rifle Division, but without any tanks to dislodge the *kampfgruppe* of XIV Panzer Corps' 16th Panzer Division from its strong defensive positions east of the Golubaia River.

Despite the weakness of Rodin's and Kravchenko's tank corps and Pliev's cavalry corps, Chistiakov's forces resumed their offensive on 25 November (see appendix 6I in the *Companion*). North of the Don, 3rd Guards Cavalry Corps, supported by 51st Guards Rifle Division and with the newly arrived 277th Rifle Division protecting its left flank, attacked east toward the towns of Akimovskii and Trekhostrovskaia on the Don. South of the river, 26th and 4th Tank Corps, cooperating with 293rd Rifle Division, drove east toward the towns of Sokarevka and Dmitrievka, which anchored the western end of Sixth Army's newly forming pocket. Pliev's cavalry corps—now short its 6th Guards Cavalry Division, which was en route to the region west of Kalach—attacked eastward against 16th Panzer Division's defenses northeast of Malonabatovskii. Heavy fighting ensued as Pliev's 5th Guards and 32nd Cavalry, supported by 51st Guards and 277th Rifle Divisions, assaulted 16th Panzer Division's defenses at Hill 169.2, 3 kilometers northeast of Malonabatovskii, and northward to about 5 kilometers east of Evlampievskii, capturing this hill.[44] When 16th Panzer withdrew southeastward across the Don during the day, it was relieved by 44th Infantry Division's 132nd Regiment, which had previously supported 14th Panzer Division but now became responsible for defending the southern half of XI Army Corps' shrinking bridgehead north of the Don. As Pliev's cavalry and infantry continued their attacks, General

Strecker reinforced 132nd Regiment's defenses with 44th Infantry's 131st Regiment.

By nightfall on 25 November, 3rd Guards Cavalry Corps' two divisions and 51st Guards Rifle Division pierced XI Army Corps' defenses northeast of Malonabatovskii and wheeled south to capture the village of Luchenskii on the Don's northern bank, 10 kilometers east of Bol'shenabatovskii. A regiment of Colonel Chudesov's 32nd Cavalry Division then forced the Don River, capturing a small bridgehead on its southeastern bank, several kilometers northwest of Peskovatka, only to be halted by 16th Panzer Division's defenses at the northern outskirts of the town. Several kilometers to the west, however, 16th Panzer managed to retain a small bridgehead on the river's northwestern bank at the village of Kartuli, where it halted the advance by 3rd Guards Cavalry Corps' 5th Guards Division. On the cavalry corps' left wing, north of the Don, 277th Rifle Division continued its advance from east of Evlampievskii and reached the region north of Kalachkin, where it was halted by 44th Infantry Division's 132nd Regiment, which by this time was little more than a reinforced battalion.

Farther south along the Don, Rodin's 26th Tank Corps moved northeastward from Kalach through Kamyshi early in the morning and advanced on Sokarevka later in the morning. It did so in tandem with the brigades of Kravchenko's 4th Tank Corps, which were attacking eastward on Rodin's right with orders to envelop German defenses at Marinovka with its right wing. Cautiously leading 26th Tank Corps' advance, Colonel Filippenko's 19th Tank Brigade captured Riumino-Krasnoiarskii, 14 kilometers northeast of Kalach, and Major Kudriashev's 157th Tank Brigade reached burial mounds +31 and +35, 5 to 6 kilometers southeast of Riumino-Krasnoiarskii, by 1000 hours. Farther south, the corps' 4th Motorized Brigade seized Hill 103.6, 10 kilometers south of Riumino-Krasnoiarskii, at midday.

On 26th Tank Corps' right and closer to Marinovka, Kravchenko's 4th Tank Corps advanced eastward from Platonovskii at about noon but immediately encountered strong defenses and extensive minefields and obstacles erected by 3rd Motorized Division. This brought Kravchenko's advance to an abrupt halt. By day's end, Kravchenko's brigades faced strong German defenses along Vaniukova *Balka*, a deep ravine that extended northward from the Karpovka River, 5 kilometers west of Marinovka, to the village of Illarionovskii, 10 kilometers northwest of Marinovka. The infantrymen of Colonel Lagutin's 293rd Rifle Division, who were supporting 26th and 4th Tank Corps' eastward thrust, also halted their advance along a line extending from west of Sokarevka southward to west of Illarionovskii.[45] Far to the rear, 21st Army's 63rd and 96th Rifle Divisions moved southeastward by forced march to rejoin their parent army. However, 21st Army's 333rd Rifle

Division, which received fresh orders after clearing Romanian forces from the region southwest of Raspopinskaia, now prepared to reinforce 5th Tank Army's advance to the Chir River.

Hard pressed by 3rd Guards Cavalry Corps' onslaught from the west and 65th Army's relentless assaults from the north and northwest, General Strecker's beleaguered XI Army Corps withdrew about half of 44th and 384th Infantry Divisions from their shrinking pocket northwest of the Don River by nightfall on 25 November. Simultaneously, General Hube withdrew XIV Panzer Corps' 14th Panzer Division back across the Don into new defensive positions in the Sokarevka region. This left 16th Panzer Division's *kampfgruppe* and two regiments each from 44th and 384th Divisions in the bridgehead to hold off the attacking Soviet 21st and 65th Armies. Hube also left his panzer corps' headquarters northwest of the Don to coordinate 16th Panzer's actions with those of XI Army Corps during the final withdrawal, which was planned for late the next day.

When 21st Army resumed its offensive at dawn on 26 November, its orders were to smash German 16th Panzer Division's defenses west of the Don once and for all, cross the river, and capture Peskovatka and Vertiachii. As before, the army's mission was to isolate and destroy the remnants of XI Army Corps and XIV Panzer Corps before they could escape southeastward across the river. However, this was not to be. Chistiakov's army was not only too weak in armor but also deficient in infantry and artillery. At this time, 63rd and 96th Rifle Divisions, with the bulk of the army's artillery, were still trudging southeastward from the Kletskaia region. Undeterred by these problems, Chistiakov resolved to rely on his infantry and cavalry, supported by whatever tanks were available, to overcome the Germans' defenses.

North of the Don River, 3rd Guards Cavalry Corps spearheaded 21st Army's advance with carefully organized assaults along two axes. Leaving one regiment of 277th Rifle Division to protect his corps' left flank from Hill 201.4 to just north of Luchenskii, Pliev dispatched the remainder of Chudesov's 32nd Cavalry Division, along with two regiments of Chernov's 277th Rifle Division, southward across the river at Luchenskii. This force was to reinforce the regiment of Chudesov's cavalry that had crossed the river the day before and, if possible, capture the town of Peskovatka. Simultaneously, Pliev sent Chepurkin's 5th Guards Cavalry and Tavartkiladze's 51st Guards Rifle Divisions southward across the river at Kartuli, 5 kilometers west of Luchenskii, to strike XIV Panzer Corps' defenses at Sokarevka from the north.[46]

After crossing the river and linking up with its regiment on the southern bank, Chudesov sent 86th Regiment, commanded by Major A. G. Bakanov, to conduct a surprise attack on Peskovatka, 5 kilometers to the south. By this time, the town was filled with German forces moving east or west to their new defensive positions. Achieving near-perfect surprise, Bakanov's regiment penetrated almost to the town's center, thoroughly disrupting the orderly German movements, before a force of tanks and motorized infantry from 14th Panzer Division counterattacked and cut off the regiment's retreat. During the ensuing fight, Major Bakanov, his chief of staff, and many of the regiment's cavalrymen perished, although a handful managed to escape the trap.[47] Despite losing almost a full regiment, 32nd Cavalry and 277th Rifle Divisions succeeded in besieging Peskovatka from two sides, rendering the position untenable to its German defenders.[48]

Meanwhile, farther south along the Don River, Chepurkin's 5th Guards Cavalry Division, followed by Tavartkiladze's 51st Guards Rifle Division, drove south across the river at Kartuli and reached the northern outskirts of Sokarevka, where they attacked 14th Panzer Division's defenses. German reports indicate that, before moving southward to the Kalach region, Colonel Belogorsky's 6th Guards Cavalry Division joined the struggle for Sokarevka, attacking the town from the northwest.[49] While 3rd Guards Cavalry Corps' cavalry and infantry divisions attacked Sokarevka from the north and northwest, a tank brigade from 26th Tank Corps assaulted the town from the south. This pressure from three sides threatened to collapse 14th Panzer's defenses until forces from 376th Infantry Division's 672nd and 767th Regiments, which had withdrawn from XI Army Corps' bridgehead south of Sirotinskaia on 24 November, reached Sokarevka. Once it was reinforced with infantry, 14th Panzer Division managed to hold 3rd Guards Cavalry Corps' forces at bay and restore the situation. However, here too, German defenses were far too tenuous to hold for long.

In 21st Army's sector south of the Don, Rodin's 26th Tank Corps had been reduced to fewer than 25 tanks and was now organized into two combat groups formed around the nuclei of 19th and 157th Tank and 4th Motorized Rifle Brigades. Nonetheless, it too took on XIV Panzer Corps' 14th Panzer Division, now supported by elements of the approaching 376th Infantry Division, in the region 6 kilometers southeast of Riumino-Krasnoiarskii and 14 kilometers north-northeast of Kalach. Rodin also dispatched one of these tank groups to join the fight on the southern outskirts of Sokarevka, 20 kilometers northeast of Kalach.

On 26th Tank Corps' right, one regiment from Colonel Lagutin's 293rd Rifle Division fought on the western outskirts of Illarionovskii, 16 kilometers east-northeast of Kalach, against elements of 3rd Motorized Division. The 293rd's other two regiments supported 4th Tank Corps' brigades fighting farther to the south. Now woefully understrength, the tank brigades of Kravchenko's 4th Tank Corps fought to overcome the defenses of XIV Panzer Corps' 3rd Motorized Division along Vaniukova *Balka*, 15 kilometers east of Kalach and 8 kilometers northeast of Sovetskii, but it recorded virtually no forward progress.

Capping Vasilevsky's first attempt to crush Sixth Army's pocket, on 27 November, Chistiakov's 21st Army, which by now had virtually all its forces on the Don's eastern bank, assaulted German defenses along the entire front from Peskovatka southward to Marinovka. By this time, however, the ferocity of the army's assaults had subsided. On the basis of orders received from the *Stavka* the previous evening, Vatutin had ordered Pliev's entire cavalry corps, together with 65th Army's 321st and 258th Rifle and 40th Guards Rifle Divisions, to deploy southward to reinforce 5th Tank Army's forces struggling to seize the German strongpoints of Oblivskaia and Surovikino on the Chir River and Rychkovskii on the Don.

Although deprived of 3rd Guards Cavalry Corps, Chistiakov continued to operate with a full complement of five rifle divisions now that 63rd and 96th Divisions had finally arrived forward. He supported his infantry with the rump elements of 26th and 4th Tank Corps. However, by this time, Chistiakov's offensive had essentially stalled opposite the ad hoc but formidable defenses erected by Sixth Army along its western front from Peskovatka southward to Marinovka. At midnight on the 27th, Vasilevsky signaled that this phase of combat was at an end when he transferred 21st Army from the Southwestern to the Don Front's control.

The subordination of Chistiakov's army to Rokossovsky's Don Front was clear evidence that Vasilevsky and the *Stavka* had finally acknowledged that their organization of forces for combat was seriously flawed. In short, they now understood why it was counterproductive to require the Southwestern Front to conduct active offensive operations simultaneously along two axes. Vatutin, it seemed, was simply incapable of being in two locations at the same time. By transferring 21st Army from the Southwestern to the Don Front, the *Stavka* unified under Rokossovsky's command all the forces attacking the northern and western perimeters of Sixth Army's Stalingrad pocket. For the time being, however, it left command relationships in the region south of Stalingrad intact.

By day's end on 27 November, Chistiakov's 21st Army had "shot its bolt" and was incapable of making substantial progress against Sixth Army's defenses. Nonetheless, just before midnight, Rokossovsky established the Don River north of Peskovatka as the boundary separating Chistiakov's 21st Army from Batov's 65th. This left Chistiakov's army with the task of operating along the 40-kilometer-wide front from the Don River southward past Peskovatka, Sokarevka, and Illarionovskii to the western approaches to Marinovka. At the time, 21st Army's 277th, 51st Guards, 96th, and 293rd Rifle Divisions were operating along this front, meaning that each division was occupying a sector roughly 10 kilometers wide. Since Chistiakov's fifth rifle division, the 63rd, was reorganizing into the new 52nd Guards Rifle Division, it would not come online until 30 November.

Chistiakov's two tank corps were also in bad shape. Rodin's 26th Tank Corps was so weak that its commander consolidated all its remaining tanks (perhaps as many as 25) in Colonel Filippenko's 19th Tank Brigade and all its motorized infantry in 4th Motorized Rifle Brigade. Kravchenko's 4th Tank Corps, which, with 30 to 35 tanks, was almost as weak, also consolidated its forces into a single brigade. The rifle and tank forces of 21st Army now faced elements of German 44th and 376th Infantry and 3rd Motorized Divisions, backed up by roughly 35 to 40 tanks subordinate to 16th and 14th Panzer Divisions. These defenses were anchored on strongpoints at Peskovatka, Sokarevka, Illarionovskii, and Marinovka, as well as the Shirokii and Vaniukova *Balkas* in between. For the moment, XIV Panzer Corps controlled these forces.

Therefore, even though 21st Army had managed to breach the Don River along its entire front, it was capable of doing little more. The only saving grace was that the Germans were just as weak and exhausted as Chistiakov's riflemen and *tankists*. Consequently, within 24 hours, the German forces opposite 21st Army's positions would conduct another withdrawal of roughly 15 kilometers to more defensible positions along the crest of a ridge extending from Marinovka northeastward to the small village of Borodin (from 20 kilometers east to 50 kilometers northeast of Kalach).

5th Tank Army
During the first phase of Vasilevsky's 25 November offensive, the most important task faced by Romanenko's 5th Tank Army was to reach the lower Chir River region and capture the Axis strongpoints at Oblivskaia, Surovikino, and Rychkovskii. The seizure of Rychkovskii was particularly important since it was the most logical location for the Germans to launch a relief operation toward Stalingrad from the west. Romanenko assigned this task to Butkov's 1st Tank Corps and the main body of Borisov's 8th Cavalry Corps, supported by whatever rifle forces could break loose from the fighting east of Chernyshevskaia and in and north of the Kurtlak River and reach the Chir Station region in time to join the attack. In addition to securing the line of the lower Chir River, 5th Tank Army had to clear XXXXVIII Panzer Corps' forces from the region east of the upper Chir, seize a bridgehead on the river's western bank at or near Chernyshevskaia, and smash Romanian Third Army's defenses in this region before they were reinforced by XXXXVIII Panzer Corps. Romanenko assigned these missions to most of 5th Tank Army's rifle divisions and 8th Cavalry Corps' 21st Cavalry Division.

Speed was of the essence in all these operations because Axis defenses along the Chir River were still pathetically weak and fragmented (see appendix 1 in the *Companion* for Romanian Third Army's order of battle on 23 November). Romanian Third Army's I and II Army Corps defended the sector along the Krivaia and Chir Rivers north of Chernyshevskaia, now under the control of ad hoc Army Group (literally, Attack Group [*Angriffsgruppe*]) Hollidt. Hollidt's attack group consisted of the following:

- German XVII Army Corps' 62nd and 294th Infantry Divisions and Romanian I Army Corps' 7th and 11th Infantry Divisions, defending along and northwest of the Krivaia River north of Bokovskaia;
- Romanian II Army Corps' 9th Infantry and 7th Cavalry Divisions, defending the Chir River front from Bokovskaia southward to Chernyshevskaia;
- XXXXVIII Panzer Corps' 22nd Panzer and Romanian 1st Armored Divisions (once they crossed to the Chir River's western bank), defending the Chir at and south of Chernyshevskaia; and
- Remnants of Romanian V and IV Army Corps' forces that withdrew westward over the Chir.

Romanian Third Army was responsible for defending the Chir River front from roughly 10 kilometers south of Chernyshevskaia southward and eastward through Oblivskaia and Surovikino to Rychkovskii on the Don; however, it was doing so under strict German supervision. This sector was defended by a dizzying array of ad hoc combat groups made up of German security forces; various "alarm" or alert groups [*alarmeinheiten*]; supply, construction, and railroad troops; rear service elements from Sixth Army and its subordinate divisions; replacement and convalescent troops; and *Luftwaffe Flak* and airfield support forces. Most of these groups took the names of the officers who commanded them.[50] The most important of these groups (deployed from left to right), together with their composition and location, were:

- Group Wandtke (to Group Spang on 24 November) (403rd Security Division's 610th Regiment)—from Chernyshevskaia southward to Ust'-Griaznovskii;
- Group Waldow (to Group Spang on 24 November) (403rd Security Division's 354th Regiment)—from Ust'-Griaznovskii southward to Lagutin, 7 kilometers southwest of Oblivskaia;
- Group VIII Air [*Flieger*] Corps (Group Fiebig) (Group Stahel by 24 November)—the Oblivskaia sector;
- Group von Stumpfeld (108th Artillery Command [ARKO])—the Surovikino sector;
- Group Adam (Group Goebel and Group Abraham on 24 November)—the Chirskii Station sector, headed by Colonel Adam, adjutant to General Paulus;

- Group Tzschöckel (the former Kalach garrison)—the Rychkovskii sector, headed by Colonel Tzschöckel, commander of 53rd Heavy Mortar Regiment;
- Group Schmidt (14th Panzer Division's rear)—east of Rychkovskii on 24 November, but to the Surovikino sector by 27 November;
- Group Korntner (to Group Selle on 28 November)—the Ostrovskii sector; and
- Group Selle (14th Panzer Division's rear)—the Nizhne-Chirskaia sector, but to the Ostrovskii sector by 30 November, headed by Sixth Army's chief of engineers.

While 26th Tank Corps readied its forces for transfer to 21st Army, on 25 November, General Butkov's 1st Tank Corps resumed operations to clear German forces from the western bank of the Don River south of Kalach and to capture both Rychkovskii and Surovikino (see appendix 6I in the *Companion*). The tank corps' understrength brigades managed to drive German security outposts from the Staromaksimovskii and Novomaksimovskii regions, 20 to 25 kilometer southeast of Surovikino, but they were thwarted in their attempts to seize Surovikino because of stubborn resistance by Group von Stumpfeld. However, the corps' reconnaissance detachments reached the northern bank of the Don River in the Samodurovka and Piatiizbianskii regions, 25 and 12 kilometers southwest of Kalach, respectively, and managed to establish contact with reconnaissance units from the Stalingrad Front's 4th Mechanized Corps on the river's southern bank. On the tank corps' right wing, its reconnaissance units reported that Surovikino was defended by two German infantry regiments and an artillery regiment. By day's end, with its strength reduced to just 20 operable tanks, the corps went over to the defense, awaiting the arrival of reinforcing rifle forces.

Roughly 30 kilometers to the west, 8th Motorcycle Regiment approached the northern outskirts of Oblivskaia by nightfall on 25 November. However, since it was clearly too weak to capture the town from the march, it too went on the defense and waited for reinforcements from 8th Cavalry Corps. In the motorcycle regiment's distant rear, 55th and 112th Cavalry Divisions of General Borisov's corps advanced southward from the Kurtlak River valley and captured the villages of Krasnoe Selo and Generalovskii, 28 kilometers north-northwest of Oblivskaia, at 1200 hours on the 25th. Thereafter, Borisov directed Colonel Chalenko's 55th Cavalry to gallop southward and reinforce 8th Motorcycle Regiment at Oblivskaia; he ordered General Shaimuratov's 112th Cavalry to march westward to the Chir River at the village of Osinovskii, 18 kilometers south-southeast of Chernyshevskaia, and seize a bridgehead across the river. Chalenko's 55th ended the day in the

Frolov and Nesterkin regions, 10 to 15 kilometers north of Oblivskaia, while Shaimuratov's 112th captured Osinovskii and a small bridgehead on the Chir's western bank.[51] Romanian Third Army's Group Waldow responded to this threat by dispatching 2nd Battalion, 354th Security Regiment, and part of the Gorlovka Alarm Battalion to contain Shaimuratov's advancing cavalry. This began a lengthy game of cat and mouse during which 5th Tank Army's cavalry and rifle forces exploited every opportunity to gain a foothold west of the river, and Romanian Third Army and Group Hollidt did all in their power to thwart such an eventuality.

Far behind the right wing of 8th Cavalry Corps' main body, General Iakunin's 21st Cavalry Division, now operating independently in 47th Guards Rifle Division's sector north of Chernyshevskaia, received orders late on 24 November to cross the Chir River and establish a bridgehead on the western bank early the next day. He left part of one regiment to help defend the village of Pichugin, 14 kilometers northwest of Chernyshevskaia, and part of another to hold the village of Rusakov, 2 kilometers east of Chernyshevskaia. The main body of Iakunin's cavalry division then crossed the Chir near the town of Chistiakovskaia, 6 kilometers northwest of Chernyshevskaia, and advanced roughly 2 kilometers deep into Romanian II Army Corps' rear. By the end of the day, 21st Cavalry had captured the villages of Stavidnianskii and Manokhin, 10 kilometers west to 10 kilometers northwest of Chernyshevskaia, and, in the process, encircled an entire regiment of Romanian 7th Cavalry Division.[52] Iakunin's cavalrymen established defenses, cordoned off the encircled Romanians, and were reinforced by a regiment from 47th Guards Division. The surprise Soviet cavalry assault across the Chir forced General Hollidt to order Group Wandtke to attempt a rescue the next day with its 610th Security Regiment and elements of Romanian 1st Armored and German 22nd Panzer Divisions, which had just escaped westward across the Chir.

Iakunin's cavalry foray on the morning of 25 November left General Fokanov's 47th Guards Rifle Division defending the more than 25-kilometer-wide sector extending from Pichugin southward to Osinovskii. Despite the fact that his division was overextended, Fokanov managed to exploit 21st Cavalry's deep thrust by sending his right-wing regiment westward across the river to occupy defenses on the eastern slope of Hill 178 on 21st Cavalry's left, 7 kilometers west of Chernyshevskaia. At the same time, the guards division's left-wing regiment supported 112th Cavalry Division's surprise advance across the Chir River at Osinovskii, 15 kilometers southeast of Chernyshevskaia. This left only 437th Regiment to defend the division's center, which included Chernyshevskaia proper and the area to its north and south.

Eager to exploit this apparent weakness in 47th Guards Division's dispositions, Romanian Third Army quickly ordered the only battle-hardened force at its disposal, the remnants of 22nd Panzer and Romanian 1st Armored Divisions, to counterattack and recapture the key Chir River town. Within hours after their harrowing escape westward to the region along the Chir, the remains of the two Axis divisions returned to action, reportedly with a force of 30 to 40 tanks and infantry mounted in up to 100 vehicles. The combined German and Romanian attack struck the rear of 47th Guards Division's 437th Regiment 2 kilometers southeast of Chernyshevskaia. According to 22nd Panzer Division's account of the battle, its *Kampfgruppe* Oppeln reached Rusakov at 0800 hours after a long overnight march from Hill 176.1, south of Bol'shaia Donshchinka, southwestward through Malaia Donshchinka, Medvezhyi, and Berezianka to the village of Rusakov. After reaching the hills northeast of Rusakov, Oppeln's group attacked at 1100 hours, led by the tanks of its 204th Panzer Regiment. Surprising the Soviets, the attacking force routed them, crossed the bridge over the Chir into Chernyshevskaia at 1230 hours, and captured it by 1500 hours.[53]

With its other two regiments out of supporting range, 473rd Regiment of Fokanov's 47th Guards Division lacked the necessary strength to retake the town. Therefore, at nightfall, General Romanenko ordered General Belov's 50th Guards Rifle Division, which was resting and refitting in the rear area after its struggle in the Bol'shaia Donshchinka region, to march southwestward to the upper Chir River in the sector from Krasnokutskaia southeastward to Rusakov. There, it was to join 47th Guards Rifle and 21st Cavalry Divisions and recapture Chernyshevskaia by enveloping it from the north.

While heavy fighting raged in the Chernyshevskaia region, 5th Tank Army's forces had cleared XXXXVIII Panzer Corps' divisions from the Bol'shaia Donshchinka and Kurtlak River regions. Once the tank army had secured the two regions and briefly rested and refitted, it was ordered to move southwestward and southward to support the army's forces already fighting along the upper and lower Chir River. These forces included Colonel Tolstov's 346th Rifle Division, Major V. G. Nikolov's 8th Guards Tank Brigade, and elements of 50th Guards and 119th Rifle Divisions. The first formation to receive new orders was 50th Guards Division, which Romanenko dispatched to the Chernyshevskaia region overnight on 25–26 November to assist the beleaguered 47th Guards Division. Records from 5th Tank Army indicate that, after ambushing and inflicting heavy losses on "a large enemy column" in the Medvezhyi region on 26 November, Nikolov's tank brigade was directed to rest and refit its forces. Tolstov's division, which had cooperated with Nikolov's tank brigade and 50th Guards and 119th Divisions in clearing the enemy, received orders to leave its second-echelon regiment and reserves in the Medvezhyi and Malaia Donshchinka regions and march southward to Petrovo and Kalach Kurtlak in the Kurtlak River valley. There, it was to relieve 47th Guards Rifle Division's regiments at and south of Chernyshevskaia and assist and then relieve 112th Cavalry Division in its bridgehead west of Osinovskii. Finally, Colonel Kulagin's 119th Rifle Division marched southward to capture Surovikino, relieve 1st Tank Corps so that it could concentrate in the Rychkovskii region, and then thrust southward across the lower Chir. Kulagin's division concentrated in the Zotovskii region, 15 kilometers southeast of Perelazovskii, at day's end.

As for 5th Tank Army's other forces, on the army's extreme right wing, Colonel Anashkin's 159th Rifle Division was to continue defending the sector along the upper Chir River from Khokhlachev on the Tsutskan' River, on 47th Guards Division's right, northwestward to Evlant'evskii, 5 kilometers southeast of Bokovskaia. Anashkin ensured that his division's right flank tied in closely with the left flank of 1st Guards Army's 14th Guards Rifle Division. Finally, 26th Tank Corps' 216th Tank Brigade, which had been detached from its parent corps to support 50th Guards (former 124th) Rifle Division, remained in 5th Tank Army's reserve until 4 December, when General Romanenko attached it to 1st Tank Corps to participate in its offensive southward across the Chir.[54]

At day's end on 25 November, General Romanenko submitted a report to Vatutin's headquaters summarizing his army's achievements during the first week of Uranus. In it, the commander declared that his tank army had advanced 140 kilometers and liberated 35,000 square miles of territory. In the process, it had destroyed Romanian 9th and 14th Infantry, 7th Cavalry, and 1st Armored Divisions; German 22nd Panzer Division; and most of Romanian 5th Infantry Division. With some exaggeration, the report claimed the tank army had killed 24,108 enemy troops; destroyed 221 tanks, 605 guns and mortars, 1,107 vehicles, 43 aircraft, and 482 carts; captured 27,632 enemy soldiers and officers, 254 tanks, 787 guns and mortars, 1,664 horses, 1,566 vehicles, 1,380 machine guns, 2 aircraft, 939 motorcycles, 101 warehouses, 289 transports, 6 locomotives, and 15 railroad cars; and liberated 5,450 Red Army prisoners of war.[55] The cost of the army's victory was 5,315 men, including 884 soldiers and officers killed and 4,187 wounded.[56] While some of these figures may have been close to reality, those applying to tanks and guns were not. For example, the assertion that 5th Tank Army had destroyed or captured a total of 475 tanks was wildly inaccurate, since the Germans lost just over 400 tanks and assault guns on the entire Eastern Front and in North Africa during November 1942.[57]

Although Romanenko did not reveal his army's overall tank strength in the report, he did note that 1st Tank Corps fielded 20 to 25 tanks and 26th Tank Corps somewhat fewer, since its 216th Tank Brigade was still attached to 50th Guards Rifle Division. The report also admitted that, while the tank army's structure was useful, it experienced serious command and control problems because of the varied nature and mobility of its component forces.[58]

What was most obvious to the Soviet chain of command late on 25 November was that the tank army had failed to accomplish its most critical missions—to capture Oblivskaia and Surovikino on the Chir and Rychkovskii on the Don and to destroy XXXXVIII Panzer Corps. However, Romanenko consoled himself with the knowledge that Borisov's cavalry had secured several bridgeheads across the upper Chir River, and the irksome German panzer corps was no longer in his rear. But he also realized that those footholds were small and tenuous, and his army would require more infantry if it was to retain those bridgeheads and drive German forces from Oblivskaia, Surovikino, and Rychkovskii. Therefore, overnight on 25–26 November, while exhorting his own forces forward, he requested infantry reinforcements from Vatutin. Responding quickly, the *front* immediately transferred 21st Army's 333rd Rifle Division to Romanenko's control and then reinforced the tank army with 321st and 258th Rifle and 40th Guards Rifle Divisions from 65th Army late on the 26th. But it would take at least another 24 hours before any of these divisions reached their final destinations along the Chir. In the meantime, Romanenko ordered his forces to continue fulfilling the missions they had received the previous day.

Butkov's 1st Tank Corps was still just a shadow of its former self, with fewer than 20 tanks, and resumed only limited offensive operations on 26 November. In an attempt to pry the stubborn Germans away from Rychkovskii, shortly after dawn, Butkov dispatched a single tank brigade reinforced by motorized infantry to attack Group Tzschöckel's defenses at the village of Skity, 6 kilometers east of Rychkovskii, as well as the railroad bridge across the Don River 5 kilometers farther south. German documents recorded the weakness of this attack, noting that infantry, supported by only four tanks, attacked the railroad bridge and that a force of 200 men and four tanks assaulted Skity.[59] After both attacks failed, 1st Tank Corps simply reported that its forces "occupied the Bol'shaia Osinovka, Novomaksimovskii, and Rychkovskii line, 15–35 kilometers southeast of Surovikino."[60]

If Butkov's 1st Tank Corps was too weak to accomplish its missions, 5th Tank Army's situation farther west along the Chir River was even worse. Because XXXXVIII Panzer Corps' resolute defense had blocked the tank army's advance for five days, most of Romanenko's forces gravitated to the Chir River sector from north of Chernyshevskaia southward to Oblivskaia. As a result, 5th Tank Army had only weak forces operating along the Chir River sector from Oblivskaia eastward through Surovikino to Rychkovskii on the Don. Appreciating this weakness, Romanenko dispatched Kulagin's 119th Rifle Division southward to fill this vacuum on 25 November and then sent the reinforcing 333rd, 321st, and 258th Rifle and 40th Guards Rifle Divisions southward as they came under his control. Until these forces reached the Chir, however, this sector of Romanian Third Army's defenses remained virtually unscathed. The ad hoc German groups defending this sector used the respite to strengthen their defenses. West of this broad gap in 5th Tank Army's attack formation, 8th Motorcycle Regiment fought in the Oblivskaia region, but it was too weak to even dent the defenses of Group Stahel's VIII Air [*Flieger*] Corps. However, the situation began to change on the afternoon of the 25th when the lead elements of 8th Cavalry Corps' 55th Cavalry Division finally reinforced the dismounted motorcycle troops, a fact duly noted by Oblivskaia's defenders.

If all was still quiet along the lower Chir River front, the same could not be said about the sector along the upper Chir River north and south of Chernyshevskaia. There, the situation ebbed and flowed as 5th Tank Army's forces fenced with those of Romanian Third Army. South of the town, 8th Cavalry Corps' 112th Cavalry Division expanded its bridgehead west of the river at Osinovskii on 26 November. Although now faced by 2nd Battalion, 354th Grenadier Regiment, and several alarm units, General Shaimuratov's cavalry succeeded in advancing north about 2 kilometers and capturing the village of Varlamovskii, 3 kilometers west of the river and 13 kilometers south of Chernyshevskaia.[61] By this time, 112th Division's axis of advance toward the north provided proof that 5th Tank Army sought to envelop Chernyshevskaia from the north and south with 112th and 21st Cavalry Divisions, supported by 47th and 50th Guards Rifle Divisions in the north and 346th Rifle Division in the south. However, this plan would work only if 50th Guards reached 21st Cavalry's sector and 346th Division reached 112th Cavalry's sector in time to bring the plan to fruition. Sadly for Romanenko, they did not.

At and north of Chernyshevskaia, 5th Tank Army's offensive slowed because the remnants of XXXXVIII Panzer Corps' 22nd Panzer and Romanian 1st Armored Divisions had recaptured the town the previous day.[62] The 5th Tank Army reported that, farther north, "after repulsing several enemy attacks," 21st Cavalry Division's forces in the bridgehead on the Chir's western bank were "halted along the Novomoskovka and Novosergeevka (8–10 kilometers northwest of Chernyshevskaia) line by day's end." In addition, on 21st Cavalry Division's left, Fokanov's 47th Guards Rifle Division "resisted enemy counterattacks against its left wing and, by day's end, occupied positions from the western outskirts of Chernyshevskaia to Hill 178.0 (7 kilometers west of Chernyshevskaia) and Osinovskii (16 kilometers southeast of Chernyshevskaia)."[63] In reality, 22nd Panzer Division's seizure of Chernyshevskaia and the counterattacks by German Group Wandtke west and northwest of the town halted any further advance by 112th Cavalry Division and the supporting regiment from 47th Guards Division.

However, 5th Tank Army's situation in the sector north of Chernyshevskaia improved significantly on 26 November when General Belov's 50th Guards Rifle Division reached the scene.[64] After completing a 20-kilometer march, 148th, 150th, and 152nd Regiments of Belov's guards division reached the Chir River between Rusakov and Illarionov, 2 kilometers east and 15 kilometers northwest of Chernyshevskaia, respectively, at about midday. Deploying for action, Belov's regiments assaulted Romanian 14th Infantry Division north of Chistiakovskaia and 22nd Panzer Division at Chernyshevskaia proper, forced their way across the river, and captured Chernyshevskaia, Leont'evskii, Novosergeevka, Novomoskovka, and Starikov, the most important villages in its sector. The division's most successful regiment, 150th Guards, pushed 6 kilometers west from Novosergeevka and captured Hill 188.0, 2 kilometers northwest of the village of Stavidnianskii. At the time, 21st Cavalry Division's right wing and the supporting regiment from 47th Guards Division were located only 4 kilometers south of Stavidnianskii. Thus, unless something was done to rescue it, a large portion of Romanian 14th Infantry Division faced possible encirclement and destruction.

To deal with this crisis, General Hollidt committed all his available forces to contain the Soviet bridgeheads at and north of Chernyshevskaia, including Group Wandtke's 610th Security Regiment, various alarm battalions, Romanian 14th Infantry and 7th Cavalry Divisions, and XXXXVIII Panzer Corps' exhausted 22nd Panzer and Romanian 1st Armored Divisions. The ensuing fight would last well into early December and end with Chernyshevskaia still in German hands. However, because XXXXVIII Panzer Corps and Romanian II Army Corps focused their attention and forces north of Chernyshevskaia, 5th Tank Army's forces south of the town were more successful than their comrades to the north. Finally, on 26 November, 159th Rifle Division, which anchored 5th Tank Army's right flank east of the junction of the Krivaia and Chir Rivers, continued to repel attacks by small groups of enemy along the Evlant'evskii and Illarionov line, 17 to 25 kilometers northwest of Chernyshevskaia.

On 27 November, the best that could be said about 5th Tank Army's offensive along the lower Chir River was that it remained stagnant. There, the absence of reserves necessary to reinvigorate offensive operations led to no progress whatsoever in the sector from Oblivskaia eastward to Rychkovskii. However, along the upper Chir, north and south of Chernyshevskaia, it was a different story. There, the ability of XXXXVIII Panzer Corps' 22nd Panzer and Romanian 1st Armored Divisions to survive as credible forces capable of fighting another day enabled Attack Group Hollidt to prevent 5th Tank Army's cavalry and infantry from expanding their bridgehead north of Chernyshevskaia. However, the arrival of 346th Rifle Division south of the town, where German and Romanian defenses were far weaker, led to modest Soviet success.

Along the lower Chir River, Butkov's 1st Tank Corps, still weak to the point of ineffectiveness, skirmished with defending German groups along the

front from the village of Zhirkov, 6 kilometers northeast of Surovikino, southeastward through the villages of Bol'shaia Osinovka and Eritskii to the northern and eastern approaches to Rychkovskii, 28 kilometers east-southeast
of Surovikino. German Group Tzschöckel reported a battalion-size attack on
its defenses at Rychkovskii from the north, and Group Schmidt was attacked
at Surovikino by an estimated battalion of infantry with only two supporting
tanks.[65] The only disconcerting news for the Germans along the lower Chir
was that a battalion of Soviet infantry with three T-34 tanks attacked the
northernmost subgroup of Group Selle, which was defending the eastern
bank of the Don opposite Nizhne-Chirskaia. Although this small Soviet force
was repelled by the 200-man group defending Selle's left wing, it turned out
to be the forward elements of a tank regiment subordinate to Vol'sky's 4th
Mechanized Corps of the Stalingrad Front's 51st Army.[66] This meant that a
new threat to German defenses along the lower Chir was materializing from
the east and southeast.

Despite 5th Tank Army's lack of success along the lower Chir River and
the relative lull in combat activity that ensued, German defenses in this region remained very weak and precarious. For example, Romanian Third
Army's records indicate that Group Schmidt's forces defending Surovikino
numbered only 4,500 men. In addition, Group Korntner, which manned
defenses in the 15-kilometer-wide sector southeast of Surovikino, counted
only 500 troops; Group Adam, which protected the 10-kilometer-wide sector from south of Novomaksimovskii to southeast of Chirskii Station, fielded
2,500 men; Group Tzschöckel at Rychkovskii numbered about 1,000 men;
and the four subgroups of Group Selle, which defended the Don River front
around Nizhne-Chirskaia, had a total of only about 750 men.[67] Although this
force of more than 9,000 troops could certainly contain the weakened 1st
Tank Corps, it would be far more difficult to do so effectively against the
three to four Soviet rifle divisions en route to the region.

More than 40 kilometers west of 1st Tank Corps' positions near Rychkovskii, the main forces of 8th Cavalry Corps' 55th and 112th Cavalry Divisions finally went into action against VIII *Flieger* Corps' defenses at
Oblivskaia on 27 November. The night before, General Shaimuratov's 112th
Cavalry Division had turned its bridgehead west of the Chir River at Osinovskii over to 346th Rifle Division and then marched southward to join
Colonel Chalenko's 55th Cavalry north of Oblivskaia. After relieving 8th Motorcycle Regiment, the two cavalry divisions launched several assaults against
the *Luftwaffe Flak* forces defending the town. At nightfall on the 26th, Borisov reported to Vatutin that his dismounted cavalry had "half encircled enemy forces [Group Stahel] in the Oblivskaia region from the west, north,
and east and reached the railroad line 2 kilometers south of Riabovskii, 5
kilometers southwest of Oblivskaia."[68] German records confirm this account,

asserting that elements of two cavalry divisions conducted a concerted assault on Hill 106.0 north of the town but were repulsed.[69] This determined defense by Group Stahel's more than 5,000 men also indicated that it would take more than dismounted cavalry to capture the strongpoint of Oblivskaia.

The heaviest fighting in 5th Tank Army's sector on 27 November took place in the vicinity of Chernyshevskaia. At the town proper and to the north, German forces assaulted the defenses of General Belov's 50th Guards Rifle Division, which had captured the town and seized a large bridgehead on the Chir's western bank north of the town the day before (see appendix 6J in the *Companion* for a Soviet description of 50th Guards Division's fight for Chernyshevskaia). The Red Army General Staff's daily summary for 27 November cryptically noted, "50th Gds. RD occupied defenses along the Krasnoiarovka, Zakharchenskii, and Novoriabukhin line (5–12 kilometers southeast of Chernyshevskaia) and fought on the eastern outskirts of Chernyshevskaia in cooperation with 47th Gds. RD."[70] The same summary recorded that "47th Gds. RD has been fighting in the Chernyshevskaia region and to the south since the morning of 27 November."[71] In neither case did the summary acknowledge that German forces had recaptured the town.

Romanian Third Army's records confirm that 22nd Panzer Division, supported on the right by Romanian 1st Armored Division, did indeed recapture Chernyshevskaia on 27 November. But they also indicate that Group Wandtke's assault against 21st Cavalry Division's defenses at Paramonov (9 kilometers west of Chernyshevskaia), which the cavalry division had captured earlier in the day, failed.[72] This failure meant that Iakunin's cavalry division and the reinforcing regiment from 47th Guards Division still held a sizable bridgehead northwest and west of Chernyshevskaia. More threatening for the Germans was the fact that Iakunin's bridgehead was now less than a kilometer away from the main road leading from the headquarters of XXXXVIII Panzer Corps and Romanian 7th Cavalry and 1st Armored Divisions in Kuteinikov, 20 kilometers to the southwest, and their troops in Chernyshevskaia. Thus, any further Soviet advance in this sector would sever XXXXVIII Panzer Corps' main supply and communications route to its divisions fighting in the Chernyshevskaia region.

Along the Chir River south of Chernyshevskaia, the single regiment of 47th Guards Division relieved 112th Cavalry Division in its bridgehead at Varlamov, west of Osinovskii and the river, permitting Shaimuratov's cavalry to march southward to Oblivskaia. However, the General Staff's daily summary also stated that "346th RD occupied defenses along the Petrovka and Golubinka line (15–28 kilometers east of Chernyshevskaia)."[73] If this is accurate, it is also likely that Colonel Tolstov's division sent advance parties to the positions along the Chir River it was supposed to deploy into that day. The obvious delay in the movement of the division's main forces may have been associated with the impending relief of Colonel Tolstov by Major General D. I. Stankevsky, which occurred officially on 28 November.[74]

Finally, on 5th Tank Army's extreme right wing along the upper Chir River, all remained relatively quiet in the sector of Colonel Anashkin's 159th Rifle Division. It still occupied defenses on the river's northern bank from Il-larionov, 15 kilometers northwest of Chernyshevskaia, through Evlant'evskii to Dulenskii, 4 kilometers east of Bokovskaia, on 50th Guards Division's right. Throughout the day, it faced the left wing of Romanian II Army Corps' 14th Infantry Division, whose main forces were locked in heavy fighting with 50th Guards Division farther south. Reportedly, Anashkin's division sent part of its left-wing regiment to help 50th Guards Division's 152nd Regiment repel several attacks by Romanian forces east of the village of Fomin, 18 ki-lometers northwest of Chernyshevskaia.

Thus, during the first three days of Vasilevsky's resumed offensive, Ro-manenko's 5th Tank Army failed to fulfill its most important mission—the sei-zure of Rychkovskii, Surovikino, and Oblivskaia and the northern bank of the lower Chir River. In mitigation, the tank army could claim that it breached Axis defenses in the Chernyshevskaia region. But even there, its gains were tenuous, largely because Romanenko's army allowed a sizable proportion of XXXXVIII Panzer Corps to escape westward across the Chir. Although no evidence exists of any official rebuke of the tank army's commander, Vasi-levsky and Vatutin could not have been pleased. The poor performance of Romanenko's army failed to eliminate the possibility of a future German relief effort east toward Stalingrad from the vital Rychkovskii bridgehead. For the time being, however, they accepted Romanenko's excuses about the weakness of his army and responded to his requests for reinforcements by sending him four more rifle divisions. They could only hope that Romanenko would employ them effectively.

1st Guards Army

While the Southwestern Front's 21st Army and 5th Tank Army were fight-ing major battles along widely separate axes along the inner and outer en-circlement fronts of the Stalingrad pocket, General Leliushenko's 1st Guards Army was fighting its own "little war" against Romanian and German forces defending the salient that formed a right angle between the Don and Krivaia Rivers. On 23 and 24 November, Leliushenko's divisions attacked to collapse the defenses of Romanian I Army Corps' 11th and 7th Infantry Divisions on the northern and eastern flanks of the salient. By doing so, they also threat-ened the right flank of Italian Eighth Army, which was defending the Don River front farther to the northwest. During these attacks, the army's 203rd and 266th Rifle and 14th Guards Rifle Divisions seized a bridgehead 5 to 16 kilometers deep on the Krivaia River's western bank. This prompted General

Hollidt, commander XVII Army Corps and his newly formed Attack Group Hollidt, to order German 62nd and 294th Infantry Divisions to launch counterattacks from the Kruzhilin and Bokovskaia regions to destroy the Soviet force west of the Krivaia River and regain the lost territory.

Early on 25 November, 1st Guards Army was deployed with its 1st, 153rd, 197th, and 278th Rifle Divisions occupying positions along the salient's northern flank, which extended from Nizhnyi Mamon south of the Don eastward to the Krivaia River south of the village of Iagodnyi. On this group's left wing, Major General D. P. Monakhov's 278th Rifle Division manned defenses extending from Hill 204.0, 2 kilometers west of Bakhmutkin on the Krivaia River, westward to Verkhnyi Krivskoi, 6 kilometers northwest of Iagodnyi. Along the salient's eastern flank, 14th Guards and 266th and 203rd Rifle Divisions defended a bridgehead west of the Krivaia River in the 28-kilometer-wide sector from Kon'kov, 4 kilometers north of Bokovskaia, northward to Hill 204.0, as follows:

- 14th Guards Division (Major General Griaznov)—from the eastern approaches to Kon'kov, 10 kilometers west of the Krivaia River and 4 kilometers north of Bokovskaia, northward 8 kilometers past Vislogubov and Nizhnyi Luchki to the southern edge of Gorbatovskii State Farm, 10 kilometers west-southwest of Dubovoi;
- 266th Rifle Division (Major General L. V. Vetoshnikov)—from the southern edge of Gorbatovskii State Farm, 10 kilometers west-southwest of Gorbatovskii on the Krivaia River, northward 8 kilometers to the southern slope of Hill 220.0, 8 kilometers west of Dubovoi; and
- 203rd Rifle Division (Major General G. S. Zdanovich)—from the eastern slope of Hill 220.0, 7 kilometers west of the villages of Rubashkin and Dubovoi on the Krivaia River, northward 12 kilometers to Hill 204.0, 2 kilometers west of Bakhmutkin.

Attack Group Hollidt struck back at 1st Guards Army's bridgehead on the western bank of the Krivaia River at dawn on 25 November. The group's records indicate that the ration strength of German XVII Army Corps at that time was 62,294 men, although it is unclear whether this included Romanian 7th and 11th Infantry Divisions.[75] The 62nd and 294th Infantry Divisions each fielded more than 12,000 men, but Romanian 7th and 11th Infantry Divisions were somewhat smaller. For comparison's sake, the ration strength of Leliushenko's 1st Guards Army was in excess of 140,000 men and 162 tanks.[76] However, 14th Guards and 266th, 203rd, and 278th Rifle Divisions operating in the sector along and west of the Krivaia River probably numbered about 40,000 men.

Group Hollidt's counterattack amounted to a double envelopment, with

62nd Infantry Division advancing eastward from Kruzhilin as its northern pincer and 294th Infantry Division thrusting northeastward from Bokovskaia as its southern. The attack caught 14th Guards and 203rd Rifle Divisions by surprise, just after they had been placed under the command of the new headquarters of 14th Rifle Corps. The two attacking German divisions forced the two Soviet divisions to withdraw behind the Krivaia River in considerable disorder, with the Germans in pursuit (see appendix 6I in the *Companion*). That evening, General Leliushenko ordered 14th Rifle Corps to counterattack on the morning of the 27th and employ its 266th Rifle Division, which had been withdrawn into the corps' reserve the night before, to spearhead its assaults (see appendix 6K in the *Companion* for 266th Division's description of the battle).[77]

Although the General Staff's description of the fighting in 1st Guards Army's sector put a "happy face" on the situation, its stark description of the first two days of fighting made it clear that Group Hollidt's 62nd and 294th Infantry Divisions had indeed made mincemeat of 1st Guards Army's defenses west of the Krivaia River; in places, the Germans had even crossed the river and driven deeply into the defenses on the army's left wing. Faced with this deteriorating situation, Leliushenko's army struck back early on 27 November, with strong counterattacks by 266th Rifle and 14th Guards Rifle Divisions. Even though the General Staff's account tacitly acknowledges that 14th Rifle Corps' counterattack failed, it provides no explanation as to why. Other sources fill in the gap by admitting that 14th Corps' counterattack was poorly organized; it committed the two divisions to combat in piecemeal fashion, several regiments at a time. As a result, the counterattack failed, and 266th Rifle Division lost an entire regiment.[78] Hollidt's 62nd Infantry Division pressed 278th and 203rd Rifle Divisions back to shallow defenses along the Krivaia River's western bank, and his 294th Infantry Division drove 14th Guards Division across the river and seized a sizable bridgehead on the east bank. The mere presence of parts of two relatively strong German divisions along and east of the Krivaia River posed an immediate threat to 5th Tank Army's right flank. If the attacks developed further, and if Hollidt's two divisions managed to continue their advance southeastward along the Chir River's northern bank, they would pose a deadly threat not only to 5th Tank Army's forces in the Chernyshevskaia region but also to the entire Southwestern Front.

To ease the pain of the disconcerting news about 1st Guards Army's troubles, the General Staff included the army's "trophy count" in its summary, noting under the heading "Trophies of the [Southwestern] Front" that "1,400 enemy troops were killed, 1,400 enemy soldiers and officers were captured, 19 guns, 44 machine guns, 30 vehicles, and 300 horses were seized, and 300 Red Army men were liberated from German captivity."[79]

Conclusions

The 21st, 5th Tank, and 1st Guards Armies of Vatutin's Southwestern Front actually accomplished very little in three days of often intense fighting. Although Chistiakov's 21st Army made it across the Don River in the Peskovatka and Sokarevka sectors, German XI Army Corps and XIV Panzer Corps were able to conduct a fairly systematic withdrawal from their bridgehead in the northwestern corner of the Great Bend of the Don. Once across the river, Chistiakov's army made pathetically slow progress in pressing the forces defending the western front of Sixth Army's Stalingrad pocket back toward the east.

Likewise, Romanenko's 5th Tank Army failed to achieve any of its major objectives. At nightfall on 27 November, the towns of Surovikino and Oblivskaia on the Chir and Rychkovskii on the Don remained firmly in German hands, along with most of the northern and southern banks of the lower Chir River. The only successes Romanenko's army registered were in the Chernyshevskaia region, and even there, Group Hollidt's defeat of 1st Guards Army's forces along the southern Krivaia River posed a deadly threat to 5th Tank Army's right wing.

However, changes were in the wind, largely because of Vatutin's decision to transfer Pliev's 3rd Guards Cavalry Corps to Romanenko's 5th Tank Army. In fact, Romanenko was so enthusiastic about the promised reinforcements that he issued an order late on 26 November indicating precisely how he planned to employ Pliev's corps. The order, which took the form of a mission statement, read, "8th Cavalry Corps, with 174th TDR and 321st RD, will occupy and firmly defend the Parshin, Oblivskaia, and Frolov sector. . . . 1st Tank Corps, with 33rd TDR, together with 3rd Cavalry Corps, will capture Verkhne-Solontsovskii [25 kilometers south of the Chir] and hold on to it firmly."[80] This order required 1st Tank and 3rd Guards Cavalry Corps to penetrate Axis defenses along the lower Chir and advance 25 to 30 kilometers south of the river. Unfortunately for Romanenko, the order was superfluous because Pliev's cavalry corps did not reach its designated assembly area along the lower Chir River until 28 November. Even then, it took another week for Romanenko to organize his new offensive.

Based on the Southwestern Front's mediocre accomplishments from 25 to 27 November, Vasilevsky had every reason to question the feasibility of assigning Vatutin's *front* objectives along axes that were so widely divergent.

The Don Front

Unlike in Vatutin's Southwestern Front, all three armies subordinate to Rokossovsky's Don Front shared a common mission—to smash the northern front of Sixth Army's Stalingrad pocket and begin liquidating the encircled army (see map 29). To fulfill that mission, Batov's 65th Army and Galanin's 24th Army were to encircle and liquidate Sixth Army's XI Army Corps and XIV Panzer Corps in the salient they occupied in the Great Bend of the Don River's northwestern corner and then collapse the northern front of Sixth Army's pocket south of the Don. Simultaneously, Zhadov's 66th Army was to smash the defenses of Sixth Army's LI Army Corps along the northeastern front of its pocket, link up with the Stalingrad Front's 62nd Army near Gorodishche, and assist in Sixth Army's destruction (see appendix 6L in the *Companion* for the Don Front's accomplishments on 25–27 November).

As simple as his missions seemed, Rokossovsky still faced two major problems that had plagued him since day one of Operation Uranus. First, relative to the two other attacking *fronts*, his armies were numerically weak; second, except for Batov's 65th, these armies were still attacking well-prepared defenses in depth manned by German troops. Within 24 hours, Rokossovsky would face a third problem: orders from Vasilevsky transferring some of his divisions to other *fronts*. Since the Southwestern Front was encountering serious difficulties in accomplishing its missions, Vasilevsky naturally reinforced Vatutin's *front* at the expense of Rokossovsky's, further weakening the latter's armies. Sixth Army contributed to Rokossovsky's problem by successfully withdrawing XI Army Corps and XIV Panzer Corps from their exposed positions in the Great Bend of the Don to more contiguous defenses south of the river. Initially, at least, this facilitated 65th Army's advance and, in turn, persuaded Vasilevsky of the wisdom of transferring forces from the Don to the Southwestern Front, where there seemed to be a greater promise of success. Coupled with the German withdrawal, the weakening of Rokossovsky's armies made it even harder for them to overcome Sixth Army's defenses south of the Don.

On the positive side of the ledger, as Sixth Army withdrew, its forces began to lose their customary high degree of cohesiveness. Many German sources describe increasing disorganization and even outright panic in the German ranks, especially in the rear services of XI Army and XIV Panzer Corps as they withdrew their forces behind the Don. Similar events took place to a lesser degree in the Orlovka sector, where the sharp defeat of 94th Infantry Division south of Erzovka on 24 November undermined the morale of its survivors, as well as soldiers in adjacent formations. However, the subsequent durability of Sixth Army's defenses around the Stalingrad pocket proves without a doubt that these reports about pervasive confusion and panic in the German ranks were significantly exaggerated.

65th Army
The divisions of Batov's 65th Army resumed their advance against Sixth Army's XI Army Corps and XIV Panzer Corps early on 25 November (see map

30 and appendix 6L in the *Companion*). The two German corps responded by systematically withdrawing their forces south toward the Don River in the sector from Peskovatka northward to Verkhnyi Akatov. Previous accounts of the fighting in this region made it difficult, if not impossible, to track which forces the Germans evacuated and which formations of 65th Army took part in this fighting and when. However, the newly released daily summaries of the Red Army General Staff issued from 26 to 28 November provide a fairly clear mosaic of 65th Army's advance.

To set the stage for the final three days of fighting in the northeastern corner of the Great Bend of the Don, German XI Army Corps, which was reinforced by XIV Panzer Corps by 23 November, had already begun transferring forces south of the Don River on 22 November. These forces, which moved southward across the river regiment by regiment, either reinforced 76th Infantry Division, which was under attack by Soviet 24th Army on the Don's eastern bank north of Vertiachii, or manned defenses on the western or northeastern fronts of Sixth Army's final Stalingrad pocket (see table 28).

On the morning of 25 November, German forces defending XI Army Corps' 18- by 18-kilometer-square bridgehead included the *kampfgruppe* from XIV Panzer Corps' 16th Panzer Division, which was defending the western sector of the bridgehead from Malonabatovskii northward to east of Evlampievskii and Golubinskii, and five infantry regiments fighting under the control of XI Army Corps' 44th and 384th Infantry Divisions, which were defending positions extending in a broad arc from east of Golubinskii northeastward to north of Kuborozhnyi and then southeastward to the Don River south of Trekhostrovskaia.[81]

Batov's army conducted its attack, more accurately described as a slow pursuit, with 24th, 304th, and 252nd Rifle Divisions deployed from left to right in the arc-shaped sector extending northwestward 14 kilometers from just south of Trekhostrovskaia on the Don River to just south of Podgorskii on the Don, and then southward 24 kilometers to the area just northeast of Golubinskii. Batov's offensive plan required Colonel Prokhorov's 24th Rifle Division, which was positioned on the army's left, to advance southward in the sector from south of Trekhostrovskaia northwestward to south of Podgorskii. On the 24th's right, but committed from the second echelon, Colonel Merkulov's 304th Rifle Division was to attack southeastward in the sector from Rodionov southward to Kubantseva *Balka*, 8 kilometers north of Evlampievskii. Finally, on the right wing of Batov's army, Colonel Shekhtman's 252nd Rifle Division was to advance eastward in the sector from Kubantseva *Balka* south to northeast of Golubinskii. To provide armor support for the advancing troops, Batov assigned 91st Tank Brigade to support Merkulov's division and 121st Tank Brigade to support Prokhorov's division. The right flank of Shekhtman's 252nd Rifle Division was closely tied in with the left

Table 28. XI Army Corps' and XIV Panzer Corps' Defense of and Withdrawal from the Sirotinskaia Bridgehead, 22–27 November 1942

22 NOVEMBER
- XI Army Corps' withdrawals:
  - 384th Infantry Division's 536th Regiment to reinforce 76th Infantry Division
  - 44th Infantry Division's 134th Regiment to south of the Don River
- Bridgehead defenses at day's end (left to right):
  - 14th Panzer Division, with 44th Infantry Division's 132nd Regiment and 384th Infantry Division's 534th Regiment
  - 376th Infantry Division's 672nd, 673rd, and 767th Regiments, with 3rd Battalion, 131st Regiment, of 44th Infantry Division
  - 44th Infantry Division's 131st Regiment (without 3rd Battalion)
  - 384th Infantry Division's 535th Regiment

23 NOVEMBER
- XI Army Corps' withdrawals:
  - 376th Infantry Division's 672nd and 673rd Regiment to XI Corps' rear area
- Bridgehead defenses at day's end:
  - XIV Panzer Corps:
    - *Kampfgruppe*, 16th Panzer Division
    - *Kampfgruppe*, 24th Panzer Division
  - XI Army Corps:
    - 14th Panzer Division, with 44th Infantry Division's 132nd Regiment and 384th Infantry Division's 534th Regiment
    - 44th Infantry Division's 131st Regiment and 376th Infantry Division's 767th Regiment
    - 384th Infantry Division's 535th Regiment

24 NOVEMBER
- XIV Panzer Corps' withdrawals:
  - 24th Panzer Division to south of the Don River and Orlovka region
- XI Army Corps' withdrawals:
  - 376th Infantry Division's 672nd and 673rd Regiments to south of the Don River
  - 14th Panzer Division to south of the Don River
- Bridgehead defense at day's end:
  - XIV Panzer Corps: *kampfgruppe*, 16th Panzer Division
  - XI Army Corps:
    - 44th Infantry Division's 131st and 132nd Regiments, with 376th Infantry Division's 767th Regiment
    - 384th Infantry Division's 534th and 535th Regiments

25 NOVEMBER
- XI Army Corps' withdrawals:
  - 376th Infantry Division's 767th Regiment to south of the Don River
- Bridgehead defenses at day's end:
  - XIV Panzer Corps: *kampfgruppe*, 16th Panzer Division
  - XI Army Corps:
    - 44th Infantry Division's 131st and 132nd Regiments
    - 384th Infantry Division's 534th and 535th Regiments

26 NOVEMBER (to 1600 hours)
- XI Army Corps' withdrawals:
  - 384th Infantry Division's 534th and 535th Regiments to south of the Don River
- Bridgehead defenses after midday:
  - XIV Panzer Corps: *kampfgruppe*, 16th Panzer Division
  - 44th Infantry Division's 131st and 132nd Regiments

Table 28. (continued)

26 NOVEMBER (after 1600 hours)
- XI Army Corps' withdrawals:
  - ° 44th Infantry Division's 131st and 132nd Regiments
- XIV Panzer Corps' withdrawals:
  - ° *Kampfgruppe*, 16th Panzer Division, to south of the Don River, protected by a company from 64th Panzer-Grenadier Regiment

Sources: Sixth Army's daily records in Florian Freiherr von und zu Aufsess, *Die Anlagenbänder zu den Kriegstagebüchern der 6. Armee, Band II* (Schwabach: Januar, 2006), 18–42; daily maps in "KTB-Karten, Nov 1942–Jan 1943, AOK 6," 30155/37 file, in NAM T-312, roll 1459.

flank of 21st Army's 76th Rifle Division, which was attacking eastward from the Evlampievskii region in tandem with 3rd Guards Cavalry Corps' 32nd Cavalry Division. In addition, Batov ordered Colonel Glebov's 27th Guards Rifle Division, in army reserve, to shift northward from its previous position behind the army's right wing and concentrate in the Zimovskii, Khmelevskii, and Karaitskii region, 4 to 9 kilometers southeast of Sirotinskaia. Glebov's guardsmen were to be prepared to conduct what Batov hoped would be the final assault on XI Corps' bridgehead on 26 November.

Attacking shortly after dawn, the three rifle divisions and two tank brigades pushed forward up to 8 kilometers during the day, meeting only light resistance by truck-mounted rear guards detailed to protect the withdrawal of 16th Panzer, 44th, and 384th Infantry Divisions.[82] General Batov later described the fighting:

> While withdrawing to the crossings, the enemy left mobile detachments behind: sub-machine gunners with tanks, antitank guns, and roaming six-barreled mortars. Now our units had to deal chiefly with the remnants of German 44th and 384th Divisions, which were being forced back from the north to the center of the great bend of the Don in trucks. The nature of the fighting was a parallel pursuit of the defeated enemy. Mobile detachments were operating in front of Shekhtman's, Prokhorov's, and V. S. Glebov's divisions. They cleaned the *balkas* and heights of firing points and intercepted the routes of the withdrawing German units. The headquarters of 252nd Division reported on 25 November: "During the day, 103 vehicles, 3 aircraft, 52 guns, and 32 antitank guns were seized."
>
> The same day Prokhorov informed me by telephone, "We have trophies—sixty vehicles and forty-five guns of various calibers. . . . You asked about prisoners? Not many, only thirty. But today we liberated 116 Red Army men from Fascist captivity. They looked strange, Comrade

commander! They were skeletons, left to decay. The clothes on them were in rags."[83]

The 65th Army's advance on 25 November reduced the size of the German bridgehead in the Don's bend by roughly half. At day's end, the four weakened regiments of 44th and 384th Infantry Divisions clung to defenses around a 6- to 10-kilometer-deep bridgehead anchored on the town of Akimovskii on the western bank of the Don, 3 kilometers northwest of Vertiachii.

While three divisions of Batov's army were engaged in the bridgehead fight, the army commander prepared many of his remaining divisions for transfer elsewhere. The night before, in accordance with an order from the *Stavka*, Rokossovsky informed Batov that he would have to transfer three divisions to the Southwestern Front's 5th Tank Army. This was in addition to 321st Rifle Division, which Vasilevsky had directed Batov to prepare for transfer to the same army late on 23 November. This meant a total of four divisions—4th and 40th Guards and 258th and 321st Rifle—would be transferred to Vatutin's *front*. These four divisions, as well 65th Army's 23rd Rifle Division, concentrated in assembly areas in the army's rear, awaiting further orders, by nightfall on 25 November.[84]

On the night of 25 November, after the fighting ended, Rokossovsky directed Batov to send 4th and 40th Guards and 258th and 321st Rifle Divisions to Romanenko's 5th Tank Army the following day. This left Batov's army with Colonel Glebov's 27th Guards Division, which was in assembly areas in the Khmelevskii and Karaitskii region, 8 to 10 kilometers southeast of Sirotinskaia, preparing to reenter the fighting on 26 November, and one division in reserve, Colonel P. P. Bakhrameev's 23rd Rifle.

Nonetheless, with its reduced complement, 65th Army resumed its pursuit early on 26 November. Actually, it began operations the night before, just after XI Army Corps' 44th and 384th Infantry Divisions carried out the next step in their withdrawal. As on previous nights, 65th Army's advancing divisions sent out forward detachments in the darkness to detect where the two German divisions would next defend. The 24th, 304th, and 252nd Rifle Divisions' main bodies resumed their advance at dawn.[85]

Given the complexity of the pursuit, even 65th Army was unable to precisely define the location of its attacking units at day's end. For example, Colonel Prokhorov's 24th "Iron" Division was supposed to advance southward through the hills south of Trekhostrovskaia, overcome 384th Infantry Division's rear guards, force its way across the Don River in the vicinity of Verkhnyi Gerasimovskii (Gerasimov) Farm, and then attack southwestward along the southern bank of the Don to capture Vertiachii. However, after beginning its assault in the morning, Prokhorov's division advanced only 4 kilometers before stalling under intense enemy fire in the vicinity of Nizhnyi Akatov, 2 to 3 kilometers north of Verkhnyi Gerasimovskii. When Prokhorov's attack stalled, Batov committed Colonel Glebov's 27th Guards Rifle Division into combat. Deploying forward 15 kilometers from the Karaitskii region, Glebov's guardsmen went into action at about 1200 hours. Their mission was to attack southeastward along the Kuborozhnyi and Kisliakov axis and capture Verkhnyi Akatov on 24th Division's right. Glebov's guardsmen did so successfully, pressing forward to the northern and western approaches to Verkhnyi Akatov by 1700 hours.

In the center of Batov's formation, Colonel Merkulov's 304th Rifle Division, with 91st Tank Brigade in support, attacked from Rodionov southeastward along the ridge midway between Antonovskii *Ovrag* and Kisliakovskii *Balka* early on 26 November. It managed to reach the northern slope of Hill 204.0, 2 kilometers south of Biriuchkov, before it was halted by heavy enemy fire from the hill. On Merkulov's right, Colonel Shekhtman's 252nd Rifle Division began its assault from the eastern slope of Hill 185.0, midway between Berezovaia *Balka* and Antonovskii *Ovrag*. Shekhtman's riflemen moved forward 4 kilometers to positions southwest of Hill 204.0, where they too stalled. To hasten his shock group's progress, later in the afternoon, Batov ordered Colonel P. P. Bakhrameev's 23rd Rifle Division to envelop the German bridgehead from the right by marching eastward south of Berezovaia *Balka* toward Kartuli. Bakhrameev's division was approaching Sukhaia *Balka*, 12 kilometers behind the army's right wing, when darkness fell.

Meanwhile, in his shrinking bridgehead, General Strecker had withdrawn 376th Infantry Division's 767th Regiment from 44th Infantry Division's southern portion of the bridgehead and sent it across the Don on 25 November. He continued withdrawing his corps, regiment by regiment, on the 26th. Next in line for evacuation were 384th Infantry Division's 534th and 535th Regiments, which withdrew from the northern half of the bridgehead and crossed the river by dawn on 26 November. By this time, the bridgehead had diminished in size to include the region from Gerasimovskii *Balka* in the north to about 2 kilometers south of Akimovskii in the south, and from Hill 204 in the west back to the western bank of the Don. The 8-kilometer-wide and 6-kilometer-deep bridgehead was defended by 16th Panzer Division's *kampfgruppe* in the Akimovskii region and by 44th Infantry Division's 131st and 132nd Regiments, deployed in positions from Hill 204.0 eastward to Nizhnyi Gerasimov, each supported by a battery of artillery.

At about noon on the 26th, 44th Infantry Division's two regiments began evacuating the northern two-thirds of the bridgehead and crossed the river, followed by most of 16th Panzer Division's *kampfgruppe*—a process that took until about 0200 hours on the 27th. The 16th Panzer Division's 64th

Panzer-Grenadier Regiment, about the size of a battalion, provided cover for the departing soldiers. When the evacuation across the river was complete by about 0330 hours, the last defending company of 64th Regiment left as well. The last few men across the bridge blew up the 328-meter-long structure at about 0340 hours.[86] Although XI Army Corps' long ordeal was over, a new and longer one was about to begin for Sixth Army as a whole.

Some accounts of XI Army Corps' evacuation of its Akimovskii bridge-head north of the Don emphasize its chaotic and frenzied nature (see appendix 6M in the *Companion* for an especially vivid but perhaps apocryphal account by German war correspondent Heinz Schröter). As harrowing as XI Army Corps' withdrawal seemed, Strecker managed to extract his forces back across the river relatively intact. But there would be no rest for the bridgehead's escaped defenders. Within hours after the last German soldier crossed the famous bridge, they would occupy new positions south of the river. Based on the ferocity of their ensuing defense, the soldiers of 44th and 384th Infantry Divisions were no longer either hysterical or panicky, if they ever had been.

Sixth Army kept close track of XI Army Corps' withdrawal with periodic reports. For example, it informed Army Group Don at 2232 hours on 26 November that XI Army Corps was being "taken back from the Don bridge-head to the Gnilowskoj [Gnilovskii]-Wertjatschij [Vertiachii]-Peskowatka [Peskovatka] line."[87] Strecker's corps reported that it was ordering the remnants of 16th Panzer Division to withdraw to the Bol'shaia Rossoshka region to become the nucleus of the army's reserve. However, heavy fighting in the Peskovatka region forced the corps to keep 16th Panzer Division's armored nucleus, a *kampfgruppe* designated Group Sikenius, well forward to provide critical armored support.

On the Soviet side of the hill, the four rifle divisions of Batov's shock group completed the reduction of XI Army Corps' bridgehead on 27 November. In Batov's words:

> The guardsmen of Glebov [27th Guards Rifle Division] and 23rd Division entered their new concentration area in Evlampievskii. Colonel Shekht-man advanced rapidly from Verkhne-Golubaia to the river and threw forward detachments to the eastern bank on the morning of 27 November. Colonel Prokhorov [24th Rifle Division] attacked from the north, and he too caught hold of the eastern bank in the Nizhne-Gerasimovka region. The 304th Rifle Division was committed into first echelon on 25 November, its forward detachments rushed up to the crossings at Peskovatka, and, during the day on 27 November, the division's main forces captured Luchenskii, and the forward units on the eastern bank abruptly turned toward the northeast and joined battle on the approaches to Vertiachii.

The shock group of 65th Army (with its regimental artillery) was already on that side of the Don.[88]

Although 65th Army's daily report to the General Staff confirmed Batov's account of the fighting, it made no mention of Colonel Prokhorov's 24th or 23rd Rifle Divisions.[89] This was because, by dawn on 26 November, Batov had ordered both to occupy assembly areas at and west of the Akimovskii Farm region as the army's new reserve. Batov's report tacitly admitted that the defending forces managed to get away virtually scot-free, since 252nd Rifle Division captured Akimovskii at 0900 hours, four and a half hours after the last soldiers from 16th Panzer Division's 64th Regiment abandoned the town and blew up the bridge.

Soon after XI Army Corps completed withdrawing its forces across the Don, late on the morning of the 27th, Sixth Army informed Army Group Don that since its defenses along the Peskovatka and Vertiachii line were becoming untenable, it intended to pull back to a new and more defensible line overnight on 28–29 November. This line, which would become the northwestern and western faces of Sixth Army's infamous Stalingrad pocket, extended as follows: "1 kilometer south of 102.3–B. Akronowa [Akronova *Balka*]–west of 115.4–126.1–west of Kosatschi [Kazachi]–117.6–131.7–Marinowka [Marinovka]."[90] In simpler terms, the line extended from the village of Borodin, 10 kilometers southwest of Kotluban' Station, westward 6 kilometers to the head of Akronova *Balka*, and then south-southwestward 5 to 6 kilometers west of the Rossoshka River to Marinovka—a total distance of 34 kilometers. Paulus chose this line because most of it was situated along the crest of the ridgeline representing the divide between the Rossoshka River and the Don River to the west. More important, the *Absicht* reported "the release and disengagement of the 384th Infantry Division and 14th Panzer Division at the disposal of the Army."[91]

At 1635 hours on 27 November, General Heitz, whose VIII Army Corps would be responsible for defending the northwestern quadrant of the Stalingrad pocket, reported to Sixth Army, "XI Army Corps has left as scheduled to go back to the intermediate defensive line. The bridge over the Don was blown up at 0400 hours. The enemy crossed the Don from Perepolni on floating rafts."[92] The report added that, as of 1715 hours, 14th Panzer Division's *kampfgruppe* was fighting at Peskovatka, 376th Infantry Division was defending the Illarionovskii sector, and 3rd Motorized Division was defending the sector from Illarionovskii southward to Marinovka.

At 2145 hours that evening, Group Heitz reported on the composition (order of battle) of XI Army Corps after it reorganized its forces south of the Don. By this time, the corps consisted of 1st and 2nd Battalions, 535th Infantry Regiment; 1st Battalion, 534th Infantry Regiment; 131st Grenadier

Regiment; 44th Bicycle Battalion [*Abteilung*]; 134th Grenadier Regiment (less its 2nd Battalion); 132nd Grenadier Regiment; and 2nd Battalion, 134th Grenadier Regiment, supported by Panzer Regiment Sikenius (from 16th Panzer Division, with about 15 tanks) and with 522nd Construction Battalion attached. At the time, 44th Infantry Division fielded 13 antitank guns (5 medium and 8 heavy), and 384th Infantry Division had 10 antitank guns (4 medium and 6 heavy).[93] For comparison's sake, as of 2155 hours on 20 November, 44th Infantry Division possessed 25 antitank guns (8 medium and 17 heavy), and 384th Infantry Division had 19 antitank guns (12 medium and 7 heavy), meaning that the two divisions had lost roughly 50 percent of their weapons during the defense of the Akimovskii bridgehead.[94]

At the same time, 376th Infantry Division's 672nd, 673rd, and 767th Regiments, together with 2nd Battalion of 384th Infantry Division's 536th Regiment and the bulk of 14th Panzer Division, were defending the Soka-revka region; the remainder of 384th Infantry Division's 536th Regiment was in Sixth Army's reserve. Paulus's defensive plan called for the withdrawal of 14th Panzer and 384th Infantry Divisions into army reserve by the time his army occupied its new defensive line overnight on 28–29 November. There-fore, although they were weaker after their withdrawal, XI Corps' 376th, 44th, and 384th Infantry Divisions survived the struggle in the Akimovskii bridgehead and fought as cohesive entities throughout the remainder of Sixth Army's siege in the Stalingrad pocket.

By day's end on 27 November, although Batov's 65th Army had succeeded in eliminating XI Army Corps' bridgehead in the northeastern portion of the Great Bend of the Don River, it utterly failed to accomplish its primary mission of destroying XI Army Corps. Despite this failure, it inflicted heavy material losses on Strecker's corps, perhaps destroying up to half of 376th, 44th, and 384th Infantry Divisions' heavy weapons and about 30 percent of their personnel. A comparison of the strengths of these divisions on 16 No-vember and 15 December underscores the adverse impact of the bridgehead struggle on their combat capabilities (see table 29).

While the total number of battalions in the divisions decreased only slightly (from 23 to 22), the number of artillery batteries decreased by al-most 50 percent (from 36 to 20), and the combat strength of their battalions decreased from average or better to weak or exhausted. However, based on their future combat performance, the divisions' morale, defensive "solid-ness," and cohesiveness did not decline commensurate with their reduced strength and combat rating (whether because of their ardor or their fear of the Russians).

Despite the damage Batov's 65th Army inflicted on XI Army Corps' forces, the stark fact was that Rokossovsky's armies had failed to fulfill their assigned mission—to encircle and destroy Strecker's corps and its three

Table 29. Combat Strength of XI Army Corps' 44th, 376th, and 384th Infantry Divisions, 16 November and 15 December 1942

Division	16 November	15 December
44th Infantry Division		
Infantry battalions	7—2 strong, 2 medium strong, 3 average	6—4 weak, 2 exhausted
Pioneer battalions	1 average	1 exhausted
Artillery batteries	11	7
Light	6	5
Heavy	3	1
Werfer°	2	1
376th Infantry Division		
Infantry battalions	7—3 medium strong, 4 average	7 exhausted
Pioneer battalions	1 average	1 weak
Artillery batteries	11	5
Light	6	2
Heavy	3	1
Werfer°	2	2
384th Infantry Division		
Infantry battalions	6 average	6 weak
Pioneer battalions	1 average	1 exhausted
Artillery batteries	14	8
Light	10	5
Heavy	3	2
Werfer°	1	1

Sources: "KR-Fernschreben an Gen. St. d. H./Org. Abt, an Gen. St. d. H. /Op. Abt., nachr.: an Heeresgruppe B (mit Anschr. Übermittlung)," and "Betr.: Zustand der Divisionen, 1200 Uhr, Armee-Oberkommando 6, Abt.-Ia, A.H.Qu., 16. November 1942," in Florian Freiherr von und zu Aufsess, *Die Anlagenbänder zu den Kriegstagebüchern der 6. Armee vom 14.09.1942 bis 24.11.1942, Band I* (Schwabach: Januar, 2006), 289–290; "Fernschreiben an Heeregruppe Don, Betr.: Sonntagsmeldung, Armee-Oberkommando 6, Abt.-Ia, A.H.Qu., 21.12.1942," in Florian Freiherr von und zu Aufsess, *Die Anlagenbänder zu den Kriegstagebüchern der 6. Armee vom 24.11.1942 bis 24.12.1942, Band II* (Schwabach: Januar, 2006), 231, 233.

° Six-barreled engineer-mortars.

combat divisions. Most Soviet critiques of the operation blame General Galanin's 24th Army for this failure.

24th Army

The mission Vasilevsky assigned to 24th Army late on 24 November was to attack southward east of the Don River early on the 25th, penetrate the defenses of German VIII Army Corps' 76th Infantry Division, capture Vertiachii and Peskovatka, and link up with 21st Army's 3rd Guards Cavalry Corps to encircle and destroy the German grouping north of the Don River (XI Army Corps and XIV Panzer Corps) in cooperation with 21st and 65th Armies. This was identical to its mission at the outset of Uranus, which it began on 22 November but failed to accomplish in three days of intense fighting. In fact, Galanin's shock group advanced only several hundred meters in those three days, penetrating 76th Infantry Division's security zone but barely reaching the forward edge of its main defensive belt. Even after committing General Maslov's 16th Tank Corps to action on the 23rd, no penetration resulted, and the tank corps' strength eroded steadily from 105 tanks on the 23rd to 59 on the 24th and 31 by dawn on the 25th.[95] By this time, the tank corps' three tank brigades were simply providing infantry support to the army's shock group, which consisted of 49th, 214th, and 120th Rifle Divisions, reinforced by 84th Rifle Division on 24 November. The failure of 24th Army's offensive continued to generate heated exchanges between 24th and 65th Armies as to who was really at fault.

Undeterred by its earlier failures, Galanin's army resumed its offensive on 25 November, with 49th, 233rd, 214th, and 120th Rifle Divisions attacking in the 10-kilometer-wide sector from 10 kilometers south-southeast to 10 kilometers south-southwest of Panshino (see appendix 6L in the *Companion*). But, as the General Staff's daily summaries indicated, these attacks essentially faltered after only minimal gains.[96] Thereafter, in two days of heavy fighting, 24th Army captured Verkhne- and Nizhne-Gnilovskii and part of Gerasimov *Balka* and reached the approaches to the village of Kislov, 1 kilometer south of Nizhne-Gnilovskii. This left its shock group still 8 kilometers north of its objective, Vertiachii.

The cost of this fighting was high, as 16th Tank Corps was reduced to fewer than 20 tanks. In fact, the corps was so debilitated that, on the night of 25–26 November, Maslov had no choice but to combine all its tanks into a single combat group formed around the nucleus of 164th Tank Brigade.[97] In the end, whatever progress 24th Army made was attributable more to 65th Army, whose forces began to cross to the Don's southern bank on 27 November, than to the ferocity of its own assault. By midday on the 27th, 65th Army's advance threatened 76th Infantry Division's left flank, forcing it to withdraw altogether from the Gnilovskii region and Gerasimov *Balka* overnight on 27–28 November and begin retrograde operations back to Paulus's new defensive line the next evening.

66th Army

Despite 66th Army's notable success the day before, when it decimated German 94th Infantry Division as it conducted its poorly planned withdrawal, Zhadov's army experienced the same problems as 24th Army on its right when it resumed its assaults on the morning of the 25th. Its attacks utterly failed (see appendix 6L in the *Companion*).

During the day, the army's 64th Rifle Division tried to exploit 94th Infantry Division's recent defeat by assaulting its defenses protecting the northeastern and eastern approaches to Orlovka. However, 64th Division suffered sharp rebuffs at the hands of 94th Division's 267th Regiment, first on the northern slope of Hill 147.6, 3 kilometers north of the town, and then on Hill 135.4, 2 kilometers east of the German stronghold. Although one assault group managed to seize a foothold on the latter, it lost it to a German counterattack. On 64th Division's right, 116th Rifle Division penetrated to the eastern slope of Hill 145.1, 3.5 kilometers northwest of Orlovka, before it too was halted by a counterattacking battalion from 16th Panzer Division's 79th Panzer-Grenadier Regiment. On 66th Army's left wing, 99th Rifle Division launched repeated assaults against 94th Infantry Division's defenses from Hill 135.4 eastward to Spartakovka in an attempt to widen its connections to 62nd Army's Group Gorokhov, which was still fighting in the Spartakovka region. Although these attacks also failed, they caused additional damage to 94th Division, prompting General Seydlitz's LI Army Corps to seek reinforcements to bolster its defenses in this region. At day's end on the 25th, 66th Army's divisions were locked in a virtual stalemate with the divisions on LI Army Corps' left wing.[98]

Despite the disappointing performance of Zhadov's 66th Army, a situation report prepared by Sixth Army's LI Army Corps at 1745 hours on 25 November vividly described the cost of victory to 94th Infantry Division and the measures the corps was taking to shore up its defenses in the vital Orlovka and Spartakovka sector:

> At daybreak, 94th Infantry Division was attacked on a broad front by enemy infantry escorted by individual tanks. Trying to widen the breakthrough point they achieved yesterday, the enemy—moving down the Erzovka road north of Spartakovka—captured the orchard and later the forested area south of there. The enemy pushed to the north-west, behind our infantry holding out along the railroad line, and captured Hill 135.4. . . . The countermeasures implemented immediately were successful, with Hill 135.4 being recaptured. . . . Fighting has not yet ended there.

Aim for 26.11: Resolution of the situation near 94th Infantry Division. For this, the remaining elements of 24th Panzer Division with Group Scheele will go into action on the right wing of 94th Infantry Division.

Casualties on 25.11 (incomplete report):

94th Infantry Division: Killed—1 officer, 15 non-commissioned officers and men. Wounded—1 officer, 28 non-commissioned officers and men.[99]

A subsequent report submitted to Sixth Army at 0700 hours the next day elaborated on what Seydlitz had done to remedy the situation:

Relief of employed elements of 94th Infantry Division south-west of Hill 135.4 by Gruppe Scheele has been smoothly carried out. On the Erzovka road, two T-34s were destroyed by 94th Infantry Division.

Casualties on 26.11 (incomplete report):

94th Infantry Division: Killed—1 officer, 51 non-commissioned officers and men. Wounded—3 officers, 128 non-commissioned officers and men.[100]

Even though LI Army Corps managed to stabilize the situation in the Orlovka and Spartakovka regions, the cost was extremely high. Including the roughly 200 personnel lost in the debacle on 24 November, 94th Infantry Division suffered another 350 casualties during the three days of fighting on 24–27 November. This was a high price to pay for a division that had numbered only 5,025 combat soldiers on 15 November.

Nor did 66th Army's prospects for success improve on 26 November. At Seydlitz's request, the night before, Sixth Army had ordered General von Lenski's 24th Panzer Division, which had failed to block the Soviet mobile corps' advance on Kalach, to return to the Orlovka region. Its mission was to take over 94th Infantry Division's defensive sector, incorporate the threadbare division's survivors into its ranks, and restore the situation in the sector between Orlovka and Spartakovka. After closing into the Orlovka region by nightfall, Lenski's troops added insult to 66th Army's injury by conducting a counterattack of its own on 27 November.

While LI Corps fought to restore its defenses between Orlovka and Spartakovka, General Zhadov threw the bulk of his army's forces into the attack, desperately trying but failing to collapse German defenses at the northeastern corner of Sixth Army's Stalingrad pocket.[101] The heaviest fighting on 26 and 27 November took place on the slopes of Hill 135.4 and to the east, where 24th Panzer Division launched a strong counterattack to regain the ground 66th Army's 64th Rifle Division had captured in the previous two days. Now organized into Group Lenski, 24th Panzer's counterattacking forces included *Kampfgruppe* Brendel, with most of 274th Grenadier Regiment, on the left and *Kampfgruppe* von Below, with the panzer division's 18 remaining tanks, reinforced by a battalion from the grenadier regiment, on the right.[102] In two days of fighting, the counterattacking forces managed to recapture much of the ground 94th Division had lost on the 25th.[103]

Although the bitter fighting in 66th Army's sector continued for several days, by month's end, Zhadov, Rokossovsky, and Vasilevsky realized there was nothing more to be gained from these costly attacks against the Germans' well-prepared defenses in the Orlovka region. Therefore, until late December, Zhadov's army was assigned to do nothing more than tie down German forces in the region with local attacks, raids, and reconnaissance actions of various scales.

Conclusions

Like its neighboring Southwestern Front, the three days of offensive action by Rokossovsky's Don Front produced mixed results. Although the offensive by Batov's 65th Army, together with the threatening if ineffectual attacks by Galanin's 24th Army, succeeded in eliminating German XI Army Corps' bridgehead north of Akimovskii on the Don River, this was a far cry from liquidation. Batov's forces inflicted heavy losses on General Strecker's XI Army Corps but did not destroy the Germans. By failing to capture Vertiachii and thereby cut XI Corps' escape routes, Galanin's 24th Army permitted Strecker to withdraw his three infantry divisions relatively intact and still somewhat combat ready. Although vastly reduced in strength, the survivors of 44th, 376th, and 384th Infantry Divisions would man credible defenses along the periphery of Sixth Army's Stalingrad pocket and, in the future, make the Soviet attackers pay dearly for every meter of ground they seized. In short, the survival of much of Strecker's force would help prolong the bloody battle for the Stalingrad pocket for another two months.

The Stalingrad Front

As was the case with Vatutin's Southwestern Front, the missions assigned to General Eremenko's Stalingrad Front late on 24 November required the *front's* forces to engage in two struggles along diametrically opposed operational axes (see maps 33 and 34). At least initially, the Stalingrad Front's 62nd, 64th, and 57th Armies, together with part of 51st Army, fought to collapse the Stalingrad pocket's eastern and southern fronts, while most of 51st Army pushed the *front's* outer encirclement front south toward Kotel'nikovo. But soon after the Stalingrad Front resumed its offensive, changing circumstances slowly but inexorably compelled Eremenko to commit all of 51st Army's forces to the struggle along the Kotel'nikovo axis.

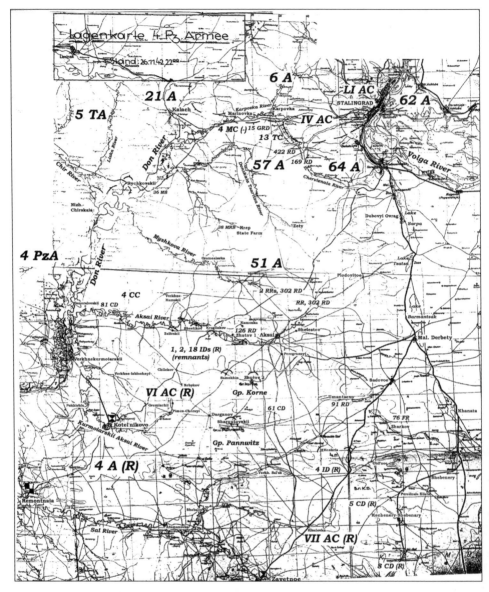

Map 33. Fourth Panzer Army's defense at 2200 hours, 26 November 1942

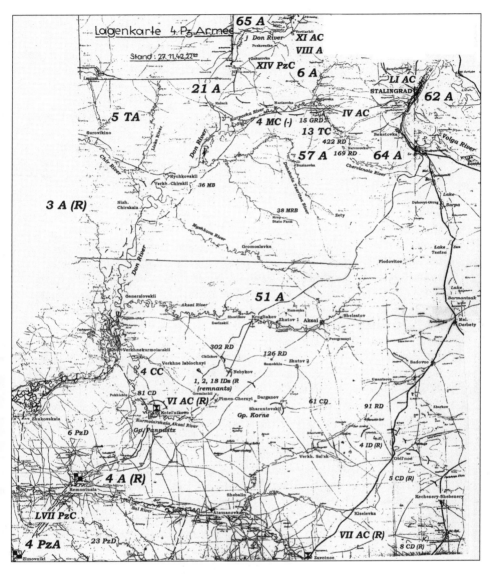

Map 34. Fourth Panzer Army's defense at 2200 hours, 27 November 1942

Similar to the Southwestern Front's 21st Army and the Don Front's 24th and 66th Armies, the Stalingrad Front's armies fighting along the inner encirclement front found themselves in a virtual stalemate with German forces—the Germans' defensive positions were simply too strong to overcome. In addition to Chuikov's 62nd Army, which played only a secondary role in the offensive from the outset, Shumilov's 64th Army would have no choice but to conduct virtual siege operations. Within two days, Tolbukhin's 57th Army would find itself in similar circumstances. Despite these stark realities, the five armies of Eremenko's *front* dutifully resumed offensive operations on 25 November (see appendix 6N in the *Companion* for the Stalingrad Front's accomplishments on 25–27 November).

64th Army

By day's end on 24 November, General Shumilov's 64th Army was operating along a relatively short front of about 22 kilometers south and southwest of Stalingrad. Its forces occupied positions extending eastward 10 kilometers from the Chervlenaia River along and north of Karavatka *Balka* to the town of Elkhi, and northeastward 12 kilometers from Elkhi to the outskirts of Stalingrad's southern suburb of Kuporosnoe. After heavy fighting on 19–23 November, during which the army's forces advanced to the *balka's* southern bank and the German stronghold of Elkhi at the *balka's* eastern extremity, Fourth Panzer Army's IV Army Corps transformed the *balka* line into a formidable fortified bastion anchored on the towns of Tsybenko in the west and Elkhi in the east. This *balka* bastion was defended by IV Corps' 371st and 297th Infantry Divisions arrayed from left (east) to right (west), reinforced by Romanian 20th Infantry Division's 82nd Regiment. The only part of IV Corps' bastion line that 64th Army had been able to breach was a 3-kilometer-wide sector adjacent to the Chervlenaia River's eastern bank, slightly south of Tsybenko. There, the army's 36th Guards Division, commanded by Colonel (promoted to major general on 27 November) Denisenko, had succeeded in seizing a small bridgehead on the *balka's* northern bank and the southern slope of nearby Hill 111.6, 2 kilometers north of the *balka*. After heavy Soviet assaults on Tsybenko from the southeast and southwest failed, fighting temporarily subsided in the region.

In an attempt to end this stalemate, late on 24 November, Vasilevsky ordered Eremenko to transfer 36th Guards Rifle Division, together with its 3-kilometer sector east of the Chervlenaia River, from Shumilov's army to Tolbukhin's 57th Army, and he directed Tolbukhin to resume his offensive. Vasilevsky assumed that opportunities for capturing Tsybenko would materially improve if Tolbukhin's army controlled and coordinated assaults against the strongpoint from the southwest and southeast.

Since Vasilevsky's order directed 64th Army to support its neighbor's offensive, Shumilov had no choice but to oblige. He did so by ordering new assaults east of Hill 111.6 and southeast of Peshchanka by elements of 7th Rifle Corps in conjunction with 57th Army's attacks on Tsybenko. However, these assaults also failed (see appendix 6N in the *Companion*).[104] Sixth Army's records confirm that the only attacks of any significance in IV Army Corps' sector during this period were a battalion-size assault with tanks southeast of Tsybenko on 25 November and an attack against 371st Infantry Division's right wing and 297th Infantry Division's left wing in the sector north and northeast of Iagodnyi on 27 November, both of which failed.[105] Although IV Corps claimed that the assault on the 27th was "multidivisional" in nature, 64th Army asserted that it was launched by only two battalions of 97th Rifle Brigade.

57th Army
Because German IV Army Corps' defenses along the Chervlenaia River were so strong, General Tolbukhin's 57th Army, like Shumilov's 64th, was forced to resort to virtual siege operations along the southern face of the Stalingrad pocket on 25 November. After Eremenko transferred 36th Guards Rifle Division and its sector east of the Chervlenaia River to 57th Army, Tolbukhin moved Colonel Ia. F. Eremenko's 169th Rifle Division eastward across the river to relieve Colonel Denisenko's division so that it could rest and refit. Beginning on 25 November, Eremenko's division spearheaded attacks against Tsybenko from the southeast. In addition, the Stalingrad Front commander supposedly transferred General Vol'sky's 4th Mechanized Corps from 51st to 57th Army's control on 25 November, although the precise time of this transfer remains unknown.[106]

Thereafter, only occasional combat occurred in 57th Army's sector for the next three days, as Tolbukhin's army sought to identify and exploit weak sectors in IV Army Corps' defenses (see appendix 6N in the *Companion*).[107] The heaviest fighting during this period took place on the army's right wing—specifically, on the approaches to Tsybenko, which IV Army Corps had transformed into a strongpoint to serve as the cornerstone of its defenses. Lighter action occurred on 57th Army's left wing and in its center, where Vol'sky's 4th Mechanized Corps (just transferred from 51st Army) conducted battalion-size probes against Groups [*Kampfgruppen*] Willig, von Hanstein, and Seidel, which manned defenses in the sector from Marinovka eastward through Voroshilov Camp to Karpovka. At the time, these small German combat groups were controlled by IV Army Corps' *Kampfgruppe* Korfes, commanded by Colonel Korfes from 295th Infantry Division.

In the Tsybenko region, 57th Army's 422nd and 169th Rifle Divisions launched repeated assaults northward along both banks of the Chervlenaia River from 25 through 27 November in an attempt to envelop IV Army

Corps' strongpoint from the west and east. West of the river, 422nd Division attacked north toward Kravtsov and against Tsybenko from the southwest. At the time, the town of Kravtsov, 2 kilometers west of Tsybenko, and the western and southwestern approaches to Tsybenko were defended by 1st and 2nd Battalions of 29th Motorized Division's 74th Panzer-Grenadier Regiment, backed up by 15 tanks from 29th Motorized Division's 129th Panzer Battalion [*Abteilung*]. East of the river, 169th Division attacked northwest toward Tsybenko from its shallow bridgehead north of Karavatka *Balka*. Tsybenko proper, together with its southeastern and eastern approaches, was defended by 1st and 2nd Battalions of 371st Infantry Division's 670th Regiment, which was now subordinate to 297th Infantry Division.[108] The 169th Rifle Division's history describes its obviously frustrating fight for Tsybenko: "The division [169th] fought to capture Tsybenko from 25 through 29 November, but failed. There were three large enemy minefields in that region. Sappers neutralized them [and] quite often attacked and destroyed the enemy along with the riflemen. . . . 680th, 434th, and 556th Rifle Regiments advanced forward a bit and occupied defenses in the vicinity of the heights in front of Tsybenko."[109]

In the sector from Marinovka eastward to Karpovka, on 57th Army's right wing and in its center, 4th Mechanized Corps reinforced by 15th Guards Rifle Division (also transferred from 51st Army on 25 November) conducted repeated probing attacks against the German *kampfgruppen* defending the vital railroad line and road between those two strongpoints. These too were unsuccessful and just as frustrating as the failed assaults on Tsybenko (see appendix 6O in the *Companion* for 4th Mechanized Corps' description of this fighting).

As it kept close track of developments along the southern face of its pocket, Sixth Army acknowledged that heavy fighting raged in the Marinovka and Karpovka sector, as well as around its strongpoints at Tsybenko and Elkhi. For example, a report dispatched to Army Group Don at 1800 hours claimed that the Soviets had suffered heavy losses, including 13 tanks, in the fighting. However, the same report admitted that the situation and the disposition of its forces fighting between Sokarevka and Marinovka farther north remained confused and unclear.[110] Reports that Sixth Army issued over the next three days confirmed intense fighting in the same regions but emphasized the Soviets' inability to make any significant gains. All these reports stressed the necessity of coordinating the actions of these diverse combat groups under more unified commands.

In addition to pounding German defenses in the Marinovka and Karpovka regions, Vasilevsky's 25 November order to 4th Mechanized Corps required Vol'sky to send part of his corps southwestward to capture crossings over the Don River in the Liapichev and Logovskii regions, 30 and 40 kilometers southwest of Sovetskii, respectively. By doing so, the *Stavka* representative hoped Vol'sky's mobile forces would be able to collapse the Germans' bridgehead on the eastern bank of the Don River opposite Rychkovskii, thereby assisting 1st Tank Corps' seizure of this key town. However, since all of 4th Corps' mechanized brigades were fighting in the sector from Marinovka to Karpovka, Vol'sky chose Lieutenant Colonel Chernyi's 158th Separate Tank Regiment to perform this task. To provide it with the necessary strength, Vol'sky reinforced Chernyi's regiment with a company of submachine gunners and armored cars from his corps' 60th Mechanized Brigade.

Chernyi's detachment moved out at dawn on 25 November but stumbled into a German minefield as it approached Liapichev on the Don. Chernyi was seriously wounded by an exploding mine and was replaced by Battalion Commissar P. D. Sinkevich, the regiment's deputy commander for political affairs. Under Sinkevich's command, the regiment reached the outskirts of Liapichev at dusk. Attacking after darkness fell, the reinforced regiment seized the town and supposedly a nearby railroad bridge over the Don from German Group Schmidt, a small force consisting of rear service units from 14th Panzer Division.[111] However, the regiment deferred any action against Logovskii, 8 kilometers to the south, because it appeared to be too strongly defended to capture. Therefore, Sinkevich requested reinforcements from Vol'sky. By this time, the Germans' bridgehead on the Don's eastern bank opposite Rychkovskii was defended by a small *kampfgruppe* led by Colonel Tzschöckel, commander of 53rd Heavy Mortar Regiment, with about 1,000 men.

Finally, between Vol'sky's 4th Mechanized Corps in the Marinovka and Karpovka regions and 422nd and 169th Rifle Divisions in the vicinity of Tsybenko, the three mechanized brigades of General Tanaschishin's 13th Tank Corps continued to fence with 29th Motorized Division's forces in the sector from Kravtsov northwestward to Staryi Rogachik for the next two days.

If the situation stabilized in the Marinovka and Karpovka sector after 25 November, the same was not the case southwestward along the Don River. There, the forces detached from Vol'sky's 4th Mechanized Corps continued their efforts to defeat German forces on the river's eastern bank and seize crossing sites. After Sinkevich decided to wait for reinforcements before assaulting German defenses at Logovskii, Vol'sky dispatched the remainder of Lieutenant Colonel Karapetian's 60th Mechanized Brigade, which was then fighting west of Karpovka, to the Logovskii region and to Ermokhinskii, 15 kilometers to the south. However, it took more than 24 hours for Karapetian's 60th Brigade to disengage from combat and regroup in the Logovskii region, where its orders were to envelop German defenses at Logovskii from the south. In the meantime, on 26 November, Sinkevich's 158th Tank Regiment captured the village of Krasnoarmeiskii, 2 kilometers north of Logovskii, but it was still too weak to expel German forces from Logovskii proper (see appendix 6N in the *Companion* for 4th Mechanized Corps' progress).

The fighting along the eastern bank of the Don River climaxed on 27 November, when 60th Mechanized Brigade and 158th Tank Regiment assaulted and penetrated Group Tzschöckel's defenses at Logovskii and captured the town. Commissar Sinkevich perished as he led his tanks into combat.[112] Despite losing Logovskii, Group Tzschöckel managed to retain a 2-kilometer-deep bridgehead on the river's eastern bank. Its forces had anchored their defenses on a series of low hills surrounded by extensive marshes that, even if only partially frozen, were virtually impenetrable by tanks. Consequently, although 60th Brigade captured the village of Nemkovskii (Nemki), 3 kilometers southwest of Logovskii, it was unable to traverse the treacherous marshes for days thereafter. This meant that 60th Brigade would have to wait for infantry support from the Stalingrad Front before it had any hope of eliminating the German bridgehead on the Don's eastern bank. Since it took another two weeks for 51st Army to send infantry to the region, the specter of a German relief effort east toward Stalingrad from the Nizhne-Chirskaia and Rychkovskii region remained a genuine threat.

All in all, despite denting German defenses in several sectors, 57th Army failed to accomplish its mission of clearing German forces from the vicinity of the railroad line and road from Marinovka eastward to Karpovka. From this point on, like Shumilov's 64th Army to the east, the operations by Tolbukhin's army would resemble a prolonged siege. In addition, because so many of its forces were tied up in the fighting for Marinovka and Voroshilov Camp, the army's newly assigned 4th Mechanized Corps could not dispatch enough of its forces southwestward to liquidate the Germans' vital bridgehead east of the Don.

51st Army

In comparison to its sister armies to the north and east, General Trufanov's 51st Army achieved the greatest degree of success on 25 November as it continued its slow advance southward from the Aksai River. Overnight on 24–25 November, Trufanov ordered General Shapkin's 4th Cavalry Corps, which was still spearheading the army's offensive along the Kotel'nikovo axis, "to advance along the Gromoslavka, Verkhne-Iablochnyi, and Kotel'nikovo march-route with 81st Cavalry Division and capture Kotel'nikovo by 27 November, in cooperation with 61st Cavalry Division attacking toward Kotel'nikovo from the east."[113] This required Colonel Baumshtein's 81st Cavalry to advance west along the Aksai River and then wheel south and march on Kotel'nikovo from the north. Simultaneously, in between the two cavalry divisions, Colonel Kuropatenko's 126th Rifle Division was to advance south toward Kotel'nikovo along the railroad from the Zhutovo region, west of the town of Aksai. This required Shapkin's cavalry corps, in tandem with 126th Rifle Division, to traverse 90 to 95 kilometers in three days and then capture the important rail center and road junction at Kotel'nikovo by attacking from three sides. Seizure of the town, Eremenko believed, would eliminate any opportunity for Romanian and German forces to restore a solid and cohesive defensive front along this important axis.

However, unknown to Eremenko and Trufanov, on 25 November, the OKH and Army Group Don reorganized Fourth Panzer Army into Army Group [*Armeegruppe*] Hoth. At Hitler's command, Hoth's new army group would control all of Romanian VI and VII Army Corps' forces in the region, and it was supposed to receive reinforcements from the West and Army Group A, which was then fighting in the Caucasus. When and if these reinforcements reached his army group, Hoth was to mount a relief effort toward Stalingrad along the Kotel'nikovo and Aksai axis. This decision suddenly elevated the importance of Kotel'nikovo in Army Group Don's offensive scheme, first and foremost because the vital communications center along the most direct route to Stalingrad from the southwest became Group Hoth's principal base of operations. This also brought 51st Army into direct conflict with German forces, beginning with a clash with Group Pannwitz on 25 November and with newly arrived 6th Panzer Division several days later.

In the meantime, General Shapkin's 4th Cavalry Corps began an initially successful but ultimately ill-fated advance toward Kotel'nikovo (see appendix 6N in the *Companion*).[114] Galloping westward from the Aksai and Peregruznyi region, 8 kilometers to the south, Colonel Baumshtein's 81st Cavalry Division advanced 25 to 30 kilometers during the day and captured the Gromoslavka and Ivanovka region, 30 to 35 kilometers northwest of Aksai, by nightfall on 25 November.

To the east, Colonel Stavenko's 61st Cavalry Division marched west toward Kotel'nikovo from its assembly area in the Umantsevo region, 18 kilometers west of Sadovoe. However, Stavenko's cavalry encountered trouble only hours after it began its advance. When the cavalry division reached the village of Sharnutovskii, 35 kilometers west of Umantsevo and 45 kilometers east of Kotel'nikovo, it stumbled into a counterattack conducted jointly by Colonel Pannwitz's ad hoc group of Cossack cavalry, infantry, and tanks and another ad hoc group built around the nucleus of Romanian 8th Cavalry Division and led by the division's commander, Colonel Korne. By this time, Stavenko's cavalry was particularly vulnerable because it was well out of range of its supporting rifle divisions. At the time, Colonel Kuropatenko's 126th Rifle Division was concentrating in the Zhutov State Farm No. 1 region, 30 kilometers north of Stavenko's cavalry, and Colonel Makarchuk's 302nd Rifle Division was in the vicinity of Kapkinskii Station, 20 kilometers northwest of Aksai and more than 40 kilometers north of Stavenko. Both rifle divisions were regrouping their forces westward and preparing to advance on Kotel'nikovo.

The results were predictable. After a fight that lasted until early the next morning and resulted in heavy losses, 61st Cavalry withdrew westward to Umantsevo in considerable disorder. There, it occupied new defenses and licked its wounds.[115] In the wake of this fighting, Group Korne exploited 61st Cavalry's eastward withdrawal by attacking north toward Aksai. Farther to the south, Army Group Hoth established its headquarters at Zimovniki, on the railroad line 80 kilometers southwest of Kotel'nikovo. Romanian Fourth Army, now re-created under the command of General Constantinescu but subordinate to Group Hoth, set up its headquarters at Remontnaia (Dubovskoe), 38 kilometers southwest of Kotel'nikovo, where it awaited reinforcements.

Paying scant attention to 61st Cavalry Division's setback at Sharnutovskii, 51st Army reorganized its forces overnight on 25–26 November and resumed its drive toward Kotel'nikovo early the next morning. Shapkin's 4th Cavalry Corps now relied primarily on Colonel Baumshtein's 81st Cavalry Division to lead its advance. The 81st Cavalry wheeled southwestward, traversed another 35 kilometers, and occupied the Novoaksaiskii and Generalovskii regions along the lower reaches of the Aksai River, about 40 kilometers north of Kotel'nikovo. This placed Baumshtein's cavalry on the left flank of Romanian VI Army Corps' forces—the remnants of 1st, 2nd, and 18th Infantry Divisions—which manned threadbare defenses along the southern bank of the Aksai River from the town of Aksai westward roughly 25 kilometers.

On 81st Cavalry Division's left, in 51st Army's center, the regiments of Colonel Kuropatenko's 126th Rifle Division fanned out westward, southwestward, and southward, reaching Zaria Station, 16 kilometers northwest of Aksai; Zhutov State Farm No. 1, 15 kilometers west of Aksai; and Il'ich Collective Farm, 4 kilometers west of Aksai, by day's end. This maneuver forced the remnants of Romanian VI Corps' 1st and 18th Infantry Divisions to give ground south of the Aksai River. Farther east, Colonel Makarchuk's 302nd Rifle Division concentrated two of its regiments in the Kapkinskii region, 15 kilometers north of Aksai, and left its third regiment in Abganerovo as a reserve.

Still farther to the east, Colonel Stavenko's 61st Cavalry Division, which had recovered its balance after being defeated by Group Pannwitz, resumed its advance and reported to 51st Army that it had captured the village of Darganov, on the Kurmoiarskii Aksai River 38 kilometers east-northeast of Kotel'nikovo, by day's end.[116] However, Army Group Hoth's records dispute this claim. Instead, Group Hoth's daily situation map shows Group Korne's Romanian 8th Cavalry Division in the Zhutov 2 region and Pannwitz's *kampfgruppe* occupying Sharnutovskii, 20 kilometers to the south.[117]

Since Stavenko's 61st Cavalry Division fled to Umantsevo, 40 kilometers east of both locations, after its defeat on 25 November, it likely remained there all day on the 26th and, at best, sent only reconnaissance parties to the Darganov region. In any case, it was clear that the eastern prong of 4th Cavalry Corps' pincer designated to capture Kotel'nikovo was essentially stalled.

Meanwhile, on 51st Army's distant left wing, General Kalinin's 91st Rifle Division spent a day resting and refitting in the Sadovoe region. Then, on 26 November, it marched west toward Umantsevo to reinforce 61st Cavalry Division's advance on Kotel'nikovo from the east. After resting in Sadovoe, the machine gun–artillery battalions of 76th Fortified Region on Kalinin's left reached the Zharkov region, 12 kilometers south of Sadovoe, where they faced Romanian 4th Infantry Division and protected 51st Army's left flank.

Regardless of whether General Shapkin knew precisely where 61st Cavalry Division was located or understood its dilapidated combat state, he ordered his corps to continue the offensive south toward Kotel'nikovo early on 27 November. Advancing southward with Lieutenant Colonel I. P. Mikhailov's 85th Tank Brigade but no rifle forces whatsoever, Colonel Baumshtein's 81st Cavalry Division advanced about 45 kilometers and reached the western and northwestern approaches to Kotel'nikovo late in the morning. There, according to Romanian sources, it was "emphatically repulsed by the German-Romanian garrison" after it attacked into the city.[118] From 51st Army's perspective, it reported late in the day that "4th CC's 81st CD concentrated 2 kilometers south of Bol'shoi Log *Balka* (8 kilometers north of Kotel'nikovo) by 1025 hours and fought to capture Kotel'nikovo from an enemy force of two infantry regiments, 50 tanks, and 5 artillery batteries."[119] A more nuanced account of 81st Cavalry Division's attempt to seize Kotel'nikovo from the march reported:

> Under the command of Colonel V. G. Baumshtein (Deputy of Political Units, G. I. Klevtsov), [81st Cavalry Division], together with 4th Separate Antitank Battalion, penetrated into the western and northwestern outskirts of Kotel'nikovo and across the railroad in a surprise raid at first light on 27 November. The enemy was seized with panic but not for long. The slow tempo of the movement into the city gave the enemy an opportunity to assemble subunits and tanks of various types located in Kotel'nikovo and launch a counterattack during the second half of the day. This succeeded in enveloping the left flank of the cavalry units, striking them from the rear, and forcing them to retreat. The Fascists were finally halted in front of the town of Verkhne-Iablochnyi.[120]

In fact, Baumshtein's cavalry, accompanied and supported by about 35 tanks from 85th Tank Brigade, attacked into the heart of Kotel'nikovo just as the lead trains carrying 6th Panzer Division on its long journey from France reached the railroad station and began unloading. Romanian forces stationed in the city apparently panicked and failed to resist Baumshtein's attack. However, Group Pannwitz, which had just returned from the fighting east of the city, reacted quickly and, cooperating with the lead elements of 6th Panzer Division, saved the town as well as the situation. After defeating Baumshtein's small force, Pannwitz's *kampfgruppe* and Romanian troops pursued it westward into the marshland along the Semichnaia River valley, 10 to 12 kilometers north-northwest of Kotel'nikovo. Meanwhile, 6th Panzer Division garrisoned the city with its lead panzer-grenadier regiment.[121] Despite Pannwitz's resolute pursuit, Baumshtein's forces escaped the trap early on 28 November and withdrew northward 20 kilometers to occupy new defenses along the northern bank of Iablochnaia *Balka* east and west of Verkhne-Iablochnyi.

The raid by 4th Cavalry Corps' 81st Cavalry Division on Kotel'nikovo outflanked Romanian VI Army Corps' defenses along the Aksai River from the west and forced the remnants of its 1st, 2nd, and 18th Infantry Divisions to withdraw southward hastily to new defenses stretching from Nebykov, 35 kilometers northeast of Kotel'nikovo, southeastward to Sharnutovskii, 50 kilometers east of the city. The 81st Cavalry's advance also enabled Colonel Stavenko's 61st Cavalry Division to advance (no doubt cautiously) once again from the Umantsevo region to the eastern approaches of Sharnutovskii. In between, 51st Army's rifle forces strove to keep up with the cavalry on their flanks. Colonel Kuropatenko's 126th Rifle Division attacked and captured the towns of Krugliakov and Kovalevka on the Aksai River, 12 to 24 kilometers west of Aksai, reportedly from a Romanian force of up to a regiment of infantry and 10 tanks, and it seized the railroad bridge northeast of Krugliakov by 1000 hours. The division then headed south toward Nebykov on the road and railroad line to Kotel'nikovo. In 126th Division's rear, Colonel Makarchuk's 302nd Rifle Division moved southwestward through Aksai and then westward, south of the Aksai River, to reach the railroad line to Kotel'nikovo, where it was supposed to advance southward on 126th Rifle Division's right.

Finally, on 51st Army's right wing, General Kalinin's 91st Rifle Division fended off several counterattacks by Romanian 4th Infantry Division in the vicinity of Hill 140.0, 9 kilometers southwest of Sadovoe. To its rear, the slower-moving machine gun–artillery battalions of 76th Fortified Region pushed Romanian 5th Cavalry Division's forces westward through Obil'noe and to the eastern approaches to Ketchener-Shebenery (today Sovetskoe), 25 kilometers south of Obil'noe.

Thus, in three days of fighting, the right wing and center of Trufanov's 51st Army pushed the forces of Romanian VI Army Corps 35 to 40 kilometers southward from the Aksai River—that is, to within one day's march from

Kotel'nikovo. During the same period, the forces on the army's left wing drove up to 20 kilometers westward and 35 kilometers southwestward from Sadovoe, posing a genuine threat to Kotel'nikovo from the east. However, the army's forward progress was deceptive. By the evening of 27 November, the army's two cavalry and three rifle divisions were stretched out across a front of well over 100 kilometers, for an average frontage of 20 kilometers per division. Against the shattered remnants of four Romanian infantry divisions and one cavalry division, this was a formidable force. But against a full-blooded German panzer division, it was not! This would become abundantly clear within a matter of days.

62nd Army

If the three armies forming the shock group of Eremenko's Stalingrad Front could appreciate the results of their offensive efforts, 62nd Army could not, despite the heavy fighting and often costly losses it endured. Instead, the battered formations of Chuikov's army did what they had been doing for more than three months. Operating in groups of well under 100 men, the army's regiments and battalions attacked, defended, and raided, measuring their successes and failures in hundreds if not tens of meters. Living with the constant threat of death or serious injury, 62nd Army's soldiers endured out of a strange mixture of hope, resignation, fear, and hatred of their tormentors. Somehow, despite the ubiquitous presence of death, they persevered, making life pure hell for their German counterparts. Sometimes, revenge was the only thing that made life livable and fighting endurable for Chuikov's soldiers.

Carrying out Vasilevsky's orders, 62nd Army's pitifully weak divisions and brigades, now fighting as mere companies, platoons, or squads, attacked across the army's entire front on 25 November, once again meeting stubborn enemy resistance and facing frequent counterattacks by groups up to company strength (see appendix 6N in the *Companion*). The results were indeed meager. Group Gorokhov's two brigades cleared German forces from most of Spartanovka, 95th Rifle Division captured a few German strongpoints in the Barrikady Factory, and 284th Rifle Division improved its positions on Mamaev Kurgan, but that was it. Undeterred, Chuikov ordered the attacks to resume on the 26th.

General Seydlitz's LI Army Corps, which faced near-constant harassing attacks along its entire front, issued an order at 2300 hours on the 25th tacitly acknowledging that its employment of assault groups made up of combat engineer battalions and special assault companies to capture well-fortified positions in the Barrikady Factory had failed. Because most of these battalions were now mere shadows of their former selves, the order simply incorporated the survivors of these units into other like units. It read: "305th

Infantry Division will disband 162nd, 294th, and 336th Pioneer Battalions and create one or two pioneer battalions from them. 389th Infantry Division will incorporate 45th Pioneer Battalion into its own pioneer battalion. The same arrangement is valid for 44th Assault Company, which will be absorbed into one of 305th Infantry Division's grenadier [infantry] regiments."[122]

Events repeated themselves on 26 and 27 November, as 62nd Army regrouped its forces and resumed its assaults, although on a somewhat smaller scale than the previous day. The sad fact was that many of Chuikov's divisions and brigades were so weak that they needed a brief respite between attacks and raids to bring up the necessary reinforcements to continue any sort of offensive action (see appendix 6P in the *Companion* for 62nd Army's daily reports). Since rest was out of the question, virtually all of the army's attacks failed.

In circumstances like these—under near-constant attack and knowing full well that Sixth Army was surrounded—the corps and division headquarters within Paulus's army had to do all in their power to bolster the troops' morale. General Seydlitz's LI Corps did so at 1900 hours on 25 November when it issued special instructions to its troops, assuring them that help was on the way, exhorting them to "hold their positions to the last," and indicating precisely how they could improve their defenses (see appendix 6Q in the *Companion*).[123] The next day, based on instructions from Sixth Army, Seydlitz's corps ordered that the soldiers' daily rations be reduced by roughly 50 percent, to include the following (the old rations are in parentheses):

> Bread—400 grams (750 grams)
> Meat or horseflesh—120 grams (250 grams)
> Vegetables—125 grams (250 grams)
> Fat—30 grams (60 grams)
> Jam—160 grams (200 grams)
> Sugar—40 grams (no change)
> Salt—7.5 grams (15 grams)
> Cigarettes—3.5 (7)
> Cigars—1 (2)[124]

If these orders were not reminder enough of Sixth Army's perilous situation, a Führer directive from Hitler was read to all of Sixth Army's soldiers on 27 November. It said in part: "The battle in Stalingrad has reached its high point. . . . Under all circumstances, you have to hold the positions in Stalingrad which you have taken with so much blood under the command of energetic Generals."[125] This directive made it abundantly clear to the *landsers* of LI Army Corps that the besiegers of Stalingrad had indeed become the besieged.

28th Army

While the bulk of the Stalingrad Front's forces were struggling to tighten the noose around German Sixth Army or push the outer encirclement front to a point of no return, on the *front*'s distant left wing, General Gerasimenko's 28th Army continued its own private war against German 16th Motorized Division in the monotonous vastness of the Kalmyk steppes (see map 32). By the end of the day on 24 November, Gerasimenko's forces had driven General Schwerin's division and its Turkestan volunteers westward through the Khulkhuta and Utta regions to the larger town of Iashkul', roughly 85 kilometers east of Elista—28th Army's ultimate objective. Withdrawing westward, Schwerin's forces had already converted Iashkul' into a veritable fortress, with imposing defensive positions spread out northward 40 kilometers to Chilgir and about 15 kilometers to the south.

Gerasimenko's army began testing the strength of 16th Motorized Division's defenses on 25 November.[126] In an order issued the previous day, he had directed 34th Guards Rifle Division and 6th Guards Tank Brigade to attack 16th Motorized Division's defenses at Oling, 8 kilometers north of Iashkul', which was situated on the left flank of 16th Motorized Division's 60th Motorized Regiment. Prior to the attack, 34th Guards Division had been resting its forces after losing about a quarter of its personnel during the previous fighting for Khulkhuta. Despite its weakened condition and the fact that the bulk of the division's and the army's artillery was still deploying westward from Utta, General Gubarevich's division moved forward, supported by tanks from Colonel M. N. Krichman's 6th Guards Tank Brigade, and deployed in attack positions at 1600 hours. Gubarevich's attack force consisted of his own division's 103rd, 105th, and 107th Regiments, with 248th Rifle Division's 899th Regiment in reserve. Although it was clearly too late to organize proper cooperation between the infantry and tanks and adjust what little artillery was available to provide support, Gubarevich attacked promptly at 1900 hours on 25 November.

The main forces of 34th Guards Division overcame the Germans' forward trenches and foxholes in the late evening, occupied Oling at 2300 hours, and then advanced 2 to 3 kilometers southwest of that point to reach within 4 kilometers of the main German defensive line around Iashkul'. Meanwhile, General Schwerin dispatched a battalion of grenadiers mounted in trucks and 10 to 12 tanks eastward, south of the main road, with orders to wheel north and strike the advancing Soviet force on its left flank. At the same time, 811th Turkestan Battalion in Chilgir was supposed to send an additional force southward to attack 34th Guards Division's right flank.

The battle began when Schwerin's motorized force advancing against 34th Guards Division's left ran into 899th Rifle Regiment near a clump of trees called Shalda Grove. In a sharp fight, 899th Regiment lost most of its supporting artillery and 220 men killed, 245 wounded, and 225 missing in action.[127] Fortunately for 248th Rifle Division, Schwerin withdrew his battalion combat group back into Iashkul's defensive lines late on 26 November, before it could inflict even more damage on the attackers. In the meantime, 34th Guards Division's main force reached positions 4 to 6 kilometers northwest of Iashkul' and 2 to 3 kilometers east of the town.

General Schwerin's main counterattack force, which consisted of 2nd and 3rd Battalions of 156th Motorized Regiment and 165th Motorcycle Battalion, supported by a panzer *abteilung*, struck back at 34th Guards Division late on the morning of the 26th and succeeded in encircling 103rd and 105th Regiments of Gubarevich's division in a loose pocket, 4 to 5 kilometers northwest of Iashkul'. After hours of heavy fighting, Gubarevich was finally able to extricate his two regiments from the pocket by punching eastward through a narrow corridor north of Oling overnight on 26–27 November, occupying new defensive positions east of Iashkul' by midday on the 27th. Understandably, Gubarevich made sure these defenses were well out of range of Schwerin's tanks and motorized infantry. According to the definitive Russian source, after suffering more than 1,000 casualties in the fight for the town, 34th Guards Division was essentially hors de combat. When it tallied its casualties and material losses for 20–30 November, they amounted to 1,625 men dead, 1,448 wounded, and 1,978 missing in action, along with 1,181 rifles, 139 PPSh submachine guns, 34 light and 6 heavy machine guns, 21 antitank rifles, 45 of the division's 60 antitank guns, and 5 mortars.[128] Obviously, it would be quite a while before 28th Army would be able to resume its advance along the Iashkul' and Elista axis.

Although accurate overall, the General Staff's daily summaries of the army's actions from 26 to 28 November tried to put a good face on what had occurred, beginning with the comment that "28th Army continued an offensive in the Oling and Iashkul' sector with its shock group against strong resistance and frequent counterattacks" (see appendix 6N in the *Companion*).[129]

Conclusions

On the surface, at least, Eremenko's Stalingrad Front seemed to accomplish far more than its sister *fronts* to the north during the fighting on 25–27 November. Although the offensives by 64th and 57th Armies against encircled German Sixth Army's southern front stalled, at least 51st Army was still advancing toward Kotel'nikovo. This differed sharply from the Southwestern Front, whose 21st Army was unable to collapse the western front of Sixth Army's pocket and whose 1st Guards and 5th Tank Armies largely failed to accomplish their missions of breaching the Chir River line. It was also more successful than the Don Front, whose 65th, 24th, and 66th Armies drove

German XI Corps from its bridgehead north of the Don River but were unable to penetrate the eastern and northern fronts of Sixth Army's main encirclement pocket.

Nevertheless, Eremenko experienced many of the same problems as Vatutin, in particular, his inability to closely supervise his armies operating along diametrically opposed axes. In fact, Eremenko's command and control problem was similar to Vatutin's, only in reverse. Whereas the latter had one army operating against Sixth Army's pocket and two along the outer encirclement front, Eremenko was employing two armies against Sixth Army and one along the outer encirclement front.

Vasilevsky, who thoroughly appreciated the awkwardness of the situation, settled matters on 26 November by asking the *Stavka* to approve the transfer of Chistiakov's 21st Army from Vatutin's Southwestern Front to Rokossovsky's Don Front and compensate Vatutin for his losses. The *Stavka* representative received an affirmative reply less than 24 hours later:

> 1. Your proposal set forth in telegram No. 1492 of 26 November 1942 is approved.
> 2. Transfer 5th MC, which is being placed at your disposal, to 5th Tank Army.
> 3. Transfer 21st Army, consisting of 4th and 26th TCs, 51st Gds., 293rd, 277th, 63rd, and 96th RDs, three tank regiments, and reinforcing units of the army, to the Don Front effective 2400 hours on 27 November 1942.
> Leave 3rd Gds. Cavalry Corps, without tank regiments, in the Southwestern Front.
> 4. Establish a boundary line between the Southwestern and Don Fronts [at]: Sukhov 2, Kletskaia, Verkhne-Buzinovka, and Kalach.
> 5. Confirm receipt. Report fulfillment.
>
> I. Stalin, A. Vasilevsky[130]

Thus, although he lost 21st Army, Vatutin retained Pliev's cavalry corps and received the new 5th Mechanized Corps, which Vasilevsky was certain would allow Vatutin's forces to reach and breach the Chir River line. The *Stavka* and Vasilevsky could make this change in command relationships with only minimal disruption since both *fronts* were situated north of Stalingrad. This left Rokossovsky with sole responsibility for attacking and crushing the northern half of Sixth Army's pocket and Vatutin with the sole task of managing the battle along the Chir and Krivaia River fronts. For the time being, however, Vasilevsky left command relationships south of Stalingrad as they were, if for no other reason than that only one *front* was operating south of the city.

Thus, Eremenko's four armies in the Stalingrad region continued to pursue two major objectives.

Above and beyond command and control problems, as mentioned earlier, the apparent success of the Stalingrad Front's 51st Army was deceptive. With 4th Mechanized Corps transferred from Trufanov's 51st Army to Tolbukhin's 57th, Trufanov's army was literally "out on a limb," despite (or perhaps because of) its offensive success. Although it could certainly deal with the remnants of Romanian forces in the region, which were now ostensibly under Romanian Fourth Army's control but actually under Group Hoth's, engaging German forces was an entirely different matter. Unbeknownst to Eremenko, Vasilevsky, and the *Stavka*, only the day before, the OKH had assured the commander of new Army Group Don, Field Marshal Erich von Manstein, that LVII Panzer Corps, with 23rd Panzer Division, would be moved from Army Group A in the Caucasus to the region southwest of Stalingrad, where it would be joined by 6th Panzer and 15th *Luftwaffe* Field Divisions under Army Group Hoth's control. In fact, the lead elements of the panzer division were reaching Kotel'nikovo at the very moment that 81st Cavalry Division of 51st Army's 4th Cavalry Corps was mounting its unsuccessful raid into the town.

Reducing the Stalingrad Pocket, the Outer Encirclement Front, and Plan Saturn, 28–30 November

SOVIET COMMAND DECISIONS: ORGANIZING OPERATION SATURN

At the same time that Vasilevsky and the *Stavka* were altering command and control arrangements to facilitate liquidation of Sixth Army's Stalingrad pocket, Stalin and Vasilevsky discussed Operation Saturn, which, according to the original strategic planning for Operation Uranus, was to begin sometime after Uranus had achieved its main goal of encircling German Sixth Army.

Prior to his exchange with Stalin on 26 November, General Vasilevsky had spent 23 and 24 November at the Southwestern Front's headquarters, where he coordinated with Vatutin and exchanged views with Rokossovsky and Eremenko by telephone. It was after these consultations that Vasilevsky issued his directive mandating a continuation of the offensive to liquidate Sixth Army and push the outer encirclement front to the west and southwest.

At this point, the fate of the larger Operation Saturn remained unresolved. After discussing Saturn with Vatutin, Vasilevsky planned to depart the Southwestern Front's headquarters on 24 November and fly to other headquarters to coordinate preparations for Saturn against the long northern flank of Army Group B. However, of the seven AN-2 light transports carrying the chief of staff's party, six of them had to make forced landings because of fog and ice. Vasilevsky ended up in a frozen farm field 30 kilometers southeast of Kalach, but he eventually reached the headquarters of the Voronezh Front at Verkhne Mamon by car on the 25th. He consulted with the Voronezh Front's commander, Lieutenant General Filipp Ivanovich Golikov, and visited the headquarters of Lieutenant General F. M. Kharitonov's 6th Army, which was supposed to cooperate closely with the Southwestern Front's 1st Guards Army during Operation Saturn. Vasilevsky then returned to the Southwestern Front's headquarters on 26 November. Consulting further with Vatutin and other senior commanders, Vasilevsky prepared a draft concept for Operation Saturn and reported its contents to Stalin later on the 26th (see map 35 and appendix 7A in the *Companion*).

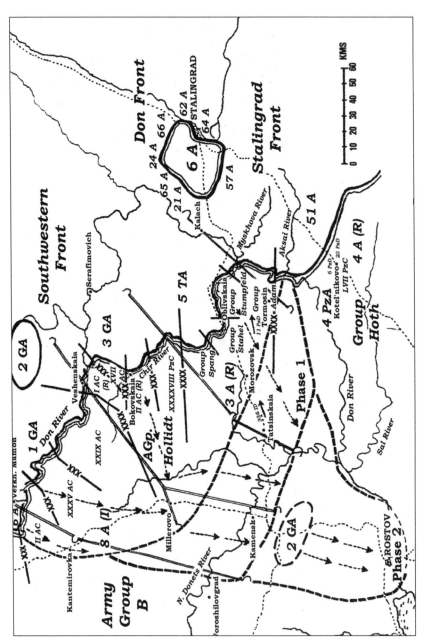

Map 35. Plan for Operation Saturn, 26 November 1942

To increase the effectiveness of command and control in the Southwestern Front during the operation, Vasilevsky proposed subdividing General Leliushenko's 1st Guards Army into two separate armies. General Kuznetsov's operational group, which was deployed along the Krivaia and Chir Rivers on the army's left wing, would become the new 3rd Guards Army under Leliushenko's command. The remainder of 1st Guards Army, positioned along the Don River on the army's right wing, would retain the designation 1st Guards and be commanded by Kuznetsov. The composition and sector of Romanenko's 5th Tank Army would remain unchanged.

The principal aim of Operation Saturn was to destroy Italian Eighth Army and Army Group Hollidt. To do so, shock groups formed in the Verkhne Mamon region, on new 1st Guards Army's right wing, and east of Bokovskaia, on new 3rd Guards Army's left, would launch concentric attacks from the north and east and link up in the Millerovo region to encircle and destroy the two Axis formations. Subsequently, mobile corps subordinate to both armies would exploit to seize crossings over the Northern Donets River in the Likhaia region and create favorable conditions for an even deeper exploitation by 2nd Guards Army to capture the Rostov region. The concept also required 6th Army, deployed on the Voronezh Front's left wing, to join the offensive and protect 1st Guards Army's right flank as it advanced south. Finally, on the Southwestern Front's left wing, 5th Tank Army would destroy Axis forces in the Chernyshevskaia, Morozovsk, and Tormosin regions to more completely isolate German Sixth Army encircled at Stalingrad, advance southwestward to capture the German airfield at Tatsinskaia and reach the Northern Donets River on 3rd Guards Army's left, and prepare to liberate the Donbas region of the eastern Ukraine in cooperation with 1st and 3rd Guards Armies.[1]

The next day, after receiving and examining Vasilevsky's concept of operations, Stalin, Vasilevsky, and Vatutin discussed its conduct in detail during a lengthy telephone conversation (see appendix 7B in the *Companion*). Since Stalin's greatest concern was completing the liquidation of encircled Sixth Army, he insisted on making a single person responsible for coordinating the Don and Stalingrad Fronts' operations to destroy Sixth Army. Therefore, at 2120 hours on 27 November, the dictator cemented the new command relationships in a curt *Stavka* directive that informed Rokossovsky and Eremenko who would coordinate their operations. The directive read: "Presently bring it to the attention of Comrades Dontsov [Rokossovsky] and Ivanov [Eremenko] that the *Stavka* of the Supreme High Command has entrusted supervision of the Stalingrad and Don Fronts' operation to liquidate the encircled enemy to Comrade Mikhailov [Vasilevsky], whose orders will be unconditionally binding for Comrades Dontsov and Ivanov. [signed] Vasil'ev [Stalin]."[2]

Secondarily, Stalin was interested in finalizing plans for Operation Saturn because, if it was successful, the question of a German effort to reinforce or rescue Sixth Army would be moot. Therefore, Stalin pressed Vasilevsky for particulars regarding Saturn, especially the reorganization of Leliushenko's 1st Guards Army into two complete armies capable of conducting Saturn's first stage. Of course, a month before, Stalin had already created the most important part of the Saturn armada—the powerful 2nd Guards Army, formed specifically to lead the exploitation to Rostov. This army, initially commanded by Major General Ia. G. Kreizer, was combat ready by 25 November.

After his conversation with Stalin, on 28 November, General Vatutin appointed his deputy, General Kuznetsov, to command an operational group on 1st Guards Army's right wing and informed him of his group's composition, missions, and other pertinent information about upcoming Operation Saturn (see appendix 7C in the *Companion*). In general, Kuznetsov's group consisted of 4th and 6th Guards Rifle Corps, 18th Tank Corps, six rifle divisions (1st, 193rd, and 195th Rifle and 38th, 35th, and 41st Guards Rifle), a motorized rifle brigade (22nd), and supporting artillery. The operational group's principal mission was to form the right pincer of the planned offensive operation designed to envelop and destroy Italian Eighth Army.[3]

When planning for Operation Saturn accelerated in early December, the *Stavka* converted Kuznetsov's operational group into a new 1st Guards Army under his command, and it converted the group of forces in 1st Guards Army's left wing into the new 3rd Guards Army under General Leliushenko's command. The fact that the first three guards armies the Red Army formed would conduct Operation Saturn (together with the Voronezh Front's 6th Army) underscored how vital the offensive was to the *Stavka*. The designation "Guards" indicated that these armies were stronger than others in terms of their personnel and weaponry and were accorded priority in the receipt of supplies and replacements. Further evidencing Saturn's importance, on 29 November, the *Stavka* appointed Lieutenant General R. Ia. Malinovsky, then deputy commander of the Voronezh Front and a former army and *front* commander, to command 2nd Guards Army in the offensive.[4]

With command relationships in the Stalingrad region sorted out and planning for Operation Saturn under way, the three *front* commanders and their subordinates approached the missions Vasilevsky had assigned to them on 24 November with renewed enthusiasm. It would not be long before naked combat would test the effectiveness of the *Stavka*'s and Vasilevsky's concept for Saturn. In the meantime, plans for conducting the offensive remained on track during the first few days of December.

THE SOUTHWESTERN, DON, AND STALINGRAD
FRONTS' OFFENSIVES

On 28 November the Southwestern Front's force repelled enemy counterattacks northeast of Bokovskaia and fought to capture Chernyshevskaia, Oblivskaia, and Surovikino.

The Don and Stalingrad Fronts' forces encountered strong enemy fire resistance and conducted offensive operations against the enemy grouping encircled in Stalingrad, while part of the Stalingrad Front's forces continued developing an offensive toward Kotel'nikovo.

> Red Army General Staff Operational Summary,
> 0800 hours on 29 November 1942[5]

On 29 November the Southwestern Front's forces continued fighting to capture the Oblivskaia, Surovikino, Verkhne-Chirskii, and Rychkovskii regions with part of their forces.

The Don Front's forces overcame enemy resistance in the strong points of Illarionovskii, Sokarevka, Peskovatka, and Vertiachii on the eastern bank of the Don River with part of their forces and pursued his withdrawing units toward the east and southeast.

The Stalingrad Front's forces continued an offensive toward Kotel'nikovo with its left wing and occupied several populated points.

> Red Army General Staff Operational Summary,
> 0800 hours on 30 November 1942[6]

On 30 November the Southwestern Front continued to fight for possession of the Oblivskaia, Surovikino, and Verkhne-Chirskii regions with part of its forces.

The Don and Stalingrad Fronts' forces continued compressing the ring around the enemy grouping encircled at Stalingrad.

> Red Army General Staff Operational Summary,
> 0800 hours on 1 December 1942[7]

When the forces of the Southwestern, Don, and Stalingrad Fronts resumed offensive operations at dawn on 28 November, they did so with basically the same missions Vasilevsky had assigned to them late on 24 November. Of course, Sixth Army's relatively successful withdrawal of its XI Army Corps and XIV Panzer Corps from the Sirotinskaia (Akimovskii) bridgehead north of the Don negated any opportunity for Soviet forces to encircle and destroy them. Nonetheless, the second part of the Don Front's mission—to collapse the western and northern fronts of Sixth Army's pocket—remained operative. The same was true of the Southwestern and Stalingrad Fronts—they were to pick up where they had left off on the evening on 27 November.

For the Germans, however, the challenge was more complex. From Paulus's perspective, the most important task was to withdraw Sixth Army's forces to the defensive lines he had designated late on 27 November and to do so without suffering undue casualties. No less of a concern to Paulus was the army's precarious supply situation, particularly with regard to ammunition, fuel, and food stocks, which the army was rapidly exhausting. Paulus also seriously doubted that the *Luftwaffe* could make good on its promise of aerial resupply. From the perspective of Army Group Don, which became operational on 26 November under the command of Field Marshal von Manstein, the most critical challenge was to somehow mount a credible effort to reinforce or rescue Paulus's army. Clearly, this could not be done unless German forces controlled the staging areas for such a relief effort—specifically, the bridgehead on the Don River's eastern bank opposite Rychkovskii and the Kotel'nikovo region southwest of Stalingrad. As a result, these two regions would remain the focal points of fighting until the issue of who controlled them was resolved. That resolution would take another two weeks of heavy fighting.

The Southwestern Front's Advance

From the *Stavka*'s perspective, the most important mission of Vatutin's *front* late on 27 November was to push 5th Tank Army's forces to and across the Chir River and capture Rychkovskii (see map 29). However, by this time, Vatutin was most concerned about the deteriorating situation on his *front's* right wing. There, German Attack Group Hollidt (XVII Army Corps) had begun a counterstroke with its 62nd and 294th Infantry Divisions, driving 1st Guards Army's 14th Guards and 278th Rifle Divisions back across the Krivaia River and seizing a lodgment on the eastern bank. Although only 4 kilometers deep, this bridgehead conjured up visions of a German thrust southeastward along the Chir River's eastern bank that could threaten 5th Tank Army's rear forces fighting in the bridgeheads on the Chir's western bank northwest of Chernyshevskaia. Therefore, Vatutin urged Leliushenko's 1st Guards Army to destroy the German bridgehead at all costs.

1st Guards Army

Leliushenko responded to Group Hollidt's counterstroke by organizing a counterattack of his own with 278th and 266th Rifle Divisions of his army's newly formed 14th Rifle Corps (see appendix 7D in the *Companion* for the Southwestern Front's accomplishments on 28–30 November). The two counterattacking divisions were to strike the Germans' bridgehead from the north and east and push German forces back to the Krivaia River. The 266th Rifle Division's history describes the assault by Group Hollidt's forces, which began at dawn on 28 November:

[The 266th Division] launched its counterstroke on the morning of 28 November in cooperation with General D. P. Monakhov's 278th Rifle Division. The division entered combat in a situation when the enemy temporarily seized the initiative and tried to exploit its success. [The situation] required a turning point in the course of battle in this sector.

Despite the absence of infantry support tanks and the small amount of artillery, which prevented suppression of the enemy's firing weapons, the attack developed successfully. . . .

The enemy launched several counterattacks during the second half of the day. More than ten "Junkers" flew in support. The regiments' advance was halted. General Vetoshnikov committed the 1010th Regiment into combat from second echelon. . . .

By day's end on 28 November, the division threw the enemy back beyond the Krivaia River and, by order of the corps' commander, went over to the defense along the line of the Dubovskii, Gorbatovskii, Ushakov, and Belavinskii Farms. The 203rd Rifle Division defended on the left, and 159th Rifle Division defended on the right.[8]

Although 1st Guards Army succeeded in containing the counterstroke by Group Hollidt's 62nd and 294th Infantry Divisions and restored the front along the Krivaia River, Soviet sources claim that Group Hollidt conducted another 19 separate attacks against 14th Corps' defenses from 1 through 9 December.[9] This proved that General Hollidt's forces were doing their part to defend the Krivaia and Chir Rivers. Romanian forces launched counterattacks of their own, prompting one source to note, "I Corps' 11th and 7th Divisions counterattacked Dubrovski [Dubovoi] seven times in late November and early December, but were repeatedly repulsed. Their 1,500 casualties were bearable, but the confidence gained by earlier defensive success was undermined."[10]

5th Tank Army
While 1st Guards Army dealt with Group Hollidt's attacks along the Krivaia River, heavy fighting also occurred in 5th Tank Army's sectors along the upper Chir River north and south of Chernyshevskaia and in the Oblivskaia and Rychkovskii regions along the lower Chir and Don Rivers. In both regions, German and Romanian forces frustrated Romanenko as his forces strove to accomplish missions that should have been fulfilled by 23 November. Try as they did, they were unable to overcome Axis defenses along the two rivers and capture the towns of Oblivskaia, Surovikino, and Rychkovskii (see map 36 and appendix 7D in the *Companion*).

However, in compensation for the Southwestern Front's loss of 21st Army to Rokossovsky's Don Front, by dawn on 28 November, Romanenko's

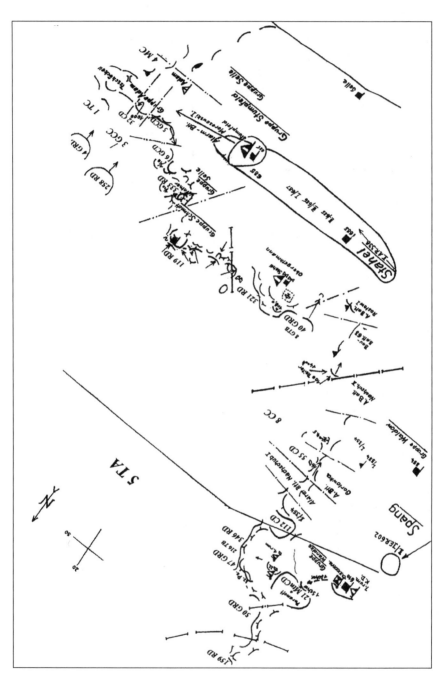

Map 36. 5th Tank Army's pursuit to the Chir River and Romanian Third Army's defenses, 30 November 1942

5th Tank Army received four rifle divisions from the Don Front's 21st and 65th Armies (333rd Rifle from 21st Army, and 40th Guards and 321st and 258th Rifle from 65th Army), as well as the three cavalry divisions of General Pliev's 3rd Guards Cavalry Corps from 21st Army. The next day, the *Stavka* alerted a fifth rifle division, 65th Army's 4th Guards, to prepare to move into 5th Tank Army's sector. In addition, the *Stavka* and the Southwestern Front took care to reinforce General Butkov's 1st Tank Corps, the only tank corps available to 5th Tank Army. After the corps' tank park dwindled to about 20 tanks on 24 November, Vatutin released enough new tanks to increase the corps' strength to 146 tanks by 29 November: 5 KVs, 75 T-34s, and 66 T-70s.[11] However, it would take several days for the corps to integrate the new tanks into its structure and conduct the necessary driver and tactical training for their employment. In the meantime, the bulk of Butkov's tank corps would remain out of action. The *Stavka* and Vasilevsky believed that these reinforcements would provide 5th Tank Army with more than enough combat power for Romanenko to accomplish both his missions.

The prolonged fighting for these two important sectors was already taking shape by the evening of 27 November. By this time, General Pliev's 3rd Guards Cavalry Corps had moved into the area north of Rychkovskii and Novomaksimovskii on 5th Tank Army's left wing, along the lower Chir River. There, it relieved 1st Tank Corps' depleted forces so they could briefly rest and incorporate their new tanks. In addition, 258th Rifle Division was completing its movement southward into assembly areas in 3rd Guards Cavalry Corps' rear, from which it could reinforce Pliev's assaults on German positions at Rychkovskii and Verkhne-Chirskii. Farther west in 5th Tank Army's center, 333rd Rifle Division had finished its march southward to the Surovikino region, where it joined 119th Rifle Division's assaults on German defenses protecting that town. To the rear, 321st Rifle Division occupied assembly areas northeast of Surovikino and was prepared to move into the sector between Surovikino and Oblivskaia. Still farther westward along the Chir, 8th Cavalry Corps' 55th and 112th Divisions assaulted German defenses at Oblivskaia, and 40th Guards Rifle Division concentrated in assembly areas north of the town, ready to join the battle.

In the Chernyshevskaia region on 5th Tank Army's right wing, where the *Stavka* and Romanenko awaited word of great victories, the army's forces had already seized sizable bridgeheads north and south of the town and were still fighting for the town proper, which was now in German hands. Romanenko intended to envelop the town from the north and south or, failing that, simply seize the town by frontal assault. To the south, 346th Rifle Division relieved 8th Cavalry Corps' 112th Cavalry Division and took over responsibility for its bridgehead on the Chir's western bank at Varlamovskii and its eastern bank southward to Klinovoi. This permitted General Borisov to concentrate two of his corps' three cavalry divisions to attack Oblivskaia. At Chernyshev-skaia proper and to the north and south, 47th and 50th Guards Rifle Divisions were engaged in intense and complex fighting against XXXXVIII Panzer Corps' 22nd Panzer Division and Romanian 1st Armored Division in the sector extending from Zakharchenskii, 10 kilometers southeast of the town, to Chistiakovskaia, 8 kilometers to the northwest. In addition, at least one regiment of 47th Guards was supporting 21st Cavalry Division's forces in a bridgehead west of the Chir River, roughly 10 kilometers west-northwest of Chernyshevskaia. Finally, on 5th Tank Army's extreme right wing, 159th Rifle Division defended the sector from Novosergeevka northwestward to Starikov, 8 to 15 kilometers northwest of Chernyshevskaia. With most of his army's forces committed forward, Romanenko held 8th Guards and 216th Tank Brigades and 8th Motorcycle Regiment in reserve positions from which they could reinforce the sector either north or south of Chernyshevskaia.

The fighting that occurred from 28 to 30 November across 5th Tank Army's entire front was inconclusive at best and was generally disappointing to Romanenko and Vatutin. The actions of 3rd Guards Cavalry Corps could best be described as a prolonged reconnaissance in force conducted to determine the strength of German defenses along the front from Rychkovskii westward to Novomaksimovskii. The corps' three cavalry divisions carried out the reconnoitering as they completed their movement into the region. To the west, however, battalion-size assaults by Colonel M. I. Matveev's 333rd Rifle Division against Group Schmidt's defenses at Surovikino forced Schmidt to withdraw his defensive perimeter roughly halfway back to the town. As the day progressed, the rifle division slid one of its rifle regiments southeast toward Golovskii, 10 kilometers southeast of the town, in an attempt to identify a weak spot in German defenses and exploit it by pushing southward across the river.

Still farther to the west, 55th and 112th Cavalry Divisions of Borisov's 8th Cavalry Corps assaulted the northern perimeter of VIII Air Corps' defenses at Oblivskaia. But the dismounted light infantry was unable to make even a dent in the strong German defenses. Clearly, the cavalry corps needed rifle reinforcements before it could hope to take the town by storm. All the while, the corps complained of intense German air strikes that had already taken a deadly toll on the cavalry and were continuing to do so. Therefore, Borisov welcomed the news that 321st Rifle and 40th Guards Rifle Divisions were closing into his rear, ready to take part in the reduction of Oblivskaia's defenses.

Farther northwestward up the Chir River, Colonel Tolstov's 346th Rifle Division moved into positions along the eastern bank, 14 to 28 kilometers south of Chernyshevskaia, and took control over the bridgehead at Varlamov from 112th Cavalry Division. The cavalry division left one regiment in the bridgehead and south along the Chir, prompting Group Wandtke's Alarm Battalion Gorlovka to report that four to five companies of Soviet infantry had seized another bridgehead on the Chir's western bank at Siniapkin, 11 kilometers south of Varlamov.[12] However, the German defenders were able to contain the small force.

In the Chernyshevskaia region proper, Major General Belov, who had been promoted from the rank of colonel the day before, shifted 50th Guards Rifle Division southward to take part in the fight for Chernyshevskaia. Two of his regiments fought to capture the town, while his third regiment defended the sector from Krasnoiarovka to Zakharchenskii, 5 to 8 kilometers to the southeast. During this fighting, elements of Romanian 14th Infantry and 7th Cavalry Divisions struck at a small bridgehead defended by 50th Guards on the western bank of the Chir at Leont'evskii. Meanwhile, 22nd Panzer Division's *Kampfgruppe* Oppeln deployed its forces in the Paramonov region, 8 kilometers west of Chernyshevskaia, to block any advance southward by 21st Cavalry Division's forces and the single regiment of 47th Guards Rifle Division occupying the sizable bridgehead on the Chir's western bank northwest of the town.[13] Although 22nd Panzer had been vastly weakened by 13 days of near-constant fighting, it was strong enough to block the cavalry division's light infantry and prevent them from cutting the road leading west from Chernyshevskaia.

While 22nd Panzer protected Chernyshevskaia from the northwest and west, Romanian 1st Armored Division moved eastward to block Soviet 346th Rifle Division in the Varlamov bridgehead south of the town. By this time, General Gheorghe's division was at 30 percent strength. Its 1st Armored Regiment fielded 9 serviceable Pz-III and Pz-IV tanks and 19 R-2 light tanks; its 1st Motorized Artillery Regiment had 11 of its authorized 12 100mm guns and 8 of 12 105mm guns. However, its 3rd and 4th Motorized Infantry Regiments fielded only one weak battalion each. As for antitank guns, its antitank battalion had two 75mm and two 47mm guns, and its antitank company fielded two 20mm guns. Fortunately for the defenders, 47th and 50th Guards Divisions had limited, if any, tank support.[14]

While General Belov's 50th Guards Division fought at Chernyshevskaia proper and southeast of the town, two regiments of Colonel Ostashenko's 47th Guards Division fought north of the town, and one of his regiments fought in support of 50th Guards Division's assault on the town. By this time, Chernyshevskaia was half encircled by Soviet cavalry to the west and northwest, infantry to the north and northeast, and still more infantry to the east and southeast. However, since neither side had sufficient forces to overcome the other, the fighting went on indecisively for days.

Thus, by day's end on 28 November, the forces of Romanenko 5th Tank Army were operating along the following axes and facing the German forces indicated:

Verkhne-Chirskii and Rychkovskii
- 3rd Guards Cavalry Corps—relieved 1st Tank Corps and deployed in the Novomaksimovskii, Rychkovskii, and Skity sector, from 10 kilometers west to 7 kilometers east of Rychkovskii, facing Groups Tzschöckel and Adam.
- 1st Tank Corps—in army reserve.
- 258th Rifle Division—in the Pogodinskii and Buratskii region in the Liska River valley, 11 to 14 kilometers northwest of Rychkovskii.

Surovikino
- 333rd Rifle Division—relieved 119th Rifle Division and fighting at and east of Surovikino, against Groups Schmidt and Korntner.
- 119th Rifle Division—fighting at and west of Surovikino against Group Stumpfeld's 108th Artillery Command (ARKO).

Oblivskaia
- 8th Cavalry Corps (55th and 112th Cavalry Divisions)—fighting at Oblivskaia against Group Stahel (VIII Air Corps).
- 321st Rifle Division—in the Mitiaevskii, Markinskii, and Zhirkov region, 7 to 15 kilometers northeast of Surovikino.
- 40th Guards Rifle Division—in the Nesterkin and Frolov region, 10 to 14 kilometers north of Oblivskaia.

Chernyshevskaia (south)
- 346th Rifle Division—fortifying the Varlamov and Klinovyi line, 14 to 28 kilometers south of Chernyshevskaia, with a bridgehead on the western bank of the Chir River at Varlamov against Group Wandtke's 2nd Battalion, 354th Grenadier Regiment, and Alarm Battalion Gorlovka.
- 112th Cavalry Division (8th Cavalry Corps)—one regiment in the Varlamov and Siniapkin regions fighting against Group Wandtke's Alarm Battalion Gorlovka.

Chernyshevskaia (north)
- 50th Guards Rifle Division—fighting on the eastern outskirts of Chernyshevskaia against XXXXVIII Panzer Corps' 22nd Panzer Division on its right wing and defending the sector from Krasnoiarovka to Zakharchenskii, 5 to 8 kilometers southeast of Chernyshevskaia, with its left wing against Romanian 1st Armored Division.

- 47th Guards Rifle Division—fighting in the sector from Chernyshevskaia to Chistiakovskaia, 6 kilometers northwest of Chernyshevskaia, with two regiments, and at Chernyshevskaia proper with one regiment against elements of Romanian 14th Infantry and 7th Cavalry Divisions and *Kampfgruppe* Oppeln of 22nd Panzer Division.

With four fresh rifle divisions in the process of reinforcing its forward positions, 5th Tank Army continued to assault the still-ragged defenses that Group Hollidt and Romanian Third Army were frantically establishing along the entire length of the Chir River. The fighting along the Chir front also intensified because Romanenko committed his last reserves into combat in the sectors where success seemed most likely. For example, he reinforced 346th Rifle Division's bridgehead in the Varlamov region with the handful of tanks available to 8th Guards and 216th Tank Brigades overnight on 28–29 November, together with two regiments from 47th Guards Rifle Division.

Despite the increasing intensity of 5th Tank Army's assaults, the German defenders were also encouraged by the arrival of fresh reinforcements. Late on 28 November, for example, the lead elements of General of Artillery Walther Lucht's 336th Infantry Division began arriving in the lower Chir valley. The first to do so were the division's 1st Battalion, 687th Regiment; 3rd Battalion, 685th Regiment; and 2nd Battalion, 686th Regiment, all of which marched eastward to fill in the front between Group Adam at Nizhne-Chirskaia and Group Schmidt at Surovikino.[15] This occurred just in the nick of time, because the forces on 5th Tank Army's left wing were about to begin a major effort to capture the entire region from Rychkovskii westward to Surovikino. In essence, a meeting engagement was about to begin between Soviet reinforcements reaching the region and, in succession, German 336th Infantry Division and 11th Panzer and 7th *Luftwaffe* Field Divisions, due to arrive over the next several days. However, rather than holding on to the Chir River line, the priority mission of these fresh forces was to form the nucleus of a reorganized XXXXVIII Panzer Corps, which was supposed to begin a relief effort toward Stalingrad from the Rychkovskii and Nizhne-Chirskaia regions during the first week of December. But fate would ordain that the old adage "first things first" still applied.

The fighting on 5th Tank Army's left wing intensified on 29 November when 5th and 6th Guards Cavalry Divisions of General Pliev's 3rd Guards Cavalry Corps, fighting side by side with several composite brigade groups from Butkov's 1st Tank Corps, assaulted German defenses along the lower Chir River in the sector from Rychkovskii westward to Novomaksimovskii. Their twin objectives were Rychkovskii, which controlled access to the Germans' bridgehead on the Don River's eastern bank, and the fortified town of

Verkhne-Chirskii, which, if captured, would leave Group Tzschöckel's forces at Rychkovskii isolated and encircled.

Leaving 32nd Cavalry Division as his corps' reserve, Pliev ordered 5th and 6th Guards Cavalry Divisions, with a handful of 1st Tank Corps' tanks in support, to attack southward from east of Chir Station and strike Group Tzschöckel's defenses at Rychkovskii. These attacks failed to even dent the Germans' well-prepared defensive positions, however. Simultaneously, the main body of Butkov's tank corps, with fewer than 20 serviceable tanks, attacked southward from jumping-off positions south and west of Chir Station in an attempt to overcome Group Adam's defenses and reach and capture Verkhne-Chirskii. However, his attack also failed, with heavy losses. Although the Red Army General Staff received no reports from Colonel Fursin's 258th Rifle Division, it likely attacked in the Novomaksimovskii sector on 1st Tank Corps' right. Like its neighbors to the right, Furson's rifle division made no progress whatsoever against Group Goebbel, which was occupying defenses on Group Adam's left wing.[16]

Romanian Third Army's daily intelligence maps duly recorded the assault, noting that it took place at 1000 hours and involved only five tanks at Rychkovskii. The sad fact was that, even if the German formations defending these positions were threadbare, the Soviet cavalry and rifle divisions were so worn down themselves by a week of fighting that they had perhaps as few as 5,000 men per cavalry division and 6,500 per rifle division.

Overnight on 29–30 November, some good news salved Romanenko's hurt feelings over the repulse at Rychkovskii. The *Stavka* informed him that it was releasing 4th Guards Rifle Division to his control and directing it to move southward to reinforce his army's shock group attacking Verkhne-Chirskii, Rychkovskii, and the adjacent German bridgehead across the Don.[17] Energized by this news, Romanenko ordered Butkov and Pliev to resume their assaults on the 30th, this time with 1st Tank Corps attacking in a sector farther west. Following their commander's orders, 3rd Guards Cavalry and 1st Tank Corps attacked the next morning. At day's end, Romanenko reported only that Butkov's corps had attacked southward from the Bol'shaia Osinovka and Staromaksimovskii region, 15 to 20 kilometers southeast of Surovikino, toward Nizhne-Chirskaia, 32 kilometers southwest of Surovikino, and that Pliev's cavalry had done so from the Novomaksimovskii and Chir Station region, 22 to 27 kilometers southeast of Surovikino, toward the same objective. No additional information had been received.[18]

When 5th Tank Army finally did receive information, it was not at all positive. The defenses of both Group Adam and Group Tzschöckel had proved too hard to crack, and the attackers once again failed to make any progress. Making matters worse, the three lead battalions from General Lucht's 336th Infantry Division had arrived to back up Group Adam's forces, in addition to 1st Morozovskaia Alarm Battalion, raised locally from German rear area units.[19] By month's end, it was clear that it would take more than 1st Tank and 3rd Guards Cavalry Corps to overcome German defenses along the lower Chir River.

Westward up the Chir valley, Colonel Kulagin's 119th Rifle Division continued its heavy assaults on Group Schmidt's defenses at Surovikino on 29 November. After 24 hours of off-and-on fighting, the division penetrated into the town's northern outskirts on the morning of the 30th, where it engaged in street fighting with the German defenders. While these assaults were under way, Colonel Matveev's 333rd Rifle Division concentrated its three regiments east of Surovikino on 29 November and then moved them 8 kilometers southeastward along the northern bank of the Chir overnight. Attacking at dawn on 30 November, Matveev's riflemen captured Dmitrievka Station, 10 kilometers southeast of Surovikino, and forced their way across the Chir River to capture the village of Golovskii on the southern bank from German Group Korntner at midmorning. Matveev's division then pushed westward 3 kilometers and captured the village of Ostrovskii, which it quickly fortified. Although the sudden attack encircled part of Group Korntner east of Ostrovskii, Group Selle quickly moved northward from its positions along the Don, rescued Korntner's force, and halted 333rd Rifle Division's advance before it could expand the bridgehead further. By this time, the bridgehead measured roughly 6 kilometers wide by 3 kilometers deep, large enough to bring additional forces across the Chir.[20]

Although Group Schmidt managed to cling to its defenses at Surovikino, the Soviet seizure of a bridgehead on the Chir River's southern bank posed a major problem for German planners. In short, they had to eliminate the bridgehead before the Soviets could move larger and stronger forces into it. Otherwise, it could become a launching point for an offensive designed to thwart any German attempt to relieve Stalingrad from the west.

While fighting flared up in the Rychkovskii and Surovikino region, it also intensified at Oblivskaia, the largest town on the northern bank of the Chir River that was still in German hands. After assaulting Oblivskaia's defenses with light cavalry for more than three days, help finally arrived on 30 November. Advancing from the north, General Makarenko's 321st Rifle Division and Major General A. I. Pastrevich's 40th Guards Rifle Division reached the Oblivskaia region, with the former concentrated in assembly areas northeast of the town and the latter northwest and west of the town. Both divisions then joined 8th Cavalry Corps' assault on VIII Air Corps' Group Stahel late on 29 November.

As the two fresh rifle divisions entered combat on 29 November, Borisov sent detachments from his corps' 55th and 112th Cavalry Divisions to conduct screening operations along the eastern bank of the Chir from the mouth of the Mashka River, 35 kilometers northwest of Oblivskaia, southward and then eastward along the bend in the river to the town of Popov, 12 kilometers west of Oblivskaia. The next day, these detachments captured several small bridgeheads on the river's western bank. According to German records, these were in Alarm Battalion Gorlovka's sector south of Georgievskii, 20 kilometers south of Varlamovskii, and in 63rd Construction Battalion's sector near Parshin and Deev, 15 to 20 kilometers northwest of Oblivskaia.[21] Both these bridgeheads were in Group Spang's area of responsibility. Although stretched to the limit, the defensive line of scattered company strongpoints erected by the motley assemblage of *kampfgruppen* in Colonel Spang's group bent, but it did not break.

With additional forces at hand, General Borisov attempted a general assault against Group Stahel's forces defending Oblivskaia on the morning of 30 November. The main forces of 8th Cavalry Corps' 55th and 112th Division attacked the defenses from the north, 321st Rifle Division struck from the east, and at least one regiment from 40th Guards Rifle Division attacked from the west. After 40th Guards Division's main forces captured the town of Frolov, 8 kilometers north of Oblivskaia, reportedly after a six-hour fight, they moved westward to relieve 8th Cavalry Corps' detachments along and west of the Chir River. Ultimately, all three regiments of General Pastrevich's 40th Guards Division manned defenses along the Chir's eastern bank from west of Oblivskaia westward and then northward to the Mashka River, which formed 346th Rifle Division's southern boundary. Despite these reinforcements, Borisov's combined infantry and cavalry assault on Oblivskaia failed, although the arrival of 40th Guards southwest of the town threatened its mainly *Luftwaffe* defenders.[22]

After receiving word of Borisov's failure, late on 30 November, an increasingly frustrated General Romanenko ordered 21st Cavalry Division, which had been fighting in the bridgehead across the Chir River north of Chernyshevskaia, to break contact, turn its sector over to 50th Guards Rifle Division, and move south to join its parent corps at Oblivskaia. However, it took almost three days of additional fighting before General Iakunin's cavalry was able to disengage from combat with 22nd Panzer and Romanian 14th Infantry Divisions, which began to conduct incessant counterattacks on 30 November.

The heavy fighting in the Chernyshevskaia area began to wind down on 29 November when Romanenko realized that, since XXXXVIII Panzer Corps' 22nd Panzer Division was on the loose in and north of the town, the best opportunity for success was in 346th Rifle Division's area of operation south of the town. Therefore, he initially decided to abandon most of the bridgehead across the Chir north of Chernyshevskaia and shift all of 47th Guards Rifle and 21st Cavalry Divisions southward—the former to reinforce

346th Rifle Division in its sector south of the town, and the latter to rejoin 8th Cavalry Corps' attacks on Oblivskaia. However, since 21st Cavalry and one regiment of 47th Guards were still involved in heavy fighting in the bridgehead, 5th Tank Army's commander settled for moving just two regiments of 47th Guards southward on 29 November.[23]

South of Chernyshevskaia, 346th Rifle Division was now commanded by Major General D. I. Stankevsky, who had replaced the hapless Colonel Tolstov several hours before. It occupied defensive positions along the eastern bank of the Chir River from the mouth of the Mashka River northward to the village of Zakharchenskii, 10 to 30 kilometers south of Chernyshevskaia. Stankevsky's forces, supported by at least a squadron of cavalry from 112th Cavalry Division, also defended three bridgeheads the cavalry had seized on the river's western bank. Two small bridgeheads were situated at Arzhanovskii, 12 kilometers south of Chernyshevskaia, and on the west bank of the river west of Osinovskii, 15 kilometers south of Chernyshevskaia; the largest, up to 5 by 5 kilometers in size, was anchored on the village of Varlamovskii, 17 kilometers south of Chernyshevskaia. The 346th Division faced small detachments from Romanian 1st Armored Division and 2nd Battalion of German 403rd Security Division's 354th Grenadier Regiment.[24]

Late on the afternoon of 29 November, two regiments from General Fokanov's 47th Guards Rifle Division, together with 8th Guards and 216th Tank Brigades, reinforced Stankevsky's forces in the bridgehead at Varlamovskii. At dawn the next day, these forces attacked westward and northwestward, capturing the village of Varlamov, 5 kilometers to the northwest. In conjunction with attacks by 346th's other regiments, 346th and 47th Guards Divisions combined their three bridgeheads west of the Chir into one large one that threatened Axis forces in the Chernyshevskaia region with envelopment from the south and southeast. General Cramer, commander of XXXXVIII Panzer Corps, responded by dispatching most of Romanian 1st Armored Division to the region, precipitating a day-long fight on 1 December during which the attacking 346th and 47th Guards Divisions were halted in positions extending from the eastern outskirts of Varlamov northward roughly 14 kilometers to the eastern outskirts of Chernyshevskaia.

The 1st Armored Division reportedly lost 26 men killed, 208 wounded, and 250 with frostbite between 27 November and 1 December. This reduced its combat strength to only 944 troops and three tanks on 2 December, although the division still counted 6,335 men in its combat support and rear service units. Conversely, the division claimed it left 690 Soviet dead on the battlefield and captured 50 prisoners and 14 antitank guns in the fighting at and southeast of Chernyshevskaia.[25] Although reliable figures are unavailable, it is likely 346th Rifle and 47th Guards Rifle Divisions numbered fewer than 6,000 men each at this stage of the fighting.

Meanwhile, at and just north of Chernyshevskaia, on 29 November, Colonel Belov's 50th Guards Rifle Division relieved the two regiments of 47th Guards Division fighting along the Chir east and southeast of Chernyshevskaia and assumed control of the sector extending from Rusakov, 2 kilometers east of the town, to Zakharchenskii, 9 kilometers southeast of the town. However, heavy attacks by Romanian 14th Infantry and German 22nd Panzer Divisions against 21st Cavalry Division's bridgehead west and northwest of Chernyshevskaia prevented it, as well as the supporting regiment from 47th Guards Division, from breaking contact and withdrawing to defenses closer to the Chir River. On 30 November, 50th Guards Division finally succeeded in relieving part of 21st Cavalry Division and 47th Guards Division's isolated regiment and, in the process, took control of the entire sector from Rusakov northward through Leont'evskii to Illarionov, from 2 kilometers east to 17 kilometers northwest of Chernyshevskaia. By this time, Belov's division and some elements of 21st Cavalry Division still retained a shallower bridgehead on the Chir's western bank from Chistiakovskaia northward to west of Starikov. However, these forces were now contained by Romanian 14th Infantry and German 22nd Panzer Divisions.[26]

As was the case south of Chernyshevskaia, 21st Cavalry Division and the supporting regiment of 47th Guards Division had likely fought themselves out and probably numbered fewer than 5,000 men between them. In essence, by 30 November, the fight around Chernyshevskaia involved divisions on both sides at regimental strength, regiments at battalion strength, and battalions at company strength. Attrition finally rendered further fighting in the region futile at best.

On 5th Tank Army's extreme right wing, as before, Colonel Anashkin's 159th Rifle Division, supported by several battalions from 21st Cavalry Division, still clung to bridgeheads on the Chir River's western bank and defended the sector on the eastern bank from Illarionov northwestward to the junction of the Chir and Krivaia Rivers and farther northward along the Krivaia to Astakhov. Anashkin's division assumed control of the 10-kilometer-wide sector of the Krivaia northward to Astakhov when 1st Guards Army concentrated its forces to conduct a counterstroke north of Astakhov. After 1st Guards Army regained the river line, 159th Rifle Division reported that it "repulsed attacks by small enemy groups along the Astakhov and Illarionov line (5 kilometers east of Bokovskaia to 17 kilometers northeast of Chernyshevskaia)" on 30 November. Thus, thanks to 14th Rifle Corps' counterattack, any threat posed by Group Hollidt to the tank army's right wing was sharply diminished.

Conclusions

The last three days of November were frustrating for General Vatutin. Despite the sizable reinforcements the *Stavka* dispatched to his *front*, none of his armies accomplished their objectives. Even though Leliushenko's 1st Guards Army successfully contained Group Hollidt's attacks, removing the fear of a counterstroke against his *front*'s right flank, Romanenko's 5th Tank Army failed to capture Rychkovskii, Verkhne-Chirskii, Surovikino, and Oblivskaia. Even in the Chernyshevskaia sector, where it appeared that Romanenko's forces might succeed in enveloping and capturing the town, XXXXVIII Panzer Corps' defenses held firm. Although 5th Tank Army controlled a sizable bridgehead south of the town, it was forced to abandon its effort to carve out a major bridgehead north of the town. With German and Romanian defenses along the Chir River intact, a German relief effort toward Stalingrad from the west remained a distinct possibility.

The 5th Tank Army failed to accomplish its assigned missions for several reasons. First and foremost, combat attrition produced by ten days of intense fighting stripped the army of much of its penetrating power. Until 1st Tank Corps was capable of operating effectively with its new complement of 146 tanks, Romanenko's army would have to subsist by depending on Pliev's cavalry corps, worn down in previous fighting, and the relatively fresh divisions Vasilevsky sent him from the Don Front. But most if not all of these divisions were also well understrength after more than a week of fighting.

Second, the Romanian and German defenses along the Chir River proved far more effective than their chaotic organization indicated. The excessive time it took to eject XXXXVIII Panzer Corps from its blocking positions north of the Kurtlak River drastically slowed 5th Tank Army's advance to the Chir. This, in turn, enabled Romanian Third Army and its German advisers to raise sufficient forces to defend key locations along the Chir and turn those locations into formidable strongpoints. In particular, the large number of German *Flak* (antiaircraft) units along the Chir, together with many antiaircraft guns (especially the vaunted 88s), made these strongpoints hard to crack. Last but not least, the fact that significant elements of XXXXVIII Panzer Corps' 22nd Panzer Division and Romanian 1st Armored and 7th Cavalry Divisions managed to escape destruction confounded 5th Tank Army's attempts to penetrate Axis defenses along the upper Chir. In short, the vexing problem of overcoming XXXXVIII Panzer Corps, which had spoiled Vatutin's initial offensive timetable from the start of his exploitation operation, also thwarted the Southwestern Front's plan to expand its offensive to and beyond the Chir River. Ironically, XXXXVIII Panzer Corps' 22nd Panzer Division, a force ridiculed for years after the German defeat at Stalingrad, proved to be the most important impediment to the operations of Vatutin's Southwestern Front throughout the first two weeks of Operation Uranus.

The Don Front's Advance

With the heavy fighting to expel German Sixth Army's XI Army Corps from the Sirotinskaia bridgehead behind them, the Don Front's 21st, 65th, and 24th Armies spent the three days from 28 to 30 November pushing their forces eastward from the Kalach region and southward and eastward from the Don River (see map 37 and appendix 7E in the *Companion* for the Don Front's accomplishments on 28–30 November). Since their axes of advance converged, they also had to regroup their forces constantly as Sixth Army withdrew to what Paulus designated as the main defensive positions of the final Stalingrad pocket. As far as command and control was concerned, Rokossovsky, the *front* commander, was satisfied that all the armies operating against the northern half of Sixth Army's pocket were now unified under his command.

On the Don Front's right wing, General Chistiakov's 21st Army, now without Pliev's 3rd Guards Cavalry Corps, fought in the sector from Peskovatka southwestward to Sokarevka and then southward to the western approaches to Marinovka. In the *front*'s center, Batov's 65th Army, now significantly reduced in size, fought in the sector from Vertiachii northeastward to Peskovatka, and Galanin's 24th Army pressed southward along the eastern bank of the Don River from Verkhne-Gnilovskii and the region to the east. On the *front*'s long left wing, Zhadov's 66th Army fought hard to collapse the northern and northeastern front of Sixth Army's pocket. Although the fighting during this period was heavy, it was by no means decisive.

Rokossovsky later summarized his armies' limited accomplishments during this period:

> In the fighting from 28–30 November, the forces of 21st and 65th Armies achieved some success: they captured Peskovatka and Vertiachii. In the remaining sectors neither we nor our neighbors achieved any results. After visiting various sectors, I became convinced that we could not hope for success in the offensive without special, serious preparations. I considered it my duty to report this to Stalin during routine conversations by enciphered teletype. I also mentioned that it would be more opportune to entrust the operation to liquidate the encircled enemy grouping force to one *front*, the Stalingrad or the Don, subordinating to it all of the troops operating in the Stalingrad region.
>
> Stalin gave no definite reply. At the time, the *Stavka* was focusing its attention on the outer encirclement front, to which all of the available reserves, and even units fighting the surrounded enemy were being directed. Thus, three rifle divisions and four antitank regiments were taken from our *front*, and almost all of the armor and motorized formations and

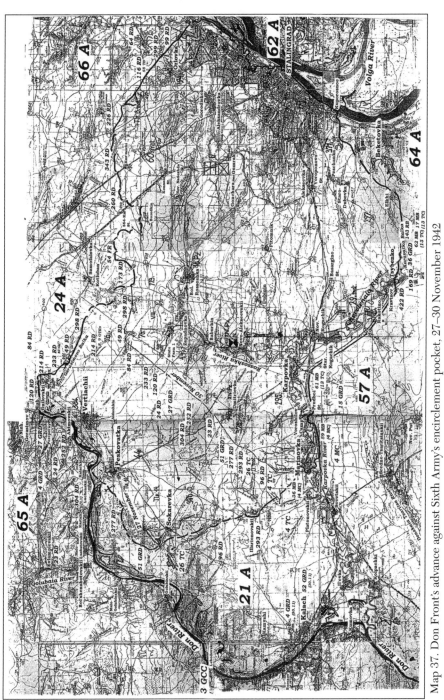

Map 37. Don Front's advance against Sixth Army's encirclement pocket, 27–30 November 1942

units were taken from the Stalingrad Front. All of this further weakened the already under-strength units engaged in continuous fighting at Stalingrad. Still, under these circumstances, these measures were correct.[27]

Nevertheless, Rokossovsky was not pleased with Stalin's decision.

21st Army

The fact that it was now fighting subordinate to the Don Front rather than the Southwestern Front did nothing to increase 21st Army's combat power or combat success. On the contrary, the transfer of Pliev's 3rd Guards Cavalry Corps to the Southwestern Front's 5th Tank Army seriously eroded the combat strength of Chistiakov's army. After the cavalry corps' departure, Chistiakov's army retained the meager remnants of Kravchenko's 4th and Rodin's 26th Tank Corps, whose tanks were consolidated into single-brigade groups capable of providing only minimal support for the army's advancing infantry. Therefore, the army's advance was slow, often measured in hundreds of meters per day. Nonetheless, Chistiakov's forces continued to pound German defenses in the sector from the western approaches to Marinovka, northward past Illarionovskii to the northern and western approaches to Sokarevka, and northeastward to the western approaches to Peskovatka (see maps 38 and 39).

The sector opposite Chistiakov's army was defended by 3rd Motorized Division and 376th and 44th Infantry Divisions of Sixth Army's XIV Panzer Corps and VIII Army Corps, supported by combat groups [*kampfgruppen*] from 14th and 16th Panzer Divisions. The 3rd Motorized, under XIV Panzer Corps, was deployed in strong defenses from Marinovka northward along the eastern bank of Vaniukova *Balka* to Illarionovskii, 9 kilometers north-northwest of Marinovka. The 376th Infantry, with a *kampfgruppe* from 14th Panzer Division, also under XIV Panzer's control, was deployed in the 12-kilometer-wide sector from just north of Illarionovskii to Sokarevka. Finally, VIII Army Corps' 44th Infantry, with its supporting *kampfgruppe* from 16th Panzer Division, manned defenses in the Peskovatka sector.

Given the slow progress of 21st Army's advance, its daily situation reports to the General Staff provide the clearest picture of its accomplishments (see appendix 7E in the *Companion*). In general, the army's 293rd Rifle Division and 4th Tank Corps captured Illarionovskii, 10 kilometers north of Sovetskii, from 3rd Motorized Division; 26th Tank Corps seized Sokarevka, 21 kilometers northeast of Kalach, from 376th Infantry and 14th Panzer Divisions; and 51st Guards Rifle Division captured Peskovatka, 31 kilometers northeast of Kalach, from 44th Infantry Division. Thereafter, Chistiakov's forces drove east toward Dmitrievka at an agonizingly slow pace because of what Soviet sources called extremely stubborn resistance.

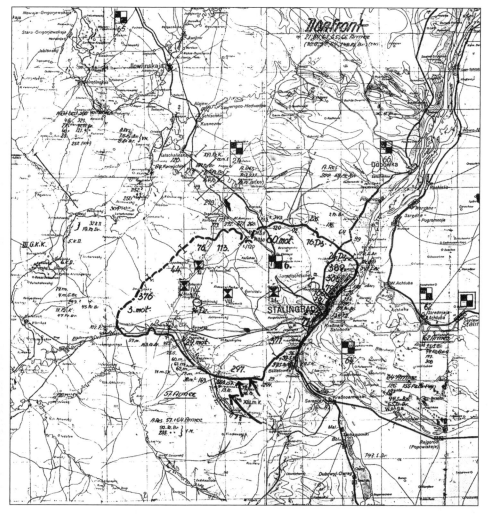

Map 38. Sixth Army's Stalingrad pocket [*Kessel*], 29–30 November 1942

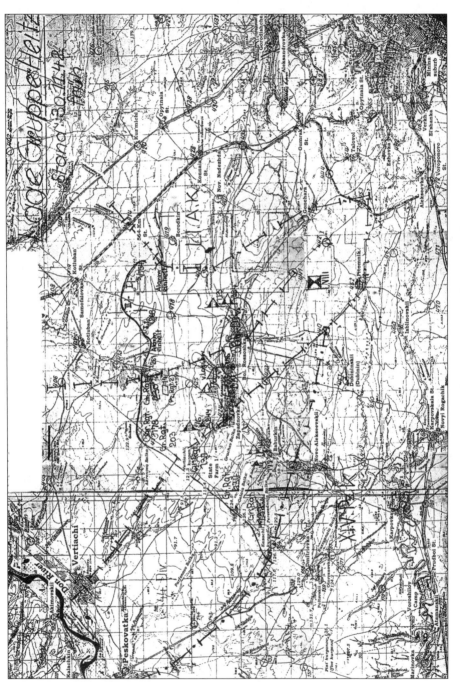

Map 39. Sixth Army's Western Front (VIII Army Corps and XIV Panzer Corps), 30 November 1942

Every unit in Chistiakov's army took part in the offensive, but most if not all were ultimately repulsed before reaching their final objectives. Although the Soviets claimed their relentless pressure forced the Germans to abandon Illarionovskii, Sokarevka, and Peskovatka, in reality, Paulus's withdrawal plan required his forces to abandon these towns by nightfall on 29 November as they withdrew to positions designated several days before. German combat reports also underscored the weakness of 21st Army's armor. For example, reports dispatched from XIV Panzer Corps to Sixth Army from 28 to 30 November mentioned attacks against 3rd Motorized Division's defenses at Hill 91.3, 2 kilometers northwest of Marinovka, by 300 Soviet infantry and 10 tanks on 28 November, as well as another assault on the same hill on 30 November by two battalions of infantry and 20 tanks.[28] Otherwise, all the corps involved in Paulus's planned withdrawal to ridgeline defenses between the Don and Rossoshka Rivers reported that they carried out the maneuver smoothly, without incident or interruption. Reports from XIV Panzer Corps stated that, as of 30 November, 3rd Motorized Division fielded 27 tanks (20 Pz-III, 3 Pz-IV short, and 4 Pz-IV long models), and 14th Panzer Division was being repositioned into Sixth Army's reserve.[29]

65th Army

As Vasilevsky's planned liquidation of Sixth Army's encirclement pocket reached its climax in late November, General Batov's 65th Army shrank drastically in size as it struggled to eliminate XI Army Corps' bridgehead around Akimovskii, north of the Don River. Quite naturally, his army's operational sector also narrowed as the axes of attack of 21st, 65th, and 24th Armies converged on the town of Vertiachii. The 65th Army's 304th, 252nd, and 27th Guards Divisions reached the northern bank of the Don at or near Akimovskii on the evening of 27 November and immediately prepared to cross the river and capture the German strongpoint of Vertiachii, several kilometers to the south. No sooner did Vasilevsky and the *Stavka* learn that Batov's forces had started crossing the Don than they stripped his army of four divisions (4th and 40th Guards and 258th and 321st Rifle), leaving him five divisions (23rd, 24th, 252nd, 304th, and 27th Guards) to continue the offensive.

Before his forces reached the northern bank of the Don, Batov had formulated a plan to send his three lead divisions across the river's icy surface to gain the Germans' flanks and rear and then attack Vertiachii simultaneously from the west, south, and north. Once the German strongpoint fell, the army would advance southeast toward Zapadnovka and Malaia Rossoshka, 18 to 20 kilometers distant.

Batov began implementing his plan at about midnight on 27 November, when two rifle battalions from 304th Rifle Division's 812th Regiment conducted a night crossing under the protective fire of 91st Tank Brigade's tanks. It was a particularly treacherous maneuver because the ice was not as firm as Batov would have liked. Nevertheless, with the help of sappers from 14th Engineer Brigade, the riflemen of Colonel Merkulov's division made it across the river safely, and soon thereafter the engineers erected a bridge (see appendix 7F in the *Companion* for Batov's description of the crossing).[30] Within hours, Batov's divisions were across the river and converging on Vertiachii, capturing the town by midnight on the 28th.

After more than 36 hours of fighting, Sixth Army's 44th and 384th Infantry Divisions completely abandoned the Peskovatka and Vertiachii regions by midday on 29 November and withdrew southeastward to the defensive line designated by Paulus several days before. The divisions of Batov's army pursued, engaging German rear guards as they advanced southeast toward Novo-Alekseevskii across the generally wide-open steppes. As they did, Batov withdrew Merkulov's 304th Division into his army's reserve and committed Colonel Sivakov's 23rd Rifle Division on his army's right wing and General Pastrevich's 24th Rifle Division on its left. By day's end on 30 November, the four divisions leading 65th Army's advance closed into positions in the roughly 14-kilometer-wide sector extending from Hill 117.6, 1.5 kilometers north of Dmitrievka, northeastward to Hill 121.3, 7 kilometers northwest of the village of Zapadnovka, on the Rossoshka River's western bank (see appendix 7E in the *Companion*).

Although 65th Army's divisions found the going relatively easy once they captured Vertiachii and began their southeastward march, the situation changed dramatically as they approached Paulus's new main defensive line. There, the pursuit ground to an abrupt halt as Batov's troops encountered intense fire and extensive fields of obstacles. To a large extent, the manner in which XI Army Corps conducted its withdrawal typified German withdrawal tactics at this time.

In addition to tracking the forward progress of Batov's army, Sixth Army's records explain how Strecker's XI Army Corps managed to withdraw its forces with the least possible harm. In this instance, while 44th and 384th Infantry Divisions carried out skillful delaying actions in the vicinity of Peskovatka and Vertiachii, 76th Infantry Division transferred its sector northeast of Vertiachii to 384th Division and then withdrew southeastward to its assigned defensive sector in the northwestern quadrant of Paulus's planned Stalingrad pocket, roughly 7 kilometers north of Zapadnovka. Thereafter, XI Corps employed two regiments from 384th Division as army rear guards and a single battalion from each of 44th and 76th Infantry Divisions' regiments as the corps' rear guards. Protected by these rearguard regiments and battalions, the corps' headquarters, together with the main bodies of all the regiments in the corps' divisions, withdrew steadily and apparently with minimal damage southeastward into their assigned defensive sectors along the western front of Paulus's "fortress" pocket. The daily report [*Tagesmeldung*] that Sixth Army issued at 2040 hours on 30 November described precisely how XI Army Corps organized its divisions for the withdrawal and subsequent occupation of its new defensive positions (see appendix 7G in the *Companion*). The same report heaped praise on 76th Infantry Division for its "outstanding" performance in the "difficult fighting in recent days," specifically stating that the division, supported by Antitank Detachment [Panzer *Jagd Abteilung*] von Lossow and 244th Assault Gun Battalion, "destroyed 64 enemy tanks and rendered 5 more immobile from 21 through 28 November."[31]

24th Army
Whereas Batov's 65th Army could claim credit for capturing Vertiachii, Galanin's 24th Army did little more than follow German XI Army Corps' withdrawing 76th Infantry Division back to its main defensive line. After the embarrassingly poor offensive performance of Galanin's army during the last week of November, this was like rubbing salt into the general's wounded pride. During the last three days of the month, his army merely advanced in the wake of the withdrawing Germans to the complex of *balkas* on the western approaches to Novoalekseevskii in the Rossoshka River valley (see appendix 7E in the *Companion*).

Thus, despite advancing up to 12 kilometers, the only thing 24th Army's divisions accomplished was to close up with the northwestern front of Sixth Army's new defensive pocket. Opposite Galanin's forces, 76th, 113th, and part of 60th Motorized Divisions were lodged in defenses that would remain impenetrable for almost six weeks.

66th Army
The history of the Don Front's 66th Army provides a starkly realistic picture of its contributions to the destruction of German Sixth Army in Operation Uranus. After detailing the army's surprise offensive on 24 November, which inflicted heavy damage on German 94th Infantry Division, it simply skips to 25 December, when the army conducted heavy attacks on German defenses in the Orlovka region (see map 37). Thus, it tacitly admits that General Zhadov's army accomplished nothing of note for about 30 days, implying that the army conducted no offensive operations whatsoever during this period. But nothing could be further from the truth. In fact, the army conducted offensive operations, albeit intermittently, right up to 12 December, all the while contending with multiple German counterattacks.[32]

The daily summaries prepared by the Red Army General Staff provide a skeletal account of 66th Army's operations from 28 to 30 November (see appendix 7E in the *Companion*). However, periodic reports in the records of German Sixth Army and LI Army Corps add flesh to this skeleton to produce a fairly clear picture of who did what to whom, along with an accurate description of the limited accomplishments of Zhadov's army. On 28 November, for example, the Red Army General Staff reported that 66th Army "resumed its offensive across its entire front at 1200 hours," but "strong enemy resistance" prevented the attacking divisions from achieving anything but "insignificant advances in several sectors."[33] Maps from the records of Sixth Army and LI Army Corps indicate that 66th Army conducted its main attack on its left wing, with 99th and 116th Rifle Divisions in first echelon and 299th Rifle Division in second echelon. The 58th Tank Brigade supported 116th Division's assault and, thereafter, both 116th and 299th Rifle Divisions. Operating on the left wing of the army's shock group, Colonel V. Ia. Vladimirov's 99th Rifle Division, with a company of tanks from Lieutenant Colonel G. I. Kalinin's 58th Tank Brigade, was to capture Hill 135.4, 2 kilometers east of Orlovka, and advance on Orlovka from the east. On the shock group's right, Colonel I. M. Makarov's 116th Rifle Division, supported by several companies of tanks from Kalinin's 58th Tank Brigade, was to capture Hills 144.2, 147.6, and 145.1, 1 to 4 kilometers north and northwest of Orlovka, and advance on the strongpoint from the north and northwest. Colonel Baklanov's second-echelon 299th Rifle Division was to commit to combat in 116th Division's sector and reinforce the assault on Orlovka.

Period maps from German records indicate that 16th Panzer Division's 16th Motorcycle Battalion; 1st Battalion, 79th Panzer-Grenadier Regiment; and 2nd Battalion, 276th Infantry Regiment (94th Division) defended the sector from Hill 146.1 southeastward to just south of Hill 147.6. At the same time, 24th Panzer Division's *Luftwaffe* Battalion Matho; 2nd and 1st Battalions, 267th Infantry Regiment (94th Division); and 1st Battalion, 21st Panzer-Grenadier Regiment defended the sector from Hill 144.2 southeastward to the approaches to Hill 135.4.[34]

The first German account of 66th Army's assault appears in Sixth Army's morning report on 28 November:

> Renewed enemy attacks against the north-eastern front of LI Army Corps. A penetration [by 99th Rifle Division] west of Rynok was straightened out by 24th Panzer Division. The enemy penetration near [Hill] 147.6 [by 116th Rifle Division and 58th Tank Brigade], which has a strength of about two battalions and more than 6 tanks and has pushed forward to the gulley 2.5 kms north-west of Orlovka, has not yet been sealed off. The elements of 16th Panzer Division that are arriving will be used to counterattack.[35]

At 1805 hours on 28 November, LI Army Corps informed Sixth Army:

> Around 1100 hours, the enemy attacked along the entire north-eastern front [with 99th and 116th Rifle Divisions], from the Erzovka-Orlovka road up to Hill 145.1 (422) with the focal point along the Erzovka-Orlovka road. The attack was repulsed by 24th Panzer Division; the enemy [99th Rifle Division] succeeded in breaking into the front-line south-west of 135.4 with 6 tanks that were subsequently forced to turn away. At 1500 hours, the enemy [116th Rifle Division and 58th Tank Brigade] attack against Hill 145.1 was renewed with 7 tanks. The enemy took the hill and pushed over the railroad to the south. Hill 147.6 is in our hands. 16th Panzer Division, which is moving into the sector, will be used to counterattack.[36]

Sixth Army's final report on 28 November summarized the day's developments:

> After an artillery preparation, the enemy advanced along a broad front with infantry and tanks. He [99th Rifle Division] was smashed back north of Spartakovka and north-east of 135.4, while he [116th Rifle Division] succeeded north-east of Orlovka and later at 1300 hours near 145.1 (west of the bend in the railway) in penetrating the main defensive area with tanks and infantry mounted on those. The penetration north-east of Orlovka was straightened out after the destruction of two T-34s. The enemy pushed forward with infantry and tanks up to Hill 147.6, where he was halted. The counterattack launched by elements of 16th Panzer Division and 60th Infantry Division (Mot.) recaptured Hill 145.1 [from 116th Rifle Division]. Fighting there has not yet ended. Near 145.1, a KV was totally destroyed, one tank was immobilized. The process of 24th Panzer Division taking over the right sector of 94th Infantry Division up to the south-east side of Hill 147.6 has started.[37]

In response to the counterattacks launched by 16th and 24th Panzer Divisions, 66th Army resumed assaults on its left wing at 1500 hours on 29 November, with the same objectives as on the previous day. This time, the General Staff described the fighting in a bit more detail, mentioning 116th Rifle Division's and 58th Tank Brigade's assault against 16th Panzer Division's 1st Battalion, 79th Panzer-Grenadier Regiment, on Hills 145.1 and 147.6, 3 to 4 kilometers northwest of Orlovka. At the same time, 99th Rifle Division attacked 24th Panzer Division's *Luftwaffe* Battalion Matho and 2nd and 1st Battalions of 94th Infantry Division but made only insignificant gains.[38] Since 66th Army's offensive on 29 November was so unsuccessful, LI Army Corps virtually ignored it. Instead, at 1730 hours, Seydlitz's corps noted, "The enemy was quiet in the morning," but "at 1200 hours, 24th Panzer Division took over the sector of 94th Infantry Division up to a point south-east of 135.4."[39]

Apparently disappointed by his army's forward progress, Zhadov committed his second-echelon 299th Rifle Division into combat on 30 November. This time, the fighting intensified enough for the General Staff to mention the actions of three rifle divisions—116th, 299th, and 99th—which reportedly captured Hills 147.6 and 135.4 but lost the latter to a German counterattack.[40] Overnight on 29–30 November, 66th Army's regrouping effort was so clumsy that German intelligence was able to detect movement and predict the direction of the impending attack. At 0600 hours, LI Army Corps reported, "Busy traffic, including tanks—at times with uncovered headlights—was seen on the road north-east of Orlovka. Our positions on Hill 147.6 and south of 111.1 lay under heavy tank- and mortar-fire for most of the night."[41] Once the Soviet attack began, LI Army Corps provided a blow-by-blow, hour-by-hour description of the day's fighting (see appendix 7H in the *Companion*).

When all was said and done, the assaults by 66th Army against the sectors of LI Army Corps' 16th and 24th Panzer Divisions would accurately reflect Soviet operations around the entire periphery of Sixth Army's encirclement pocket for the next six weeks. By this time, as Hitler demanded, Paulus had converted Sixth Army's defensive perimeter around its encirclement pocket into a virtual "fortress." Although fighting continued along the periphery of the Stalingrad pocket for days, by now, Rokossovsky and Eremenko realized it would take far more than their tired and depleted armies to crack Sixth Army's defenses. The *Stavka* itself would soon acknowledge this reality.

Conclusions

During the last three days of November, Rokossovsky's Don Front continued to be the sacrificial lamb of Operation Uranus. Like Chuikov's 62nd Army fighting in the rubble of Stalingrad, the real mission of 65th, 24th, and 66th Armies' understrength divisions was to attack and die—although this was couched in terms of tying down German forces. Ostensibly, 65th and 24th Armies were to conduct an envelopment of their own, but as the bloody fighting at Kotluban' many months before indicated, the likelihood of the two armies succeeding was remote at best. Moreover, Rokossovsky's incessant criticism of what he considered faulty command and control relationships indicated that the Don Front's commander inherently understood this reality. In the end, even 65th Army's success in driving XI Corps from its bridgehead north of the Don River was due as much to the Germans' deliberate withdrawal as to the ferocity and effectiveness of the Soviet assaults.

Ultimately, the combat operations conducted by Rokossovsky's three armies against the northern half of Sixth Army's encirclement pocket from 19 to 30 November served as a precursor to subsequent operations around the perimeter of the pocket in early December. At the very least, these operations proved that it would take a major offensive, perhaps commensurate with a full-scale siege, to liquidate Paulus's encircled Sixth Army. This also meant that the three Soviet *fronts* and nine armies operating in the Stalingrad region were insufficient to conduct simultaneous offensive operations along Stalingrad's inner and outer encirclement fronts. Although Rokossovsky realized this, it would take two more weeks for Stalin and the *Stavka* to acknowledge this reality.

The Stalingrad Front's Advance

While Vasilevsky solved the most serious command and control problem north of Stalingrad by assigning the Southwestern and Don Fronts distinctly different missions, the *Stavka* representative failed to do the same south of the city (see map 40). There, he left Eremenko fighting battles in two separate directions: while the Stalingrad Front's 62nd, 64th, and 57th Armies were conducting virtual siege operations against the southern and eastern fronts of Sixth Army's pocket, its 51st Army was continuing its headlong offensive south toward Kotel'nikovo. As developments would soon indicate, 51st Army was not up to its task.

By the evening of 27 November, two of the three armies that had once constituted the Stalingrad Front's main shock group were stalled in positions along the southern front of Sixth Army's Stalingrad pocket. On the right wing of the *front's* main shock group, General Shumilov's 64th Army manned positions stretching eastward along Karavatka *Balka* to Elkhi and then northeastward to the outskirts of Stalingrad's southern suburb of Kuporosnoe. On the shock group's left wing, Tolbukhin's 57th Army was deployed from the southern approaches to Marinovka eastward, south of the Karpovka River; southeastward, west of the Chervlenaia River, to just south of Tsybenko; and then across the river into a roughly 4-kilometer-wide sector north of Karavatka *Balka*. The only formation in 57th Army enjoying freedom of action and maneuver was General Vol'sky's 4th Mechanized Corps; two of its three mechanized brigades still faced north, opposite the Stalingrad pocket, and its third brigade faced the German bridgehead on the eastern bank of the Don River, opposite Rychkovskii and Nizhne-Chirskaia. Regardless of the static nature of 64th and 57th Armies' positions, both armies attacked obediently in accordance with Vasilevsky's plan.

Based on the importance of its mission, the third army in Eremenko's former shock group, General Trufanov's 51st, constituted a shock group in its own right. It alone was responsible for projecting the Stalingrad Front's

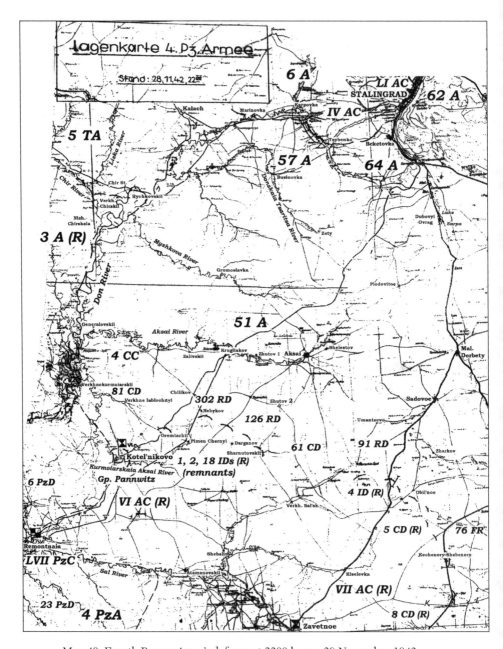

Map 40. Fourth Panzer Army's defense at 2200 hours, 28 November 1942

outer encirclement front as far southwestward as possible. It was also responsible for preempting, containing, or defeating any relief forces the Germans might dispatch toward Stalingrad from the southwest. Therefore, in this sense, 51st Army's mission was similar to that assigned to General Romanenko, commander of the Southwestern Front's 5th Tank Army. Unlike Romanenko, however, Trufanov faced two major problems. First, he lacked a neighboring army, such as 1st Guards on 5th Tank Army's right, that was capable of supporting his operations. Second, 51st Army lacked a powerful tank force, such as 5th Tank Army's 1st Tank Corps, to spearhead its operations. Instead, Trufanov had to rely on the tankless 4th Cavalry Corps as its maneuver force—a slender reed indeed.

In addition to these three armies, Eremenko's *front* included Chuikov's 62nd, which was still serving the dual role of bait and sacrificial lamb in the rubble of Stalingrad, and Gerasimenko's 28th Army, now in virtual suspended animation in its private war with German 16th Motorized Division in the depths of the Kalmyk steppes on the *front's* far left wing.

64th Army

In many ways, the situation confronting General Shumilov's 64th Army was the same as that faced by the Don Front's 66th Army. However, unlike 66th Army, whose official history essentially ignores this period, 64th Army's history treats the struggle in late November as a logical consequence of its earlier failure to defeat Sixth Army on the open battlefield. Thus, it candidly states: "Having encircled the enemy, the forces of 64th Army, together with the *front's* other formations, fulfilled only part of their missions. Now it was necessary to compress the encirclement ring tightly, dismember the Hitlerite forces that found themselves in the ring, and, if they failed to surrender, completely destroy them unit by unit as rapidly as possible. The enemy resisted stubbornly."[42]

The only documentary evidence regarding 64th Army's operations during the last three days of November is contained in the Red Army General Staff's daily operational summaries (see appendix 7I in the *Companion* for the Stalingrad Front's accomplishments on 28–30 November). These assert that the army captured Hill 145.5, 2 kilometers southwest of Zelenaia Poliana, from IV Army Corps' 371st Infantry Division on 28 November but accomplished little more in three days of frustrating fighting.[43] However, German operational maps and reports challenge this assertion by describing in detail a far more powerful Soviet attack launched by several rifle divisions, supported by one or probably two tank brigades, against two separate sectors of IV Army Corps' defenses. The first effort was a major attack on a fairly broad front north and west of the town of Iagodnyi; the second, farther east, was probably a diversionary attack southwest of Peschanka.

Sixth Army's daily operational maps indicate that the lesser of these two attacks took place southwest of Zelenaia Poliana, where elements of 93rd and 97th Rifle Brigades of 64th Army's 7th Rifle Corps, supported by 10 to 15 tanks, struck 371st Infantry Division's defenses and captured Hill 145.5. By virtue of its scale, this attack appears to have been designed to divert German attention and forces away from 64th Army's main attack, which took place along Karavatka *Balka*, north and west of Iagodnyi, in conjunction with an attack by 57th Army on the German strongpoints of Tsybenko and Kravtsov from the west, south, and southeast.

The 64th Army launched its main attack with 38th and 157th Rifle Divisions, supported by 50 to 60 tanks from 56th and 235th Tank Brigades and likely 154th Naval Rifle Brigade in second echelon. It occurred early on the morning of the 28th in a roughly 6-kilometer-wide sector of 297th Infantry Division's defenses along Karavatka *Balka*, north and northwest of Iagodnyi. Simultaneously, on 64th Army's left, 57th Army's 169th, 36th Guards, and 422nd Rifle Divisions assaulted German defenses at Tsybenko from the south and southwest and at Kravtsov, 2 kilometers west of Tsybenko, from the southwest. The combined attack by 64th and 57th Armies' shock groups struck German IV Army Corps' defenses in the 11-kilometer-wide sector extending from north of Iagodnyi westward to the Chervlenaia River and then northwestward to the approaches to Kravtsov. The objective was to collapse IV Army Corps' defensive front by capturing Tsybenko and Kravtsov.

The sector attacked by 64th Army was defended by Romanian 82nd Infantry Regiment, flanked on the left by 297th Infantry Division's Bicycle [*Radfahr*] *Abteilung* and 3rd and 1st Battalions, 523rd Regiment, and on the right by *Kampfgruppe* Pickel and 371st Infantry Division's 670th Regiment, all under 297th Division's control. The 670th Regiment was also defending Tsybenko and its eastern approaches with its 1st and 2nd Battalions. West of the Chervlenaia River, 29th Motorized Division defended the strongpoint at Kravtsov with 1st and 2nd Battalions of its 71st Motorized Regiment. During two days of what the Germans described as very intense fighting, 64th Army's 157th Rifle Division apparently penetrated the Romanians' defenses along the *balka* to a depth of about 1 to 2 kilometers but was driven back by a counterattack supported by a handful of tanks provided by 14th Panzer Division. According to the only reference to the fighting in 64th Army's history, a company from 157th Rifle Division's 716th Regiment was encircled in the Iagodnyi region by the counterattack but succeeded in fighting its way back to Soviet lines after suffering heavy casualties.[44]

Surviving reports prepared by Sixth Army and its IV Army Corps confirmed the 28 November attack and underscored its ferocity. For example, Sixth Army's morning report, sent to Army Group Don at 1420 hours on 28

November, said the attacks were "delivered by two Russian divisions with tanks against 297th Infantry Division and the western wing of 371st Infantry Division, with the point of main effort [*schwerpunkt*] on both sides of Iagodnyi."[45] A more complete description of the attack sent by IV Army Corps to Sixth Army at 1650 hours said the Russians attacked north of Iagodnyi with several infantry regiments and 50 tanks in an apparent attempt to envelop Tsybenko from the east, but they lost 15 tanks and were driven back. After bringing up fresh forces, the Soviets attacked again with about three regiments in the same region, accompanied by a battalion-strength assault with tank support against the left wing of 29th Motorized Division west of the Chervlenaia River and by shock group attacks against 371st Division's right wing. These assaults were supported by Soviet aircraft that bombed and strafed the German defenses north of Iagodnyi.[46] It was likely during this fighting that a German counterattack cut off and nearly destroyed 4th Company of 157th Rifle Division's 716th Regiment.

A final report dispatched by IV Army Corps to Sixth Army at 2200 hours on 28 November stated that the Soviets had lost at least 330 dead, with 19 tanks destroyed and another 21 damaged. An attachment to the report noted that 297th Infantry Division employed 4 tanks (3 Pz-III and 1 Pz-IV) provided by 14th Panzer Division and 13 88mm guns in its defense and that 29th Motorized Division fielded 39 tanks and 10 88mm guns, as well as 9 tanks sent by 14th Panzer Division.[47]

General Jänecke's IV Army Corps continued to report on 64th and 57th Armies' assaults on 29 November, noting at midmorning that "Russian IV and XIII Motorized Corps had about 100 tanks south of Iagodnyi," apparently supporting or preparing to exploit 64th Army's offensive.[48] The fact that there is no further mention of these tanks is indicative of the offensive's failure by day's end on 29 November. However, the same report noted renewed assaults against 297th Infantry Division's left wing and 371st Division south of Peschanka, during which another 10 enemy tanks were knocked out. Finally, IV Army Corps' report at 2150 hours on the 29th confirmed that the attacks were decreasing in frequency and strength; it also noted that 297th Infantry Division was employing 2 assault guns, 30 antitank guns [*Paks*] (11 heavy and 19 medium), and 12 88mm guns and that 29th Motorized Division's armored strength had decreased to 36 tanks.[49]

Thus, although Soviet sources de-emphasize the importance of 64th Army's attacks south of Stalingrad, these documents make it crystal clear that the Stalingrad Front was deadly serious about achieving a penetration on Sixth Army's southern front. It is also apparent that 64th and 57th Armies' attacking forces paid a high price in this effort in terms of human casualties and tank losses.

57th Army

Similar to 64th Army, Soviet sources readily admit that Tolbukhin's 57th Army participated in Vasilevsky's offensive on 28–29 November but provide precious little detail about the intensity of the fighting. In general, Soviet and German records agree that 57th Army conducted strong attacks against 29th Motorized Division's left wing in the Kravtsov region and against 297th Infantry Division's right wing at Tsybenko and also conducted spoiling attacks against 29th Motorized Division's right wing in the Karpovka region. They also confirm that, despite the intense fighting, none of these attacks succeeded (see appendix 7I in the *Companion*).

During its offensive on 28 and 29 November, 57th Army conducted its main attack against German 29th Motorized Division and 297th Infantry Division at Kravtsov and Tsybenko. West of the Chervlenaia River, the army's 422nd Rifle Division attacked Kravtsov from the south and southwest; east of the river, 36th Guards and 169th Rifle Divisions attacked northwest toward Tsybenko from the bridgehead they controlled on the northern bank of Karavatka *Balka*. Although not apparent from Soviet sources, German operational maps indicate that Tolbukhin supported this attack with tanks and motorized riflemen from 13th Tank Corps' 17th Mechanized Brigade and 44th Tank Regiment, as well as elements of 38th and 68th Motorized Rifle Brigades.[50] But Tolbukhin's efforts were to no avail. His offensive expired late on 29 November without denting IV Army Corps' defenses.

In addition to the reports from Sixth Army and IV Army Corps cited above, the two headquarters noted some activity in the Karpovka region and farther south along 29th Motorized Division's front at Skliarov but mentioned no attacks of major consequence in either area. That was also the case in 3rd Motorized Division's front from west of Karpovka to Marinovka, where only light action took place. The records noted, however, that 3rd Motorized Division fielded 28 tanks, 33 antitank guns, and 5 88mm guns on 30 November.[51]

While 57th Army was conducting its futile assaults against IV Army Corps' defenses from Karpovka southeastward to Tsybenko, elements of 4th Mechanized Corps continued to try to clear German forces from the eastern bank of the Don River, 45 kilometers to the west. The 60th Mechanized Brigade of Vol'sky's corps finally reinforced 158th Tank Regiment in this region on 28 November. The next day, the combined force succeeded in capturing the village of Ermokhinskii, 15 kilometers south of Logovskii. However, even though 60th Brigade now held Nemkovskii and Ermokhinskii, the two most important villages on the eastern bank of the Don opposite Rychkovskii and Nizhne-Chirskaia, its forces remained scattered across a 25-kilometer-wide front from Liapichev in the north to Ermokhinskii in the south. Worse still, the brigade still lacked sufficient infantry to clear the small German forces from their bridgehead in the marshlands on the Don's eastern bank opposite Rychkovskii.

51st Army

While the Stalingrad Front's 64th and 57th Armies remained mired in positional fighting along the southern front of Sixth Army's encirclement pocket, General Trufanov's 51st Army tried to continue its pursuit southwestward along the Kotel'nikovo axis, simultaneously licking the wounds inflicted on it when the Germans defeated the raid by 4th Cavalry Corps' 81st Cavalry Division on Kotel'nikovo (see map 31 and appendix 7I in the *Companion*). This severe and unexpected defeat after so many days of unfettered advance had a sobering effect on the army's commander. Trufanov, who already acknowledged the army's weakness in armor, now realized that a cavalry corps with two weak divisions lacked sufficient strength to spearhead sustained offensive operations. He also recognized that any large enemy armored force could decimate his cavalry, just as it had done in the streets of Kotel'nikovo. It was one thing to engage an ad hoc formation such as that assembled by Colonel Pannwitz at Sharnutovskii several days before. It was an entirely different matter when the Stalingrad Front's Intelligence Department informed Trufanov that the lead elements of German 6th Panzer Division were rolling into Kotel'nikovo. Rather than a hastily formed ad hoc tank group, the 6th was a full-blooded panzer division arriving from the West with a force of more than 150 tanks. Nor was 51st Army's commander certain that 6th Panzer was the only fresh German formation being dispatched to the region. In any case, he was sure that if 6th Panzer went into action, his army would be unable to continue its offensive. In fact, he doubted his army could contain a concerted counterstroke should the Germans launch one.

Despite this air of uncertainty, Trufanov's army resumed its offensive on 28 November—minus its formations shattered at Kotel'nikovo. In the wake of that defeat, General Shapkin withdrew 4th Cavalry Corps' headquarters, along with 81st Cavalry Division and 85th Tank Brigade, pell-mell to a new defensive line along the northern bank of the Iablochnaia River, 18 to 20 kilometers north of Kotel'nikovo. There, he was supposed to erect new defenses along the river in the 15-kilometer sector from Verkhne-Iablochnyi westward through Nizhne-Iablochnyi to Verkhne-Kurmoiarskii on the Don River's eastern bank. In reality, once Shapkin ascertained that the Germans were not pursuing his forces, he reassembled them north of the designated defensive line and cautiously resumed his southward advance.

Egged on by Eremenko, Trufanov's army initiated a slow, painstaking, and very tentative advance southward into positions extending from Nebykovskii Station, 25 kilometers northeast of Kotel'nikovo, southeastward through Samokhin and Sharnutovskii to the Verkhne-Sal and Kanukovo (Kenkrua) regions southwest of Sadovoe. From Trufanov's perspective, his army's most important achievement on the 28th was the "liberation" of a gold mine of logistical stocks in Romanian warehouses at Krugliakov (now Oktiabr'skaia), situated on the railroad line 25 kilometers west of Aksai.

As a cascade of new intelligence reached Trufanov's headquarters hour by hour, providing details of the menacing new German troop concentrations in the Kotel'nikovo region, 51st Army slowed its advance to a snail's pace on the 29th as the army commander positioned his forces to contend with the possible appearance of fresh German panzers. Since he knew 6th Panzer was arriving in Kotel'nikovo—his army's ultimate objective—at nightfall he laagered his forces a safe distance from the town. Evidencing Trufanov's newfound caution, on 30 November, he ordered his army to go over to the defense in positions roughly midway between the Aksai River and Kotel'nikovo and await further German actions. However, an impatient Eremenko soon prodded the reluctant Trufanov into advancing again, this time with distinctly unpleasant results.

During the last three days of November, Army Group Don assigned Army Group Hoth—consisting of Fourth Panzer Army's remnants, plus those of Romanian VI and VII Army Corps combined in a new Romanian Fourth Army—the twin tasks of delaying the Soviet advance on Kotel'nikovo and organizing a force capable of reinforcing or rescuing encircled Sixth Army (see chapter 9 in book 2 of this volume). Operating under direct German supervision, Romanian Fourth Army was to delay the Soviet advance on Kotel'nikovo long enough for Group Hoth to assemble a strike force in the vicinity of the town. By this time, Hitler had ordered the formation of two groups to conduct relief operations toward Stalingrad—the first in Kotel'nikovo, subordinate to Group Hoth's LVII Panzer Corps, and the second south of the lower Chir River, under the control of Group Hollidt's XXXXVIII Panzer Corps. The former was to advance northeast toward Stalingrad from Kotel'nikovo, and the latter was to move east toward Sixth Army's pocket from the Rychkovskii bridgehead.

Group Hoth's LVII Panzer Corps consisted of Lieutenant General Erhard Raus's 6th Panzer Division, dispatched to the region from France on 24 November; Lieutenant General Hans *Freiherr* von Boineburg-Lengsfeld's weak 23rd Panzer Division, sent by Army Group A in the Caucasus; and Lieutenant General Fridolin von Senger und Etterlin's 17th Panzer Division, dispatched southward from the Orel region. Once it had assembled in the Kotel'nikovo region under the control of General of Panzer Troops Friedrich Kirchner's LVII Panzer Corps (also from Army Group A), this force of about 240 tanks and assault guns was to mount a relief operation codenamed *Wintergewitter* (Winter Tempest) toward Stalingrad. Scheduled to begin on 8 December, the operation ultimately kicked off on 12 December without 17th Panzer Division because Hitler refused to release it to Group

Hoth. Nevertheless, when LVII Panzer Corps unleashed its panzers, it was more than a match for Trufanov's 51st Army.

For the time being, however, there would be no German relief effort unless and until Group Hoth assembled the necessary forces. According to General Raus, who arrived in Kotel'nikovo with the lead trains transporting his 6th Panzer Division, the situation in the region in late November was far too dangerous to conduct any sort of offensive operation. In fact, he asserted, "Had the Russians been more enterprising, they could have compelled Fourth Panzer Army to locate its assembly areas behind the Sal River—fifty kilometers farther to the rear." If they had, according to Raus, "This would have substantially reduced the probability of any successful relief attack."[52] Of course, at this point, Raus did not know how weak Trufanov's army really was. Instead of attacking, as General Kirchner wished, to gain a more favorable jumping-off position along the Aksai River, Raus insisted that he defend Kotel'nikovo until the region was secure and reinforcements had arrived. And so he did.

As 51st Army slowed its advance on Kotel'nikovo, General Constantinescu's Romanian Fourth Army did its best to halt the Soviet advance. But it was in no shape to do so for long. By late November, the strength of Romanian VI Army Corps' 1st, 2nd, and 18th Infantry Divisions had decreased by about 80 percent, leaving only 2,000 to 3,000 men in each and fewer than 1,000 men in their combat units. Therefore, the Romanians were able to defend only a narrow sector along the Aksai River. When 4th Cavalry Corps' 81st Division enveloped its defenses along the river from the west, VI Corps was forced to withdraw southward along the railroad to Kotel'nikovo. Withdrawing along separate axes because they were too weak to erect consecutive defensive lines, VI Corps' three divisions ultimately converged on Kotel'nikovo from the north and northeast.

Operating to the southeast of VI Corps, Romanian VII Army Corps' three divisions were in far better condition. The 4th Infantry Division, at about 30 percent strength, fielded roughly 4,000 men; the nearly full-strength 5th Cavalry Division operated with a complement of about 7,000 men; and 8th Cavalry Division, at 85 percent strength, fielded about 6,000 men. Fighting in unison, these forces could certainly delay the advance of several Soviet rifle divisions. However, they could not do so along their entire front of well over 70 kilometers.[53] All this meant that Trufanov's 51st Army could advance at will unless and until it encountered substantial German forces. Then, however, it would be in serious trouble.

62nd Army
It probably came as no surprise to General Chuikov that the Don and Stalingrad Fronts' armies were having significant difficulty overcoming Sixth

Army's defenses. After struggling for three months in the rubble of Stalingrad, 62nd Army's troops were used to brutal and bloody fighting. They, more than anyone else in the Red Army, understood what it would take to crush Sixth Army's defenses and liquidate its resistance. Therefore, while Vasilevsky searched for an elusive formula for victory, Chuikov's 62nd continued its nasty little war in the ruins of Stalingrad. Although 62nd Army's grim, thrice-daily reports formed a monotonous mosaic of deadly Soviet attacks and German counterattacks that produced a steady stream of dead and maimed on both sides, they confirmed that 62nd Army's soldiers were slowly squeezing the lifeblood from the German defenders. According to 62nd Army's report, as LI Army Corps of Paulus's Sixth Army was frantically shuffling its troops to counter relentless Soviet assaults from every point of the compass, it was bleeding to death in the streets and ruined buildings of Stalingrad.

Complying with Eremenko's orders with almost robot-like determination, 62nd Army's skeletal formations conducted operations in the bowels of the city that mirrored those of other armies in the steppes along the periphery of Sixth Army's fortress pocket. In concert with the other armies deployed around the pocket, 62nd Army attacked on 28 and 29 November but went over to the defense on the 30th (see map 41 and appendix 7J in the *Companion*). At day's end on the 28th, for example, Chuikov reported that his army had held and improved its positions, while recording only insignificant gains in assaults within the Barrikady and Krasnyi Oktiabr' Factories and in the vicinity of Bannyi Ravine and Mamaev Kurgan. As requested by the Stalingrad Front, Chuikov noted that 39 German transport aircraft had landed, but ice on the Volga prevented resupply of 138th Rifle Division's defending troops isolated on so-called Liudnikov's Island east of the Barrikady Factory.[54]

Sixth Army's records confirm this action, adding that Russian assault groups conducted seven attacks in the Krasnyi Oktiabr' Factory, and 30 to 40 boats managed to cross the icy Volga and reach the factory.[55] The next morning, LI Corps reported that Group Sanne, formed around the nucleus of 100th Jäger Division, had lost 6 men killed and 64 wounded in the fighting on Mamaev Kurgan; 79th Infantry Division lost 9 killed, 22 wounded, and 1 missing in the fighting on the grounds of Krasnyi Oktiabr' Factory.[56] Grimly persistent, Chuikov ordered his formations to resume their assaults from the Krasnyi Oktiabr' Factory and Bannyi Ravine toward Hill 107.5, beginning after midday on the 29th. Their objective was to clear all German forces from Krasnyi Oktiabr' village and, if possible, seize all of Mamaev Kurgan.

A memorandum issued by General Seydlitz's LI Army Corps at 2240 hours on 28 November made it abundantly clear that Sixth Army was

Map 41. Situation in Stalingrad, 28 November 1942

experiencing severe logistical problems associated with the immense expenditure of ammunition in the fighting inside Stalingrad:

> Because the operational measures of OKH require a certain amount of time, the fate of the army depends, in the first instance, on ammunition. Together with the supply expected to arrive via aerial transport, ammunition stocks must be conserved by extreme thriftiness so that there is enough to last until the ring of encirclement is broken open. If that does not happen, then a state of defenselessness will arise, that is, the army will be destroyed. Everyone must be made clear about that. It is therefore essential to achieve the greatest possible benefit with the smallest usage of ammunition. This must be instilled in every soldier.[57]

Chuikov's forces continued to batter the defenses of Sixth Army's LI Army Corps on 29 November, striking the same objectives as the day before and exchanging artillery, mortar, and machine gun fire with the Germans across the entire front. Once again, however, the army's actual gains were few and far between, while the cost in dead and wounded rose inexorably on both sides. Attesting to this grim toll, 95th Rifle Division, which was struggling to break through to 138th Rifle Division's troops isolated on Liudnikov's Island, lost 6 men out of its overall strength of 773 combatants, and 284th Division suffered 105 men killed and wounded on a day when 62nd Army reported killing an obviously inflated figure of roughly 450 Germans.[58] On the other side of the lines, LI Army Corps' Group Sanne (100th Jäger Division) lost 4 men killed and 29 wounded, and 79th Infantry Division lost 5 killed and 25 wounded. As a whole, Seydlitz's corps reported 120 casualties (20 killed and 100 wounded).[59]

The most significant developments for 62nd Army on the 29th involved supplies, especially food and ammunition, which had been cut off for several days by ice on the Volga. In the evening, Chuikov's headquarters reported that Soviet transport aircraft had delivered 45 boxes of ammunition, 33 sacks of food, and a single sack of newspapers to its forces, although 2 of the sacks fell into the Volga, and several sacks of dry rations that had been dropped without parachutes burst open. In a more positive vein, a "relaxation" in ice conditions on the river permitted the evacuation of 150 wounded by ship, although Chuikov complained that far more ships were required. Finally, as was the case in the other armies besieging Sixth Army, Chuikov ordered his forces to cease their futile assaults and go on the defense on the 30th.

Therefore, on 30 November, 62nd Army enjoyed a lull, defending and improving its positions, conducting reconnaissance, and exchanging fire with "an inactive enemy who continued heavy mortar and machine gun fire on our positions." It also reported that "about 30 transport aircraft were observed landing in the vicinity of Severnaia Bazisnaia."[60] The 62nd claimed that it had killed as many as 350 Germans, including 120 due to artillery fire, although it failed to note how these casualties were determined. The army's soldiers likely welcomed Chuikov's new orders to "hold your positions, reinforce reconnaissance, and destroy and suppress enemy firing points by artillery and mortar fire." Sixth Army's documents confirm the lull in action on 30 November and, for the first time in several days, make no mention of any casualties in LI Army Corps' divisions.

As monotonous and deadly as their lives in Stalingrad were, it would still be weeks before Chuikov and his soldiers would become genuine "besiegers" rather than the besieged.

28th Army

General Gerasimenko's 28th Army suffered a stinging defeat on 25 November when it attempted to capture the town of Iashkul' from 16th Motorized Division and its battalions of Turkestan volunteers. It endured an even sounder drubbing in the counterattack delivered by General Schwerin's forces on 26 and 27 November. Thereafter, relative quiet supposedly prevailed around the German fortress town until mid-December (see map 32 and appendix 7I in the *Companion*).

In fact, 16th Motorized Division conducted two more sorties against 28th Army on 28 and 29 November (although the army's history claimed the first of these took place on the 27th rather than the 28th). The first attack, by motorized infantry and 16 tanks, occurred against 34th Guards Rifle Division's 107th Regiment on 28 November, but it was repulsed. The second, conducted on 29 November by the same-size force at the boundary between 34th Guards Division and 6th Guards Tank Brigade, was also repulsed.

The most interesting information about 28th Army during this period involved its heavy losses. Archival documents indicate that the 1,000 casualties 34th Guards Rifle Division suffered in the fight for Iashkul' brought its total losses for the period 20–30 November to 1,625 men killed, 1,448 wounded, and 1,978 missing (many of whom were killed or captured). The division's logistical section also reported the loss of 1,181 rifles, 139 PPSh submachine guns, 34 light and 6 heavy machine guns, 21 antitank rifles, 45 guns (out of 60), and 5 mortars—appalling losses, especially for a Guards division. Although returnees ultimately reduced the number of missing in action from 1,978 to 999 men, this was small consolation, considering that overall losses amounted to well over half of 28th Army's total (see appendix 7K in the *Companion*).[61]

During the same period, 28th Army's Operations Department claimed that up to 2,000 Germans were killed and 12 captured, although the author added sarcastically, "If this were so, 16th Motorized Division would have ceased to exist."[62] In addition, the army asserted that it collected 10 tanks, 18 guns, 39 mortars, 14 heavy and antiaircraft machine guns, 118 light machine guns, and more than 1,000 rifles in the steppes, including some Soviet equipment captured and employed by the Germans.[63]

All things considered, 28th Army had a very difficult time in late November, whereas German 16th Motorized Division had every reason to celebrate. But most Germans probably wished there were reason to celebrate in Stalingrad, where there clearly was not.

Conclusions

The operations conducted by the Stalingrad Front during the last three days of November represent extreme examples of the two most daunting problems faced by the *Stavka* and its representative, Vasilevsky. Rokossovsky's Don Front confronted one problem—its inability to overcome Sixth Army's defenses with the forces at its disposal. Vatutin's Southwestern Front had a similar problem along the Chir River. Eremenko's Stalingrad Front, however, had two problems: first, he had to invigorate his stalled offensive against Sixth Army's encirclement pocket, and second, he had to contend with a genuine and potentially deadly threat to his *front*'s left wing.

In part, Eremenko's difficulties were the direct result of long-standing command and control problems: specifically, he had to pay attention to two completely separate operational axes—Stalingrad and Kotel'nikovo—and do so simultaneously. In a Red Army where command presence was necessary for any force to succeed, Eremenko could not be in two places at one time. Worse still, Eremenko lacked the requisite forces to conduct major operations along two axes. In its present form, Trufanov's 51st Army was far too weak, especially in armored and mechanized forces, to capture the Kotel'nikovo region and contain a major German counterstroke. Therefore, within a matter of days, what had been a spectacularly successful offensive would become a potential military debacle.

THE BATTLE IN THE SKIES, 19–30 NOVEMBER

Throughout the first five days of Operation Uranus, the air forces on both sides were forced to limit their operations because of bad weather, low ceilings, and poor visibility associated with a cold front that passed through the Stalingrad region. The horrid weather curtailed most of the air activity by the Southwestern and Don Fronts' 17th and 16th Air Armies from 19 through 23 November and by the Stalingrad Front's 8th Air Army from 20 through 23 November. Of course, the same weather conditions plagued German Fourth Air Fleet's VIII Air Corps, denying the Germans their most powerful defensive instrument at the worst possible time. Fourth Air Fleet emphasized this problem in an entry in its war diary on 19 November:

Rain, snow, and ice-forming have completely prevented air operations, and the VIII Air Corps, from its command post at Oblivskaia, can direct only a few single aircraft to the attack. It is impossible to close the Don bridges by bombing. It is not even possible to gain any insights into the situation by aerial reconnaissance. We can only hope that the Russians will not reach our rail route. . . .

Urgently needed transfers [of air units] are as yet impossible because of the miserable weather. We must have good weather soon, otherwise there is no longer any hope.[64]

Despite the poor flying conditions, the Germans were able to put some aircraft into the skies, operating singly, in pairs, or, on rare occasions, as full flights. As evidence of this ability, Soviet reports mention instances of air strikes hindering their operations, particularly in the case of their exploiting tank and cavalry corps. For example, General Fiebig's VIII Air Corps [*Fliegerkorps*], which was headquartered in Oblivskaia, managed to send up some Stukas and other aircraft of the 1st Group of 2nd Dive-Bomber Wing from airfields and airstrips in the Karpovka region. These made up the bulk of the 120 sorties German pilots flew on the 19th.[65] However, these flights were not enough to impede the Southwestern Front's 5th and 21st Armies from carrying out their penetration and exploitation operations against outgunned Romanian Third Army.

Colonel Hans-Ulrich Rudel, a future ace flier who commanded a Stuka squadron, lamented his inability to affect the outcome of the fighting:

One morning after the receipt of an urgent report, our Wing takes off in the direction of the bridgehead at Kletskaya. The weather is bad; low lying clouds, a light fall of snow, the temperature probably around 20° below zero [−4° Fahrenheit]; we fly low. What troops are those coming toward us? We have not gone more than halfway. Masses in brown uniforms—are they Russians? No. Rumanians! Some of them are even throwing away their rifles in order to run faster: a shocking sight, we are prepared for the worst! We fly the length of the column emplacements. The guns are abandoned, not destroyed. Their ammunition lies beside them. We have passed some distance beyond them before we sight the first Soviet troops.

They find all the Rumanian positions in front of them deserted. We attacked with bombs and gun-fire—but how much use was that when there was no resistance on the ground?

We are seized with a blind fury—horrid premonitions rise in our minds: how can this catastrophe be averted? Relentlessly I drop my bombs on the enemy and spray bursts of M.G. fire into these endless yellow-green attack waves of oncoming troops [from Asia and Outer Mongolia]. . . . I haven't a bullet left, even to protect myself against the contingency of a pursuit attack. Now quickly back to rearm and refuel. With these hordes, our attacks are merely a drop in the bucket, but I am reluctant to think of that now.

On the return flight, we again observe the fleeing Rumanians; it is a good thing for them that I have run out of ammunition to stop this cowardly rout.[66]

With regard to Soviet air activity from 19 through 23 November, the Southwestern Front's 17th Air Army reported that its aircraft flew 546 sorties during this period, primarily against Romanian ground troops south of Raspopinskaia and motorized forces in the Akimovskii and Luchenskii region; the latter were probably XIV Panzer Corps' 24th and 16th Panzer Divisions as they moved west toward the Kalach region. At the same time, 16th Air Army, operating in support of the Don Front, reported that it carried out 238 sorties.[67] Finally, the Stalingrad Front's 8th Air Army supposedly conducted 438 air sorties from 20 to 23 November: 170 bombing and assault strikes against enemy objectives, 150 sorties to protect their own forces and to accompany bombers and assault aircraft, and 118 for reconnaissance. It claimed these strikes destroyed 110 enemy vehicles and 12 tanks, dispersed up to 2 enemy infantry companies, and killed about 250 enemy soldiers and up to 70 cavalrymen.[68]

The 17th Air Army's history reports that, on the evening of 19 November, the commander directed, "Because of the bad weather conditions, operate on 20 November by means of methodical 'hunting' with the best crews against enemy withdrawal routes and [troop] concentrations."[69] The 8th Air Army's history offers an even more detailed description of weather conditions on 19 and 20 November, along with an assessment of the impact of air operations on the ground offensive:

On the eve [of the offensive] the skies were overcast with dense low clouds, freezing rain was falling, and the visibility did not exceed 2–3 kilometers. The SB, Il-4, and R-5 night bombers of 270th Bomber Division could not operate in such weather conditions. Only the Po-2 aircraft of 272nd Night Bomber Division flew, bombing and strafing enemy forces in the "Barrikady" region from heights of 200–300 meters. Sixteen Po-2 transported ammunition, food, and medicine to the forces of 62nd Army located north of the Tractor Factory and to the east of the northern part of "Barrikady," as well as units situated on the Volga islands of Zaitsevskii and Spornyi.

By the morning of 20 November, the clouds lowered to up to 50–100 meters and visibility decreased to up to 200–800 meters, and there was fog in places. Only during the second half of the day, aircraft from 206th Assault Division completed 24 combat sorties, singly or in pairs in the Plodovitoe, Tinguta, and Abganerovo region [south of Stalingrad]. In the same region, two Iak-1 aircraft of 268th Fighter Division conducted close air reconnaissance.

The unfavorable weather conditions did not improve in subsequent days. Because of this, the pilots were forced to operate in small groups and singly within the limits of low heights. The fighters of 2nd Mixed Aviation Corps, as had been agreed, protected the operations of the *front's* ground forces and assault aircraft opened routes for them in the enemy's defense by bombing strikes and destroyed enemy forces moving toward the penetration regions with assault strikes. The bombers conducted long-range reconnaissance and detected enemy reserves approaching the penetration sectors from the depths.[70]

When weather conditions began to improve on 24 November, the air forces on both sides took to the skies with a vengeance. For example, according to reports from 5th Tank Army's 8th Cavalry Corps, German and Romanian aircraft plagued its operations in the Oblivskaia region and along the Chir River for 10 days beginning late on the evening of 22 November. As a result, "During the course of 25 November, the enemy conducted no fewer than 800 aircraft sorties, preventing the cavalry from advancing. . . . On one day alone, [airpower] knocked out 4 regimental commanders, a division chief of staff, 12 squadron commanders and more than 500 personnel and up to 1,500 horses."[71]

Overall, the three Soviet air armies recorded 5,760 combat sorties in the Stalingrad region during the seven-day period from 24 through 30 November, for an average of roughly 800 sorties per day.[72] That was five times more than German and Romanian air units flew during the same period. German and Romanian aircraft were less active in November than they had been in October, not only because of poor weather but also because the German command had to transfer many aircraft to new airfields after their bases were overrun by advancing Soviet forces. The ensuing Soviet air superiority significantly eased the task of the ground forces and facilitated their rapid advance. Throughout the entire period, the priority mission of Soviet aircraft was to provide air support for the ground forces.

Careful study of the recently released daily operational summaries prepared by the Red Army General Staff provides fresh data on the intensity and sometimes the effectiveness of the air support provided to the three *fronts* conducting the initial phases of the Uranus offensive (see appendix 7L in the *Companion* for the number of air sorties conducted across the entire Soviet-German front immediately before and during the initial stage of Uranus). A comparison of the data in appendix 7L with other sources indicates that, from 24 to 30 November, the Soviet Air Force conducted a total of 9,510 air sorties across the entire front and 5,760 (60 percent) in the Stalingrad region—a reasonable figure, given the importance of that sector.[73] In addition, based on the sources cited above, 17th, 16th, and 8th Air Armies conducted a total of 1,240 aircraft sorties during the five-day period from 19 to 23 November. According to German sources, the *Luftwaffe*'s VIII Air Corps conducted 361 sorties during the first four days of the Soviet offensive.[74] Even if the German figure is increased by one-quarter to account for the fifth day, the three Soviet air armies still conducted more than twice as many sorties as the Germans in the Stalingrad region.

With regard to aircraft losses, according to the Red Army General Staff, the *Luftwaffe* and the Romanian Air Force lost 257 aircraft from 15 through 30 November, compared with 217 aircraft lost by the Soviet Air Force. The fact that the bulk (220) of these losses occurred from 24 through 30 November is indicative of heavy losses of slow-flying German bombers delivering supplies to encircled Sixth Army and aircraft destroyed during bombing or outright seizure of German and Romanian airfields. However, like the Soviet claims of German tank losses, the figures for German aircraft losses are also highly inflated.

THE SITUATION LATE ON 30 NOVEMBER

Axis Dispositions

The disposition of Axis forces in the Stalingrad region at the end of November was a direct result of the Soviets' successful encirclement operation. During the initial stage of Operation Uranus, the attacking Southwestern and Stalingrad Fronts tore an immense, 250-kilometer-wide hole in the Axis front extending from the Krivaia River north of Bokovskaia southeastward across the Don River to the Aksai and Sadovoe regions. The two attacking *fronts*, together with the Don Front, shattered the defenses of Romanian Third Army and German Fourth Panzer Army's IV Army Corps and Romanian VI Army Corps, drove their remnants southward to the Chir and Aksai Rivers, and surrounded German Sixth Army and the German half of Fourth Panzer Army in what soon became the Stalingrad pocket. West of Stalingrad, German and Romanian headquarters that remained outside the encirclement pocket worked frantically to cobble together new defensive lines along

the Krivaia, Chir, Don, and Aksai Rivers. Initially, they did so with a dizzying array of hastily assembled security, alarm, and logistical units whose
parent formations were either encircled in Stalingrad or scattered along German lines of communication west and southwest of Stalingrad.[75] Soon, these
forces were joined by the remnants of formations that had been defeated and
broken up in the encirclement fight and found themselves outside the Stalingrad pocket, such as the divisions of XXXXVIII Panzer Corps and Romanian
IV and V Army Corps northwest of Stalingrad and Romanian VI Army Corps
south of the city.

By the end of November, better-organized and better-equipped German
forces from other sectors of the Eastern Front or the West reinforced those
units already in position along the Krivaia, Chir, and Aksai Rivers, including 62nd and 294th Infantry Divisions of Group Hollidt (XVII Corps) along
the Krivaia River, the lead elements of 336th Infantry Division along the
Chir River, and 6th Panzer Division in the Kotel'nikovo region. It was these
forces that stabilized the Axis's front, albeit temporarily, along the Krivaia,
Chir, Don, and Aksai Rivers. Well to the rear, other formations such as 11th,
17th, and 23rd Panzer Divisions and the newly formed 7th and 8th *Luftwaffe*
Field Divisions were either heading toward the Stalingrad region, on Hitler's
orders, or awaiting orders to do so.

The Stalingrad Pocket's Inner Encirclement Front

The most apparent legacy of Operation Uranus was the infamous Stalingrad
pocket (see maps 38 and 39). Occupied primarily by German Sixth Army and
Fourth Panzer Army's IV Corps, together with the remnants of Romanian
1st Cavalry and 20th Infantry Divisions, the pocket also contained a host of
units temporarily attached to Sixth Army and under Army Group B's direct
control, some *Luftwaffe* airfield or antiaircraft [*Flak*] forces, and a variety of
Todt Organization construction units.

The Stalingrad pocket itself began to form immediately after the Soviet
counteroffensive started. The battle lines in Stalingrad city, which existed
before the Soviet operation began, became the eastern or Volga front of the
pocket. Since the Don Front's 24th and 66th Armies did not participate in
the initial counteroffensive, the battle lines northeast and north of the city,
from Rynok on the Volga River northwestward past Orlovka and Konnaia
Station to the Don River near Kachalinskaia, became the Stalingrad pocket's
northern front. Subsequently, the eastern portion of the northern front fell
back a bit on 24 November as a result of LI Army Corps' ill-advised withdrawal of 94th Infantry Division. The Stalingrad pocket's southern front also
took shape by 24 November, when the offensive by the Stalingrad Front's
64th, 57th, and 51st Armies stalled along the Marinovka, Karpovka, Tsybenko, Elkhi, and Kuporosnoe line.

The final stage in the formation of Sixth Army's Stalingrad pocket occurred from 26 to 29 November, when Sixth Army's XI Army Corps and XIV Panzer Corps completed their withdrawal from the Akimovskii bridgehead; abandoned the strongpoints at Sokarevka, Peskovatka, and Vertiachii; and pulled back to what became the pocket's western front. Although no single order created the Stalingrad pocket, a Sixth Army order [*Absicht* (intention)] issued on 27 November 1942 defined the pocket's western front as follows: "Withdrawal [*Zurücknahne*] of the Western Front to the line: unchanged to 1 kilometer south of [Hill] 102.3 [10 kilometers south of Kotluban']–B. Akronowa [Akronova *Balka*]–west of [Hill] 115.4–[Hill] 126.1–west of Kosatschi [Kazachi]–[Hill] 117.6–[Hill] 131.7– Marinowka [Marinovka]."[76] This meant that, after the withdrawal, the pocket's defensive front was unchanged from the Volga River westward to 1 kilometer south of Hill 102.3, 10 kilometers south of Kotluban'. Thereafter, it extended westward 6 kilometers to the upper reaches of Akronova *Balka* and then southwestward 28 kilometers to Marinovka. The line from Akronova *Balka* to 8 kilometers north of Marinovka ran from northeast to southwest along the crest of the ridgeline divide 5 to 8 kilometers west of the Rossoshka River and 15 to 25 kilometers east of the Don River. The purpose of the withdrawal was to shorten the pocket's western front and thus free up 384th Infantry and 14th Panzer Divisions to serve as Sixth Army's reserve. Any mention of the word "withdrawal" always had to be carefully weighed, because Hitler had categorically forbidden any such action.

Headquartered at Gumrak airfield, 15 kilometers west of Stalingrad and several kilometers northwest of Gumrak Station, Paulus initially organized Sixth Army's pocket into six fronts (sectors) subordinate to XI, VIII, IV, and LI Army Corps and XIV Panzer Corps, each of which consisted of several infantry or panzer divisions. On 30 November, Sixth Army reorganized the pocket's defense into Group [*Gruppe*] Seydlitz, which included Seydlitz's own LI Army Corps, Group Strecker's XI Army Corps, and VIII Army Corps, XIV Panzer Corps, and IV Army Corps, with an army reserve consisting of 384th Infantry and 14th Panzer Divisions, minus their forces left in the pocket's forward defenses (see tables 30 and 31). Despite this reorganization, through 9 January 1943, the Stalingrad pocket included six fronts (sectors), designated Volga, Northeast, North, West, South, and Southwest.[77]

Since many if not most of Sixth Army's divisions were understrength and had either consolidated their forces into fewer battalions or attached their battalions to other divisions, the composition and sector of each corps and division frequently changed as the situation developed. For example, by 1 December, Sixth Army's defenses included 5 corps and 17 divisional or group sectors (see appendix 7M in the *Companion*).

Table 30. Sixth Army's Command Structure and Operational Fronts (Sectors), 0800 Hours, 2 December 1942

GROUP SEYDLITZ (LI ARMY CORPS)
- **Volga Front**—from Reference Point 510 (El'shanka) to Point 729 (2 kilometers west of Rynok), with:
  - 71st Infantry Division
  - Group Sanne (295th and 100th Jäger Divisions)
  - 79th Infantry Division
  - 305th Infantry Division
  - 389th Infantry Division
- **Northeast Front**—from Point 729 to 2 kilometers west of Point 419 (Borodkin)—Group Strecker (XI Army Corps) with:
  - 24th Panzer Division (Group von Lenski) (part)
  - 16th Panzer Division (part)
  - 60th Infantry Division (Motorized) (remnants)
  - 94th Infantry Division, attached to 24th and 16th Panzer Divisions

VIII ARMY CORPS
- **North and West Fronts**—from Point 419 to the road from Points 143 to 154 (Kazachi), with:
  - 113th Infantry Division
  - 76th Infantry Division
  - 44th Infantry Division

XIV PANZER CORPS
- **Southwest Front**—from the road from Points 143 to 154 (Kazachi) to Karpovka (inclusive), with:
  - 376th Infantry Division
  - 3rd Infantry Division (Motorized)

IV ARMY CORPS
- **South Front**—from Karpovka (exclusive) to Point 510 (El'shanka), with:
  - 29th Infantry Division (Motorized)
  - 297th Infantry Division
  - 371st Infantry Division

ARMY RESERVE
- 384th Infantry Division (5 weak battalions) (Bol'shaia Rossoshka)
- 14th Panzer Division (Dubinskii)

Source: "Funkspruch an Heeresgruppe Don, Befehlsgliederung 2.12., 08.00 Uhr, Armee-Oberkommando 6, Abt.-Ia, A.H.Qu., 30. November 1942," in Florian Freiherr von und zu Aufsess, *Die Anlagenbänder zu den Kriegstagebüchern der 6. Armee vom 24.11.1942 bis 24.12.1942, Band II* (Schwabach: Januar, 2006), 66.

Table 31. Sixth Army's Order of Battle and Senior Command Cadre, 1 December 1942

Sixth Army (German)—General of Panzer Troops Friedrich Paulus
  IV Army Corps—General of Engineers Erwin Jänecke
    371st Infantry Division (669th and 671st Regiments)—Lieutenant General Richard Stempel
    297th Infantry Division (522nd, 524th, and 523rd Regiments; 20th Infantry Division's [R] 82nd Regiment; and 371st Infantry Division's 670th Regiment)—General of Artillery Max Pfeffer
    29th Motorized Division (71st and 15th Regiments and 71st Infantry Division's 1st Battalion, 191st Regiment)—Major General Hans-Georg Leyser

  XIV Panzer Corps—General of Panzer Troops Hans-Valentin Hube
    295th Infantry Division (Group Korfes)—Major General Dr. Otto Korfes
    Group Domaschk
    Group Grahms
    Group von Hanstein (1st and 2nd Battalions, *Luftwaffe* Regiment [I and II/*Luftwaffe* Regiment])
    Group Willig (60th Motorized Division's 10th Company, 120th Regiment, and 5th Company, 92nd Regiment, and 2nd Battery, 2nd Mortar Regiment)
    3rd Motorized Division (8th and 29th Regiments)—Lieutenant General Helmuth Schlömer
    376th Infantry Division (672nd, 673rd, and 767th Regiments and 384th Infantry Division's 2nd Battalion, 536th Regiment)—Lieutenant General Alexander Edler von Daniels

  VIII Army Corps—Colonel General Walter Heitz
    44th Infantry Division (131st, 132nd, and 134th Regiments and 177th Assault Gun Battalion)—Lieutenant General Heinrich Deboi
    76th Infantry Division (178th, 203rd, and 230th Regiments; 16th Panzer Division's 2nd Panzer Regiment; and 244th Assault Gun Battalion)—General of Artillery Maximilian de Angelis
    113th Infantry Division (1st Battalion, 261st Regiment; 1st and 3rd Battalions, 268th Regiment; and 3rd Company, 754th Pioneer Battalion)—Lieutenant General Hans-Heinrich Sixt von Arnim

  XI Army Corps—Colonel General Karl Strecker
    60th Motorized Division (160th Pioneer and Motorcycle Battalions; 9th Machine Gun Battalion; 1st and 2nd Battalions, 120th Regiment; and 1st and 3rd Battalions, 92nd Regiment)—Major General Hans-Adolf Arenstorff
    16th Panzer Division (71st Infantry Division's 71st Pioneer Battalion; 41st Pioneer Battalion; 1st Battalion, 64th Motorized Regiment; 2nd Company, 16th Motorcycle Battalion; and 1st Battalion, 79th Motorized Regiment; and 94th Infantry Division's 2nd Battalion, 276th Regiment)—Major General Günther Angern
    24th Panzer Division (Group Lenski) (*Luftwaffe* Battalion Matho, 94th Infantry Division's 2nd and 1st Battalions, 267th Regiment, and 274th Regiment, plus 4th Motorcycle Battalion and Group von Below's 21st and 26th Motorized Regiments)—Lieutenant General Arno von Lenski

  LI Army Corps—General of Artillery Walter von Seydlitz-Kurzbach
    389th Infantry Division (544th, 545th, and 546th Regiments)—Major General Erich Magnus
    305th Infantry Division (576th, 577th, and 578th Regiments)—Lieutenant General Bernhard Steinmetz
    79th Infantry Division (208th, 212th, and 226th Regiments)—Lieutenant General Richard Schwerin

Table 31. (continued)

100th Jäger Division (54th and 227th Jäger and 369th Croat Infantry Regiments)—
  Lieutenant General Werner Sanne
295th Infantry Division (516th, 517th, and 518th Regiments)—Major General Dr. Otto
  Korfes (part with Group Korfes)
71st Infantry Division (191st, 194th, and 211th Regiments)—Lieutenant General
  Alexander von Hartmann
245th Assault Gun Battalion

Reserve
14th Panzer Division (36th Panzer and 103rd and 108th Panzer-Grenadier Regiments)—
  Colonel Martin Lattmann
384th Infantry Division (–) (534th, 535th, and 536th Regiments) (to XIV Panzer Corps in
  mid-December)—Lieutenant General Eccard Freiherr von Gablenz

Source: Based on all of the primary sources listed in the Bibliography

Based on the way Paulus organized and tailored Sixth Army's defensive sectors, each of its five corps (army or panzer) faced one to two Soviet armies; each German division or special group opposed three to six Soviet rifle divisions or rifle (mechanized) brigades; and, on average, each German regiment operated against one rifle division or rifle or mechanized brigade. Moreover, each Soviet army was supported by one or two tank brigades from Soviet tank corps, and each mechanized corps was supported by its own organic tank regiments. Rokossovsky and Eremenko sought to achieve the greatest possible superiority in infantry and tanks in every army sector in the Stalingrad and Don Fronts (see table 32 and appendix 1 in the *Companion*).

Ostensibly, table 32 provides a rough correlation of opposing forces, which in this case appears to be between two and three to one in the Soviets' favor. However, relying on force symbols can be misleading because of the varying strength of each force at any given time. Since most Soviet rifle divisions began the operation at 50 to 70 percent of their authorized personnel strength, many if not most were operating at well under 50 percent strength (4,500 to 5,000 men) by 1 December. For example, 5th Tank Army's rifle divisions averaged roughly 8,800 men on 19 November but only about 7,000 men by 1 December. Similarly, the average personnel strength for the Don and Stalingrad Fronts' rifle divisions decreased from 4,500 and 5,850 men, respectively, on 19 November to about 3,800 and 5,000 men, respectively, on 1 December. Similarly, German Sixth Army's divisions fighting outside of Stalingrad proper (376th, 44th, 384th, 76th, 113th, 371st, and 297th) ranged in strength from 8,100 to 10,600 men, for a weighted average of roughly 9,300 men per division on 18 November. Based on Sixth Army's estimate of 34,000 men lost from 19 to 23 November and the likelihood that this number rose to over 40,000 by month's end, and assuming that these divisions suffered half of Sixth Army's total casualties, the average strength of

Table 32. Opposing Forces around Sixth Army's Stalingrad Pocket, 1 December 1942

STALINGRAD FRONT

64th Army
7th Rifle Corps
  96th Rifle Brigade
  93rd Rifle Brigade
  97th Rifle Brigade
29th Rifle Division
204th Rifle Division
157th Rifle Division
38th Rifle Division
66th Naval Rifle Brigade
154th Naval Rifle Brigade
56th Tank Brigade
235th Tank Brigade

57th Army
169th Rifle Division
36th Guards Rifle Division
17th Mechanized Brigade (13th Tank Corps)
422nd Rifle Division
90th Tank Brigade
62nd Mechanized Brigade (13th Tank Corps)
61st Mechanized Brigade (13th Tank Corps)

15th Guards Rifle Division
59th Mechanized Brigade (4th
  Mechanized Corps)
36th Mechanized Brigade (4th
  Mechanized Corps)

DON FRONT
21st Army
52nd Guards Rifle Division
96th Rifle Division, with 4th Tank Corps
293rd Rifle Division, with 26th Tank Corps

51st Guards Rifle Division
277th Rifle Division
65th Army
23rd Rifle Division

SIXTH ARMY

IV Army Corps
371st Infantry Division
  669th Regiment
  671st Regiment

297th Infantry Division
  522nd Regiment
  524th Regiment
  523rd Regiment
  82nd Regiment (Romanian)
  670th Regiment

29th Motorized Division
  71st Regiment
  15th Regiment
  129th Panzer *Abteilung*
  1st Battalion, 191st Regiment (71st
    Infantry Division)

XIV Panzer Corps
Group Korfes
  Group Domaschk
  Group Grahms
  Group von Hanstein
  Group Willig

3rd Motorized Division
  8th Regiment
  29th Regiment
  103rd Panzer *Abteilung*
376th Infantry Division
  672nd Regiment
  673rd Regiment
  767th Regiment

Table 32. (continued)

VIII Army Corps

252nd Rifle Division
27th Guards Rifle Division
91st Tank Brigade
121st Tank Brigade
304th Rifle Division (second echelon)
24th Rifle Division (second echelon)
24th Army
120th Rifle Division

233rd Rifle Division
84th Rifle Division
49th Rifle Division
214th Rifle Division (second echelon)

298th Rifle Division
273rd Rifle Division
54th Fortified Region
173rd Rifle Division

44th Infantry Division
  132nd Regiment
  134th Regiment
  131st Regiment
  2nd Battalion, 268th Regiment (113th
    Infantry Division)
  2nd Battalion, 2nd Panzer Regiment
    (16th Panzer Division)
  177th Assault Gun Battalion
76th Infantry Division
  203rd Regiment
  178th Regiment
  230th Regiment
  244th Assault Gun Battalion
113th Rifle Division
  1st Battalion, 261st Regiment
  268th Regiment
  260th Regiment

XI Army Corps

260th Rifle Division
66th Army
343rd Rifle Division
226th Rifle Division
64th Rifle Division
116th Rifle Division

299th Rifle Division
99th Rifle Division

60th Motorized Division
  120th Regiment
  92nd Regiment
  160th Panzer *Abteilung*
16th Panzer Division
  1st Battalion, 64th Panzer-Grenadier
    Regiment
  79th Panzer-Grenadier Regiment
24th Panzer Division
  267th Regiment (384th Infantry
    Division)
  21st Panzer-Grenadier Regiment
  274th Regiment (384th Infantry
    Division)

STALINGRAD FRONT

62nd Army
Group Gorokhov
138th Rifle Division
95th Rifle Division
45th Rifle Division
39th Guards Rifle Division
92nd Rifle Brigade
284th Rifle Division

13th Guards Rifle Division

LI Army Corps
389th Infantry Division
305th Infantry Division

79th Infantry Division

Group Sanne
  100th Jäger Division
  295th Infantry Division
71st Infantry Division

Source: Based on all of the primary sources listed in the Bibliography

these divisions likely fell to about 7,500 men per division or 2,500 men per regiment.

Given these numbers, the correlation of forces in most sectors favored the Red Army by a factor of roughly 2.5 to 1. Since defenders have a clear advantage over attackers, this explains why the besiegers encountered difficulty overcoming the besieged.

The Stalingrad Pocket's Outer Encirclement Front

The situation along the outer encirclement front differed significantly from that along the inner front for two reasons. First, by design, Red Army forces along the outer encirclement front tended to be stronger and better equipped because, originally, they formed part of the Southwestern and Stalingrad Fronts' main shock groups. Second, with the exception of forces arriving in the Stalingrad region from other fronts (such as the two divisions of XVII Army Corps), Axis forces defending along the outer encirclement front were either the remnants of forces defeated in previous operations or troops cobbled together from rear services or lines of communication. In addition, Vatutin's Southwestern Front included large forces in reserve earmarked for employment in Operation Saturn, while Eremenko's Stalingrad Front did not.

THE DON, KRIVAIA, AND CHIR RIVER FRONT

The Southwestern Front encountered three problems as it attempted to push its forces forward and across the Krivaia and Chir Rivers (see map 42). First, during the last weeks of November, its advance was far slower than anticipated. This was due primarily to the resistance offered by XXXXVIII Panzer Corps, but it was exacerbated by the slow deployment forward of rifle divisions involved in liquidating Romanian Third Army's forces encircled south of Raspopinskaia, as well as the slow regrouping of the five rifle divisions transferred to 5th Tank Army from 21st and 65th Armies. This permitted Romanian Third Army to erect hasty but effective defenses along both river lines. Second, the successful escape of XXXXVIII Panzer Corps' 22nd Panzer Division and Romanian 1st Armored Division across the Chir in relatively decent fighting condition materially strengthened these hasty defenses. Third, still later in the month, the arrival of General Hollidt's XVII Corps, with 62nd and 294th Infantry Divisions along the Krivaia and 336th Infantry Division along the Chir, blocked the Southwestern Front's advance unless and until it received fresh reinforcements.

However, the virtual stalemate that developed along the Krivaia and Chir Rivers by the end of November would last for only a few days. Thereafter, the arrival of sizable reinforcements enabled the Southwestern Front to resume offensive operations because Vatutin's reinforcements were more than

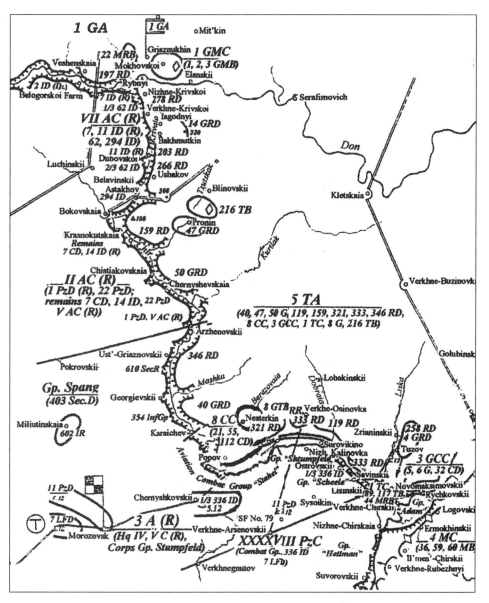

Map 42. Situation along the Krivaia and Chir Rivers, early December 1942

enough to outgun those received by Romanian Third Army. Two weeks later, when the Southwestern Front finally employed the large forces its had been husbanding for Operation Saturn, Group Hollidt's forces would also be significantly outgunned. Tables 33 and 34 show the composition of Axis forces deployed along the two rivers as of 1 December and the Soviet forces they opposed.

It is difficult to determine the balance of forces in any given sector of the Krivaia and Chir River fronts. The various groups and detachments subordinate to Romanian Third Army ranged in strength from 300 to 2,800 men each, and many of the 83,000 men subordinate to Romanian Third Army who escaped encirclement were thoroughly disorganized. It is safe to say, however, that Army Group Hollidt fielded roughly 75,000 men, including 25,000 German and 50,000 Romanian troops. These troops faced 1st Guards Army and one rifle division of 5th Tank Army—a force of about 160,000 men, including the reserves earmarked for Operation Saturn. As of 24 November, Romanian Third Army's Groups Spang, Stahel, and Stumpfeld fielded roughly 2,500, 3,500, and 9,000 men, respectively. However, reinforcements reaching the front by 30 November increased their strength to about 3,500, 5,000, and more than 10,000 men, respectively, with another 30,000+ Romanian troops assembling in the rear. Thereafter, 336th Infantry Division added another 10,000 men to Group Stumpfeld, and 7th *Luftwaffe* Division added about 9,000 men. This is why it was so important for 5th Tank Army to concentrate its forces quickly and capture Oblivskaia, Surovikino, and Rychkovskii before Axis reinforcements reached the region. The fact that 5th Tank Army's forces failed to do so saved the day for Romanian Third Army, at least temporarily.

The Kotel'nikovo Axis

At least initially, it appeared as if the Stalingrad Front's outer encirclement front was safe and secure in the hands of General Trufanov's 51st Army (see map 43). It is true that, throughout the last week of November, Trufanov's forces were more than a match for Romanian Fourth Army's VI and VII Army Corps. However, Group Pannwitz's victories over 4th Cavalry Corps' 61st Cavalry Division at Sharnutovskii on 25 November and its 81st Cavalry Division at Kotel'nikovo on 28 November were harbingers of things to come. These two defeats, coupled with the arrival of 6th Panzer Division in Kotel'nikovo on 28–29 November, shifted the correlation of forces in the Germans' favor (see tables 35 and 36). As subsequent combat would indicate, the cavalry and rifle divisions of Trufanov's 51st Army were no match for one German panzer division, let alone two.

Table 36 graphically portrays the balance of forces before and after the arrival of 6th Panzer Division and, later, 23rd Panzer and 15th *Luftwaffe*

Table 33. Composition of Army Group Hollidt and Romanian Third Army, 1 December 1942

ARMY GROUP HOLLIDT [*Angriffsgruppe*—Attack Group Hollidt]—General of Infantry Karl Hollidt
XVII Army Corps (headquarters only)—General of Infantry Dietrich von Choltitz on 7 December
I Army Corps (R)—Lieutenant General Teodor Ionescu
    7th Infantry Division (14th, 18th, and 36th Infantry Regiments) (R)—Brigadier General Constantin Trestioreanu
    9th Infantry Division (36th, 60th, and 84th Infantry Regiments) (R)—Major General Constantin Panaitiu and Major General Costin Ionaşcu in December or January
    11th Infantry Division (2nd, 3rd, and 19th Infantry Regiments) (R)—Brigadier General Savu Nedelea (captured in December) and Major General Romulus Ioanovici
II Army Corps (R)—Lieutenant General Nicolae Dăscălescu
    7th Cavalry Division (9th *Călărasi* and 11th and 12th *Rosiori* Regiments) (R)—Brigadier General Gheorghe Munteanu
    14th Infantry Division (6th, 13th, and 39th Infantry Regiments) (R) (remnants)—Major General Gheorghe Stavrescu
    62nd Infantry Division (164th, 183rd, and 190th Infantry Regiments) (G)—Major General Richard-Heinrich von Reuss
    294th Infantry Division (513th, 514th, and 515th Infantry Regiments) (G)—General of Infantry Johannes Block
XXXXVIII Panzer Corps (G) (to Army Group Hoth by 3 December)—Major General Hans Cramer and General of Panzer Troops Otto von Knobelsdorff on 4 December
    1st Armored Division (R) (remnants)—Major General Radu Gheorghe
    22nd Panzer Division (G) (remnants)—Colonel Eberhard Rodt
    5th Infantry Division (R) (remnants)
    6th Infantry Division (R) (remnants)—Brigadier General Traian Stanescu

ROMANIAN THIRD ARMY—General Petre Dumitrescu (as of 4 December)
    Detachment [*Abschnitt*] Spang (Group Spang by 4 December)—Lieutenant General Willibald Spang (chief of Sixth Army's Rear)
    Group Wantke (610th Security Regiment, 403rd Security Division)
        Detachment, 44th Infantry Division (80 men)
        Detachment, 7th Cavalry Division (R) (350 men)
        Pioneer Battalion, z.b.V. 10 (267 men)
        1st Alarm Battalion, Army Group B (300 men)
    Group Waldow (354th Security Regiment, 213th Security Division)
        2nd Battalion, 354th Security Regiment
        1st Alarm Battalion of Supply Troops (345 men)
        Alarm Battalion Gorlowka (200 men)
        1st Battalion, 354th Security Regiment
        2nd Alarm Battalion of Supply Troops (300 men)
    Reserve:
        2nd Battalion, 602nd Infantry-Engineer Battalion
        3rd Battalion, 354th Security Regiment
    Detachment, 13th Infantry Division (R)—Brigadier General Gheorghe Ionescu-Sinaia
    Detachment [*Abschnitt*] Stahel (former Group Fiebig) (headquarters VIII *Luftwaffe* Air [*Flieger*] Corps)—Major General Reiner Stahel (commander, 99th *Flak* Regiment)
    63rd Construction [*Bau*] Battalion (450 men)
    3rd Company, 177th Security Regiment (403rd Security Division) (46 men and 93 *Hiwis*)
    1st Alarm Battalion Rostow (400 men)
    1st Battalion, 8th *Luftwaffe* Field Division
    Group Obergehtmann (2,000 men) (99th *Flak* Battalion)
    Group von Stumpfeld (108th ARKO—Corps Artillery Command) (half to XXXXVIII Panzer Corps by 3 December)
    Group Colonel Schmidt (520th Pioneer Battalion) (2,800 men)

Table 33. (continued)

Group Weicke:
  301st Panzer Battalion [*Abteilung*]
  Military Leave Battalion
  36th Front Battalion
  1st Company, 301st Panzer Battalion
Group Colonel Selle (Sixth Army's engineers) (2,500 men)
2nd Alarm Battalion Charkow (550 men) (2 December from Group Stahel)
1st Alarm Battalion Stalino (270 men)
Group Colonel Adam (former Group Abraham in late November; to XXXXVIII Panzer Corps
    on 3 December)—Colonel Adam (aide-de camp to the commander of Sixth Army)
  Group Colonel Erdmann (450 men)
  Group Captain Göbel (800 men)
  Group Colonel Mikosch (600 men)
  1st Alarm Battalion Morozovskaia (300 men)
  Group Colonel Tzschöckel (600 men) (commander, 53rd Heavy Mortar Regiment)
    2nd Heavy Mortar Regiment (part)
    Headquarters and 1st Battalion, 53rd Heavy Mortar Regiment
  Group Dellinger
Group Colonel Heilmann (528 men) (to XXXXVIII Panzer Corps on 3 December)
  Group Sedmaier (detachment, 14th Panzer Division)
  Group Eichner (detachment, 29th Motorized Division)
336th Infantry Division (685th, 686th, and 687th Infantry Regiments) (G) (to XXXXVIII
    Panzer Corps on 3 December)—General of Artillery Walther Lucht
7th *Luftwaffe* Field Division (three infantry battalions) (G) (to XXXXVIII Panzer Corps on
    3 December)—Major General Wolf Freiherr von Biedermann
Reserve:
  Group Major von Klein
  4th Alarm Battalion Morozovskaia
  IV Army Corps (R) headquarters
    5th Infantry Division (R) (remnants)
    6th Infantry Division (R) (remnants)—Brigadier General Traian Stanescu
    14th Infantry Division (6th, 13th, and 39th Infantry Regiments) (R) (remnants)—
      Major General Gheorghe Stavrescu
  V Army Corps headquarters (R)—Lieutenant General Aurelian Son
    13th Infantry Division (R) (remnants)—Brigadier General Gheorghe Ionescu-Sinaia
    15th Infantry Division (R) (remnants)—Brigadier General Alexandru Nicolici
XXXXVIII Panzer Corps (G)—(on 3 December)
  7th *Luftwaffe* Field Division (three infantry battalions) (G) (from Romanian Third Army
    on 3 December)—Major General Wolf Freiherr von Biedermann
  11th Panzer Division (15th Panzer and 4th, 110th, and 111th Panzer-Grenadier
    Regiments) (G)—Lieutenant General Hermann Balck
  336th Infantry Division (685th, 686th, and 687th Infantry Regiments) (G) (from
    Romanian Third Army on 3 December)—General of Artillery Walther Lucht
  Group Adam (3 December)
  Group Heilmann (3 December)

**Subordinate to Army Group B but en route to Romanian Third Army's operational
    region**:
3rd Stalino Detachment
17th Panzer Division (39th Panzer and 40th and 63rd Panzer-Grenadier Regiments) (G)—
    Lieutenant General Fridolin von Senger und Etterlin
304th Infantry Division (573rd, 574th, and 575th Infantry Regiments) (G)—Major General
    Ernst Seiler
306th Infantry Division (579th, 580th, and 581st Infantry Regiments) (G)—General of
    Artillery Georg Pfeiffer
11th Panzer Division (15th Panzer and 4th, 110th, and 111th Panzer-Grenadier Regiments)
    (G)—Lieutenant General Hermann Balck

Source: Based on all of the primary sources listed in the Bibliography

Table 34. Opposing Forces along the Don, Krivaia, and Chir Rivers, 1 December 1942

SOUTHWESTERN FRONT	ARMY GROUP HOLLIDT
1st Guards Army	**I Army Corps (R) and XVII Army Corps (German)**
197th Rifle Division	7th Infantry Division (R)
278th Rifle Division	14th Regiment
	18th Regiment
	16th Regiment
	One regiment, 62nd Infantry Division
14th Rifle Corps	11th Infantry Division (R)
203rd Rifle Division	2nd Regiment
266th Rifle Division (to 6th Guards Rifle Corps)	3rd Regiment
	19th Regiment
4th Guards Rifle Corps (reserve)	Two regiments, 62nd Infantry Division
35th Guards Rifle Division	9th Infantry Division (R) (remnants)
41st Guards Rifle Division	
195th Rifle Division	
22nd Motorized Rifle Brigade (reserve)	
14th Guards Rifle Division	294th Infantry Division
6th Guards Rifle Corps (reserve)	513th Regiment
38th Guards Rifle Division	514th Regiment
44th Guards Rifle Division	515th Regiment
266th Rifle Division	
1st Guards Mechanized Corps (reserve)	
5th Tank Army	**II Army Corps (R)**
159th Rifle Division	14th Infantry Division
216th Tank Brigade (second echelon)	6th Regiment
	13th Regiment
	39th Regiment
50th Guards Rifle Division	7th Cavalry Division
	9th *Călărasi* Regiment
	11th *Rosiori* Regiment
	12th *Rosiori* Regiment
	XXXXVIII Panzer Corps (to 3 December)
One regiment, 47th Guards Rifle Division	22nd Panzer Division
One regiment, 21st Cavalry Division	
	1st Armored Division (R)
346th Rifle Division	**ROMANIAN THIRD ARMY**
	Group Spang
Two regiments, 47th Guards Rifle Division	Group Wandtke
21st Cavalry Division (8th Cavalry Corps) (en route)	610th Security Regiment (403rd Security Division)
	Detachments and alarm battalions
8th Cavalry Corps (en route)	Group Waldow
112th Cavalry Division (en route)	354th Grenadier Regiment (213th Security Division)
55th Cavalry Division (en route)	Alarm battalions
40th Guards Rifle Division (en route)	**Group Stahel** (VIII Air Corps)
40th Guards Rifle Division	3rd Battalion, 177th Regiment (403rd Security Division)
8th Cavalry Corps	
55th Cavalry Division	63rd Construction Battalion
112th Cavalry Division	1st Battalion, 8th *Luftwaffe* Field Division
321st Rifle Division (en route)	Group Obergehtmann (99th *Flak* Battalion
8th Guards Tank Brigade	

Table 34. (continued)

Group Stumpfeld (108th ARKO)

321st Rifle Division	Group Schmidt (520th Pioneer Battalion)
119th Rifle Division	301st Panzer Battalion
	36th Front Battalion
333rd Rifle Division	Group Selle
	Alarm battalions
258th Rifle Division	Group Adam
1st Tank Corps	Group Erdmann
89th Tank Brigade	Group Göbel
117th Tank Brigade	Group Mikosch
159th Tank Brigade	Group Tzschöckel
44th Motorized Rifle Brigade	Group Dellinger
3rd Guards Cavalry Corps	
5th Guards Cavalry Division	
6th Guards Cavalry Division	
32nd Cavalry Division	
60th Mechanized Brigade (4th Mechanized	Group Heilmann
Corps)	Group Sedmaier (14th Panzer Division)
	Group Eichner (29th Motorized Division)
	En route:
	306th Infantry Division
	304th Infantry Division
	ARMY GROUP HOTH (3 December)

(3–4 December)	**XXXXVIII Panzer Corps (3 December)**
4th Guards Rifle Division	336th Infantry Division
3rd Guards Cavalry Corps	685th Regiment
5th Guards Cavalry Division	686th Regiment
6th Guards Cavalry Division	687th Regiment
32nd Cavalry Division	
258th Rifle Division	7th *Luftwaffe* Field Division (three battalions)
333rd Rifle Division	11th Panzer Division (3 December)
1st Tank Corps	
89th Tank Brigade	
117th Tank Brigade	
159th Tank Brigade	
216th Tank Brigade (26th Tank Corps)	
44th Motorized Rifle Brigade	
119th Rifle Division	
***Front* Reserves:**	
5th Mechanized Corps	
18th Tank Corps	
57th Army	

4th Mechanized Corps	Group Adam (3 December)
59th Mechanized Brigade	Group Heilmann (3 December)
60th Mechanized Brigade	
36th Mechanized Brigade (en route)	
158th Tank Regiment	
55 Tank Regiment (en route)	
	En route:
	17th Panzer Division

Source: Based on all of the primary sources listed in the Bibliography

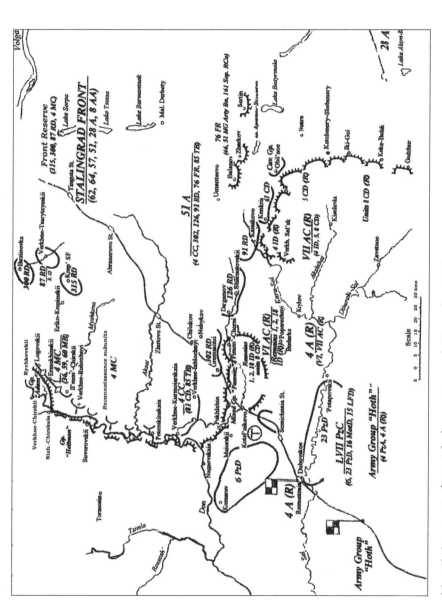

Map 43. Situation in the Kotel'nikovo region, early December 1942

Table 35. Composition of Army Group Hoth, 1 December 1942

ARMY GROUP HOTH (former Fourth Panzer Army)—Colonel General Hermann Hoth
   Headquarters, Fourth Panzer Army (with headquarters, Fourth Romanian Army)
   Group Korne (R)—Brigadier General Radu Korne
   Group von Pannwitz (cavalry group) (G)—Colonel Helmuth von Pannwitz
   VI Army Corps (R)—Lieutenant General Corneliu Dragalina
      2nd Infantry Division (1st, 26th, and 31st Infantry Regiments) (R)—Brigadier General
         Dumitru Tudose
      18th Infantry Division (18th, 90th, and 92nd Infantry Regiments) (R)—Brigadier General
         Radu Băldescu
      1st Infantry Division (85th and 93rd Infantry Regiments) (R)—Major General Barbu
         Alienescu and Brigadier General Ioan Dumitriu in December
   VII Army Corps (R)—Lieutenant General Florea Mitrănescu
      4th Infantry Division (5th, 20th, and 21st Infantry Regiments) (R)—Major General Barbu
         Alienescu and Brigadier General Ioan Dumitriu in December
      5th Cavalry Division (7th and 8th *Rosiori* Regiments) (R)—Colonel Dumitru Popescu
      8th Cavalry Division (2nd and 3rd *Călărasi* and 4th *Rosiori* Regiments) (R)—Brigadier
         General Radu Korne
      16th Panzer-Grenadier Division (60th and 156th Panzer-Grenadier Regiments, 116th
         Panzer Battalion, and 450th, 782nd, and 811th Turkestan Volunteer Battalions)
         (G)—General of Panzer Troops Gerhard Graf von Schwerin

Subordinate to Army Group Don but en route to Army Group Hoth
   LVII Panzer Corps—General of Panzer Troops Friedrich Kirchner
      6th Panzer Division (arrived in Kotel'nikovo on 28–29 November)
      23rd Panzer Division (en route to Kotel'nikovo)
      15th *Luftwaffe* Field Division

Source: Based on all of the primary sources listed in the Bibliography

Divisions. These arrivals tipped the scale in favor of LVII Panzer Corps until the *Stavka* remedied things by dispatching sizable reinforcements to the
region.

CONCLUSION

Occurring as it did on the heels of a dramatically successful counteroffensive
and encirclement operation, the fighting in the Stalingrad region from 24
through 30 November marked an important watershed in Operation Uranus
as a whole. After the striking successes achieved by the Southwestern and
Stalingrad Fronts from 19 through 23 November, the multiple difficulties
encountered by all three Soviet *fronts* during the final week of November
made it abundantly clear that the way they had organized their forces for
combat during the successful penetration and encirclement operation no
longer suited the existing situation in several important respects. First and
foremost, the two *fronts* conducting the pincer operation encircled far more

Table 36. Opposing Forces along the Kotel'nikovo and Elista Axes, 1 December 1942

STALINGRAD FRONT	RMY GROUP HOTH (3 December)
51st Army	**I Army Corps (R)**
4th Cavalry Corps	1st Infantry Division (R) (remnants)
81st Cavalry Division	Group Pannwitz
85th Tank Brigade	
302nd Rifle Division	2nd Infantry Division (R) (remnants)
	18th Infantry Division (R) (remnants)
126th Rifle Division	Group Korne (regiment, 8th Cavalry Division [R])
300th Rifle Division (reserve)	**LVII Panzer Corps** (en route)
315th Rifle Division (reserve)	6th Panzer Division
87th Rifle Division (*front* reserve)	23rd Panzer Division (en route)
	15th *Luftwaffe* Division (en route)
	VII Army Corps (R)
61st Cavalry Division (4th Cavalry Corps)	4th Infantry Division (R)
91st Rifle Division	5th Cavalry Division (R)
76th Fortified Region	8th Cavalry Division (R) (–)
28th Army	**16th Motorized Division**
34th Guards Rifle Division	60th Motorized Regiment
248th Rifle Division	156th Motorized Regiment
152nd Separate Rifle Brigade	116th Panzer *Abteilung*
6th Guards Tank Brigade	450th Turkestan Battalion
	782nd Turkestan Battalion
	811th Turkestan Battalion

Source: Based on all of the primary sources listed in the Bibliography

forces than the *Stavka* anticipated—that is, roughly 284,000 men rather than the estimated 90,000.[78] As subsequent combat indicated, even if they drastically reduced the strength of their forces on the outer encirclement front, the three Soviet *fronts* would probably not be strong enough to liquidate the larger Axis force in the Stalingrad pocket.

Second, even though Vasilevsky was able to identify serious command and control difficulties by 26 November and start to remedy them, such as by transferring 21st Army from the Southwestern to the Don Front, these problems would persist as long as the armies of Eremenko's Stalingrad Front operated along diametrically opposed axes. And there was no quick solution to this problem, because Eremenko's *front* lacked enough field armies to accomplish its two assigned missions.

Third, by husbanding large forces to conduct Operation Saturn—specifically, 2nd Guards Army; 7th, 17th, 18th, 24th, and 25th Tank Corps; 5th, 1st, and 2nd Guards Mechanized Corps; and 4th and 6th Guards Rifle Corps—the *Stavka* and Vasilevsky deprived its three *fronts* operating in the Stalingrad region of the necessary forces—in particular, armored and mechanized forces—to accomplish either of their two important missions. Without sizable reinforcements, they could neither liquidate Sixth Army nor fend off likely German relief operations from the Kotel'nikovo and Aksai regions or from the confluence of the Chir and Don Rivers in the Rychkovskii and Verkhne-Chirskaia regions.

Fourth, faced with these new problems, the *Stavka*, Vasilevsky, and the three *front* commanders had to determine the fate of Operation Saturn. And if they did not conduct it as planned, they had to decide where and how to employ the large strategic and operational reserves in the Stalingrad region: first and foremost, General Malinovsky's 2nd Guards Army. How they answered these and other lesser questions would shape the nature and ultimately the outcome of the struggle along the Stalingrad axis throughout December 1942.

On the German side, Hitler's decisions to forbid the withdrawal of Sixth Army and to order the *Luftwaffe* to supply the army by air were critical to the survival of Paulus's army, if not to the entire German war effort. First and foremost, these decisions resulted from Hitler's perception that the "stand fast" order he had issued to Army Group Center at the gates of Moscow in December 1941 had been successful in preventing the collapse of Bock's army group and, more important, in maintaining the German will to prevail in the war. Second, like many German commanders, Hitler could not believe that the previously inept Red Army could accomplish so bold a feat as to encircle, much less destroy, an entire German army. Even if he harbored hidden doubts about Göring's assurances that the *Luftwaffe* could sustain Sixth Army (and there is no evidence that he did), it was unimaginable that Soviet forces could actually liquidate such a powerful and famous force as Paulus's army. Besides, German panzer divisions had accomplished Herculean feats the previous winter when they rescued multiple encircled or isolated German forces, and they could certainly do so again. Thus, Hitler's arrogance, confidence, and belief in his own Nazi ideology and propaganda conditioned the decisions he reached during the last ten days of November.

Second, Manstein exercised what turned out to be a fatal influence on Hitler when he seemed to confirm Hitler's decision to order Paulus to stand fast. After Manstein's first conference with Weichs at Starobel'sk and on many occasions thereafter, Manstein broke up what had been a unanimous assessment of the perils of Sixth Army's situation by Weichs, Paulus, and many other German generals and did not explicitly favor an immediate breakout from the pocket. This would become even clearer after mid-December, when Manstein proved either unable or unwilling to give Paulus the break-out order.

All this set the stage for a harrowing race between the forces of German Army Group Don and the Red Army's Southwestern and Stalingrad Fronts during the first week of December 1942. The outcome of the race would determine whether Paulus's Sixth Army was saved or destroyed, with immense strategic implications for both winner and loser. Stated more precisely, Army Group Don's objective was to mount relief operations from the west and southwest to save Sixth Army, while the *Stavka's* goal was to block and defeat those relief attempts. At stake was not only the survival of Sixth Army but also the reputation, if not the ultimate fate, of Hitler's *Wehrmacht*.

As for the human cost of the fighting during the initial stages of Operation Uranus, the most recent Russian official history of the battle for Stalingrad asserts that German and Romanian forces lost a total of 145,000 soldiers and officers from 19 to 30 November, including 65,000 prisoners of war.[79] The same source places Axis material losses at 3,600 machine guns, 2,900 guns, 700 mortars, more than 300 tanks, more than 250 aircraft, 7,500 vehicles of various types, up to 1,500 motorcycles, and vast amounts of other military equipment and supplies. Additionally, Soviet forces "liberated" about 700 captured Soviet tanks from German hands, as well as 6,000 recently captured Red Army prisoners of war. On the other side of this grim ledger, the same source acknowledges that the three attacking *fronts* lost 79,400 men, including 18,400 killed in action; 359 tanks (145 irrevocably); and 125 aircraft. Subdivided by *front*, the Southwestern Front lost 38,400 men (including 8,200 dead), the Don Front lost 22,800 men (including 5,800 killed in action), and the Stalingrad Front suffered 18,200 casualties (including 4,400 dead). Since all three *fronts* were on the offensive, their losses in artillery and rifle weaponry were minimal. For example, the Stalingrad Front reported losing only 15 guns, 15 mortars, and 13 machine guns.[80]

Axis sources generally confirm the high personnel losses, admitting that Romanian Third Army and the two Romanian corps fighting south of Stalingrad lost about 90,000 men, while Sixth Army and Fourth Panzer Army suffered about 34,000 casualties by 23 November and another 14,000+ by month's end. Although the Russian estimate of Axis tank losses is close to the mark, as previously indicated, the number of "liberated" Soviet tanks is clearly inflated. Nonetheless, all in all, the second half of November was a profitable period for Soviet arms.

Notes

Abbreviations

BA-MA   *Bundesarchiv Miltärarchiv* (German Military Archives)
NAM   National Archives Microfilm
TsAMO   *Tsentral'nyi arkhiv Ministerstva Oborony* [Central Archives of the Ministry of Defense]
VIZh   *Voenno-istoricheskii zhurnal* [Military-historical journal]
VMI   *Vestnik voennoi informatsii* [Herald of military information]

Chapter 1. Framework for Disaster

1. G. F. Krivosheev, ed., *Soviet Casualties and Combat Losses in the Twentieth Century*, trans. Christine Barnard (London: Greenhill Books; Mechanicsburg, PA: Stackpole Books, 1997), 94. To this total must be added several million civilians killed or kidnapped into forced labor. For an updated and expanded version of this book, see G. F. Krivosheev, ed., *Velikaia Otechestvennaia bez grifa sekretnosti. Kniga poter'* [The Great Patriotic (War) without the secret classification. A book of losses] (Moscow: Veche, 2009).

2. Horst Boog, Werner Rahm, Reinhard Stumpf, and Bernd Wegner, *Germany and the Second World War*, vol. 6, *The Global War: Widening of the Conflict into a World War and the Shift of the Initiative 1941–1943*, trans. Ewald Osers et al. (Oxford: Clarendon Press, 2001), 126–130.

3. See, for example, Joel Hayward, "Hitler's Quest for Oil: The Impact of Economic Considerations on Military Strategy, 1941–42," *Journal of Strategic Studies* 18, 4 (December 1995): 94–135.

4. Führer Directive No. 41 is contained in Hugh R. Trevor-Roper, ed., *Blitzkrieg to Defeat: Hitler's War Directives 1939–1945* (New York: Holt, Rinehart, and Winston, 1964), esp. 117, 119.

5. See, for example, Rolf-Dieter Müller and Gerd R. Ueberschar, *Hitler's War in the East, 1941–1945: A Critical Assessment*, trans. Bruce D. Little (Providence, RI: Berghahn Books, 1997), 113.

6. "Gruppirovka i sostav 3 Rumynsko i 8 Ital'ianskoi armii na Donu" [The grouping of 3rd Romanian and 8th Italian Armies on the Don], in *Sbornik materialov po izucheniiu opyta voiny, No. 8 (avgust-oktiabr' 1943 g.)* [Collection of materials for the exploitation of war experiences, No. 8] (Moscow: Voenizdat, 1943), 24–36; Mark Axworthy, Cornel Scafeş, and Cristian Craciunoiu, *Third Axis Fourth Ally: The Romanian Armed Forces in the European War, 1941–1945* (London: Arms and Armour Press, 1995); *L '8' Armata Italiana nella Seconde Battaglia Difensiva Del Don (11 Decembre 1942–31 January 1943)* [The 8th Italian Army in the second defensive battle

of the Don] (Roma: Ministero della Guerra, Stato Maggiore Esercito-Ufficio Storico, 1946); *Le Operationi della Unita Italiane Al Fronte Russo (1943–1944)* (Roma: Ministero della Guerra, Stato Maggiore Esercito-Ufficio Storico, 1977).

7. Geoffrey Jukes, *Hitler's Stalingrad Decisions* (Berkeley: University of California Press, 1985), 70–72; Boog et al., *Germany and the Second World War*, 6:990–991.

8. Earl F. Ziemke and Magna E. Bauer, *Moscow to Stalingrad: Decision in the East* (Washington, DC: U.S. Army Center of Military History, 1987), 377–378; Boog et al., *Germany and the Second World War*, 6:1057–1058.

9. Zeitzler briefing to Hitler, mid-October 1942, quoted in Seymour Frieden and William Richardson, eds., *The Fatal Decisions*, trans. Constantine Fitzgibbon (New York: William Sloane Associates, 1956), 139.

10. Ibid., 137–139.

11. Boog et al., *Germany and the Second World War*, 6:1084–1086.

12. Jukes, *Hitler's Stalingrad Decisions*, 83–88; Zeitzler's report in Frieden and Richardson, *Fatal Decisions*, 142–143; George E. Blau, *The German Campaign in Russia: Planning and Operations (1940–1942)*, Department of the Army Pamphlet No. 20-261a (Washington, DC: Department of the Army, 1955), 170–171; Boog et al., *Germany and the Second World War*, 6:1114–1118.

13. David M. Glantz and Jonathan M. House, *When Titans Clashed: How the Red Army Stopped Hitler* (Lawrence: University Press of Kansas, 1995), 30–33. For the Germans' dependence on horses, see Richard L. DiNardo, *Mechanized Juggernaut or Military Anachronism: Horses and the German Army of World War II* (Westport, CT: Greenwood Press, 1991), esp. 40–43.

14. Klaus Reinhardt, *Moscow—The Turning Point: The Failure of Hitler's Strategy in the Winter of 1941–42*, trans. Karl Keenan (Oxford: Oxford University Press, 1992), 367–370. This total included 4,262 antitank guns, 5,990 mortars, 1,942 howitzers, and 1,411 infantry support guns. This discussion of the *Wehrmacht*'s recovery draws heavily from Reinhardt.

15. Ziemke and Bauer, *Moscow to Stalingrad*, 177, 293–295; Franz Halder, *The Halder War Diary, 1939–1942*, ed. Charles Burdick and Hans-Adolf Jacobsen (Novato, CA: Presidio Press, 1988), 613–615; Timothy A. Wray, *Standing Fast: German Defensive Doctrine on the Russian Front during World War II, Prewar to March 1943* (Ft. Leavenworth, KS: Combat Studies Institute, 1986), 112–113.

16. Ziemke and Bauer, *Moscow to Stalingrad*, 296; Williamson Murray, *Luftwaffe* (Baltimore: Nautical & Aviation Publishing Company of America, 1985), 112–119.

17. Jason D. Mark, *Death of the Leaping Horseman: 24. Panzer-Division in Stalingrad, 12th August–20th November 1942* (Sydney, Australia: author, 2002), 333–334.

18. Boog et al., *Germany and the Second World War*, 6:1091–1095; troop shortages are calculated from the table on 1106.

19. Joel S. A. Hayward, *Stopped at Stalingrad: The Luftwaffe and Hitler's Defeat in the East, 1942–1943* (Lawrence: University Press of Kansas, 1998), 195.

20. A. A. Grechko, *Bitva za Kavkaz* [The battle for the Caucasus] (Moscow: Voenizdat, 1973), 211. See also Wilhelm Tieke, *The Caucasus and the Oil: The*

German-Soviet War in the Caucasus 1942/43, trans. Joseph G. Welsh (Winnipeg, Canada: J. J. Fedorowicz, 1995), esp. 231–237.

21. Boog et al., *Germany and the Second World War*, 6:1114–1115.

22. See an essay on Manstein by Richard Carver in Correlli Barnett, ed., *Hitler's Generals* (New York: Grove Weidenfeld, 1989), 221–246. Manstein's memoir, *Lost Victories*, trans. Anthony G. Powell (Chicago: Henry Regnery, 1958), 261–386, predictably blames Hitler for the failures of the 1941–1943 campaign.

23. See the essay by Samuel W. Mitcham Jr. in Barnett, *Hitler's Generals*, 249–263.

24. Krivosheev, *Soviet Casualties and Combat Losses*, 123–126.

25. See tables 45 and 46 in David M. Glantz and Jonathan M. House, *Armageddon in Stalingrad, September–November 1942: The Stalingrad Trilogy*, vol. 2 (Lawrence: University Press of Kansas, 2009), 707, 719–780.

26. *Stavka* Directive Nos. 9954275 and 994276, 23 October 1942, quoted in V. A. Zolotarev, ed., *Russkii arkhiv: Velikaia Otechestvennaia: Stavka VGK: Dokumenty i materially 1942 god, T. 16 (5-2)* [The Russian archives: The Great Patriotic [War]: *Stavka* VGK: Documents and materials 1942, vol. 16 (5-2)] (Moscow: Terra, 1996), 442–443; hereafter cited as Zolotarev, "*Stavka* 1942," with appropriate pages. These orders also formed the new 1st and 2nd Guards Mechanized Corps in the two new guards armies.

27. O. A. Losik, *Stroitel'stvo i boevoe primenenie Sovetskikh tankovykh voisk v gody Velikoi Otechestvennoi voiny* [The formation and combat use of Soviet tank forces in the years of the Great Patriotic War] (Moscow: Voenizdat, 1979), 44–77.

28. Iu P. Babich and A. G. Baier, *Razvitie vooruzheniia i organizatsii Sovetskikh sukhoputnykh voisk v gody Velikoi Otechestvennoi voiny* [The development of the armament and organization of the Soviet ground forces in the Great Patriotic War] (Moscow: Frunze Academy, 1990), 44–45. See also David M. Glantz, *Colossus Reborn: The Red Army at War 1941–1943* (Lawrence: University Press of Kansas, 2005), 218–236.

29. Glantz, *Colossus Reborn*, 297. On antitank losses, see A. N. Ianchinsky, *Boevoe ispol'zovanie istrebitel'no-protivotankovoi artillerii RVGK v Velikoi Otechestvennoi voine* [The combat employment of destroyer antitank artillery of the *Stavka* Reserve in the Great Patriotic War] (Moscow: Voroshilov Academy, 1951), 25–26; classified secret.

30. Glantz, *Colossus Reborn*, 290–291. See also Babich and Baier, *Razvitie vooruzheniia*, 53.

31. See, for example, Geoffrey Roberts, *Stalin's Wars: From World War to Cold War, 1939–1953* (New Haven, CT: Yale University Press, 2006), 27, 123, 159.

32. Ibid., 133.

33. The Presidium decree justifying Order No. 307 is quoted in Ziemke and Bauer, *Moscow to Stalingrad*, 438–439. See the full text of NKO Order No. 307 in V. A. Zolotarev, ed., *Russkii arkhiv: Velikaia Otechestvennaia: Prikazy narodnogo komissara oborony SSSR 22 iiunia 1941 g.–1942 g. T.13 (2-2)* [The Russian archives: The Great Patriotic [War]: Orders of the People's Commissar of Defense of the USSR, vol. 13 (2-2)] (Moscow: Terra, 1997), 326–327; hereafter cited as Zolotarev, "NKO 1941–42," with appropriate pages. See also John Erickson, *The Road to Stalingrad*

(New York: Harper & Row, 1975) 452; Kenneth Slepyan, *Stalin's Guerrillas: Soviet Partisans in World War II* (Lawrence: University Press of Kansas, 2006), 244.

34. Louis C. Rotundo, ed., *Battle for Stalingrad: The 1943 Soviet General Staff Study* (Washington, DC: Pergamon-Brassey's International Defense Publishers, 1989), 78–79; Richard N. Armstrong, *Red Army Tank Commanders: The Armored Guards* (Atglen, PA: Schiffer Military/Aviation History, 1994), 21–22; Erickson, *Road to Stalingrad*, 450–453.

35. On Zhukov's background and role, see the general's "authorized" memoirs in G. Zhukov, *Reminiscences and Reflections*, vols. 1 and 2 (Moscow: Progress Publishers, 1985); Georgi K. Zhukov, *Marshal Zhukov's Greatest Battles*, trans. Theodore Shabad (New York: Cooper Square Press, 2002); and Otto Preston Chaney, *Zhukov* (Norman: University of Oklahoma Press, 1996). See also Viktor Anfilov, "Georgy Konstantinovich Zhukov," in *Stalin's Generals*, ed. Harold Shukman (New York: Grove Press, 1993), 343–360; David M. Glantz, *Zhukov's Greatest Defeat: The Red Army's Epic Disaster in Operation Mars, 1942* (Lawrence: University Press of Kansas, 1999); and, for an analysis of his generalship, M. A. Gareev, *Marshal Zhukov: Velichie i unikal'nost' polkovodcheskogo iskusstva* [Marshal Zhukov: The greatness and uniqueness of a commander's art] (Moscow: Eastern University, 1996).

36. Geoffrey Jukes, "Alexander Mikhailovich Vasilevsky," in Shukman, *Stalin's Generals*, 275–285. See also Aleksandr M. Vasilevsky, *A Lifelong Cause* (Moscow: Progress Publishers, 1976), and the Russian unedited version: A. M. Vasilevsky, *Delo vsei zhizni* [A life's work], 2 vols. (Moscow: Izdatel'stvo politicheskoi literatury, 1989).

37. For an abridged version of Eremenko's memoirs, see A. Eremenko, *The Arduous Beginning* (Moscow: Progress Publishers, 1966); for the unabridged versions, see A. I. Eremenko, *V nachale voiny* [In the beginning of the war] (Moscow: Khranitel', 2006) ,and *Gody vozmezdiia* [Years of retribution] (Moscow: Nauka, 1969). For his vital role in the battle for Stalingrad, see A. I. Eremenko, *Stalingrad: Zapiski komanduiushchego frontom* [Stalingrad: The notes of a *front* commander] (Moscow: Voenizdat, 1961). Eremenko's works, published during Khrushchev's "thaw" in historical censorship, are remarkable for their accuracy and candor.

38. For an abridged version of Rokossovsky's memoirs, see K. Rokossovsky, *A Soldier's Duty* (Moscow: Progress Publishers, 1970, 1985); the unabridged and uncensored version is K. K. Rokossovsky, *Soldatskii dolg* [A soldier's duty] (Moscow: Golos, 2000). A recent biography is Vladimir Daines, *Rokossovsky: Genii manevra* [Rokossovsky: A genius of maneuver] (Moscow: Iauza Eksmo, 2008). For a shorter biographical essay, see Richard Woff, "Konstantin Konstantinovich Rokossovsky," in Shukman, *Stalin's Generals*, 177–198.

39. Sadly, Vatutin left no memoir because he was killed by Ukrainian partisans in early March 1944. His best biographies include Iu D. Zakharov, *General Armii N. F. Vatutin* [Army general N. F. Vatutin] (Moscow: Voenizdat, 1985); S. Kulichkin, *Vatutin* (Moscow: Voenizdat, 2001); and David M. Glantz, "Nikolai Fedorovich Vatutin," in Shukman, *Stalin's Generals*, 287–300.

40. For example, because liquidating large pockets of German troops encircled in the vicinity of major cities required well-organized and sustained firepower, the *Stavka* appointed Voronov to plan and coordinate Operation Ring [*Kol'tso*] in the Stalingrad region.

Chapter 2. Soviet Strategic Planning

1. For a succinct description of the controversy over the "second front," see Erickson, *Road to Stalingrad*, 394–402.

2. G. K. Zhukov, *Vospominaniia i razmyshleniia* [Reminiscences and reflections] (Moscow: Izdatel'stvo agentstva pechati Novosti, 1970), 382; hereafter cited as *Reminiscences and Reflections*. See the English translation, Georgi Zhukov, *Reminiscences and Reflections*, vol. 2 (Moscow: Progress Publishers, 1985), 94.

3. A. I. Eremenko, *Stalingrad: Zapiski komanduiushchego frontom* [Stalingrad: The notes of a *front* commander] (Moscow: Voenizdat, 1961), 325–326.

4. Ibid.

5. Roberts, *Stalin's Wars: From World War to Cold War, 1939–1953*, 149, citing "Posetiteli Kremlevskogo Kabineta I.V. Stalina," *Istoricheskii Arkhiv* 2 (1996): 35–38.

6. In the case of Khar'kov, this involved penetrating the defenses of Romanian units; in the Crimea, it was based on smashing the defenses of both German and Romanian covering forces in the eastern Crimea, while the bulk of Manstein's Eleventh Army besieged Soviet troops in city of Sevastopol' in the western Crimea.

7. The Russian phrase *inoe reshenie* can be variously translated as "a different [or another] solution" or "a different [or another] decision [or plan]."

8. At Moscow, for example, the Soviet counteroffensive began with counterattacks born of outright desperation in early December. When these succeeded (to the Soviets' surprise), Zhukov, with Stalin's approval, expanded them into a counterstroke in mid-December and a full-scale counteroffensive in January 1943.

9. S. M. Shtemenko, *The Soviet General Staff at War, 1941–1945*, book 1, trans. Robert Daglish (Moscow: Progress Publishers, 1985), 121. According to Stalin's daily calendar, Bokov's first meeting with him took place from 1935 to 2030 hours on 23 July, along with Major General P. G. Tikhomirov, temporary chief of the Operations Directorate. See A. A. Chernobaev, ed., *Na prieme u Stalina. Tetradi (zhurnaly) zapisei lits, priniatykh I. V. Stalinym (1924–1953gg.). Spravochnik* [Received by Stalin. The notebooks (journals) of entries of those persons admitted by I. V. Stalin (1924–1953)] (Moscow: Novyi khronograf, 2008), 379.

10. S. Mikhalev, "O razrabotke zamysla i planirovanii kontrnastupleniia pod Stalingradom" [About the concept and planning of the counteroffensive at Stalingrad], *VMI* 8 (August 1992): 1.

11. Chernobaev, *Na prieme u Stalina*, 384. In fact, Stalin held no meetings from 10 to 12 September and did not meet with Zhukov on the 13th. For a recent attempt by Russian historians to square the contradictions between Zhukov's assertions and the actual archival evidence, see V. A. Zolotarev, ed., *Velikaia Otechestvennaia voina 1941–1945: Voenno-istoricheskii ocherki v chetyrekh knigakh, Kniga 2: Perelom* [The Great Patriotic War 1941–1945: Military-historical survey, book 2: The turning point] (Moscow: Nauka, 1998), 36. This account accepts Zhukov's assertions regarding who suggested Operation Uranus and when, stating: "The strategic plan of operations of the Armed Forces on the southern wing of the Soviet-German front began to be formulated in the *Stavka* of the Supreme High Command in mid-September and for the winter campaign of 1942–43 as a whole—in November and December. Its

bases were proposals expressed by Zhukov and Vasilevsky as early as 12 September in meetings with Stalin. The essence of these included the delivery of powerful concentrated blows with the forces of three–four *fronts* against both flanks of the enemy grouping which had wedged into the defenses of Soviet forces at Stalingrad with the aim of its successive encirclement and destruction, with the simultaneous creation of an actively operating external front. This preliminary concept was then defined more precisely, rendered concrete, and developed with consideration of the thoughts of the Red Army General Staff and the proposals of the *front* commanders. The fully worked-out plan for the Stalingrad counteroffensive, under the code-name Uranus, was submitted to the Supreme High Commander on 13 October for his scrutiny. At this time, Stalin, who had learned from bitter experience, did not intrude with his ideas, but instead entirely agreed with his military leaders. On the map submitted to him with the counteroffensive plan, he wrote one single word: 'Agreed.' A month later, after more precise definition on the basis of conducted personal reconnaissances, the plan was once again examined in meetings in the *Stavka*. And again, Stalin approved the final timing for the beginning of the counteroffensive without any sort of objection and also agreed with the proposals of Zhukov and Vasilevsky about the preparation of offensive operations along other axes, first and foremost, north of Viaz'ma." Therefore, this account attempts to satisfy all parties in the dispute over responsibility for planning by ignoring the entries in Stalin's daily calendar and accepting Zhukov's assertion that he proposed the "different solution" to Stalin on 12–13 September. But it then skirts the issue entirely by admitting that the plan was sharply revised by 13 October, based on input from *front* commanders. It also recognizes that Operation Mars, which was to be conducted north of Viaz'ma, was an integral part of the overall strategic plan. The sources on which this judgment is based include Zhukov's and Vasilevsky's memoirs, but no other archival citations. The underlying note states: "The initial transition of Soviet forces to the counteroffensive was intended to be on 9–10 November. At a meeting on 13 November, it was determined that the Southwestern and Don Fronts would go over to the offensive on 19 November and the Stalingrad Front—a day later."

12. Zolotarev, "*Stavka* 1942," 440–441; archival citation *TsAMO*, f. 148a, op. 3763, d. 107 l. 240. For details on the creation of the Southwestern Front, see chapter 4 of volume 2 of this trilogy.

13. For references to Rokossovsky's temporary appointment to command the Stalingrad Front for roughly one week, see Shukman, *Stalin's Generals*, 185–186; K. K. Rokossovsky, *Soldatskii dolg* [A soldier's duty] (Moscow: Golos, 2000), 187; and *Kirill Konstantinov Rokossovsky: Pobeda ne liuboi tsenoi* [Kirill Konstantinovich Rokossovsky: Victory at any cost] (Moscow: Eksmo Iauza, 2006), 153, which erroneously states, "On 1 October, the representatives of the *Stavka* [Zhukov] ordered Rokossovsky to take command of the Stalingrad Front (soon renamed Don)." Zhukov actually dispatched Rokossovsky to the Stalingrad region to take over the four armies on the Stalingrad Front's right wing and lead them in the counterstroke from the Kotluban' and Erzovka region. In this sense, he was just replacing Gordov, who no longer inspired Zhukov's trust. In *Soldatskii dolg*, 185, Rokossovsky criticizes Gordov as a "cuss commander" who berated his subordinates but makes no reference to the report that he temporarily displaced Eremenko in the defensive battle.

14. Dmitri Volkogonov, *Stalin: Triumph and Tragedy*, trans. and ed. Harold Shukman (Rocklin, CA: Prima Lifestyles, 1992), 461–463; S. Mikhalev, "O razrabotke zamysla i planirovanii kontrnastupleniia pod Stalingradom" [About the concept and planning of the counteroffensive at Stalingrad], *VMI* 8 (August 1992): 1–5. The earlier, 1976 version of Vasilevsky's memoirs, *A Lifelong Cause*, 188–189, follows Zhukov's account. See also Glantz, *Zhukov's Greatest Defeat*, 19–20.

15. Mikhalev, "O razrabotke zamysla," 1.

16. A. I. Eremenko, *Stalingrad: Uchastnikam Velikoi bitvy pod Stalingradom posviashchaetsia* [Stalingrad: A participant in the great battle for Stalingrad explains] (Moscow: Khranitel', 2006), 352–353.

17. "Direktiva Stavki VGK No. 170644 komanduiushchemu Donskim frontom T. Rokossovskomu [*Stavka* VGK Directive No. 170644 to the commander of the Don Front, Comrade Rokossovsky], in *Stalingradskaia bitva. Khronika, fakty, liudi: v 2-kh.* [The Battle of Stalingrad. Chronicles, facts, and people, in 2 books], ed. V. A. Zhilin (Moscow: Olma-Press, 2002), book 1, 694; archival citation *TsAMO RF*, f. 48a, op. 1640, d. 27, ll. 246–247.

18. "Doklad komanduiushchego voiskami Stalingradskogo fronta No. 2889 Verkhovnomu Glavnokomanduiushchemu o plane operatsii po ob'edineniiu s voiskami, oboroniaiushchimisia v Stalingrada" [Report of the commander of the forces of the Stalingrad Front No. 2889 to the supreme high commander on a plan of operations for uniting with the forces defending in Stalingrad], in Zhilin, *Stalingradskaia bitva*, book 1, 707–709; archival citation *TsAMO RF*, f. 48a, op. 1161, d. 6, ll. 259–264; telegram, copy no. 3.

19. Ibid.

20. Aleksei Isaev, *Stalingrad: Za Volgoi dlia nas zemli net* [There is no land for us behind the Volga] (Moscow: Iauza Eksmo, 2008), 270, states: "In general, it is impossible not to recognize A. I. Eremenko as one of the movers of the planned counteroffensive at Stalingrad. But, as a whole, his proposal to conduct the operation with cavalry seems completely feeble. In such a variant, it was not so much a counterstroke as a raid with the aim of destroying enemy communications."

21. Zolotarev, "*Stavka* 1942," 549–550; archival citation *TsAMO RF*, f. 48a, op. 1159, d. 2, ll. 339–345; telegram, copy no. 2. The seven formations referred to by Rokossovsky were the 226th, 219th, 252nd, 62nd, 277th, 293rd, and 333rd Rifle Divisions. All of these had been withdrawn from combat for rest and refitting during the spring and early summer of 1942 after suffering heavy losses; they were now returning to the front as full unit reinforcements. For example, on 15 June 1942, 293rd Rifle Division numbered 1,374 men, with six field guns and three antitank guns. By 24 October 1942, after refitting, the 293rd included 10,420 men, as opposed to the authorized (*shtatnyi*—TO&E or establishment) strength of 10,868 men. See Isaev, *Stalingrad*, 267.

22. Vasilevsky, *Delo vsei zhizni*, 219.

23. Zolotarev, "*Stavka* 1942," 440–441; archival citation *TsAMO*, f. 148a, op. 3763, d. 107 l. 240. The *front's* right boundary (with the Voronezh Front) extended from Rtishchevo, Povorino, Novokhopersk, Verkhnyi Mamon, and Kantemirovka to Lisichansk; its left boundary (with the Don Front) stretched from Atkarsk, Balanda, Rakovka, Kletskaia, and Selivanov to Evseev. Lieutenant General Golikov replaced Vatutin as commander of the Voronezh Front.

24. V. A. Zolotarev, ed., *Russkii arkhiv: Velikaia Otechestvennaia. General'nyi shtab v gody Velikoi Otechestvennoi voiny: Dokumenty i materialy. 1942 god. T. 23 (12-2)* [The Russian archives: The Great Patriotic (War). The General Staff in the years of the Great Patriotic [War]: Documents and materials. 1942. Vol. 23 (12-2)] (Moscow: Terra, 1999), 379; hereafter cited as "General Staff 1942," with appropriate pages. Archival citation *TsAMO*, f. 48a, op. 3408, d. 99, ll. 280, 279.

25. Zolotarev, "*Stavka* 1942," 441–442; archival citation *TsAMO*, f. 48a, op. 3408, d. 72, ll. 355–357.

26. Ibid.; archival citation *TsAMO*, f. 96a, op. 1711, d. 7a, l. 195.

27. Mikhalev, "O razrabotke zamysla," 5.

28. Zolotarev, "*Stavka* 1942," 442; archival citation *TsAMO*, f. 148a, op. 3763, d. 111, l. 38.

29. Zolotarev, "General Staff 1942," 380–381; archival citation *TsAMO*, f. 48a, op. 3408, d. 99, ll. 282–283.

30. Zolotarev, "*Stavka* 1942," 443–444; archival citation *TsAMO*, f. 48a, op. 3408, d. 72, ll. 351–354.

31. Zolotarev, "General Staff 1942," 382; archival citation *TsAMO*, f. 48a, op. 3408, d. 113, l. 297.

32. Zolotarev, "*Stavka* 1942," 445–446; archival citation *TsAMO*, f. 148a, op. 3763, d. 126, ll. 189–190.

33. Leliushenko had earned hero status while leading the 1st Guards Rifle Corps' successful fight with Guderian's Second Panzer Group at Mtsensk in October 1941 and for his role as commander of 30th Army in the battle for Moscow.

34. Zolotarev, "*Stavka* 1942," 446–447; archival citation *TsAMO*, f. 148a, op. 3763, d. 124. ll. 291–292.

35. Ibid., 447; archival citation *TsAMO*, f. 48a, op. 3408, d. 72. ll. 358–359.

36. Ibid., 448; archival citation ibid., l. 360.

37. Ibid.; archival citation *TsAMO*, f. 148a, op. 3763, d. 126. l. 192.

38. Mikhalev, "O razrabotke zamysla," 5, citing *TsAMO*, f. 232, op. 590, d. 73.

39. Zhukov makes no mention of the 6 November meeting with Stalin in his memoirs, nor does a published version of his wartime calendar, "Khronika deiatel'nosti Marshala Sovetskogo Soiuza G. K. Zhukova v period Velikoi Otechestvennoi voiny 1941–1945 gg." [A chronicle of the activities of Marshal of the Soviet Union G. K. Zhukov during the period of the Great Patriotic War 1941–1945], in "Vekhi frontovogo puti" [Landmarks of a front path], *VIZh* 10 (October 1991): 25. See the entry on Stalin's 6 November meeting with Zhukov and others in *Tetradi (zhurnaly) zapisei lits, priniatykh I. V. Stalinym (1924–1953gg.)*, 389.

40. Zolotarev, "General Staff 1942," 383–384; archival citation *TsAMO*, f. 48a, op. 3408, d. 113, l. 413.

41. Zhilin, *Stalingradskaia bitva*, book 1, 856; archival citation *TsAMO RF*, f. 48a, op. 1640, d. 180, ll. 361–362.

42. Zolotarev, "General Staff 1942," 385–386; archival citation *TsAMO*, f. 48a, op. 3408, d. 113, ll. 446–447. The message indicated that 129th Rifle Brigade and 350th Rifle Division would reach the *front* on 13 and 15 November, respectively; 172nd Rifle Division would reach it on 17 November; and 267th Rifle Division and 106th Rifle Brigade would do so on 19 November.

43. Mikhalev, "O razrabotke zamysla," 5, citing *TsAMO*, f. 220, op. 451, d. 3, ll. 327–331 and d. 92 (a map).

44. Zhukov, *Reminiscences and Reflections*, 404.

45. Zolotarev, "*Stavka* 1942," 448–449; archival citation *TsAMO*, f. 148a, op. 3763, d. 126. l. 193. See also Zhukov, *Reminiscences and Reflections*, 404–405.

46. Zolotarev, "General Staff 1942," 388–389; archival citation *TsAMO*, f. 48a, op. 3408, d. 114, l. 8.

47. Ibid., 389; archival citation ibid., ll. 11–13. Later the same day, the General Staff directed 10th Reserve Army to dispatch 87th and 315th Rifle Divisions to the Stalingrad Front without delay and with all their required manpower and equipment. See ibid., 390; archival citation ibid., ll. 17–18.

48. Zolotarev, "*Stavka* 1942," 449–450; archival citation *TsAMO*, f. 148a, op. 3763, d. 126, l. 195.

49. In *Reminiscences and Reflections*, 405, Zhukov wrote: "The morning of 13 November we saw Stalin. He was in a cheerful mood; he asked us to detail the state of affairs at Stalingrad and the progress being made in preparing for the counteroffensive." Vasilevsky, *Delo vsei zhizni*, 222, echoes Zhukov's assertion about the 13 November meeting. However, neither general appears on the list of attendees at Stalin's meetings on 13, 14, or 15 November. Zhukov's first attendance after midmonth was on 16 November, and Vasilevsky's first appearance was on the 17th. Both then met with Stalin on 18 November before returning to the front the next day. See Chernobaev, *Na prieme u Stalina*, 390–391.

50. Zhukov, *Reminiscences and Reflections*, 407, agrees with Stalin's daily schedule with regard to this decision.

51. Zolotarev, "General Staff 1942," 392; archival citation *TsAMO*, f. 48a, op. 3408, d. 114, l. 30.

52. Ibid., 393; archival citation ibid., l. 50.

53. Ibid., 392; archival citation ibid., l. 38.

54. Ibid., 394; archival citation ibid., ll. 61–62.

55. Ibid., 393–394; archival citation ibid., l. 56.

56. Ibid., 396; archival citation ibid., ll. 68–69.

57. Zolotarev, "*Stavka* 1942," 450; archival citation *TsAMO*, f. 48a, op. 3408, d. 72, l. 365.

58. Rokossovsky, *Soldatskii dolg*, 194. Rokossovsky's comments in this unexpurgated version of his memoirs are identical to those in the original version published by Voenizdat in 1970.

59. Ibid., 195–196. The unexpurgated version of Rokossovsky's memoirs alters the date of this meeting from 3 to 4 November.

60. Vasilevsky, *Delo vsei zhizni*, 224–225. Interestingly, the editors of the English-language version of Vasilevsky's memoirs, *A Lifelong Cause*, omitted this incident entirely. See an even more detailed account in Isaev, *Stalingrad*, 285–286, which recounts the exchange between Stalin and Vasilevsky as recorded by historian K. Simonov in an interview with Vasilevsky in 1967. Isaev observes: "In this account of the event, V. T. Vol'sky looks like an alarmist at best who basically did not bear the stresses of the preparatory period of a large-scale operation. But if we understand that the *tankists* of Vol'sky's corps were still wet behind the ears and had little

experience in driving, the letter of the corps commander to the Supreme High Commander looks altogether different. Archival documents permit us to doubt the so carefully depicted scene of A. M. Vasilevsky's astonishment after his perusal of V. T. Vol'sky's letter. It is doubtful whether he had no idea about the principal completeness [strength] of the formations participating in Operation 'Uranus.' Accordingly, the conversation with I. V. Stalin cited above appears fabricated from beginning to end. Most likely, the decision was simply reached that it will do as it is against the Romanians. As subsequent events demonstrated—so it was." However, Stalin's daily calendar confirms the meeting to which Vasilevsky referred. The fact that Stalin met with Zhukov and with Molotov, Beriia, and Malenkov (members of the GKO [State Defense Committee]) from 1800 to 2350 hours and with Tiulenev, Maslennikov, Vasilevsky, and Bokov from 1800 to 2230 hours on 18 November tends to confirm Vasilevsky's account. See Chernobaev, *Na prieme u Stalina*, 391.

Chapter 3. Gathering the Troops

1. V. A. Zolotarev, ed., *Velikaia Otechestvennaia, Deistvuiushchaia armiia 1941–1945 gg.* [The Great Patriotic (War), The operating army 1941–1945] (Moscow: Animi Fortitudo Kuchkovo pole, 2005), 587.

2. For additional details on the specific organizations that provided strategic direction to the Soviet Union's armed forces during wartime, as well as their functions, see David M. Glantz, *Colossus Reborn: The Red Army at War, 1941–1943* (Lawrence: University Press of Kansas, 2005), 369–465.

3. See General Vatutin's full biographical sketch on pp. 155–156 of volume 1 of this trilogy.

4. See Romanenko's biographical sketch on p. 529, n. 40, of volume 1 of this trilogy. The Kozel'sk offensive is also described in volume 1.

5. See A. M. Samsonov, *Stalingradskaia bitva* [The battle of Stalingrad] (Moscow: Nauka, 1983), 569, for the order of battle in the Southwestern, Don, and Stalingrad Fronts as of 19–20 November 1942.

6. See Butkov's biographical sketch on pp. 487–488 of volume 1 of this trilogy.

7. The 26th Tank Corps was awarded the designation 1st Guards Tank Corps on 8 December 1942 because of its outstanding performance at Stalingrad. The corps' history is contained in M. F. Panov, *Na napravlenii glavnogo udara* [On the axis of the main attack] (Moscow: Shcherbinskaia Tipografiia, 1993). The 26th Tank Corps spent several weeks forming and re-forming before being assigned to 5th Tank Army on 5 August 1942. It remained in the *Stavka* Reserve, training with the tank army, until its movement into the Stalingrad region in November. Its commander, General A. G. Rodin, was an artilleryman who transferred to the mechanized forces after attending the Stalin Academy of the Mechanization and Motorization of the Red Army in 1937. Chief of armor for 50th Rifle Corps in the Soviet-Finnish War, Rodin later became deputy commander of 10th Mechanized Corps' 24th Tank Division, a position he held through the fighting along the Luga River during the initial stages of Operation Barbarossa. When his corps was disbanded, he commanded 13th Tank Brigade from September 1941 through February 1942 and 54th Army's 124th Tank Brigade until May 1942, when he became the army's chief of armored forces.

He received command of 26th Tank Corps in September 1942. Because of his corps' stellar performance in Operation Uranus, Rodin was awarded the title Hero of the Soviet Union on 7 February 1943 and was given command of the Central Front's 2nd Tank Army, which he led during the advance on Sevsk and Orel in February and March 1943 and in the Battle of Kursk in July and August 1943. After his army seized Sevsk in September 1943, Rodin was elevated to the post of commander of armored and mechanized forces of the Western and, later, the 3rd Belorussian Front through early 1945. After the war, Rodin commanded the armored and mechanized forces of several military districts and taught at the Voroshilov General Staff Academy until he retired into the reserves in 1954. In poor health after late 1943, Rodin died in 1955. See his complete biographical sketch in M. G. Vozhakin, ed., *Velikaia Otechestvennaia Komandarmy: Voennyi biograficheskii slovar'* [Great Patriotic army commanders: A military-biographical dictionary] (Moscow-Zhukovskii: Kuchkovo pole, 2005), 291–293; hereafter cited as *Komandarmy*.

8. See Borisov's full biographical sketch in *Velikaia Otechestvennaia Komkory: Voennyi biograficheskii slovar' v 2-kh tomakh, Tom 2*] [Great Patriotic corps commanders: A military-biographical dictionary, vol. 2] (Moscow-Zhukovskii: Kuchkovo pole, 2006), 44–45; hereafter cited as *Komkory*.

9. The 8th Cavalry Corps was awarded the designation 7th Guards Cavalry Corps on 14 February 1943 for a raid it conducted to Debal'tsevo in the Donbas region. The corps' history is in M. S. Dokuchaev, *V boi shli eskadrony* [The squadrons went into battle] (Moscow: Voenizdat, 1984).

10. Zolotarev, *Velikaia Otechestvennaia, Deistvuiushchaia armiia*, 582–583. See the history of 21st Army, which was awarded the designation 6th Guards Army on 16 April 1943, in I. M. Chistiakov, ed., *Po prikazu Rodiny: Boevoi put' 6-i Gvardeiskoi armii v Velikoi Otechestvennoi voine, 1941–1945 gg.* [By order of the Motherland: The combat path of 6th Guards Army in the Great Patriotic War, 1941–1945] (Moscow: Voenizdat, 1971). General Chistiakov's memoir, *Sluzhim otchizne* [We serve the Motherland] (Moscow: Voenizdat, 1975), is, in essence, another history of the army.

11. Samsonov, *Stalingradskaia bitva*, 569.

12. The 4th Tank Corps was awarded the designation 5th Guards Tank Corps on 7 February 1943. See Kravchenko's biographical sketch on pp. 488, 499, and 539, n. 44, of volume 1 of this trilogy.

13. Samsonov, *Stalingradskaia bitva*, 405. See also Anna Stroeva, *Komandarm Kravchenko* [Army commander Kravchenko] (Kiev: Politicheskoi literatury Ukrainy, 1984).

14. Among Pliev's many autobiographies, see I. A. Pliev, *Pod gvardeiskimi znamenem* [Under a guards banner] (Ordzhonikidze: IR, 1976). See his biographical sketch on pp. 383–384 and 568, n. 54, of volume 1 of this trilogy.

15. Zolotarev, *Velikaia Otechestvennaia, Deistvuiushchaia armiia*, 582–583.

16. See Leliushenko's biographical sketch on pp. 584–585, n. 145, of volume 1 of this trilogy.

17. The two guards rifle corps did not join 1st Guards Army initially because of delays in their formation.

18. Samsonov, *Stalingradskaia bitva*, 569.

19. Zolotarev, *Velikaia Otechestvennaia, Deistvuiushchaia armiia*, 582–583. It

is important to distinguish the 5 November formation of 1st Guards Army from other iterations of the army. Specifically, the *Stavka* formed the first iteration of the army on 6 August 1942 in the Southeastern Front but then transferred the army to the Stalingrad Front on 18 August and to the Don Front on 28 September. This first iteration of 1st Guards Army fought in the Kotluban' region under the command of Generals Moskalenko and Chistiakov until it was withdrawn into the *Stavka* Reserve on 16 October and disbanded on 25 October, when its forces were assigned to new 24th Army (see volume 2 of this trilogy for the army's record during this period). After forming the second iteration of 1st Guards Army on 5 November under Leliushenko's command, the *Stavka* split the army in two on 8 December, creating a third iteration of 1st Guards Army under the command of Lieutenant General Vasilii Ivanovich Kuznetsov and a new 3rd Guards Army under the command of Leliushenko. These two armies fought in Operation Little Saturn subordinate to the Southwestern Front.

20. Ibid. In addition, the Southwestern Front had the headquarters of 14th Rifle Corps and 4th and 6th Rifle Corps (with 35th and 41st Guards Rifle Divisions in the former and 38th and 44th Guards Rifle Divisions in the latter) waiting in the wings to reinforce 1st Guards Army.

21. See General Eremenko's full biographical sketch on pp. 280–281 of volume 1 of this trilogy.

22. Zolotarev, *Velikaia Otechestvennaia, Deistvuiushchaia armiia*, 584.

23. Samsonov, *Stalingradskaia bitva*, 570.

24. See General Tolbukhin's biographical sketch on pp. 279 and 554, n. 22, of volume 1 of this trilogy.

25. For 13th Tank Corps' history, see V. F. Tolubko and N. I. Baryshev, *Na iuzh-nom flange* [On the southern flank] (Moscow: Nauka, 1973). The corps was awarded the designation 4th Guards Mechanized Corps on 9 January 1943. For Tanaschishin's biography, see *Komkory*, 2:187–189, and pp. 492–493 of volume 1 of this trilogy. Tanaschishin was promoted to the rank of major general on 7 December 1942.

26. Zolotarev, *Velikaia Otechestvennaia, Deistvuiushchaia armiia*, 584.

27. The history of 51st Army can be found in S. M. Sarkis'ian, *51-ia Armiia* [51st Army] (Moscow: Voenizdat, 1983).

28. Born in 1900, Trufanov joined the Red Army in 1919 and fought as a private and chief of a field telephone station in the Russian Civil War. He rose through the ranks of the cavalry in the interwar years, commanding at the platoon and squadron levels and serving in a variety of staff positions before becoming chief of staff of 4th Rifle Division during the Soviet-Finnish War, deputy commander of 23rd Rifle Corps in early 1941, and chief of staff of 28th Mechanized Corps on the eve of Operation Barbarossa. Trufanov served as chief of staff, chief of the rear, and deputy commander of the Trans-Caucasus Front's 47th Army until April 1942, when he received command of 1st Guards Rifle Corps. After commanding at the corps level successfully, he took command of 51st Army in July 1942 and, after an extended illness, resumed command in October 1942. After distinguishing himself during Operation Uranus, Trufanov served successfully as deputy commander of 5th Guards Tank Army at Kursk in July 1943, deputy commander of 69th Army from late July 1943 to March 1945, and commander of 25th Rifle Corps during the Berlin operation. After the war, Trufanov served in the Soviet administration in East Germany and

in a variety of senior staff positions in the Far East before retiring in 1960. He died in 1982. For additional information, see *Komandarmy*, 229–230.

29. Samsonov, *Stalingradskaia bitva*, 570.

30. For a history of 4th Mechanized Corps, see A. M. Samsonov, *Ot Volgi do Baltiki* [From the Volga to the Baltic] (Moscow: Nauka, 1963). The corps was awarded the designation 3rd Guards Mechanized Corps on 18 December 1942 for its excellent performance in Operation Uranus; specifically, it blunted the advance by Fourth Panzer Army's LVII Panzer Corps in the four days of fighting in and around Verkhne-Kumskii. See General Vol'sky's biography on p. 502 of volume 1 of this trilogy.

31. Samsonov, *Stalingradskaia bitva*, 406n136. The corps' commander, General Shapkin, was a rare exception in the Red Army officer cadre. Unlike most of his colleagues, he had served in the Tsar Imperial Russian Army as a Don Cossack cavalryman from 1907 to October 1917, seeing service on the Western Front in World War I. Later, he served as a junior officer leading Cossack cavalry in General Denikin's White Volunteer Army in the Ukraine during the Russian Civil War. He and his entire *sotnia* (a unit of 100 men) deserted to the Red Army in March 1920. Shapkin then served as regimental and brigade commander in Budenny's famed 1st Cavalry Army in the Soviet-Polish War in 1920 and in the campaign against Baron Wrangel's White Army, where he rose to division command. During the interwar years, Shapkin commanded the 2nd Cavalry and 7th Mountain Cavalry Divisions against insurgents in Central Asia, attended the Frunze Academy in 1935–1936, led the 3rd and 20th Mountain Cavalry Divisions in the Far East and Central Asia, and rose to command 4th Cavalry Corps in January 1941, where he remained until his corps was summoned to the Stalingrad region in October 1942. After his corps' outstanding performance in Operation Uranus and the ensuing offensive to Rostov, Shapkin fell ill and died of blood poisoning in March 1943. See Shapkin's full biography in *Komkory*, 2:91–92. After Shapkin's death, 4th Cavalry Corps, now under the command of Major General M. F. Maleev, was incorporated into 7th Guards Cavalry Corps; as 8th Cavalry Corps, this unit had lost its commander, General Borisov (who was captured by the Germans), and many of its men in the famous advance to Debal'tsevo in the eastern Donbas region.

32. Zolotarev, *Velikaia Otechestvennaia, Deistvuiushchaia armiia*, 584.

33. See General Gerasimenko's biographical sketch on pp. 375 and 567, n. 102, of volume 1 of this trilogy.

34. For details on 34th Guards Rifle Division's formation and combat record, see V. F. Margelov, ed., *Sovetskie vozdushnoi-desantnye: Voenno-istoricheskii ocherk* [Soviet airborne: A military-historical survey] (Moscow: Voenizdat, 1986), 158, 175–176.

35. Zolotarev, *Velikaia Otechestvennaia, Deistvuiushchaia armiia*, 584.

36. The 62nd Army was awarded the designation 8th Guards Army on 5 May 1943. Chuikov's several volumes of memoirs serve collectively as the history of 62nd Army.

37. Samsonov, *Stalingradskaia bitva*, 571.

38. See General Chuikov's full biographical sketch on p. 188 and pp. 536–537, n. 30, of volume 1 of this trilogy.

39. Zolotarev, *Velikaia Otechestvennaia, Deistvuiushchaia armiia*, 584.

40. See volume 2, p. 701. This does not count the newly assigned 160th Rifle Brigade.

41. For a history of 64th Army, see D. A. Dragunsky et al., eds., *Ot Volgi do Pragi* [From the Volga to Prague] (Moscow: Voenizdat, 1966). The 64th Army received the designation 7th Guards Army on 1 May 1943.

42. Samsonov, *Stalingradskaia bitva*, 571.

43. See General Shumilov's complete biographical sketch on pp. 245 and 556, n. 54, of volume 1 of this trilogy.

44. Margelov, *Sovetskie vozdushnoi-desantnye*, 156–157.

45. Zolotarev, *Velikaia Otechestvennaia, Deistvuiushchaia armiia*, 584.

46. Samsonov, *Stalingradskaia bitva*, 571.

47. Zolotarev, *Velikaia Otechestvennaia, Deistvuiushchaia armiia*, 582.

48. See Rokossovsky's full biographical sketch on pp. 155, 249–250, and 548–549, n. 64, of volume 1 of this trilogy.

49. Specifically, 24th Army disbanded its 207th, 221st, 292nd, and 316th Rifle Divisions, and 66th Army its 62nd, 212th, and 231st Rifle Divisions.

50. See General Batov's full biographical sketch on pp. 41 and 789, n. 125, of volume 2 of this trilogy. Batov's memoir, *V podkhodakh i boiakh* [In marches and battles] (Moscow: Golos, 2000), serves as a history of 65th Army.

51. *Boevoi sostav Sovetskoi Armii, chast' II (Ianvar'–dekabr' 1942 goda)* [The combat composition of the Soviet army, part 2 (January–December 1942)] (Moscow: Voenizdat, 1966), 215; classified secret.

52. Samsonov, *Stalingradskaia bitva*, 570.

53. Zolotarev, *Velikaia Otechestvennaia, Deistvuiushchaia armiia*, 583.

54. The first 24th Army was destroyed in the Viaz'ma encirclement in October 1942, the second was converted into 1st Reserve Army in May 1942, and the third 24th Army was disbanded in August 1942 after being severely damaged by German forces conducting Operation Blau. After several mutations from 1 February through March 1942, the fourth formation of 24th Army received the designation 4th Guards Army on 5 May 1943.

55. For full details of General Galanin's career, see pp. 588–589, n. 150, of volume 1 of this trilogy and pp. 446 and 792–793, n. 141, of volume 2. For General Kozlov, see pp. 55 and 516, n. 46, of volume 1 and pp. 19 and 726, n. 33, of volume 2.

56. Samsonov, *Stalingradskaia bitva*, 570.

57. See the biographical sketch of General Maslov on p. 489 of volume 1 of this trilogy.

58. Zolotarev, *Velikaia Otechestvennaia, Deistvuiushchaia armiia*, 583.

59. For a history of 66th Army, see I. A. Samchuk, P. G. Skachko, Iu. N. Babikov, and I. L. Gnedoi, *Ot Volgi do El'by i Pragi* [From the Volga to the Elbe and Prague] (Moscow: Voenizdat, 1970). The 66th Army was awarded the designation 5th Guards Army on 5 May 1943.

60. See the biographical sketch of General Zhadov on pp. 596 and 814–815, n. 144, of volume 2 of this trilogy.

61. Samsonov, *Stalingradskaia bitva*, 570.

62. Zolotarev, *Velikaia Otechestvennaia, Deistvuiushchaia armiia*, 583.

63. Samsonov, *Stalingradskaia bitva*, 570.

64. Zolotarev, *Velikaia Otechestvennaia, Deistvuiushchaia armiia*, 582.

65. Ibid., 585.

66. For details of the planning and conduct of Operation Mars, see Glantz, *Zhukov's Greatest Defeat*, esp. 20–22. For additional planning documents on the operation, see the Russian-language edition: David Glantz, *Krupneishee porazhenie Zhukova. Katastrofa Krasnoi Armii v operatsii "Mars" 1942 g.* [The greatest defeat of Zhukov. The catastrophe of the Red Army in operation "Mars" 1942] (Moscow: Astrel', 2006), 404–602.

67. V. A. Zolotarev, ed., *Velikaia Otechestvennaia voina 1941–1945: Voenno-istoricheskie ocherki v chetyrekh knigakh, Kniga 2, Perelom* [The Great Patriotic War 1941–1945: A military-historical survey in four books, Book 2, The turning point] (Moscow: Nauka, 1998), 38. In addition to these offensives, during October, the *Stavka* also organized supporting offensives by the Leningrad and Volkhov Fronts in the Leningrad region (Operation Spark), by the Northwestern Front in the Demiansk region, and by the Trans-Caucasus Front in the Mozdok region, all timed to roughly coincide with Operations Uranus and Mars. Like the Kalinin Front's 3rd Shock Army, the Northwestern Front's 11th and 1st Shock Armies actually began their offensive on 24 November; the rest of the two armies joined the assault on 27 and 28 November. However, within days, the offensive faltered in the face of determined German resistance. For details, see David M. Glantz, *Forgotten Battles of the German-Soviet War (1941–1945)*, vol. 4, *The Winter Campaign (19 November 1942–21 March 1943)* (Carlisle, PA: self-published, 1999), 67–82.

68. Glantz and House, *When Titans Clashed*, 136–138. See also Glantz, *Zhukov's Greatest Defeat*, 22–30. In addition to these "planetary" code names, the assault on the city of Rzhev proper was code-named Venus [*Venera*]. See Zolotarev, "*Stavka* 1942," 394, 543–544.

69. For a thorough discussion of the strategic concept for Operation Uranus, the missions of the Soviet *fronts* and armies conducting the operation, and the course and outcome of the counteroffensive, see K. K. Rokossovsky, ed., *Velikaia pobeda na Volge* [The great victory on the Volga] (Moscow: Voenizdat, 1965). Among the many studies on the battle for Stalingrad, with the few exception noted in this study, Rokossovsky's remains the most through and accurate. Whereas Rokossovsky's is the best analysis of the entire Stalingrad operation from a military point of view, the best history of the battle by a civilian historian is Samsonov, *Stalingradskaia bitva*. Both these studies owe their accuracy and relative candor to the historical "thaw" instituted by Khrushchev in the early 1960s. However, as this study makes evident, all works published in the Soviet Union contain certain biases. The most accurate study written by a Russian historian since 1991 is Aleksei Isaev, *Stalingrad: Za Volgoi dlia nas zemli net* [Stalingrad: There is no land for us beyond the Volga] (Moscow: Iauza Eksmo, 2008), which, on the basis of fresh archival evidence, courageously challenges some of the errors in previous Soviet and Russian studies of the battle.

70. The contents of all of the directives and orders issued by the *Stavka*, the People's Commissariat of Defense (NKO), and the Red Army General Staff during the preparatory period for Operation Uranus and other offensive operations along the Soviet-German front are found in V. A. Zolotarev, ed., *Russkii arkhiv: Velikaia Otechestvennaia: Stavka VGK: Dokumenty i materially 1942 god, T. 16 (5-2)* [The

Russian archives: The Great Patriotic (War): *Stavka* VGK: Documents and materials 1942, vol. 16 (5-2)] (Moscow: Terra, 1996), 442–443, hereafter cited as Zolotarev, "*Stavka* 1942"; V. A. Zolotarev, ed. *Russkii arkhiv: Velikaia Otechestvennaia: Prikazy narodnogo komissara oborony SSSR 22 iiunia 1941 g.–1942 g. T.13 (2-2)* [The Russian archives: The Great Patriotic (War): Orders of the Peoples Commissar of Defense of the USSR, vol. 13 (2-2)] (Moscow: Terra, 1997), 326–327, hereafter cited as Zolotarev, "NKO 1941–1942"; and V. A. Zolotarev, ed., *Russkii arkhiv: Velikaia Otechestvennaia. General'nyi shtab v gody Velikoi Otechestvennoi voiny: Dokumenty i materialy. 1942 god. T. 23 (12-2)* [The Russian archives: The Great Patriotic (War): The General Staff in the years of the Great Patriotic War: Documents and materials. 1942. Vol. 23 (12-2)] (Moscow: Terra, 1999), hereafter cited as Zolotarev, "General Staff 1942."

The specific directives requiring *fronts* to send formations to the *Stavka* Reserve were issued at 0745 hours on 31 August and included the following numbered directives to the following *fronts*: No. 994180 to the Volkhov Front, No. 994181 to the Northwestern Front, No. 994182 to the Western Front, No. 994183 to the Briansk Front, No. 994184 to the Voronezh Front, and No. 994185 to the Stalingrad Front. See Zolotarev, "*Stavka* 1942," 380–381.

The directives creating new reserve armies were also issued at 0745 hours on 31 August and included the following: No. 994187 for 4th Reserve Army, No. 994188 for 10th Reserve Army, No. 994196 for 3rd Reserve Army, and No. 994199 for 2nd Reserve Army. See Zolotarev, "*Stavka* 1942," 382–383.

The directives withdrawing 3rd and 5th Tank Armies into the *Stavka* Reserve included No. 994176 on 30 August for 5th Tank Army and No. 170606 on 9 September for 3rd Tank Army. See Zolotarev, "*Stavka* 1942," 376, 389.

71. Directive Nos. 994203 and 994204, in Zolotarev, "*Stavka* 1942," 395, 1396.

72. Directive Nos. 994207 and 994208, in Zolotarev, "General Staff 1942," 336–337.

73. Directive No. 170627, in Zolotarev, "*Stavka* 1942," 403.

74. Directive No. 994212, dated 0315 hours 29 September, and No. 94213 dated 30 September, in Zolotarev, "General Staff 1942," 339, 342.

75. Directive Nos. 994214 and 994215, in Zolotarev, "*Stavka* 1942," 406–407.

76. Directive No. 994216, ibid., 407–408.

77. Directive Nos. 994217 and 994218, in Zolotarev, "General Staff 1942," 347–348.

78. Unnumbered directive issued at 2100 hours on 3 October, ibid., 348–349.

79. Directive No. 170647, in Zolotarev, "*Stavka* 1942," 423; Directive Nos. 990157 and 990154, in Zolotarev, "General Staff 1942," 358, 360.

80. Directive No. 203974, in Zolotarev, "*Stavka* 1942," 425.

81. Directive No. 994273, ibid., 440–441; Directive No. 990373, in Zolotarev, "General Staff 1942," 379.

82. Directive No. 170678, in Zolotarev, "*Stavka* 1942," 441–442. See also Rokossovsky, *Velikaia pobeda na Volge*, 224–228.

83. NKO Order No. 00220, in Zolotarev, "NKO 1941–1942," 346–347, contains the specific composition and strength of the first two guards mechanized corps. These corps ultimately included the 1st, 2nd, and 3rd in the Kalinin Front; the 1st

Guards and 5th in the Southwestern Front; the 4th in the Stalingrad Front; the 2nd Guards in the *Stavka* Reserve; and the 6th in the Moscow Military District. See *Boevoi sostav*, pt. 3, 230–253.

84. *Stavka* Order Nos. 994275 and 994276, in Zolotarev, "*Stavka* 1942," 442–443.

85. Directive No. 170679, ibid., 443–444.

86. See Rokossovsky, *Velikaia pobeda na Volge*, 225, citing archival reference Arkhiv MO USSR, f. 220, op. 451, d. 82, ll. 79–114. This directive is not included in Zolotarev's collection of documents.

87. Directive No. 157704, in Zolotarev, "General Staff 1942," 382.

88. For details of Zhukov's and Vasilevsky's itineraries during their visits to the *fronts* during the first week of November, see G. K. Zhukov, *Vospominaniia i razmyshleniia* [Reminiscences and reflections] (Moscow: Agenstva pechati Novosti, 1974), 402–403; the English translation of this memoir, G. K. Zhukov, *Reminiscences and Reflections*, vol. 2 (Moscow: Progress, 1985), 116–117; Harrison E. Salisbury, ed., *Marshal Zhukov's Greatest Battles* (New York: Harper & Row, 1969), 165, 166; "Khronika deiatel'nosti marshala Sovetskogo Soiuza G. K. Zhukova v period Velikoi Otechestvennoi voiny 1941–1954 gg." [A chronicle of the activities of Marshal of the Soviet Union G. K. Zhukov in the period of the Great Patriotic War], *VIZh* 10 (October 1991): 23–33; A. M. Vasilevsky, *Delo vsei zhizni* [Life's work] (Moscow: Politizdat, 1983), 222–223; the English translation of Vasilevsky's memoir, A. M. Vasilevsky, *A Lifelong Cause* (Moscow: Progress, 1981), 192–193; and Stalin's wartime schedule of meetings in Chernobaev, *Na prieme u Stalina*, 389–390.

89. M. E. Morozov, ed., *Velikaia Otechestvennaia voina 1941–1945 gg. Kampanii i strategicheskie operatsii v tsifrakh v 2 tomakh. Tom 1* [The Great Patriotic War 1941–1945. Campaigns and strategic operations in 2 volumes. Vol. 1] (Moscow: Ob'edinennaia redaktsiia MVD Rossii, 2010), 481.

90. Rokossovsky, *Velikaia pobeda na Volge*, 226.

91. Ibid.

92. Ibid., 227.

93. See the General Staff's complaint about this problem in Zolotarev, "General Staff 1942," 389.

94. For further details on the effort to expand the railroad network supporting the Uranus force, see G. A. Kumanov, *Voina i zhelznodorozhnyi transport SSSR 1941–1945* [War and the USSR's rail transport 1941–1945] (Moscow: Nauka, 1988), 130–149.

95. Ibid., 149.

96. Rokossovsky, *A Soldier's Duty*, 138–140.

97. See the complete set of planning documents for 5th Tank Army and its subordinate formations and units in I. M. Kravchenko, *Nastupatel'naia operatsiia 5-i Tankovoi Armii v kontrnastuplenii pod Stalingradom (19–25 noiabria 1942 g.)* [The offensive operation of 5th Tank Army in the counteroffensive at Stalingrad (19–25 November 1942)] (Moscow: Voroshilov Academy of the General Staff, 1978); classified secret. This contains, as attachments, the portion of the Southwestern Front's directive pertaining to the overall situation and 5th Tank Army and the initial combat orders of 5th Tank Army, 26th Tank Corps, 47th Guards Rifle Division, and 1st

Mixed Aviation Corps. Detailed summaries of the initial directives and orders of the Southwestern Front's other armies and of the Don and Stalingrad Fronts and their subordinate armies are contained in Rokossovsky, *Velikaia pobeda na Volge*, 228–246; Samsonov, *Stalingradskaia bitva*; and appropriate sections of *Sbornik materialov po izucheniiu opyta voiny, Nos. 6–8 (aprel'–oktiabr' 1943 g.)* [Collection of materials for the study of war experience, Nos. 6–8 (April–October 1943)] (Moscow: Voenizdat, 1943).

98. Kravchenko, *Nastupatel'naia operatsiia 5-i Tankovoi Armii*, appendices.

99. Rokossovsky, *Velikaia pobeda na Volge*, 228–229.

100. Ibid., 229–230; Kravchenko, *Nastupatel'naia operatsiia 5-i Tankovoi Armii*, 6–9.

101. Rokossovsky, *Velikaia pobeda na Volge*, 230–231; Chistiakov, *Po prikazu Rodiny*, 32–33.

102. Rokossovsky, *Velikaia pobeda na Volge*, 231–232.

103. At this time, the official Soviet term for the element (force) in the operational formation of a *front* or an army designated to develop or exploit success in an offensive operation—that is, convert a tactical penetration into an operational exploitation—was an echelon for the development (exploitation) of success [*echelon razvitiia uspekha*]. The more common term for this element is mobile group [*podvizhnaia gruppa*]. This element was the antecedent of the operational maneuver group [*operativnaia manevrennaia gruppa*] of the 1970s and 1980s and the operational mobile reserve [*operativnii mobil'nyi reserv*] of more recent years.

104. Rokossovsky, *Velikaia pobeda na Volge*, 233–234.

105. Ibid., 234–235. For additional details, see "Artilleriia v nastupatel'nykh operatsiiakh pod Stalingradom" [Artillery in offensive operations at Stalingrad], in *Sbornik materialov po izucheniiu opyta voiny, No. 6*, 115–123.

106. The 17th Air Army, which was formed on 15 November 1942 under Krasovsky's command and fielded 447 combat aircraft, received its baptism of fire in Operation Uranus. See the air army's history in N. M. Skomorokhov et al., eds., *17-ia Vozdushnaia Armiia v boiakh ot Stalingrada do Veny* [The 17th Air Army in battles from Stalingrad to Vienna] (Moscow: Voenizdat, 1977). Krasovsky, an airman throughout his career, joined the Red Army in 1918, served as chief of communications and commissar in an aviation regiment during the Civil War, and commanded an aviation detachment, brigade, and corps from 1927 through 1939. After participating in the Soviet-Finnish War as commander of the Murmansk Aviation Brigade, he rose to command the North Caucasus Military District's air forces in June 1941. During wartime, he led the air forces of the Southern Front's 56th Army until January 1942, when he received command of the air forces of the Briansk Front. When the first air armies were formed in May 1942, Krasovsky took command of 2nd Air Army, formed in the Briansk Front, where he amassed significant experience during the fighting in the Voronezh region in July and August 1942. After commanding 17th Air Army from October 1942 to March 1943, he commanded 2nd Air Army until the war's end. In the postwar period, Krasovsky commanded the air forces of several military districts and 2nd and 26th Air Armies before becoming a marshal of aviation and chief of the Air Force Academy. Pensioned in October 1968, apparently for political

reasons, he was restored to service as a special adviser in the General Inspectorate in July 1970. He died in 1983. For further details, see *Komandarmy*, 376–378.

107. Rokossovsky, *Velikaia pobeda na Volge*, 235. For additional information about Soviet air operations in Uranus, see "Deistviia VVS v bor'be za Stalingrad" [Actions of the air force in the struggle for Stalingrad], in *Sbornik materialov po izuche-niiu opyta voiny, No. 6*, 147–154.

108. Samsonov, *Stalingradskaia bitva*, 569.

109. Rokossovsky, *Velikaia pobeda na Volge*, 236. For additional details on engineer support, see S. Kh. Aganov, ed., *Inzhenernye voiska Soverskoi Armii 1918–1945* [Engineer forces of the Soviet Army 1918–1945] (Moscow: Voenizdat, 1985); and A. D. Tsirlin, P. I. Biriukov, V. P. Istomin, and E. N. Fedoseev, *Inzhenernye voiska v boiakh za Sovetskuiu Rodinu* [Engineer forces in battles for the Soviet Motherland] (Moscow: Voenizdat, 1970).

110. Rokossovsky, *Velikaia pobeda na Volge*, 237.

111. Ibid., 237–238. See also Dragunsky et al., *Ot Volgi do Pragi*, 37–60.

112. Rokossovsky, *Velikaia pobeda na Volge*, 238–239. See also Tolubko and Baryshev, *Na Iuzhnom flange*, 51–52, for 13th Tank Corps' mission in the operation.

113. Rokossovsky, *Velikaia pobeda na Volge*, 239–240; Sarkis'ian, *51-ia Armiia*, 97–100. For 4th Mechanized Corps' mission, see Samsonov, *Ot Volgi do Baltiki*, 25–28.

114. Rokossovsky, *Velikaia pobeda na Volge*, 241.

115. Ibid.

116. Ibid., 240–241.

117. Ibid., 241–242.

118. See 8th Air Army's history in B. A. Gubin and V. A. Kiselev, *Vos'maia vozdush-naia: Voenno-istoricheskii ocherk boevogo puti 8-i Vozdushnoi armii v gody Velikoi Otechestvennoi voiny* [Eighth Air: A military-historical survey of the combat path of 8th Air Army in the tears of the Great Patriotic War] (Moscow: Voenizdat, 1986), 83–114. The army was formed on 13 June 1942 on the base of the Southwestern Front's air forces. General Khriukin was only 32 years old when he assumed command of 8th Air Army. A pilot who served as a volunteer on the Republican side in the Spanish Civil War from August 1936 to March 1937, Khriukin later led an aviation squadron and fought in China during 1938 as a squadron and bomber group commander, where he was awarded the title Hero of the Soviet Union. He then took part in the Soviet-Finnish War and commanded the air forces of the Kiev Special Military District's 12th Army from May 1941 through the outbreak of the Soviet-German War. During the Soviet-German War, he led the Karelian Front's air forces in the defense of the Murmansk railroad in 1941 and received command of the Southwestern Front's air forces (and 8th Air Army) in June 1942. After leading 8th Air Army until July 1944, he commanded 1st Air Army until the war's end, supervising air operations in East Prussia and during the siege of Konigsberg. After serving as a deputy commander in chief of the Soviet Air Force, Khriukin retired in the early 1950s and died in 1953. For additional details, see *Komandarmy*, 393–394.

119. Rokossovsky, *Velikaia pobeda na Volge*, 242–243.

120. Samsonov, *Stalingradskaia bitva*, 570–571.

121. Rokossovsky, *Velikaia pobeda na Volge*, 243. See also, "Inzhenernoe obe-spechenie operatsii Stalingradskogo fronta" [Engineer support of the Stalingrad Front], in *Sbornik materialov po izucheniiu opyta voiny, No. 6*, 158–172.

122. Rokossovsky, *Velikaia pobeda na Volge*, 243–244. See also Rokossovsky, *Soldatskii dolg*, 195–199.

123. See Rokossovsky, *Velikaia pobeda na Volge*, 244, and P. I. Batov, *V podkhodakh i boiakh*, 165–176, for details of 65th Army's missions and planning.

124. Rokossovsky, *Velikaia pobeda na Volge*, 244–245.

125. See ibid., 245, and Samchuk et al., *Ot Volgi do El'by i Pragi*, 32–33, for 24th Army's limited missions.

126. Rokossovsky, *Velikaia pobeda na Volge*, 245; Samsonov, *Stalingradskaia bitva*, 570.

127. Rokossovsky, *Velikaia pobeda na Volge*, 245–246.

128. The 16th Air Army was formed on 16 August 1942 and supported the Stalingrad Front during its defense of Stalingrad city. For a biographical sketch of General Rudenko, see p. 559, n. 75, of volume 1 of this trilogy. See also Rudenko's memoir, *Kryl'ia pobedy* [Wings of victor] (Moscow: Mezhdunarodnye otnosheniia, 1985).

129. Rokossovsky, *Velikaia pobeda na Volge*, 246.

130. Samsonov, *Stalingradskaia bitva*, 570.

131. Rokossovsky, *Velikaia pobeda na Volge*, 246.

132. Khrulev was promoted to the rank of colonel general in November 1942. Born in 1892, Khrulev had joined the Tsar's army in 1918 and then shifted to the Red Army, becoming chief of the political section of 1st Cavalry Army's 11th Cavalry Division in December 1919. Rising fast through the ranks, he served as military commissar in a cavalry regiment and division in the 1920s, as deputy chief of the Moscow Military District's Political Directorate from 1928 to 1930, and in a series of high-level administrative positions dealing with financial and logistical matters in directorates of the NKO and Red Army (RKKA). His prewar service culminated with his assignment as chief of the RKKA's Supply Directorate in October 1939, a post he occupied until August 1940; he then served as chief intendant (quartermaster) from August 1940 through the first few months of the war. Stalin appointed Khrulev chief of the Red Army's Directorate of the Rear in August 1941, as well as a deputy people's commissar of defense. In February 1942, he added the post of chief of the People's Commissariat of Communications to his portfolio, becoming, in effect, the Soviet Union's wartime logistical tsar. Thereafter, Khrulev served as chief of the Directorate of the Rear and chief of the Red Army Rear, a position he retained through the end of the war and into the postwar years. Retiring in 1953 after Stalin's death (the two had been closely associated), he returned to high-level logistical service later that year, becoming the USSR's deputy minister for construction in 1956. He retired into the inspectorate in 1958 and died in 1962. See his full biography in *Voennaia entsiklopediia v vos'mi tomakh, Tom 8* [Military encyclopedia in eight volumes, vol. 8] (Moscow: Voenizdat, 2004), 340.

133. For further details on Soviet weapons and ammunition production in 1942, see G. A. Kumanev, ed., *Sovetskii tyl v pervyi period Velikoi Otechestvennoi voiny* [The Soviet rear in the first period of the Great Patriotic War] (Moscow: Nauka, 1988), 232–299.

134. See G. A. Kumanov and L. M. Chuzavkov, "Sovetskii soiuz i lend-liz 1941–1945 gg." [The Soviet Union and Lend-Lease 1941–1945], in *Lend-liz i Rossiia* [Lend-Lease and Russia], ed. M. N. Supron (Arkhangel'sk: OAO IPP Pravda Severa, 2006), 92–123.

135. Ibid.

136. For additional details on this controversial matter, see V. A. Zolotarev, ed., *Velikaia Otechestvennaia voina 1941–1945: Voenno-istoricheskii ocherki v chetyrekh knigakh, Kniga 4: Narod i voina* [The Great Patriotic War 1941–1945: A military-historical survey in four books, Book 4: The people and the war] (Moscow: Nauka, 1999), 205–217.

Chapter 4. The Balance of Opposing Forces on 18 November

1. Rokossovsky, *Velikaia pobeda na Volge*, 252–253; Samsonov, *Stalingradskaia bitva*, 369–371.

2. See M. E. Morozov, ed., *Velikaia Otechestvennaia Voina 1941–1945 gg. Kampanii i strategicheskie operatsii v tsifrakh, Tom 1* [The Great Patriotic War] (Moscow: Ob'edinennaia redaktsiia MVD Rossii, 2010), 481.

3. Rokossovsky, *Velikaia pobeda na Volge*, 253.

4. Ibid.

5. While the overall tank strengths of the Southwestern, Don, and Stalingrad Fronts are reliably known, the actual operating strengths of many of the tank and mechanized corps and tank brigades, regiments, and battalions are not. Although table 13 includes the most accurate information available, there are gaps and other inconsistencies primarily because many of these forces had tanks in various stages of repair or were unable to put them into action at the designated time. This applies in particular to the Stalingrad Front's 13th Tank Corps and 4th Mechanized Corps, which fielded close to their authorized 205 and 220 respective tanks but brought only about two-thirds of them into action initially; the remainder reinforced the corps over subsequent hours and even days. The most detailed descriptions of the strengths of specific tank corps are contained in Isaev, *Stalingrad*, 316, 319, which cites archival sources to indicate 4th and 16th Tank Corps' tank strengths on 19 and 23 November 1942:

4th Tank Corps

	Type of Tank			
Brigade	**KV**	**T-34**	**T-70**	**Total**
45th Tank	22	—	26	48
102nd Tank	—	30	18	48
69th Tank	—	28	19	47
Total	22	58	63	143

Archival citation: *TsAMO RF*, f. 3403, op. 1, d. 7, l. 39.

16th Tank Corps

| | Type of Tank | | | | |
Brigade	KV	T-34	T-70	T-60	Total
107th	32/29	—	—	17/11	49/40
109th	8/6	19/17	—	14/14	41/37
164th	—	28/20	10/5	12/3	50/28
Total	40/35	47/37	10/5	43/28	140/105

Archival citation: *TsAMO RF*, f. 3414, op. 1, d. 25, l. 22.
Note: On hand/operable.

6. Blau, *German Campaign in Russia*, 168.

7. Quoted in Vasily S. Grossman, *A Writer at War: Vasily Grossman with the Red Army, 1941–1945*, ed. and trans. Anthony Beevor and Luba Vinogradova (New York: Pantheon Books, 2005), 162. Grossman's real name was Iosif Solomonovich Grossman, but he used the pseudonym Vasilii Semenovich when writing for the army newspaper *Krasnaia zvezda* (Red Star).

8. For a thorough discussion of Axis relations, see Richard L. Dinardo, *Germany and the Axis Powers: From Coalition to Collapse* (Lawrence: University Press of Kansas, 2005), 136–157.

9. From June through December 1941, the frontages of Army Groups North, Center, and South increased from 200 to 400 kilometers, 400 to 600 kilometers, and 350 (360, including Romanian sectors) to 600 kilometers, respectively. This indicated that *Wehrmacht* overextension became a major factor in the defeat of Operation Barbarossa. In late June 1942, Army Groups North, Center, and South operated on frontages of 400, 500, and 600 kilometers, respectively. The excessive width of Army Group South's frontage at the outset of Operation Blau forced Hitler to subdivide it into Army Groups A and B, but in reality, the two new army groups contained the same number of major German formations as the former Army Group South. Consequently, when Army Group B's frontage reached over 800 kilometers in September and October, Hitler remedied the situation by pushing four allied armies forward into the front lines. In essence, he was creating a new but highly vulnerable army group.

10. Rokossovsky, *Velikaia pobeda na Volge*, 253, places Axis strength in this sector at 49 divisions and 2 brigades, including 36 infantry, 5 tank, 4 motorized, and 4 cavalry divisions. According to Rokossovsky, this force included 5 Italian divisions and 2 brigades and 18 Romanian divisions; the rest were 26 German divisions, including 2 security divisions.

11. On 9 November, in an attempt to shore up Romanian Third Army's defenses, Sixth Army dispatched a support group (Group Simon) consisting of one antitank company, one motorized infantry battalion, and one section of heavy assault artillery and 823 men into the Romanian army's rear. The next day, XXXXVIII Panzer Corps received orders to concentrate in the Third Army's rear. Ultimately, it consisted of 22nd Panzer Division, Romanian 1st Armored Division, an antitank battalion (less Simon's company), and a panzer artillery battalion. The 14th Panzer Division's force at Verkhne-Buzinovka was supposed to be attached to XXXXVIII

Panzer Corps on 20 November, but by then, this was a futile gesture. See Walter Goerlitz, *Paulus and Stalingrad: A Life of Field-Marshal Friedrich Paulus with Notes, Correspondence, and Documents from His Papers*, trans. R. H. Stevens (New York: Citadel Press, 1963), 197–199.

12. For the German order of battle in Army Group B's sector, see William Mc-Crodden's five-volume unpublished study, *The Organization of the German Army in World War II: Army Groups, Armies, Corps, Divisions, and Combat Groups*. Romanian order of battle information is in Axworthy et al., *Third Axis, Fourth Ally*.

13. Rolf Grams, *Die 14. Panzer-Division 1940–1945* (Eggolsheim, Germany: Dörfler, 2002), 56. By this time, 14th Panzer was able to muster 4th Panzer Artillery Regiment, 4th Panzer *Jagd Abteilung*, and 4th Panzer Reconnaissance *Abteilung*. The division's 103rd and 108th Panzer-Grenadier Regiments were able to field a battalion each, and 64th Motorcycle Battalion (K-64) managed only a company. After participating in heavy fighting in Stalingrad, 103rd Regiment's remnants (one weak battalion) were in Karpovka with a company of 36th Panzer Regiment and 64th Motorcycle Battalion and would ultimately form a *kampfgruppe* under Senior Lieutenant Seydel. The headquarters of 108th Regiment, with a single grenadier battalion, 36th Panzer Regiment, and the division's service elements, was near Kamenskaia.

14. Rokossovsky, *Velikaia pobeda na Volge*, 253.

15. Ibid.

16. For a detailed map of the dispositions of Italian Eighth and Romanian Third Armies on 15 November 1942, see David M. Glantz, *Atlas of the Battle of Stalingrad* (Carlisle, PA: self-published, 2000), map 7. For details on the organization and defenses of the two armies, see "Gruppirovka i sostav 3 Rumynskoi i 8 Italianskoi armii na Donu" [The grouping and composition of 3rd Romanian and 8th Italian Armies on the Don], in *Sbornik materialov po izucheniiu opyta voiny, No. 8, avgust–oktainbr' 1943 g.* [Collection of materials for the study of war experience] (Moscow: Voenizdat, 1943), 24–36; and *L "8" Armata Italiana*.

17. For an extended discussion of the Romanians' efforts to deal with this situation, see Axworthy et al., *Third Axis, Fourth Ally*, esp. 85–87. For Soviet perceptions of organization, strength, and dispositions of Romanian forces, see "Gruppirovka i sostav 3 Rumynskoi i 8 Italianskoi armii na Donu."

18. See the Report by General Ferdinand Heim, the German liaison with Romanian Third Army, in Goerlitz, *Paulus and Stalingrad*, 196; and Boog et al., *Germany and the Second World War*, 6:1113.

19. Goerlitz, *Paulus and Stalingrad*, 195–196.

20. Rolf Stoves, *Die 22. Panzer-Division, 25. Panzer-Division, 27. Panzer-Division und die 233. Reserve Panzer-Division: Aufstellung, Gliederung, Einsatz* (Friedberg, FRG: Podzun-Pallas-Verlag, 1985), 45–49; Paul Carell [pseudo. Paul Schmidt], *Stalingrad: The Defeat of the German 6th Army*, trans. David Johnston (Atglen, PA: Schiffer Publishing, 1993), 154–155; Goerlitz, *Paulus and Stalingrad*, 218–219; Samuel W. Mitcham Jr., *The Panzer Legions: A Guide to the German Army Tank Divisions of World War II and Their Commanders* (Westport, CT: Greenwood Press, 2001), 165–166. The story of the mice immobilizing 22nd Panzer Division has become a minor legend, but the same problem also affected the Soviet forces in a more insidious manner. On the eve of the Uranus offensive, 16th Air Army, assigned

to support Rokossovsky's attack on the Romanians, found that rodents had damaged the wiring in a number of aircraft. Worse, mice infected the aircrews with tularemia, a blood-borne bacterial fever. See Rokossovsky, *A Soldier's Duty*, 139. Reports differ on 14th Panzer Division's strength: "Morgenmeldung LI. A.K. meldet 06.00 Uhr 18.11.42," in Florian *Freiherr* von und zu Aufsess, *Die Anlagenbänder zu den Kriegstagebüchern der 6. Armee vom 14.09.1942 bis 24.11.1942, Band I* (Schwabach: Januar, 2006), 294, states the division had 5 Pz-II, 9 Pz-III short, 17 Pz-III long, 5 Pz-IV short, 12 Pz-IV long, 2 command, and 5 Pz-III 75mm, for a total of 55 tanks. In contrast, "Tagesmeldung XXXXVIII. Pz. K. vom 16.11. 1945 Uhr und vom 18.11.1942, 2100/2200 Uhr" states the division had 36 tanks, including 29 Pz-IIIs and 7 Pz-IVs. At the time, the division's 103rd and 108th Grenadier Regiments, each fielding one battalion, and 13th Pioneer Battalion were fighting in Stalingrad as Group Seydel.

21. Goerlitz, *Paulus and Stalingrad*, 197–199; Alexander Statiev, "The Ugly Duckling of the Armed Forces: Romanian Armour 1919–1941," *Journal of Slavic Military Studies* 12, 2 (June 1999): 220–244. Goerlitz provides a different account of the strength and composition of XXXXVIII Panzer Corps, but it does not accord with other sources.

22. "Betr.: Zustand der Divisionen, Armee-Oberkommando 6, Abt. Ia, A.H.Qu., 16. November 1942, 12.00 Uhr," in *Die Anlagenbänder zu den Kriegstagebüchern der 6. Armee*, book 1, 285–290. On 13 November, as an addendum to a lengthier report issued on 24 October concerning the numerical strength of its divisions, Sixth Army prepared an assessment of the strength of 389th Infantry Division. Whereas the division had a ration strength of 8,604 and a combat strength of 2,736 men (with 979 infantry and sappers) on 24 October, by 13 November, its ration strength had fallen to 7,540 men and its combat strength had risen to 4,021 men (2,279 infantry and sappers), by virtue of the combat engineer forces transferred from Army Group B and other personnel transfers from combat support units to fighting units. See "Betr: Verpflegungs-und Gefechstärkem, Armee-Oberkommando 6, Ia Nr. 4548 /geh., A.H.Qu., 13. November 1942," ibid., 269.

23. "Betr.: Zustand der Divisionen, Armee-Oberkommando 6, Abt. Ia, A.H.Qu., 09. November 1942, 16.20 Uhr" and "Betr.: Zustand der Divisionen, Armee-Oberkommando 6, Abt. Ia, A.H.Qu., 16. November 1942, 12.00 Uhr," ibid.

24. Joachim Lemelsen, Walter Fries, and Wilhelm Schaeffer, *29. Division: 29 Infanteriedivision, 29. Infanteriedivision (mot), 29. Panzergrenadier-Division* (Bad Nauheim, FRG: Podzun-Verlag, 1960), 204.

25. According to Isaev, *Stalingrad*, 295, 29th Motorized Division's 59 tanks included 7 Pz-II, 23 Pz-III long, 9 Pz-III 75mm, 18 Pz-IV long, and 2 command tanks.

26. According to ibid., 16th Motorized Division's 43 tanks included 8 Pz-II, 16 Pz-III long, 7 Pz-III 75mm, 11 Pz-IV long, and 1 command tank.

27. See Manfred Kehrig, *Stalingrad: Analyse und Dokumentation einer Schlacht* (Stuttgart: Deutsche Verlag-Anstalt, 1974), 662–663, citing reports dated 11 and 19 November 1942.

28. "Betreff.: Meldung über personellen Fehlbestand vom 01.11.42 getrennt, Anlage 1, Armee-Oberkommando 6, Abt. Ia, Nr. 4534/42 geh, A.H.Qu., 12. November 1942," in *Die Anlagenbänder zu den Kriegstagebüchern der 6. Armee*, book 1, 284–296.

29. Isaev, *Stalingrad*, 289–290.

30. "Deistviia i gruppirovka protivnika za period s 20.10 po 1.11.42" [The operations and grouping of the enemy during the period from 20 October through 1 November 1942], in 62nd Army's Combat Journal. This reports places German equipment strengths at 17,550 rifles, 340 mortars, 1,800 automatic weapons, 20 six-barreled mortars [*Werfers*], 228 heavy guns, 92 light guns, and 230 antitank rifles. It also provides the precise grouping of forces in each sector of the city.

31. These numbers are based on the following calculations of the personnel strength of Sixth Army on 18 November 1942:

Personnel Category	Line Divisions (17)	Army [*Heere*] Troops	Total
Authorized	265,246	32,430	297,676
Deficit	115,414 (44%)	6,486 (20%)	121,900 (41%)
Ration (on hand)	149,832 (57%)	25,944 (80%)	175,776 (59%)

32. The ration and combat strengths of German infantry divisions are based on the strength returns of 14 out of 16 divisions, excluding 62nd and 298th Infantry Divisions. The number of *Hiwis* and attached troops [*Zugeteilte*] is based on 12 divisions, excluding 62nd, 297th, 298th, and 371st Infantry Divisions. Rokossovsky, *Velikaia pobeda na Volge*, 253, asserts that Axis infantry divisions ranged in strength from 10,000 to 12,000 men. The ration and combat strengths of German panzer and motorized divisions include all 8 divisions. The number of *Hiwis* and attached troops in panzer and motorized division excludes 22nd Panzer and 16th and 29th Motorized Divisions.

33. Axworthy et al., *Third Axis, Fourth Ally*, 39, 85–86, 89.

34. Ibid., 85, 89.

35. V. T. Minov, *Nastupatel'naia operatsiia 5-i Tankovoi armii v kontrnastuplenii pod Stalingradom (19–25 noiabria 1942 goda)* [The offensive operation of 5th Tank Army in the counteroffensive at Stalingrad (19–25 November 1942)] (Moscow: Voroshilov Military Academy of the General Staff, 1979), 5.

36. Illustrative of the wide-ranging Soviet estimates of the strength of Romanian divisions, Rokossovsky, *Velikaia pobeda na Volge*, 253, claims that Romanian divisions fielded up to 18,000 men. This obviously includes reinforcements provided by army and corps, with a separate infantry battalion per division and supporting artillery. In contrast, the secret Soviet assessment contained in "Gruppirovka i sostav 3 Rumynskoi i 8 Italianskoi armii na Donu," 25–26, which was prepared by the Red Army General Staff's Department for the Exploitation of War Experience, correctly estimates that Romanian Third Army consisted of eight infantry, two cavalry, and one armored divisions, with a total strength of about 130,000 men and a ration strength of 13,000 to 14,000 men per division. However, simple arithmetic indicates that, despite disparities in the strength of infantry, cavalry, and armored divisions, a force of 11 divisions averaging 13,000 to 14,000 men per division would total 143,000 to 154,000 men, not counting nondivisional forces at the army and corps levels. This figure is clearly too high. This study also asserts that Third Army included four heavy artillery regiments (2nd, 4th, 5th, and 8th) and one heavy artillery battalion (41st) and fielded

4,500 machine guns, 1,100 mortars, 680 antitank guns, 480 field guns, 92 heavy guns, 140 to 150 antiaircraft guns, and 130 tanks.

37. Axworthy et al., *Third Axis, Fourth Ally*, 89. A report by Lieutenant General Ferdinand Heim, chief of the German Military Mission to Romania, asserts that 1st Armored Division consisted of 108 tanks, including 87 Czech T-38 (t) models. See Goerlitz, *Paulus and Stalingrad*, 199.

38. Boog et al., *Germany and the Second World War*, 6:1118–1119.

39. For details, see David Glantz, *Soviet Military Deception in the Second World War* (London: Frank Cass, 1989), 109–110.

40. Blau, *German Campaign in Russia*, 170–171; Goerlitz, *Paulus and Stalingrad*, 198–199, 227.

41. V. A. Zhilin, ed., *Stalingradskaia bitva: Khronika, fakty, liudi v 2 kh.* [The battle of Stalingrad: Chronicles, facts, and people in 2 books] (Moscow: Olma, 2002), book 1, 849–850, citing KTB OKW, Bd. II, hb. II, 1305–1306. See a condensed version of Gehlen's report in David Kahn, "An Intelligence Case Study: The Defense of Osuga, 1942," *Aerospace Historian* 28, 4 (December 1981): 248. Gehlen's *The Service: The Memoirs of General Reinhard Gehlen*, trans. David Irving (New York: World Publishing, 1972), omits any mention of the 6 November report.

42. Goerlitz, *Paulus and Stalingrad*, 218.

43. Quoted in Ziemke and Bauer, *Moscow to Stalingrad*, 466.

44. Ibid., 464. For employment of these battalions, see chapter 9 of volume 2 of this trilogy.

45. Hoth quoted in Carell, *Stalingrad: Defeat of German 6th Army*, 158. For German signals intelligence concerning the Red Army buildup, see *Concentration of Russian Troops for Stalingrad—Offensive*, Historical Division, European Command, Study MS P-096, 1952.

46. Blau, *German Campaign in Russia*, 171–172. On Soviet deception, see M. Kozlov, "Strategy and Operational Art at Stalingrad," *VIZh* 11 (November 1982): 9–16.

Chapter 5. The Penetration Battle, 19–20 November

1. Numerous sources confirm the poor weather conditions on the morning of 19 November, including the Red Army General Staff's daily operational summaries; Soviet classified (secret) studies on the operation, such as Kravchenko, *Nastupatel'naia operatsiia 5-i Tankovoi Armii*, 26; analytical studies of the battle, such as Rokossovsky, *Velikaia pobeda na Volge*, 261; Sixth Army's surviving records; studies based primarily on German sources, such as Ziemke and Bauer, *Moscow to Stalingrad*, 468; and more popular studies such as Antony Beevor, *Stalingrad: The Fateful Siege: 1942–1943* (New York: Viking, 1989), 239. The Soviets deliberately chose to attack in bad weather to deprive the Germans and Romanians of their usually deadly air support.

2. For example, in the Don Front's 65th Army, 304th Rifle Division conducted a reconnaissance in force on 10 November that reportedly captured 31 prisoners from Romanian 1st Cavalry Division. Two days later, 24th Rifle Division conducted a raid that supposedly bagged 30 soldiers from German 376th Infantry Division. See

Batov, *V podkhodakh i boiakh*, 180–181. Batov claims that, because of these and other reconnaissance activities, his intelligence department and the Don Front's Intelligence Directorate identified a concentration of German tanks and infantry in the Verkhne-Buzinovka region behind Sixth Army's left wing. Specifically: "Information obtained on 13 November [indicated] 40 tanks (14th Panzer Division) were located in Tsimlovskii and Orekhovskii [15 kilometers south and southeast of Kletskaia], 30 tanks—in Logovskii [15 kilometers east of Kletskaia], 12—in Osinki [20 kilometers east-southeast of Kletskaia], and 10 tanks each—in Sirotskii and Kamyshinka. From 14–16 November, reconnaissance determined that 14th Panzer Division's 32nd Regiment was transferred from the Volga to Verkhne-Buzinovka." Although some of these reports were erroneous and others simply reflected multiple sighting of the same group of tanks, they were indicative of Sixth Army's ultimate dispatch of 14th Panzer Division to the Verkhne-Buzinovka region. At the time, the panzer division's 36th Regiment (erroneously identified by Batov as the 32nd) mustered 50 to 55 tanks, but not all of them were operational at any given time.

3. Rokossovsky, *Velikaia pobeda na Volge*, 260–261.

4. Kravchenko, *Nastupatel'naia operatsiia 5-i Tankovoi Armii*, 26.

5. Rokossovsky, *Velikaia pobeda na Volge*, 261.

6. Ibid., 260–262.

7. "Izvlechenie iz operativnoi svodkoi No. 324 General'nogo shtaba Krasnoi Armii na 8.00 20. 11. 42 g." [Excerpts from Operational Summary No. 324 of the Red Army General Staff at 0800 hours on 20 November 1942], in V. A. Zhilin, ed., *Stalingradskaia bitva. Khronika, fakty, liudi: v 2-kh.* [The Battle of Stalingrad. Chronicles, facts, and people, in 2 books] (Moscow: Olma-Press, 2002), book 2; archival citation *TsAMO RF*, f. 16, op. 1072ss, d. 11, ll. 125–131.

8. V. E. Tarrant, *Stalingrad: Anatomy of an Agony* (London: Leo Cooper, 1992), 105. The author cites no source for this message.

9. The most detailed timelines and accounts of the Soviet assaults are found in Rokossovsky, *Velikaia pobeda na Volge*, 261–265; Kravchenko, *Nastupatel'naia operatsii 5-i Tankovoi Armii*, 26–29; Chistiakov, *Po prikazu Rodiny*, 36–38; and Axworthy et al., *Third Axis, Fourth Ally*, 89–92. For maps detailing the fighting from 19 through 21 November and thereafter, see David M. Glantz, *Atlas of the Battle of Stalingrad: Red Army Offensive Operations, 19 November 1942–2 February 1943* (Carlisle, PA: self-published, 2000).

10. Goerlitz, *Paulus and Stalingrad*, 201; Heinz Schröter, *Stalingrad* (New York: Ballantine Books, 1958), 61–62. Schröter, a journalist with Sixth Army who wrote his book in 1948, is considered less than reliable.

11. See "Tagesmeldung, XXXXVIII Pz. K., 18.11.1942 2100/2200 Uhr," in XXXXVIII Pz. K. Ia, 26 775/2 file. See differing figures in Axworthy et al., *Third Axis, Fourth Ally*, 89. Heim's report, in Goerlitz, *Paulus and Stalingrad*, 199, asserts that 22nd Panzer Division fielded 40 tanks, including 5 Czech 38 (t) models, and that 1st Armored Division's total strength was 108 tanks, including 87 38 (t) models. In fact, the bulk of these Romanian tanks were R-2 models built under license for the T-35 (t).

12. The tank strength of 14th Panzer Division is also subject to debate. For example, Heim, cited in Goerlitz, *Paulus and Stalingrad*, 199, places the division's strength at 51 tanks; Axworthy et al., *Third Axis, Fourth Ally*, 89, states it had 36

tanks; and Sixth Army's records indicate it had 55 tanks on 18 November: 5 Pz-II, 9 Pz-III short-barreled, 17 Pz-III long, 5 Pz-IV short, 12 Pz-IV long, 5 Pz-III 75mm, and 2 command tanks. See "Morgenmeldung LI. A.K. A.O.K. 6, I.a, 0600 Uhr, 18.11-42," in *Die Anlagenbänder zu den Kriegstagebüchern der 6. Armee*, book 1, 296.

13. Zeitzler sent the order to Army Group B, requiring XXXXVIII Panzer Corps to halt and wheel to the left, at 1150 hours, after he had discussed the matter with Hitler. See "HGr B/Ia an XXXXVIII Pz. K. vom 19.11.1942, 1150 Uhr," in XXXXVIII Pz. K./Ia, 26 775/2 file.

14. For details of 21st Army's offensive, see Chistiakov, *Po prikazu Rodiny*, 36–37; Samsonov, *Stalingradskaia bitva*, 371; and Axworthy et al., *Third Axis, Fourth Ally*, 91.

15. K. K. Rokossovsky, *Soldatskii dolg* [A soldier's duty] (Moscow: Golos, 2000), 200.

16. Batov, *V podkhodakh i boiakh*, 190.

17. Kravchenko, *Nastupatel'naia operatsii 5-i Tankovoi Armii*, 27.

18. Confusion reigns in Soviet sources with regard to the commander of 157th Tank Brigade. The official secret source, *Komandovanie korpusnogo i divizionnogo zvena Sovetskikh vooruzhennykh sil perioda Velikoi Otechestvennoi voiny, 1941–1945 gg.* [Commanders at the corps and division levels of the Soviet armed forces in the period of the Great Patriotic War, 1941–1945] (Moscow: Main Cadre Directorate of the USSR's Ministry of Defense, 1964), 448, shows Major A. S. Shevtsov as the brigade's commander from 6 June to 8 December 1942 (hereafter cited as *Komandovanie*). However, the history of 26th Tank Corps, M. F. Panov, *Na napravlenii glavnogo udara* [On the axis of the main attack] (Moscow: Shcherbinskaia, 1995), 14–20, states that Lieutenant Colonel I. I. Ivanov replaced Shevtsov on the eve of the offensive and was, in turn, replaced by Major P. S. Makhur, the brigade's chief of staff, after being killed by German artillery fire while his brigade was assaulting State Farm 86, roughly 8 kilometers north of Ust'-Medveditskii, on the night of 19–20 November.

19. Samsonov, *Stalingradskaia bitva*, 368, citing TsAMO SSSR, f. 331, op. 5041, d. 20, l. 31.

20. The Romanian strongpoint at Blinovskii was supposedly defended by two artillery regiments and a reserve infantry battalion from Romanian 14th Infantry Division. See Kravchenko, *Nastupatel'naia operatsii 5-i Tankovoi Armii*, 27.

21. Ibid. According to General Heim's report in Goerlitz, *Paulus and Stalingrad*, 200, Romanian 9th Infantry Division's 36th Regiment defended Blinovskii (called Blinov by the Germans), and artillery units from 9th Division manned strongpoints to the east. Heim also asserts that antitank elements of 22nd Panzer Division reached the Peschanyi region at 1330 hours and engaged 1st Tank Corps' forces later in the afternoon and that the lead elements of Romanian 7th Cavalry Division, deploying forward from the Pronin region, counterattacked against 47th Guards Rifle Division's forces in Blinovskii but managed to seal off the village for only a short period before being forced to withdraw.

22. Ust'-Medveditskii State Farm was a sprawling complex of farms roughly 2 to 5 kilometers north of the village of Peschanyi.

23. Goerlitz, *Paulus and Stalingrad*, 200.

24. Axworthy et al., *Third Axis, Fourth Ally*, 91–92.

25. Chistiakov, *Po prikazu Rodiny*, 36–37.

26. I. A. Pliev, *Pod gvardeiskim znamenem* [Under a guards banner] (Ordzhonikidze: Izdatel'stvo IR, 1976), 120. Like many Soviet memoirs written during the 1970s, General Pliev routinely exaggerates his corps' accomplishments and overstates German losses.

27. Ibid., 121.

28. General Heim's report in Goerlitz, *Paulus and Stalingrad*, 199–200, accurately sums up the Romanians' action in the Kletskaia region as follows: "The 1 Cavalry Division held on to its positions throughout the 19th and during the afternoon was placed under the command of Sixth Army. On 13 Division front, the 87th Infantry Regiment was forced to withdraw at 0700 hours, but very quickly what remained of it halted and fought on. The 1 Infantry Regiment maintained its position and was eventually surrounded [west of Kletskaia] with the Lascar Group. Twenty-five enemy tanks were destroyed on 13th Division's front on 19th. The counter-attack by 15 Division was eventually driven off by enemy tanks [4th Tank Corps], which remained in possession of the commanding high ground previously re-gained by the counter-attack. 15 Division held on to the second position allotted to it, to the west of Gromki, against all subsequent attacks. At 1400 hours, twenty-five enemy tanks reached Gromki, and a little later a few isolated tanks got as far as Kalmykov [30 kilometers southwest of Serafimovich]. IV Rumanian Corps, to which 14th Panzer Division had been attached during the course of the day, was not able to initiate any effective counter-measures. On the evening of the 19th the remnants of 13 Division were attached to 6 and 15 Divisions, and command of all troops to the east of a line Kletskaya–Yevstratovskiy was assumed by Sixth Army. The enemy had succeeded in breaking through to a depth of seven or eight kilometres on an eighteen-kilometre front. In addition, in the Gromki sector, the Rumanian front had been breached on a front the extent to which was not yet known."

29. Axworthy et al., *Third Axis, Fourth Ally*, 91, describes the action in the Kletskaia sector and asserts that General Sion's 15th Infantry Division also destroyed 8 of 15 Soviet tanks that were trying to wheel westward into 6th Infantry Division's rear. However, according to this account, the supposedly armor-piercing shells from Romanian 75mm field guns simply bounced off the Soviet tanks.

30. Isaev, *Stalingrad*, 317. Isaev's work is the most complete and accurate account of the battle written since the fall of the Soviet Union in 1991.

31. Pliev, *Pod gvardeiskim znamenem*, 124.

32. Ibid., 125; *Komandovanie*, 367. Brikel' served as temporary commander of the division until appointed permanent commander on 1 January 1943. He was promoted to the rank of major general on 22 February 1944 and became a Hero of the Soviet Union later in the war.

33. The Romanian infantry and tanks fighting at Selivanov and Vlasov were apparently from Colonel Voicu's detachment, which by this time consisted of the remnants of one regiment of 15th Infantry Division, fragments of 13th Infantry Division, and a battalion of motorized 100mm howitzers, possibly with some R-2 tanks, detached from Romanian 1st Armored Division. See Axworthy et al., *Third Axis, Fourth Ally*, 93.

34. Chistiakov, *Po prikazu Rodiny*, 38.

35. Samsonov, *Stalingradskaia bitva*, 405n107, citing I. Wieder, *Katastrofa na Volge* [Catastrophe on the Volga] (Moscow: Voenizdat, 1965), a Russian translation of Joachim Wieder, *Die Tragödie von Stalingrad. Erinnerungen eines Überlebenden* (West Germany: Deggendorf, 1955).

36. Actually, Army Group B issued the order to halt XXXXVIII Panzer Corps and wheel it toward the north and northwest only after Weichs received the order from Zeitzler at the OKH, who had discussed the matter with Hitler. See "H.Gr. B, Ia an XXXXVIII. Pz.K. vom 19.11.1942, 1150 Uhr," in *KTB XXXXVIII. PzK Ia, BA-MA*, RH 26 775/2. At this time, Hitler was wearing two hats: commander of the *Wehrmacht* [*Oberbefehlshaber der Wehrmacht*] and commander of the army [*Oberbefehlshaber des Heeres*].

37. Paul Carell, *Stalingrad: The Defeat of German 6th Army* (Atglen, PA: Schiffer Military/Aviation History, 1993), 159. Carell's book is flamboyantly pro-German, with many exaggerations of German successes, and must be read with extreme caution. While he states that 22nd Panzer fielded 20 tanks, it is likely it had closer to 30.

38. Hitler quoted (thirdhand) by Zeitzler in Seymour Frieden and William Richardson, eds., *The Fatal Decisions* (New York: William Sloane Associates, 1956), 155; Horst Boog, Jürgen Forster, Joachim Hoffmann, et al., *Germany and the Second World War*, vol. 6, *The Attack on the Soviet Union*, trans. Dean S. McMurray, Ewald Osers, and Louise Wilmot (Oxford: Clarendon Press, 2001), 1123–1124; Ziemke and Bauer, *Moscow to Stalingrad*, 471. See also Friedrich Schulz, *Reverses on the Southern Wing (1942–1943)*, Military Study No. T-15 (Headquarters, U.S. Army, Europe, n.d.), 25–30. This last source is somewhat suspect, having been written after the fact and clearly intending to blame Hitler for the entire defeat.

39. G. Dërr, *Pokhod na Stalingrad* [The approach to Stalingrad] (Moscow: Voenizdat, 1957), 69. This is a Russian translation of Hans von Dörr [Doerr], *Der Feldzug nach Stalingrad* (Darmstadt, West Germany: E. S. Mittler und sohn, GmbH, 1955). A colonel when the war began, von Dörr served, successively, as chief of staff of LII Army Corps, chief of the second German liaison staff to Romanian Fourth Army, commander of 384th Infantry Division, and chief of staff of XVII Army Corps before being assigned as military attaché in Madrid, Spain, in August 1943, where he ended the war as a major general.

40. Schröter, *Stalingrad*, 62.

41. "KR-Fernschreien an AOK.6," Oberkommando der Heeresgruppe B, 19.11.1942 21.30 Uhr," in *Die Anlagenbänder zu den Kriegstagebüchern der 6. Armee*, book 1, 302.

42. Ibid., 300–301.

43. Samsonov, *Stalingradskaia bitva*, 378, quoting from a Russian translation of Wilhelm Adam, *Der schwere Entschluss* (East Berlin, 1965). This account of deliberations in Sixth Army's headquarters was written by Paulus's former adjutant.

44. Ziemke and Bauer, *Moscow to Stalingrad*, 470.

45. V. Adam, *Trudnoe reshenie: Memuary polkovnika 6th Germanskoi armii* [A difficult decision: The memoirs of a colonel in 6th German Army] (Moscow: Voenizdat, 1967), 167–168. This is a Russian translation of Wilhelm Adam, *Der schwere*

Entschluss (East Berlin, 1965). Because Adam was captured by the Soviets at Stalingrad and lived in communist East Germany after the war, his account is a favorite of Soviet and Russian historians. Although he is kinder to the Soviets than most German chroniclers of the battle, Adam treats Paulus in a favorable light and is strident in his criticism of Hitler.

46. Samsonov, *Stalingradskaia bitva*, 378.

47. Untitled message, in *Die Anlagenbänder zu den Kriegstagebüchern der 6. Armee*, book 1, 300–301.

48. Jason D. Mark, *Island of Fire: The Battle for the Barrikady Gun Factory in Stalingrad, November 1942–February 1943* (Sydney: Leaping Horseman Books, 2006), 256.

49. Ibid., 257.

50. Dërr, *Pokhod na Stalingrad*, 69.

51. "Izvlechenie iz operativnoi svodkoi No. 325," in *Stalingradskaia bitva*, book 2, 36; archival citation *TsAMO RF*, f. 16, op. 1072ss, d. 11, ll. 132–136.

52. "KR-Fernschreiben an Gen. Kdo. XI. A.K. nachr: O.Q./AOK. 6, Armee-Oberkommando 6, Abt. Ia, A.H.Qu., 20.11.1942 00.55 Uhr," in *Die Anlagenbänder zu den Kriegstagebüchern der 6. Armee*, book 1, 302.

53. "Funkspruch an 14. Pz. Div. bei XI. A. K. uber AOK. 6, rum. V. A. K., 20.11.1942 02.00 Uhr," ibid., 303.

54. Ibid. This Kalmykovskii should not be confused with another village named Kalmykovskii situated 30 kilometers southwest of Serafimovich in 5th Tank Army's sector.

55. General Heim's report in Goerlitz, *Paulus and Stalingrad*, 201–202, causes considerable confusion because it misidentifies exactly when XXXVIII Panzer Corps received its conflicting orders of 19 and 20 November. Ultimately, however, it made no difference: XXXXVIII Panzer Corps' forces were decisively engaged in the Peschanyi region from 20 through 23 November.

56. "Morgenmeldung XI. A.K. 0600 Uhr, A.O.K. 6 Ia., 20.11.1942," in *Die Anlagenbänder zu den Kriegstagebüchern der 6. Armee*, book 1, 304.

57. Ibid.

58. "Funkspruch an AOK. 6, rum. IV. A.K., 20.11.1942," ibid., 306.

59. "Zwischenmeldung, Armee-Oberkommando 6, Abt. Ia., A.H.Qu., 20.11. 1942, 0750 Uhr," ibid., 307–308.

60. "LI. AK/Ia an Gruppe Schwerin vom 20.11.1942 0945 Uhr (79. ID/Ia, 33 077/2)," as quoted in Mark, *Island of Fire*, 258.

61. The most definitive account of 22nd Panzer Division's composition and fight from 19 to 24 November is Rolf Stoves, *Die 22. Panzer-Division, 25. Panzer-Division, 27. Panzer-Division und die 233. Reserve-Panzer-Division* (Friedberg, West Germany: Podzun-Pallas-Verlag, 1985), 53–66. On 19 November, the division consisted of its headquarters, 140th Panzer Reconnaissance Company [*Pz. Späh-Kp.* 140], 204th Panzer Regiment [*Pz. Rgt.* 204] (four panzer companies), 129th Panzer-Grenadier Regiment [*Pz. Gren. Rgt.* 129] (two battalions), 24th Motorcycle Battalion [*Kradshutz. Btl.* 24], 140th Panzer Artillery Regiment [*Pz. Art. Rgt.* 140] (three mixed artillery *abteilung*), 289th (Motorized) *Flak Abteilung* (antiaircraft battalion; with two 88mm batteries and 1 mixed *Flak* battery), 140th Panzer Reconnaissance

Abteilung [*Pz. Nachr. Abt.* 140] (with three companies), 140th Panzer Antitank *Abteilung* [*Pz.* Jäger-*Abt.* 140] (with four companies), 140th Panzer Pioneer Company [*Pz. Pi. Kp.* 140] (with five platoons and 1 *Werfer* platoon), and various smaller support elements.

62. Kravchenko, *Nastupatel'naia operatsiia 5-i Tankovoi Armii*, 30–31, describes 5th Tank Army's operations on 20 November in considerable detail.

63. Stoves, *Die 22. Panzer-Division*, 56.

64. Kravchenko, *Nastupatel'naia operatsiia 5-i Tankovoi Armii*, 31.

65. See Panov, *Na napravlenii glavnogo udara*, 22; and Kravchenko, *Nastupatel'naia operatsiia 5-i Tankovoi Armii*, 31, for details on the fight for Perelazovskii.

66. Panov, *Na napravlenii glavnogo udara*, 22–23.

67. General Lascar was an exceptionally skilled and tenacious combat commander and had been awarded a German *Ritterkreuz* (Knight's Cross) for his service during the Siege of Sevastopol'. See Axworthy et al., *Third Axis, Fourth Ally*, 95.

68. Ibid., 94.

69. Ibid.

70. Kravchenko, *Nastupatel'naia operatsiia 5-i Tankovoi Armii*, 48.

71. "Deistviia podvizhnoi gruppy 5 Tankovoi armii v proryve" [The actions of 5th Tank Army's mobile group in the penetration], in *Sbornik materialov po izucheniiu opyta voiny No. 6, aprel'–mai 1943 g.* [Collection of materials for the study of war experience, No. 6, April–May 1943] (Moscow: Voenizdat, 1943), 57. This report was prepared by the General Staff of the Red Army and classified secret.

72. For the situation in the Kletskaia region on 20 November, see Samsonov, *Stalingradskaia bitva*, 374–376; Rokossovsky, *Velikaia pobeda na Volge*, 268–269; and Axworthy et al., *Third Axis, Fourth Ally*, 92–93.

73. Axworthy et al., *Third Axis, Fourth Ally*, 92–93.

74. Ibid.

75. Pliev, *Pod gvardeiskim znamenem*, 126. Given the strength of the Romanian force, these figures are likely exaggerated.

76. For details about the fighting for Gromki, see Chistiakov, *Po prikazu Rodiny*, 39–40. Before expanding the Kletskaia penetration, Chistiakov referred to the penetration bridgehead as a "puffed pastry" because, by this time, the enemy's defenses were artificially overextended and ripe for destruction.

77. See Batov, *V podkhodakh i boiakh*, 193–195, for a description of 65th Army's operations on 19 November.

78. Ibid., 196–202. Other sources describing the raid by 65th Army's mobile group provide little detail. For example, Rokossovsky confirms Batov's account of Anisimov's raid in his memoirs but provides no details; nor does he do so in *Velikaia pobeda na Volge*. For the German perspective, see Sixth Army's and XI Army Corps' situation maps for 21 and 22 November and partial information about 65th Army's assault in "Fernspruch an Heeresgruppe B, Morgenmeldung, 0710 Uhr, Armee-Oberkommando 6 Abt. Ia, A.H.Qu., 20.11.1942," "Fernschreiben an Heeresgruppe B, Zwischenmeldung, 0750 Uhr, Armee-Oberkommando 6 Abt. Ia, A.H.Qu., 20.11.1942," and "Fernschreiben an Heeresgruppe B, Tagesmeldung. 2155 Uhr,

Armee-Oberkommando 6 Abt. Ia, A.H.Qu., 20.11.1942," in *Die Anlagenbänder zu den Kriegstagebüchern der 6. Armee*, book 1, 306–307, 314.

79. Axworthy et al., *Third Axis, Fourth Ally*, 94.

80. Rolf Grams, *Die 14. Panzer-Division 1940–1945* (Eggolsheim, West Germany: Dörfler in Nebek Verlag, GmbH, 2004), 56.

81. See "Fernschreiben an Gen. Kdo. XIV. Pz.K, Gen. Kdo. LI. A.K., Grn. Kdo. VIII. A.K., Gen. Kdo. XI. A.K., nachr.: VIII. Fliegerkorps, 1445 Uhr, Armee-Oberkommando 6, Abt. Ia, A.H.Qu., 20.11.1942," in *Die Anlagenbänder zu den Kriegstagebüchern der 6. Armee*, book 1, 311–312.

82. Mark, *Island of Fire*, 262.

83. "Izvlechenie iz operativnoi svodkoi No. 324," in *Stalingradskaia bitva*, book 2, 29–31; archival citation *TsAMO RF*, f. 16, op. 1072ss, d. 11, ll. 125–131.

84. "Izvlechenie iz operativnoi svodkoi No. 325," ibid., 36; archival citation, ibid., ll. 132–136.

85. For details on the Stalingrad Front's offensive, see Rokossovsky, *Velikaia pobeda na Volge*, 268–270; Samsonov, *Stalingradskaia bitva*, 382–385; and A. I. Eremenko, *Stalingrad: Zapiski komanduiushchego frontom* [Stalingrad: The notes of a *front* commander] (Moscow: Voenizdat, 1961), 325–351.

86. For details of 64th Army's assault, see Samsonov, *Stalingradskaia bitva*, 284; D. A. Dragunsky et al., *Ot Volgi do Pragi* [From the Volga to Prague] (Moscow: Voenizdat, 1966), 42–43; and Axworthy et al., *Third Axis, Fourth Ally*, 101–102.

87. For details of 57th Army's assault, see Rokossovsky, *Velikaia pobeda na Volge*, 270; Samsonov, *Stalingradskaia bitva*, 384. For a detailed account of 13th Tank Corps' operations, see V. F. Tolubko and N. I. Baryshev, *Na iuzhnom flange: Boevoi put' 4-go Gvardeiskogo mekhanizirovannogo korpusa (1942–1945 gg.)* [On the southern flank: The combat path of the 4th Guards Mechanized Corps (1942–1945)] (Moscow: Nauka, 1973), 49–57.

88. Isaev, *Stalingrad*, 326, asserts that 57th Army began its artillery preparation at 0930 hours and its ground assault at 1030 hours.

89. From left to right in its roughly 15-kilometer-wide sector from Khara-Uson to 3 kilometers southwest of Bol'shaia Chapurniki, 2nd Infantry Division defended with 2nd and 1st Battalion, 1st Infantry Regiment with 1st and 2nd Battalion, and 26th Infantry Regiment with one separate company defending the railroad sector on its left flank. See VI Army Corps' operations map dated 14 November 1942 in *D.V.K. 16, 114/42 g. Kdes.*

90. See Isaev, *Stalingrad*, 325.

91. For details about 13th Tank Corps' plan and attack, see Tolubko and Baryshev, *Na iuzhnom flange*, 52.

92. Isaev, *Stalingrad*, 328, asserts that 13th Tank Corps began its advance at 1330 hours. The discrepancy probably reflects the difference between the commitment of the corps' lead elements and the commitment of its main forces, since it took several hours for Tanaschishin's force to join battle.

93. German and Soviet accounts of 29th Motorized Division's counterattack sharply disagree. For example, Rokossovsky, *Velikaia pobeda na Volge*, 270, states that 29th Motorized Division simply "slowed its [13th Tank Corps'] advance on

Nariman," which is essentially correct but masks the scope of 13th Tank Corps' initial defeat. In contrast, 13th Tank Corps' history (Tolubko and Baryshev, *Na iuzhnom flange*, 56–57) puts a far "happier face" on the engagement, although it asserts the action took place on 21 November rather than the 20th (see also appendix 5K in the *Companion*). By focusing on the fighting on 21 November, Tolubko and Baryshev simply cover up 13th Tank Corps' initial setback late on 20 November.

94. Isaev, *Stalingrad*, 327. Soviet records indicate 422nd Rifle Division suffered 7 men killed and 129 wounded on 20 November, while 143rd Rifle Brigade lost 7 men killed and 174 wounded.

95. Ibid.

96. V. A. Zolotarev, ed., *Velikaia Otechestvennaia voina, Kniga 2: Perelom* [The Great Patriotic War, book 2: The turning point] (Moscow: Nauka, 1998), 59; hereafter cited as *VOV*. This account claims, erroneously, that 422nd Rifle Division captured Nariman; Colonel Eremenko's 169th Division actually captured the town.

97. Ziemke and Bauer, *Moscow to Stalingrad*, 470.

98. Kehrig, *Stalingrad*, 148. Reinforcing this judgment is Axworthy et al., *Third Axis, Fourth Ally*, 103, which asserts that the situation of VI and VII Corps was "catastrophic" and that the bulk of Romanian 18th and 2nd Divisions was surrounded between Tinguta and Tinguta Station and "largely destroyed by following rifle divisions the next day. . . . The only still-intact elements of VI Corps outside the developing encirclement were now the southernmost regiment of 1st Division around Tundutovo, which swung its front round to face north and repulsed local attacks, and 4th Division, which was not attacked."

99. Isaev, *Stalingrad*, 325.

100. For details of 57th Army's operations, see S. M. Sarkis'ian, *51-ia Armii* [The 51st Army] (Moscow: Voenizdat, 1983), 101–102; and A. M. Samsonov, *Ot Volgi do Baltiki: Ocherk istorii 3-go Gvardeiskogo mekhanizirovannogo korpusa 1942–1945 gg* [From the Volga to the Baltic: A study of the history of 3rd Guards Mechanized Corps 1942–1945] (Moscow: Nauka, 1963), 40–45.

101. Samsonov, *Ot Volgi do Baltiki*, 40, claims the attacking forces lost two T-34 tanks that were burned and two more that were knocked out in the fighting for Hill 87.0. Most of the hill's defenders ultimately surrendered.

102. Isaev, *Stalingrad*, 325, notes that 158th Separate Tank Regiment reported it destroyed 8 guns and 23 bunkers with their defenders on 20 November, and 55th Tank Regiment claimed it destroyed 12 guns and 42 bunkers, many of them on Hill 87.0. In addition, the two regiments reported destroying 18 antitank guns, including several "88s." The 158th Regiment reported losing 8 T-34 tanks (5 burned and 3 blown up by mines), 4 T-70 tanks, and 6 T-34s that got stuck in the swamps. The 55th Regiment lost 2 T-34s and 3 T-70s to enemy fire and 3 that got stuck in the marshes.

103. Samsonov, *Ot Volgi do Baltiki*, 43. Some German sources assert that Vol'sky delayed his attack because he feared that after successfully attacking 13th Tank Corps to the north, German 29th Motorized Division would head south and engage his corps. However, the delayed commitment of 4th Mechanized Corps (from 1120 to 1300 hours) occurred before 29th Motorized Division went into action, making this explanation is implausible.

104. Ibid., 46.

105. For details of 28th Army's operations, see Oleg Shein, *Neizvestnyi front Velikoi Otechestvennoi* [The unknown front of the Great Patriotic (War)] (Moscow: Eksmo Iauza, 2009).

106. This forward detachment consisted of two 45mm antitank guns, six antitank rifles, two heavy machine guns, and three 82mm mortars. The next day, the rifle brigade found 50 dead and 2 wounded on the battlefield. The German force numbered 200 men, 13 tanks, and 8 to 10 armored personnel carriers. See an account of the engagement in Shein, *Neizvestnyi front*, 166–167, and the Red Army General Staff's rebuke in Zolotarev, "General Staff 1942," 393.

107. Shein, *Neizvestnyi front,* 170.

108. Ibid., 171. According to Soviet archival records, 16th Motorized Division fielded 43 tanks: 8 Pz-IIs, 23 Pz-IIIs, 11 Pz-IVs, and 1 command tank. The 28th Army numbered 47,891 men, 1,196 guns and mortars, and 80 tanks.

109. Wilhelm Tieke, *The Caucasus and the Oil: The German-Soviet War in the Caucasus 1942–43* (Winnipeg, Canada: J. J. Fedorowicz, 1995), 134–135.

110. Shein, *Neizvestnyi front*, 185. Shein provides a very detailed account of the fighting on 20 November based on both Soviet and German sources.

Chapter 6. The Encirclement Closes, 21–23 November

1. Adam, *Trudnoe reshenie: Memuary polkovnika 6th Germanskoi armii*, 170.

2. Ibid.

3. N. I. Krylov, *Stalingradskii rubezh* [The Stalingrad position] (Moscow: Voenizdat, 1979), 302–303.

4. Boog et al., *Germany and the Second World War*, 6:1139.

5. Frieden and Richardson, *The Fatal Decisions*, 147–150.

6. Geoffrey Jukes, *Hitler's Stalingrad Decisions* (Berkeley: University of California Press, 1985), 104–105; John Erickson, *The Road to Berlin; Continuing Stalin's War with Germany* (Boulder, CO: Westview Press, 1983), 7.

7. See Army Detachment Hollidt's *Anlagen zu KTB I, Tagl. Meldungen*, in *BA-MA*, RH 20-6/249, box 56/222, which records the army detachment's operations beginning on 23 November 1942.

8. See the excellent discussion of the airlift decision in Joel S. A. Hayward, *Stopped at Stalingrad: The Luftwaffe and Hitler's Defeat in the East, 1942–1943* (Lawrence: University Press of Kansas, 1998), 234–239.

9. "H. Gr. B/Ia, Funkspruch Nr. 1352 an AOK 6 vom 21.11.1942," in *BA-MA*, RH 20-6/241.

10. Tarrant, *Stalingrad*, 112–113; Antony Beevor, *Stalingrad: The Fateful Siege, 1942–1943* (New York: Viking, 1998), 245.

11. "Izvlechenie iz operativnoi svodkoi No. 326," in *Stalingradskaia bitva*, book 2, 41–42; archival citation *TsAMO RF*, f. 16, op. 1072ss, d. 11, ll. 137–142.

12. Samsonov, *Stalingradskaia bitva*, 386, quoting *TsAMO SSSR*, f. 331, op. 5041, d. 20, l. 1.

13. For details about 22nd Panzer Division's movements and actions on 21 November, see Stoves, *Die 22. Panzer-Division*, 57–59. After claiming that it destroyed 26 enemy tanks, presumably from 1st Tank Corps, on 19 and 20 November,

the division asserted that it killed 6 more tanks near Hill 192.4, several kilometers east of Medvezhyi. By this time, 22nd Panzer had only a handful of tanks at its disposal.

14. For further details and a sharp critique of 1st Tank Corps' operations, see Kravchenko, *Nastupatel'naia operatsiia 5-i Tankovoi Armii*, 33; Rokossovsky, *Velikaia pobeda na Volge*, 271; "Deistviia podvizhnoi gruppy" and "Nekotorye vyvody po ispol'zovaniiu tankovykh i mekhanizirovannykh korpusov dlia razvitiia proryva" [Some conclusions regarding the employment of tank and mechanized corps in the penetration], in *Sbornik materialov po izucheniiu opyta voiny, No. 8, avgust–oktiabr' 1943 g.* [Collection of materials for the study of war experiences, No. 8, August–October 1943] (Moscow: Voenizdat, 1943), 48–80. See English translations of these two critiques in David M. Glantz, *Soviet War Experiences: Tank Operations* (Carlisle, PA: self-published, 1998).

15. Samsonov, *Stalingradskaia bitva*, 386, quoting *TsAMO SSSR*, f. 1st Guards Tank Corps, op. 33764, d. 2, l. 3.

16. Panov, *Na napravlenii glavnogo udara*, 23.

17. Axworthy et al., *Third Axis, Fourth Ally*, 95–96, describes Romanian Third Army's actions on 21 November in detail.

18. Kravchenko, *Nastupatel'naia operatsiia 5-i Tankovoi Armii*, 34.

19. See "Tagesmeldung, Armee-Oberkommando 6, Abt.-Ia, A.H.Qu. 20.11.1942," in *Die Anlagenbänder zu den Kriegstagebüchern der 6. Armee*, book 1, 314, which was transmitted by Sixth Army's Ia to Army Group B at 2155 hours on 20 November. This describes the situation in XI Army Corps' sector, the position and strength of 14th Panzer Division, and the status of forces marching to reinforce 14th and 24th Panzer Divisions, whose forward forces were deployed in the Verkhne-Buzinovka and Sukhanov regions.

20. See a full account of the operations of *Kampfgruppe* Don (24th Panzer Division) in F. M. von Senger und Etterlin Jr., *Die 24. Panzer-Division vormals 1. Kavallerie-Division 1939–1945* (Neckargemund: Kurt Vowinckel Verlag, 1962). The 24th Panzer Division's *kampfgruppe* consisted of division headquarters; part of 86th Panzer Reconnaissance Battalion [*Abteilung*]; 1st Squadron, 4th Motorcycle Battalion (K-4); two weak panzer battalions under Colonel Winterfeld; 4th Battalion, 89th Panzer Artillery Regiment; and 40th Panzer Antitank Battalion [*Jägt Abteilung*] (less one platoon), equipped with about 45 tanks. The *kampfgruppe's* mission was to man defenses along the Liska River from Suchanow (Sukhanov), where its headquarters was located, southward through Jerusslanowskij (Eruslanovskii) to Skworin (Skvorin), and then send out security forces to the Werknij Businowka (Verkhne-Buzinovka)–Jerik (Erik) line, in coordination with 14th Panzer Division to the north.

21. Isaev, *Stalingrad*, 317. It is very unlikely Kravchenko's corps captured these aircraft.

22. See "Morgenmeldung, Korüch 593, 0530 Uhr, A.O.K. 6 I.a, 21.11.42," "KR-Fernschreiben an Heeresgruppe B, nachr.: Fernscrib. an Stab Don usw, 0740 Uhr, Armee-Oberkommando 6, Abt.-Ia, A.H.Qu., 21.11.1942," and "Morgenmeldung, XIV. Pz. K., 0619 Uhr, A.O.K. 6 I.a, 22.11.42," in *Die Anlagenbänder zu den Kriegstagebüchern der 6. Armee*, book 1, 318, 320, 326.

23. The 3rd Guards Cavalry Corps' operations on 21 November are described in Pliev, *Pod gvardeiskim znamennem*, 126–128.

24. Ibid., 128–129.

25. "KR-Fernschreiben an Heeresgruppe B, nachr.: Fernscrib. an Stab Don usw, 0740 Uhr, Armee-Oberkommando 6, Abt.-Ia, A.H.Qu., 21.11.1942," in *Die Anlagenbänder zu den Kriegstagebüchern der 6. Armee*, book 1, 320.

26. "Lagenmeldung, VIII. A.K. meldet 1725 Uhr, A.O.K. 6 I.a, 21.11.42," ibid., 321.

27. "Zwischenmeldung, LI. A.K. meldet 2030 Uhr, A.O.K. 6 I.a, 21.11.42," ibid., 320–323. According to the midday reports [*Zwischenmeldung*] of LI Army Corps, Group von Hanstein, which ended up defending in the Karpovka region, included one grenadier battalion, the headquarters of the artillery regiment, one light battery, and an antitank platoon [1 *Zug Pz. Jg.*] from 3rd Motorized Division and one grenadier battalion, the headquarters of an artillery detachment [*abteilung*], one antitank platoon, and a panzer company with 10 tanks from 60th Motorized Division.

28. Batov, *V podkhodakh i boiakh*, 202.

29. For sparse commentary on 65th Army's operations on 21 November, see ibid. and Rokossovsky, *Soldatskii dolg*, 200–201.

30. "Morgenmeldung XI. A.K., 0522 Uhr, A.O.K. 6 I. a, 21.11.42," in *Die Anlagenbänder zu den Kriegstagebüchern der 6. Armee*, book 1, 318.

31. "Morgenmeldung XI. A. K., 0540 Uhr, A.O.K. 6 I. a, 22.11.42," ibid., 325.

32. Axworthy et al., *Third Axis, Fourth Ally*, 96; General Heim's report in Goerlitz, *Paulus and Stalingrad*, 201–203.

33. Kehrig, *Stalingrad*, 158–159.

34. Dërr, *Pokhod na Stalingrad*, 70.

35. Adam, *Trudnoe reshenie*, 174–175, as quoted in Samsonov, *Stalingradskaia bitva*, 387–389. Adam used the term "fled" rather than "moved" because he was writing in Communist East Germany after the war. Although an important source, Adam tends to hold people other than Paulus—certainly Hitler, but other generals as well—responsible for the fate of Sixth Army.

36. Ibid.

37. Colonel Adam recorded that Sixth Army's headquarters column, together with the headquarters of VIII Army Corps, passed through Kalach at midday on 22 November, where it assisted Sixth Army's quartermaster in destroying equipment it was unable to evacuate due to a shortage of transport. See Adam's vivid description of the scene in Samsonov, *Stalingradskaia bitva*, 389 (quoted in full in appendix 5P in the *Companion*).

38. "Izvlechenie iz operativnoi svodkoi No. 326," 41–42.

39. For a general description of 64th Army's operations on 21 November, see K. S. Belov et al., eds., *Ot Volgi do Pragi* [From the Volga to Prague] (Moscow: Voenizdat, 1966), 43–44; this is a history of 7th Guards (64th) Army. The figure of 50 to 70 tanks was an exaggeration by 64th Army because 29th Motorized Division, the only German panzer force in the region, fielded 52 operational tanks (4 Pz-III and 48 Pz-IV models) at the outset of the Soviet offensive and certainly lost at least several thereafter. Nonetheless, Rokossovsky, *Velikaia pobeda na Volge*, 272–273, supports 64th Army's contention, stating, "On the right wing [on 21 November], the shock group of 64th Army was forced to repel a strong counterattack by the enemy 297th Infantry Division. As a result of one of the counterattacks, in which, besides the infantry, 60–70 tanks took part, the enemy succeeded in pushing back this army's 38th

Rifle Division in the region north of Nariman." Likewise, Samsonov, *Stalingradskaia bitva*, 397, asserts, "The German command undertook measures to disrupt our offensive; during the night, a division, reinforced by 70 tanks, was thrown into 64th Army's sector, and it launched a counterattack against 38th Rifle Division on the morning of 21 November. Simultaneously, strong counterattacks were undertaken against 204th and 157th Rifle Divisions in the Iagodnyi region [to the northeast]. After repulsing the fierce enemy onslaught, as a result of heavy losses, 38th Rifle Division was forced to withdraw to the Hill 128.2 region by the end of the day. The right-wing 169th Rifle Division of 57th Army also had no success on this day." These comments, together with the silence of German sources about 29th Motorized Division's activities on 21 November, underscore the likelihood that all or part of the division's panzer detachment supported 297th Infantry Division's counterattack. It likely did so along with assault and antitank guns [*Paks*], which the Soviets probably misidentified as tanks. In any event, the strong German counterattacks against 64th Army enabled IV Army Corps to withdraw its forces in good order to what would become the southern face of Sixth Army's Stalingrad pocket.

40. Tolubko and Baryshev, *Na iuzhnom flange*, 57.

41. "Tagesmeldung, Armee-Oberkommando 6, A.H.Qu., 23.11.1942," in *Die Anlagenbänder zu den Kriegstagebüchern der 6. Armee*, book 1, 331.

42. For the Stalingrad Front's operations, see Rokossovsky, *Velikaia pobeda na Volge*, 270–271. For details about 51st Army's operations, see Sarkis'ian, *51-ia Armiia*, 101–102.

43. The 4th Mechanized Corps' operations on the 20th are detailed in Samsonov, *Ot Volge do Baltiki*, 48–49.

44. See the daily reports of these divisions on 21 November, as well as 62nd Army's Combat Journal.

45. Ibid.

46. Shein, *Neizvestnyi front*, 187.

47. Ibid., citing archival document *TsAMO*, f. 382, op. 8465, d. 81.

48. Ibid.

49. Ibid.

50. Ibid., 191–192.

51. Wilhelm Tieke, *The Caucasus and the Oil: The German-Soviet War in the Caucasus 1942/43* (Winnipeg, Canada: J. J. Fedorowicz, 1995), 135.

52. Shein, *Neizvestnyi front*, 193, citing Wilhelm Tieke, *Marsh na Kavkaz. Bitva za neft', 1942–1943* [The march into the Caucasus: The battle for oil, 1942–1943] (Moscow: 2005), 165, a translation of Wilhelm Tieke, *Der Kaukasus und das Öl: Der Deutsch-sowjetische Krieg in Kaukasien 1942/43* (Osnabruck: Munin Verlag, 1970).

53. Tieke, *The Caucasus and the Oil*, 135.

54. See Axworthy et al., *Third Axis, Fourth Ally*, 103; and Fourth Panzer Army's *Lagenkarte* (daily situation map) as of 2200 hours on 21 November 1942.

55. "Izvlechenie iz operativnoi svodkoi No. 327," in *Stalingradskaia bitva*, book 2, 47; archival citation *TsAMO RF*, f. 16, op. 1072ss, d. 11, ll. 143–150.

56. Panov, *Na napravlenii glavnogo udara*, 23.

57. Kravchenko, *Nastupatel'naia operatsiia 5-i Tankovoi Armii*, 38. Actually,

26th Tank Corps ultimately engaged elements of 16th Panzer Division in the Lozhki region, 12 kilometers northwest of Kalach, as well as German and Romanian security and rear service units, some from 3rd Motorized Division and bits and pieces of other forces, at *Pobeda Oktiabriia* (October Victory) and *10 Let Oktiabriia* (10 Years of October) State Farms, 15 to 17 kilometers west of Kalach. It is also possible that *Kampfgruppe* von Hanstein from 3rd Motorized sent some smaller units to stiffen the defenses west of Kalach. But Hanstein had only two grenadier battalions available to his *kampfgruppe*, and most of them were securing the railroad from Marinovka eastward to Karpovka.

58. Panov, *Na napravlenii glavnogo udara*, 25–26. Although previous accounts of this raid asserted that Filippov's force included five tanks from Major Makhur's 157th Tank Brigade, Panov, who wrote 26th Tank Corps' history, and Filippov himself claimed that, although Makhur was at the meeting where Rodin ordered the formation of the forward detachment, nothing was said about assigning it a platoon of tanks. Instead, Makhur's tanks reinforced the forward detachment during its raid.

59. Adam, *Trudnoe reshenie*, 167–168.

60. Dërr, *Pokhod na Stalingrad*, 70–71.

61. "Morgenmeldung, XIV. Pz.K. 0615 Uhr, A.O.K. 6, Ia, 22.11.42," in *Die Anlagenbänder zu den Kriegstagebüuchern der 6. Armee*, book 1, 326.

62. "Funkspruch an Heeresgruppe B, 1900 Uhr, Armee-Oberkommando 6 Abt.-Ia, A.H.Qu., 22.11.1942," ibid., 327.

63. Panov, *Na napravlenii glavnogo udara*, 27–28, and Samsonov, *Stalingradskaia bitva*, 391, provide details on 19th and 157th Tank Brigades' actions west of Kalach.

64. Panov, *Na napravlenii glavnogo udara*, 27.

65. Ibid., 27–28.

66. Kravchenko, *Nastupatel'naia operatsiia 5-i Tankovoi Armii*, 35–37.

67. Ibid., 37.

68. For details on 55th Cavalry Division's fight with Romanian 1st Armored Division, see ibid., 35–36, and Axworthy et al., *Third Axis, Fourth Ally*, 96.

69. See *Sbornik materialov po izucheniiu opyta voiny, No. 6, aprel'–mai 1943 g.* [Collection of materials for the study of war experiences, No. 6, April–May 1943] (Moscow: Voenizdat, 1943), 91; classified secret.

70. Axworthy et al., *Third Axis, Fourth Ally*, 96.

71. Kravchenko, *Nastupatel'naia operatsiia 5-i Tankovoi Armii*, 36.

72. For details on 22nd Panzer Division's dispositions and movements on 22 November, see Stoves, *Die 22. Panzer-Division*, 61–62. General Heim (cited in Goerlitz, *Paulus and Stalingrad*, 202) asserts that, at least in part, the Romanians escaping southwestward from Group Lascar's pocket actually joined 22nd Panzer Division.

73. Kravchenko, *Nastupatel'naia operatsiia 5-i Tankovoi Armii*, 36–37. This study does not explain exactly why the motorcycle regiment decided to conduct diversionary operations instead of seizing Oblivskaia. However, the most rational explanation is the strong defense the *Luftwaffe*'s VIII Air Corps [*Fliegerkorps*] established around the town, along with 108th Artillery Command [*ARKO* 108], which soon became Group Stahel.

74. Ibid., 37.

75. At least initially, Army Group B viewed XVII Army Corps' arrival along the Krivaia and upper Chir Rivers as a potential means to rescue all or part of encircled Romanian Third Army, as well as Sixth Army once it was encircled. However, it soon became clear that a force of two German infantry divisions was inadequate to the task.

76. Axworthy et al., *Third Axis, Fourth Ally*, 96. See also Rokossovsky, *Velikaia pobeda na Volge*, 277–278.

77. Axworthy et al., *Third Axis, Fourth Ally*, 97.

78. Ibid.

79. Ibid.

80. Ibid.; Kravchenko, *Nastupatel'naia operatsiia 5-i Tankovoi Armii*, 38–39.

81. Axworthy et al., *Third Axis, Fourth Ally*, 97. See also Chistiakov, *Po prikazu Rodiny*, 42–44, for details about the final reduction of the Romanian pockets.

82. Rokossovsky, *Velikaia pobeda na Volge*, 278; Samsonov, *Stalingradskaia bitva*, 391.

83. Von Senger und Etterlin, *Die 24. Panzer-Division*, 129–130, provides details on 24th Panzer Division's engagements on 22 November. By this time, 24th Panzer Division's *Kampfgruppe* von Below consisted of 2nd Battalion, 21st Panzer-Grenadier Regiment; 1st Battalion, 89th Panzer Artillery Regiment; 3rd Company, 40th Panzer Pioneer Battalion; 2nd Company, 4th Motorcycle Battalion; and the headquarters of 24th Panzer Regiment and 89th Panzer Artillery Regiment.

84. The 16th Panzer Division numbered 34 tanks on 20 November (23 Pz-III long and 11 Pz-IV long) and, according to its next mention in Sixth Army's records, 15 tanks on 26 November (in Group Sikenius). See "Zwischenmeldung XIV. Pz. K., 1810 Uhr, A.O.K. Ia, 26.11.42," in *Die Anlagenbänder zu den Kriegstagebüchern der 6. Armee*, book 2, 24.

85. Anna Stroeva, *Komandarm Kravchenko* [Army commander Kravchenko] (Kiev: Politicheskoi literatury Ukrainy, 1984), 38. Isaev, *Stalingrad*, 318, points out that "the strategy of Paulus to hold on to bridgeheads on the western bank of the Don River, with detachments sent from his mobile formations, worked against him," because many of the Don River bridges remained undestroyed.

86. Pliev, *Pod gvardeiskim znamenem*, 129.

87. Ibid., 130. Here, Pliev once again exaggerates German losses severalfold.

88. Axworthy et al., *Third Axis, Fourth Ally*, 98.

89. See Army Group B's message, "Ia Nr. 4018/42.g. Kdos, Chefsache, Heeresgruppe B, O. Qu., 22.11.1942," in *Die Anlagenbänder zu den Kriegstagebüchern der 6. Armee*, book 1, 326–327.

90. For details on 65th Army's attack, see Batov, *V pokhodakh i boiakh*, 202–204.

91. See Isaev, *Stalingrad*, 319, and chapter 3 for the distribution of tanks in Maslov's 16th Tank Corps.

92. Rokossovsky, *Soldatskii dolg*, 201.

93. "Funkspruch an Heeresgruppe B, 1900 Uhr, Armee-Oberkommando 6 Abt.-Ia, A.H.Qu., 22.11.1942," in *Die Anlagenbänder zu den Kriegstagebüchern der 6. Armee*, book 1, 327.

94. "Izvlechenie iz operativnoi svodkoi No. 327," 50–51. The entry that reads "completing the operational encirclement of German Fourth Panzer and Sixth Armies on the Stalingrad axis" causes some confusion about when the linkup and

encirclement were complete. Although the physical linkup by 4th Tank and 4th Mechanized Corps did not take place until the afternoon of 23 November, the General Staff considered the crossing of the Don River at Kalach by 26th Tank Corps and one brigade of 4th Tank Corps and the capture of Sovetskii by 4th Mechanized Corps to be equivalent to linkup and encirclement because it severed Sixth Army's rail and road communication with its deep rear area.

95. K. V. Amirov, *Ot Volgi do Al'p: Boevoi put' 36-i Gvardeiskoi strelkovoi Verkhnedneprovskoi Krasnoznamennoi ordenov Suvorova i Kutuzova II stepeni divizii* [From the Volga to the Alps: The combat path of the 36th Guards Verkhne-Dnepr, Red Banner, and orders of Suvorov and Kutuzov Rifle Division] (Moscow: Voenizdat, 1987), 47.

96. For a very sketchy account of 64th Army's operations on 22 November, see Belov, *Ot Volgi do Pragi*, 44, and German IV Army Corps' daily operational map for 22 November 1942.

97. "Izvlechenie iz operativnoi svodkoi No. 327," 50–51.

98. Rokossovsky, *Velikaia pobeda na Volge*, 277; Tolubko and Baryshev, *Na iuzhnom flange*, 57; German IV Army Corps' daily operational map for 22 November 1942.

99. "Izvlechenie iz operativnoi svodkoi No. 327," 50–51.

100. For details on 51st Army's operations, see ibid.

101. Sarkis'ian, *51-ia Armiia*, 102.

102. Samsonov, *Ot Volgi do Baltiki*, 51, citing Eremenko's memoirs.

103. Ibid., citing Popov's memoirs.

104. Ibid., 52.

105. Ibid.

106. Isaev, *Stalingrad*, 329–330.

107. Samsonov, *Ot Volgi do Baltiki*, 55.

108. See IV Army Corps' daily operational map for 22 November 1942.

109. Samsonov, *Ot Volgi do Baltiki*, 55–56.

110. Ibid., 55, citing archival documents in *TsAMO*, f. 605, op. 64614, d. 1, l. 7.

111. "Izvlechenie iz operativnoi svodkoi No. 327," 50–51. For details about the operations of 51st Army's 76th Fortified Region, see "Polevye ukreplennye raiony v srazhenii za Stalingrad" [Field fortified regions in the battles for Stalingrad], in *Sbornik materialov po izucheniiu opyta voiny, No. 7 iiun'–iiul' 1943 g.* [Collection of materials for the study of war experience, No. 7, June–July 1943] (Moscow: Voenizdat, 1943), 54–59; prepared by the Department for the Exploitation of War Experience on the Red Army General Staff and classified secret. The 76th Fortified Region consisted of 46th and 51st Separate Machine Gun–Artillery Battalions, 161st Mortar Company, 376th Signal Company, and an attached rifle company from 302nd Rifle Division's 827th Regiment. The fortified region's former 45th Battalion was left in 57th Army's reserve, and 49th Battalion had been disbanded after heavy fighting in September 1942.

112. See 62nd Army's daily operational summary for 22 November 1942 and "Izvlechenie iz operativnoi svodkoi No. 327," 50.

113. "Direktiva General'nogo shtaba no. 158028 nachal'niku shtaba Stalingradskogo fronta o merakh po ustraneniiu nedostatkov v soedineniiakh 62-i Armii"

[General Staff directive no. 158028 to the chief of staff of the Stalingrad Front about measures to eliminate shortcomings in 62nd Army's formations], in Zolotarev, "General Staff 1942," 397; archival citation *TsAMO*, f. 48a, op. 3408, d. 114, l. 102.

114. Details on 28th Army's operations on 22 November are in Shein, *Neizvestnyi front*, 193–194.

115. See "Lagenkarte 16. I.D. (Mot), Stand 25.11.42. 2200 Uhr," in Fourth Panzer Army's daily situation maps.

116. "Funkspruch an Heeresgruppe B, 1900 Uhr, Armee-Oberkommando 6 Abt.-Ia, A.H.Qu., 22.11.1942," in *Die Anlagenbänder zu den Kriegstagebüchern der 6. Armee*, book 1, 327.

117. Ibid.

118. "Izvlechenie iz operativnoi svodki No. 328," in *Stalingradskaia bitva*, book 2, 57; archival citation *TsAMO RF*, f. 16, op. 1072ss, d. 11, ll. 151–158.

119. Kravchenko, *Nastupatel'naia operatsiia 5-i Tankovoi Armii*, 39–40. See also Rokossovsky, *Velikaia pobeda na Volge*, 278–280.

120. Panov, *Na napravlenii glavnogo udara*, 29.

121. Ibid., 40. Rodin's claim is an exaggeration, because 24th Panzer Division had no such quantity of tanks to lose. However, this figure no doubt pertains to German losses during the fighting at *Pobeda Oktiabriia* and *10 Let Oktiabriia* State Farms and may have included Russian T-34 tanks that the Germans defending west of Kalach had previously captured and were now employing.

122. "Izvlechenie iz operativnoi svodki No. 328," 58.

123. Ibid.

124. Axworthy et al., *Third Axis, Fourth Ally*, 98–99.

125. For details on 22nd Panzer Division's fight on 23 November, see Stoves, *Die 22. Panzer-Division*, 62–63.

126. Axworthy et al., *Third Axis, Fourth Ally*, 99.

127. Rokossovsky, *Velikaia pobeda na Volge*, 281. Colonel Tolstov was replaced as commander of 346th Rifle Division by Major General D. I. Stankevsky on 28 November, perhaps because of the division's defeat at Bol'shaia Donshchinka.

128. "Izvlechenie iz operativnoi svodki No. 328," 58.

129. Traiain Stanescu was one of several generals with the same surname who served in the Romanian army. He should not be confused with the Stanescu who later commanded Romanian Fourth Army.

130. Samsonov, *Stalingradskaia bitva*, 392.

131. Ibid., 393. See also Chistiakov, *Po prikazu Rodinu*, 44–47, for a detailed description of the liquidation of Romanian forces west and southwest of Raspopinskaia.

132. Samsonov, *Stalingradskaia bitva*, 392; Rokossovsky, *Velikaia pobeda na Volge*, 280–281.

133. Stroeva, *Komandarm Kravchenko*, 39.

134. Ibid., 40.

135. Pliev, *Pod gvardeiskim znamenem*, 130–131.

136. Ibid., 131.

137. "Izvlechenie iz operativnoi svodki No. 328," 58.

138. Pliev, *Pod gvardeiskim znamenem*, 130–131.

139. "Izvlechenie iz operativnoi svodkoi No. 328," 59.

140. Rokossovsky, *Soldatskii dolg*, 201.

141. Isaev, *Stalingrad*, 320–321, covers each day of 24th Army's offensive.

142. "Izvlechenie iz operativnoi svodkoi No. 328," 59.

143. Ibid.

144. Ibid.; Belov, *Ot Volgi do Pragi*, 44.

145. Amirov, *Ot Volgi do Al'p*, 48–49.

146. The headwaters of the Chervlenaia (sometimes spelled Chervlennaia) and Karpovka Rivers were near Staryi Rogachik and Karpovka Station, respectively. The former flowed southeastward past the western end of Karavatka *Balka* to the Volga River, and the latter flowed westward past Karpovka into the Don.

147. S. I. Vasil'ev and A. P. Dikan', *Gvardeitsy piatnadtsatoi: Boevoi put' Piatnadtsatoi Gvardeiskoi strelkovoi divizii* [The 15th Guards: The combat path of the 15th Guards Rifle Division] (Moscow: Voenizdat, 1960), 69.

148. "K.R. Funkspruch, Geh. Kdos.! An Heeresgruppe B—Ia, 23.12.42," in *Die Anlagenbänder zu den Kriegstagebüchern der 6. Armee*, book 1, 328.

149. See "Lage IV. A. K. vom 23.11.1942" and "Lage IV. A. K. vom 25.11.1942," KTB-Karten, Nov 1942–Jan 1943, AOK 6, 30155/37, in NAM T-312, roll 1459.

150. Samsonov, *Ot Volgi do Baltiki*, 58.

151. Ibid., 58–59.

152. Ibid., 59.

153. Ibid., 60. Although Tanaschishin was promoted to the rank of major general on 7 December, this and other sources refer to him as a general days earlier, probably as a courtesy.

154. Sarkis'ian, *51-ia Armiia*, 104. See also the entries about 51st Army in "Izvlechenie iz operativnoi svodkoi No. 328," 59, which confirm other accounts of the fighting on 23 November.

155. See the daily combat report in 62nd Army's Combat Journal.

156. Ibid.; see also entries in the combat journals of 62nd Army's subordinate divisions.

157. Mark, *Island of Fire*, 282–283.

158. "Izvlechenie iz operativnoi svodkoi No. 328," 59.

159. See Sixth Army's situation map for late on 23 November in AOK 6, 30155/37, in NAM T-312, roll 1459; and "Funkspruch an Heeresgruppe Don, Tagesmeldung, Armee-Oberkommando 6, Abt. Ia, A.H.Qu., 23.11.1942," in *Die Anlagenbänder zu den Kriegstagebüchern der 6. Armee*, book 1, 331.

160. Axworthy et al., *Third Axis, Fourth Ally*, 104.

161. Ibid., 101, 109. The Soviets reported capturing 37,000 Romanian troops.

162. Zolotarev, *VOV*, book 2, 66.

163. Tarrant, *Stalingrad*, 123. Although Tarrant cites no source for his numbers, they are credible when compared with existing archival data.

164. "Funkspruch an Heeresgruppe B, Armee-Oberkommando 6, Abt.-Ia, A.H.Qu., 22.11.1942, 1900 Uhr," in *Die Anlagenbänder zu den Kriegstagebüchern der 6. Armee*, book 1, 327–328.

165. Ibid.

166. "Führer-Spruch Nr. 1368 an 6. Armee, 2200 Uhr, 21.11.42," ibid., 329.

167. Weichs's radio message to OKH/GenstdH/OpAbt fur Chef GenStdH, dated 1845 hours 23 November, in Kehrig, *Stalingrad*, 561.

168. Ibid.

169. For details of these discussions, see Goerlitz, *Paulus and Stalingrad*, 208–212.

170. See also Mark, *Island of Fire*, 282–283.

171. "Funkspruch geh. Kdos., Chefsache! An OKH, 2345 Uhr, 23.11.42," in *Die Anlagenbänder zu den Kriegstagebüchern der 6. Armee*, book 1, 333.

172. For details on the discussions among Zeitzler, Sodenstern, and Hitler overnight on 23–24 November, see Bernd Wegener, "Der Krieg gegen die Sowjetunion 1942/43," in *Das Deutsche Reich und der 2. Weltkrieg, Band 6* (Stuttgart: Militärgeschichtlichen Forschungsamt, 1990), 1028–1029, with relevant footnotes.

173. "Funkspruch an AOK 6, 0540 Uhr, Heeresgruppe B, O. Qu., 24.11.1942," in *Die Anlagenbänder zu den Kriegstagebüchern der 6. Armee*, book 2, 5–6; sent to Army Group B by OKH/GenStdH/OpAbt. (I/SB) Nr. 420 960/42.

174. "Funkspruch an AOK 6, 1830 hours, OKH, 24.11.1942," ibid., 6.

175. Army Group B, "Funkspruch an AOK 6, Q. Qu., 23.11.1942 1338 Uhr," ibid., 5, with the notation Ia Nr. 4199/42 geh. Kdos.

176. Mark, *Island of Fire*, 283.

177. Ibid., 284.

Chapter 7. Reducing the Stalingrad Pocket and Forming the Outer Encirclement Front, 24–27 November

1. The West (capitalized) refers to the German homeland and Western European theater of operations, as opposed to the simple direction west (lowercase).

2. Rokossovsky, *Velikaia pobeda na Volge*, 284–286; Samsonov, *Stalingradskaia bitva*, 399.

3. "Izvlechenie iz operativnoi svodkoi No. 329, in *Stalingradskaia bitva*, book 2, 67–69; archival citation *TsAMO RF*, f. 16, op. 1072ss, d. 11, ll. 159–168.

4. Ibid., 68.

5. Kravchenko, *Nastupatel'naia operatsiia 5-i Tankovoi Armii*, 42.

6. Axworthy et al., *Third Axis, Fourth Ally*, 99–100, records that 1st Armored Division fielded 9 Pz-III and Pz-IV tanks and 19 R-2 tanks after its escape. It goes on to say that 35 of its trucks reached 22nd Panzer Division on the night of 23–24 November and were used during the panzer division's escape westward across the Chir.

7. For details on 216th Tank Brigade's role in the fighting at Bol'shaia Donshchinka, see Panov, *Na napravlenii glavnogo udara*, 31–32, which asserts that 346th Rifle Division and its supporting forces killed or wounded up to 2,600 Romanian and German soldiers, captured 900 more, and seized 15 guns and significant quantities of other equipment in the fighting. Further, Panov reports that 216th Heavy Tank Brigade was attached to Butkov's 1st Tank Corps on 4 December and took part in the subsequent fighting for Surovikino and State Farm No. 79 through 4 January 1943, after which it returned to its parent corps just before it was reorganized as 1st Guards Tank Corps.

8. For details on 22nd Panzer Division's escape, see Stoves, *Die 22. Panzer-Division*, 70–73.

9. Axworthy et al., *Third Axis, Fourth Ally*, 99. Romanian sources claim that this column lost 400 men, 2 tanks, 6 antitank guns, and 59 trucks in the escape, while Soviet sources confirm that 8th Cavalry Corps lost 2,100 men in the fighting, most of them to German air attacks.

10. Since this order has yet to be released, these missions are inferences based on 8th Cavalry Corps' subsequent operations.

11. Rokossovsky, *Velikaia pobeda na Volge*, 290.

12. For details on 203rd Rifle Division's attack, see G. S. Zdanovich, *Idem v nastuplenie* [We went on the offensive] (Moscow: Voenizdat, 1980), 32–33.

13. "Izvlechenie iz operativnoi svodkoi No. 329," 67.

14. For details on this action, see K. E. Naumenko, *266-ia Artemovsko-Berlinskaia: Voenno-istoricheskii ocherk boevogo puti 266-i strelkovoi Artemovsko-Berlinskoi Krasnoznamennoi, Ordena Suvorova II stepeni divizii* [The 266th Artemovsk-Berlin: A military-historical study of the combat path of the 266th Red Banner and Order of Suvorov II Degree Rifle Division] (Moscow: Vownizdat, 1987), 6. Strangely enough, Rokossovsky emphasizes 1st Guards Army's offensive operations, seconded by 266th Rifle Division's history, while Samsonov speaks only of the army's defensive mission. The General Staff's daily summary splits the difference, noting only that 14th Guards Rifle Division attacked successfully but the other divisions remained in their current positions at day's end, probably because their attacks failed.

15. "Izvlechenie iz operativnoi svodkoi No. 329," 68.

16. For these and other movements, see Paulus's order, "Armeebefehl für die Weiterführung des Kampfes, Armee-Oberkommando 6, Abt.-Ia, A.H.Qu., 24.11.1942," in *Die Anlagenbänder zu den Kriegstagebüchern der 6. Armee*, book 2, 4.

17. Rolf Grams, *Die 14. Panzer-Division 1940–1945* (Eggolsheim, West Germany: Dörfler, in Nebek Verlag, GmbH, 1957), 57–58; Von Senger und Etterlin, *Die 24. Panzer-Division*, 130–132.

18. Pliev, *Pod gvardeiskim znamenem*, 133, citing archival document TsAMO, f. 335, op. 5113, d. 123, l. 22.

19. "Izvlechenie iz operativnoi svodkoi No. 329," 68.

20. Pliev, *Pod gvardeiskim znamenem*, 134.

21. "Izvlechenie iz operativnoi svodkoi No. 329," 68.

22. Batov, *V podkhodakh i boiakh*, 208.

23. Isaev, *Stalingrad*, 321.

24. Ibid., citing archival document TsAMO RF, f. 3414, op. 1, d. 25, l. 31.

25. Mark, *Island of Fire*, 282–283.

26. "Izvlechenie iz operativnoi svodkoi No. 329," 69.

27. For details on 94th Infantry Division's ordeal, see Adelbert Holl, *An Infantryman in Stalingrad: From 24 September 1942 to 2 February 1943* (Sydney, Australia: Leaping Horseman Books, 2005), 148–159. See Sixth Army's references to the incident in "Morgenmeldung LI. A.K. [no time indicated], A.O.K. 6, I.a, Datum 25.11.42," "Funkspruch an Heeresgruppe B, Morgenmeldung, 1006 Uhr, Armee-Oberkommando 6, Abt.-Ia, A, A.H.Qu., 25.11.1942," and "Zwischenmeldung, LI.

A.K. meldet 1745 Uhr, A.O.K. 6, I.a, Datum 25.11.42," in *Die Anlagenbänder zu den Kriegstagebüchern der 6. Armee*, book 2, 7–10.

28. Samsonov, *Stalingradskaia bitva*, 401.

29. Rokossovsky, *Velikaia pobeda na Volge*, 288.

30. "Izvlechenie iz operativnoi svodkoi No. 329," 70.

31. Indicative of 64th Army's stalled offensive, few Soviet or more recent Russian sources cover the army's operations from 24 to 30 November. Sixth Army's daily records in *Die Anlagenbänder zu den Kriegstagebüchern der 6. Armee*, book 2, 4–75, contain numerous entries regarding IV Army Corps' defensive efforts, all of which confirm 64th Army's complete lack of success.

32. "Izvlechenie iz operativnoi svodkoi No. 329," 70. Sixth Army's records speak only of an attack by two companies of Soviet infantry and 10 to 15 tanks against 29th Motorized Division's right wing. See "Morgenmeldung, IV. A.K., A.O.K. 6, I.a, 25.11.42," in *Die Anlagenbänder zu den Kriegstagebüchern der 6. Armee*, book 2, 6.

33. Ibid.

34. "Funkspruch an Heeresgrupe B, Morgenmeldung [no time indicated], Armee-Oberkommando 6, Abt.-Ia, A.H.Qu., 24.11.1942," ibid., 4.

35. Samuel J. Newland, *Cossacks in the German Army, 1941–1945* (London: Frank Cass, 1991), 105–107.

36. "Funkspruch an AOK 6 an 6. Armee, Führerentscheid, 0540 Uhr, Heeresgruppe B, O. Qu., 24.11.1942" and "Funkspruch an AOK. 6 an 6. Armee, Heeresgruppe B, Heeresgruppe Don (über Heeresgruppe B), OKH, Gen. Stab des Heeres, Op. Abt. (I S/B) Nr. 420964) vom 24.11.42, 1830 Uhr," in *Die Anlagenbänder zu den Kriegstagebüchern der 6. Armee*, book 2, 5–6. Citing the first Führer order (No. 420960), the second message (OKH Order No. 420964) demanded an answer as to why the North Front was withdrawn and said that Hitler categorically forbade any withdrawal from any front sector in the pocket.

37. "Izvlechenie iz operativnoi svodkoi No. 329," 70. See also Shein, *Neizvestnyi front*, 195–196, for an excellent description of 16th Motorized Division's defenses at Iashkul'.

38. See "Lagenkarte 16. I.D. (Mot), Stand: 25.11.42, 2200 [uhr]," in Fourth Panzer Army's Combat Journal.

39. "Izvlechenie iz operativnoi svodkoi No. 330," in *Stalingradskaia bitva*, book 2, 79; archival citation *TsAMO RF*, f. 16, op. 1072ss, d. 11, ll. 169–175.

40. "Izvlechenie iz operativnoi svodkoi No. 331," ibid., 87; archival citation, ibid., ll. 176–182.

41. "Izvlechenie iz operativnoi svodkoi No. 332," ibid., 98; archival citation, ibid., ll. 183–191.

42. Panov, *Na napravlenii glavnogo udara*, 31.

43. Pliev, *Pod gvardeiskim znamenem*, 133.

44. "Morgenmeldung, XI. A.K. [no time indicated], A.O.K. 6, Ia, 25.11.42," in *Die Anlagenbänder zu den Kriegstagebüchern der 6. Armee*, book 2, 8, confirmed this attack, stating, "16th Pz. Div.: Energetic attack by 80 Russians and 4 tanks on our position on Hill 169.2 early in the morning. The hill was lost. Heavy enemy vehicular movement between [reference points] S. 115 and S. 116 [northeastward from Malonabatovskii]. Heavy enemy artillery and rocket fire throughout the division's entire

sector. Expect an enemy attack with its focal point east of Hill 169.2. According to testimony from a prisoner, one strong division with tanks and strong artillery." Sixth Army's subsequent midday [*Zwischenmeldung*] and evening [*Tagesmeldung*] reports to Army Group B confirmed strong Soviet attacks against the Don bridgehead northwest of Luchenskii and Nymino Krasnojarskij (this should read Riumino Krasnoiarskii), 5 kilometers west of Sokarevka, by then calling the situation in the bridgehead a crisis. See *Die Anlagenbänder zu den Kriegstagebüchern der 6. Armee*, book 2, 10–11, 18.

45. "Izvlechenie iz operativnoi svodkoi No. 330," 80.

46. "Izvlechenie iz operativnoi svodkoi No. 331," 88.

47. Pliev, *Pod gvardeiskim znamenem*, 134.

48. This fighting is confirmed by Sixth Army's reports, including, "Zwischenmeldung, VIII. A.K. 1745 Uhr, A.O.K. 6, I.a Datum 26.11.42," which confirms the cavalry thrust into Peskovatka and its subsequent withdrawal; "Zwischenmeldung, XIV. Pz.K. 1810 Uhr, A.O.K. 6, I.a Datum 26.11.42"; and "Funkspruch an Heeresgruppe Don, Tagesmeldung, 2232 Uhr, Armee-Oberkommando 6, Abt.-Ia, A.H.Qu., 26.11.1943," in *Die Anlagenbänder zu den Kriegstagebüchern der 6. Armee*, book 2, 23–24, 27.

49. See Sixth Army's situation maps dated 2000 hours on 26 November 1942 and 2000 hours on 29 November 1942, in War Journal—Maps (KTB-Karten), November 1942–January 1943, AOK 6, 30155/37, NAM T-312, roll 1459. These maps display intelligence information as of several days earlier, including 6th Guards Cavalry Division's presence at the battle for Sokarevka. These maps imply that 6th Guards Cavalry Division reached Sokarevka either by following 5th Guards Cavalry across the Don River at Kartuli or by moving eastward across the Don somewhere farther south. In any event, 3rd Guards Cavalry Corps as a whole began to disengage from combat in the Sokarevka region the next day, when it received orders to move south and participate in efforts to capture Rychkovskii on the Don.

50. For the daily intelligence maps of Romanian Third Army's forces along the Chir River, which also show the names and composition of the various defending groups, see War Journal—Maps (KTB-Karten), November 1942–January 1943, AOK 6, 30155/37, NAM T-312, roll 1459. The structure and dispositions of these groups changed frequently and sometimes daily.

51. M. S. Dokuchaev, *V boi shli eskadrony: Boevoi put' 7-go gvardeiskogo ordena Lenina, Krasnoznamennogo, ordena Suvorova korpusa v Velikoi Otechestvennoi voine* [The squadrons went into battle: The combat path of the 7th Guards Order of Lenin, Red Banner, and Order of Suvorov (Cavalry) Corps in the Great Patriotic War] (Moscow: Voenizdat, 1984), 27.

52. Ibid., 26.

53. For additional details, see the account of 22nd Panzer's escape in Stoves, *Die 22. Panzer-Division*, 69–70.

54. Panov, *Na napravlenii glavnogo udara*, 32.

55. Kravchenko, *Nastupatel'naia operatsiia 5-i Tankovoi Armii*, 46.

56. Ibid. Presumably, the remaining 244 lost consisted of sick, self-maimed, or deserters.

57. Rolf-Dieter Müller, "Albert Speer und die Rüstenspolitik im totalen Krieg,"

in *Das Deutsches Reich und der Zweite Weltkrieg, Band 5, Zweiter Halbband* (Stuttgart: Militärgeschichlichen Forschungsamt, 1999), Farbtafel gegenüber 570.

58. See "Izvlechenie iz operativnoi svodkoi No. 330," 79; and Kravchenko, *Nastupatel'naia operatsiia 5-i Tankovoi Armii*, 46–47.

59. See annotations on "Lage 26.11.42, Skizza 3a, Anlage zu KTB I, Skizzen, Armee Abt. Hollidt," in 26624/5 file; a copy of the original.

60. "Izvlechenie iz operativnoi svodkoi No. 331," 88.

61. Ibid. See also Romanian Third Army's "Lage, 26.11.42," AOK 6, 30155/57, in NAM T-312, roll 1459, which shows both German and Romanian force dispositions and enemy action that day.

62. Axworthy et al., *Third Axis, Fourth Ally*, 100, claims that 1st Armored Division's 1st Armored Regiment had 9 Pz-III and Pz-IV and 19 R-2 tanks, 1st Motorized Artillery Regiment had 11 of its 12 100mm Skoda howitzers and 12 Schneider 105mm guns, and the AT Battalion had 2 75mm and 2 47mm guns. The division as a whole retained about 30 percent of its authorized strength. This was certainly enough to counter a Soviet cavalry division and rifle regiment.

63. "Izvlechenie iz operativnoi svodkoi No. 331," 88.

64. For a detailed account of 50th Guards (124th Rifle) Division's fighting along the Chir, see A. V. Tuzov, *V ogne voiny: Boevoi put' 50-i Gvardeiskoi dvazhdy Krasnoznamennoi ordena Suvorova i Kutuzova strelkovoi divizii* [In the flames of battle: The combat path of the 50th twice Red Banner and Orders of Suvorov and Kutuzov Rifle Division] (Moscow: Voenizdat, 1970), 65–67.

65. See annotations on "Lage 27.11.42, Skizza 4, Anlage zu KTB I, Skizzen, Armee Abt. Hollidt," in 26624/5 file; a copy of the original.

66. Ibid.

67. See Romanian Third Army's "Lage, 27.11.42," AOK 6, 30155/57, in NAM T-312, roll 1459, which shows both German and Romanian force dispositions and enemy action on 27 November.

68. "Izvlechenie iz operativnoi svodkoi No. 332," in *Stalingradskaia bitva*, Book 2, 99.

69. "Lage, 27.11.42," AOK 6, 30155/57, in NAM T-312, roll 1459.

70. Ibid.

71. Ibid. The entry for 21st Cavalry Division simply states, "Received no information about the positions of 21st Cavalry Division."

72. "Lage, 27.11.42," AOK 6, 30155/57, in NAM T-312, roll 1459.

73. Ibid.

74. The General Staff had officially reprimanded Tolstov for his division's poor performance during the fighting in the Bol'shaia Donshchinka region several days before.

75. Axworthy et al., *Third Axis, Fourth Ally*, 100.

76. Morozov, *Velikaia Otechestvennaia voiny 1941–1945*, 495–496. Although 1st Guards Army's ration strength was 142,869 men, Vasilevsky was reserving the bulk of the army and its tanks for Operation Saturn.

77. Naumenko, *266-ia Artemovsko-Berlinskaia*, 7.

78. Ibid., 8.

79. "Izvlechenie iz operativnoi svodkoi No. 332," 99.

80. See extract from "Combat Order No. 0010, Headquarters, 5th TA, on 26 November 1942," in *Boevye prikazy 1 Tankovoi korpusa* (1942) [Combat orders of 1st Tank Corps (1942)]; archival citation *TsAMO MO RF*, f. 3398, op. 1, d.3, l. 37. A copy of the original, this directive was signed by the commander of 5th Tank Army, Lieutenant General Romanenko; the army's member of the Military Council, Division Commissar Tumanian; and the chief of staff of 5th Tank Army, Major General Danilov.

81. These five regiments were 131st and 132nd Regiments; 376th Infantry Division's 767th Regiment, fighting under 44th Infantry Division's control; and 384th Infantry Division's 534th and 535th Regiments. However, 767th Regiment crossed to the Don's south bank in the morning.

82. "Izvlechenie iz operativnoi svodkoi No. 330," 80. See an account of 24th Rifle Division's role in the fighting in I. N. Pavlov, *Legendarnaia Zheleznaia: Boevoi put' motostrelkovoi Samaro-Ul'ianovskoi, Bedichevskoi, Zheleznoi ordena Oktiabr'skoi Revolutsii, trizhdy Krasnoznamennoi, ordena Suvorova i Bogdana Khmel'nitskogo divizii* [The legendary iron: The combat path of the Samara-Ul'ianovsk and Berdichev, Order of the October Revolution, thrice Red Banner, and Orders of Suvorov and Bogdan Khmel'nitsky Iron Motorized Rifle Division] (Moscow: Voenizdat, 1987), 106–107.

83. Batov, *V pokhodakh i boiakh*, 208–209.

84. "Izvlechenie iz operativnoi svodkoi No. 330," 80.

85. "Izvlechenie iz operativnoi svodkoi No. 331," 89.

86. Antony Beevor, *Stalingrad: The Fateful Siege:1942–1943* (New York: Viking, 1998), 261–262. Following in the footsteps of William Craig's classic *Enemy at the Gates: The Battle for Stalingrad* (New York: E. P. Dutton, 1973), Beevor's book provides an excellent overview based largely on the recollections of soldiers from both sides.

87. "Funkspruch an Heeresgruppe Don, Tagesmeldung, Armee-Oberkommando 6, Abt.-Ia, A.H.Qu., 26.11.1942, 22.32 Uhr," in *Die Anlagenbänder zu den Kriegstagebüchern der 6. Armee*, book 2, 27.

88. Batov, *V pokhodakh i boiakh*, 210.

89. "Izvlechenie iz operativnoi svodkoi No. 332," 99.

90. "Funkspruch an Heeresgruppe Don, Tagesmeldung, Armee-Oberkommando 6, Abt.-Ia, A.H.Qu., 27 November 1942," in *Die Anlagenbänder zu den Kriegstagebüchern der 6. Armee*, book 2, 32.

91. Ibid.

92. "Gr. Heitz, meldet 16.35 Uhr, Zwischenmeldung, A.O.K. 6, I.a, Datum 27.11.42," ibid., 33.

93. For the strength of Group Sikenius, see "IV. A.K., meldet 21.20 Uhr, A.O.K. 6, I.a, Datum 27.11.42," ibid., 39.

94. "KR-Fernschreiben an Heeresgruppe B, nachr.: Fernschrb. and Stab Don usw., 2155 Uhr, Armee-Oberkommando 6, Abt.-Ia, A.H.Qu., 20.11.1942," in *Die Anlagenbänder zu den Kriegstagebüchern der 6. Armee*, book 1, 315.

95. Isaev, *Stalingrad*, 320–321.

96. "Izvlechenie iz operativnoi svodkoi Nos. 330, 331, 332," 80, 89, 99.

97. Isaev, *Stalingrad*, 321.

98. "Izvlechenie iz operativnoi svodkoi No. 330," 80.

99. Holl, *An Infantryman in Stalingrad,* 151. See the original German, "Zwischenmeldung LI. A.K. meldet 1745 Uhr, A.O.K. 6, I.a, Datum 25.11.42," in *Die Anlagenbänder zu den Kriegstagebüchern der 6. Armee,* book 2, 9–10.

100. Holl, *An Infantryman in Stalingrad,* 151; "Morgenmeldung, LI. A.K. 0700 Uhr, A.O.K. 6, I.a, Datum 26.11.42," in *Die Anlagenbänder zu den Kriegstagebüchern der 6. Armee,* book 2, 19. The 24th Panzer Division's Group Scheele consisted of 2nd Battalion, 26th Panzer Grenadier Regiment, and 4th Motorcycle Battalion. It was led by Colonel von Scheele, commander of 26th Panzer-Grenadier Regiment. For details about its operations, see Von Senger und Etterlin, *Die-24. Panzer-Division,* 136–137.

101. "Izvlechenie iz operativnoi svodkoi Nos. 331, 332," 89, 99–100.

102. For details on 24th Panzer Division's march to Orlovka and subsequent fighting in the region, see Von Senger und Etterlin, *Die 24. Panzer-Division,* 137.

103. Sixth Army's records indicate that Lenski's division suffered at least 76 and probably as many as 100 casualties in the fighting on 27 and 28 November.

104. "Izvlechenie iz operativnoi svodkoi Nos. 330, 331, 332," 81, 89, 100.

105. "Morgenmeldung, Armee-Oberkommando 6, Abt.-Ia, A.H.Qu, 28.11.42," in *Die Anlagenbänder zu den Kirigstagebüchern der 6. Armee,* book 2, 43. Later reports from IV Army Corps corrected the initial report by adding Peschanka as one of the objectives.

106. Samsonov, *Ot Volgi do Baltiki,* 64, states that 4th Mechanized Corps became operationally subordinate to 57th Army beginning on 25 November. The General Staff's daily operational summaries include 4th Mechanized Corps in 51st Army through 0800 hours on 27 November; their first mention of the corps' subordination to 57th Army was at 0800 hours on the 28th.

107. "Izvlechenie iz operativnoi svodkoi Nos. 330, 331, 332," 81, 89, 100.

108. "Morgenmeldung IV. A. K. meldet 28.11.05.00 Uhr an A.O.K. 6/Ia.," in *Die Anlagenbänder zu den Kriegstagebüchern der 6. Armee,* book 2, 41. The 29th Motorized Division's 15 tanks consisted of 2 Pz-II, 2 Pz-III long, 5 Pz-III short, 2 Pz-IV long, 3 Pz-IV short, and 1 command tank.

109. V. P. Kachur and V. V. Nikol'skii, *Pod znamenem Sivashtsev: Boevoi put' 169-i strelkovoi Rogachevskoi Krasnoznamennoi ordena Suvorova II stepeni i Kutuzova II stepeni divizii (1941–1945)* [Under the name Sivash. The combat path of the 169th Rogachev, Red Banner, and Orders of Suvorov II Degree and Kutuzov II Degree Rifle Division (1941–1945)] (Moscow: Voenizdat, 1989), 80.

110. "Zwischenmeldung, 1800 Uhr, Armee-Oberkommando 6, Abt.-Ia, A.H.Qu., 25.11.1942," in *Die Anlagenbänder zu den Kriegstagebüchern der 6. Armee,* book 2, 11.

111. Samsonov, *Ot Volgi do Baltiki,* 65–67. Samsonov asserts that Liapichev was defended by a small German force occupying bunkers and dugouts, with a significant number of heavy weapons, and that it took several hours of fighting for Sinkevich's forces to overcome those defenses. In addition, Romanian Third Army's daily intelligence map for 26 November shows a Soviet tank force of undetermined strength attacking its defenses on the eastern bank of the Don River north of Logovskii and notes that, before retreating, the defenders destroyed four Russian tanks. However, the railroad bridge actually crossed the Don 4 kilometers north of Logovskii and about 7 kilometers south of Liapichev.

112. Ibid., 67–68, describes the assault on Logovskii in considerable detail and states that the defenders of the bridgehead (Group Tzschöckel) consisted of railroad troops and soldiers from a pontoon bridge unit, supported by a few tanks and artillery pieces. The assault force that penetrated the group's defenses was made up of three rifle companies, two platoons of antitank riflemen, a company of submachine gunners, and 158th Regiment's tanks, supported by two artillery batteries. After Sinkevich perished, he was succeeded as commander of the tank regiment by Major Brizhinev. Interestingly, Romanian Third Army's situation map for 26 November shows Group Tzschöckel's forces conducting a planned withdrawal from the Logovskii bridgehead overnight on 26–27 November. Thus, 60th Brigade's assault likely engaged German rear guards rather than Tzschöckel's entire force. See Romanian Third Army's daily maps for this period, which basically confirm Samsonov's account, in "Lage, 25–27.11.42," AOK 6, 30155/57, in NAM T-312, roll 1459.

113. Sarkis'ian, *51-ia Armiia*, 105.

114. See ibid., 105–106, for details of 4th Cavalry Corps' advance.

115. "Izvlechenie iz operativnoi svodkoi No. 330," 81. Sarkis'ian, *51-ia Armiia*, 105, states that during the fighting in Sharnutovskii, 61st Cavalry Division was commanded by Major General Ia. Kuliev; other sources list Colonel Stavenko as its commander. Sarkis'ian characterizes German efforts at Sharnutovskii as "fierce resistance" that inflicted "heavy losses" on Stavenko's division. Axworthy et al., *Third Axis, Fourth Ally*, 104, claims that Pannwitz's and Korne's forces captured more than 500 prisoners, 10 antitank guns, and a complete field artillery battery. If this is true, 61st Cavalry Division lost much of its combat effectiveness in the battle.

116. See "Izvlechenie iz operativnoi svodkoi No. 330."

117. See the daily maps in Fourth Panzer Army, "Lagenkarten zum KTB. Nr. 5 (Teil IV.), PzAOK 4, Ia, 21 Nov Dec 1942. PzAOK. 4," 28183/13 file, in NAM T-313, roll 359, for Axis dispositions along the Kotel'nikovo axis during this complex fighting.

118. Axworthy et al., *Third Axis, Fourth Ally*, 105.

119. "Izvlechenie iz operativnoi svodkoi No. 332," 100.

120. Sarkis'ian, *51-ia Armiia*, 105–106.

121. For 6th Panzer Division's role in the defense of Kotel'nikovo, see Wolfgang Paul, *Brennpunkte: Die Geschichte der 6. Panzerdivision (1. leichte) 1937–1945* (Osnabrück: Biblio Verlag, 1984), 232–233.

122. Mark, *Island of Fire*, 286, citing LI Army Corps' Order No. 119.

123. Ibid., 290–291, citing LI Army Corps' Order No. 120. This order was extracted from a far longer message Seydlitz dispatched to Paulus the same day. For the full text of this message, see "Geheime Kommandosache, An den Herrn Oberbefehlshaber der 6. Armee, Der Kommandierende General des LI. A.K. Nr. 603/42 g. Kdos, O.U., den 25.11.1942," in *Die Anlagenbänder zu den Kriegstagebüchern der 6. Armee*, book 2, 12–16.

124. Mark, *Island of Fire*, 297–298. For the full text of this message, see "Versorgungslage des LI. A.K. Stand 23.11. abends, Anlage zu 603/42 g. Kdos," in *Die Anlagenbänder zu den Kriegstagebüchern der 6. Armee*, book 2, 16–17.

125. See the full text of this Führer directive in "Armee-Oberkommando 6, Abt.-Ia, A.H.Qu., 27 November 1942," in *Die Anlagenbänder zu den Kriegstagebüchern der*

6. Armee, book 2, 30. This was forwarded by the OKH under the rubric OKH/GenStdH /Op.Abt. (Is/b) Nr. 48/42g. Kdoes.

126. Shein, *Neizvestnyi front*, 202–205.

127. Ibid., 201.

128. Ibid., 205.

129. "Izvlechenie iz operativnoi svodkoi No. 331," 89.

130. "Direktiva Stavki VGK No. 170694 komanduiushchim voiskami Iugo-zapadnogo i Donskogo frontov o perepodchinenii 21-i Armii" [*Stavka* VGK Directive No. 170694 to the commanders of the forces of the Southwestern and Don Fronts about the resubordination of 21st Army], in Zolotarev, "*Stavka* 1942," 453; archival citation *TsAMO MD RF*, f. 148a, op. 3763, d. 124, l. 299.

Chapter 8. Reducing the Stalingrad Pocket, the Outer Encirclement Front, and Plan Saturn, 28–30 November

1. Vasilevsky, *Delo vsei zhizni*, 230–231.

2. Direktiva Stavki VGK No. 170695 komanduiushchim voiskami Donskogo i Stalingradskogo frontov o koordinatsii deistvii frontov [*Stavka* VGK Directive No. 170695 to the commanders of the forces of the Don and Stalingrad Fronts about the coordination of the operations of the *fronts*], in Zolotarev, "*Stavka* 1942," 457; archival citation *TsAMO MD RF*, f. 132a, op. 2642, d. 13, l. 140.

3. "Iz direktivy Voennogo Soveta Iugo-Zapadnogo fronta zamestiteliu komanduiushchego general-leitenantu Kuznetsovu" [From a directive of the Military Council of the Southwestern Front to the deputy commander, Lieutenant General Kuznetsov], in *Razgrom Italo-Nemetskikh voisk na Donu (Dekabr' 1942 r.): Kratkii operativno-takticheskii ocherk* [The destruction of Italian-German forces on the Don (December 1942): A brief operational-tactical summary] (Moscow: Voenizdat, 1945), 115–116; classified secret and prepared by the Military-Historical Department of the Red Army General Staff.

4. "Prikaz Stavki VGK No. 0912 o naznachenii komanduiushchego 2-i Gvardeiskoi Armii i zamestitelia komanduiushchego voiskami Voronezhskogo fronta" [*Stavka* VGK Order No. 0912 about the appointment of the commander of 2nd Guards Army and the deputy commander of the forces of the Voronezh Front], in Zolotarev, "*Stavka* 1942," 458; archival citation *TsAMO*, 148a, op. 3763, d. 126, l. 197.

5. "Izvlechenie iz operativnoi svodkoi No. 333," in *Stalingradskaia bitva*, book 2, 106–109; archival citation *TsAMO RF*, f. 16, op. 1072ss, d. 11, ll. 192–205.

6. "Izvlechenie iz operativnoi svodkoi No. 334," ibid., 113–116; archival citation ibid., ll. 206–215.

7. "Izvlechenie iz operativnoi svodkoi No. 335," ibid., 120–123; archival citation *TsAMO RF*, f. 16, op. 1072ss, d. 12, ll. 1–9.

8. Naumenko, *266-ia Artemovsko-Berlinskaia*, 8–9. Naumenko records that 266th Rifle Division's 1010th Regiment lost 40 percent of its personnel and most of its artillery during the German counterattack on 26–27 November. However, Naumenko fails to mention which type of Junker aircraft conducted the strikes.

9. Ibid., 9.

10. Axworthy et al., *Third Axis, Fourth Ally*, 100.

11. Vitalii Belokon' and Il'ia Moshchansky, *Na flangakh Stalingrada: Operatsii na Srednem i Verkhnem Donu, 17 iiulia 1942–2 fevralia 1943 goda* [On the flanks of Stalingrad: Operations on the Middle and Upper Don, 17 July 1942–2 February 1943] (Moscow: PKV, 2002), 52.

12. "Lage am 28.11.42, Anlagen zu K.T.B. I, Armee Abt. Hollidt," 26624/6 file, in NAM T-312, roll 1452.

13. Stoves, *Die 22. Panzer-Division*, 72, indicates that *Kampfgruppe* Oppeln consisted of part of 204th Panzer Regiment; 2nd Battalion, 129th Panzer-Grenadier Regiment; and a platoon of 15cm "assault panzer" self-propelled infantry guns. These "assault panzers" were likely 12 StuIG 33B infantry assault guns, which were constructed on the chassis of the StuG III and dispatched to Stalingrad but were "lost" to 22nd Panzer Division. These should not be confused with the assault panzer [*Sturmpanzer*] IV "Brummbär," which entered operational service in 1943.

14. Axworthy et al., *Third Axis, Fourth Ally*, 100.

15. Track the forward deployment of 336th Infantry Division in "Lagenkarten, Anlagen zu K.T.B. I, Armee Abt. Hollidt," 26624/6 file, in NAM T-312, roll 1452.

16. The only Soviet accounts of this fighting appear in the Red Army General Staff's daily operational summaries for 29 November and 1 December, "Izvlechenie iz operativnoi svodkoi Nos. 334 and 335," in *Stalingradskaia bitva*, book 2, 114, 121. The daily dispositions and intelligence assessments of Romanian Third Army's defenses along the Chir River, including the multitude of groups and subgroups subordinate to it, are found in "Anlage zu KTB 1, Armee Abteilung Hollidt, Lagenkarten" [Appendix to War Journal 1, Armee Abteilung Hollidt, Situation Maps], December 1942, AOK 6, 22624/6, in NAM T-312, roll 1452. The subgroups subordinate to Group Adam, arrayed from left to right in the 10-kilometer-wide sector from Blizhne-Mel'nichnii and Kul'pinskii on the Chir River, 18 to 22 kilometers southeast of Surovikino, eastward to Verkhne-Chirskii, were subgroups Daiber, Kolb, Plog, Gluch, and Jakel; each was the size of a small battalion and named after its commander. Groups Goebel and Mikosch defended Verkhne-Chirskii, and Group Tzschöckel defended Rychkovskii and the nearby bridgehead across the Don River. All remained subordinate to Group Stumpfeld until XXXXVIII Panzer Corps moved its headquarters to Nizhne-Chirskaia on 4 December. Major General Hans Cramer succeeded General Heim as commander of XXXXVIII Panzer Corps late on 19 November and commanded the corps until he was replaced by General of Panzer Troops Otto von Knobelsdorff on 4 December. However, Major General Heinrich Eberbach led the corps temporarily on 28–29 November.

17. N. Z. Kadyrov, *Ot Minska do Veny: Boevoi put' 4-i Gvardeiskoi strelkovoi Apostolovsko-Venskoi Krasnoznamennoi divizii* [From Minsk to Vienna: The combat path of 4th Guards Apostolova-Vienna Red Banner Rifle Division] (Moscow: Voenizdat, 1985), 4.

18. See "Izvlechenie iz operativnoi svodkoi Nos. 334 and 335," 114, 121, for a summary of all of 5th Tank Army's operations on 29 and 30 November.

19. "Stand v. 30.11.42, Lagenkarten, Anlagen zu K.T.B. I, Armee Abt. Hollidt," 26624/6 file, in NAM T-312, roll 1452.

20. Ibid.

21. Ibid.

22. "Izvlechenie iz operativnoi svodkoi No. 335," 121.

23. The progress of the fighting north of Chernyshevskaia is shown on Attack Group Hollidt's daily maps for 30 November and 1 December 1942.

24. For Romanian Third Army's daily dispositions in this and other actions along the Chir, see "Lagenkarten, Anlagen zu K.T.B. I, Armee Abt. Hollidt," 26624/6 file, in NAM T-312, roll 1452.

25. Axworthy et al., *Third Axis, Fourth Ally*, 100.

26. For details on 22nd Panzer Division's operations from 28–30 November, see Stoves, *Die 22. Panzer-Division*, 76–77.

27. Rokossovsky, *Soldatskii dolg*, 204.

28. See "A.O.K. 6/I.a, Zwischenmeldung 28.11.1942 XIV. Pz. K, 1755 Uhr" and "A.O.K. 6/I.a, Zwischenmeldung 30.11.1942 XIV. Pz. K, 1740 Uhr," in *Die Anlagenbänder zu den Kriegstagebüchern der 6. Armee*, book 2, 47, 72.

29. "A.O.K. 6/I.a, Tagesmeldung 30.11.1942 XIV. Pz. K. 2010 Uhr," ibid., 74.

30. Batov, *V boiakh i pokhodakh*, 212–214.

31. "Tagesmeldung, XI. A.K. [no time indicated], A.O.K. 6, Abt. I.a, Datum 29.11.42," in *Die Anlagenbänder zu den Kriegstagebüchern der 6. Armee*, book 2, 60.

32. Four principal sources exist that describe in varying detail the operations in 66th Army's sector: General von Senger und Etterlin's excellent history of 24th Panzer Division; the newly reconstructed and released records of Sixth Army, which frequently mention the fighting in the Orlovka sector; the recently released Red Army General Staff's operational summaries for the period; and the recently published memoirs of Adelbert Holl, an infantryman who served in German 94th Infantry Division.

33. "Izvlechenie iz operativnoi svodkoi No. 333, 0800 hours, 29 November 1942," in *Stalingradskaia bitva*, book 2, 108.

34. The daily maps are found in Holl, *An Infantryman in Stalingrad*, 154–157, and "Lage 28.11.42, KTB-Karten, Nov 1942–Jan 1943, AOK 6," 30155/37 file, in NAM T-312, roll 1459.

35. Holl, *An Infantryman in Stalingrad*, 154; "Funkspruch an Heeresgruppe Don, 2. Morgenmeldung, Armee-Oberkommando 6, Abt.-Ia, A.H.Qu., 28.11.1942," in *Die Anlagenbänder zu den Kriegstagebüchern der 6. Armee*, book 2, 43.

36. Holl, *An Infantryman in Stalingrad*, 155; "Zwischenmeldung, LI. A.K., 1805 Uhr, A.O.K. 6, I.a, Datum 28.11.42," in *Die Anlagenbänder zu den Kriegstagebüchern der 6. Armee*, book 2, 47.

37. Holl, *An Infantryman in Stalingrad*, 156–157. As an interesting side note, this report also stated that Romanian 1st Cavalry Division and Group Voicu, a total of 3,000 men, were now subordinate to LI Army Corps. See "Tagesmeldung, LI. A.K., meldet [no time indicated], A.O.K 6, I.a, Datum 28.11.42," in *Die Anlagenbänder zu den Kriegstagebüchern der 6. Armee*, book 2, 49. A report issued the next day showed that 24th Panzer Division had 14 tanks—1 Pz-II, 5 Pz-III short, 2 Pz-III long, 3 Pz-IV short, 2 Pz-IV long, and 1 command tank—and suffered 74 losses on 28 November (6 killed and 68 wounded). See "Morgenmeldung, LI. A.K., 0630 Uhr, A.O.K. 6, I.a, Datum 29.11.42," ibid., 54–55.

38. "Izvlechenie iz operativnoi svodkoi No. 334, 0800 hours, 30 November 1942," in *Stalingradskaia bitva*, book 2, 115.

39. Holl, *An Infantryman in Stalingrad*, 157; "Zwischenmeldung, LI. A.K.

meldet 1730 Uhr, A.O.K. 6, I.a, Datum 29.11.42," in *Die Anlagenbänder zu den Kriegstagebüchern der 6. Armee*, book 2, 58.

40. "Izvlechenie iz operativnoi svodkoi No. 335, 0800 hours, 1 December 1942," in *Stalingradskaia bitva*, book 2, 122.

41. "Morgenmeldung, LI. A.K., 0600 Uhr, A.O.K. 6, I.a, Datum 30.11.42," in *Die Anlagenbänder zu den Kriegstagebüchern der 6. Armee*, book 2, 64; Holl, *An Infantryman in Stalingrad*, 157.

42. Belov, *Ot Volgi do Pragi*, 45.

43. "Izvlechenie iz operativnoi svodkoi No. 333," 108.

44. Belov, *Ot Volgi do Pragi*, 45–46.

45. "Funkspruch an Heeresgruppe Don, 2. Morgenmeldung, Armee-Oberkommando 6, Abt.-Ia, A.H.Qu., 28.11.42," in *Die Anlagenbänder zu den Kriegstagebüchern der 6. Armee*, book 2, 43.

46. "Zwischenmeldung IV. A. K. meldet 1650 Uhr, A.O.K. 6, I.a, Datum 28.11.42," ibid., 46–47.

47. "Tagesmeldung, IV A.K. 22.00 Uhr, A.O.K 6, I.a, Datum 28.11.42," ibid., 50–51. The 29th Motorized Division's 39 tanks consisted of the following: 6 Pz-II, 15 Pz-III long, 5 Pz-III short, 12 Pz-IV long, and 1 Pz-IV command tank. The 14th Panzer Division's 9 tanks were 7 Pz-III, 1 Pz-IV long, and 1 Pz-III short models.

48. "Funkspruch an Heeresgruppe Don, Armee-Oberkommando 6, Abt.-Ia, A.H.Qu., 29.11.42," ibid., 56.

49. "Tagesmeldung IV A.K. 21.50 Uhr, A.O.K 6, I.a, 29.11.42," ibid., 62. The 29th Motorized Division's 36 tanks consisted of the following: 6 Pz-II, 13 Pz-III long, 5 Pz-III short, 11 Pz-IV, and 1 Pz- IV command tank.

50. "K.T.B. 29.XI, KTB-Karten, Nov 1942–Jan 1943," AOK 6, 30155/37 file, in NAM T-312, roll 1459.

51. "Tagesmeldung XIV. Pz. K. 2215 Uhr, A.O.K. 6, I.a, Datum 29.11.1942," in *Die Anlagenbänder zu den Kriegstagebüchern der 6. Armee*, book 2, 63. The 3rd Motorized Division's 28 tanks consisted of the following: 20 Pz-III long, 4 Pz-IV short, and 4 Pz-IV long models.

52. Erhard Raus, *Panzer Operations: The Eastern Front Memoir of General Raus, 1941–1945*, trans. Steven H. Newton (n.p.: Da Capo Press: 2003), 145.

53. Axworthy et al., *Third Axis, Fourth Ally*, 109.

54. Ibid.

55. "Tagesmeldung LI. A.K. [no time indicated], A.O.K. 6, I.a, Datum 28.11.42," in *Die Anlagenbänder zu den Kriegstagebüchern der 6. Armee*, book 2, 49.

56. "Morgenmeldung, LI. A.K., 0630 Uhr, A.O.K. 6, I.a, Datum 29.11.42," ibid., 53.

57. Mark, *Island of Fire*, 298.

58. "Opersvodka Nr. 303, 304, Boevoe donesenie Nr. 245" [Combat summaries No. 303 and 304 and combat report No. 245], dated 29 November 1942, in 62nd Army's Combat Journal for November 1942.

59. "Morgenmeldung, LI. A.K., 0600 Uhr, A.O.K. 6, I. a, Datum 30.11.42," in *Die Anlagenbänder zu den Kriegstagebüchern der 6. Armee*, book 2, 65.

60. "Boevoe donesenie 246" [Combat report No. 246], dated 30 November 1942, in 62nd Army's Combat Journal for November 1942.

61. Shein, *Neizvestnyi front*, 206–207.

62. Ibid., 207.

63. Ibid.

64. Lieutenant General Herman Plocher and Harry R. Fletcher, eds., *The German Air Force versus Russia, 1942*, USAF Historical Studies No. 154 (USAF Historical Division, Aerospace Studies Institute, Air University, June 1966), 252, quoting an entry in the Richthofen diary for 19 November 1942, 369.

65. Hayward, *Stopped at Stalingrad*, 229.

66. Ibid. This translation leaves out the bracketed words "from Asia and Outer Mongolia," apparently because of their racial overtones. These words are found in a translation of Rudel's remarks in an older study by Plocher and Fletcher, *The German Air Force versus Russia, 1942*, 253–254, which also claims that VIII Air Corps and Romanian pilots flew 150 sorties on 19 November.

67. S. I. Rudenko et al., eds., *Sovetskie voenno-vozdushnye sily v Velikoi Otechestvennoi voine, 1941–1945 gg.* [The Soviet Air Force in the Great Patriotic War, 1941–1945] (Moscow: Voenizdat, 1968), 139. This source states that 8th Air Army conducted 340 sorties from 20 through 23 November, significantly fewer than the 438 sorties claimed by 8th Air Army's history.

68. Ibid., 99.

69. N. M. Skomorokhov et al., eds., *17-ia Vozdushnaia Armiia v boiakh ot Stalingrada do Veny: Voenno-istoricheskii ocherk a boevom puti 17-i Vozdushnoi Armii v gody Velikoi Otechestvennoi voiny* [The 17th Air Army in combat from Stalingrad to Vienna: A historical survey of the combat path of 17th Air Army in the Great Patriotic War] (Moscow: Voenizdat, 1977), 14.

70. B. A. Gubin and V. A. Kiselev, *Vos'maia Vozdushnaia: Voenno-istoricheskii ocherk boevogo puti 8-i Vozdushnoi Armii v gody Velikoi Otechestvennoi voiny* [The 8th Air: A historical survey of the combat path of 8th Air Army in the Great Patriotic War] (Moscow: Voenizdat, 1986), 98.

71. Dokuchaev, *V boi shli eskadrony*, 28.

72. M. N. Kozhevnikov, *Komandovanie i shtab VVS Sovetskoi Armii v Velikoi Otechestvennoi voine 1941–1945 gg.* [The commands and headquarters of the Air Force of the Soviet Army in the Great Patriotic War 1941–1945] (Moscow: Nauka, 1977), 110.

73. Ibid.

74. Hayward, *Stopped at Stalingrad*, 254. In his diary, General Richthofen cites a higher figure of 400 sorties, but this does not alter the Soviets' favorable ratio.

75. Alarm forces were variously sized units consisting of German or indigenous volunteers that were hastily assembled in cities and towns.

76. "Funkspruch an Heeresgruppe Don, Tagesmeldung, Armee-Oberkommando 6, Abt.-Ia, A.H.Qu., 27 November 1942," in *Die Anlagenbänder zu den Kriegstagebüchern der 6. Armee*, book 2, 32. This order also placed 384th Infantry and 14th Panzer Divisions in Sixth Army's reserve.

77. Sixth Army's 2 December order actually called the Southwest Front (from Kazachii through Marinovka to Karpovka) the Southeast Front, probably due to a typographical error.

78. Virtually all Soviet and Russian sources claim that the *Stavka* underestimated the size of the forces that would be encircled, blaming the error on faulty Soviet intelligence assessments. Thus, according to Rokossovsky, *Velikaia pobeda na Volge*, 289, the *Stavka* estimated that 80,000 to 90,000 enemy would be encircled, but the actual total was about 330,000 men. Citing Vasilevsky's postwar memoirs, Samsonov, *Stalingradskaia bitva*, 398, 423, asserts that Soviet planners estimated that 85,000 to 90,000 men would be encircled, but more than 300,000 men ultimately found their way into the encirclement pocket. Isaev, *Stalingrad*, 289, 341, cites both Vasilevsky's figures and the erroneous intelligence reports and concludes that 284,000 German and Romanian troops were encircled, all of them ending up under Sixth Army's control.

79. Zolotarev, *VOV*, 2:71.

80. Ibid.

Selected Bibliography

Abbreviations

BA-MA	*Bundesarchiv Miltärarchiv* (German Military Archives)
JSMS	*Journal of Slavic Military Studies*
NAM	National Archives Microfilm
TsAMO	*Tsentral'nyi arkhiv Ministerstva Oborony* [Central Archives of the Ministry of Defense]
TsPA UML	*Tsentral'nyi partiinyi arkhiv Instituta Marksizma-Leninizma* [Central Party Archives of the Institute of Marxism and Leninism]
VIZh	*Voenno-istoricheskii zhurnal* [Military-historical journal]
VVI	*Vestnik voennoi informatsii* [Herald of military information]
VV	*Voennyi vestnik* [Military herald]

Primary Sources

German Combat Journals [*Kriegstagebuch*]

Army Detachment Fretter-Pico. *Kriegstagebuch Nr. 1, Armee-Abteilung Fretter-Pico, 18.12. 1942–2.2. 1943. BA-MA XXX A.K.* 31783/1 file. Copy of the original.

Army Detachment Hollidt. (*Anlagen zu K.T.B. 1, Armee Abteilung Hollidt, Skizzen, Nov 1942*), AOK 6, 26624/5 file. NAM series T-312, roll 1452.

———. *Anlagen zu K.T.B. 1, Armee Abteilung Hollidt, Lagekarten, Dez. 1942.* AOK 6, 22624/6 file. NAM series T-312, roll 1542.

———. *Anlagen zu K.T.B. 1., Armee Abt. Hollidt, Tagl. Meldungen, Teil A: 23–27.11.42, Teil B: 28.11–31.12.42. BA-MA RH* 20-6/249. Copy of the original.

———. *Kriegstagebuch Armee Abteilung Hollidt, 23.11.42 bis 27.12.42, Deutscher Generalstab bei 3. rum. Armee, 27.12.42 bis 31.12.42 Armeegruppe Hollidt. BA-MA RH* 20-6/246. Copy of the original.

Army Group Don. *Heeresgruppe Don Kriegstagebuch vom 22.12.42 -31.1.43, Anlagen Band 6.* NAM series T-311, roll 270.

———. *Kriegstagebuch Nr. 1, Oberkommando der Heeresgruppe Don/Süd, 20 November 1942–23 März 1943. BA-MA* [number illegible]. Copy of the original.

Fourth Panzer Army. *Lagenkarten zum KTB. Nr. 5 (Teil III.), PzAOK 4, Ia, 21 Oct–24 Nov 1942. PzAOK. 4.,* 28183/12 file. NAM series T-313, roll 359.

———. *Lagenkarten zum KTB. Nr. 5 (Teil IV.), PzAOK 4, Ia, 21 Nov–Dec 1942, PzAOK. 4,* 28183/13 file. NAM series T-313, roll 359.

Romanian Third Army. *Anlagen zu K.T.B 1, Armee Abt. Hollidt, Befehl und sonst. Anlagen, Teil A: 1–29 & Teil B: 30–143).* AOK 6/2624/2 file. NAM series T-312, roll 1452.

———. *Anlagen zu. K.T.B. 1, Armee Abt. Hollidt, Skizzen, Teil A: 1–5, Teil B: 6–26.* AOK 6/26624/5. NAM series T-312, roll 1452.

———. *Tatigkeitsbericht 5.–31. Dez. 1942, Ic, Rum. AOK. 3, der Chef des Deutschen Gen.-Stabes, dann Armeegruppe Hollidt, 1. Text, 2. Anlagen, 1-11 Feindlagenkarten, 3. Zwischen u. Tagesmeldungen.* AOK 6, 26624/7 and 26624/9 files. Activities Report, Romanian Third Army. NAM series T-312, roll 1452.

Sixth Army [*6. Armee*]. NAM series T-312, roll 1453.

———. *K.T.B.–AOK. 6, Ia., Karten, Nov 1942–Jan 1943.* AOK 6, 30155/37 file. NAM series T-312, roll 1459.

XXX Army Corps. *K.T.B. Gen. Kdo. XXX. A.K. vom 6.11.42–13.12.42.* 31296/1-2 file, *BA-MA* [number missing]. Copy of the original.

XXXXVIII Panzer Corps. *Generalkommando XXXXVIII. Pz. Korps., Lagenkarten, 16.11.1942–31.12.1942. BA-MA* RH 26775/6. Copy of the original.

———. *Kriegs-Tagebuch, Dezember 1942., Gen. Kdo. XXXXVIII. Panzer Korps. BA-MA* RH 26-776/3. Copy of the original.

11th Panzer Division. *K.T.B. 11th Panzer-Divizion.* Copy of the original.

22nd Panzer Division. *Kriegstagebuch Nr. 3 vom .12.42-5.3.43 d. 22. Pz. Division Ia. BA-MA* RH 27-22/15. Copy of the original.

———. *Kriegstagebuch Nr. 3 Anlagenband I der 22 Panzer Division vom 1.12.42–5.3.43. BA-MA* RH 27-22/16. Copy of the original.

———. *Kriegstagebuch Nr. 3 Anlagenband II der 22 Panzer Division vom 1.12.42–5.3.43. BA-MA* RH 27-22/17. Copy of the original.

62nd Infantry Division. *62. I.D., K.T.B. Nr. 7, Buch 2 vom 1.8.42 bis 28.2.43. BA-MA* RH 26-62/70. Copy of the original.

294th Infantry Division. *Anlagenband. 1, Kriegstagebuch Nr. 4, 294. I.D. vom 1.12.42–21.12.42, Nr. 1559–1683. BA-MA* 26-294/34. Copy of the original.

———. *Anlagenband. 2, Kriegstagebuch Nr. 4, 294. I.D. vom 22.12.42–14.1.43, Nr. 1685–1819. BA-MA* 26-294/35. Copy of the original.

Soviet Combat Journals [*Zhurnal boevykh deistvii*]

62nd Army, September–November 1942.

5th Shock Army (15 December 1942–31 March 1943). F. 333, op. 4885, d. 25, ed. khr. 24.

5th Tank Army (1942). F. 333, op. 5041, d. 130.

7th Tank Corps (25 August 1942–20 January 1943). F. 3401, op. 1, d. 8.

2nd Guards Mechanized Corps (1942–1943). F. 3426, op. 1, d. 6.

3rd Guards Mechanized Corps (December 1942). F. 3428, op. 1, ed. khr. 3.

7th Guards (8th) Cavalry Corps (1942–1943). F. 3475, op. 1, ed. khr. 12.

9th Guards (5th) Mechanized Corps (1942). F. 3443, op. 1, d. 11.

95th Rifle Division.

112th Rifle Division.

138th Rifle Division. *138-ia Krasnoznamennaia strelkovaia diviziia v boiakh za Stalingrada* [The 138th Red Banner Rifle Division in the battle for Stalingrad]

284th Rifle Division.

308th Rifle Division.

37th Guards Rifle Division.
39th Guards Rifle Division.
10th Rifle Brigade.
42nd Rifle Brigade.

German Sixth Army's Rediscovered Daily Records

Aufsess, Florian *Freiherr* von und zu. *Die Anlagenbänder zu den Kriegstagebüchern der 6. Armee vom 14.09.1942 bis 24.11.1942, Band I.* Schwabach: Januar, 2006.
————. *Die Anlagenbänder zu den Kriegstagebüchern der 6. Armee vom 24.11.1942 bis 24.12.1942, Band II.* Schwabach: Januar, 2006.
————. *Die Anlagenbänder zu den Kriegstagebüchern der 6. Armee vom 24.12.1942 bis 02.02.1943, Band III.* Schwabach: Januar, 2006.

Other Primary Sources

Boevoi sostav Sovetskoi armii, chast' 2 (Ianvar'–dekabr' 1942 goda) [Combat composition of the Soviet Army, part 2 (January–December 1942)]. Moscow: Voenizdat, 1966.
Boevoi sostav Sovetskoi armii, chast' 3 (Ianvar'–dekabr' 1943 goda) [Combat composition of the Soviet Army, part 3 (January–December 1943)]. Moscow: Voenizdat, 1972.
Dushen'kin, V. V., ed. *Vnutrennye voiska v Velikoi Otechestvennoi voine 1941–1945 gg.: Dokumenty i materially* [Internal troops in the Great Patriotic War 1941–1945: Documents and materials]. Moscow: Iuridicheskaia literatura, 1975.
GKO [State Defense Committee] Decrees. *TsPA UML*, f. 644, op. 1, d. 23, ll. 127–129, and f. 644, op. 1, d. 33, ll. 48–50.
"Ia, Lagenkarten Nr. 1 zum KTB Nr. 1, November 1942–January 1943." AOK 6, 30155/37. NAM series T-312, roll 1459.
Kommandovanie korpusnovo i divizionnogo svena Sovetskikh vooruzhennykh sil perioda Velikoi Otechestvennoi voiny 1941–1945 g. [Commanders at the corps and division level in the Soviet armed forces in the period of the Great Patriotic War, 1941–1945]. Moscow: Frunze Academy, 1964.
Kriegstagebuch der Oberkommandes der Wehrmacht/Wehrmachtfuhrungsstab: 1940–1945, Bd. II. Frankfurt, 1963.
Organy gosudarstvennoi bezopastnosti SSSR v Velikoi Otechestvennoi voine: Sbornik dokumentov, Tom chetvertyi, Kniga 1: Sekrety operatsii "Tsitadel'," 1 ianvaria-30 iiunia 1943 goda [Organs of state security of the USSR in the Great Patriotic War: A collection of documents, vol. 1, book 1: The secrets of operation "Citadel"]. Moscow: Izdatel'stvo Rus', 2008.
Pogranichnye voiska SSSR v Velikoi Otechestvennoi voine 1942–1945: Sbornik dokumentov i materialov [Border guards troops of the USSR in the Great Patriotic War 1942–1945: A collection of documents and materials]. Moscow: Nauka, 1976.
Sbornik materialov po izucheniiu opyta voiny, No. 6 (Aprel'–mai 1943 g.) [Collection of materials for the study of war experiences, no. 6 (April–May 1943)]. Moscow: Voenizdat, 1943. Originally classified secret.
Sbornik materialov po izucheniiu opyta voiny, No. 7 (Iun'–iul' 1943 g.) [Collection of materials for the study of war experiences, no. 7, (June–July 1943)]. Moscow: Voenizdat, 1943. Originally classified secret.

Sbornik materialov po izucheniiu opyta voiny, No. 8 (Avgust–oktiabr' 1943 g.) [Collection of materials for the study of war experiences, no. 8 (August–October 1943)]. Moscow: Voenizdat, 1943. Originally classified secret.

Sbornik materialov po izucheniiu opyta voiny, No. 9 (Noiabr'–dekabr' 1943 g.) [Collection of materials for the study of war experiences, no. 9 (November–December 1943)]. Moscow: Voenizdat, 1944. Originally classified secret.

Sbornik voenno-istoricheskikh materialov Velikoi Otechestvennoi voiny, Vypusk 18 [Collection of materials of the Great Patriotic War, issue 18]. Moscow: Voenizdat, 1960. Originally classified secret.

Stalingradskaia epopeia [Stalingrad epoch]. Moscow: Evonnitsa-MG, 2000. (A collection of NKVD documents.)

Zhilin, V. A., ed. *Stalingradskaia bitva: Khronika, fakty, liudi v 2 kn.* [The Battle of Stalingrad: Chronicles, facts, people in 2 books]. Moscow: OLMA, 2002.

Zolotarev, A. M., ed. "General'nyi shtab v gody Velikoi Otechestvennoi voiny: Dokumenty i materially, 1942 god" [The General Staff in the Great Patriotic War: Documents and materials, 1942]. In *Russki arkhiv: Velikaia Otechestvennaia [voina], 23 (12-2)* [The Russian archives: The Great Patriotic (War), vol. 23 (12-2)]. Moscow: Terra, 1999.

———. "General'nyi shtab v gody Velikoi Otechestvennoi voiny: Dokumenty i materially, 1943 god" [The General Staff in the Great Patriotic War: Documents and materials, 1943]. In *Russki arkhiv: Velikaia Otechestvennaia [voina], 23 (12-3)* [The Russian archives: The Great Patriotic (War), vol. 23 (12-3)]. Moscow: Terra, 1999.

———. "Preliudiia Kurskoi bitvy: Dokumenty i materialy 6 dekabria 1942 g.–25 aprelia 1943 g." [Prelude to the Battle of Kursk: Documents and materials 6 December 1942–25 April 1943]. In *Russkii arkhiv: Velikaia Otechestvennaia [voina], T. 15 (4-3)* [The Russian archives: The Great Patriotic (War), vol. 15 (4-3)]. Moscow: Terra, 1997.

———. "Prikazy narodnogo komissara oborony SSSR, 22 iiunia 1941 g.–1942" [Orders of the People's Commissariat of Defense of the USSR, 22 June 1941–1942]. In *Russkii arkhiv: Velikaia Otechestvennaia [voina], 13 (2-2)* [The Russian archives: The Great Patriotic (War), vol. 13 (2-2)]. Moscow: Terra, 1997.

———. "Prikazy narodnogo komissara oborony SSSR, 1943–1945 gg." [Orders of the People's Commissariat of Defense of the USSR, 1943–1945]. In *Russkii arkhiv: Velikaia Otechestvennaia [voina], 13 (2-3)* [The Russian archives: The Great Patriotic (War), vol. 13 (2-3)]. Moscow: Terra, 1997.

———. "Stavka VGK: Dokumenty i materialy 1942" [The *Stavka* VGK: Documents and materials, 1942]. In *Russkii arkhiv: Velikaia Otechestvennaia [voina], 16 (5-2)* [The Russian archives: The Great Patriotic (War), vol. 16 (5-2)]. Moscow: Terra, 1996.

———. "Stavka VGK: Dokumenty i materialy 1943" [The *Stavka* VGK: Documents and materials, 1943]. In *Russkii arkhiv: Velikaia Otechestvennaia [voina], 16 (5-2)* [The Russian archives: The Great Patriotic (War), vol. 16 (5-2)]. Moscow: Terra, 1999.

Secondary Sources

Books

Abrosimov, G. H., M. K. Kuz'min, L. A. Lebedev, and N. F. Poltorakov. *Gvardeiskii Nikolaevsko-Budapeshtskii: Boevoi put' 2-go gvardeiskogomekhanizirovannogo korpusa* [The guards Nikolaev-Budapest: The combat path of 2nd Guards Mechanized Corps]. Moscow: Voenizdat, 1976.

Adam, V. *Trudnoe reshenie: Memuary polkovnika 6th Germanskoi armii* [A difficult decision: The memoirs of a colonel in 6th German Army]. Moscow: Voenizdat, 1967. A translation of Wilhelm Adam. *Der schwere Entschluss*. East Berlin, 1965.

Afanas'ev, N. I. *Ot Volgi do Shpree: Boevoi put' 35-i gvardeiskoi strelkovoi Lozovskoi Krasnoznamennoi, ordena Suvorova i Bogdan Khmel'nitskogo divizii* [From the Volga to the Spree: The combat path of 35th Guard Lozovaia, Red Banner, and Orders of Suvorov and Bogdan Khmel'nitsky Rifle Division]. Moscow: Voenizdat, 1982.

Aganov, S. Kh., ed. *Inzhenernye voiska Soverskoi Armii 1918–1945* [Engineer forces of the Soviet army 1918–1945]. Moscow: Voenizdat, 1985.

Amirov, K. V. *Ot Volgi do Al'p: Boevoi put' 36-i gvardeiskoi strelkovoi Verkhnedneprovskoi Krasnoznamennoi, ordenov Suvorova i Kutuzova II stepeni divizii* [From the Volga to the Alps; The combat path of 36th Guards Upper Dnepr Red Banner and Orders of Suvorov and Kutuzov II Degree Rifle Division]. Moscow: Voenizdat, 1987.

Armstrong, Richard H. *Red Army Tank Commanders: The Armored Guards*. Atglen, PA: Schiffer Military/Aviation History, 1994.

Axworthy, Mark, Cornel Scafeș, and Cristian Craciunoiu. *Third Axis, Fourth Ally: The Romanian Armed Forces in the European War, 1941–1945*. London: Arms & Armour Press, 1995.

Babich, Iu P., and A. G. Baier. *Razvitie vooruzheniia i organitzatsii Sovetskikh sukhoputnykh voist v gody Velikoi Otechestvennoi voiny* [Development of the armament and organization of the Soviet ground forces in the Great Patriotic War]. Moscow: Frunze Academy, 1990.

Barnett, Correlli, ed. *Hitler's Generals*. New York: Grove Weidenfeld, 1989.

Bartov, Omar. *The Eastern Front, 1941–45: German Troops and the Barbarization of Warfare*. New York: St. Martin's Press, 1986.

Batov, P. I. *V pokhodakh i boiakh* [In marches and battles]. Moscow: Golos, 2000.

Beevor, Antony. *Stalingrad: The Fateful Siege: 1942–1943*. New York: Viking, 1998.

Bekker, Cajus. *The Luftwaffe War Diaries*. New York: Doubleday, 1968.

Belokon', Vitaliy, and Il'ia Moshchansky. "Na Flangakh Stalingrada: Operatsi na Srednem i Verkhnem Donu 17 iiulia 1942–2 fevralia 1943 goda" [On the flanks of Stalingrad: Operations on the middle and upper Don, 17 July 1942–2 February 1943]. In *Voennaia Letopis'* [Military chronicle]. Moscow: PKV, 2002.

Beshanov, V. V. *God 1942—"Uchebnyi"* [The year 1942—educational]. Minsk: Harvest, 2002.

Biriukov, N. I. *Trudnaia nauka pobezhdat'* [Hard science conquers]. Moscow: Voenizdat, 1975.

Bitva pod Stalingradom, chast' II: Kontranastuplenie Sovetskikh voisk [The battle at

Stalingrad, part II: The counteroffensive of Soviet forces]. Moscow: Voroshilov Academy of the General Staff, 1956. Originally classified secret.

Bitva za Stalingrad [The battle for Stalingrad]. Volgograd: Nizhne-Volzhskoe knizhnoe izdatel'stvo, 1973.

Blau, George E. *The German Campaign in Russia: Planning and Operations (1940–1942)*. Department of the Army Pamphlet No. 20-261a. Washington, DC: Department of the Army, 1955.

Boog, Horst, Jurden Forster, Joachim Hoffmann, et al. *Germany and the Second World War.* Vol. 4. *The Attack on the Soviet Union.* Trans. Dean S. McMurry, Ewald Osers, and Louise Wilmot. Oxford: Clarendon Press, 2001.

Boog, Horst, Werner Rahm, Reinhard Stumpf, and Bernd Wegner. *Germany and the Second World War.* Vol. 6. *The Global War: Widening of the Conflict into a World War and the Shift of the Initiative 1941–1943.* Trans. Ewald Osers et al. Oxford: Clarendon Press, 2001.

Bradley, Dermot, Karl-Friedrich Hildebrand, and Markus Rövekamp. *Die Generale des Heeres 1921–1945.* Osnabruk: Biblio Verlag, 1993.

Carell, Paul. *Stalingrad: The Defeat of the German 6th Army.* Trans. David Johnston. Atglen, PA: Schiffer Publishing, 1993.

Chernobaev, A. A., ed. *Na prieme u Stalina. Tetradi (zhurnaly) zapisei lits, priniatykh I. V. Stalinym (1924–1953gg.). Spravochnik* [Received by Stalin. The notebooks (journals) of entries of those persons admitted by I. V. Stalin (1924–1953)]. Moscow: Novyi khronograf, 2008.

Chistiakov, I. M. *Sluzhim otchizne* [In service to the Fatherland]. Moscow: Voenizdat, 1975.

———, ed. *Po prikazu Rodiny: boevoi put' 6-i gvardeiskoi armii v Velikoi Otechestvennoi voine* [By order of the Motherland: The combat path of 6th Guards Army in the Great Patriotic War]. Moscow: Voenizdat, 1971.

Chuikov, Vasili I. *The Battle for Stalingrad.* Trans. Harold Silver. New York: Holt, Rinehart & Winston, 1964.

———. *Ot Stalingrada do Berline* [From Stalingrad to Berlin]. Moscow: Voenizdat, 1980.

Concentration of Russian Troops for Stalingrad—Offensive. Historical Division, European Command, Study MS P-096, 1952.

Craig, William. *Enemy at the Gates: The Battle for Stalingrad.* New York: Reader's Digest Press, E. P. Dutton, 1973.

Daines, Vladimir. *Rokossovsky: Genii manevra* [Rokossovsky: A genius of maneuver]. Moscow: Iauza Eksmo, 2008.

Demin, V. A., and R. M. Portugal'sky. *Tanki vkhodiat v proryv* [Tanks enter the penetration]. Moscow: Voenizdat, 1988.

Dërr, G. *Pokhod na Stalingrad* [The approach to Stalingrad]. Moscow: Voenizdat, 1957. A translation of Hans von Dörr. *Der Feldzug nach Stalingrad: Versuch eines operativen Überblickes.* Darmstadt: E. S. Mittler und Sohn GmbH, 1955.

Dinardo, Richard L. *Germany and the Axis Powers: From Coalition to Collapse.* Lawrence: University Press of Kansas, 2005.

———. *Germany's Panzer Arm.* Westport, CT: Greenwood Press, 1997.

———. *Mechanized Juggernaut or Military Anachronism: Horses and the German Army of World War II.* Westport, CT: Greenwood Press, 1991.

Dokuchaev, M. S. *V boi shli eskadrony: Boevoi put' 7-go gvardeiskogo ordena Lenina, Krasnoznamennogo, ordena Suvorova korpusa v Velikoi Otechestvennoi voine* [The squadrons went into battle: The combat path of 7th Guards Order of Lenin, Red Banner, and Order of Suvorov (Cavalry) Corps in the Great Patriotic War]. Moscow: Voenizdat, 1984.

Domnikov, V. M., ed. *V nastuplenii gvardiia: Ocherk o boevom puti 2-i Gvardeiskoi Armii* [Guards on the offensive: A study of the combat path of 2nd Guards Army]. Moscow: Voenizdat, 1971.

Dragunsky, D. A., ed. *Ot Volgi do Pragi* [From the Volga to Prague]. Moscow: Voenizdat, 1966.

Egorov, Aleksandr Vasilevich. *V Donskiky Stepyakh* [In the Don steppes]. Moscow: DOSAAF, 1988.

Eremenko, A. I. *Stalingrad: Uchastnikam Velikoi bitvy pod Stalingradom posviatshchaetsia* [Stalingrad: A participant in the great battle at Stalingrad dedicates]. Moscow: AST, 2006.

———. *Stalingrad: Zapiski komanduuishchevo frontom* [Stalingrad: The notes of a *front* commander]. Moscow: Voenizdat, 1961.

Erickson, John. *The Road to Stalingrad: Stalin's War with Germany.* Vol. 1. New York: Harper & Row, 1975.

———. *The Road to Berlin: Continuing Stalin's War with Germany.* Boulder, CO: Westview Press, 1983.

Friedin, Seymour, and William Richardson, eds. *The Fatal Decisions.* New York: William Sloane Associates, 1956.

Gehlen, Reinhard. *The Service: The Memoirs of General Reinhard Gehlen.* Trans. David Irving. New York: World Publishing, 1972.

Geroi Sovetskogo Soiuza, tom 1 [Heroes of the Soviet Union, vol. 1]. Moscow: Voenizdat, 1987.

Glantz, David M. *After Stalingrad: The Red Army's Winter Offensive 1942–1943.* Solihull, West Midlands, England: Helion, 2008.

———. *Atlas of the Battle of Stalingrad: Red Army Offensive Operations, 19 November 1942–2 February 1943.* Carlisle, PA: self-published, 2000.

———. *Colossus Reborn: The Red Army at War, 1941–1943.* Lawrence: University Press of Kansas, 2005.

———. *Forgotten Battles of the German-Soviet War (1941–1945).* Vol. 4. *The Winter Campaign (19 November 1942–21 March 1943).* Carlisle, PA: self-published, 1999.

———. *From the Don to the Dnepr: Soviet Offensive Operations December 1942–August 1943.* London: Frank Cass, 1991.

———. *Krupneishee porazhenie Zhukova. Katastrofa Krasnoi Armii v operatsii "Mars" 1942 g.* [The greatest defeat of Zhukov. The catastrophe of the Red Army in Operation "Mars" 1942]. Moscow: Astrel', 2006.

———. *Red Army Command Cadre (1941–1945).* Vol. 1. *Direction, Front, Army, Military District, Defense Zone, and Mobile Corps Commanders.* Carlisle, PA: self-published, 2002.

———. *The Role of Intelligence in Soviet Military Strategy in World War II.* Novato, CA: Presidio Press, 1990.

———. *Soviet Military Deception in the Second World War*. London: Frank Cass, 1989.

———. *Soviet War Experiences: Tank Operations*. Carlisle, PA: self-published, 1998.

———. *The Strategic and Operational Impact of Terrain on Military Operations in Central and Eastern Europe*. Carlisle, PA: self-published, 1998.

———, ed. *1984 Art of War Symposium, From the Don to the Dnepr: Soviet Offensive Operations, December 1942–August 1943: A Transcript of Proceedings*. Carlisle, PA: Center for Land Warfare, U.S. Army War College, 1985. Reprinted with additional maps by Foreign Military Studies Office, U.S. Army Combined Arms Command, Fort Leavenworth, KS, 1992. Reissued as a self-published, unbound copy by David M. Glantz, Carlisle, PA, 1999.

———. "Nikolai Fedorovich Vatutin." In *Stalin's Generals*, ed. Harold Shukman, 287–300. London: Weidenfeld & Nicolson, 1993.

———. *1941–1943 Sovetskoe boennoe chudo: Vozrozhdenie Krasnoi Armii* [1941–1943 Soviet military miracle: The rebirth of the Red Army]. Moscow: Iauza Eksmo, 2008.

Glantz, David M., and Jonathan House. *When Titans Clashed: How the Red Army Stopped Hitler*. Lawrence: University Press of Kansas, 1995.

Goerlitz, Walter. *Paulus and Stalingrad: A Life of Field-Marshal Friedrich Paulus with Notes, Correspondence, and Documents from His Papers*. Trans. R. H. Stevens. New York: Citadel Press, 1963.

Golikov, S. *Vydaiushchiesia pobedy Sovetskoi Armii v Velikoi Otechestvennoi voine* [The distinguished victory of the Soviet army in the Great Patriotic War]. Moscow: Voenizdat, 1954.

Gorshkov, S. G. *Na Iuzhnom flange, osen' 1941 g.–vesna 1944 g.* [On the southern flank, fall 1941–spring 1944]. Moscow: Voenizdat, 1989.

Grams, Rolf. *Die 14. Panzer-Division 1940-1945*. Eggolsheim, West Germany: Dörfler in Nebek Verlag, GmbH, 2004.

Grechko, G. A., ed. *Bitva za Kavkaz* [The battle for the Caucasus]. Moscow: Voenizdat, 1973.

———. *Istoriia Vtoroi Mirovoi voiny 1939–1945 v dvenadtsati tomakh, Tom shestoi: Korennoi perelom v voine* [A history of the Second World War 1939–1945 in 12 volumes, volume 6: The fundamental turning point in the war]. Moscow: Voenizdat, 1976.

Grossman, Vasily S. *A Writer at War: Vasily Grossman with the Red Army, 1941–1945*. Ed. and trans. Anthony Beevor and Luba Vinogradova. New York: Pantheon Books, 2005.

Gubin, B. A., and V. A. Kiselev. *Vos'maia vozdushnaia: Voenno-istoricheskii ocherk boevogo puti 8-i Vozdushnoi armii v gody Velikoi Otechestvennoi voiny* [Eighth Air: A military-historical survey of the combat path of 8th Air Army in the years of the Great Patriotic War]. Moscow: Voenizdat, 1986.

"Gurov Kuz'ma Akimovich." In *Voennaia Entsiklopediia v vos'mi tomakh, 2* [Military encyclopedia in 8 volumes, vol. 2], ed. P. S. Grachev, 534. Moscow: Voenizdat, 1994.

Gvardeiskaia Chernigovskaia: Boevoi put' 76-i gvardeiskoi strelkovoi Chernigovskoi Krasnoznamennoi divizii [The guards Chernigov: The combat path of 76th Guards Chernigov Red Banner Rifle Division]. Moscow: Voenizdat, 1976.

Halder, Franz. *The Halder War Diary, 1939–1942*. Edited by Charles Burdick and Hans-Adolf Jacobsen. Novato, CA: Presidio Press, 1988.

Hardesty, Von, and Ilya Grinberg. *Red Phoenix Rising: The Soviet Air Forces in World War II*. Lawrence: University Press of Kansas, 2012.

Haupt, Werner. *Army Group South: The Wehrmacht in Russia 1941–1945*. Trans. Joseph G. Welsh. Atglen, PA: Schiffer Press, 1998.

Hayward, Joel S. A. *Stopped at Stalingrad: The Luftwaffe and Hitler's Defeat in the East, 1942–1943*. Lawrence: University Press of Kansas, 1998.

Heiber, Helmut, and David M. Glantz. *Hitler and His Generals: The Military Conferences 1942–1945*. New York: Enigma Books, 2002.

Historical Study: Small Unit Actions during the German Campaign in Russia. Department of the Army Pamphlet No. 20-269. Washington, DC: Department of the Army, July 1953.

Holl, Adelbert. *An Infantryman in Stalingrad: From 24 September 1942 to 2 February 1943*. Trans. Jason D. Mark and Neil Page. Sydney, Australia: Leaping Horseman Books, 2005.

Ianchinsky, A. N. *Boevoe ispol'zovanie istrebitel'no-protivotankovoi artillerii RGVK v Velikoi Otechestvennoi voine* [The combat employment of destroyer antitank artillery of the *Stavka* Reserve in the Great Patriotic War]. Moscow: Voroshilov Academy, 1951.

Iminov, Lieutenant Colonel V. T. *Nastupatel'naia operatsii 5-i Tankovoi Armii v kontrnastuplenii pod Stalingradom (19–25 noiabria 1942 g)* [The offensive operation of 5th Tank Army in the counteroffensive at Stalingrad (19–25 November 1942)]. Moscow: Voroshilov Academy of the General Staff, 1979. Originally classified secret.

Irving, David. *Hitler's War*. London: Papermac, 1977.

Isaev, Aleksei. *Stalingrad: Za Volgoi dlia nas zemli net* [Stalingrad: There is no land for us beyond the Volga]. Moscow: Iauza Eksmo, 2008.

Istoricheskii podvig Stalingrada [The historical victory at Stalingrad]. Moscow: Mysl', 1985.

Jentz, Thomas L. *Panzertruppen: The Complete Guide to the Creation & Combat Employment of Germany's Tank Force, 1943–1945*. Atglen, PA: Schiffer Publishing, 1996.

Jukes, Geoffrey. "Alexander Mikhailovich Vasilevsky." In *Stalin's Generals*, ed. Harold Shukman, 275–286. London: Weidenfeld & Nicolson, 1993.

———. *Hitler's Stalingrad Decisions*. Berkeley: University of California Press, 1985.

Kachur, V. P., and V. V. Nikol'skii. *Pod znamenem Sivashtsev: Boevoi put' 169-i strelkovoi Rogachevskoi Krasnoznamennoi ordena Suvorova II stepeni i Kutuzova II stepeni divizii (1941–1945)* [Under the name Sivash: The combat path of 169th Rogachev, Red Banner, and Orders of Suvorov II Degree and Kutuzov II Degree Rifle Division (1941–1945)]. Moscow: Voenizdat, 1989.

Kadyrov, N. Z. *Ot Minska do Veny; Boevoi put' 4-i gvardeiskoi strelkovoi Apostolovsko-Venskoi Krasnoznamennoi divizii* [From Minsk to Vienna; the combat path of 4th Guards Apostolovo-Vienna Red Banner Rifle Division]. Moscow: Voenizdat, 1985.

Kehrig, Manfred. *Stalingrad: Analyse und Dokumentation einer Schlacht*. Stuttgart: Deutsche Verlag-Anstalt, 1974.

Keilig, Wolf. *Die Generale des Heeres*. Bad Nauheim: Podzun-Pallas, 1983.

Keitel, Wilhelm. *In the Service of the Reich*. Trans. David Irving. New York: Stein & Day, 1966.

Kirill Konstantinov Rokossovsky: Pobeda ne liuboi tsenoi [Kirill Konstantinovich Rokossovsky: Victory at any cost]. Moscow: Eksmo Iauza, 2006.

Kolomiets, Maksim, and Il'ia Moshchansky. "Oborona Kavkaz (iiul'–dekabr' 1942 goda)" [The defense of the Caucasus (July–December 1942)]. In *Frontovaia illiustratsiia* [Front illustrated]. Moscow: Strategiia KM, 2000.

Komandarmy. Voennyi biograficheskii slovar' (Velikaia Otechestvennaia) [Army commanders. Military-bibliographical dictionary (The Great Patriotic [War])]. Moscow: Institute of Military History, Russian Federation's Ministry of Defense, OOO Kuchkovo pole, 2005.

Komandovanie korpusnogo i divizionnogo zvena Sovetskikh Vooruzhennykh Sil perioda Velikoi Otechestvennoi voiny, 1941–1945 gg. [Commanders at the corps and division level in the Soviet armed forces in the period of the Great Patriotic War, 1941–1945]. Moscow: Frunze Military Academy, 1964.

Komkory. Voennyi biograficheskii slovar' (Velikaia Otechestvennaia), Tom 1 and 2 [Corps commanders. A military-biographical dictionary (The Great Patriotic [War]), vols. 1 and 2]. Moscow: Institute of Military History, Russian Federation's Ministry of Defense, OOO Kuchkovo pole, 2006.

Kozhevnikov, M. N. *Komandovanie i shtab VVS Sovetskoi Armii v Velikoi Otechestvennoi voine 1941–1945 gg.* [The commands and headquarters of the air force of the Soviet army in the Great Patriotic War 1941–1945]. Moscow: Nauka, 1977.

Kozlov, M. M., ed. *Velikaia Otechestvennaia voina 1941–1945: Entsiklopediia* [The Great Patriotic War 1941–1945: An encyclopedia]. Moscow: Sovetskaia entsiklopediia, 1985.

Krasnoznamennyi Chernomorskii Flot [The Red Banner Black Sea Fleet]. Moscow: Voenizdat, 1987.

Kravchenko, I. M. *Nastupatel'naia operatsii 5-i Tankovoi Armii v kontrnastuplenii pod Stalingradom (19–25 noiabria 1942 g)* [The offensive operation of 5th Tank Army in the counteroffensive at Stalingrad (19–25 November 1942)]. Moscow: Voroshilov Academy of the General Staff, 1978. Originally classified secret.

Krivosheev, G. F., ed. *Grif sekretnosti sniat: Poteri vooruzhennykh sil SSSR v voinakh, boevykh deistviiakh, i voennykh konfliktakh* [The classification secret is removed: The losses of the USSR's armed forces in wars, combat operations, and military conflicts]. Moscow: Voenizdat, 1993.

———. *Rossiia i SSSR v voinakh XX veka: Poteri vooruzhennykh sil, Statisticheskoe issledovanie* [Russia and the USSR in wars of the twentieth century: Armed forces losses, a statistical investigation]. Moscow: OLMA, 2001.

———. *Soviet Casualty and Combat Losses in the Twentieth Century*. London and Mechanicsburg, PA: Schiffer Books, 1997.

———. *Velikaia Otechestvennaia bez grifa sekretnosti. Kniga poter'* [The Great Patriotic (War) without the secret classification. A book of losses]. Moscow: Veche, 2009.

Krull, Albert. *Das Hannoversche Regiment 73: Geschichte des Panzer-Grenadier-Regiments 73 (vorm. Inf. Regt. 73), 1939–1945*. Published by the 73rd Regiment's Kameradschaft, ca. 1967.

Krylov, N. I. *Stalingradskii rubezh* [The Stalingrad line]. Moscow: Voenizdat, 1984.

Kuhn, George W. S. *Ground Forces Casualty Rate Patterns: The Empirical Evidence, Report FP703TR1.* Bethesda, MD: Logistics Management Agency, September 1989.

Kulichkin, S. *Vatutin.* Moscow: Voenizdat, 2001.

Kumanov, G. A., ed. *Sovetskii tyl v pervyi period Velikoi Otechestvennoi voiny* [The Soviet rear in the first period of the Great Patriotic War]. Moscow: Nauka, 1988.

———. *Voina i zhelznodorozhnyi transport SSSR 1941–1945* [War and the USSR's rail transport 1941–1945]. Moscow: Nauka, 1988.

Kumanov, G. A., and L. M. Chuzavkov. "Sovetskii soiuz i lend-liz 1941–1945 gg." [The Soviet Union and Lend-Lease 1941–1945]. In *Lend-liz i Rossiia* [Lend-Lease and Russia], ed. M. N. Supron. Arkhangel'sk: OAO IPP Pravda Severa, 2006.

Kuznetsov, I. I. *Sud'by general'skie: Vysshie komandnye kadry Krasnoi Armii v 1940–1953 gg.* [The fates of the generals: The higher command cadre of the Red Army 1940–1953]. Irkutsk: Irkutsk University Press, 2002.

Laskin, I. A. *Na puti k perelomu* [On the path to the turning point]. Moscow: Voenizdat, 1977.

L '8' Armata Italiana nella Seconde Battaglia Difensiva Del Don (11 Decembre 1942–31 January 1943). Rome: Ministero della Guerra, Stato Maggiore Esercito-Ufficio Storico, 1946.

Lebedev, Ia. A., and A. I. Maliutin. *Pomnit dnepr-reka: Vospominaniia veteranov 193-i strelkovoi Dneprovskoi ordena Lenina, Krasnoznamennoi, ordena Suvorova i Kutuzova divizii* [Remember the Dnepr River: Recollections of veterans of 193rd Dnepr Order of Lenin, Red Banner, and Orders of Suvorov and Kutuzov Rifle Division]. Minsk: Belarus', 1986.

Lemelsen, Joachim, Walter Fries, and Wilhelm Schaeffer. *29. Division: 29. Infanteriedivision, 29. Infanteriedivision (mot), 29. Panzergrenadier-Division.* Bad Nauheim, BRD: Podzun-Verlag, 1960.

Le Operationi della Unita Italiane Al Fronte Russo (1943–1944). Rome: Ministero della Guerra, Stato Maggiore Esercito-Ufficio Storico, 1977.

Liudnikov, I. I. *Doroda dlinoiu v zhizn'* [The long road in life]. Moscow: Voenizdat, 1969.

———. *Doroga dlinoiu v zhizn'* [The long road of life]. Moscow: Vysshchaia shkola, 1985.

Loser, Jochen, ed. *Bittere Pflicht: Kampf und Untergang der 76.Berlin-Brandenburgischen Infanterie-Division.* Osnabruck: Biblio Verlag, 1988.

Losik, O. A. *Stroitel'stvo i boevoe primenenie Sovetskikh tankovykh voisk v gody Velikoi Otechestvennoi voiny* [The formation and combat use of Soviet tank units in the years of the Great Patriotic War]. Moscow: Voenizdat, 1979.

Madej, W. Victor, ed. *German Army Order of Battle.* New Martinsville, WV: Game Marketing, 1978.

Manstein, Field Marshal Erich von. *Lost Victories.* Edited and translated by Anthony G. Powell. Chicago: Henry Regnery, 1958. From the German version *Verlorene Siege.* Bonn: Athenäum-Verlag, 1955.

Margelov, V. F., ed. *Sovetskie vozdushnoi-desantnye: Voenno-istoricheskii ocherk* [Soviet airborne: A military-historical survey]. Moscow: Voenizdat, 1986.

Mark, Jason D. *Death of the Leaping Horseman: 25. Panzer-Division in Stalingrad, 12th August–20th November 1942.* Sydney, Australia: Leaping Horseman Books, 2003.

———. *Island of Fire: The Battle for the Barrikady Gun Factory in Stalingrad, November 1942–February 1943.* Sydney, Australia: Leaping Horseman Books, 2006.

Martynov, V., and S. Spakhov. *Proliv v ogne* [The straits in flames]. Kiev: Izdatel'stvo politicheskoi literatury Ukrainy, 1984.

Maslov, Aleksander A. *Fallen Soviet Generals.* London: Frank Cass, 1998.

McCroden, William. *The Organization of the German Army in World War II: Army Groups, Armies, Corps, Divisions, and Combat Groups.* 5 vols. Draft manuscript, n.d.

Mellenthin, Friedrich W. von. *German Generals of World War II as I Saw Them.* Norman: University of Oklahoma Press, 1977.

———. *Panzer Battles.* Trans. H. Betzler. Norman: University of Oklahoma Press, 1956.

Melvin, Mungo. *Manstein: Hitler's Most Controversial Commander.* Draft manuscript, 2009.

Milch, Erhard. *Taschenkalender.* David Irving microfilm series, Records and Documents Relating to the Third Reich. Microfilm [Wakefield] Ltd.

Minov, V. T. *Nastupatel'naia operatsiia 5-i Tankovoi armii v kontrnastuplenii pod Stalingradom (19–25 noiabria 1942 goda)* [The offensive operation of 5th Tank Army in the counteroffensive at Stalingrad (19–25 November 1942)]. Moscow: Voroshilov Military Academy of the General Staff, 1979. Originally classified secret.

Mirzoian, Suren. *Stalingradskoe Zarevo* [The Stalingrad conflagration]. Erevan: Izdatel'stvo Anastan, 1974.

Mitcham, Samuel W., Jr. *Hitler's Legions: The German Army Order of Battle, World War II.* New York: Stern & Day, 1985.

Morozov, I. K. "Na iuzhnom uchaske fronta" [In the *front*'s southern sector]. In *Bitva za Volge* [The battle for the Volga]. Stalingrad: Knizhnoe izdatel'stvo, 1962.

———. *Ot Stalingrada do Pragi: Zapiski komandira divizii* [From Stalingrad to Prague: The notes of a division commander]. Volgograd: Nizhnyi-Volzhskoe knizhnoe izdatel'stvo, 1976.

Morozov, M. E., ed. *Velikaia Otechestvennaia Voina 1941–1945 gg.. Kampanii i strategicheskie operatsii v tsifrakh, Tom 1* [The Great Patriotic War 1941–1945: Campaigns and strategic operations in figures, vol. 1]. Moscow: Ob'edinennaia redaktsiia MVD Rossii, 2010.

Moskalenko, K. S. *Na iugo-zapadnom napravlentii* [On the southwestern axis]. Vol. 1. Moscow: Nauka, 1969.

Müller, Rolf-Dieter, and Gerd R. Ueberschar. *Hitler's War in the East 1941–1945: A Critical Assessment.* Providence, RI: Berghahn Books, 1997.

Murray, Williamson. *Luftwaffe.* Baltimore: Nautical & Aviation Publishing Company of America, 1985.

Mutovin, B. I. *Cherez vse ispytaniia* [Through all ordeals]. Moscow: Voenizdat, 1986.

Nasha 252-ia: Veterany divizii vospominaiut [Our 252nd: Veterans of the division remember]. Perm: Permskoe knizhnoe izdatel'stvo, 1983.

Naumenko, Iu. A. *Shagai pekhota!* [By the steps of infantry]. Moscow: Voenizdat, 1989.

Naumenko, K. E. *266-ia Artemovsko-Berlinskaia: Voenno-istoricheskii ocherk boevogo puti 266-i strelkovoi Artemovsko-Berlinskoi Krasnoznamennoi, Ordena Suvorova II stepeni divizii* [The 266th Artemovsk-Berlin: A military-historical study of the combat path of 266th Red Banner and Order of Suvorov II Degree Rifle Division]. Moscow: Voenizdat, 1987.

Neidhardt, Hanns. *Mit Tanne und Eichenlaub: Kriegschronik der 100. Jäger-Division vormals 100. leichte Infanterie-Division.* Graz-Stuttgart: Leopold Stocker Verlag, 1981.

Nikoforov, N. I., et al., eds. *Velikaia Otechestvennaia voina 1941–1945 gg.: Deistvuiushchaia armiia* [The Great Patriotic War 1941–1945: The operating army]. Moscow: Animi Foritudo, Kuchkovo pole, 2005.

Oleinikov, A. I. *Rozhdennaia na zemliahk zaporozhskikh* [Born on the lands of Zaporozhe]. Kiev: Izdatel'stvo politicheskoi literatury Ukrainy, 1980.

Operatsii Sovetskikh vooruzhennykh sil v Velikoi Otechestvennoi Voine 1941–1945: Voenno-istoricheskii ocherk, Tom II: Operatsii Sovetskikh vooruzhennykh sil v period korennogo pereloma v khode Velikoi Otechestvennoi voiny (19 noiabria 1942 g.–dekabr' 1943 g.) [Operations of the Soviet armed forces in the Great Patriotic War 1941–1945: A military-historical survey, vol. 2, Operations of the Soviet armed forces in the period of a fundamental turning point in the Great Patriotic War (19 November 1942–December 1943)]. Moscow: Voenizdat, 1958. Originally classified secret.

Panin, A., and S. Pereslegin. *Stalingrad: Tsena pobedy* [Stalingrad: The cost of victory]. Moscow: AST, 2005.

Panov, M. F. *Na napravlenii glavnogo udara* [On the axis of the main attack]. Moscow: Shcherbinskaia tipografiia, 1993.

Paul, Wolfgang. *Brennpunkte: Die Geschichte der 6. Panzerdivision (1. leichte) 1937–1945.* Osnabruck: Biblio Verlag, 1984.

Pavlov, I. N. *Legendarnaia zheleznaia: Boevoi put' motorstelkovoi Samaro-Ul'ianovskoi, Berdichevskoi Zheleznoi, ordena Oktiabr'skoi Revolutsii, trizhdy Krasnoznamennoi, ordenov Suvorova i Bogdana Khmel'nitskogo divizii* [The legendary iron: The combat path of the Samara-Ul'ianovsk, Berdichev Iron, Order of the October Revolution, and Orders of Suvorov and Bogdan Khmel'nitsky Motorized Rifle Division]. Moscow: Voenizdat, 1987.

Pliev, I. A. *Pod gvardeiskim znamenem* [Under a guards banner]. Ordzhonikidze: Izdatel'stvo IR, 1976.

Plocher, Herman, and Harry R. Fletcher, eds. *The German Air Forces versus Russia, 1942.* USAF Historical Studies No. 154. Aerospace Studies Institute, Air University, USAF Historical Division, June 1966.

Pod gvardeiskim znamenem: Boevoi put' 66-i gvardeiskoi strelkovoi Poltavskoi Krasnoznamennoi divizii [Under a guards banner: The combat path of 66th Guards Poltava and Red Banner Rifle Division]. Moscow: Voenizdat, 1992.

Popov, P. P., A. V. Kozlov, and B. G. Usik, *Turning Point: Recollections of Russian Participants and Witnesses of the Stalingrad Battle.* Trans. James F. Gebhardt. Sydney, Australia: Leaping Horseman Books, 2008.

Portugal'sky, R. M. *Analiz opyta nezavershennykh nastupatel'nykh operatsii Velikoi Otechestvenoi voyny. Vyvody i uroki* [An analysis of the experience of uncompleted offensive operations of the Great Patriotic War. Conclusions and lessons]. Moscow: Izdanie akademii, 1991.

Pospelov, P. N., ed. *Istoriia Velikoi Otechestvennoi voiny Sovetskogo Soiuza 1941–1945 v shesti tomakh, tom vtoroi* [History of the Great Patriotic War 1941–1945 in 6 vols., vol. 2]. Moscow: Voenizdat, 1961.

Ramanichev, N. M., and V. V. Gurkhin. "Rzhevsko-Sychevskie operatsii 1942" [The Rzhev-Sychevka operation 1942]. In *Voennaia entsyklopidiia v vos'mi tomakh*, 7 [Military encyclopedia in 8 vols., vol. 7], ed. S. B. Ivanov, 233–234. Moscow: Voenizdat, 2003.

Raus, Erhard. *Panzer Operations: The Eastern Front Memoir of General Raus, 1941–1945*. Compiled and translated by Steven H. Newton. N.p.: De Capo Press, 2003.

Razgrom Italo-Nemetskikh voisk na Donu (Dekabr' 1942 r.): Kratkii operativno-takticheskii ocherk [The destruction of Italian-German forces on the Don (December 1942): A brief operational-tactical summary]. Moscow: Voenizdat, 1945. Originally classified secret.

Rebentisch, Ernst. *The Combat History of the 23rd Panzer Division in World War II*. Mechanicsburg, PA: Stackpole Books, 2012.

Reinhardt, Klaus. *Moscow—The Turning Point: The Failure of Hitler's Strategy in the Winter of 1941–42*. Trans. Karl Keenan. Oxford: Oxford University Press, 1992.

Roberts, Geoffrey. *Stalin's Wars: From World War to Cold War, 1939–1953*. New Haven, CT: Yale University Press, 2006.

Rokossovsky, K. K. *Soldatskii dolg* [A soldier's duty]. Moscow: Golos, 2000.

———, ed. *Velikaia pobeda na Volge* [Great victory on the Volga]. Moscow: Voenizdat, 1965.

Rotmistrov, Pavel A. *Stal'naia gvardiia* [Steel guards]. Moscow: Voenizdat, 1984.

Rozhdennaia v boiakh: Boevoi put' 71-i gvardeiskoi strelkovoi Vitebskoi, ordena Lenina, Krasnoznamennoi divizii [Born in battle: The combat path of 71st Guards, Vitebsk, Order of Lenin, and Red Banner Rifle Division]. Moscow: Voenizdat, 1986.

Rudenko, S. I. *Kryl'ia pobedy* [Wings of victor]. Moscow: Mezhdunarodnye otnosheniia, 1985.

———, et al., eds. *Sovetskie voenno-vozdushnye sily v Velikoi Otechestvennoi voine, 1941–1945 gg.* [The Soviet Air Force in the Great Patriotic War, 1941–1945]. Moscow: Voenizdat, 1968.

Ruef, Karl. *Odysee einer Gebirgsdivision: Die 3. Geb. Div. im Einsatz*. Graz and Stuttgart: Leopold Stocker Verlag, 1976.

Sadarananda, Dana V. *Beyond Stalingrad: Manstein and the Operations of Army Group Don*. New York: Praeger Publishers, 1990.

Samchuk, I. A. *Gvardeiskaia Poltavskaia: Kratkii ocherk o boevom puti 97-i gvardeiskoi Poltavskoi Krasnoznamennoi, ordenov Suvorov i Bogdan Khmel'mitskogo strelkovoi divizii* [Poltava guards: A short survey about the combat path of 97th Guards Poltava, Red Banner, and Orders of Suvorov and Bogdan Khmel'nitsky Rifle Division]. Moscow: Voenizdat, 1965.

———. *Trinadtsataia gvardeiskaia* [The 13th Guards]. Moscow: Voenizdat, 1971.

Samchuk, I. A., P. G. Skachko, Iu. N. Babikov, and I. L. Gnedoi. *Ot Volgi do El'by i Pragi (Kratkii ocherk o boevom puti5-i Gvardeiskoi Armii)* [From the Volga to the Elbe and Prague (A short study of the combat path of 5th Guards Army)]. Moscow: Voenizdat, 1970.

Samsonov, A. M. *Ot Volgi do Baltiki: Ocherk istorii 3-go gvardeiskogo mekhanizirovannogo korpusa 1942–1945 gg.* [From the Volga to the Baltic: A study of the history of 3rd Guards Mechanized Corps 1942–1945]. Moscow: Nauka, 1963.

———. *Stalingradskaia bitva* [The battle for Stalingrad]. Moscow: Nauka, 1983.

———. *Stalingradskaia bitva* [The battle for Stalingrad]. Moscow: Academy of Science of the USSR, 1960.

———, ed. *Stalingradskaia epopeia* [Stalingrad epic]. Moscow: Nauka, 1968.

Sarkis'ian, S. M. *51-ia Armiia* [The 51st Army]. Moscow: Voenizdat, 1983.

Schadewitz, Michael. *Panzerregiment 11/Panzerabteilung 65 1937–1945, Panzerersatz- und Ausbildungabteilung II 1939–1945.* Lünen, FRG: Schmidt-Verlag, 1987.

Scheibert, Horst. *Nach Stalingrad—48 Kilometers! Der Einsatzvorstoss der 6. Panzerdivision. Dezember 1942.* Neckargemünd: Kurt Vowinckel Verlag, 1956.

———. *Zwischen Don und Donez—Winter 1942/43.* Neckargemünd: Kurt Vowinckel Verlag, 1961.

Schneider, Franz, and Charles Gullans, trans. *Last Letters from Stalingrad.* Westport, CT: Greenwood Press, 1974.

Schneider, Major I. G. Heinz. "Breakthrough Attack by the V Russian Mechanized Corps on the Khir River from 10–16 December 1942: The Defensive Engagement by the 336th Infantry Division and the 11th Panzer Division on the Khir River against the V Mechanized Corps from 10 to 16 December 1942." In *Project #48. Small Unit Tactics: Tactics of Individual Arms, Part II,* MS P-060 f. Mueller-Hillebrand, ed. Major General Burkhart, Chief of Staff, Third Panzer Army. Koenigstein, Germany: Historical Division European Command, Foreign Military Studies Branch, 3 February 1951.

Schröter, Heinz. *Stalingrad.* New York: Ballantine, 1958.

———. *Stalingrad: ". . . bis letzten Patrone."* Lengerich: Kleins Druck- und Verlagsanstalt, n.d.

Schulz, Friedrich. *Reverses on the Southern Wing (1942–1943).* Military Study No. T-15. Headquarters, U.S. Army, Europe, n.d.

Senger und Etterlin, Ferdinand von. *Die 24. Panzer-Division vormals 1. Kavallerie-Division 1939–1945.* Neckargemünd: Kurt Vowinckel Verlag, 1962.

Senger und Etterlin, Frido von. *Neither Fear nor Hope: The Wartime Career of General Frido von Senger und Etterlin, Defender of Cassino.* New York: E. P. Dutton, 1964.

Seth, Ronald. *Stalingrad: Point of Return: The Story of the Battle August 1942–February 1943.* New York: Cowrad-McCann, 1959.

73-ia Gvardeiskaia: Sbornik vospominanii, dokumentov i materialov o boevom puti 73-i gvardeiskoi strelkovoi Stalingradsko-Dunaiskoi Krasnoznamennoi divizii [The 73rd Guards: A collection of recollections, documents, and materials about the combat path of 73rd Guards Stalingrad-Danube Red Banner Rifle Division]. Alma-Ata: Kazakhstan, 1986.

Shein, Oleg. *Neizvestnyi front Velikoi Otechestvennoi* [The unknown front of the Great Patriotic (War)]. Moscow: Eksmo Iauza, 2009.

Shtemenko, S. M. *The General Staff at War, 1941–1945*. Moscow: Progress, 1970.

———. *The General Staff at War, 1941–1945*. Book 1. Trans. Robert Daglish. Moscow: Voenizdat, 1985.

Shukman, Harold, ed. *Stalin's Generals*. New York: Grove Press, 1993.

Skomorokhov, N. M., et al., eds. *17-ia Vozdushnaia Armiia v boiakh ot Stalingrada do Veny: Voenno-istoricheskii ocherk a boevom puti 17-i Vozdushnoi Armii v gody Velikoi Otechestvennoi voiny* [The 17th Air Army in combat from Stalingrad to Vienna: A historical survey of the combat path of 17th Air Army in the Great Patriotic War]. Moscow: Voenizdat, 1977.

Slepyan, Kenneth. *Stalin's Guerrillas: Soviet Partisans in World War II*. Lawrence: University Press of Kansas, 2006.

Soviet Documents of the Use of War Experience. Vol. 3. *Military Operations 1941 and 1942*. Trans. Harold S. Orenstein. London: Frank Cass, 1993.

Speer, Albert. *Inside the Third Reich*. Trans. Richard Winston and Clara Winston. New York: Macmillan, 1970.

Spielberger, Walter J., and Uwe Feist. *Panzerkampfwagen IV: "Workhorse" of the German Panzertruppe*. Berkeley, CA: Feist Publications, 1968.

Stalingrad: Tsena pobedy [Stalingrad: The cost of victory]. Moscow: AST, 2005.

Stalingrad: Zabytoe srazhenie [Stalingrad: The forgotten battle]. Moscow: AST, 2005.

Stalingradskaia epopeia: Vpervye publikuemye dokumenty, rassekrechennye FSB RF [Stalingrad epoch: Declassified documents of the Russian Federation's FSB published for the first time]. Moscow: Evonnitsa-MG, 2000.

Stoves, Rolf. *Die Gepanzerten und Motorisierten Deutschen Grossverbande, 1935–1945*. Friedberg: Podzun-Pallas-Verlag, 1986.

———. *Die 22. Panzer-Division, Die 25. Panzer-Division, Die 27. Panzer-Division, und die Die 233. Reserve-Panzer-Division*. Friedberg: Podzun-Pallas-Verlag, 1985.

Stroeva, Anna. *Komandarm Kravchenko* [Army commander Kravchenko]. Kiev: Politicheskoi literatury Ukrainy, 1984.

Sukharev, A. Ia., ed. *Marshal A. M. Vasilevsky—strateg, polkovodets, chelovek* [Marshal A. M. Vasilevsky—strategist, military leader, and the man]. Moscow: Sovet Veteranov khigoizdaniia, 1998.

Sydnor, Charles W., Jr. *Soldiers of Destruction: The SS Death's Head Division, 1933–1945*. Princeton, NJ: Princeton University Press, 1977.

Tarrant, V. E. *Stalingrad: Anatomy of an Agony*. London: Leo Cooper, 1992.

3. Infanterie-Division, 3. Infanterie-Division (Mot.), 3. Panzergrenadier-Division. Cuxhaven: Gerhard Dieckhoff, 1960.

Tieke, Wilhelm. *The Caucasus and the Oil: The German-Soviet War in the Caucasus 1942/43*. Trans. Joseph G. Welsh. Winnipeg, Canada: J. J. Fedorowicz, 1995. A translation of Wilhelm Tieke. *Der Kaukasus und das Öl: Der Deutsch-sowjetische Krieg in Kaukasien 1942/43*. Osnabruck: Munin Verlag, 1970.

Timokhovich, I. V. *Operativnoe iskusstvo Sovetskikh VVS v Velikoi Otechestvennoi voine* [The operational art of the Soviet air forces in the Great Patriotic War]. Moscow: Voenizdat, 1976.

Tolubko, B. F., and N. I. Baryshev. *Na iuzhnom flange: Boevoi put' 4-go gvardeiskogo mekhanizirovanogo korpusa (1942–1945 gg.)* [On the southern flank: The combat path of 4th Guards Mechanized Corps (1942–1945)]. Moscow: Nauka, 1973.

Trevor-Roper, Hugh R., ed. *Blitzkrieg to Defeat: Hitler's War Directives 1939–1945*. New York: Holt, Rinehart & Winston, 1964.

Tsirlin, A. D., P. I. Biriukov, V. P. Istomin, and E. N. Fedoseev. *Inzhenernye voiska v boiakh za Sovetskuiu Rodinu* [Engineer forces in battles for the Soviet Motherland]. Moscow: Voenizdat, 1970.

Tuzov, A. V. *V ogne voiny: Boevoi put' 50-i Gvardeiskoi dvazhdy Krasnoznamennoi ordena Suvorova i Kutuzova strelkovoi divizii* [In the flames of battle: The combat path of 50th Twice Red Banner and Orders of Suvorov and Kutuzov Rifle Division]. Moscow: Voenizdat, 1970.

Two Hundred Days of Fire: Accounts by Participants and Witnesses of the Battle of Stalingrad. Moscow: Progress Publishers, 1970.

Vasil'ev, I., and A. P. Likan'. *Gvardeitsy piatnadtsatoi: Boevoi put' Piatnadtsatoi Gvardeiskoi strelkovoi divizii* [The guardsmen of the 15th]. Moscow: Voenizdat, 1960.

Vasilevsky, A. M. *Delo vsei zhizni* [Life's work]. Moscow: Izdatel'stvo politicheskoi literatury, 1983.

———. *A Lifelong Cause*. Moscow: Progress Publishers, 1976.

Velikaia Otechestvennaia Komkory: Voennyi biograficheskii slovar' v 2-kh tomakh [Great Patriotic corps commanders: A military-biographical dictionary in 2 vols.]. Moscow-Zhukovskii: Kuchkovo pole, 2006.

Venkov, B. S., and P. P. Dudinov. *Gvardeiskaia doblest': Boevoi put' 70-i gvardeiskoi strelkovoi glukhovskoi ordena Lenina, dvazhdy krasnoznamennoi, ordena Suvorova, Kutuzova i Bogdana Khmel'nitskogo diviziii* [Guards valor: The combat path of 70th Guards Glukhov, Order of Lenin and Order of Suvorov, Kutuzov and Bogdan Khmel'nitsky Rifle Division]. Moscow: Voenizdat, 1979.

Vider, Ioakhim. *Stalingradskaia tragediia: Za kulisami katastrofy* [The Stalingrad tragedy: Behind the scenes of a catastrophe]. Trans. A. Lebedev and N. Portugalov. Moscow: Iauza, Eksmo, 2004.

Vinogradov, I. N. *Oborona, shturm, pobeda* [Defense, assault, victory]. Moscow: Nauka, 1968.

Voennaia entsiklopediia v vos'mi tomakh, 1 [Military encyclopedia in 8 vols., vol. 1]. Edited by I. N. Rodionov. Moscow: Voenizdat, 1997.

Volkogonov, Dmitri. *Stalin: Triumph and Tragedy*. Translated and edited by Harold Shukman. Rocklin, CA: Grove, 1992.

Volostnov, N. I. *Na ognennykh rubezhakh* [In firing positions]. Moscow: Voenizdat, 1983.

Vorob'ev, F. D., and V. M. Kravtsov. *Pobedy Sovetskikh vooruzhennykh sil v Velikoi Otechestvennoi voine 1941–1945 (kratkii ocherk)* [The victory of the Soviet armed forces in the Great Patriotic War 1941–1945 (a short summary)]. Moscow: Voenizdat, 1953.

Voronov, N. N. *Na sluzhbe voennoi* [In military service]. Moscow: Voenizdat, 1963.

Vovchenko, I. A. *Tankisti* [Tankists]. Moscow: DOSAAF SSSR, 1976.

Vyrodov, I. Ia., ed. *V srazheniakh za Pobedy: Boevoi put' 38-i armii v gody Velikoi Otechestvennoi voyny 1941–1945* [In battles for the Fatherland: The combat path of 38th Army in the Great Patriotic War 1941–1945]. Moscow: Nauka, 1974.

Warlimont, Walter. *Inside Hitler's Headquarters 1939–1945*. Trans. R. H. Barry. Novato, CA: Presidio, 1964.

Werthen, Wolfgang. *Geschichte der 16. Panzer-Division 1939–1945*. Bad Nauheim: Podzun-Pallas-Verlag, 1958.

Wieder, I. *Katastrofa na Volge* [Catastrophe on the Volga]. Moscow: Voenizdat, 1965. A translation of Joachim Wieder. *Die Tragödie von Stalingrad. Erinnerungen eines Überlebenden*. West Germany: Deggendorf, 1955.

Wijers, Hans J. *The Battle for Stalingrad: Operation "Winter Storm"—The Relief Operation of LVII Panzer Corps*. Self-published, 2003.

Woff, Richard. "Chuikov." In *Stalin's Generals*, ed. Harold Shukman, 67–76. London: Weidenfeld & Nicolson, 1993.

———. "Rokossovsky." In *Stalin's Generals*, ed. Harold Shukman, 177–198. London: Weidenfeld & Nicolson, 1993.

Wray, Timothy A. *Standing Fast: German Defensive Doctrine on the Russian Front during World War II, Prewar to March 1943*. Fort Leavenworth, KS: Combat Studies Institute, 1986.

Wüster, Dr. Wigand. *An Artilleryman in Stalingrad: Memoirs of a Participant in the Battle*. Trans. Torben Laursen, Jason D. Mark, and Harald Steinmüller. Sydney, Australia: Leaping Horsemen Books, 2007.

Zakharov, Iu. D. *General armii N. F. Vatutin*. Moscow: Voenizdat, 1985.

Zalessky, Konstantin. *Vermacht: Sukhoputnye voiska i Verkhovnoe komandovanie* [The *Wehrmacht*: Ground forces and the High Command]. Moscow: Iauza, 2005.

Zaloga, Steve, and Peter Sarson. *T-34/76 Medium Tank, 1941–1945*. London: Osprey/Reed Publishing, 1994.

Zhadov, A. S. *Chetyre goda voyny* [Four years of war]. Moscow: Voenizdat, 1978.

Zhukov, G. *Georgi K. Marshal Zhukov's Greatest Battles*. Trans. Theodore Shabad. New York: Cooper Square Press, 2002.

———. *Reminiscences and Reflections*. Vol. 2. Moscow: Progress Publishers, 1985.

Ziemke, Earl F. *Stalingrad to Berlin: The German Defeat in the East*. Washington, DC: U.S. Army Office of the Chief of Military History, 1968.

Ziemke, Earl F., and Magna E. Bauer. *Moscow to Stalingrad: Decision in the East*. Washington, DC: Center of Military History U.S. Army, 1987.

Zolotarev, V. A., ed. *Velikaia Otechestvennaia Deistvuiushchaia armiia 1941–1945 gg.* [The Great Patriotic (War): The operating army 1941–1945]. Moscow: Animi Fortitudo Kuchkovo pole, 2005.

———. *Velikaia Otechestvennaia voina 1941–1945: Voenno-istoricheskii ocherki v chetyrekh tomakh, Kniga 1: Surovye ispytaniia* [The Great Patriotic War 1941–1945: A military-historical study in 4 vols., book 1: A harsh education]. Moscow: Nauka, 1998.

———. *Velikaia Otechestvennaia voina 1941–1945: Voenno-istoricheskii ocherki v chetyrekh tomakh, Kniga 2, Perelom* [The Great Patriotic War 1941–1945: A military-historical study in 4 vols., book 2, The turning point]. Moscow: Nauka, 1998.

Zvartsev, A. M., ed. *3-ia gvardeiskaia tankovaia armiia* [The 3rd Guards Tank Army]. Moscow: Voenizdat, 1982.

Articles

Domnikov, V. "Protiv 'Zimnei grozy'" [Against "Winter Tempest"]. *VIZh* 7 (July 1969): 35–44.

Eliseev, Vladimir, and Sergei Mikhalev. "Liudskie poteri v Stalingradskoi bitva" [Personnel losses in the battle for Stalingrad]. *VVI* 12 (December 1992): 1–4.

Glantz, David M. "Soviet Mobilization in Peace and War, 1924–42: A Survey." *JSMS* 5, 3 (September 1992): 345–352.

Gurkin, V. V. "Liudskie poteri Sovetskikh Vooruzhennykh sil v 1941–1945 gg.: Novye aspekty" [Personnel losses of the Soviet armed forces in 1941–1945: New aspects]. *VIZh* 2 (March–April 1999): 2–13.

Hayward, Joel. "Hitler's Quest for Oil: The Impact of Economic Considerations on Military Strategy, 1941–1942." *Journal of Strategic Studies* 18, 4 (December 1995): 94–135.

I'lenkov, S. A. "Concerning the Registration of Soviet Armed Forces' Wartime Irrevocable Losses, 1941–1945." *JSMS* 9, 2 (June 1996): 440–442.

Il'in, P. "Boi za Kalach-na-Donu" [The battle for Kalach-on-the-Don]. *VIZh* 10 (October 1961): 70–81.

Isaev, S. I. "Vekhi frontovogo puti" [Landmarks of a front path]. *VIZh* 10 (October 1991): 24–25.

Ivanov, V., N. Pavlenko, and N. Fokin. "Klassicheskaia operatsiia na okruzhenie" [A classic encirclement operation]. *VIZh* 11 (November 1969): 26–37.

Kahn, David. "An Intelligence Case Study: The Defense of Osuga, 1942." *Aerospace Historian* 28, 4 (December 1981): 242–252.

"Khronika deiatel'nosti Marshala Sovetskogo Soiuza G. K. Zhukova v period Velikoi Otechestvennoi voiny 1941–1945 gg." [A chronicle of the activities of Marshal of the Soviet Union G. K. Zhukov during the period of the Great Patriotic War 1941–1945]. In "Vekhi frontovogo puti" [Landmarks of a front path]. *VIZh* 10 (October 1991): 23–33.

Kozlov, M. "Strategy and Operational Art at Stalingrad." *VIZh* 11 (November 1982): 9–16.

Kuz'michev, I. V. "Shtafniki" [Penal troops]. *Serzhant* [Sergeant] 14 (2006): 25–34.

Lashchenko, P. N. "Prodiktovan surovoi neobkhodimost'iu" [Severe measures are dictated]. *VIZh* 8 (August 1988): 76–80.

Lenskii, A. "Stalingrad—konets i probuzhdenie" [Stalingrad—The end and the awakening]. *VIZh* 3 (March 1961): 85–90.

Mikhalev, S. "O razrabotke zamysla i planirovanii kontrnastupleniia pod Stalingradom" [About the concept and planning of the counteroffensive at Stalingrad]. *VVI* 8 (August, 1992): 1–7.

Ogarev, P. "Boi u Verkhne-Kumskovo (15–19 dekabria 1942 goda)" [The battle at Verkhne-Kumskii (15–19 December 1942)]. *VIZh* 5 (May 1959): 51–59.

Popov, Markian M. "Iuzhnee Stalingrada" [South of Stalingrad]. *VIZh* 2 (February 1961): 67–98.

Rokossovsky, K. "Pobeda na Volge" [Victory on the Volga]. *VIZh* 2 (February 1968): 64–76.

Rokossovsky, K. K. "Soldatskii dolg" [A soldier's duty]. *VIZh* 2 (February 1990): 47–52.

Rotmistrov, P. "O Sovetskom voennom iskusstve v bitve na Volge" [About Soviet military art in the battle for the Volga]. *VIZh* 12 (December) 1962: 1–14, and 1 (January 1963): 9–20.

Runov, V. "Ot oborony–k reidu" [From defense to a raid]. *VV* 5 (April 1991): 42–46.

Runov, V. A. "Boevye deistviia 87-i strelkovoi divizii v Kotel'nikovsko operatsii (15–31 dekabria 1952 g.)" [The combat actions of 87th Rifle Division in the Kotel'nikovo operation (15–31 December 1942)]. *VIZh* 11 (November 1987): 72–76.

Shaposhnikov, M. "Boevye deistviia 5-go mekhanizirovannogo korpusa zapadnee Surovikino v dekabre 1942 goda" [The combat operations of 5th Mechanized Corps west of Surovikino in December 1942]. *VIZh* 10 (October 1982): 32–38.

Statiev, Alexander. "The Ugly Duckling of the Armed Forces: Romanian Armour 1919–41." *JSMS* 12, 2 (June 1999): 225–240.

———. "When an Army Becomes 'Merely a Burden': Romanian Defense Policy and Strategy (1918–1941)." *JSMS* 13, 2 (June 2000): 67–85.

Vasilevsky, A. M. "Nezabyvaemye dni" [Unforgettable days]. *VIZh* 1 (January 1966), 13–33, and 3 (March 1966): 24–44.

Vorob'ev, F. "Ob operatsii 'Kol'tso'" [About Operation Ring]. *VIZh* 11 (November 1962): 52–58.

Voronov, N. "Operatsiia 'Kol'tso'" [Operation Ring]. *VIZh* 5 (May 1962): 71–84, and 6 (June 1962): 68–76.

Websites

Axis Biographical Research. http://geocities.com/~/orion/.

Axis Fact Book—*Des Heeres.* http://www.axishistory.com/index.

Die Generale des Heeres. http://balsi.de/Homepage-Generale/Heer/Heer-Startseite .html.

Index